# AGE OF THE FRENCH REVOLUTION
*by Claude Manceron*

# AGE OF THE FRENCH REVOLUTION
## IV

MAP
OF
FRANCE
Before the Revolution

# *Toward the Brink* 1785-1787

## CLAUDE MANCERON

*Translated from the French by Nancy Amphoux*

A TOUCHSTONE BOOK
Published by Simon & Schuster Inc.
New York · London · Toronto · Sydney · Tokyo

Touchstone
Simon & Schuster Building
Rockefeller Center
1230 Avenue of the Americas
New York, New York 10020

10   9   8   7   6   5   4   3   2   1   Pbk.

Library of Congress Cataloging in Publication Data
Manceron, Claude.
    [Révolution qui lève. English]
    Toward the brink, 1785–1787/Claude Manceron: translated from the French
by Nancy Amphoux.—1st Touchstone ed.
        p.   cm.—(Age of the French Revolution; v. 4)
    Translation of: La révolution qui lève.
    Reprint. Originally published: 1st American ed. New York: Knopf, 1983,
© 1982. Originally published in series: The French Revolution; 4.
    "A Touchstone book."
    Includes bibliographical references.
    1. France—History—Louis XVI, 1774–1793—Biography.   2. France—
History—Revolution, 1789–1799—Biography.   3. France—History—
Revolution, 1789–1799—Causes.   4. France—Biography.   I. Title.
II. Series: Manceron, Claude. Hommes de la liberté. English (Simon and
Schuster, Inc.); 4.
    [DC145.M3513   1989 vol. 4]
    [DC137.5.A1]
    944.04′092′2   s—dc20
    [944′.035′0922]                                          89-21620
                                                                 CIP
    ISBN 0-671-68022-6 Pbk.

ILLUSTRATION CREDITS

*Anderson-Giraudon:* page 93; *Bibliothèque Nationale:* pages 3, 8, 13a, 26, 47, 60,
67, 72, 77, 81, 123a, 130, 137, 142, 149, 155, 163, 169a, 233, 250, 257,
274, 309, 356, 370, 378; Caisse Nationale des Monuments Historiques: pages
88b, 364; Collection Viollet: page 21; Documentation Tallandier: pages 98, 289;
Editions Robert Laffont-Service Iconographique: pages 13b, 42, 123b, 169b,
193, 200, 214, 225, 237, 250, 266, 283, 304, 315, 327, 342; Françoise Foliot:
pages 155, 186, 334; Giraudon: pages 35, 320; Musées Nationaux: page 106;
New York Public Library: frontispiece; Photographie Bulloz: pages 54, 88a.

*Most of the illustrations were provided through the courtesy of the Service Iconographique of
Editions Robert Laffont.*

*To the Inseparables:*
*Pierre, Janine, and Charlotte*
*Viansson-Ponté*

One minute of the world is passing. . . . To paint it, as it is! And forget everything for that.

—PAUL CEZANNE


The history of the French Revolution is an anthology of prophesies.

—JEAN-PAUL RABAUT SAINT-ETIENNE


When all is said and done, it was a way of seeing clearly in the past what seems unclear in the present. We tend to be nearsighted when we look at the present: we have to hold it at the right distance in order to get it into focus. Or we can use a lens. For me, the right distance (or the lens) is a historical account. Its sole function is to make the past become present.

—LEONARDO SCIASCIA


These facts prove what a mistake it was to date the beginning of the Revolution from the opening of the Estates-General. For a number of years the Revolution was not only imminent but had already commenced, and there was as much energy in it then as has been deployed by it since. Even in those years, were not the elements of the old monarchy already disintegrating? Was it not the scandals, the want of money, and, in short, the impending disorganization of the body politic, that impelled the convening of the Estates-General?

—ALEXANDRE DE LAMETH


Today, May 18, 1787, I hear from Paris that the Chevalier de Fabri, a distinguished man in the navy whose name is surely not unknown to you, has just perished in a most unfortunate fashion indeed. He had made his chief seaman run the gauntlet; the man was wild with rage, and determined upon revenge. A few days later, seeing the Chevalier de Fabri walking alone on the bridge, he put a cannonball in each of his pockets and, drawing near, threw his arms around the chevalier, clasped him tight, and dragged them both into the sea where they soon drowned: surely what could be called a cruel vengeance. I am also told that it is not known when the Assembly of Notables will end; it is still discussing schemes of improvement and reform.

—Letter from the COMTESSE DE SABRAN
to the CHEVALIER DE BOUFFLERS

# Contents

# Acknowledgments

Robert Laffont and his team have added a new dimension—patience—to the support they have been lavishing upon me from the start. All I can do is stammer out the same old thanks, especially to the Laffont iconographic and production departments. This series is increasingly becoming a collective venture and I sometimes feel that infinitely discreet hands are helping me to hold my pen when my own fingers would let it drop from exhaustion.

I am a poor correspondent and have not thanked all the people who have written their encouragement or criticism. I would like them to know that every one of those echoes reaches my heart, however; and every page of this book is an attempt to answer them.

Max Gallo, the expert in significant titles, came up with the original for this one, and I thank him for it, from the bottom of our friendship.

—C.M.

# *Preface*

The main idea of the *Age of the French Revolution* is to explore the roots of the Revolution by the method of intersecting biographies. In each volume, we make or renew our acquaintance with the characters who will become the leading actors of 1789–1797.

They don't know each other. Unawares, they will approach one another during the fifteen-year reign which rejected the Revolution, thereby endowing it with its messianic character: a cleavage in time to serve all time. Once under way, the Revolution will set the stage for their meeting: they will love, unite, defy, tear to shreds, destroy each other—or survive now and then owing to luck, betrayal, or patience. From 1789–1797 they will enact a *chanson de geste,* each episode of which is part of our existence, destined to become the very tissue of it: the Peters, Johns, and Magdalens, the Pontius Pilates and Judases bearing the glad tidings of liberty. Whenever possible I shall try to bring them out of obscurity to personify them, to capture the reality of their daily lives.

Over a thousand people, then, a hundred of whom we shall stalk. Their biographies are woven into the main thread of chronological events.

Running heads at the top of each page show the reader where he is at all times. On the left is the date of the incident, on the right its contents in a nutshell. The names used in the titles are those of History: "Louis Phillipe and His Cousins," for example, shows the future King of the French—then only Duc de Valois—in the care of his new "governor," Félicité de Genlis. In running heads the spelling of names is that of the revolutionary period; in the narrative, however, it is that of the period to which the episode belongs. Thus the title "Dumouriez, a Privileged Prisoner" refers to the adventures in 1774 of Colonel du Mouriez, and "Biron Courts the Queen" deals with the person known as the Duc de Lauzun in 1775.

The alphabetical index at the end of the book will help those who prefer to follow the thread of a single biography straight through the series.

The numbered notes toward the end of the book contain bibliographic references and details of use to students and researchers. Asterisks and daggers refer to the footnotes on the page—of which I am as sparing as possible— required for an immediate understanding of the text, especially where approximate equivalents of sums and measurements are concerned.

Instead of chapters, sequences. A guiding rule: objective truth as to dates, facts, acts, spoken and written words. A bias: the desire to enter into the psychology of each person, whatever his role in the Revolution—hence respect for Charette as well as Marceau—in an attempt to reconstitute his inner movement. A technique: combining anecdotal material with events to provide the background for a portrait and to make a figure live again in his own times through simultaneous sensations and impressions. The Revolution was also David, Talma, Gossec, Ledoux, balloons, visual telegraphy, and Fulton's experiments, just as the liberation of France was also Aragon, Eluard, Camus, Giacometti, Gérard Philipe, and Le Corbusier. An ambition: to steer a course midway between the analysis of economic and social spheres that shape mankind and the study of a particular person's unpredictable influence on those spheres, thereby exploding the framework of determinism. Napoleon and revolutionary Europe; Lenin and the Russia of 1917; De Gaulle and the French Resistance.

Finally, an explanation: my sifting through thousands of episodes resulted in retaining (trifling as they may seem—an operatic aria, an epigram, an academic reception, a love letter) only those things which enhance the understanding of a quarter-century containing all centuries. A conceivable, if insufferable, subtitle comes to mind: "Poetic and historic manual for bringing about instant total change in myself and others."

—Claude Manceron
from *Twilight of the Old Order*

# A Note:
# Johann-Heinrich Pestalozzi
# on Europe Before 1789

"There was less hanging and more pardoning, objections were viewed with greater leniency—so long, of course, as they offered no challenge to authority. In fact, laws were made as though men actually had a few rights, occasionally they were allowed to express themselves, it was accepted that not every creature believed exactly the same as his prince; there were even one or two restrictions on hunting privileges. In short, here and there a few liberties were conceded to subjects who nevertheless continued to possess the status of slaves. These derogations in no way impinged upon the privileges of the lords or the advantages of their servants. Property was allowed to go to ruin when it served the interests of some higher authority. Subjects were even permitted to leave the country, if the canton or signorial recruitment officers made no objection.

"A man had to be nothing but be capable of doing anything; like an ass, he had to bear, and like the captain's steed, he had to prance. In order to obey blindly, he had to remain as witless as a Polish peasant; in order to pay the *accise* [a tax levied on wine and beer in some northern regions], he had to drink like a fish; in the concert hall he had to sing like a castrato, in the army he had to stand up straight as a phallus. He had not to concern himself with his rights. His knowledge had to embrace all things general, as though his brain were that of a philosopher; but in the particulars of first import to himself, it had to remain as blinkered as that of a German day laborer. . . .

"In most of the states of Europe the clergy had fallen so low that they rejected every request addressed to them; worse, they conspired to smother the truth and prolong the moral servitude of the people; they trucked with pernicious gambling, they nodded at murder. They preached mute and abso-

Johann-Heinrich Pestalozzi (1746–1827), a man of liberty, Swiss educator and promotor of universal education; made an honorary citizen of France by the Legislative Assembly on August 26, 1792, at the proposal of Marie-Joseph Chénier.

lute obedience. They combined the love of God and Christ with the obligation to obey; for 7 kreutzers a day they persuaded people that God expected the same total compliance of them as was exacted by his anointed priests. All demands or even aspirations to liberation must be eschewed, none must seek to escape this abject condition, or free himself from this unnatural slavery, or strive for justice, or cry out for the freedom his fathers had known. . . .

"Why must the truth be silenced? The world is not governed on Christian principles; governments, when governing, are not Christian; and the state, as state, behaves, where its fundamental principles are concerned, in a way that is the very antithesis of Christianism. A Christian army, a Christian battle, Christian chaplains, Christian finances, Christian acts of government, Christian customs barriers, and Christian weights and measures: all to ensure the blind obedience of subjects and inferiors and the incommensurable rights of the lords and powerful, over us, our children, and our children's children; and all these, like the man in the moon, have no reason for being or justification except in the minds of lunatics."

> *Considerations on the Opinion of a Citizen*
> *of Mankind Established in the Greater and*
> *Lesser States of Europe*
> BY A FREE MAN, *February 1793*
> (quoted by Alfred Rufer,
> in *La Suisse et la Révolution française*)

# The Situation
## at the Beginning of This Book

In France, Louis XVI has just turned thirty and is tranquilly presiding over the nobiliary clampdown by means of which families with hereditary privileges have been enabled to monopolize all officers' ranks in the military service, all high church or civil functions, and all real estate. After the failure of the reformers Turgot and Necker, Calonne, the latest minister of finance, is inventing a new form of acrobatics in his efforts to plug the holes in the royal treasury which began to gape so alarmingly during the recent American war.

That has now been won, but England has quickly regained her former strength and prestige. There is talk of coming wars, both in the east, between Russia and Turkey, and in the west, involving Holland. Europe is uneasy. The new American republic is looking for its identity. In both worlds, the Spirit of Enlightenment is becoming more and more firmly entrenched in the emerging classes of the bourgeoisie, which is demanding its place in the sun. The embryonic proletariat in the manufactures is beginning, like the peasants, to hear messages that will precipitate the first working-class uprisings.

Readers are reminded that sums of money have been altered to take into account the differences in the cost and value of goods or products under Louis XVI and today—what one might call the shift in life styles and standards. On the advice of the Duc de Castries, who has studied the question at length and whom I thank for his assistance, I have adopted a coefficient of between 7 and 10, depending on the case, when converting the franc or livre of 1786 to that of 1979.

*Toward the Brink*

# I

## MARCH 1785

### *I Shall Not Sleep at Home This Night*

In those days arrests were fairly discreet affairs, or at least the arrests of people who were likely to cause a scandal—such as Beaumarchais, since his triumph with the *Mariage de Figaro*. Who could have dreamed that less than a year later . . .

. . . On March 7, 1785, he dines at home, in the company of his extensible and ill-defined tribe. His friend (and bookseller, ergo occasional publisher) Nicolas Ruault is there, along with two or three habitués of his table (including Abbé Sabatier de Castres, who sat through the opening performance of the *Mariage* with him), and his inseparable secretary and chum Gudin de la Brenellerie. The honors are agreeably performed by Marie-Thérèse de Willermawlaz, the partner, in every sense of the word, whom he's been "forgetting to marry" for more than ten years, but hope springs eternal, and patience is her cardinal quality anyway. Their daughter Eugénie, already eight, a small person dressed up in tons of petticoats to look like a big one, is also there. Her every whim is indulged, he positively dotes upon her. And Julie de Beaumarchais too, the perfect sister-daughter-mummy. If she never married—but didn't remain a virgin either, that's for sure—it may be because of him. He makes the people who share his board so gay! There's a fullness in being together, a shared smile . . . It's impossible to imagine Beaumarchais alone at a dinner table.

The dishes are choice and the setting superb, between the "Cabinet of Zephyrs," where he planted his bed, and the "Salon de Flora," on the first floor of the "Hôtel of the Ambassadors of Holland."* This level shows you

---

*Which, in all likelihood, was never inhabited by any representative of the Low Countries; it was built a century earlier and rented out in separate apartments, its owners adding glamor to it by this usurped name. The bulk of the house had been leased to Beaumarchais—or rather to

the prettified lair of the author and "Parisian personality." But downstairs you find yourself wandering through a maze of offices and chambers furnished with odds and ends, some of them sublet to other people (Ruault lives there when he feels like it), and vast warehouses containing nothing but cobwebs. Roderigue, Hortalez and Co., which he tried to make into a sort of underground ministry of supplies to the Insurgents, has been losing momentum since the peace (of 1783) and even before it—since his best ships were sunk or captured and the Americans began refusing to pay their debts.

A mixture of intelligent comfort and empty space for hire: a perfect image of the life of Beaumarchais.

On March 7, around nightfall, Gudin relates,

> We were still at table when Commissioner Chenu was announced; the commissioner asked to speak to him privately. Beaumarchais went to his study. We knew that this commissioner was well disposed toward him, yet although the hour was not late this conference worried us; and the longer it lasted the more anxious we became. At last they emerged together. Beaumarchais embraced us; he told us that he was obliged to go out then and possibly spend the night away, begged us not to worry, and said that we should have news of him on the morrow.
>
> Far from allaying our fears, these words only intensified them. We had little doubt that he was being arrested. But why? And where was he being taken? Perhaps to the Bastille![1]

Ruault confirms:

> We were at supper when Chenon* came in with a long face and asked to speak to him in his study. He was not away long. He returned to the room a short while later, asked his wife for his nightcap, two shirts, and his dressing gown, telling us, "I shall not sleep at home this night, and it is by order of the King that I sleep elsewhere. . . ." The commissioner had not told him where he was being taken; we supposed it was to the Bastille, as that was the customary place of punishment for men of letters who displeased the government.[2]

Sangfroid and self-control in the face of adversity are typical of him too. He had them back in the days of his famous censure by the Parlement of Louis XV eleven years before, and his arrest by Maria Theresa in Vienna in 1774. Chin up.

---

"La Maison Roderigue, Hortalez et Cie"—by Le Tellier, an architect, since 1776, for 6,600 livres, or 40,000 modern francs [$10,000], a year.

*Chenon or Chenu? On the assumption that either Gudin or Ruault is a bad speller, we checked through the *Almanach royal,* only to discover that there were one Chenu and two Chenons on the Châtelet payroll.

| | |
|---|---|
| Toujours, toujours, il est toujours le même, | [He is ever and ever, forever the same |
| . . . Le temps sombre ou serein, | . . . Whether the weather be ice or flame, |
| Les jours gras, le carême, | |
| Le matin ou le soir, | Fat days or lean, |
| Dîtes blanc, dîtes noir, | Morning or e'en, |
| Toujours, toujours, il est toujours | Call fame, call shame, He's ever and ever, forever |
| le même.*3 | the same.] |

In this case there is some justification for his serenity. Commissioner Marie-Joseph Chenon, Junior (if it was he), is not just any policeman. The gentlemen in the Châtelet have dispatched a person of tact and sensitivity, one of the ten or twelve officers in the sort of "high-society squad" whose business is to keep tabs on the shenanigans of the aristocrats, and who are instructed to intervene when it is deemed on high that one of them has overstepped the bounds. Years before, for instance, there was de Bruguières, who tracked Mirabeau and Sophie into Holland, and in 1774 there was Inspector Goupil, who trudged up the steep slopes of La Coste to the château of the Marquis de Sade . . . This is a kind of copper who knows how to treat a "customer." Chenon found the words, or half-words, that would prevent Beaumarchais from rousing the neighborhood or frightening the family. But where is he being taken? And, more to the point, what for? Well might he ask, with all the love and money problems he has hanging over his head; is it a creditor's suit, some nobleman's tantrum about the abduction of a chambermaid? And even if it is Louis XVI himself, having a snailfit of temper eight months after allowing the *Mariage* to be performed, where's the harm, who cares, he's only giving Beaumarchais the patina of his century—a few weeks in the Bastille. A new order of chivalry could have been founded on behalf of the authors whose success their kings have certified by stuffing them in the clink.

So, a little dose of the Bastille for Figaro . . . Beaumarchais is almost whistling as he goes, and tosses back a reassuring "See you soon!" to his friends.

He should have known better.

The triumph of the *Mariage de Figaro,* unlike so many others, was not a case of short-lived, soon-forgotten mass hysteria; it has lasted for sixty-eight performances and eight months. Except for a few fleeting moments in Molière's

---

*Beaumarchais himself wrote this song in 1774, when he had been released from his Austrian internment at the behest of Louis XVI and was on his way back to his next round of adventures in France.

day, this is the first time in the history of French theater that genius has been rewarded by success without a time lag. But as Gudin de la Brenellerie* sighs, "The numbskulls who would have burned Molière would also have strangled Beaumarchais with a smile. The same merit engendered the same mutterings. Their tableaus were true: the wicked were outraged."

And when, regretfully, the French Acting Company closes the run on January 10, 1785, to meet its other commitments, the Italians from the boulevard are already rehearsing *Il barbiere di Siviglia,* an opera buffa written in 1782 by Paisiello,† one of the last great Neapolitan composers, who has just spent eight triumphant years in St. Petersburg.

Beaumarchais can't help it if copies of his *Mariage* are sprouting like dandelions: the Société des Auteurs recently founded by himself (and operating only in Paris at this point) is having trouble enough defending its members' profits on their own works. So a *Repentir de Figaro* by somebody named Pariseau was performed at the Ambigu-Comique[4] on June 28, 1784, and an *opéra comique* "combined with arietta and vaudevilles" called *Les Amours de Chérubin* by one Des Fontaines, with a score by a son of Piccini, was acted by the Italians. And a woman called Olympe de Gouges, who "came up" to Paris from Montauban, they say, because she was stage-struck, is rushing through the press a *Mariage inattendu de Chérubin,* a "comedy in three acts and in prose," in time to go on sale at the end of 1785 "in Paris, at Cailleau's and from the novelty-sellers"[5] because she can't get any acting company to take it. For her this is the beginning of a long train of misfortune. Not all the women who fancy themselves playwrights have such strong protectors as Mme de Genlis.** Olympe de Gouges is not the only unlucky one: an anonymous *Mariage de Glogurrio,* a parody of the *Mariage de Figaro,* has just been printed; and the Cailleau person commits a further offense with his *Veuvage de Figaro, ou la fille retrouvée*—which remains equally unperformed.

Beaumarchais doesn't like any of this, but shrugs: it is the price he pays for his success. His play is even being translated "into all languages. It is being

*No mean writer himself, Gudin has left precious *Mémoires inédits* on the life of Beaumarchais, whom he followed like a shadow almost everywhere in the course of his peregrinations, even to England.

†Napoleon's favorite composer under the Empire. Born 1740, died 1816. His *Barber* has been eclipsed by that of Rossini, but nevertheless has some very good features.

**Whose plays, moreover, were virtually never performed, at least in her time, except "in society." We shall meet Olympe de Gouges again; she becomes one of the most interesting female figures of the Revolution, although her only moment of fame comes with the guillotine (during the Terror) and is followed by a century and a half of neglect from historians of all persuasions. This will now cease: Olivier Blanc, a gifted young researcher and journalist, has devoted several years to a fascinating study of Olympe de Gouges, and I thank him for showing me his manuscript.

performed in every theater in Europe."[6] Or almost. Late in 1784, "private" actors were performing some of the twelve (!) German versions[7] for the princes of Liechtenstein, Auersperg, Odescalchi, and the Comte de Fries, but Joseph II had vetoed any official production in his theater.[8] His eyesight's no worse than that of Louis XVI and he's rather better at making up his mind; also, he hasn't had the author and his own family laying siege to him for years. In which of the great homes, one wonders, did Mozart, who's been living in Vienna since 1783 and is now twenty-nine, first see the play? Or perhaps he never did? In any event, his library contained one of the 1785 translations,[9] which proves that Beaumarchais's opus was covering Europe as fast as horses could carry it. "He received some new translation daily," purrs Gudin; "there is one by which he would have been most flattered but which he never saw. . . . It is a translation which some English made into their Hindustani language [*sic*], and I am told that the *Mariage de Figaro* is performed in that language on those same shores where the ancient Greeks went in search of wisdom."[10]

But even if he'd followed Figaro up the Ganges, Beaumarchais would not have been left in peace; sometimes, when the climate remains so relentlessly chilly, nothing scares an intuitive person more than success. Throughout the latter part of 1784, paradoxically, he had been on his guard. At the same time as the *Mariage* was inching the minds of the Parisian petits bourgeois toward a realization that nobiliary privilege was obsolete, it was also provoking wrath and a desire for vengeance among those whom the fifth-act tirade had finally pilloried: "What did you ever do to deserve so much? You gave yourself the trouble to be born and that is all." Hearing it once or twice was quite enough—but sixty times! And hearing it in the streets, skipping from mouth to mouth. His noble friends were cutting him. For once they had been slower on the uptake than their sovereign, they had needed almost a year to see what a load of dynamite Beaumarchais was stocking their cellars with.

The lit. crits. were also slow to get started but, after letting the first wave of acclamation roll off their backs, they began to build up steam in the summer. Beaumarchais heard the wasps buzzing in his ears. "In the past the great have been made to laugh at the expense of the small; this time, on the contrary, it is the small who are made to laugh at the expense of the great, and as the small exist in very considerable numbers there is nothing surprising in this prodigious concourse of spectators of every quality whom Figaro has aroused. They look as though they were coming to seek solace in their misery."[11] That was Métra, and he is almost an accomplice! But Garat: "Although many found Figaro a good comedy, nobody found it a good morality." And Duruflé: "Beaumarchais may be criti-

cizing morals with laughter but the criticism is too strong, for they are
injured. . . ."*

But who launched that flood of "little papers," handouts or tracts we'd call
them, the lines of doggerel drifting down from the flies into balcony and
parquet at the fifth performance?

>      In this shameful play every actor is a vice,
>      Distinctly personified in all its horror . . .

The Parisian whisper was, "That's Suard's work! Suard did it!" Like so
many others, the pedant is making his way into history by mudslinging.

SUARD

# 2

MARCH 1785

## *Let's Club That Mangy Figaro!*

Jean-Baptiste Antoine Suard was born in Besançon in 1732 (the same year as
Beaumarchais) in a sticky, starchy, academic, and therefore right-minded†
circle, and slipped quietly into the front row of armchairs in the Parisian
literary salons of Mme du Deffand, Julie de Lespinasse, and especially Mme
Geoffrin. There he met and flattered a couple of old men who could open the
doors of the century to him—Montesquieu (can you imagine!) and Fontenelle.
He knew English and had produced a few respectable translations; thanks to
him the French of his day could savor Hume or Bolingbroke.

This man, "very tall but slight, weak-voiced, fragile in movement,
spiritual and mild of mien, dressed always in fashion but never ahead of it,"[1]
was obsessed with the idea of immortality, and in his eyes immortality had long
since taken the form of the Académie. Seek and ye shall find. If ever perseverance was rewarded, it was his. He had inched up every ladder, gone through
every ritual. For example, he had posed as a "secular moralist," like Vauve-
nargues but without his genius—it was the latest fad; and he had been en-

---

*Both men were drama critics for the *Variétés Littéraires.*

†Suard's father was secretary of the University of Besançon, so his son could complete his
schooling—including the "humanities"—without leaving the paternal roof. The Suards play a
rather special role on the margins of the Revolution, chiefly during Condorcet's last hours.

dorsed by "forward-looking" people through cautious friendships with Condorcet and the Neckers (although the former loathed the latter). He contrived to stand in the good graces of both princes and court priests—a beanpole balancing act.

At the right moment, marriage settled him on the conformist side of the fence. "Of Mr. Panckoucke's* two sisters, both very young upon their arrival in Paris, only the younger was pretty; she was also the only one to have cultivated her mind to any degree, although exclusively among the books to be found in her own house, which was steeped in the tastes, principles, and reasoning of Fénelon, Massillon. . . ."[2] An ideal morsel for a young scribe who could shine neither too dimly nor too brightly, who would nod diffidently behind the erudite warblings of his pretty little wife and defend, in the proper gazettes, the works published by his Croesus-like father-in-law. The Suards and their "little family," who were capable of putting on Rousseauist airs of devotedness into the bargain (at least in public; Diderot had much to say on the subject), became household names for years to come; taking over from the glorious early salons of impertinence, they offered the end of their century the first salon in which absolutely nothing was said.

Two gems from their biographer (Garat): "Mr. Suard was neither slave nor republican, and like all who meditate or dream he wanted to fashion individuals and peoples in his own image."[3] "By avoiding the opposing extremes of severity and facility, Mr. Suard always proved how much more fertile a wise mind is than an audacious one."[4] Suard was appointed "censor of entertainments" in 1774, when Louis XVI first came to the throne, and the following year he was elected to the Académie. Garat's third gem explains Commissioner Chenon's intrusion into the Beaumarchais family dinner: "Appointed to functions in which it was then so difficult to satisfy all three—authority, audience, and authors—at once, a single voice was raised against him: that of Beaumarchais. Mr. Suard had not approved the *Mariage de Figaro*" in 1782, and apparently had the courage to stick to his guns despite the tidal wave of success in 1784.

He had his reasons: the support of the second "authority" at court, who was no less a person than Monsieur, Comte de Provence.

Monsieur had bought Suard—cheap, with promises and presents befitting the style of the "little family," who lived modestly, being more avid for prestige than for money (another point in their favor in the eyes of the stingiest prince in France). The lines that fluttered down from the flies during that perform ance of the *Mariage* were inspired by Monsieur, who may even have taken a hand in their composition. It was he who suggested that Suard make use of

*This is according to Suard's biographer Garat, his companion critic and platitudinist.

his address welcoming the Comte de Montesquieu into the Académie eight months earlier to spray some acid on the subject of "the relationship between taste and morals" in Beaumarchais's direction. And it was Monsieur who gave Suard the go-ahead to vent four columns of spleen against the *Mariage* in the *Journal de Paris* on February 21, 1785.

What's gotten into Provence? He's no more prudish than the next man, he's got Mme de Balbi just down the hall in the Luxembourg Palace; he's more the agnostic type, indulging in small doses of vaguely risqué Latin verse. And the new theater in which the *Mariage* took the town by storm was known as the Théâtre de Monsieur (now the Odéon).

But these days, as doubts about Louis XVI's ability to stay the course begin to rise, the positions of the various coteries are hardening, and they're starting to resemble so many feudal clans. Are we really going to have pure nothingness, a vacuum on the throne of France for the next fifty years? If Calonne's efforts can't bail out the treasury . . . historians of monarchies know that a palace revolution often "economizes," as they like to call it, the expense of a real one. Louis XVI has two sons, so Provence can hardly hope to sit on the throne himself; but why not a regency that would give him *de facto* power, if he could just get rid of the "Queen's party" that was so libertine and so expensive, with all those Vaudreuils and Coignys in it, and even his own brother, Artois the will-of-the-wisp. This arrangement would also short-circuit the Orléanses, those dynamic second-stringers, because they were a lot lower down in line for the throne, and it would put paid to any hankerings of the Condés, however much they trace their lineage back to St. Louis. The Court of France is becoming like a big recreation field on which a bunch of overgrown boys are playing capture the flag. Back in the days of Henri IV you could lose your princely head if you were on the wrong team.

The leaders were picking their champions: no doubt Monsieur, like everybody else, had thought of Beaumarchais. Maybe that was why the theater was suddenly available. But in this case one good turn did not beget another. Beaumarchais doesn't care for weasels. Sure, he'll sell all right, but not for nothing and not to any buyer. He doesn't fancy Provence and his mixture of cunning, Voltairean piousness, and smutty iciness. The Orléanses look a little shaky. Underneath it all, and down some very twisting byways, it is the Queen whom Figaro's been serving for the last ten years, fraternizing with her gilded gang of scatterbrains. And with every passing year the Queen and Provence drift a little further into enmity, beneath their smiles.

Since February, it's been open warfare. Suard had sailed into the blessed wind exhaled by the new Archbishop of Paris, Antoine-Eléonor-Léon Le Clerc de Juigné (the deliquescent Beaumont having finally expired at almost the same time as Maurepas). His Lenten letter showed no propensity for trifling. "The

Archbishop of Paris promises to be a stern and rigorous prelate. In connection with eggs, the use of which is permitted this Lent,* he bitterly railed in his letter against the corruption of morals, the obscenity of theaters, the proliferation of small entertainments, and the government's tolerance for the propagation of writings which torment the true servants of God."[5] In particular, he mentioned the *Mariage* (no longer running) and threatened to excommunicate the entire population of Paris for going to see it. Suard went him one better, by adopting an ecclesiastical alias and addressing himself to the author of the play in an open letter in the *Journal de Paris:*

> The sound of your name and your successes has reached as far as Les Halles [markets] and the Port Saint-Nicolas.† There is not a single day laborer or laundress of any pretensions but has seen the *Mariage de Figaro* at least once, and culled from it a few witticisms with which they are continually enlivening their conversation. . . . A great many of these good people, who had never even heard of the Théâtre Français, wanted to see your play and, as they understood not a word of it the first time, went back to see it again. . . . The name of Figaro has become immortal in the mouths of the people, like that of Tartuffe in the mouths of people of quality. But Tartuffe is used only to refer to hypocrites, whereas Figaro is applied to every manner of undesirable thing: the name is given to dogs, cats, and coach horses. The other day I heard a chair bearer say, upon seeing a mongrel cur barking at all the passersby, "Let's club that mangy Figaro!"[6]

Suard had the unwitting merit of placing the quarrel of the *Mariage* at its proper level, that of a cultural battle between classes. Figaro made Caliban laugh—a bad sign. As long as the people only growl, they can be muzzled; but when they open their jaws to guffaw . . .

Beaumarchais was a perfect friend, but he never could go halfway with his enemies—another sign of his class "inferiority." People of base extraction could neither accept nor return a blow in moderation, as Goëzman had learned in 1773. This time, too, Pierre-Augustin did not quail before the storm but gave back as good as he got, mainly in the preface to the *Mariage* written ten months after its first performance and still unpublished. In this text, some grit gets mixed with his laughter:

> The author has been uninterruptedly attacked and persecuted with verbal, written, and printed insult. The resources of calumny itself have been exhausted in the attempt to damn me in the minds of all who have any influence upon the citizen's tranquillity in France.** Fortunately, my work is before the eyes of the

*This was an exception, made for 1785 and not repeated until the Revolution.

†First sign of the contempt with which aristocrats—and bourgeois—treated "the dregs of the people"—symbolized by the women of Les Halles and the stevedores—during the Revolution.

**Both "citizen" and "nation," thus, were in current use in 1785.

nation, which, in the past ten months, has seen, judged, and appreciated it. Allowing it to be performed so long as it gave pleasure is the sole vengeance I have permitted myself. I do not write this for those who will read me today; the tale of a woe too well known brings few tears. But in eighty years it will bear fruit. The authors of those days will compare their lot with ours, and our children will learn what it cost to entertain their fathers.[7]

If only the blighter had known enough to enlist the support of a few friendly magistrates. But on March 10, 1784, he had sent a sharp jolt of his pen to the excellent Président du Paty, the most liberal man in Bordeaux, who had asked for a box with a screen in front so that "a mother and her daughters" might see the *Mariage.* Beaumarchais's blood boiled:

> I have no consideration at all, Monsieur le Président, for women who allow themselves to see a play they deem improper but insist that they must see it without being seen. I will have no traffic with such absurdities. I have given my play to the public, to entertain and edify it, and not to afford half-lapsed prudes the pleasure of thinking well of it inside a private box on condition that they may speak ill of it in society. The pleasures of vice and honors of virtue: such is the prudery of this century. There is nothing equivocal about my play; it must be taken as it is or avoided. Please accept my respects; I shall keep my box for myself.*

A man needs to be sure of his reinforcements if he's going to start tilting at windmills like that. And Beaumarchais was mother-naked. But that's how he's always fought his battles—with plenty of friends ready to dump him and no protector he could count on. "I hope, after this declaration, to be left in peace: AND NOW I HAVE DONE."†

That was just the beginning.

Suard, wearing his wall-colored surplice, answered back in the *Journal de Paris.* And Beaumarchais kept on having to "have done." Not react, him? They'd have had to tear out his tongue and his quill both. On March 6, 1785, he sent a counterretort to the poorly disguised priest in a short letter, in which he informed the editors "that he would no longer answer anonymous attacks," and immediately added:

"I have had to overcome lions and tigers to have a play put on the stage; and do you imagine, now that it is a success, that you will reduce me to the

---

*The worst of it was that Beaumarchais thought the world of this little sermon and circulated it—and society thought it was meant for the Duc de Villequier, an uptight old courtier who had just written a letter of complaint to the King.

†Closing sentence of the preface; Beaumarchais's capitals.

status of the Dutch servant girl who must beat the mattress every morning to shake out the vile bugs of the night?"[8]

He thought that would get Antoine Suard out of his hair—instead of which, he's being scalped.

The carved wooden door of the little townhouse with its smiling bas-relief sun and moon closes behind the narrow coupé. Inside, Pierre-Augustin sits alone with the commissioner; their carriage, quickly joined by two more, does not turn left onto the rue des Francs-Bourgeois, where it would reach the Bastille in a few turns of the wheels, but right and then right again, through the Porte Saint-Denis and on into the faubourg, then toils up the hill cluttered with flower and vegetable gardens that was dedicated to St. Lazare.

"Where the devil are you taking me? That is not the way to the Bastille."

"I never said you were being imprisoned in the Bastille, sir. I regret to inform you that my instructions are to remit you to the gentlemen of Saint-Lazare."

Family and friends would soon hear the news. They "secretly had the police carriages followed by a lackey, who came to tell us at one in the morning that his master had gone into Saint-Lazare."[9]

Calm or not, this was a blow. Saint-Lazare! A reform school for harum-scarum pages, Little Red Ridinghoods of the Bois de Versailles whose parents wanted to give them a lesson, a granary for the bad seeds that had been separated from the chaff at birth.

Who on earth told them to put Figaro in a prison for Chérubins?

SAINT-LAZARE

LENOIR

# 3

MARCH 1785

## *Like a Schoolboy*

Who? Why, Louis XVI, that's who. The King, our good King Louis himself gave the order to inflict the absurdity of Saint-Lazare upon Beaumarchais. He did it suddenly, out of the blue, in the evening of March 6; it was one of those brainstorms that hit him after a good meal with plenty of wine. His brother Provence runs him to earth at the gaming table, where Louis XVI never lingers long—not like that other table a few feet away, at which the Queen sometimes wagers the price of a regiment. These "intimate" evenings at Versailles, with a mere twenty or thirty courtiers in attendance, are his brothers' best opportunity for slipping him a word to the wise or begging some favor—one of the advantages of living under the same roof, even a roof as capacious as that of Versailles.

Monsieur reads his brother Beaumarchais's reply, hot off the presses of the *Journal de Paris.* He gives it just the right emphasis in that beautiful resonant voice that the notables will find so attractive when it harangues them. Of the three brothers (and the same is true of the Orléans branch), Provence is the only one who knows how to place his voice. This time, all he has to do is underline two words: "I have had to overcome *lions* and *tigers. . . .*" When Beaumarchais wrote that, he had certainly not been thinking of the royal pair, for the very good reason that the Queen has always been more or less on his side, and as for trying to see Louis XVI as a lion! His real grudge was against lawyers and censors and "authorities" in general. But this year the King's personality is changing: suspicion and outbursts of ill-humor are beginning to corrode his carapace of bonhomie, and the success of the *Mariage* has further shortened his temper. He's cross with himself for not holding out against the play, and cross with Beaumarchais for having achieved such a durable triumph. The lion: why, that's me! He feels almost pleased by this touch of counterflattery.

Then and there, without leaving the gaming table, he scribbles a note to the chief of police ordering him to incarcerate the impudence which he thinks is finally giving him an opening in an act he can construe as incipient lèse majesté. The Comte d'Artois is on the scene, looking a shade embarrassed; but he does manage to spare his "friend" Beaumarchais the worst blow of all, by changing Louis XVI's first destination for him, which was Bicêtre!

"Sire, you do not know what Bicêtre is like! Only scoundrels are imprisoned there."

"Where else should he be imprisoned, then?"

Monsieur intimated that there was an establishment in Paris known as Saint-Lazare, where bad boys were put.

"Fine, let it be Saint-Lazare!"[1]

Having no paper at hand, the King apparently wrote his order to Lenoir on the back of a seven of spades;* in any case, official confirmation does not come until five days after the arrest, in the hand of Breteuil, minister of the King's Household (and whims):†

---

*The card was never found; Nicolas Ruault the bookseller, always well up on the latest gossip, affirmed its existence on March 10.

†This "list of orders," which is all that remains of the documents in the case, was found and published by Manuel, the first revolutionary "administrator" of police, in 1789.

Please find enclosed, Sir [to Lenoir], the orders of the King as required to authorize the capture [*sic*] of the Sieur de Beaumarchais and his detention in Saint-Lazare.

I am, Sir, etc.,

The Baron de Breteuil.[2]

"The lion took his revenge like a rat."*

The bones of Vincent de Paul reposed there, in a silver reliquary behind the high altar of the great Gothic church towering over a group of four-story buildings that were put up without any governing plan or idea a century earlier, on the site "of a former lepers' hospital served by leprous monks,"[3] the lazar-house of St. Ladre—whence its remoteness from Paris and location among the cornfields. "The area of the place is immense; it is the biggest in all the faubourgs," and the church is its only link with the past. With Vincent de Paul as the base, the place became an ecclesiastico-constabulary agglomerate comprising convent, hospital, old-age home, prison, and children's "enclosure."[4] "To dispel the disorder which had become prevalent there [during the Fronde] and in almost every religious community, it was decided to assign the buildings to the respectable Vincent de Paul and the congregation he instituted in 1625,"[5] whose members, since taking possession of the place, have commonly been known as Lazarists; and in 1785 they, with their assorted "boarders,"† are almost its only inhabitants.

Vincent could accordingly be seen all over the church walls, "preaching to the poor of the Hospital of the Name of Jesus, which he had established; instituting the foundlings' home, and blessing the general superiors of the order who succeeded him in this congregation (in the background are the Sisters of Charity, similarly founded by Vincent de Paul)." There are a dozen or so more testimonials in a similar style—diluted Louis XIII with lots of draperies and ecstatic postures—all portraying Vincent, "the galley chaplain."

Less then two centuries after its attribution to the Lazarists, Vincent's dream, the great earthbound ship of peace, had become a very golden galley, "a prison in which priests who had violated the laws of the church were imprisoned [by order of the Archbishop of Paris], together with youths and even men of good family found guilty of libertinage, dissipation, the passion of gambling, or a desire to misally themselves [*sic*]—by order of the *lettre de cachet* [i.e., the King]. . . . But Saint-Lazare was a prison of distinction, accessi-

---

*The expression is used by Frédéric Grendel in his *Beaumarchais* (Flammarion, 1973).

†The official name of the order is "Congrégation des Prêtres de la Mission." The premises occupied an area (in the 10th arrondissement) now circumscribed by the rues du Faubourg Saint-Denis, Poissonnière, de Paradis, and de Dunkerque. No connection with the site of the future Saint-Lazare railway station. The buildings were pillaged and burned in 1789; the prison remained standing and was used for a century more.

ble only to persons of means."[6] And indeed, the inmates paid dearly for the honor of residing in this somewhat irregular hotel:

"The smallest pensions were 600 livres,* for which one got food, light, and bed linen; but the rest of one's expenses, and heat, and medicines had to be paid for by the family. It is true that there were boarders who paid 1,000 or 1,200 livres and received services commensurate with the agreed arrangement." Saint-Lazare was certainly a horse of a very different color from Bicêtre.†

Yes, but even a drunkard from the gutter got a less stinging welcome to Bicêtre than did the gentry interned in Saint-Lazare, where a "flogger father," chosen for his biceps and enthusiasm, administered "a copious thrashing to the fleshy part of their persons; this was deemed to be unparalleled as a means of calming them." Beaumarchais will be wearing his prison halo round his rump**—at least if Louis XVI and Monsieur get their way. There must have been quite a little ripple of amusement at the King's gaming table on March 7.

The next day, the whole town is giggling.

| | |
|---|---|
| Un Lazariste inflexible, | [A Lazarist intransigent, |
| Ennemi de tout repos, | To rest a deadly foe, |
| Prend un instrument terrible | Plies his dreaded instrument |
| Et l'exerce sur son dos, | From nape to very toe, |
| Par ce châtiment horrible | And by this searing punishment |
| Caron est anéanti. . . .[7] | Is Caron [Beaumarchais] now |
| | brought low. . . .] |

Revenge. The kill. For two or three days, people hurl themselves upon Beaumarchais like a pack of hounds; it's as though they are thrown into panic by the smell of humiliation, like horses by the smell of blood. Grimm, licking his lips, gathers up every morsel of insult from the hastily run-off prints and improvised comic turns. But that kind of treatment costs money—it wasn't the ragpickers who were obsessively bawling:

| | |
|---|---|
| Quoi, c'est vous, mon pauvre père, | [Oh father dear, is that you, poor chap, |

---

*Annually, about 4,000 modern francs [$1,000]. The most expensive ones could be twice that amount.

†For 1785, the mission fathers' books record the incarceration of forty-eight individuals, "including twelve children" (age not specified).

**Corporal punishment existed in several other places, in particular the Hôpital des Vénériens (for persons having contracted venereal disease), where patients were given a daily spanking before their dose of mercury, to punish them for having caught syphilis. Caning, etc., was left to the schoolmaster's discretion in most of the "little schools."

| | |
|---|---|
| Dit Figaro ricanant, | Says Figaro between his snickers, |
| Qu'avec grands coups d'étrivières | They're flogging with a stirrup strap |
| On punit comme un enfant! | Like a schoolboy with lowered knickers!] |

Or, even more inspired, and more indicative of what's really bothering them, there's this *Chanson nouvelle,* possibly written by the Duc de Fronsac—a friend of success, i.e., of last summer, who's now eager to have the fact forgotten:

| | |
|---|---|
| Tes bons mots effaçaient les nôtres; | [You were so clever, we looked like fools; |
| Mais, par un trop juste retour, | Still, every dog has its day: |
| On te fait la barbe à ton tour | With us you'd play? Then you must pay, |
| Comme tu la fis à tant d'autres. | Is one of the primary rules.] |

But it isn't quite so simple. Soon something like a shock wave surges back to confound the confounders. Many magistrates, increasingly exasperated by the subservience in which the third estate is being held, raise indignant voices in protest against this new instance of arbitrary procedure. At the Club des Echecs, where a few of them meet for ostensibly peaceful purposes, Duval d'Esprémesnil* is cheered for "having disapproved of this severity. . . . The King strikes but must not stigmatize."[8] La Fayette returns an unpaid bill of exchange to Beaumarchais with the words, "Heaven forbid!"[9]

In the bookshops, the first series of caricatures beget countercaricatures. Whether financed by Beaumarchais's true friends or a spontaneous emission of the presses of underground printers, one of them bearing the date March 1785 on an anonymous engraving shows Beaumarchais being "led into Saint-Lazare by two French guardsmen" beneath the irate headline, "WHAT WE ARE REDUCED TO BY THE ARISTOCRACY."[10] Jean Arnault, a middle-class onlooker, pricks up his ears and later remembers that month: "Everyone felt threatened by Beaumarchais's arrest; it was a menace not only to freedom but also to a man's good name."[11] The March issue of the *Nouvelles à la Main* simply enquires "whether anyone can be assured of sleeping in his bed this night."

Even the people of Paris react—and because of an author? Yes, even the people of Paris, where nobody stirred when Voltaire, Diderot, and the senior Mirabeau were thrown in the Bastille or Vincennes. But there was good

---

*A young lawyer, always eager to lead the field by opposing it.

reason for that: the people of Paris had never heard of them. Beaumarchais, on the other hand, is becoming a symbol.*

Is this something new? On that scale, it certainly is.

Meanwhile, Pierre-Augustin is not yet on the rack, nor, in fact, has he been subjected to the indignity everybody's singing about. In his case there is no flagellation, as he proclaims the moment he gets out of jail and steadfastly maintains thereafter. There is a guardian intercessor, or a mediator at least, watching over him, ready to screen and soften the blows, in the person of Lenoir, that very curious chief of police who did all he could to spare Mirabeau (the son, of course) at Vincennes five years before and who seems to be mellowing like a vintage wine with every passing year. One begins to wonder why Turgot hated him so much and moved him out of the way after the Grain War. There is quite a body of convergent evidence, for his last years in office at any rate, in support of the hypothesis that Lenoir was not a cruel man, at least not to outspoken writers and lawyers.

Gudin, for instance:

> When we learned where Beaumarchais was being detained, we were also informed that he was being accorded unprecedented treatment in that place of desolation. In the chamber assigned to him he found a good fire and a good bed, a servant to wait on him, and an antechamber for his private use. M. Lenoir, lieutenant of police, had come less to interrogate than to comfort him, and asked him no questions at all. He even deigned to transmit three letters which the prisoner had written, one to the minister,† one to the Marquis de La Fayette, and the third to Mme de Beaumarchais,[12]

although that wasn't officially her name at this point, but people wrote it as if it were.

Was it the effect of the letter? Or an approach by Lenoir, after taking the city's pulse? Or the courage of one or two courtiers in the "Queen's party" who remained loyal to Beaumarchais? Or the fear that he might spill a few details concerning his secret missions? Whatever the reason, on March 15 Louis XVI relapses into his jolly-good-(or indifferent)-fellow role and consents to release Pierre-Augustin, who will consequently have served a total of five days' imprisonment in considerable comfort. "The shame of it will be a lesson to him."

*Even back in 1774 his censure by the Parlement of Louis XV had prompted demonstrations of sympathy, but mainly among progressive bourgeois and craftsmen, who were not trying to be heard by the King.

†Breteuil, minister of the King's Household, which included his châteaus for compulsory residence.

People are also beginning to understand that government by fits and starts is another aspect of Louis XVI.

Gudin, Marie-Thérèse, and little Eugénie (accompanied by Commissioner Chenon—another executioner who's fallen in love with his victim) rush off to Saint-Lazare, anticipating a euphoric reunion. They find Beaumarchais metamorphosed.

A five-day growth of beard—he has deliberately refused to shave. He took to his bed on the night of his incarceration and has hardly been out of it since. A man in nightshirt and nightcap, ageless, limp, his cheeks darkened by the incipient beard and his eyes turned inward: Figaro defeated. In this, Louis XVI was right: the humiliation of Saint-Lazare, however symbolic and fleeting, is experienced by Pierre-Augustin as a death wound. His whole life long he has been trying to make people forget that he was born the son of clockmaker Caron. Twelve years ago he served one term in For l'Evêque, the jail for deserters and actors, after a scuffle with a half-mad nobleman, the Duc de Chaulnes. It had cut deep (but that was before the *Barbier* and *Mariage*): "In pursuance of a letter without cachet known as a *lettre de cachet,* and signed Louis, I have since this morning been placed in For l'Evêque,[13] in a room with bare walls where I am given to hope that I shall want for nothing, apart from the essentials. . . . Thus it is that in all well-policed countries those who cannot be charged by justice are harassed by authority." Does that mean that under Louis XVI everything is exactly the same as under Louis XV? All the kicks and slaps received at the hands of the powerful swim up to the surface of the mind of the man they insist upon seeing as a clown. Ten secret missions, a Herculean effort to help the Americans on the sidelines of official French assistance, two plays that can stand up to the centuries—all so that the pulp papers can show him being spanked by some flunkey in the booksellers' windows? And what about his magnificent edition of the works of Voltaire, in the press at Kehl on the other side of the Rhine, where it can be printed without interference on the land of the Grand Duke of Baden, seventy volumes at least: is he going to be stuck with it? And what about the 3 million livres the Americans owe him?*

He wriggles further under the bedclothes.

"Freedom? I refuse it. I did not deserve to lose it. I cannot leave this place until I have been judged and cleared."[14]

Arms are thrown up in despair. Now he's starting to treat the King of France the way he treated the Empress of Austria. The prisoner's revenge! "At

---

*20 million modern francs [$5 million]—if, that is, we take Beaumarchais's word in this complicated affair. The exact amount of his bill to Congress, most of which had been lent to him by financiers or the royal treasury, approaches that figure, and is an indication of the scope of his ambitions as "purveyor of arms" after 1777.

length, we urged him to leave while the gates were still open to him; not to expose himself to the risk of seeing them close upon him again and precipitate a fresh outburst of anger, the effect of which would be to have him transferred to Pierre-en-Scize or the Sainte-Marguerite Islands,* the châteaus of oblivion where the voices of innocence cannot be heard through the walls."

He plays hard to get, you'd think he was demonstrating a scene to his actors, he's talking of nothing less than attacking the King himself, and in the King's courts! His wife and daughter are in tears, Gudin groaning, Chenon threatening . . . Virtually by force, he is "wrapped in his *videchoura*," a Turkish-style dressing gown,[15] and hustled into the carriage. After being arrested with kid gloves, he has to be virtually hauled back to freedom.

And once home, he barricades himself in. On April 2 he writes Louis XVI a letter, a precarious balance of dignity and provocation, complaining of the injury that has been done to him. A stream of unofficial go-betweens are dispatched to soften him, by Lenoir, Vergennes, Calonne, and finally Breteuil himself, his chief persecutor; but he sends them all packing. He demands public reparation, and he obtains the seizure of the engravings depicting his spanking; he neglects all his work for weeks.† He's stopped writing.

He's losing the wit that was the force of his last two plays. Saint-Lazare breaks Beaumarchais. He leafs apathetically through the material for his next play, *Tarare,* a comic opera in which, after calling the tune for an age, he bows to the dance of a day.

*Or any of the twenty-one other state prisons, not counting the Bastille and Vincennes: the Château du Taureau in Brittany, Saumur, Trompette in Bordeaux, the Mont-Saint-Michel, the fortresses of Joux and Brehon, the châteaus of Ham, Bicêtre, Charenton, Angers, Nancy, Rouen, Tanlay, Amboise, Armentières, Lille, Château-Thierry, Romans, Candillac, Pontorson, and Poitiers.

†Basing themselves on Loménie's useful but confused book, most of Beaumarchais's historians have mistakenly claimed that he received full reparation from the Court at once. It is untrue that the ministers attended a performance of the *Mariage* (which was no longer running) in a body (something they never did). As for his invitation to Trianon, where the Queen and princes put on a performance of the *Barbier:* that doesn't take place until five months later. The only immediate compensation he received, in April, was the payment of a substantial amount of money, expedited by Calonne in order to loosen his creditors' grip.

# 4

## MAY 1785

### *Freedom Tower*

Youth dies, in Mme de Sade's household, on May 23, 1785—"Youth" being the Figaro of her husband, Marquis Donatien-Alphonse, prisoner of the state since February 1777.* His real name was Carteron and the alias "La Jeunesse" [youth—*Trans.*] was the nickname customarily assigned to servants and soldiers. He came to work for the Sades in 1772 and seems rapidly to have equaled and then outstripped his predecessor Latour in the practice of that form of sordid but respectful intimacy between master and man which has just been immortalized by Beaumarchais.

Youth doesn't get much chance to share his master's white bread—a bare five years—before having to share the black bread of his mistress in the Convent of Sainte-Aure in Paris, where she becomes a boarder in order to be near her husband and her mother and persecutor, Présidente de Montreuil, after the old lady has finally managed to bury her accursed son-in-law alive. For the last eight years Renée-Pélagie de Sade has been precariously hanging on by the side of a husband whose companion she continues to be now in his hell on earth as she was before in his debauchery, clinging with respectable right-minded bourgeois fidelity, like one bewitched. He has borne her with him beyond all limits, so far beyond that she can't come back. Even so, she still hopes that her presence may one day soften her mother's heart, since it was the Montreuils who obtained the *lettre de cachet* and who could, if they would, have it revoked . . . But for the time being, they won't.

So the marquise almost never returns to the eyrie at La Coste near the foot of the Lubéron, except to pay an occasional call on their friend and helper Gaufridy, the notary of Apt. Penny by penny he gouges her pittance out of the olive trees and the few flocks left on their land. Without that, how could she keep up a decent appearance? She wasn't giving the nuns enough as it was,

---

*His first servant-accomplice was for many years his valet Latour, who was also a participant in his Provençal mischief; but Latour apparently contrived to lose himself shortly before his master's arrest, thereby avoiding an even harsher fate, because he was co-accused and sentenced to death in absentia in "the case of the Marseilles prostitutes."

so they "took away her suite of rooms" in September, "to convert it into cubicles, and gave her other rooms in the attic. A veritable hole. What a mockery for a marquise who has three châteaus which [according to her] are falling into ruins for want of being lived in. Nevertheless, Mme de Sade would undergo ten thousand such vexations if only her husband could have justice."*[1]

In her "hole" she writes to Gaufridy, on May 24, that "poor Youth has died, after an illness lasting six weeks . . ., long and cruel indeed. His palate had to be cut. . . . He went in full possession of his faculties and in a properly religious frame of mind. . . . With all his faults I miss him greatly, for he was attached [sic]. I cannot yet bring myself to replace him, and it will not be an easy matter to do so."[2] Somebody should see about making an inventory of his possessions back at La Coste, and find out how they could be passed on to his children. The sale of the deceased's wardrobe in Paris produces 36 livres.† With rare exceptions, servants own no property. How many of them are there in France—more and more all the time—living this rootless existence? Over a million men and women at any rate, most of whom do not belong to the battalions of the princes and millionaires but form a horde of unattached "Youths" or "Mignonnes" (the name of the Phlipons' maid).

Numbering two, three, or four in the "average households" of the lesser nobility, rising bourgeois, or rich farmers, the "domestics"—boarded, bedded, shod (a semi-luxury in the country), hatted (the gentlemen of the poor), clothed, and laundered—constitute the forgotten class of the age, for the very good reason that there is no structure of solidarity among them. They are a host of solitudes condemned to both subservience and individualism. Some, like Youth, become their masters' intimates and live on the same footing as the old spinster cousin at the far end of the dinner table; and they often know many more secrets.[3] Their wages consist of a more or less regularly paid sum of "pocket money" determined by verbal agreement and varying in relation to the "employer's" fortune.

Employer or owner? The law does not expressly forbid a servant to leave his place (and abundantly permits his master to throw him out whenever he pleases), but the out-of-work domestic is looked upon with suspicion. It's his tough luck if his record book is not filled with glowing testimonials; he can odd-job his way to death in the gutter. If he hangs on and digs into the family of his first place, however (as de Sade's valet with the eloquent nickname did), he will be able to die there, lacking every superfluity but seldom the essentials, and benefiting from the "family security" which holds him up like the rope

---

*According to Gilbert Lély, whose *Vie du marquis de Sade* must be followed like a breviary where Sade's wife is concerned.

†About 250 modern francs [$62].

around a hanged man's neck. By the way, what's happened in the last two years to the 800-odd servants of both sexes whose dismissal was an unavoidable consequence of the Rohan-Guéménée bankruptcy?

Sade hears the news in his chamber in the Bastille, where he was transferred in February 1784, over a year ago, through six feet of snow in the middle of the winter that killed Diderot. The King had finally decided to deconsecrate the prison in the tower in which Mirabeau was recently ground to a pulp, and his compulsory "tenants" at Vincennes have been rehoused in various other establishments. The state-subsidized pensioners in the nearby château had long been complaining of the prisoners' proximity, our daughters can't even look out the windows anymore, although some of them seem to spend the best part of their time standing in front of the window in hopes of a glimpse of the obscene gesticulations of the gallowsbait across the way.

A few can still remember the songs Mirabeau used to bellow for their benefit during his constitutional walks. But now the tower has been opened to the public, who can parade through and be convinced that the King's prisoners are really quite decently treated. The premises are being converted into a "philanthropic bakery" and manufactory of gun hammers.[4] But the police administration is grumbling and hopes to get the tower back again, once the "emollient craze" is over—their prisons in Paris are overflowing.

Meanwhile, Sade is eating better than before, three meals a day, served at seven and eleven in the morning and six in the evening. "Many and copious dishes, palatable wine, although the periodicity* of the menu has a painfully adverse effect upon some imaginations. In fact, the diet in the Bastille may be said to be too succulent for the sedentary and confined lives people are compelled to live there."[5] In Sade's case the grub is paid for by the Montreuils, the people who asked the King for a *lettre de cachet* in order to have him put away. They gladly disburse 800 livres a quarter† to keep their irrepressible son-in-law under lock and key. Do they imagine a diet of fat pork is going to tranquilize him? "Exercise is more essential to me even than food,"[6] and the only exercise he can get is in the evenings** in one of the inner courtyards that divide up the Bastille like a hollow checkerboard, "an enclosed space," he writes, "in which the only air one can breathe smells of guards and kitchens," "a square 32 yards long [according to Linguet] with walls over a hundred feet high that have not a single window in them, so that in reality it is

---

*He means monotony; this optimistic declaration is to be taken with a grain of salt because it was written by Launay, the governor of the Bastille, who is massacred on July 14, 1789.

†Approximately 6,000 modern francs [$1,500].

**Beginning November 24, 1785, Sade is also entitled, occasionally, to "one hour of fresh [?] air in the morning on the towers."

a sort of huge well, unbearably cold in winter because the wind whirls round and round in it, and no better in summer because the air does not circulate and the place becomes a veritable oven in the sun."[7]

Most of the time Sade treads round and round in the cage of "the second freedom"—big joke!—which is the appellation given to the second floor of "freedom tower"; there's no shortage of humor in the King's prisons. Each of the tower's six stories is composed of a single eight-sided room, quite large but higher than it is long, with a brick floor. Three steps in a recess lead up to a window which is always shut behind triple bars. The actual rooms are not too bleak, because prisoners of note may send for their own furniture—whence his bed with green serge curtains, tables with handy drawers, comfortable armchairs, and, on the whitewashed walls, "long and brightly colored hangings."[8]

Sade writes. That's about all he does do. Many creators after him will dream of a Bastille like his, far from creditors and time-wasters . . . But he's in no condition to enjoy it, he's a slow-burning disease. When they locked him up they locked up a living powder keg, a volcano of wrath. The news of Youth's death hits him like another blow from his executioners. There had been a kind of love between the two men, and something of Sade's gift for shattering the molds of morals and language had passed into the writing of this manservant, whom the marquis also nicknamed "le Chevalier Quiros" and whom he had encouraged, with his customary cynicism, to abandon his wife and three children at Langres before leaving the serving woman Gothon at La Coste to languish among her memories of unforgettable nights. Sade kept a handful of letters in which the "Chevalier Quiros" addresses his master in tones that even Figaro would not have dared use with Almaviva. In one letter, for example, he describes his master seated in the stern of a gondola during a trip to Venice,

> Wolfing down food and smoking your pipe like a pirate, giving orders like an admiral. . . . I have heard tell, Sir, that you have been to some pains to learn the art of writing, but I see that it's the same there as with everything else, a swarm of bees seems to have been grazing on your paper; at the very least, if you must compare me to my cousin Don Quixote, then you must also allow me, if you please, to compare you to Sancho, as far as your handwriting is concerned. I know you used to tell me that only underlings should know how to write. No temper, now, above all, no temper. . . .[9]

But he wanted that temper, he was courting it. Sade's withering reply heralded the hatching of one of the greatest French prosaists. Oh delectable wrath! The servant was well served:

> Martin Quiros, you're being cheeky with me, my boy; if I were there I should thrash you, I should rip off that godforsaken *toupet* of yours which you refurbish

every year with hair from the tails of every nag on the road from Courthezon to Paris. . . . Come now, do try to pipe down a little, I implore you, for one wearies of being insulted at such length by riffraff. Verily, I do as the mastiff does; when I see such a pack of mongrel curs and pups yapping at my heels, I lift my leg and piss on their noses.[10]

The only consolation Sade can get is pen in hand; his prison walls recede when he can let off steam like this, and nobody after him will be capable of it for a long time to come. Beaumarchais himself would have been embarrassed:

> You flittery old monkey with the face of a scrub brush smeared with blackberry juice, you prop of Noah's vine, you bone from the spine of Jonah's whale, you old match from a bordello tinderbox, you rancid candle from a four-a-penny packet, you evil-smelling girth strap from the he-donkey of my wife . . ., you aged pumpkin candied in bedbug juice, you third horn on the devil's head, you cod's head stretched like the two ears of an oyster, you fetid bedslipper of a procuress, you hank of rag soiled with the red things of Milli Printemps,* if I had you here, oh how I'd rub your face in it, your dirty baked-apple snout that looks like burning chestnuts. . . .

Donatien-Alphonse will never again have anyone to write to in these tones. The death of Youth wraps him a little more tightly into himself. He's been struggling for over eight years now, in vain. Sixteen months in Vincennes. A crazy escape attempt in July 1778, improvised during a trip to the south where he had been sent to "surrender himself" to the law at Aix-en-Provence. After his death sentence had been commuted to a mere censure, he thought his troubles were at an end. But no matter what the law courts said, the *lettre de cachet* was still there and still in force, so back to Vincennes he was brought. Wild with rage, he escaped from the "convenience" of an inn in Valence and spent forty days on the run before going to stick his neck in the noose at La Coste—at home, out of sheer fecklessness and provocation. There he saw himself "definitively arrested, with a rage, ferocity, brutality, and insolence that would not be employed upon the basest of scoundrels from the dregs of the people,† dragged bound and pinioned through his province and the very places in which his [relative] innocence had just been proclaimed in the decree confirming it."[11]

What's the point? He got another five and a half years of Vincennes ("Well, you can believe me, Mister Quiros,** prison is the monarchy's finest institution"); then there was the squabble through the window with his cousin

---

*A folk expression meaning a sanitary napkin which has just been used.

†His own words, of course; Sade is, as we have already seen, a perfect exponent of the attitudes of his own class.

**From a Niagara of a letter to Youth in January 1780.

Mirabeau; then a fit of jealousy directed against his wife, spread over three months of epistles, based on precious little and stupefying in such a man; and finally, his transfer to the Bastille, where he is now convinced he will die but not before he shouts the towers down.

He returns to his writing table, he clings to it like a shipwrecked man to the mast of his lifeboat. In three months he's going to write *Les Cent Vingt Journées de Sodome, ou l'école de libertinage* ["One hundred and twenty days in Sodom, or the school of libertinage"—*Trans.*].* Four millionaires who have made their fortunes in murder and extortion, as distinguished as they are sordid, assemble a cast of willing or abducted characters in a hidden château in the Black Forest, to engage in a methodical orgy in which six hundred sexual, scatological, and criminal perversions will transcend, page by page, the farthest limits of what can be done and said—well beyond the bounds of contemporary exploration in the field. In the end, thirty people die of lovemaking or torture.

Sadism is born.

BARÈRE

# 5

## MAY 1785

## *The Study of Politics*

On the 14th of that same month of May, 1785, way down in the southwestern part of France, so close to Spain that you hardly know which side of the Pyrenees you're on, an event occurs which is not the fruit of Sade's imagination in one of its wilder moments, although he might have found the situation promising enough—the wedding of a child of twelve with a lawyer almost thirty. Oh, the nasty man! However, the marriage of Bertrand Barère† has

---

*On October 22, 1785, he begins transcribing a clean copy, in microscopic script, onto a role of ultra-thin paper. It takes him twenty evenings. Prisoners of "quality" were allowed to write pretty much what they pleased; even so, a manuscript like this was likely to drag Sade in front of the judges again. In 1789 it is lost to its author forever, and in 1904, mysteriously but unmistakably found by a bibliophile. The complete text was not published until 1931, in Paris.

†Born September 10, 1755, a member of the Constituent Assembly, the Convention, and the An II Committee of Public Safety—the committee of Robespierre, whom he abandons in Thermidor in the nick of time. He plays a leading role on the speaker's platform and in the corridors of revolutionary power.

nothing to do with any perversion except, possibly, money. Through parental intermediaries and other agents, a representative of the solid middle class of the comte of Bigorre has purchased a virgin possessing similar qualifications. From top to bottom of the social ladder the rules of marriage are the same: lord, lawyer, and landsman take a wife as they would choose a chair.

But Catherine-Elisabeth Monde—really, she's only twelve . . .* The folks in Vic-en-Bigorre are used to girls marrying young, but even they will have something to talk about this time, while participating, according to their class, as actor or spectator in the traditional wedding festivities on which both families have spent lavishly.[1]

The mass is celebrated at midnight in the old church of Saint-Martin, illuminated by tapers and lanterns, a sleepless night between two days of partying: that was the custom in the Lavedan, a nine- or ten-league valley following the course of the Gave on the far side of Tarbes toward Spain—a custom which had lately crossed the Adour to invade the country north of the little metropolis of Vic. These people can pay for a bang-up feast, though. The Barère family owns "quite a considerable quantity of noble properties [*sic*] at Anclades near Lourdes† and Vieuzac, where I also [according to Barère] had feudal rights extending to Aisac, Préchac, and Ozouf."[2] "Although this land is surrounded by mountains, it has everything required for life. Above all, there is an abundance of excellent pastureland, thick with animals."[3] Barère has never known need or the shadow of it. For a nickel he'd regard himself as a noble, but in the hearts of the rich bourgeois that nickel is becoming a malignant growth. Bertrand proved that he was not exempt from it a couple of years ago** when he spoke of hereditary titles the way the fox in the fable talks about grapes. He had been asked to give the commemorative oration for one of his seniors in the profession, and hadn't had the stomach to refer to his breeding. "I leave it to the slaves of human vanity who care only for genealogies to speak of the origins of Maître [i.e., Attorney] Furgole. What is nobility, commonalty? What are these vain distinctions between man and man, when knowledge or virtue are at stake? Merit has no need of ancestors."[4]

His child bride is apparently of "higher extraction": "the Mondes and Briquets, allied to the Marmogets, Biezes, and Belocs, belonged to the lesser

---

*Plus nine months and twenty-three days; call it "going on thirteen." She is known as both "Monde" and "de Monde," and so are her father Antoine and her mother Thérèse, depending on whether or not the speaker grants them the courtesy of the particle to which they have absolutely no right.

†Lourdes is the chief town of the Lavedan, but it was demoted after its annexation by the counts of Bigorre who ruled in Tarbes; at this point, all it has left is the pride of its fortress, to which the King occasionally sends a prisoner to rot.

**On September 6, 1783, in a closing speech at the "conference of charity of MM. the advocates of the Parlement of Toulouse," a philanthropic association founded a short time before on his initiative.

nobility of the province.''⁵ It is true that Bertrand's mother was called nothing less than Catalaine Marrast de Neys and descended from the counts of Lavedan, ''but not in such a way that she could boast of it.'' Deeper and stronger were the roots of his paternal grandparents, in the upper strata of the third estate of Bigorre. His father Jean Barère ''would have had no difficulty in proving four quarters* of bourgeoisie.''⁶ An entire network of attorneys, advocates, notaries, and priests for good parishes. The Barères stood for something long before Jean, himself the first counselor to the merchants and municipal magistrates of Tarbes, gave substance to their pretensions in 1776 by acquiring, for 12,000 livres,† the position of King's counselor to the seneschalsy court of Bigorre for his boy Bertrand. The age requirement had to be waived by special dispensation—twenty-seven was the minimum age for the job, and Jean's youngster was only twenty-one. This constituted the scarcely needed inducement to the son to jump the hurdle of fictitious nobility, especially now that Jean had bought the fief of Vieuzac. On his wedding day his son styles himself Barère de Vieuzac, without the slightest authorization but with universal tolerance. Such is the progress of the slow-motion revolution of the third estate, by usurpation of particles and titles. Anyway, when you're on the spot, is there really such a big difference between the ''false'' nobleman and the true? When his father dies Barère will inherit not just a communal flour mill and fulling mill (there is no fortress or big farm at Vieuzac) but also the right to enthrone the village priest, who will in a sense be his local chaplain, Bertrand himself bearing the title of lay abbé** and receiving the collection plates from masses at Ascension, Assumption, All Saints, and Christmas in the box reserved for his family ''in the most honorable and distinguished place,'' where it is sprinkled with holy water before any other. The Barères carry the front poles of the dais in processions and are buried in the choir of the church, in return for which they keep the edifice in good repair and feed its incumbent on the tithes of grain, wine, sheep, hides, etc.⁷ that the parishioners are obliged to furnish annually.

Since 1774 the Barères have been nothing less than lords of Vieuzac; what else could you call them?

In Vic, then, a few leagues to the north, things are done according to the Bigourdine ritual. On May 13 the bride and groom tour the dignitaries of the little town and some of the big farmers in the neighborhood in an ox cart paid for by Elisabeth's parents, polished and repainted for the occasion in the brightest hues and surmounted by a huge spindle and distaff. Behind come the

*Four generations.
†80,000 modern francs [$20,000].
**In other words, chief person of the parish after the priest.

young cousins and friends who went with Bertrand to fetch the little girl in her parents' handsome white house, also newly whitewashed, a large square under a steep-pitched roof. Their arms were loaded with presents from Bertrand, among which he slipped a beautiful doll dressed in yellow satin. They chanted the words of the ritual dialogue, which was centuries old and the same for bourgeois and shepherds, between the suitor's friends on one side and, on the other, the young village women barring the door. In Bigorre you don't just barge into a girl's house. They recited their list of gifts in vain, the door stood fast until the very end:

"The jewels of love I bring to thee, O bride!"

Thereupon the door swings wide and a wild scramble ensues, searching through the house for the bride, who is solemnly hidden in a clothes cupboard during the serenade. The ox cart, already containing her "promised" in black and white belted in red, with a wide-brimmed flat hat on his head, is awaiting her at the door. And then, of course, they have to eat and drink themselves to death everywhere because otherwise the whole town would be offended, and they'll have to do the same tomorrow.[8] In some cases, a midnight mass can be a relief.

No organ, but tambourines and shepherds' horns, the men's choir on the right of the altar alternating with the women standing in the three-pillared Romanesque nave. Latin, incense, and great clusters of lights. In the depths of the spring night, symbolic of the groping adventure of human marriage, Father Jean-Pierre Barère, Bertrand's own younger brother,* leans toward the mature man and the first-communion child at his side and speaks:

*"Ego conjungo vos in matrimonium . . ."*

A roulette-table hush falls and, as the priest's blessing rings out like a croupier's call, two destinies begin to roll along an endless track. In that instant of deep silence, every wedding guest smiles nostalgically over his and her own loves, even the Princesse and Prince de Rohan-Rochefort—lieutenant general of the King's armies for the Béarn†—who have dropped by for the wedding, even the elite from Toulouse, the men of the parlement and the church dignitaries standing before the society of Tarbes ranged in descending sociological strata to the very back of the nave, which is occupied by a mob who speak not French but "a mixture of Catalonian, Provençal, and French,"[9] or so it seems to the superficial ears of outsiders. In fact, three-quarters of the people of the Béarn speak and understand nothing but a mingled offshoot of Basque and Gascon, the Pyrenean idiom so firmly entrenched for centuries that the Estates of the Béarn, which votes the annual tax, still drafts the minutes

---

*He has no others. Another similarity to, or imitation of, nobility: the Barère parents traditionally sent their younger sons into the church so as to leave the elder a clear path to the wig and long gown, there being no hope of the sword.

†A cousin of the Cardinal de Rohan.

of its proceedings in that tongue,[10] and the catechism is taught in it, and actors in the fairground farces perform in it. Any "distinguished" Bigourdans like the Barère family are forced to be bilingual: to the peasants of Vieuzac and Vic it is the ladies and gentlemen who talk peculiarly, some incomprehensible jargon, Latin or French, it's all the same anyway.

The Bigorre is governed by a small minority who, by speaking French, reveal their complicity in the appropriation of land and offices. In this respect, there's not much difference between some of the kingdom's mainland provinces and the Leeward Islands.

Elisabeth is overpowered by her black woolen gown under a lambswool shawl. For her the wedding is a game. Bertrand, on the other hand, is not the life of the party tonight, not his usual vivacious self. Here's another bourgeois who, like Buzot in Caen last year, is the very image of gloom on the day of compulsory joy.

> Not enough attention is paid to the preliminaries to the great events of life; and yet they are warnings given us by Providence, though we seldom heed them, perhaps because we do not perceive them, or because they come too late. In 1785, at the time of my marriage, which was a great family feast in Vic and Tarbes, I went to the altar with my young fiancée in the dead of night; the church was dazzling bright, we were surrounded by a numerous crowd of friends and relatives. A deep sorrow gripped my heart, and when I uttered the solemn *I do*, involuntary tears flowed down my blanched cheeks. Only my mother saw them; after the ceremony she took my hand and pressed it to her breast.
>
> For my mother, whom I cherished more than life, the memory remained a melancholy one; she had a presentiment that I should not be happy in this bond, contracted in the interests of convenience rather than sentiment.[11]

Oh come now! Tomorrow Bertrand will be dancing with the rest. His mother reacts like many another mother-in-law in similar circumstances. She herself married at fourteen, is forty-five today, and imagines herself an old woman because she's "losing" her son. How could she know that she herself will die a year later? It won't be "losing" him that kills her, at any rate, because he remains very much his *maman*'s little boy and speaks of her at every important moment in his life. It was she who chose his name, in honor of St. Bertrand, the great semi-legendary bishop of A.D. 1000 from nearby Comminges. But there was nothing unusual in that; every third boy in this part of the country is named Bertrand.

And his melancholy does not prevent him from meeting the gaze of the rest of the world with "his customary pretty airs of ease and nonchalance, his light and unconstrained ways." "He was tall, slender, and shapely and all his movements, as his attitudes, expressed genuine distinction," according to Félicité de Genlis, in whose drawing room he subsequently makes a few appearances; and his presence does not go unremarked, thanks to a teasing gentleness of expression in the eyes beneath firm brows as black as his hair, a gentleness that contrasts with the ironic line of his mouth. "He is the only man," Félicité writes, "whom I have ever seen arrive from the depths of his province possessing manners and a tone that would have passed muster in the great world or at Court."[12]

Barère himself couldn't agree with her more, and although he may have doubts about happiness, he has none where his person is concerned. "Tone and manners"—that's him.

> I was born in the Pyrenees, that is, the land of freedom: the character of those excellent mountain people . . . , living far removed from the corruption and servitude of capitals and large cities, is formed by love of independence. . . .[13]
>
> In his capacity as counsel-*échevin** for the city of Tarbes, my father distinguished himself defending the rights of the people in the Assembly of the Estates of Bigorre, where he was chairman of the municipal representatives. He was banished by the intrigues of a treasurer of the Estates, whose accounts he wanted to inspect in order to reveal a deficit. A bishop, who was then chairman of the Estates, was an accomplice in this miscarriage of justice. . . .†

There are the grounds for his resentment of the great and powerful, intensified by his pride in a father of Roman stature. As for the matrix of eternal return, "my mother adored me beyond all power of speech, owing, no doubt, to my physical and emotional resemblance to her. She was fifteen when she gave birth to me and when, in my early youth following my return from Toulouse, I would walk out with her to take the waters of Cauterets, Saint-Saveur, and Bagnères, strangers would mistake us for brother and sister."

The reputation of these spas has been mounting for two or three centuries. Back in the days of Henri IV the mountain folk were observed to be "more robust, corpulent and longer-lived than those of the plains, and [were] cured of a number of ailments** without the aid of any physician, simply by drinking and bathing in the hot water of the baths at Bagnères, Cauteretz [*sic*], or Barèges."[14] Now Barère's fellow citizens eagerly await the ten to fifteen thousand wheezers and gaspers who drift in from every part of France

---

*An elected position arising primarily in merchant or craft societies, with a term of office that varied according to the town; beginning in the late Middle Ages, it gradually became widespread. The *échevins* were something like aldermen, with limited powers.

†The "banishment" amounted to no more than Jean Barère's permanent exclusion "from the administration of the town and municipal functions" after 1762. But there was also a *lettre de cachet*, which the chief dignitaries of the Bigorre had extorted from the ineffable Saint-Florentin, future Duc de la Vrillière, who was their patented manufacturer under Louis XV. It was presumably as a retort to this that Jean Barère bought his son's position in the seneschalsy court at such an early age.

**"Paralyses, ulcers, and diseases caused by a cold humor."

during the summer months, and welcome them with a hospitality the zealousness of which may be partly attributable to the fact that the involuntary tourists leave over 100,000 livres* a year in the hands of the "porters, caterers, landlords, and physicians" of the region.[15]

Throughout his life those waters keep running through his head; the most violent tempests fail to part him from them. "For such a region," he writes in the days of his political eclipse, "one can but long to see accomplished one day the projects which have already been proposed [largely by himself] for the improvement of our agriculture and thermal establishments."[16]

He himself, meanwhile, is becoming the wellspring of an unending flood of eloquence.

> As a pupil I was singled out by my rhetorics master [at home], and my father was encouraged to enter me in a literary competition in eloquence and history, so that my dissertation could be dedicated to a Comte de Gontault-Biron, whose only remarkable feature was the name of his forebears, and who was delighted to see his name and titles printed on a Latin dissertation.
>
> I was sent to the renowned law faculty of Toulouse at the age of fifteen. To be admitted I needed a dispensation, as the law required entrants to have passed their sixteenth birthday.

Toulouse—what a platform from which to launch a lawyer! In fact, that's about all it is; the pink city is bursting at the seams from its one and only activity.

> Although no town in the kingdom† is more advantageously situated for commerce than Toulouse, almost none takes place there. The special genius of the inhabitants leads them, if they are prosperous, to acquire some judiciary office or aspire to the *capitoulat;*** thus it is that Toulouse, one of the largest towns of the realm, is one of the poorest and least populous. There are presidial and seneschalsy courts and jurisdictions, a mint, a *généralité,* a parlement and university, but all these fine names bring in no wealth. Its academy is as it was in the days of the troubadours; its [literary] prizes consist of a golden amaranth, a dog-rose,‡ a violet, and a silver marigold.[17]

The local lawyers get plenty of business from defending the members of religious minorities condemned by birth to poverty or humiliation. "The

---

*Not far from 1 million modern francs [$250,000].

†According to Jaucourt, in the *Encyclopédie.*

**The *capitouls* (whose name comes from the fact that they sat in the Capitol) administered the city; they were elected, like *échevins,* but since the time of the Albigensian war their election had to be confirmed by the bishop.

‡The future actor and member of the Convention, Fabre, who comes from Limoux, attaches the name d'Eglantine to his own [*églantine* being the French for dog-rose—*Trans.*] and claims to have won the poetry prize for which the silver dog-rose was awarded.

Dominicans continue to have a monk of their order appointed by the King to the office of inquisitor in Toulouse, because certain emoluments go with the position." When young Barère studied law there it was only ten years since the Protestant Calas, innocent of his son's suicide, had been broken alive upon the wheel by *capitoul*-administered justice outside his own house.

Bertrand had landed in a hornet's nest:

> I came to this town [in 1772] at a time when a despotic minister, Chancellor Maupeou, had just destroyed the last vestiges of public freedom, i.e., the right of remonstrance and the right to register tax laws—rights which chance, far more than the nation's mandate, had granted to the parlements ever since the Bourbon Louis XIII [*sic*] suspended the convening of the Estates-General during the minis- try of the Cardinal de Richelieu. Toulouse was in mourning for its famous parle- ment. . . . My first three years in the town were spent in the center of this concert of hostility toward the despotism of ministers combined with admiration for the courage of the magistrates, defenders of the people's rights.

Barère's youth thus reflected the features of Louis XVI at twenty, when the death of Louis XV and the reinstatement of the parlements had made almost everyone giddy with hope.

During those years he studied "Roman legislation, the decretals,* and French law with the most celebrated professors. . . . I had always passionately loved the noble profession of lawyer." Having stepped straight into the uni- verse of fine speech, finely spoken at the age of twenty and forever after, he is now a fully fledged member of the tribe who will plead for himself and the rest of his species. "I took my oath in the profession on July 8, 1775, in the midst of the celebrations and joy occasioned by the restoration of the Parle- ment. Hatred of despotism was instilled in every young attorney of the day, as though it were a sacred tradition."

He has successfully contrived not to become a full-time magistrate; "I had a natural aversion to the functions of a judge." When are people going to understand that all he wants to do is talk, dispute, argue, express himself? "To avoid being recalled to Tarbes in my capacity as counselor to the seneschalsy court, I accelerated my studies and quickly became involved in a few minor cases." He defended the appeal, in Toulouse, of a poor girl named Catherine Ribes who had killed her own child and been sentenced to death by the seneschalsy court of Limoux, "in pursuance of the pitiless edict handed down by Henri II in a century of religious fanaticism and hypocrisy." In reality, she had thrown the body of a stillborn infant into some water. Barère had only to read the surgeon's report and run to show it to Villars, an eminent professor of anatomy and surgery: "The woman is saved, my friend, she is innocent: her

---

*An anthology of writings by civil and ecclesiastical authorities which constituted the jurisprudence of that time.

child never breathed, it was stillborn! I saw her when she emerged from prison; she came running to thank me. . . . Never in my life have I experienced a pleasure so intense and pure. . . . That settled it: I was a lawyer for life, having enlisted in the honorable ranks of the *chevaliers ès-lois,* who also wage battles, in their own way."*

What with a prod here and a push there, he hasn't wasted his time. He won the Toulouse Académie des Jeux Floraux prize for eloquence, for a eulogy of Louis XII, "the only king whose Institute [*sic*] remained alive, as Mercier said, in the memory of the people," followed by another prize from the Academy of Montauban for a eulogy of the Sully of Louis XII, i.e., the Cardinal d'Amboise. He defended another young woman who had been seduced and abducted in Avignon by one Chevalier Desroys, who now wanted to repudiate her in order to buy a commandership in the Order of Malta. "Desroys was able to arouse all the sons of the *capitouls,* magistrates and old nobles infatuated with their coats of arms, in his defense. It became a case of nobility against commoner, aristocracy against the third estate, and the pride of birth against the useful professions," or at least that's how Barère saw it. He won; the suborning repudiator was convicted of abduction and the marriage lawfully annulled. "After the hearing, the Archbishop de Brienne† had me invited to the archbishopric, where he made me welcome in the most distinguished manner possible and told me I might ask him anything within his power either in the province of Languedoc or in Paris."

Bertrand does not mean to rest on his budding laurels. He wants to divide his time between academy, bar, and Freemasonry, of which Toulouse is a bastion. "The most important of the twelve lodges in the town was the 'Encyclopédique,' most of whose members were lawyers, doctors, or professors. According to their aptitudes, they sat on one or another of the seven committees which studied various questions relating to government, education, philanthropy, propaganda on behalf of [tolerance]. . . . These committees were named after the colors of the prism. Barère was in the violet section."[18] "Every evening we [his best friend, a man named Taverne, and he] prepared excerpts from Tacitus and Montesquieu, di Baccaria** and Machiavelli, Gravina‡ and Bacon. I devoted half of each week to the study of politics. I never foresaw that this career, so arduous and perilous, would one day be my sole passion."

*In passages quoted from Barère's *Mémoires,* I follow him word for word, including his italics (as in *chevaliers ès-lois* ).

†Loménie de Brienne, Archbishop of Toulouse, had great influence in the Assembly of Bishops of France, and was rising in favor at Court.

**The publication in Milan of his famous *Treaty on Offenses and Punishments* had recently mobilized opinion in enlightened Europe against torture and even capital punishment.

‡An Italian jurisconsult and man of letters who died in Rome in 1718.

He may not have foreseen, but he behaves as though he did. Monsignor de Brienne has dangled Paris before his eyes, but for the time being Bertrand Barère will make do with Toulouse. Now he's married. On November 15 he will officially take up his duties at Tarbes, ten years after being appointed to them. He will spend as little time as possible there, shuttling between Tarbes and Toulouse to defend cases and his place in society while keeping his back firmly propped up by the beloved Pyrenees of his childhood. On clear days you can see them from the bridge Mansart built across the Garonne, "one of the handsomest in Europe."[19] A few stages down the road: Toulouse, L'Isle-Jourdain, Gimont, Aubiet, Miélan, Rabastens, Tarbes, and he's home again. He often rides on to Vic-en-Bigorre, where he has left his baby wife to be nursed by his parents-in-law, whom he prudently got to sign a contract undertaking, "should he continue to practice his profession in Toulouse and not reside with them, or his wife either, to pay an annual sum of fifteen hundred livres."* When they were both at Vic, on the other hand, the parents were pledged, "to accommodate and board them and their servants in both sickness and in health, in their own house, at the same kettle and hearth."[20]

BENJAMIN FRANKLIN

# 6

JULY 1785

## *I Took Leave*

Franklin's going. People were beginning to think he was French, even Parisian, he'd been living in Passy so long—almost nine years. It was he who gave Europe its first image of the United States. In the unfocused eyes of the public he is the chief midwife of their birth and the peace of 1783. During the term of his embassy in France he will have seen the deaths of Voltaire, Rousseau, d'Alembert, and Diderot; and to those who are agitatedly seeking a guide to lead them through the fog of these new times, Franklin's departure seems almost like the second death of those other four giants. The eighteenth century's last agent provocateur is going home to end his days in his lair.

One more octogenarian (less a year) having a brush with suicide by traveling in a perilous state of health; and yet he witnessed Voltaire's self-

---

*10,000 modern francs [$2,500].

destruction in 1778, and blamed him for it, back in the days when he himself was still bathing in the Seine and could, with a little effort, believe he was yet in his prime.

But now fatigue and lack of exercise have turned him into an atoll of drollery beaten by seas of trouble. He doesn't leave his house these days, not even in a carriage, because his poor bladder, tortured by a stone for the last three years, can't take any more jolts and jars. He's drinking less wine, too— but more tea. When he does emerge from the Hôtel de Valentinois, part of which has been lent to him by the wealthy Le Ray de Chaumont, to call on his favorite neighbors, the Brillons, another family of villa-owning lordlings in Passy, the miniature Capua climbing up one bank of the Seine, he no longer even tries to stretch his legs on the "fine flight of a hundred and fifty steps which lead from the terrace down to the lawn. . . . You have sat on the terrace, praised the fine view, and looked at the beauties of the gardens below; but you have never stirred a step to descend and walk about in them. On the contrary, you call for tea and the chessboard,"*[1] which has become so exclusively the royal alibi for his protracted immobility that he has written a treatise on *The Morals of Chess.* † The other day he was reminded of an old song from his youth in Philadelphia (he always has a headful of songs), when he hoped to achieve complete mastery over his passions and suffer from neither gout nor bladder stones. "But what signifies our wishing? Things happen, after all, as they will happen. I now find at fourscore that the three contraries [to the wishes of his youth] have befallen me, being subject to the gout and the stone and not yet being master of all my passions. Like the proud girl in my country who wished and resolved not to marry a parson nor a Presbyterian nor an Irishman and at length found herself married to an Irish Presbyterian parson."[2]

The Citizen of Two Worlds, having come into that limpid shadow-sculpting light of the sun setting over broad rivers, is well aware that he has just enough time left to decide in which of his worlds he wants to die. A few more months and travel will become an impossibility. Which will it be, the Old or the New? France or America? Paris or Philadelphia? Having been mummified alive in his homeland of the last ten years, he already feels himself a prisoner "of the verdant gardens and tenderness of his French friends." To die a Parisian, all he needs to do is let go.

But he's been badgering Congress with his requests to be recalled, especially since Thomas Jefferson has arrived as the new "ordinary" ambassador of the United States, making Franklin an increasingly "extraordinary" one, and you can say that again; in other words, he has nothing more to do. Not

*Text by Franklin, writing about himself in the second person.

†Printed for a few friends on his private presses around 1779, *The Morals of Chess* is first published in Philadelphia in 1786 in the *Columbian Magazine,* before being translated into several languages; it is consulted until this day by practitioners of the sport, as they like to call it.

that he's bored—he's incapable of that. But from the depths of his hardworking past a sort of remorse has been clawing at his heart, a desire to make himself useful again. Back there they are hard at it, building the first modern democracy. And there is the pull of his roots too. And the ship's bells in the mist. His nomad side is awakening. And then, there's his eternal need to do the opposite of what people want him to do.

"At your age, in your condition, really now, you could not even tolerate the post!"

In the end, they make him want to prove them wrong, and thus to embark upon one last long voyage before the inevitable, ultimate one.

On May 2, 1785, the letter from Congress arrives that gives him his freedom. Ten years before he had sneaked out of London on his grandson's arm, to face the perils of the sea and a war of independence that was off to a bad start. At eighty, in contrast, he will travel like a prince. He'll have to waste a little time pacifying his friends, yes, yes, I promise to stop on the road and turn back if I am feeling really unwell, and first I shall cross the Channel to try out my old body at sea. All the of-course-it-wills, indeed-I-won'ts, the lies that take the edge off final partings. Meanwhile, he supervises the preparation of his belongings. So many gifts, so many books given or bought, and such lovely furniture, and physics instruments, and paintings—he who had come ashore at Quiberon with nothing but the shirt on his back! And he doesn't want to leave his wine cellar behind, because where will he ever find Burgundy like that again? Notwithstanding the sour comments of the puritan John Adams, he has managed to invest his salary and indemnities wisely without yielding to corruption. Like so many men with deprived childhoods, Franklin has never been one to sneer at earthly possessions; when he turned poor again, it was to indulge his sense of honor and for as short a time as possible.

He finally assembles 128 crates and a portrait of Louis XVI set with 408 diamonds, which the King sends on the eve of his departure.* The baggage is to go down the Seine in barges before being embarked directly at Le Havre for Philadelphia. Vergennes and Castries offer one of the King's frigates as a conveyance for the most cumbersome item of all—Franklin's heavy, pain-racked body; but Franklin says no. He sticks to his idea of a trial run across the Channel, which will enable him to breathe a little more of the air of that England he has decried so fiercely, as is often the way with people and things one has too much loved. He will also see the Comte de Mirabeau, an odd fellow whose hired pen is producing a pamphlet for him against the Order of

---

*Such "little gifts" were presented as a conventional courtesy to every ambassador leaving a court—unless there had been a quarrel. Their value, however, was proportional to the diplomat's personality and the size of the mark of esteem the host country wanted to show him.

the Cincinnati, which was attempting to sow the seeds of hereditary nobility in the United States. It is a better pleasure for that pure scion of the aristocracy, now vegetating in London for want of funds in France, to take up the cudgels against the very concept of aristocracy.

Then, on July 12, "I took leave of the Court and my friends and set out on my return home, leaving Passy with my two grandsons* at 4 P.M.; arrived about eight o'clock at St. Germain."[3] A cautious little earthbound hop around Paris by the west, through the Bois de Boulogne and Saint-Germain. Franklin has put a toe in the water and decides it's not too cold: "I found that the motion of the litter, lent me by the Duke of Coigny, did not much incommode me. It was one of the Queen's,† carried by two very large mules, the muleteer riding another; M. Le Veillard and my children in a carriage. We drank tea and went early to bed."

He travels like Richelieu before him, half-reclining on mountains of pillows in a large painted wooden box in which he can sleep or dream as he pleases to the measured pace of the mules, protected by a complicated system of springs designed to digest the acidities of the road. By Saint-Germain the worst is almost over—the wrench, the amputation of the heart to which an old man of long experience is almost inured. He has peeled away his second skin of friends, the cortege of adorers who followed him through the Bois de Boulogne, mobilizing the village men to cheer and their womenfolk to weep as he passes. In Passy Mme Helvétius, his chaste vamp, has already begun to write him a real love letter—now that he's safely out of sight; it's always the way: "I see you in your litter, every step taking you further from us." . . .

"It is no one's fault but yours, Madame, if things did not turn out otherwise,"[4] is the sharp retort of Franklin's last French lady friend, Mme Brillon, the pretty wife of the neighbor with the great garden staircase. She's still ravishing to look at, married to a man old enough to be her father and almost in love with Franklin, who is old enough to be her grandfather. Caroline Brillon couldn't even face the idea of saying good-bye to him. Two days before she wrote, "All the days of my life I shall remember that a great man, a sage, wished to be my friend," and not platonic either. It was a close shave some afternoons, during those long tea parties in the gardens when the husband was

---

*William Temple, the natural child of Franklin's only son by a Miss Temple, who had been adopted by his grandfather and accompanied him everywhere these last ten years; and Benjamin Bache, the son of one of Franklin's daughters who had married and stayed behind in Pennsylvania. Benjamin Bache, less than twenty years old, had been sent to his grandfather for a taste of the Paris air; hardworking and diligent, he has just learned, like Franklin, the printer's trade in Didot's handsome workshop in Paris. As for William Temple, nicknamed "Franklinet" by the Parisians, he has become a young "red-heel" (fop) and sires in due course a natural child of his own, by a Mademoiselle Caillot.

†In his capacity as *grand-écuyer* the Duc de Coigny, father of the marquis on whom the Queen was showering so many favors, had free run of the King's stables and carriages.

going about his business. Once again, it was not Franklin's fault if things didn't quite . . .

She tried to gain time without entirely compromising the future, by referring him to a better world:

"In Paradise* we shall be reunited, never to leave each other again. We shall there live on roast apples only; the music will be made up of Scotch airs; all parties will be given over to chess. . . ."

This tableau was not quite enough for him:

"The idea of an eternity in which I shall be favored with no more than permission to kiss your hands, or sometimes your cheeks, and to pass two or three hours in your sweet society on Wednesdays and Saturdays, is frightful."

She, however, prudently stuck to the Beyond:

"I give you my word of honor that I will become your wife in Paradise, on condition, however, that you do not make too many conquests among the heavenly maidens while you are waiting for me. I want a faithful husband when I take one for eternity."[5]

Perhaps the patriarch's stately withdrawal is not unmixed with the relief of escape . . . God keep you, complicated Frenchwomen!

July 13. Emboldened, they cover four or five leagues of a road that flirts along the loops of the Seine. They lunch in an inn at Meulan, at the end of the long nine-arched stone bridge. This is real country; Paris is a world away. "A messenger from the Cardinal de La Rochefoucauld meets us there, with an invitation to stop at his house at Gaillon the next day, acquainting us at the same time that he would take no excuses. . . . We consented. Lodged at Mantes," in the shadow of the towers of another Notre Dame built in one short stretch in the twelfth century, girt with a range of big gargoyles at the base of two towers that soar almost as high as those in Paris. "Found myself very little fatigued with the day's journey."

July 14. Off at dawn, traveling before and after the heat of the day. They sit down to "breakfast"—four courses—at Vernon where "the French navy can command incorruptible stores [of wheat] in a great flour mill" creaking and hanging crookedly over the river with "its four mills on boats, and the mill race tearing at the piers of the bridge like a mountain torrent."[6] The people around here are protected from famine in the event of a bad harvest "thanks to the mill's storehouses, which contain enough to feed 20,000 mouths for three months." Then a long nap—you know what you're in for when you call on a prince, and what a prince! The Cardinal-Archbishop of Rouen in his Norman Versailles . . . "Arrived at the cardinal's without dining, about six in the afternoon."

But when Franklin's caravan reaches Gaillon, more or less level with

---

*Excerpts from letters exchanged by Mme Brillon and Franklin.

Louviers on the west and the Andelys on the northeast, and almost a league from the Seine, which still bathes the countryside in fresh bright green here, even in mid-July, he is much farther from Rouen than Versailles is from Paris. What beautiful trees, what plump herds of cattle, and the smell of new-mown hay! Freshly painted barriers, well-combed meadows, well-beaten paths, and farmhouses with well-maintained thatch all bespeak a great estate.

Then, on the side of a wide hill, crowds of yokels standing with hat in hand, scurrying footmen in livery, senior servants garbed in black. "One enters this château* by a large courtyard leading to another and still larger, square one, in the middle of which is a splendid fountain. The château is formed of four wings of buildings and has a flanked chapel in one of the corner angles."[7]

At the foot of the ceremonial staircase, shrouded in purple and the ribbons of the great orders, a stately sixty-year-old conjugates and declines the ritual of lordly welcome as perfected by three centuries of training. François-Philippe de La Rochefoucauld, Archbishop of Rouen since 1759, is the chief scion of a family whose members are princes, of church or sword, from the womb. At this moment one La Rochefoucauld is Bishop of Bourges, another of Beauvais, and a third of Saintes.† The family is one of the best organized in France, as far as the rapid accumulation of real estate is concerned. Saint-Simon observed many years before that

> the Ducs de La Rochefoucauld were long accustomed to prefer a single successor, who would inherit all the property and fortune of the father; they married neither the daughters nor the younger sons (whom they accounted as nothing) and cast them all to Malta or the church. . . . The second Duc de La Rochefoucauld, who played such a part in the troubles under Louis XIV and was so renowned for his wit [one should hope so; he was the author of the *Maximes*], had five sons and three daughters. Three of the four younger sons were Knights of Malta and the fourth a priest, but all four had numerous abbeys. The three daughters died sibyls** in the corner of the La Rochefoucauld house to which they had been relegated.[8]

And that is how one noble family tribe can spread like an oil slick from the Charentes to Normandy, taking in the Île-de-France and Paris on the

---

*Built by the Cardinal d'Amboise, a powerful minister of state under Louis XII and an Archbishop of Rouen who left a deep mark upon that city, the château was further enlarged and embellished by Nicolas Colbert, another Archbishop of Rouen by virtue of the influence of his uncle, the famous minister of Louis XIV. The château was partly destroyed in the Revolution before serving as a prison in the nineteenth century.

†The last two are brothers; they are massacred in the prison of Carmes in September 1792. We will meet their cousin the Archbishop of Rouen again, at the Estates-General; he emigrates.

**From the name of the prophetesses of ancient Greece; "a woman who grows old without marrying" (Littré).

way,* thanks to the system of compulsory celibacy. Those who were sacrificed
—the men at least—could find consolation in power and opulence. The family
bishops, and especially this one, ruled over more land than most of the peers
of the realm. Franklin's a long way from his Pennsylvania Quakers here.

What's the attraction for him in this meeting? A touch of snobbery? The
study of a human phenomenon in total contradiction to his philosophy? For
him every experience is worth having; he proceeds, as through a zoo, while
the archbishop shows him

> the two great ceremonial suites of rooms one above the other, the lower of the
> two being composed of several large rooms, a gallery at the end facing the
> orangery, and a colonnade which is a sort of open salon. Above it, at the end of
> the gallery corresponding to the one below, is one of the most beautiful salons,
> from which one enters the hothouse leading in turn straight to a flower bed.
> . . . The orangery is in the shape of an amphitheater and one may see over three
> hundred orange trees in it. . . . The grounds, of 800 arpents,† are divided by an
> infinity of roads. . . . The view from the château is one of the finest in France:
> from the four galleries of the corridor one can see more than two leagues of
> country. On the right there are slopes covered with vineyards and small woods,
> and on the left is the river Seine, which winds back and forth and looks rather
> like a large canal that nature has made expressly to embellish the château.

This hierarchized kingdom, its blood sucked for centuries by a few dozen
families, gave the pioneer of the great Republic a last symbolic vision in which
the very river was tamed. He doesn't linger over it. "We supped early. We
were allowed to go early to bed, on account of our intention to depart early
in the morning. The cardinal pressed us to stay another day with him; offering
to amuse us with hunting in his park," where the game, at his mercy and no
one else's, possessed "a special flavor famous throughout the region." He
doesn't know that Franklin hasn't shot so much as a rabbit for fifty years. But
they could not lose a day and risk coming late to Le Havre. Nevertheless, "the
entertainment was kind and cheerful."

Benjamin never says quite all he thinks; but he must have had to answer
the queries of the noble archbishop. What France are you leaving behind you,
Mr. Franklin?

*Already in these volumes there have been La Rochefoucaulds from the Angoumois (in
connection with Jacques Roux) and from La Roche-Guyon in Normandy (in connection with
Alexandre de Beauharnais); a La Rochefoucauld-Liancourt witnessed Louis XV's death, and the
Duc de La Rochefoucauld-d'Enville is a friend of Franklin and will play a part in the Revolution.
†About 1,000 acres.

# 7

## MARCH–JULY 1785

## *White Bread That Made Our Mouths Water*

Lord, but it's hot! The Frenchmen Mr. Franklin is leaving behind him, at any rate, are being parched by a spring drought so long and fierce that the oldest inhabitants cannot remember its like, although Paris itself is nothing but one long party, from Carnival to Easter to the Queen's churching after the birth of her second male child.* Never, no doubt, have the "little people" of Paris been so much in harmony with the highest lady of the land, sharing her attitude of life's-such-a-ball-who-cares-what-it's-all-about, in defiance of the gods of drought and dullness.

> For the last few days† we have been in the throes of the most brilliant festivities. Both God and man could find pleasant enough ways of making us pass the time, if only we had a drop of water to slake our thirst. A few cross-minded bigots are criticizing Marie Antoinette for forsaking Sainte-Geneviève** for the Opéra. These upstart malcontents pretend that this is what has held back the clouds that would otherwise have burst upon our dry and burning land—as though it were not perfectly natural for a young woman who is bored almost all year long at her Court to seek a little distraction and enjoyment when the opportunity arises! To the profane among us this is proof that she has not yet become pious. For a time, people in Paris believed that Her Majesty's prayers to the patron saint of idlers, combined with those of the holy monks who serve and minister to her, would bring us the health-giving rain we have so long been awaiting; large, heavy clouds were drifting over the town, people were drinking them in with eye and mouth, but the wind carried them afar.[1]

At the other extremity of what is commonly called the "social ladder," almost the bottom rung, a little villein of eight similarly finds what distraction she can during the great drought of 1785. To escape from her boarding school and

*The Duc de Normandie, future Louis XVII.
†From Ruault's diary for May 26, 1785.
**The future Pantheon; the huge church was still unfinished, but the Queen visited it to pay homage to the patron saint of Paris.

get back home to her family, Marie-Victoire Monnard* hitches a ride from a religious procession. She was asking for a good hiding, and all she gets in the way of freedom is the right to stay tied to her mother's apron strings for a long time to come.†

Her father had put her to board "with Madame [illegible] at Verneuil," two leagues from home, i.e., in another world, light-years away from her tiny legs in their wooden clogs. She doesn't own any real shoes anymore; the great luxury of her seventh year, "my shoes with the beautiful silver buckles on them that all the little girls who saw them longed to have,"[2] were stolen from her by a brat of her own age one day when in defiance of her mother's prohibition, they hid in a cart under a big walnut tree to "see the pig's throat cut."

It was "almost immediately after this incident" that she had been sent to Madame X, "who had five or six boarders and as many day pupils" in one of that pullulation of "little schools," the only form of primary education existing in those days, where anybody could teach anybody provided they had the backing of the parish priest.

I stayed there eight months, at the end of which I had learned nothing. I was dying of boredom in that house and to round off my torment I was given eight lines of the *Civilité puérile et honnête*** to learn by heart. I had to recite them the next evening after a procession which I was supposed to attend and which was to go toward Creil, and if I didn't I would get a beating. The procession gave me the idea of escaping from my boarding school. I went to bed but not to sleep, worked out my plans, and made up my mind to carry them out. When the procession that was to go toward Creil stopped before turning back in this direction, I would hide in a ditch or behind a tree.

There are many people at these religious prayers asking God to make the rain fall when it is too dry; it was one of those that was to take place on this occasion.

I supposed that my schoolmistress, with her eyes on her book, would not see that one of her pupils was missing. Delighted with my resolution, I set out with the mistress and my fellow pupils, determined not to come back with them. On the way I prayed to God and the Holy Virgin to make my plan work. My prayers weren't long because I have never been able to learn anything by heart; but I do

---

*Born at Creil on October 4, 1777, the daughter of Jean Monnard, a small farmer in Vaux (an outlying hamlet of Creil), and Marie-Geneviève-Victoire Jourdain. Baptized the 6th of the month in the "royal and collegial church of Saint-Evremond of Creil."

†The tale of her escape and return home has been taken from the sixty-page handwritten notebook in which the young peasant woman, whom we meet in Paris during the Revolution, pours out the story of her life without the assistance of either spelling or punctuation, both of which have been inserted here.

**A general title for all the textbooks of good conduct—anonymous civil catechisms of sorts, like religious manuals—that had been circulating since the sixteenth century. They were printed in "civility" type resembling the round cursive script taught to children.

have a memory for what I feel; whatever is natural and goes to the heart strikes my imagination so that I cannot get rid of it again. I am not patient and maybe lack understanding to make stick in my head what is agreed between men when I don't understand it; but if I read or see something done I never forget.

No, she doesn't forget the essentials; even at night her head is full of her fair town of Creil, one thousand inhabitants if you please, "in a most pleasant site on the left bank of the Oise, on the road between Senlis and Beauvais, some ten leagues from Paris"; and the bridge over the Oise, "most singular in construction, the view from which is highly picturesque," especially when you're "in the middle of the river, on a delightful little island where you can see the ruins of quite a formidable château. . . . In the fourteenth century one of those vultures that used to be called lords had its lair there, and from it would send out detachments of men to loot the travelers in the plains,"[3] but in 1567 the "Calvinists" burned everything, including the venerable relics of St. Evremond, patron saint and Bishop of Creil, whose skull alone was saved . . . thanks to six canons of the collegiate church, "who hid it so well that it was never found again afterwards."

These were the bedtime stories of her childhood, with its terror of the werewolf that emerged from the forest of Compiègne every Advent and came prowling around to carry off little girls who did not obey their parents, and "the band of Cartouche, of whom we had heard tell so many times."* Her childhood was the typical one of an eldest daughter of a peasant who was skillful enough to make his land work for him but not rich enough to own it.

> My father and mother worked hard and were not happy. Everything was hardship for them in their lives; the land belonging to the farm was poor and my father too good a farmer not to improve it. He spent money so that it would produce more, but spending money on land that is only leasehold means ruining oneself and enriching the landlord; and that is what happened. Again he lost his horses from a sickness called glanders and the year after that his flock of sheep was taken off by another called *claviot*. He had all these losses in the first seven years after he set up as a farmer, but he became rich in progeny because he also had five children.

Five, at least, who managed to survive and could work. Marie-Victoire's family, like that of the Restifs out in the Morvan, was a kid factory. "My mother had, including me, eight girls, one after the other; a boy came ninth and then five more girls and another boy, which meant they had fifteen children in seventeen years of married life. Eight was the most we ever were

---

*Louis-Dominique, alias Cartouche, was broken on the rack in Paris in 1721, after leading one of the gangs of starving layabouts who were looting the countryside. Marie-Victoire's upbringing seems to have transformed Cartouche into another werewolf.

alive at one time," all kept firmly in line by the father—he's not the one she wants to go home to. He has already punished her once for skipping school and she is not about to forget it:

> When he came in my father asked me where I had been to school the day before. Before I had time to answer he had already pulled up my skirts and was whipping me, so hard that I thought he would beat my behind off. I thought it would be better to be eaten by a wolf than get another punishment like that. The reason he gave for it was that a child who dissembles or lies will surely turn into the antiphon of a thief [sic]. From that time on I feared him like lightning and never told him a lie or disobeyed. His will was law to me; he had only to make one sign or gesture and I would do what was wanted instantly.
>
> It was not the same with my mother.* When she ordered me to do something I didn't fancy I would run away, and she would run after me like a little girl, and say, "I'll tell your father."

However, it's the tale-telling but beloved mother, and the little sister Angélique who is disabled because she fell "in the huge boiling hot cauldron full of potatoes† that we cooked to feed the pigs," and the farmyard full of feathers and cackling, and the fairs at Creil that turned the town into a proper little Paris with all the noise and people, the horses shod outdoors and the stalls hawking gleaming porcelain from the new factory, and the bigarreau cherries of Mme Honoré Saint-Homère that she bought with 2 sols stolen from the mantelpiece at home: it's all of them that are pulling Marie-Victoire away from Verneuil, where there's nothing but fields and houses built above the terrifying underground passages of the château destroyed by some fearsome ogre.

> So I followed the procession, looking ahead to see if I could make out the Creil church tower, which should give me the direction to take in order to reach Vaux, when all of a sudden I heard a whisper:
> "The clergy of Creil are coming this way."
> "There's a bit of luck!" I exclaimed, "I'll go back with them."
> It was excessively hot and then, in 1785, it was the custom for great numbers of parishioners from each place to go out to the fields with the priests, to pray and call upon the Supreme Being to do them the grace to suspend the ardor of the sun's rays that were drying out the earth and causing fears for the harvest. To make my happiness complete, the two processions joined and the priests paused for a station; all the parishioners mixed together, and when they separated each person followed his own cross and banner. I went off with the ones from Creil, who would pass by Vaux on their way back, and I let the procession from Verneuil go its way, often looking behind me to see if anyone was leaving it and coming to fetch me back. When I was reassured enough not to have any more fears on

---

*Who was eighteen when Marie-Victoire was born; her father was twenty-five.

†A novelty; potatoes were just beginning to make their way, via Germany, into the peasant life of northern and eastern France.

that account, another worry arose: how would I go about getting into my mother's house and what would I tell her? I would tell her that I made a mistake when I followed the cross of Creil, taking it for the cross of Verneuil. When I reached home my heart was thumping with fear of being scolded by my parents for my escapade; but the pleasure of seeing them again outweighed my terrors, and I entered the farm. My father, whom I feared most, was away; my mother was delighted to see me. I told her my story and she repeated it to my father, who was very displeased that the mistress of the boarding school did not keep better watch over her pupils. It was decided that I should not go back to her. I was overjoyed at this and was kind and nice to my mother for a while, so that she would keep me; and she did.

For at least one little girl in all of heat-prostrated France, the drought was a good thing. Marie-Victoire thought she was as happy as Marie Antoinette, although her life was not going to be that of a queen:

My father's lease on the farm was expiring and we went to live in Creil. Three horses and a very few other animals were all he had left. He rented a little land, farmed it, and carried wood and other goods for the public. How many times I saw him set out for Paris at nine in the evening, and in the harshest weather, driving his cart laden with flour! I was very young but even so I felt a secret pain in the depths of my heart, to see how hard he worked to keep us; which did not prevent my sisters and me from stealing bits of old iron, which we traded for an equal weight of sweet cherries. My sister Angélique ate the proceeds of the stolen iron along with the rest of us, but that didn't stop her from telling on us, and my mother put an end to our thievery by locking up the iron.

We only went to school in the winter;* during the summer all the children of the small farmers worked in the fields, so they had time to forget what they learned during the rainy season; they were not given what is called a careful education. It cost six sols a month for each of us.

Our parents did all they could, each in his way, to make the most of what they had. My mother had the idea of selling her cows' milk, thinking to get more for it that way than if she made it into butter. She bought us each a jug that held twelve sols' worth and a cup to measure it out with. I was to carry my jug around one side of town and my sister the other; we set out, going from door to door, asking who wanted to buy any milk.

We lived in a sort of cul-de-sac. Across from us were people who had young ladies eighteen to twenty years old, and we went to pay calls on them. They ate white bread that made our mouths water.[4]

---

*The parish school of Saint-Evremond at Creil, kept by a "master" under the supervision of the parish priest. Parents were asked to pay the equivalent of 2 modern francs [50 cents] per child per month.

# 8

MARCH–JULY 1785

## The Policy of Tyranny and Commerce

Franklin's convoy is hauling four or five "dress trunks," as they were then called, full of manuscripts and first drafts, scraps of paper plowed to the corners by the furrows of his careful handwriting, readable despite the thick strokes of his goose-quill pen. The lines slant slightly downwards to the right, showing mild pessimism, and the letters are firmly attached to each other within the words, indicating a deductive rather than an intuitive mind.* One of these tatters of a great thought stuffed away in a crate, undated but drafted shortly before his departure, refers to the condition of millions and millions of French whose fate is that of the Monnards, near whose home the old gentleman's coach has just passed.

> The low price of wages is one of the greatest vices of the political societies of Europe, or rather the Old World.
>
> If the word "wages" is given the fullest extension of which it is capable, almost all the citizens of a great state will be found to receive and give wages; but here I refer only to one kind of wages, the only kind with which a government must be concerned and which has need of its care; I mean the lowest order of wage earners, men without property or capital, who have only their arms for a living. This class is always the most numerous in a nation; and consequently one cannot call happy the society in which, owing to the smallness and inadequacy of wages, the wage earners have so narrow an existence that, being hardly able to satisfy their first needs, they have means neither to marry nor raise a family and are reduced to begging whenever work is short or age and illness force them to abstain from it. . . .
>
> Unfortunately, in all the policed states of the Old World a numerous class of citizens have nothing but their wages to live on, and those wages are insufficient. This, truly, is what causes the misery of so many journeymen working in the country or town manufactures, the mendicity, an evil growing daily more

---

*American archivists in Philadelphia and Washington have taken almost two centuries to catalogue them, but they were not racing against the clock: Franklin's fame lapsed throughout much of the nineteenth century.

extensive because the only remedies governments use against it are impotent; the moral depravation; and almost all crimes.

The policy of tyranny and commerce has ignored and disguised these truths. The horrible maxim which says that a people must be poor in order to remain submissive is still that of many hardhearted and false-minded people.[1]

There is little likelihood that Franklin raised this question during the supper for thirty that is served and stage-managed by the fifty relatively privileged wage earners who are responsible for the day-to-day management of the Château de Gaillon. But the Cardinal de La Rochefoucauld, following the example of his cousin Liancourt, sets himself up as a liberal aristocrat and hobnobs with both Physiocrats and Freemasons, so Franklin gives him a copy of a book he had had printed at his own expense five years before; he didn't write it himself, but he's as proud of it as if he had. This book is the only one of its kind on earth: *Le Conciliateur de toutes les nations de l'Europe* ["The conciliator of all the nations of Europe"—*Trans.* ],[2] written by a galley convict named Pierre Gargaz* who spent twenty years of forced labor meditating, beneath his red cap, upon a scheme for universal and perpetual peace. The moment he was free, he walked from Toulon to Paris, intending to submit his project to ministers, prelates, and other "right people." Their footmen, inevitably, ejected him—except Franklin's. Benjamin read Gargaz's manuscript and found in it "many reasonable things which should be printed." But how could the poor devil get them printed himself, having used up the few coins of his earnings on his trek from the coast? So Franklin became his publisher and, as a sort of publisher's advance, gave the ex-convict as many copies as he wanted. In 1785 Gargaz is still scraping along, selling a book now and then to people whose names Benjamin gives him.

The worldly varnish of the dinner-table conversation is unchipped by Gargaz, however; it moves on to festivities and academies, at both of which the archbishop and the savant are often fellow guests these days—except that Franklin is not content just to receive the honors and actually interests himself in the most original of their activities when they relate to his own fields: the sciences of today and tomorrow. He dares to commit and even overcommit himself, as last year when he helped to annihilate Mesmer.

Franz Anton Mesmer left Paris two weeks before Franklin, in one of those fits of indigestion that mark his life like a saw-toothed range of Capitoline and Tarpeian Rocks—Vienna, Paris, Spa, Lyons, Paris again, London, and maybe

---

*I have tried in vain to learn more about him than the little that Franklin tells his friends. The archives of the Toulon prison contain nothing but a mention of his arrival in December 1761 and his departure in December 1781. The notion of "time off for good behavior" did not exist in those days—not even for stool pigeons. They simply got more money when they were discharged, but paid secretly.

Paris once more tomorrow.* Mesmer has already walked out once before, in 1781; for him it wasn't enough to treat the Princesse de Lamballe and a horde of faddists, he wanted to be regarded, and remunerated, as a prince, but the powers didn't see it that way. At the end of 1782 he returned in triumph, supported, borne aloft, fed, and enriched by an association named the "Société de l'Harmonie Universelle," which was a mixed bag of the credulous and the profiteering—the lawyer Bergasse and the Alsatian banker Kornmann;† the aristocratic—the Duc de Chartres and La Fayette (who wanted to convert Washington to "animal magnetism"); the judiciary—Duport and d'Esprémesnil (although the latter has just noisily turned his coat); and the scholarly—Court de Gébelin, historian of the ancient world. The crowds come surging back; Mesmer catches on again in public opinion.

But not at Court. The Polignacs don't like him because Mme de Lamballe and La Fayette are clients of his, and the Queen has not forgiven his impertinent letter. The Academy of Sciences is by nature opposed to all forms of pioneering research. It condemned Marat's "medical electricity" even though Franklin made a few gestures in its defense; and this time Breteuil, minister of the King's Household, instructs the Academy to smash Mesmer before he becomes one of those Parisian forces which Versailles has sworn to neutralize ever since the Fronde. And also, his disagreeable personality and "democratic" ideas are public knowledge. A committee chaired by the increasingly influential astronomer Bailly and led by Lavoisier, the learned tax-farmer general and senior civil servant who may be creeping up toward the office of comptroller general, invites Franklin to attend some magnetism experiments.

Among the members of the same committee, Benjamin meets a fellow Freemason from the "Nine Sisters" lodge, the "arts and literature" lodge to which Voltaire also belonged: Doctor Joseph-Ignace Guillotin,** who seems destined for a distinguished career in medicine and philanthropy. A professor of anatomy, pathology, and physiology who is also doctor-regent of the medical faculty, he is an imposing combination of mildness and firmness of character, "his eye keen, his physiognomy expressive, his conversation charming and often merry but without pedantry,"[3] supplemented by beautifully polished manners acquired in his native province of Charentes; he wears a long-tailed coat, powdered wig, and cocked hat.

He treats many poor people for nothing. On account of its prophylactic properties, he dissuades Calonne from levying a tax on vinegar. He tells

---

*As indicated earlier in this series, Mesmer was not the charlatan he has been cast as; he was establishing, more or less unconsciously, the rudiments of psychosomatic medicine.

†Whom we shall soon be meeting as Beaumarchais's adversaries in one of the author's last great *affaires*.

**Son of a lawyer in Saintes, Guillotin was born there on May 28, 1738; "doctor-regent" is roughly equivalent to "dean" today.

Franklin about his scheme for draining the swamps of the Poitou and Sain-tonge, in the hope of alleviating the deadly fevers they discharge from time to time, which impartially mow down hundreds of starvelings and Comte Charles-François de Broglie, the disgraced possessor of the King's secrets who trails away to die in an inn at Saint-Jean-d'Angély. Guillotin's schemes are supported by some of the archbishop's cousins, the Rochefoucaulds who rule over the homeland of Ravaillac and Jacques Roux, which includes the town that bears the family name. Franklin's real meeting with them takes place in the world of science and technology; the pope himself is draining swamps outside Rome. As for Guillotin, bursting with ideas beneath his academic phlegm, he's been badgering Franklin for a year about an emigration scheme somewhere in the forests of Pennsylvania, dreamed up by a group of small financiers and merchants with a yen for the exotic, all of whom belong to another masonic lodge, the "Concorde Fraternelle," which specializes in businessmen.* They want to build a phalanstery, give jobs to the Indians, found a sort of new masonic Athens.

In the meantime, Guillotin and Franklin both ally themselves mercilessly with Lavoisier, Bailly, and the rest, to demolish Mesmer, or rather the doctrine and practices he invented—because Franz Anton himself (out of calculation? bravado?) refuses to take part in the experiments and the investigating com-mittee has to content itself with d'Eslon, his best-established French disciple, whose rooms are almost as well patronized as the Hôtel de Coigny on the rue du Coq-Héron, where Mesmer himself has been officiating since his return. Master and disciple spend their time quarreling and making up again. In 1784 Mesmer disclaimed everything d'Eslon was doing and filed suit against him for scientific plagiarism. He even tried to intimidate Franklin, as he had tried to intimidate the Queen before:

> My discovery is of concern to all nations and it is for all nations that I wish to prepare both my story and my defense. My voice can be silenced here, as it has been in the past: but that will only make my claims the more imposing and redoubtable elsewhere.
>
> Like you, Sir, I am one of those men who cannot be kept down without risk; those who, because they have done great things, wield shame as powerful men wield authority. Whatever others may try, Sir, I can, like you, call upon the world to judge; and although the good I have done may be forgotten and that I wish to do prevented, I shall have posterity to avenge me.[4]

His tone—the "German tone" they call it, when he begins to rant like this—is not calculated to put Franklin on his side. However much of a philan-thropist one may be, one's tolerance usually does not stretch to the point of

---

*They continue corresponding about this plan until the Revolution puts an end to it.

smiling when one is told off—even in royal terms—particularly when the rest of the world tends to take one for a pope. Benjamin therefore approved the committee's report, dated August 11, 1784; it was promptly printed, and the run of 80,000 copies* was distributed by the royal booksellers. In it the authors pretend to condemn d'Eslon but are actually playing billiards, aiming, on the rebound, at "animal magnetism" and their real target, Mesmer, who is a dead man in France from that day forth.

> The members . . . unanimously concluded, on the question of the existence and utility of magnetism, that nothing proves the existence of the animal magnetic fluid; that this nonexistent fluid is therefore without utility; that the violent effects observed in the course of public treatment derive rather from touch, stimulated imagination, and that automatic form of imitation which leads us to repeat whatever has struck our senses, in spite of ourselves. At the same time they feel compelled to add, as a capital observation, that the touching and the repeated action of the seizure-inducing imagination may be deleterious.[5]

To this text—from which there could already be no appeal—the commissioners appended another, designed more particularly to shock the prudish Louis XVI, but not without first giving him a few pleasurable thrills, of the kind he liked to savor in his police reports, by establishing and insisting upon an arbitrary link between magnetism and eroticism. Might they be just a trifle voyeur around the edges, the staid and solemn MM. Bailly, Lavoisier, and Guillotin? Franklin, at any rate, never tries to hide his penchant for this kind of scientific observation:

> Most of the women who go for magnetic treatments are not truly ill. Many come for distraction and amusement. . . . Their faculties are quite sound, their youth has lost none of its sensibility. They have grace enough to affect the physician and health enough to be affected by him; so the danger is twofold. . . . The practice is for the man who is magnetizing to hold the knees of the woman within his own; hence the knees and all the lower parts of the body are touching. The hand is applied to the hypochondrium and sometimes lower, to the ovaries; contact therefore takes place at a great number of points at once, and all in the vicinity of the most sensitive parts of the body. Often the man, with his left hand thus placed, passes his right hand behind the woman's body; the movement of both is to lean forward, to facilitate this double touch. The proximity could hardly be greater; face almost touches face, breath breathes breath, all physical impressions are instantly shared, and the reciprocal attraction between the sexes must operate with all its force.

---

*Sold for 10 sols apiece, the equivalent of 4 modern francs [$1], it was stocked by many booksellers and dispatched in bales, gratis, to all the provincial academies. This run, exceptionally large for those days, shows the place that "animal magnetism" was beginning to occupy in public opinion—the opinion of its critics, at least.

Oh, I say, I say!

So much for Mesmer, d'Eslon, and their disciples, now papered with the dual label of quacks and libertines.

The chief of police cleverly takes advantage of the Carnival festivities in Paris to destroy Mesmer's image and deal his fad a deathblow. What a Carnival that was, a sort of hysteria witnesses will never forget; the whole of 1785 has the devil in its flesh. Franklin can't get over it—he who has never known any headier form of release, as a prelude to the dour Lent of Anglo-Saxon countries, than a slightly less stringy piece of beef on the Shrove Tuesday dinner table.

But that year Paul Thiébault, a lad of sixteen, is discovering Paris at the dawn of a long military career,* and the Carnival of 1785 hits him full in the face like a bursting balloon:

> It was as though the entire population had gone mad. The middle and even the upper classes of society did not confine their masquerades to a few drawing-room gatherings but took a public part in this delirium; anyone able to lay hands on some article of costume disguised or rather disfigured himself, for the poorest people simply painted their faces and covered themselves with rags, to which they tried to give a grotesque air. Thus it was not by couples, by small groups, or by isolated carriages that one perceived a few homely masks now and then; it was by the hundreds, by the thousands that they filled the streets and squares, most of them on foot, to be sure, but countless numbers in coaches and more or less splendid carts. On Sunday and Shrove Tuesday the masquerades began with the day and did not end until late the next night, continuing by the light of torches or candles borne by masked figures on carts, astride horses, or perched before, behind, and atop carriages and multitudes of cabs![6]

Louis-Sébastien Mercier, the anatomist of Paris of that age, would soon have disabused young Thiébault and old Franklin of their wonderment. According to him, it was "the police themselves, attentive to all outward manifestations of public joy, especially in times of acute poverty, who bear the cost of many of the masquerades. All their spies and other employees go to a warehouse where there are costumes for two or three thousand maskers. Then, costumed, they roam through the districts and go in dirtied bands to the Faubourg Saint-Antoine, where they feign a mendacious popular merriment."[7] If that is true, then this year's main tableau, a satire on Mesmerism, may have been one of the last brainchildren of M. Lenoir, who is about to step down as chief of police in favor of de Crosne, another Châtelet magistrate. They leave nothing to chance in the city where ridicule kills.

---

*A future general and baron of the Empire; he writes copious, wordy *Mémoires* which are gossipy and confused but full of anecdotes. In 1785 he had newly arrived from Berlin, where his father taught literature at the military academy.

Beneath his own windows Mesmer heard cheering. A johnny* was coming up lantern in hand, with fife and drums on either side. Behind him a Pierrot was holding a sort of Chinese banner adorned with bells and an inscription in tall gold letters: HARMONICA.† A physician followed, riding backwards on an ass with his head facing the tail of his mount. Behind them came a crowd of maskers representing patients. They were all quite wild, simulating transports and fits and uttering animal noises. While this weird procession was going through the streets of Paris, the aeronaut Homond launched, from a window in the Tuileries (obligingly opened by the royal household, thus), a little balloon in the shape of a vintner bearing a tub on his head, on which was written, ADIEU BAQUET, VENDANGES SONT FAITES[8] ["Farewell tub, the harvest's over," the Tub being the symbol of Mesmer's experiments—*Trans.*].

Farewell, Mesmer.

Good evening, Mr. Franklin. When the conversation turns to the sublime trivia of French politics, he asks the Cardinal de La Rochefoucauld to forgive him for retiring so early. What's the point of descanting about things upon which one has no leverage? In Europe's eyes the great French event that spring, far more than Mesmer's mortification, has been the death of Choiseul. Franklin, saturated with distinguished utterances, spends three more days reaching Le Havre, where he embarks with M. Houdon, the great sculptor who was so overjoyed to have been able to make a nude statue of Voltaire and who is now on his way to Philadelphia to make another statue, this time of General Washington fully attired.

*According to Littré, *jeannot* [johnny—*Trans.*] is derived from the name John and used to designate a ninny. The wisecracking clowns who caper about on fairground trestle stages are known as "johnnies."

†Mesmer was also a music lover and had been friendly with the Mozart family; he had invented a "glass organ" and baptized it "harmonica."

DUC DE CHOISEUL

# 9

## MAY 1785

## Blue Ribbons into Infinity

Etienne-François, Duc de Choiseul-Amboise, *né* de Stainville, dies at sixty-six years of age exactly when and as he should. He had worn himself out carrying all the hopes of all those people who were still mumbling about history and dreaming of his comeback. The granddad had dismissed him over fourteen years before, and ten years ago he knew the grandson would never call him back,* and so he has used the intoxication of his debts to drug his despair. He wasn't ill and he still stood up straight, despite his embonpoint and the network of wrinkles encircling his small, upturned nose. But he was coming to the last page, the one you have to know how to turn. Another few months and the Choiseul bankruptcy would be public knowledge and cause even more of a furor than that of the Rohan-Guéménées. Suicide was not in fashion and Choiseul, although a skeptic, did believe in some kind of a vague Supreme Being; so all that was left for him was to let the works run down. They'll say he died like a monarch, but his feet were very much of clay.

To the bitter end, he goes on squandering his 800,000 livres of annual income,† minus the amount saved from the disaster by the separation awards to his duchess in 1772 and reinvested with a view to subsequent repayments: between 100,000 and 200,000 livres a year, to which Louise-Honorine has every right, especially as it was she—or rather her parents, she herself being less than fifteen at the time—who contributed the major share of the capital to their marriage thirty-five years ago. The Crozat du Châtels, after making millions in two generations from plantations in the Antilles and the slave trade, had slipped under their son-in-law's feet the first rung of the ladder to a destiny which his alliance with Mme de Pompadour made into one of the brightest meteors of the century: the embassy in Rome, followed by an assortment of ministries, followed *de facto*, if not officially, by the prime minister's post.

---

*His hopes and those of his coterie (hopes encouraged by Marie Antoinette) at the time of Louis XVI's accession, the reasons for the new King's antagonism, and the details of his retirement at Chanteloup and his curious "family life" have been covered in previous volumes.

†Around 550,000 modern francs [$136,000], from pensions, investments, and estates.

France at his discretion for eleven years, and Louis XV virtually reduced to the role of Louis XIII, until the day in 1770 when Choiseul tripped on little Jeanne Bécu, the Comtesse du Barry, because he imagined he could toss her away like a pebble in the stream. It was Richelieu's good fortune that Louis XIII had cared so little about women.

The Duchesse de Choiseul had stuck by her husband's side ever since, bittersweet, like a submissive reproach, a rose that had crumpled before it opened. With her pretty tired smile and a wit acquired by hard work, she presided over the lordly train at Chanteloup as she presided over the magnificent right bank mansion in Paris, which might better be known as the inn of gratitude to 200 potential guests.* She cohabited with two old harpies to whom her husband had insisted upon leaving suites of rooms after his demise. They were Choiseul's sister and nevertheless ex-mistress, the Duchesse de Gramont, who always wants to give all the orders or at least have it look that way, the female forever frustrated of one royal night, much longed for and narrowly missed; and the woman of Choiseul's declining years, his mistress for the last ten, a Rohan-Rochefort who was the widow of a Comte de Brionne, a former property of his cousin the cardinal; it's easy to lose your way among the alcoves of Stainvilles and Rohans in the subterranean labyrinths of Lorraine.

Three women at once were a bit much for one small man who refused to admit defeat. Three twilight sentinels, bringing him daily reminders of the catastrophe: his wife's silence, his sister's agitation, Mme de Brionne's appetites . . .

In 1781 the edifice began to fall apart, the terraces were caving in, the temple pillars got the shudders. In 1780 the creditors had worked themselves into such a frenzy that the family had to resort to the ultimate milch cow: the King, whom the more extravagant wing of the nobility has stuck up on the skyline of their playground as supreme banker. Swallowing his pride for once, Choiseul let his wife beg for him and obtained a loan of 4 million,† which Louis XVI was only too glad to give to the person whom his Queen had made into a perpetual conjugal reproach. See that? I've got nothing against your Choiseul, whatever you may think![1] Especially when he's begging.

But even rocks that size can't fill an abyss like Choiseul's. Lot by lot they sold off the grounds of the mansion on the rue de Richelieu; they were known as "the other Tuileries" and speculators had had their eyes on them ever since the Orléanses began developing their land at the nearby Palais Royal. But what the sellers took in with one hand was taken from the other because they

---

*Two hundred and ten to be exact—those who had defied Louis XV and called on Choiseul during his disgrace; it was also to them that he dedicated the famous "pagoda" at Chanteloup.

†25–8 million modern francs [$6.25–7 million].

then became embroiled in real estate intrigues. "By Act dated August 26, 1781 the Duc and Duchesse de Choiseul hereby undertake to have built, for the King's acting company, the playhouse known as the Comédie Italienne.* It is formally stipulated that the Duc and Duchesse shall have, together with the Duchesse de Gramont, the ownership of one eight-person box next to that of the King."[2]

They'll never use it. Work on the theater has hardly started when the mansion itself has to be sold and the family is forced to retreat to a miserable thirty-room apartment on the rue de la Grande Batelière and begin thinking about selling Chanteloup. There's one man alive in France who can afford to collect imperiled Versailleses: the Duc de Penthièvre, last descendant of the bastards of Louis XIV, father-in-law of the Princesse de Lamballe, and, virtually, lord of upper Brittany. Living quietly on his estate, he has prospered, while the rest were pouring sand into the desert. They say he could buy France; however that may be, he doesn't refuse Chanteloup. Negotiations are put in hand; but Choiseul will not live to see the outcome. Since the beginning of the heat wave the duke has had a sort of lingering "drought cold" that turns into a catarrh—bronchitis, people will call it later. He ignores it. "The humors have fallen upon the entire chest; a fluxion. From the chest they have penetrated into the rest of the body and especially the organs of evacuation," sagely declare the eleven physicians summoned to his bedside in Paris, where he had gone on business; their unending bickering makes his death a caricature of that of Louis XV. Molière couldn't have improved upon them. In the end, nobody knows whether Choiseul is dying of pneumonia or intestinal occlusion; whatever the medical term may be, he's dying in order not to lose face.

Like the admission of a new member of the Académie or the first night of a Beaumarchais play, the demise of one of the century's great men is an event not to be missed. Beginning on May 5 the rue de la Grande Batelière is blocked by a death-agony traffic jam.

> In those days it was the custom in society to move in on sick friends. To show proof of one's concern one invaded their rooms, perturbed the service, and made it impossible for them to receive the care they required. . . . After May 6 there were thirty persons sleeping in the house every night, ten of them women of the highest rank, including [I should think so!] the Comtesse de Brionne. The most illustrious names in Paris were littered around the periphery of the house. The door was besieged from morning to night; carriages had to queue up to reach the door.[3]

*The "second company" (the Comédie Française being the first) subsidized by the King was badly cramped on the narrow rue de Mauconseil. The new building, financed with money paid out by the Choiseuls in compound interest, became what is now the Opéra Comique.

"Four secretaries were constantly occupied issuing [health] bulletins. There was a vast concourse, a special etiquette was established among the crowd; there were the first and second antechambers, drawing room and bedroom, each person had a place in a particular room and only a chosen few were admitted to the last. . . . Every evening more than eighty people supped in the house,"[4] at the dying man's expense, of course; even at this extremity he goes on accumulating debts, because after all, you've got to be decent to freeloaders too.

One of them, in the front row in the drawing room, is Comte Valentin Esterhazy de Galantha and de Frakno; camp marshal,* Knight of the Order of the Holy Ghost, governor of Rocroi, and one of the Queen's four or five special intimates, he is a Hungarian who would far rather serve France than the House of Hapsburg, that awkward "protectress" of his country. This distinguished member of the international nobility-of-the-sword set has just shelved a playboy's life for future reference when writing his *Mémoires,* by marrying, at forty-six and as though it were the most ordinary thing in the world, a rich heiress of seventeen to whom he writes laboriously enamored letters when parted from her in the King's service. Loyal to the Choiseuls, if only out of his commitment to the "Paris-Vienna axis" and the Queen, Esterhazy duly comes running and keeps a little conjugal diary of the event.

On May 6, "M. de Choiseul was in a very bad way until three in the after-dinner.† He sees Barthès but does not do what he orders.** There is one little surgeon in the house who hates him and undoes whatever he does in his very presence. They say, in short, that the house is a hotbed of medical intrigue, and this dissension among the faculty is even more alarming than the illness, although that is serious enough. . . .

"Yesterday the patient took English powders; their effect is not yet known. They were not prescribed by Barthès; he said he would not prescribe them because he did not know them‡ and preferred the emetic in a wash,[5] i.e., an enema."

On May 7, "M. de Choiseul felt worse; he called for Barthès, people galloped through Paris to find him, he came. The patient told him that he felt

*Equivalent in rank to a general of a division today. Esterhazy emigrates and ends his military career in the service of Catherine II in Russia.

†Afternoon.

**The famous Montpellier physician who had abandoned all hope of curing Charles de Buonaparte in February chanced to be in Paris at the time. He was apparently consulted out of courtesy but not really "mobilized," and the family's regular doctors blocked him at every turn.

‡An instance of the Anglomania that was becoming fashionable again, now that the war was over: drugs were brought across the Channel, along with horses, furniture and clothes, even when nobody knew what they were good for.

he had not been properly treated, nothing had been done for him, but that he had complete faith in him [Barthès] and would do nothing thereafter unless he prescribed it. He also asked for his man of business. . . . At four o'clock M. de Choiseul made his will," which he dictates in a firm voice, asking to be buried "at Amboise in the parish of Saint-Denis, which is my parish, in the cemetery I had made for the inhabitants," and requesting the priest of Saint-Eustache (the parish in which he will die) to have one hundred masses said for the repose of his soul. He gives life pensions, which there is no money to pay, to fifty of his servants, but mentions only two of the multitude of women he has loved: Mme de Brionne will have "the rose-colored diamond at the top of the cord on my Golden Fleece" and Mme de Gramont will be his universal heir and legatee. Is this a dig at his wife, who sits dissolved in glacial tears, unmoving, by his bedside? Most likely not: she has her own money, as we know, and the dying man's sister sagely refuses this anti-inheritance in order to avoid the liability for his debts.*

He stops asking for treatment. He doesn't want to die in a scrimmage of apothecaries. Barthès's gaze was enough for him, the truthful eyes of the great doctor who ennobles a nobleman's death. "He saw the fatal moment approaching without a qualm, and himself comforted those around him. To the very last he behaved as though giving an audience."

Two long nights of vigil in the gilded drawing room have injected strange tremors into the pages on which Esterhazy records his grief, and also his apprehensions. Why on earth should a noble Hungarian sitting at the bedside of a decomposing ex-millionaire worry about the troubles of the common people of Rocroi or Amboise, or of Countess Esterhazy's estates in Burgundy and Picardy?

"What is more, the times are ominous. The price of wood is going up. Butter costs 44 sols, meat will soon be at 12,† and if there is no rain, the worst is to be feared." But not for you, surely, M. le Comte? If Famine scares the rich it's only because of her sister, Riot, who had already reared her ugly head in Choiseul's day. On May 7 Esterhazy goes on: "My sister tells me that there is consternation in her country [the Beauvais region, where she married] owing to fears for the harvest; last year's failed and the farmers cannot pay; indeed, they need assistance and are in straits. I sent 600 francs ** straightaway, in place of the New Year's present I give her every year and hadn't yet sent this year." As long as charity survives, then, everything else survives, is

---

*The Choiseuls had no children but had adopted their nephew, a Stainville, who accordingly inherits the title without the fortune, and naturally serves in the army. We shall meet him again on the path of the King's flight in June 1791.

†Both prices are for a pound; in other words, 15 modern francs [$4] for a pound of butter and more than 4 [$1] for a pound of meat—but he's talking about pork only.

**Approximately 4,200 modern francs [$1,050].

that it?—from Louis XVI to Choiseul, and from Esterhazy to the villeins on his sister's land. But what if there is no more charity?

Fleeting wingbeats in the night of death; Choiseul goes in broad daylight. At nine in the morning of May 8, "never was there a desolation comparable to that of the Château de Choiseul [*sic*]; beginning at six yesterday his state worsened, he has been extremely weak and sinking continually. It was thought he would not live the night and he is still alive, but that is all that can be said." At 11:45 "he is not dead yet but can take nothing more. We await only the moment," which comes a quarter of an hour later, just at noon.

On May 10 the coffin is "presented" for a service at Saint-Eustache, before the transfer of the body to Amboise. "Never had a more numerous and brilliant cortege been seen. There were blue ribbons into infinity, and red ones, and foreign decorations; old men bent by the weight of their years seemed ready to descend into their own tombs after paying their last respects to the dead."[6]

One of Choiseul's more noteworthy neighbors (a neighbor of the Polignacs, too, who were ensconced at Chambord) and the possessor of a superb château on the Loire, Jean Dufort—who naturally styled himself Dufort de Cheverny*—was, he said, "so attached to the duke that my heart was broken. Upon reaching Blois [from Paris, where he too had stuck it out to the end], I was walking mournfully, lost in thought, in the garden of the bishopric, when I noticed two vehicles on the road, a German coach and a berlin, with a single courier. It was the duke being carried to the cemetery at Amboise. The Maréchal de Stainville and Duc du Châtelet followed in a berlin; there was a priest with the coffin."[7]

The duchess is not following. The day after her husband's death she leaves for a long-awaited rest, alone, in the Convent of the Recollects on the rue du Bac, "with one servant and a dog named Chanteloup." Every week she receives an army of businessmen. She wants to pay up, to the last penny. The Duc de Penthièvre buys Chanteloup (the château, not the dog) for 4 million livres a few months from now. The duchess will gradually placate the creditors and, in two years, even repay Louis XVI.

So if Marie Antoinette wants—and she does want—to have some say in politics at last, she's going to have to change her tack and find a new front man outside her own circle of featherweights. She's going to have to bring forth another Choiseul and play Queen-Pompadour. Her grief, and even more her anxiety, are sincere; they last all of thirty-six hours, which is a long time at Versailles, until they are blown away by a drawing-room fart:

*The son of a successful magistrate, Dufort de Cheverny, born in 1731, held an honorary position at Court: he was "introducer of ambassadors" on the day they presented their letters of accreditation. He leaves two volumes of *Mémoires* before dying in 1801.

On Sunday evening she was presiding over her table with a stricken air when a trivial incident destroyed the general atmosphere of grief and restored everyone to gaiety. The Marquis de Lau, who was playing at lansquenet, forgot himself for an instant; startled by this unexpected noise, the entire company stared at one another; then the ladies began fanning themselves furiously to hide their laughter. But the Queen could not keep from bursting out, and everyone else did too.[8]

JEANNE DE VALOIS

# 10

## APRIL–AUGUST 1785

## *Where Have You Been?*

After playing on the rooftops of all the neighboring houses and knocking down an occasional Choiseul or Guéménée, lightning strikes the French monarchy, as it had to one day, on the morning of August 15, 1785.

Prelude number 1—Louis XVI takes his Easter communion. *Gazette de France,* * April 1:

"Yesterday the King went, in ceremonial procession, to the Church of Notre Dame parish [in Versailles], where he took communion from the hands of the Cardinal Prince de Rohan, Grand Almoner of France. The Duc de Coigny and Maréchal de Mouchy held the cloth on the King's side; the Bishop of Senlis, His Majesty's first almoner, and the duty almoner, held the cloth on the altar side."†

Prelude number 2—*Correspondance secrète,* March 24:

"The Sieur Aubert, jeweler to the Crown, having had an attack of apoplexy that paralyzed half his body, the Queen has appointed to replace him the Sieur Böhmer,** onetime jeweler to the King of Poland and then to La du Barry,

---

*The unofficial organ of the royal government. Ministers and princes inserted in it anything they wanted to make public.

†The Duc de Coigny is there as the King's *écuyer;* Roquelaure, Bishop of Senlis, aged sixty-five, received his Court title in 1764; the Duc de Mouchy, seventy, has been maréchal since 1759. The names of the real almoners, the eight men who are on "duty by quarters," that is, three months at a time, are seldom mentioned.

**This is the correct spelling of the man's name; others, showing the hesitation that was customary in those days, indicate that it was pronounced "Buhmare" or "Boaymare." The King

whose fall from favor nearly ruined him. He is a likable man, highly regarded for his taste, talents, and a degree of polish seldom encountered among the men of his profession";[1] were jewelers supposed to be boors, then? Böhmer, in any event, will soon need all the suavity he can command. When Marie Antoinette made the grand tour of Paris for her churching on May 24, from Notre Dame to the Opéra by way of Sainte-Geneviève, "Her Majesty was sumptuously bejeweled, and wore a pair of earrings costing 800,000 livres.* She asked that all the ladies accompanying her be dressed in gowns of silver."[2]

Third prelude:

Paris showed so little interest in this parade that both the courts and gazettes of Europe noticed the fact: one young queen was losing ground in the popularity polls. "The people expressed so little enthusiasm that the Princess, who has an exceedingly kind heart,† was quite affected by it and said in great distress, upon her return to the Tuileries, 'What have I done to them?' "[3]

And at that point the lightning had not yet struck. It hits Versailles first on Tuesday, August 15, Assumption Day, and we shall see how.** But who could imagine that one of the crannies of France into which it snakes only two days later, on the evening of the 17th, would be one of the most forgotten and untroubled areas in the whole country: the glorious Abbey of Clairvaux in the diocese of Langres in Champagne, where St. Bernard reformed the Cistercians in 1115? And what possible connection could there be between Clairvaux, the upheaval at Versailles, and this young-old man of twenty-four, Jacques-Claude Beugnot,‡ a provincial lad to whom, in theory, nothing should ever have happened? If "accidents" ever do occur in history, this must be one.

A nice fellow, with big lively eyes set in a mildly pleasant face, he's the son of Edme Beugnot, notary at Bar-sur-Aube, and an equally Champenois woman

---

of Poland was Stanislas Leczynski, Queen Marie's father, a refugee who "reigned" in Nancy until his death.

*More than 5 million modern francs [$1,250,000].

†Again according to the anonymous author of the *Correspondance secrète,* whose confidential bulletin was dispatched to the rulers in Warsaw or St. Petersburg, or possibly both.

**I earnestly hope the reader will see the point of my approach to the "Necklace Affair," one of the most significant in the reign of Louis XVI and one involving many circles. I have chosen to move from obscurity to illumination because that was how the event was experienced by contemporaries; this explains my unchronological detour beginning August 17 and ending August 15, after a long flashback to the preliminaries.

‡J.-C. Beugnot, Comte d'Empire (1761–1835), is subsequently a moderate delegate to the Legislative Assembly, joins the Council of State during the Consulate, and holds major administrative positions during the Empire, before becoming an ephemeral minister of the navy under Louis XVIII. His *Mémoires* make wonderful reading.

named Elisabeth Janson. No problems in childhood or youth; he was born to be a lawyer. The ABCs he got from a tutor at home, followed by a smidgen of law at Troyes and a lot of the law in Paris. Life looks all right, for now: he needs security, and what could be more tranquilizing than the sight of this lawyer's-office walls stretching out to the crack of doom? He's fond of orating and even fonder of writing, although it takes him too long, as became clear during the three years of his initiation into his profession in Paris and, when court was not in session, back home working for the kindly folks who were giving him sweets and chucking him under the chin fifteen years earlier. In Bar-sur-Aube, though, people can afford to take their time. "It is in the nature of my character to be totally engrossed in whatever I do and to hate interruption. Even though I spent whole nights in my office I became known as slothful, and not without some justification, for all the time I was busy with my pleadings and reports, the briefs were piling up around me."[4]

All right; but what about women, Jacques-Claude? Yes, it's true, women do bring the one breath of fresh air into his life, the rest of which is spent closeted with heavy tapestries and folios of Roman law. He loves the ladies and they, in response to the appeal of a large sensual mouth and an aquiline nose, reciprocate without much persuading. Mostly he sees them in Paris—students will be students—and around the Palais Royal, but when he gets home again . . . ? Beugnot doesn't go in for debauchery, and besides, how could he in this burg? Here it has to be one woman at a time, accessible and discreet, more than a servant and less than a wife, "the usual thing," as he was taught in his world.

But what has happened, to his consternation, ecstasy, and misery, is that this village rooster has chanced upon a very extraordinary hen. Six years ago he met one of those indefinable young women who turn whole provinces upside down when they inhabit them—Jeanne de Saint-Rémi de Luz, Comtesse de La Motte-Valois—and he has gradually become her faithful swain, that is, her lover, when she feels like it and when she has some time to spend, with or without her husband, in the handsome house the couple have just bought in Bar-sur-Aube. Actually, she's quite fond of little Beugnot with his spaniel eyes. He is so good at listening, and she's got so much to tell! After all, she's a friend, a real, true, intimate friend of the Queen. Sometimes Beugnot can almost believe he's sleeping at Trianon.

What about the husband? He doesn't bother them, he's an indulgent type, often off God knows where, a captain in the gendarmerie who had a brief whirl at the head of the "Burgundians' company" before finding a safe berth with the Comte de Provence's Life Guards. He's not too proud for the country lasses himself. The little lawyer, with his Paris-sur-Aube level of sophistication, is fascinated by the pair of them. Most of their nobility flows in Jeanne's blood. La Motte acts and looks like a gendarme; whereas she *is* a Valois. A real one?

A descendant of our old kings, the ones before the Bourbons? Absolutely. In a direct line from Henri II.

Beugnot has got Jeanne de Valois, as she styles herself just to simplify matters, very much on his mind, but her influence there is upsetting, disquieting. Sometimes Jacques-Claude is almost weary of her, as on this August 17, when she asks him to accompany her to the Duc de Penthièvre's; she's been invited to a reception at his place at Châteauvillain, over toward Chaumont. A Valois dining in the home of a direct descendant of Louis XIV* is a sight worth a few hours of jolting over rough roads and a return journey in the middle of the night; even so, Beugnot won't go. He's shy, and he also has the honest pride of the bourgeois who doesn't like to be seen hanging around people who are too big for him. People should know their places and stay in them. Just once he let himself be dragged along by the La Mottes to the home of another illustrious neighbor, the Comte de Brienne,† and he came back very sore indeed. Why, the best society of Champagne spent the whole evening sneering at the Comte de La Motte, who decidedly has the manners of a parvenu. His wife, at least, behaved like a lady, but the husband "was the focal point of malevolent lorgnettes which passed from hand to hand with scornful titters or shrugs of the shoulders. He gave them just cause: he had dressed with the most studied elegance and, what was in the worst possible taste, had contrived to incorporate diamonds into his toilette at a time when simplicity of dress was beginning to be the rule."[5]

"But what can you have to fear this time? My oaf of a husband will be out hunting all day long. I don't want him as a companion any more than you do; he makes me too ashamed. You will be my gallant."[6]

Beugnot, mulish: "The wound of Brienne was still bleeding and I had sworn an oath never to be taken in again.

" 'Madame, I have no ground for being admitted by the Duc de Penthièvre, and I have nothing to ask of him. Besides, no Beugnot would be allowed to sit at his table, with or without you. I should be relegated to the table of his gentlemen of honor and might perhaps be tolerated in the grand salon for coffee. Don't you know that etiquette is more scrupulously observed in Penthièvre's home than in that of any of the princes of the blood?' " A tradition among great bastards: the "legitimate" Bourbons can ease up on the rules, but not they. No commoner knocks at the door of Châteauvillain unless he is of the prince's Household or has a favor to ask.

She pouted; but "I held out against Mme de La Motte. I proposed merely that she should set me down at Clairvaux, which is on the road from Bar-sur-

---

*The duke is the heir of the Comte de Toulouse, legitimized bastard of Louis XIV and Mme de Montespan; in addition to his vast holdings in Brittany, he also received the very substantial estate of Châteauvillain in Champagne from his father.

†Brother of the Cardinal-Archbishop of Toulouse who is angling for *the* ministry.

Aube to Châteauvillain, and pick me up again there in the evening, after her visit." A deal; away rolls the La Motte coach, leaving Bar-sur-Aube at eight in the morning of August 17, 1785, "a day I shall never forget."[7]

We next find Jacques-Claude deposited for safekeeping in one of the kingdom's religious pinnacles. More than six hundred years before, Hugues, Comte de Troyes, bequeathed to St. Bernard the valley of Absinthe with everything pertaining to it, and the bequest was subsequently enriched by many a count of Champagne or Flanders, and by the kings themselves. This is the real Champagne, by which Parisians are so bemused—the *campana,* or countryside, woods stretching away to the horizon, the scent of pines, roads that send up clouds of chalk. In it the order of Cîteaux grew like another forest: "The walls of the house of Clairvaux measure [in 1785, that is] more than a thousand fathoms around* and encompass two complete monasteries."[8] Moving from one to the other of them, Beugnot can measure the centuries of decadence and observe the rotting of a great monastic order, the end of the path down which the church had led it. "The old monastery is as it was built by St. Bernard, that is, quite small and simple, in accordance with the precept of religious poverty; it has been preserved in memory of the founders." Even it, however, could accommodate five hundred monks by the time of its founder's death. Now, on the other hand, there are only fifty or sixty monks, twenty lay brothers, and forty servants or thereabouts, "in the eighteenth-century abbey which is divided into several main buildings, all built with great splendor and set in superb formal gardens; the chief occupants [the "monks," that is] have an income of 120,000 livres,† part in money, part in wheat, and the rest in wine and wood." Especially wine: in one cellar stands the biggest cask in the kingdom, the Clairvaux Tun they call it, which can be filled "to a capacity of 800 barrels."

Are these monks of St. Bernard or St. Bernardin? Dom Rocourt, the Abbot of Clairvaux, is more like the ones in the song: his eminent dignity has enabled him to reign, by procuration, over a dozen more affiliated abbeys, all equally anemic from the religious point of view, but juicy enough as far as income is concerned—the lion's share of which goes to him without his ever setting foot in them. Beugnot duly pays his court to this Champenois mini-despot, who "commanded [for himself alone, counting all his sources

*Generally a fathom was equal to six feet in length, with variations depending on the country.

†Approximately 800,000 modern francs [$200,000]. After the monks are dispersed in the Revolution, Clairvaux becomes a paper mill, then a glassworks, and is finally converted (!), under Louis-Philippe, into a prison. Today it is one of the most notorious penitentiaries of France.

in the order] an income of 300,000 or 400,000 livres,* had splendid carriages, and never went out with fewer than four horses and an outrider in
front."

Oh, grandiose is the abbot, "tall, with a handsome and gracious face," and
he wears the habit of his order with such a noble mien "that the Queen
exclaimed, 'What a fine-looking monk!' on the day of his presentation at
Versailles."⁹ Naturally, when he's here he lives in the modern abbey—we
might better call it a château—where he is bored stiff despite his grand prelate's retinue, and delights, for relief, in entertaining the "people of his court,"
in the words of Beugnot, who boasts of being "a habitué of the house." He's
turned up at just the right moment, the Most Reverend Father is looking for
chums to help him bear the tedium of one of his official chores: "St. Bernard's
feast day [August 20] was a great occasion at Clairvaux; the poor who came
to the abbey doors were given distributions [*sic*] and the bourgeois of Bar-sur-
Aube and vicinity were let in to dine in the refectory with Monsignor Abbot
presiding—a thing that happened but once in the year." Beugnot rather
wanted "to be present at this dinner in order to make a little fun of the abbot,
who spoke of the custom as an ancient vestige which he meant to abolish and
treated with contempt the guests who came of their own accord," but not those
who were invited, and warmly invited, like Jacques-Claude: a lawyer with a
future in Bar-sur-Aube could always come in handy. "The abbot pledges me
to spend three days with him, if I am not frightened away by the Feast of St.
Bernard, and promises, as a reward, that I shall hear Abbé Maury, who is
arriving the same evening to preach the saint's panegyric." Who, Maury, the
King's own preacher? Yes indeed, Clairvaux will have none but the best, even
when it means a showman of Maury's class, who is noted for the size of his
fees,† especially since his recent election to the Académie Française in compliance with strong pressure from the King's aunts and in opposition to a nasty
"modern" playwright named Sedaine.

The dishes at supper tonight will be choice, in honor of one of the great
tenors of the Church of France, and of the countess, whose return from
Châteauvillain we shall of course await before sitting down to consume them.
After all, she is also one of the mistresses of the Grand Almoner, Cardinal de
Rohan, who is responsible for the distribution of every ecclesiastical benefice
in the country. Beugnot knows about it; she makes no effort to hide the fact.
And it would be in extremely poor taste to be jealous of such a rival. This

*Between 2 and 3 million modern francs [$500,000–$750,000].

†The son of a cobbler in the Comtat Venaissin, Maury has been preaching to the King for
ten years and will be an important figure in the Royalist group in the Constituent Assembly; he
ends his days a cardinal, after occupying the archbishopric of Paris under Napoleon without being
appointed to the post.

*de facto* complicity with a Rohan is the little lawyer's entrée, for want of any better, into the nobility of the boudoir.

The countess turns up at eight, "in a brilliant toilette, covered in diamonds." There's fire enough in her without them, though, to set the whole abbey burning. A beauty she is not, but the dash and spice in her more than make up for any physical imperfections; she's "middling in height but slender and well-shaped, with expressive blue eyes beneath black, well-arched brows, the face a little long, a large mouth but admirably garnished, and an enchanting smile.* Her hands are beautiful, her feet very small. Her complexion is of remarkable whiteness. By some strange whim, nature, when forming her bosom, stopped halfway through the work, and the half that was there made one long for the other half."[10] She's close to thirty but looks younger.† For years youth has been her only trump card, and as she's determined to be a winner, she likes to keep all her weapons within reach.

Her small face, always a little strained, lights up as she tells about her reception at Châteauvillain, where the Duc de Penthièvre "walked with her to the doorway of the second drawing room leading to the grand staircase, an honor he did not bestow upon duchesses and reserved only for princesses of the blood."[11] The Abbot of Clairvaux immediately "fell over himself with protestations of respect and adoration. Beyond any doubt the abbot was aware of the intimate relations obtaining between the Cardinal de Rohan and Mme de La Motte, and treated her as a princess of the church."

Maury's late. Of course, it's a rough trip, with twenty-two changes of horses, even if he left Paris at dawn by the straightest road, through Charenton, Nangis, Provins, and Troyes.[12] They while away the time waiting for him "in a walk and a game," gambling being a regular feature of the abbot's drawing room. There are dozens of other provincial micro-societies chasing their tails like this one, from Châteauvillain to Brienne or Clairvaux.** At last carriage wheels are heard in the distance. There's still a smear of red in the August sky,[13] they're just sitting down to eat, it's after half-past nine, the superior rises, "hurries to meet the panegyrist of St. Bernard and brings him by force into the dining room without giving him time to remove his traveling robe." This kind of unceremonial bustle suits Maury well enough, with his air of being a Hercules of the church, jutting out his chin to let you know, "It's me, Maury, the cobbler's son, just see how well I've caught the trick of your

---

*Portrait by Beugnot.

†Jeanne de Saint-Rémi de Valois was born at Fontette in Champagne on July 22, 1756.

**We have already met those of Pontarlier, Dijon, and Aix, as revealed through Mirabeau; of the Chateaubriands in Brittany, of Laclos or Barnave in Grenoble (from which Stendhal is to emerge), of Arras (Robespierre, Carnot) and Toulouse (Barère, Fabre); and will subsequently become acquainted with those of Lyons, Bordeaux, Clermont, etc.

mannerisms"; but there's a shade too much nonchalance about him, a tinge of insincerity . . .

"The napkins had hardly been unfolded" when the Abbot of Clairvaux asks the ritual question: "So, tell us what's happening in Paris. What are people saying, what are they doing? Is there any news?"

For once, there is. Maury is confident of his effect:

"What do you mean, news? But where have you been? There certainly is news, but nobody can make head or tail of it; it has amazed and staggered the entire city of Paris. On Tuesday, Assumption Day, the Cardinal de Rohan was arrested, in his pontifical robes, as he came out of the King's private apartments."

So much for that castle in Spain . . . Beugnot was presumably not the only one, "the moment the news struck his ears," to stare at Mme de La Motte, "who had let her napkin fall from both hands, and whose face, pale and motionless, remained perpendicular to her plate." The questions fly: How did it happen? What does it mean? Does anyone know the reason for his arrest?

"No, not precisely. There is talk of a diamond necklace which the cardinal was supposed to have bought for the Queen and did not buy. It is unthinkable that the Grand Almoner of France could be arrested for such a trifle [*sic*]— in his pontifical robes, you hear me, in his pontifical robes . . ."

She rises from her chair. It's too much; she leaves the room stammering excuses and no one raises an eyebrow, any more than when Beugnot, loyal escort to the end, stumbles after her, abandoning the Feast of St. Bernard. One of the household officials accompanies them to the door. "She had already ordered the horses put in. We left." Can they get back to Bar-sur-Aube in time?

BEUGNOT

# I I

## AUGUST 1785

## *So Loyal a Man*

BARRAS

So there they are, in a brand new pearl gray berlin (its form designed primarily for comfort) sporting a coat of arms copied from those of the Valois and bearing the motto of the Saint-Rémis: *Rege ab avo sanguinem, nomen et lilia*

(From the King I hold blood, name, and lily). They've got two leagues to cover in pitch dark, from Clairvaux to Bar-sur-Aube, but that's no great problem; the four bob-tailed English mares can trot smartly along, thanks to the oil lanterns that light up the road for twenty feet ahead. Two footmen sit behind and, next to the driver, "a Negro covered in silver from head to foot" is there to lower the step.

"The weather was magnificent, moonlight as clear as very day."* But inside the vehicle, between the dashboard and the white leather cushions, confusion is degenerating into dispute. Jacques-Claude wants to know the whole story. By now Jeanne has recovered her sangfroid, however, and is "affecting tranquillity," her only worry being the idea that she might have been impolite to her hosts:

"Perhaps I was wrong, especially with Abbé Maury there?"[1]

"Not at all! Your association with the cardinal is known and almost publicly admitted. His life may be in danger. Your role is to make haste and await letters, messengers, news. . . . But have you yourself any explanation of his arrest?"

She rambles and wanders and almost seems to be talking about something else—why, Beugnot, it's nothing for you to get upset about—but as usual, under the mask she is thinking hard. How many hours does she have in which to improvise some sort of safety scaffolding in case the Rohan floor should give way beneath her feet? But is it really going to? She has been leaning on a pillar of the high clergy, yes; and nothing has yet proved to her that it has collapsed. There may be a crack, because of some earthquake at Versailles, but the Court has seen so many . . . And even if her cardinal is a dead man, Jeanne has already staked out plenty of claims elsewhere. Lots of men have made sheep's eyes at her in the last few months. At the beginning of August, for example, there was that handsome eagle-beaked snob trailing in the wake of the Baron de Breteuil, who sat next to her at Versailles in the home of the old notary Jean-Pierre de La Fresnaye; Rohan was there too, as a matter of fact, "and several of his friends."[2] What was the fellow's name? Baron?—no, Comte de Barras, that was it, another card in Jeanne's hand.

Rohan, Maury, Barras . . . In 1785, Jeanne de La Motte is holding hands with three generations of putrescence†—that of today, tomorrow, and the day after. Her image has marked them; Paul de Barras has not forgotten that dinner party on August 5, ten days before the big blowup. There was even a scheme to make a match between the ex-officer of the Languedoc regiment

*Beugnot remembers the moonlight and refers to it again in a note written on August 17, 1834, shortly before his death and forty-nine years after the event.

†Ten years from now, taking over from the men of liberty, Barras will govern France; he will be one of the decisive figures of 9 Thermidor and, until 18 Brumaire, the most influential member of the Directoire.

and Jeanne's sister, Marie-Anne de Saint-Rémi—twenty-seven, fair, and good-natured, a wide-eyed witness to the blazing career of her sister and brother-in-law, who would like to take advantage of their own meteoric rise to connect her to some desirable family.

They were not discouraging the approaches of the "Baron" de Barras, as he calls himself, without the least justification, pending the day when he can more defensibly claim the title of "comte" after his father's demise. He too is a first-class bluffer, but nothing is easier than for one fake to take in another, it's almost a game, and both La Mottes were appreciative of his polish and his hot-off-the-presses and highly seasoned reminiscences of his two campaigns in India, first in the retrenchments of Pondicherry and then at sea in the Bailli du Suffren's little fleet. In fact, Barras has wasted seven or eight years out there without a promotion and now he hasn't even got an assignment; in other words, he's retired before the age of thirty. Ragged but proud he left his native Provence, and proud but ragged he has returned, and is finding it rather confining. Paul, the eldest of four surviving children (out of ten), has no taste for agriculture and no wish to wrest from the hands of his younger brethren the meager fields of Fox and Amphoux. He bounded up from Marseilles* to Paris to seek his fortune in the intricate labyrinth of drawing rooms and offices where another lost aristocrat, Mirabeau, was also striving to feather his nest and not rejecting contributions from the distaff side. "Deprived of any military activity, I had few resources for life in Paris; I was supported by an old female relative who lived in Marseilles." Not much gold to be gouged from this newly coined comte, thus, but to the La Mottes his escutcheon is worth regilding: three bars (*barras* in Provençal) on a shield fesse in gold and azure would make a pretty balcony overlooking the nobility of Aix and Marseilles, and one of his uncles, Barras de la Penne, led de Grasse's winning squadron in the Chesapeake at the decisive moment. On his mother's side, moreover, Paul de Barras is allied to Breteuil's cousin the Marquis de Créqui, the rising minister in charge of the King's prisons. Paul boasts of having angered the Marquis de Castries, the present minister of the navy, whose popularity wanes when that of Breteuil waxes, by informing him of the mismanagement of some of the ships' commanders that caused Suffren's Indian strategy to misfire; in one of his frequent fits of temper Castries "armed himself with a book with the apparent design of hurling it at my head." Diverting chap, Barras, who drives ministers to attempt manslaughter when they're not on his side. Mme de La Motte-Valois has an eye for men, and this one, as brother-in-law, would not be too loathsome a person to encounter in my dear little sister's house. Has

---

*Where, in 1779, the ship that brought him and part of his regiment back from the Indies the first time—a ship named the *Sartines* in honor of the ex-minister of the navy—gave birth to the famous tale of the sardine so big that it blocked the entrance to the Vieux Port. It actually did land athwart the roadway after a wrong maneuver.

Jeanne sensed his other side, his love of authority, his art of circumstance? He himself rapidly understood that if he wanted to marry one sister he would have to pay court to the other who already had a husband. Their brother, Jacques de Saint-Rémi de Valois, a fellow naval officer, had told his mate Barras about both girls while they were campaigning with Suffren,* and even gave him a letter of recommendation to the older sister.

"I confess that the life of a young man who tended not to be very particular about his acquaintances brought me into the society of the Lamotte [sic] woman." . . . That evening in August, things had gone well enough for Barras to wangle the right to take her home when, "at midnight, the guests departed. On the way she felt faint and oppressed and invoked my friendship which, she told me in very vague terms, she might well need. Never had she known so loyal a man as I; indeed, my loyalty went to the point of candor."

In other words, he might have become her latest investment in human capital; but their relations went no further. Barras has had a close shave.†

When the sky actually falls, Beugnot happens to be the unlucky man beneath it. As they approach their hometown he begins to panic. Maybe he's had suspicions all along and is terrified to think that he may have turned too blind an eye. A lawyer is a man who knows jurisprudence, and where lèse majesté is concerned jurisprudence is full of gallows. And he had been planning such a quiet career! Already he can see his name being dragged through the gazettes. He challenges her head-on:

"What is this about a necklace which the cardinal was supposed to buy for the Queen? And how does it happen that a cardinal should be chosen to make such a purchase? And how came the Queen to hit upon Prince Louis [de Rohan], whom she openly detests, to make this purchase for her?"[4]

She brushes his questions away like flies, she tries to pretend that the whole thing is the fault of that curious character who has got his claws into the cardinal and became his magi, wizard, director of conscience, you know who I mean, his evil genius, that Cagliostro who claims to be a contemporary of Moses, a sort of Mesmer with less knowledge and more nerve. There, that's what she needs, just the thing:

*The brother, therefore, was not involved in the La Mottes' intrigues, although he had been glad enough to accept a pension and the title of Baron de Valois, thanks to Jeanne. He has just died (on May 9, 1785) of fever, in Port Louis (Île-de-France, now Mauritius), where he was captain of a frigate. Presumably Jeanne has not yet heard the news; in August, at any rate, she is not in mourning.

†After Rohan's arrest, he takes the precaution of leaving Paris for a few weeks, "on the advice," he writes, "of the protector of his youth, the Duc d'Orléans." In 1797 Marie-Anne de Saint-Rémi, the sister they were trying to marry to Barras, seeks an interview with Barras, the all-powerful Director, who most certainly does not answer her letter—but he does keep it among his papers.[3]

"It's Cagliostro from start to finish."

But she can't keep the chasm from yawning wide in Beugnot's mind, and his contagious anxiety finally affects her too:

"It's true that if the prince really is in trouble, he is perfectly capable of saying all sorts of nonsense to clear himself."

In other words, of implicating herself and her husband. Beugnot breaks out:

"Madame de La Motte, you have just said far more than I should have wished to hear. I have one last favor to ask of you. It is ten o'clock in the evening. I know a reliable person who lives close by. I shall entrust you to his care. I shall accompany your carriage back to Bar-sur-Aube, and shall warn M. de La Motte, who can come for you within the hour in a gig behind your two best horses. He can bring your most precious possessions, and this very night you can both set out by the Chalons road, because the Troyes road will not be safe for you. You can reach Picardy or Normandy. Do not show yourself at either Boulogne or Calais or Dieppe, where you may already be looked for; but there are a score of places between those ports from which you may cross for 10 louis and be set down in England."

"Sir, you will put me out of patience if you continue; I have let you talk on because I was thinking of other matters. How many times must I tell you that this business has nothing to do with me?"

At that, all Beugnot can do is sulk. "We rode in silence for half an hour." A bitter silence, the acerbity of their ruminations unsoftened by the lake of moonlight spreading over the countryside. Beugnot may well, in that half-hour, have taken an oath never to come within fifty miles of such a woman again.

How could he have foreseen? When the two sisters, looking like Cinderella and the Goose Girl, had first fluttered into the wretched inn "La Tête Rouge" six years before, after escaping from the Abbey of Longchamp in which they were determined not to be buried alive, the whole of Bar-sur-Aube, you might say, fell in love with them. "Each of them had one fat écu in her pocket, and their entire wardrobe consisted of a single chemise." People knew their story here, because they had been born and had endured their suffering childhood in that miserable hovel of Fontette in the canton of Essoyes four leagues from Bar-sur-Aube, "with a little trapdoor opening onto the street, through which people took turns bringing them a bowl of soup or some coarse morsels of food." Beugnot's father remembered them well.

"I saw it with my own eyes," he had said to Jacques-Claude, "and the priest himself did not dare open the door of those naked children who were fed like some sort of wild animals."

Their mother? A trollop, Marie Josselle, the laborer's daughter who had been a servant in the château of Fontette before subsiding into prostitution and drink. "Jeanne liked to lie in bed in the morning, and sometimes her mother chased after her with a pitchfork all the way to her pallet, to make her get up."[5] Marie also reduced her husband to shreds—the half-tamed gentleman, part forester, part poacher with a touch of brigand thrown in, who perpetuated the name of Saint-Rémi and eventually married her. People respected him while keeping well clear of him, because this brute "of imposing stature" was a genuine Valois. There had been Saint-Rémis living at Fontette since the days of Henri II, as the old wives had been saying by the fireside for two centuries. This pigsty was the last vestige of the great estate of Fontette which King Henri gave to the bastard he had had by Nicole de Savigny and had recognized: the first of the Saint-Rémi de Valois, who was also governor of Châteauvillain . . . In the end, Henri II's three legitimate sons, and the Bourbon kings who came after them, forgot their embarrassing cousins, leaving them to rot in Champagne.

In the spring of 1760 the last tatters of this human wreckage piled onto a farm wagon, their raft, and set out to beg from the good-hearted Parisians. "The Baron and Baronne de Saint-Rémi" disappeared from the "fief of Fontette," whose last crumbs they had tossed to their creditors.* They bore their children away over the ocean of indigence, one unexpected wave of which flung their two daughters back up onto the native shores twenty years later. As moving as Venus, and almost as naked.

BAR-SUR-AUBE

# 1 2

AUGUST 1785

## In This Gilded Cavern

The "young de Saint-Rémi ladies" did not long remain at "La Tête Rouge." The Beugnots (father and son) hastened to their side; and a woman named de Surmont, the arbiter of society in Bar-sur-Aube, took them in at the risk of a marital crisis (her husband the provost, whom a later age would call

---

*A few traces of the earlier buildings can be seen today, in the thickness of certain walls, a farm courtyard, and the outline of the château's round towers in the flooring of the houses subsequently built on its site.

"commissioner," promptly succumbed to Jeanne's spell) and a drawing-room revolution. "The de Saint-Rémi girls brought life and movement into the home of Mme de Surmont. The young men who were entertained there soon observed that the demoiselles had a number of features in common with fairy-tale princesses and were no less obliging. All things considered, they would have yielded to any bourgeois who was truly infatuated and aspired to the honor of their hand,"[1] and Jacques-Claude saw this clearly enough to embark upon a mournful little fairy tale of his own. "I admired, without understanding the danger of it, her bold spirit [Jeanne's] that would stop at nothing. . . . I never wearied of singing her praises. The year the de Saint-Rémi girls came to live in Bar-sur-Aube, my father, for the first time in his life, began trying to hasten my departure for Paris."

Six years have now passed and he can thank his father, although Jeanne would never have consented to become Mme Beugnot. Her declared intention was nothing less than to reconquer "her vast family estates," especially Essoyes, Fontette, and Verpillières, "which had fallen into the King's hands," or in other words had been scooped up for the Crown by the intendant of Troyes, to the detriment of Jeanne's father. Since her entire fortune consisted of one écu she had no time to waste, and she needed allies with long arms. She came to such a good understanding with the Surmonts' nephew Nicholas de La Motte that on June 6, 1780, she married him, before giving birth—on July 6 of the same year—to twin boys.* To Beugnot this came almost as a relief: "This latter circumstance brought a union which had previously seemed quite inexplicable down to the level of the exceedingly commonplace." Jeanne, who was a good sport, quickly provided the young lawyer with equally "commonplace" consolations, in return for his drafting of pleadings and documents in support of the revenge of the Valois.

At first she seemed to be getting nowhere fast. Court and bureaucrats made no response to Beugnot's brilliant (at least he was sure it was) memorandum, "replete with the philosophical considerations that were then in vogue," requesting the Bourbons "to pay the natural debt of those whose magnificent inheritance had fallen to them." Jeanne and her husband spent two or three years vegetating in a couple of pokey rooms in "La Ville de Reims," a third-rate hostelry on the rue de la Verrière in Paris. "Her credit had fallen to an exceedingly low ebb and two loans of 10 louis each† that I made her did little to improve it." Was she about to go under, like her parents?

Suddenly her sails filled. There were mysterious and increasingly lengthy disappearances, followed by reappearances of a metamorphosed Jeanne. "I thought I could see something reassured in her features and manner; there was

---

*They lived only a few days and the La Mottes had no other children.

†About 3,000 modern francs [$750] in all; this is Beugnot speaking, of course.

already a glimmer of hauteur in her deportment."[2] Cinderella had found the coach that could convey her to the top of the hill—to the Cardinal-Prince-Bishop Louis de Rohan. But not only there; she also "had an audience with M. le Maréchal de Richelieu, who, amiable and sensitive as ever to the fair sex, treated her charmingly. She had some hopes in that quarter as well." At the age of eighty-four Richelieu has just remarried, his bride being a pretty woman from the lesser nobility of Lorraine, only fifty years his junior, who cannot contrive, with all her vigilance, "to drive away the flies that were still buzzing around the old libertine's brow."[3] Out of injured pride, as always, Beugnot begins to backpedal: "There was Mme de La Motte, hovering between the oldest and the most graceless courtiers of the century! That left scant room in the middle for a mere lawyer." But she kept her grip on him too, out of friendship, calculation, and her need of a willing ear. To hear her tell it, she had progressed well beyond the Rohans and Richelieus and was now "running" in higher, much higher circles; there was nothing elevated about their morals, however, and Beugnot sat with mouth agape, afraid to ask any more questions lest he be compelled to understand what she was making all too clear already: the Queen, I tell you, the Queen and I . . . He plugged his ears, but only halfway.

The La Mottes took rooms at Versailles—in a mere hotel, it is true—but they also rented a house on the rue Neuve Saint-Gilles in the Marais in Paris, "with porter's lodge, bread oven, sheds, large and small stables, three stories, and high windows decorated with wrought-iron balustrades representing flowers and other motifs,"* and when they first came back to spend a few days at Bar-sur-Aube you can imagine how flabbergasted the locals were to see them preceded by "a very heavily loaded wagon pulled by a handsome team and followed by two costly thoroughbred horses."[4] No more putting up in the inn, be it dirty or clean. "The owner of a good-sized house was promptly turned out (for a price, of course), and the rooms hastily made ready. A butler who came with the wagon requisitioned more provisions than would be needed to feed the best house in town for six months. People stared at each other in the streets, wondering what this new chapter out of the *Thousand and One Nights* could possibly mean. . . ."

Beugnot clasped her secret to his bosom: He knew. This was Favor with a capital *F.* In Paris, when he went to the rue Neuve Saint-Gilles, he always dressed "in black, with long hair [stuffed into a little snood], and the comtesse much appreciated this sign of respect. She never failed to introduce me as a young magistrate and placed me immediately after her titled guests."[5]

Rohan he never saw; the cardinal called only when he could see Jeanne alone in her room. But he very much wanted to make the acquaintance of

---

*Later number 10, rue Saint-Gilles.

another person, and eventually did see, touch, and hear the man—"rather middling in size and quite stout, with an olive complexion, a very short neck and round face adorned with two large, protruding eyes and a flaring, turned-up nose"—called Cagliostro, the great sorcerer of the day, who wore a "French-style coat, iron gray with gold braid, a scarlet jacket, red trousers, a sword poking through the tails of his coat, an embroidered hat with a white plume in it," not to mention the lace cuffs, precious rings, and shoe-buckles of an earlier age that looked as though they were made of fine dia-monds; in short, all the paraphernalia that enabled Cagliostro to mystify the top Christians who no longer believed in their own God and keep them hanging on his words when, as that evening, he talked about "the skies, the stars, the great arcana* of Memphis, the hieroglyphant [sic], transcendent chemistry, giants, enormous animals, a city in the African interior ten times larger than Paris, where he had correspondents; he punctuated his speech with humorous asides to Mme de La Motte, whom he called his doe, his gazelle, his swan, his dove. . . ."

Beugnot's basic bourgeois self was rather shaken by it all; he walked back home alone that mild spring night and, pausing at the corner of the Place Royale,† was

> filled with pity for the poor human race, reflecting that such tawdry ravings were a refuge, for the powerful of this earth, from the surfeit of possessions which the social order had inflicted [sic] upon them from birth. I thought of the unfortunate Cardinal de Rohan, caught between Cagliostro and Mme de La Motte, who, it is plain to me, have conspired to lead him into the abyss; and as for my own curiosity: is it really so innocent? What business have I in this gilded cavern inhabited by people for whom I feel nothing but contempt, when they ought properly to inspire me with horror?

One can sympathize with Beugnot—a nice, ordinary guy, a standard mixture of weakness and honesty . . . He is our best witness to 1785.** And, once or twice, he has recoiled from the quicksands of his own life.

He is at any rate inspired with sufficient horror not to return to the rue Neuve Saint-Gilles after "the last supper I ate in her house,"[6] which went on far, far into the night because the La Mottes, who were not expecting him (he was a close enough friend to turn up whenever he felt like it), did not come home themselves until sometime between midnight and one in the morning, accompanied by one of their new playmates, Marc-Antoine Rétaux de Villette. Beugnot positively writhes at the fatuousness of this "handsome fellow of

---

*Universal remedy, dream of Illuminism.

†Place des Vosges today.

**And will be our best witness to Napoleon's downfall in 1813 and to some of the episodes of the Hundred Days.

thirty, well-formed, with fair hair in which a few strands of silver could already be seen, blue eyes, a fresh and ruddy complexion";[7] and his loathing is fully justified. This time, really, Jeanne is going a bit too far, flaunting a *ménage à trois* in front of her little lawyer, it's plain to see that she has been bewitched by this ladies' man—another former officer brought home by her husband. Well, why should they bother about appearances?—this is Paris.

Beugnot's definitive nausea is caused less by Villette, however, than by the girl they had along with them. He's never seen her before, and she is so reserved and shy that he takes her for a mute or a moron until the meal is over. Beautiful, though,

> extremely beautiful, between twenty-five and thirty years old, and with an exceptionally fine figure. . . . From the very first glance this woman's features had given me that slightly puzzled, anxious feeling that one has when looking at a face one is sure one has seen somewhere before but can't remember when or where. I hoped I should be able to solve the mystery when I accompanied her home. I plied her with questions, trying to find a lead, but could get nothing out of her. . . . I let my fair mute out on the rue de Cléry,

and went home to nurse a stomach sickened by the meal, or rather by the way in which the people partaking of it had "raved and sung, unable to stand on their feet." They were clearly having victory hysterics, but over whom or what? Life, no doubt; but which aspect of it? Villette, three sheets to the wind, almost let the cat out of the bag, but

> Mme de La Motte, who was next to him at table, swiftly placed a hand over his mouth and said, in the most imperious tone:
> "Hush. M. Beugnot is too proper a person to hear our secrets."
> I should have been flattered by the compliment if Mme de La Motte had not been in the habit, in her ordinary speech, of using "proper" as a synonym for "stupid."

And she may not have been far wrong, either, Beugnot bitterly muses as the first houses of Bar-sur-Aube rise up in the moonlight—the hometown of them both, full of legends and old stones. St. Germaine had the priory church built, it was named after her; you can see it in the distance "at the top of the hill near the town, among the ruins of an ancient city allegedly called Florence. . . . Germaine helped build the church with her own hands, carrying water in a jug, so that painters often show her with a jug in either hand." She was martyred "by order of Attila, behind the church of Saint-Macrou in a field which is said to have remained sterile ever since and in which absolutely nothing will grow."[8]

St. Germaine has been neglecting her town of late, though, and has allowed its population to fall to a mere three or four thousand souls. "Most of the woolen manufacturers have ceased operating and only a few are left, employing a very small number of workers." Where are the days "of the four free fairs that were attended by merchants from all parts of Europe? . . . In those days there were separate districts in the town, one for the Dutch, another for Germans and another for the people of Lorraine, and there was even a district for merchants from the Principality of Orange. There were Jews living in the town, and they had a fine synagogue there. . . ."

Dead and gone, all of them, swept away by time and growing competition from Troyes. Because of Jeanne de La Motte-Valois, however, the kingdom of France is about to remember Bar-sur-Aube.

DE LA MOTTE

# 13

AUGUST 1785

## *My Bastille Bag*

Beugnot:

"As we came into town, I begged her at least to burn any papers that might compromise herself or the cardinal: 'It is a measure dictated by honor on the one hand, and by your own safety on the other.'

"To this she consented."[1]

The coach clatters to a halt in a flurry of half-asleep stable-boys, before "the capacious bourgeois house, two wings, a main building and its ancillaries,* standing in the center of town."[2] The La Mottes bought it last November,† as though to confer a certificate of authenticity upon their *Thousand and One Nights*. They have twelve horses and five more vehicles in the stables, including "the light cabriolet that was Jeanne's favorite, in the shape of a balloon over ten feet high"; the upper windows of the house look onto the Aube, the old bridges, and, in the distance, the countryside with its thickets

---

*In French, *basse-cour,* now "farmyard," which corresponded in those days to the outbuildings, usually only one or two stories tall, where the servants lived above the chickens and other domestic fowl.

†In July 1797 the Comte de La Motte himself, who emerges from the Terror unscathed and wearing the becoming halo of martyr to the monarchy, sells it to a local philanthropist, Nicholas Armand, whose name is given to the street that subsequently bisects the main body of the house. Its two wings became numbers 1, 3, 5, and 2, 4, and 6 of that street, and 37 and 38 of the rue Nationale.

of alder and willow, its rows of poplars, and the vines on which "St. Germaine's wine" is ripening . . . No time to stand dreaming in front of them now. Seconds count.

"I offered to help her; she did not refuse, and, leaving the coach, we went up to her rooms. Her husband, who had gone out hunting that morning with a party, was not yet returned." They'll be working amidst the dazzling array of objects in the impressive convoy of forty-two carters' wagons that delivered "a vast quantity of furnishings" last June: "fabrics, hangings, and carpets from Texier worth 50,000 francs,* *meubles meublants†* from Gervais, Hericourt and Fournier of the Faubourg Saint-Antoine, including a crimson velvet bed garnished with gold braid and fringe and strewn with sequins and pearls," and the bronze statues by Chevalier, the Adams marbles, the Sikes crystal . . . She moves to "a large sandalwood casket" from which she extracts "papers of all colors and dimensions."

Why does she insist upon reading them all?

"Have you any bearer bonds there, or notes from the discount bank, any securities to keep? No? Then throw the whole lot into the fire and let that be an end of it."

But she must needs look through them, at least, and so we did, she most painstakingly and I in great haste. It was then, casting a rather fleeting glance upon one or two of the thousand [*sic*] letters of M. le Cardinal de Rohan, that I saw and pitied the havoc wrought upon that unhappy man by the madness of love, intensified by the madness of ambition. It is fortunate for the memory of M. le Cardinal that those letters were destroyed. Their loss is a loss to the history of human passion, no doubt; but what was this century in which a prince of the church openly wrote, signed, and sent, to a woman he knew so little and so ill, letters which in our day a man with any inkling of self-respect might begin to read, but would never finish?

We can well see why she was so unwilling to burn them, in the big log fire that was always laid in these parts, even in August, to warm the old stones. What a cover it had been, that purple mantle draped over a bed! And also, what perfect material for blackmail, to use against the cardinal and his family . . . Meanwhile, there is further edification in store for Beugnot. Leafing through the heap he discovers "multitudes of bills, some receipted, others not, offers of land for sale, announcements concerning precious objects and new inventions." At last they reach the bottom of the pile, and there lay what he knew had to be there: "letters from Böhmer and Bassenge** referring to a

---

*350,000 modern francs [$87,500].

†"The words *meubles meublants* apply solely to furniture intended to serve in and adorn living apartments" (Civil Code, article 534); what might be called "luxury furniture."

**Bassenge, Böhmer's son-in-law and associate, was the more active partner in the firm of jewelers, and was supposed to inherit it.

necklace and overdue payments, acknowledging receipt of certain sums and demanding larger ones. . . ." They scorch his fingers. But he does consult her about them, he realizes their potential value in her defense if Rohan should try to lay all the blame on her. She now becomes increasingly uncertain, which shows that she was not expecting arrest or even a public scandal. This time it's Beugnot who makes the decision. He's far more terrified than she is, and if worst comes to worst, it's better to leave no traces at all than such double-edged ones. "I took the safest way; that is, I threw everything into the fire."

It's half past three in the morning. He leaves for home on foot, not before having once more begged Jeanne to go, go this very minute, don't even wait for dawn; there's still time . . . Ah Beugnot, you great ninny, what a spineless creature you are! The only promise she will make is to go straight to bed.

"So I left her in her rooms, reeking of burning papers and twenty different kinds of sealing wax."

Poor Jacques-Claude doesn't get much rest that night and is soon rubbing his eyes and peering over the blankets as his parents' aged serving woman opens the door with a grumble to admit a caller as unlikely as he is unexpected, in the "somewhat rumpled year-round velvet coat which he wore out hunting and had not taken off since the day before"—Nicholas de La Motte.

What on earth time is it? Six in the morning! Beugnot guesses the news before the comte delivers it, "in a self-satisfied, calm tone."

"My wife has been arrested. Two officers of the King came for her at four in the morning, to take her to Paris. Some business I know nothing about, the Cardinal de Rohan, the Queen, a necklace. . . ."

"But I was with her at half past three!"

"I know, I came in earlier but she had given orders that the two of you were not to be disturbed. I obeyed, I waited, and just as I was on the point of going to bed myself I heard the officers' carriage."

He is so calm, so unconcerned, or at least appears to be, that Beugnot positively snaps at him, "Sir, let me inform you that this very night I advised your wife to leave with you for England by the quickest route. If she had listened to me she would not now be on the high road to the Bastille. I would advise you to undertake alone what I hoped you both would do."

The other fellow almost yawns, placidly settling his "ugly but well-formed" person into an armchair. His body is "skilled in all physical exercises," the very model of the patented seducer; "despite his ugliness, his features have an amiable and mild expression [long face, pale complexion, black eyebrows, a rather thick lower lip], and he is not totally lacking in wit, but uses whatever gifts he may possess in that direction for unworthy purposes."[3] His nonchalance—feigned, no doubt, but to perfection—propels poor Jacques-Claude out of bed in his long white nightshirt:

"I know enough about your position to tell you frankly that you are behaving like an idiot or a fool."

"Goodness, what an extraordinary way to talk to a person! What can Mme de La Motte have told you?"

"She told me nothing. All the more reason for me to urge you to withdraw without a moment's delay, do you hear, without a moment's delay!"

"M. de La Motte shrugged and humming a tune, left me,"[4] walking "with the rather heavy lurch that caused him to be called 'Momotte' by his comrades in the gendarmerie."

But the very next day finds him in England all the same, together with what was left of their compromising papers and negotiable securities. "This was August 18. It was not until four days later that they came back to Bar-sur-Aube to arrest him."

Beugnot and the rest of the townspeople can hardly believe the incompe-
tence of the investigators, as well as of their superiors: the Baron de Breteuil, Thiroux de Crosne (the new chief of police), all those officials who have orders to rush proceedings in the case of the century and who need four days to realize that if the wife is implicated in all the accusations made on August 15, they'd better grab the husband too.

Beugnot—to finish his part of the story—is scared out of his wits. He has not yet plumbed the full depths of the authorities' inefficiency. Having gotten hold of one end of the skein—Jeanne—they must, he reasons, unwind it up to me, and then farewell, carefree youth!

> I could not guess the lengths to which the Baron de Breteuil would carry inepti-
> tude or malevolence in this matter and, having deduced what he *would* do by
> considering what he *ought* to do, I anticipated my arrest. I then remembered the
> secret horror I had always felt when I passed the Bastille, and took it for a
> presentiment. I dared not leave Bar-sur-Aube, yet dreaded to remain there,
> imagining all too clearly the despair of my family if I were to be forcibly removed
> from the house in which I had been born to be conducted to the entrance of the
> Faubourg Saint-Antoine.[5]

Thus we learn that the shadow of the Bastille was longer than the faubourg itself, and fell even upon the provinces. It had become the symbol of arbitrary arrest for the people of Champagne as well.

How far can he count on Jeanne's silence, once her tongue has been loosened? If she discloses her "intimate" relations with him he can say good-bye to his reputation. If she says he burned papers pertaining to the case and advised her to leave the country, he'll be implicated in the proceedings, especially if anybody finds out that he read some of them before throwing them into the fire.

As he neither can nor even wants to run away himself—Beugnot is not a man to live outside his own life—he eventually returns to Paris and tries to make himself as inconspicuous as possible among the ranks of the black-robed armies of the law. He sets to work on an important case for the town of Bar-sur-Aube. He prudently chooses "to cut himself off from all society." But the fear of arrest haunts him so that it becomes his constant companion:

> Once I convinced myself of what would happen, I tried to come to terms with the idea of sudden disappearance. I packed my Bastille bag; it consisted of small editions of our best authors, called "Cazins" after the name of the bookseller who published them, to which I added a set of drawing instruments, an atlas, a sufficient supply of paper, quills, ink, and underclothes. I placed these things in a trunk which I kept at the foot of my bed, like a friend standing sentry, ready to follow me at whatever hour I might have to depart. I did more: I went two or three times to the entrance of the Faubourg Saint-Antoine and the Arsenal garden, to accustom myself to the sight of the Bastille and scrutinize it as closely as I could from a distance. Counting the narrow slits in its walls that did duty for windows, I tried to guess which one would be assigned to bring the light of day to me. In this way, little by little, I familiarized myself with the idea that had initially struck such terror to my soul.

Practical training for apprentice convicts. But Beugnot won't have to apply it, or at least not in the King's lockups. The loyal Jeanne does not give her little lawyer away, and he never is put in the Bastille. He almost seems to regret it.

CARDINAL ROHAN

# 14

## AUGUST 1785

## *A Fine-looking Prelate, Not Religious at All*

Jeanne was so sure she'd won! She was so certain she had flummoxed the lot of them, from the hicks of her childhood to the fancy punks out there in Versailles, and Böhmer and Bassenge, celebrated jewelers to the courts of Europe, in the bargain. Had anybody else ever started with so little and made so much of it?

Until they actually came to arrest her she was convinced that once Rohan realized how she had diddled him he would pay for the necklace and shut up. But the rub was that she had diddled him too well, her trick was too perfect: Rohan hadn't paid for the very good reason that he hadn't seen through her. He believed Jeanne right to the end, that is, five or six days too long.

There is no mystery about the Queen's necklace. The whole business is a tangle of misunderstandings entwined by the protagonists' credulity, with Jeanne de La Motte alone being wittingly deceitful. The rest misled each other as to their intentions, but in good faith. Böhmer truly believed that Marie Antoinette had bought herself a necklace through the agency of the cardinal; the cardinal truly believed he had been commissioned to make the purchase, and was seeing himself as prime minister in another month or so; the Queen, followed by the King, truly believed that Rohan had stolen the necklace, using their names as cover; and on August 15 in Versailles, instead of explaining themselves, they all start screaming at one another. Jeanne and her husband might have slipped through the net like a pair of minnows while the bigger fish were floundering around inside, but instead they were caught by their own cleverness. They had based their entire scheme on the stupidity of Louis de Rohan, and even there they underestimated him: he's not just stupid, he's an imbecile. But he is also an *honnête homme*.

Jeanne does not feel now, and never will, the least remorse. The trick she played on him is her revolution, the only kind she can imagine. Tit for tat. She is a Valois, and to her fingertips she feels herself a member of a superior race, or at least equal to the flashiest among them. Her chance was stolen from her in her cradle, and she is simply taking it back, using the only weapons at her command: cunning and seduction. She has probably thought of little else since the day that wagon from Bar-sur-Aube dumped her and her parents into the gutter of Paris.

Boulogne, to be exact—a pretty village hidden in the woods on the banks of the Seine, downstream from Paris. The parish priest took them in in the spring of 1760. He gave them a bed; for board, Jeanne's parents had already taught her how to beg, hands outstretched, for "two orphans of royal blood."[1] It was a profitable come-on. Her father and mother had not stayed together long: Marie was still in good enough shape to satisfy the soldiers, but Jacques de Saint-Rémi was decomposing on his feet. His wife threw him out and he went and died at the Hôtel-Dieu in February 1762, in one of those beds into which they stuffed the ailing two or three at a time. His place at home had already been taken by Jean-Baptiste Raimond, a sergeant in the French Guards and a brute with rather special tastes, starting with naked seven-year-old girls. Sade didn't really invent much.

Unmoved by my tears, my pitiless mother shut the door and, after forcing me to remove the wretched rags that scarce covered my body, she fell upon me furiously and flayed my skin off with great lashes of her stick. That was not all. Raimond had tied me to the foot of the bed and if, in the course of the cruel operation, I ventured to utter a cry, she would begin striking me afresh and with redoubled strength. Often her rod broke in her hands, so heavily had her brutal anger fallen upon me.[2]

The Boulogne parish priest saved the two little girls in the nick of time by recommending them to a local benefactress, the Marquise de Boulainvilliers, wife of the provost of Paris.* A Valois, did you say a Valois? The good lady in her château at Passy was all atwitter. For the first time Jeanne saw what an "open sesame" her name could be. It enabled her to change families, for instance, just as her mother, abandoned by the sergeant, was going back to Champagne to die under the weight of peasants and wagon drivers. She simply vanished, nobody knew where, and was transformed by the wave of a magic wand into the Marquise de Boulainvilliers, a lady all in gold and silver like you read about in fairy tales, the adoptive mother of thirty children who see her from a distance and who can count on her without loving her. In Passy, doing good is part of one's toilette.

Five years in the home of a Dame Leclerc, who taught them their manners. At fourteen she "went into service" as an apprentice seamstress in the Faubourg Saint-Germain. After all, another Jeanne started the same way and ended up as the Comtesse du Barry. But ours was not called Bécu, and you don't shove a Valois in the back of the shop to be worked over by aging libertines. "I was tyrannized by an uncrushable pride which I had received from nature and which the kindness of Mme de Boulainvilliers, holding out the promise of a more brilliant future, had rendered all the more demanding."[3] She irritated her superiors. "I became by turns a laundress, water carrier, cook, ironer, linen maid, anything and everything except happy and respected."[4] Mme de Boulainvilliers—"open sesame" again—didn't scold her too much for her instability and took her to live in her own home as a sort of companion, a servant in all but name, for two years.

Yes; but she was going on twenty and the benefactress's husband wanted a share in the good works; the incident with François Henri de Boulainvilliers, sixty-two at the time, added the adolescent's hatred of anyone having power to the child's resentment. One inevitable evening, in the château in Passy,

everybody had retired to rest and deep silence reigned on all sides, when M. de Boulainvilliers, who had not gone to bed and had taken every precaution to

---

*Not to be confused with the provost of merchants, who was actually the mayor of Paris, elected, as a formality, by the bourgeois but in reality appointed by the King's Household. The provost of Paris was something like a director of police, with more dignity than real power.

ensure that he would meet no obstacle, crept softly out of his rooms and into mine.
. . . But the noise he could not prevent himself from making awoke me, and I
parted the curtains of the bed.

Heavens! what should I see but the Marquis de Boulainvilliers, in dressing
gown and slippers, with a lantern in his hand, which he placed upon a console. . . .

In an instant, the scales fell from my eyes; I no longer saw, in the man I had
loved as a father and looked upon as my protector and the guardian of my
innocence, anything but a cruel foe, a vile creature bent upon my destruction.
. . . With such feelings as these, it took no great effort of virtue to resist him.[5]

According to Jeanne, her resistance was the cause of a series of domestic
persecutions, including the replacement of wax with tallow candles in her
room.[6] But did she really resist all that much? Perhaps, instead, her distinguished benefactress deemed it expedient to remove her. At any rate the two
sisters, Jeanne and Marie-Anne, were dispatched to the Abbey of Yerres as
boarders, where they had nothing to do and no life to live, and were surrounded by commoners to boot. But their luck was about to turn. An inquiry
which had been instigated by the Marquise de Boulainvilliers and was carried
out by the famous d'Hozier, judge-at-arms of nobility, certified, on May 6,
1776, "that the Demoiselles de Saint-Rémi de Valois descend from Henri
II."[7] In those days, when the illicit appropriation of titles was almost a major
industry, a genuine patent from d'Hozier was worth its weight in gold. One
word from him could have tarnished a ducal lineage. Boulainvilliers, who
turns out to be not such a cad after all, secures for each of the girls, almost
automatically, a yearly income of 800 livres,* which was immediately invested
in their board at another abbey, at Longchamp, "where only girls of quality
were accepted."

Accepted as novices, that is, because they were going to have to choose,
at twenty-five, a lifetime in gray and black. To hell with "quality"; the nunnery
is not for us. "They went over the hedge that fenced in the abbey, with one
small bundle under their arm and 12 écus in their pockets."[8]

Bar-sur-Aube. The Beugnots. The Surmonts. La Motte. Marriage. The
twins. And they were off.

A few months in the barracks town of Lunéville, La Motte's last garrison. Now,
there's a man who would be well advised not to submit his lineage to M.
d'Hozier for verification: he had no shadow of a right to be called a count,
which only made him call himself one all the more. Since the Treaty of

*About 5,500 modern francs [$1,375]. The allowance was paid out of the King's privy
purse, and the payment order was signed by him on presentation of the certificate of nobility by
Breteuil or Calonne. For a moment, at least, Louis XVI came in contact with the name of Jeanne
de Valois.

Versailles the army had become redundant, so he had no difficulty obtaining what was known as a "leave of distinction," or early retirement.[9] It wasn't much in the way of wealth—another 150 livres.* But Jeanne had already begun to make plans. She would get the Boulainvilliers to forgive her for running away from Longchamp and, duly married, allegedly a countess, definitely a Valois, she would use them as a launching pad for a shot at Court.

In September 1781 the marquis and his wife were in Strasbourg, two days from Lunéville—an excellent opportunity to cast Mme de Boulainvilliers in the role of benefactress one last time. The marquise had been invited by the Cardinal de Rohan to his château at Saverne. She took along the La Mottes, to introduce them to the mighty and potent lord. If he would consent to give them a hand . . .

Cinderella found her coach, Sleeping Beauty met her Prince Charmer, if not Charming. One foot in the stirrup. The Boulainvilliers could drop dead —which they obligingly did, within months.

Saverne. An ideal setting for the opening lines of a fairy tale. The château, which had burned in 1779, had been almost completely rebuilt—a new Versailles rising out of the pink Alsatian sandstone. Four stories, each thirty-five windows long. A masterpiece of late eighteenth-century architecture, with a few baroque allusions, lots of forward-looking antiquity, fluted pilasters brightening up the vast façades, one of which overlooked the town square while the other gave onto terraced gardens of Babylonian proportions at the foot of a monumental staircase. Inside, row upon row of sparkling, glittering rooms, all rosewood, gilt, and encrusted panels, physics and natural history laboratories, several libraries . . .

The opulence of the more advanced disciples of Holy Poverty, as subsequently savored by Franklin in the La Rochefoucaulds' place at Gaillon, is still several degrees inferior to this "sovereign state" over which Prince Louis reigns supreme. But where does he get the "prince"? From the Holy Roman Empire, to which the bishopric of Strasbourg has become so closely annealed that many of its flock can hardly tell whether they are ex-German or neo-French. The Rohans (who have been handing the miter down from generation to generation over a century of organized nepotism) "seemed to have undertaken to represent France to Germany."[10] They hobnobbed as equals with the princes of Baden, Darmstadt, and Zweibrücken. The Elector of Cologne went home in a pet when it became plain to him that he was not keeping up with this Jones. "The Fair Eminence lives on a grander scale in Saverne than any prince of Germany, or even the ecclesiastical electors."[11] Not hard to believe: the Saverne estate is something like the ultimate summer home, the pinnacle

*7,000 modern francs [$250].

of the ultra-luxurious hotel trade that is bleeding the whole system to death. "The entire province hastened to accept the invitations of the prince-bishop, who could offer his guests seven hundred beds; even then they sometimes ran out of space. There were 124 horses in the stables, and more carriages than anyone could desire. A butler went through the rooms every morning and inquired who wished to be served there; at the stipulated hour [of the early afternoon], an exquisite collation would be brought. In the evening, however, everyone assembled for supper. There was the greatest freedom imaginable at Saverne"; for some people it was a—relative—release from the straitjacket of etiquette reigning at Versailles or among the princes of the blood, "and a Latin verb, *suadere,* * inscribed like a device over every door, indicated that persuasion was the sole means employed to attract and retain guests."

"There was no woman of decent background who did not long to go to Saverne."[12] There Jeanne really felt like a Valois, right down to the supreme refinement of throwing bones to the peons.

> The ladies took part in the great hunts. Six hundred peasants, with keepers, stationed at regular intervals, formed a chain a league long and went running over vast expanses, shouting and beating the bushes and woods. The huntsmen waited at the foot of the hills for the game that was being driven from all sides, and had more than their choice of shots. Three beats were held before one in the afternoon. At that hour the entire company assembled under a fine tent pleasantly situated at the side of a stream. The repast was a gay affair, and since nobody could be allowed to be sad, benches and tables were dug in the grass for the peasants, each of whom was given a pound of meat, two of bread, and half a bottle of wine.

Jeanne didn't spend much time mooning about the landscape; she had not come to unwind. She immediately singled out the only objective worthy of her attention—the tall, empty, vague man with the incipient spare tire who was the sun of this solar system, the spiritual and temporal master of Strasbourg. "M. le Cardinal often graced the supper-table by his presence. The comeliness of his affable face inspired confidence; he had the true physiognomy of the man destined to represent [*sic*]; his features, taken as a whole, always gave him that mien that inspires adoration;† a look that cost him nothing was a gesture of courtesy."

Louis-René-Edouard, Cardinal de Rohan, Grand Almoner of France, Commander of the Order of the Holy Ghost, Superior General of the royal hospital of the Quinze-Vingts (for the blind) in Paris, incumbent of the richest bishopric in France, Prince of the Holy Roman Empire, Superior of the two large abbeys of St. Vaast (Arras) and La Chaise-Dieu (Auvergne), Provost of

---

*"To advise, persuade, as distinct from enjoin."

†According to the *Mémoires* of one of his semi-permanent guests, the Marquis de Valfons, who must have been particularly well treated.

the Sorbonne, member of the Académie Française (since 1761), was also Landgrave of Alsace and hence lord of fourteen square leagues and 25,000 souls in the communities of Ruffach, Dachstein, Mutzig, Schirmeck, Marckolsheim, Benfeld, Wasselone, Kochersberg, and Saverne—not to mention a sort of secondary supremacy over eighty towns, villages, and hamlets of the margravate of Baden, acquired in pursuance of the territorial tangle of the treaties of Westphalia. His face was handsome but somehow babyish, round, smooth and doll-like, with a florid complexion, whitish gray hair receding from the forehead, excellent carriage, and a supple stride. He bore his fifty years with the majesty of budding obesity.[13] Affable, amiable, and comely, everybody agreed as to that; but his first meetings with women were always complicated by a special look, whose consequences were favorable or otherwise, depending on the case—depending on the woman. The assault of female by male, the English "leer" [in English in the original—*Trans.*], the heavy, thick, lingering stare that sometimes obviates all further preliminaries. Even Mme d'Oberkirch, that most respectable baroness, recognized it: "He is a fine-looking prelate, not religious at all but much addicted to women."[14] Young as she had been in 1770, when Rohan had come to meet her at the gates of France on her way to marry the dauphin, Marie Antoinette had, with one shudder of her beautiful shoulders, brushed away that look. A trifle too long, too hard, it had presumed to linger over even her exalted person, and perhaps over every part of it. Who did this bishop think he was? Rohan's undoing was the weakness of the man of slender wit who is incapable of deciphering character, who was born in silk to live in purple and who ends by taking himself for a demigod. He believed himself, that was all.

For Jeanne, the cast of mind and mood of such a man as this was the opening of Ali Baba's cave. With him, her "open sesame" could not fail. He had had, and was still having, prettier women than she; perhaps in the anonymity of his drawing rooms he would scarcely have noticed her. But a Valois, heh, heh!

At his very first interrogation by a counselor from the law court,* he gave full particulars of their meeting. Odd that this man who met so many people should remember it so well. "He met Mme de Boulainvilliers on the high road; she ordered her carriage to stop, he came up, and she introduced to him a person who was seated in front, whom she told him was named Mlle de Valois, adding that that great name was hers by right, that she had no fortune at all, and that she [the marquise] commended her to me."[15]

"Rohan expressed great eagerness to hear the amazing events that must have transpired in the life of so pretty a woman."[16] A few weeks later La Motte

---

*Jean-Pierre Titon, who questioned him in "one of the rooms in the château of the Bastille" on January 11, 1786.

obtained, through him, a post as supernumerary captain of Monsieur's dragoons, where his unmerited title of comte resounded pleasingly. After one nibble, a reassuring bite. The Lunéville debts were paid to the last farthing, and the couple set out for Paris by stagecoach. The cardinal spent a considerable portion of his time in the city and had invited Jeanne to call on him any time.

MARIE ANTOINETTE
AND HER CHILDREN

CARDINAL ROHAN'S HOME,
THE HÔTEL SOUBISE

# 15

AUGUST 1785

## The Queen Has Taken a Fancy to You

It had not been smooth sailing all the way. When she got to Paris, Jeanne realized that Rohan had almost forgotten her; all the preliminaries had to be gone through again. Between their furnished rooms on the rue de la Verrerie in Paris and their furnished rooms, owned by the Goberts, on the Place Dauphine in Versailles, the La Mottes lived from hand to mouth. "This period of her life is obscure.* It shows the motley of an existence that was precarious, uncertain, a mixture of opulence and indigence: a footman, a jockey,† chambermaids, a hired carriage, but also rented furniture, quarrels with the landlady, 1,500 livres of debts for food, and mendicity."[1] High-society mendicity, that is.

She laid siege to the cardinal in his superb mansion on the rue Vielle du Temple,** one of the five or six handsomest "châteaus of Paris," if you count the complex gardens and buildings of the adjoining Palais de Soubise as part of it. A mere fifty-two English mares in the stables. Rooms in the latest fashion, with risqué decorations on the piers parading as mythology, several landscapes by Boucher, and, above all, Christophe Huet's "monkey drawing room," a

---

*According to Target, Rohan's counsel at the trial.

†Meaning "a young servant whose chief duty was to drive a carriage mounted postilion" (Littré). Another instance of double borrowing; this was a French term, *un jacques* (the name having become synonymous with the function, as with Jeeves), which had gone to England, been deformed, and come back again.

**Now the home of the Archives nationales, where the "monkey room" is still to be seen.

lavish splurge of chinoiserie that made the very walls flutter like fans. There she undertook to divert the prince anew and arouse him with her half-insolent, half-victimized availability. Beginning in May 1782, he was already doling out small sums as emergency relief, 5 or 6 louis here and there, that were charged against "the Grand Almoner's funds." In September she got 25 louis in one go,* enough to rent the house on the rue Neuve Saint-Gilles—within walking distance of Rohan—not knowing where the next quarter's rent would come from, and with nothing left to furnish the rooms. The creditors were buzzing like flies.

It was a hard winter. The fire alternately flared up and froze. Rohan was still hanging back, but melting. In February 1783 he agreed to stand surety for a loan of 5,000 francs from the soundest usurer in Nancy, "the Jew Cerf-Beer," as he was contemptuously called by so many noble personages who came knocking at his door.† The "count" sold the rights to their two pensions under a sort of lifehold arrangement to a man named Hubert Gautier, "bourgeois of Paris," for a lump payment of 9,000 livres.** They could set up house. Their circle of acquaintances began to widen; they treated themselves to a little house in Fontainebleau, where "many proper gentlemen would come in turn to call on Mme la Comtesse, while M. le Comte went to warm himself in the other rooms of the château. . . . Officers and lawyers liked to visit her, and leave her tokens of their generosity."[2]

As last she was sufficiently firmly entrenched to indulge in a little court of love. A few middle-aged financiers, a couple of abbots, a "Minim brother" named Father Loth who was straight out of Rabelais, officers bored with Paris, and, most important of all, an official lover recruited among her husband's colleagues: Marc-Antoine Rétaux de Villette, a good-looking man of thirty, son of the director general of tolls in Lyons. "Of ardent temperament,‡ he pursues women avidly and indiscriminately, and occasionally seeks them in the lowest ranks of the prostitutes. It was his physical prowess which induced Mme de La Motte to choose him as her lover."[3] But also as her agent and factotum. His verve and spirit of adventure made up for the flabbiness of La Motte, who was too much of a Milquetoast to carry out the grand maneuvers of a wife who, by the end of 1783, was finally in a position to board the admiral galley of

---

*About 3,500 modern francs [$875].

†In her *Mémoires justificatifs* published in London in 1789, Jeanne de La Motte amusingly miscalls him "the Jew Cerbère [French for Cerberus—*Trans.* ]." He was in fact an important man in the town, and represented the Jewish community of Lorraine during the Revolution.

**More than 60,000 modern francs [$15,000]. This shows the extent to which "honorary rewards" had degenerated into objects of commerce, even speculation.

‡According to a report by Inspector Quidor, chief of the "prostitutes brigade" of the Paris police.

France. Gallery, rather—the Gallery of Mirrors at Versailles. "The public, with the exception of people dressed in the manner of the lowest class,* went in and out of the gallery and main suites of Versailles as though they were a park."4

Seemly in attire, distinguished in manner, known to the familiars of the Boulainvilliers and of Rohan, Jeanne could now station herself along the paths of the great. She opted for the princesses, in preference to the men; Rohan was enough in that line. She did not want to be accused of mass soliciting among the mighty. In December 1783 she conveniently fainted at the feet of Mme Elisabeth, the King's sister, and repeated the performance in January in front of the Comtesse d'Artois. This caused a little stir, intensified by the fact that she was a Valois—that "open sesame" again—and therefore "one of us," poor thing, in a milieu where it is readily understood that one can prefer to starve to death in order to "keep up appearances." She stirs their consciences; she incites them to good deeds. On the initiative of Elisabeth's almoner a little collection is taken up then and there, and Elisabeth sends her physicians to call on Jeanne at home.5 She is given a new pension, this time for 1,500 livres. They grow accustomed to the sight of their little pang of remorse. The other Madame, i.e., the Comtesse de Provence, is also made to take a vague interest in her fate. And then, on February 2, 1784, Jeanne puts on one last fainting act—but this time in the presence of Marie Antoinette.

The Queen is hardly aware of the incident and doesn't even pause, but she asks what it is about, "tsks" sympathetically, and forgets. No matter; Jeanne has won the first round. Now, without too great a stretch of credibility, she can make the cardinal believe that the Queen has taken notice of her. The second round lies ahead: she has to persuade the poor man, and a few others, that the Queen has taken *particular* notice of her. By spring, it's done. As Abbé Georgel, Rohan's grand vicar and a sort of Figaro in surplice, delicately puts it, "She undertook to persuade the cardinal that she had succeeded in insinuating herself into circumstances of the most intimate familiarity with Her Majesty."6

At this point, we really must stop beating around the bush; at bottom, it's so simple! Jeanne de La Motte, who is in a position to tell Rohan whatever she pleases because she has been his mistress for the last few months, convinces him, beginning in March 1784, that she is sleeping with the Queen.†

*The expression is Mme Campan's, and her reservation sets clear limits upon the much-vaunted (by some historians) accessibility of the sovereigns. Dress was a mark of wealth, if not of blood; and the "lowest class of people" was the people.

†The prudery of the historians of the necklace affair, a consequence of the morbid self-censorship of the nineteenth century in all matters even remotely sexual, has obscured this obvious fact, which provides the key to all Jeanne's machinations; whether believed—as it was by Rohan and those who were defaming the Queen—or not, this was her essential lie.

We now call on Jeanne de La Motte-Valois:* "I kept nothing from him; he kept nothing from me. We read in each other's souls the secret of our ambitions. His is known to all, he wanted to be prime minister; mine was merely to be the lady of Fontette."[7] In her galloping mythomania she tries to make believe that it was Rohan who drove her to Marie Antoinette's boudoir; she puts her own fantasies in the cardinal's mouth.

> Nothing can equal the amazement into which he precipitated me one day when, I having been near as the Queen was passing, her Majesty deigned to honor me with one of those smiles which are so very hard to resist. I recall how, the next moment, having chanced to look up at him, I saw the joyful sparkle in his eyes.
> "Do you know, Countess, that my fortune is in your hands, as is your own? . . . I have discovered beyond all doubt that the Queen has taken a fancy to you."
> "A fancy? . . . You mean she is kindly disposed, feels compassion?"
> "You may call the sentiment with which she honors you by whatever name you please. All you need to know is that she likes your looks. . . . Therefore, place yourself entirely in her hands."

Whence, according to her, the motive for her fainting act of February 2, followed . . . by a summons to the presence, issued by the Queen and transmitted by Mme de Mizery, her first lady-in-waiting, who "gave me to understand from the very first moment that the honor I was to have, of being presented to Her Majesty, was to be kept secret from everyone, warning me that the slightest indiscretion on my part would be the end of all my hopes." This finesse worked; to carefully selected auditors she could boast of being "intimate" with the Queen, without anyone ever seeing them together. "Thus conversing, I waited until eleven, for the Queen to leave her cards. At last she appeared. Lord, how beautiful I thought her! . . .

"Her Majesty smiled and her expression at that moment told me many things, the explanation of which lies in my letters to the cardinal."†

Yes, but if this really is a grand passion, why doesn't the Queen lift one little finger and order the Valois estates in Champagne to be restored to the La Mottes before the year is out? No sooner asked than answered—Jeanne may have been a little short on scruples, but not on imagination. Marie Antoinette was being subjected to so much criticism already for her presents to Yolande de Polignac that she must keep the existence of any other favorite absolutely hidden. At their very first interview she warns Jeanne:

"I cannot reconcile my desire to serve you publicly with my desire to see

---

*From her *Mémoires justificatifs;* this tissue of fabrications is a warmed-over version of the tales she told Rohan.

†Faked love letters which Jeanne hands to Rohan as though coming from the Queen; the cardinal destroyed them when he was first arrested, and she issues her "reconstituted" version of them as an appendix to her *Mémoires.*

you privately. But I can, indirectly, perform the good offices you may expect of me. . . ."

Clear enough? The Queen can do virtually nothing for Jeanne herself, but a great deal for the friends her darling may discreetly recommend to her. In this way the comtesse becomes all-powerful for them, not for herself. And if they have any decency at all, the people she edges close to the source from which all bounty flows will be pleased to show their gratitude to this sister of charity of Lesbos. Starting with Rohan.

"Her Majesty ended by making me a present of a purse and honoring me with her first kiss, enjoining me to remain at Versailles. . . . It was said that we should meet again." And they did, says Jeanne, "a few days later, between eleven and midnight, at the Petit Trianon," of course. "This second interview was devoted purely to business matters; it was then explained to me what the cardinal had tried to make me understand when he spoke of *fancy* and *looks.* . . . Verily, I thought myself more than a mere mortal."

And on she piles it, and will pile it even higher:

> Her Majesty brought our long conversation to a close, showing her munificence by the gift of a wallet containing 10,000 livres in treasury notes. Her last words were,
> "Farewell, we shall meet again!"
> And indeed we did meet again, and often, and at length, and always on the same footing. This admission darkens my soul, my heart contracts, the quill falls from my fingers! O my august sovereign, it is to you alone that I speak now;* remember those moments of intoxication which I hardly dare describe. Then you raised me up to you; you lowered yourself to me. But in vain did you deign to divest yourself in my presence of that imposing majesty; I saw it in your very abandon. I said to myself: this is the goddess Flora, trifling with a meadow flower.

How can Rohan swallow all this malarkey, and how can one or two others who hear hints of it credit what they hear? The answer is that the ground has been very thoroughly prepared, not only in their minds but in the most "informed circles" of Versailles, partly by the irresponsible conduct of Marie Antoinette herself, who is drowning herself in desperate frivolity and the unconscious provocation of a husband for whom she feels nothing but contempt which she makes little effort to hide; but also by that enormous gilded cage of a Court that has imprisoned her, spies on her, and is beginning to mass forces against her because of what in the end is the poor woman's best quality: her irrepressible spontaneity.

When Jeanne de La Motte first came to Court she was not intending to

---

*In 1789, that is; at a time when Jeanne can still hope that her sizzling "revelations" will get her back to France to resume her intrigues.

pass herself off as a favorite in such a very specific sense; but she was swept along by the great whisper. Deeply embittered and inclined to spitefulness, she probably believed that Marie Antoinette actually was a lesbian. Well, then, why not me? She went angling in the lowest depths of murky waters, and landed the logical outcome of the process of calumny that had comprised the immediate environment of the Queen of France for several years.

MADAME VIGÉE-LEBRUN

# 16

## AUGUST 1785

### "Antoinette's Pastimes"

Louis XVI himself set the tone. For some time he had been telling anyone who'd listen "that all he saw in the Queen's entourage were nonentities and whores."[1] True, he served his own brothers the same sauce—it was his way of showing affection for them, with great blundering swipes of his bear-paw. But there were plenty of others who hadn't waited for the King's permission to splatter mud on that beautiful white muslin gown, called a *gaulle*, in which Marie Antoinette is having her portrait painted by a young woman exactly her age, whose career is getting off to a promising start thanks to the Queen's favor: Louise Elisabeth Vigée, the (unhappy and soon separated-from) wife of the owner of an art gallery named Lebrun.

It was a pretty frock, "with cross-pleated but quite close-fitting wristbands; when the painting was exhibited at the Salon,* the spiteful did not fail to observe that the Queen had had her portrait painted in her chemise, for calumny was already beginning to spread about her";[2] nor did it spare the dress, which had "neither waist nor belt, [and was] a poor compromise between the *robes à l'enfant* of the Regency and the Greek-inspired frocks which the Queen hoped to bring into fashion again. It was not so much a gown as a sort of loose sack, such as chambermaids wear in the morning," sourly comments one of the "readers" who ply Marie Antoinette with their envious attentions and almost all of whom owe their jobs to Abbé de Vermond, the

---

*In 1786; the commentary is by Mme Vigée-Lebrun, who had become the "in" painter at Court since the famous portrait exhibited at the Salon of 1783, in which she painted the Queen in a much more spectacular satin gown with broad paniers, holding a rose.

adviser-spy-in-chief she had inherited from her mother.[3] This charitable memorialist goes on to say that

> so inexpensive a fashion was ill-suited to Court proprieties. Above all, it enabled women of low condition to compete with our ladies; . . . in the past, only women of quality had been able to dress all day long like princesses.
>
> The Queen, a thousand times more graceful still in these airy creations, aroused swarms of desires of which she had not the slightest idea. Young men, with the presumptuousness of their years, fixed upon any chance look as a distinction with which she had honored them. Hosts of rumors arose . . . and when the Queen, apprised of them, feigned no longer to see those who had boasted of attracting her attention, their injured vanity prompted them to insinuate that some other, more fortunate man had taken their place, and, even more often, that Marie Antoinette's friendship for La Polignac was such as to put them all out of the running.

Poor Yolande de Polignac (*née* de Polastron), called "la Comtesse Jules" to distinguish her from her sister-in-law—the face of an angel, the brain of a bird, and an accredited lover in the person of comely Vaudreuil, and all the good they did her was to add fuel to very different fires. Not just anybody's fires, either. The Comte d'Artois, for example, came upon the Queen once when the two women had been bickering over a trip to Fontainebleau and were making up.

> The Queen wept, embraced the countess, clasped her hands, implored, urged, threw her arms about her neck. The door was ajar. Entering, M. le Comte d'Artois saw this tableau. He burst out laughing and left, saying,
> "Pray don't let me disturb you!"
> And told everybody how he had interrupted the two friends.[4]

While from the Abbé de Véri, the sidelines witness to the whole early part of the reign who had followed Turgot's fall step by step, we get this:

> Last month [October 1783], the Queen was to sup at Saint-Hubert, a hunting lodge five leagues from Versailles. That morning the King had said, with his air of rude cheeriness, "This evening we shall have ladies to supper." Changes of horses were accordingly posted along the road and the Life Guards sent out to relieve those accompanying the Queen from Versailles.
> That day she learned that the Comtesse Jules de Polignac, still her favorite at the time, had returned to Paris from her course of treatment at a spa. Her desire to see the countess outweighed all other considerations. She was informed that the relief horses and guards could no longer be transferred to the Paris road, but in vain. "I shall go," said she, "without horses and without guards!" No one dared tell her what a sense of propriety in regard to the King dictated that she should do, and this thought did nothing to dissuade her. All was forgotten for her favorite, and she did not go to Saint-Hubert. . . .
> The public's suspicions regarding her alleged affections for some lover have

been dispelled; there is no longer any illusion on that score. However, evil tongues can always find solace somewhere: affections of the same type are now being ascribed to her, in respect of persons of her own sex.[5]

Rumor, starting from this very undeniable—but platonic—"particular friendship," had a field day. Any woman anywhere within hailing distance of Marie Antoinette was labeled, not to speak of others whom she hardly knew. "The Queen was very openly criticized for practices which history has attributed to several empresses. Mme de Marsan made representations to the King. The Queen considered herself outraged; soon, wearying of Mme de Guéménée, as of Mme de Lamballe before her, she became attached to Mme Jules de Polignac. . . . She was alleged to have secret commerce with Mme Bertin, the capital's celebrated seamstress, and with the demoiselles Guimond, Renaud, and Gentil,"[6] who were singers in the chorus of the Opéra. And why not? Princes, after all, displayed them like choice trophies in their lifelong hunt; why shouldn't a lesbian queen play the same game?

Similar rumors were emanating from "Mesdames Tantes," Louis XV's two surviving daughters at—or rather on the edges of—Court, huddled inside their pious fortress at Bellevue after Louise took orders with the Carmelites and Sophie died (in 1782; if ceasing not to live can be called dying). The redoubtable Adélaïde and the insignificant Victoire added their vinegary flutes to the score. They had always loathed the little Austrian who had robbed them of the leading role in the drawing rooms, and even of a share of their father's ambiguous affection. Since she didn't seem eager to be chaperoned by them, they had dropped her, and were now pelting her with cushion-shot pellets of calumny via the withered courtiers who called on them to reminisce about the good old days. They had joined forces with the two Piedmontese, the wives of Provence and Artois, who couldn't bear to read the reflection of their homeliness on people's faces in circles where their presence would merely set off the beauty of Marie Antoinette. Not that all these women had much affection for each other: "Can you believe it? the five princesses [three aunts* and two sisters-in-law] detested each other so passionately that they willingly divulged every detail of the private life of the Queen. What one suggested another confirmed, while the third princess then rendered the anecdote incontrovertible."[7]

When scandalous allegations of this type are manufactured in a family factory and bear the brand names of aunts, brothers-in-law, sisters-in-law, cousins (Orléanses and Condés), and even the husband himself, it is not surprising that by the time Jeanne de La Motte entered the picture the entire Court was a-seethe with scabrous gossip about the Queen. As in Basile's

---

*This text was written by Soulavie and describes the general atmosphere around 1780, when Mme Sophie was still alive.

monologue, calumny perspired through every pore of the château of Versailles, was augmented by the embellishments of delivery boys, tavern-keepers, and coachmen, and overflowed in the gutters of Paris. On June 8, 1785, the *Correspondance secrète* notes that

> clandestine and calumnious writings and licentious songs made at the Court itself have soured the French virtues of mildness and amiability, and it is no service to render a nation, to sow the seeds of a most regrettable and ominous coldness between it and its sovereigns. Never has the government shown such severity toward public writings, and never have so many clandestine satires been published. These couplets, songs, and satires have traveled and done incalculable harm, by teaching people to feel less respect for what they formerly revered.[8]

> The guard mounted around the Queen while she had the measles at Trianon, by MM. Esterhazy, de Guines, Coigny, and Besenval, seemed to confirm a myriad of vague hopes which M. de Lauzun's blustering had given out as painful truths. The King's long impotence having convinced the world of his sterility, people were saying audibly that the Comte d'Artois was not unconnected with [the paternity of] Mme Royale, nor was M. de Coigny with [that of] the dauphin. The Queen's demonstrations of affection for La Polignac at the time of her confinement seemed like expressions of a mutual complicity.[9]

Thus the gentlemen stamped on the paving stones and libel issued forth. That year the police seized a long list of publications at the frontiers or in the printers' shops; and to cut others off at the source, the secret agents of M. Lenoir or M. de Crosne bought them up wholesale, including the plates, in London or Holland. Some thirty titles on the list for the year were concerned primarily with the Queen. They included *Le Pou; Le Procès des trois rois; Essais sur la vie d'Antoinette; Les Amours de Charlot* [meaning Charles, Comte d'Artois] *et d'Antoinette; Le Portefeuille d'un talon rouge; La Malle cachetée du lord North; La Préface de l'histoire de Louis XVI* ["The louse"; "The trial of the three kings"; "Essays on the life of Antoinette"; "The loves of Charlie and Antoinette"; "The portfolio of a red heel"; "Lord North's sealed trunk"; "Preface to the history of Louis XVI"—*Trans.* ].[10] Why stop there? Educated bourgeois and big tradesmen with pretensions to sophistication read as much of this tripe as they did of the libertines, and there was the added thrill that you had to acquire it surreptitiously.

In 1784, when Brissot was at his lowest ebb and got his taste of the Bastille,* he received a visit, on the third day of his incarceration, from the lieutenant of police in person (still Lenoir at that point).

_____
*For reasons which will be explained later.

He informed me that I was accused of having composed libels in London against the Queen. I was outraged at this calumny, and retorted heatedly. He quoted from a dozen such libels, to see if I could at least identify the authors. There was *La Naissance du Dauphin* ["The dauphin's birth"—*Trans.*], in which the infamy had been committed, he said, of attributing the paternity of the royal child to a royal prince who was not the King; there were *Les Amours du Vizir de Vergennes; Les Petits Soupers à l'hôtel de Bouillon; Réflexions sur la Bastille; La Gazette noire; Les Rois de France jugés au tribunal de la raison; Les Rois de France dégénérés*, and finally *Les Passe-Temps d'Antoinette* ["The loves of Vergennes's vizier"; "Little suppers in the Bouillon house"; "Reflections upon the Bastille"; "The black gazette"; "The Kings of France tried by the court of reason"; "The Kings of France degenerate"; and "Antoinette's pastimes"—*Trans.*].[11]

The poor fellow fought like a tiger, shifting suspicion onto out-and-out rotters like the eternal Théveneau de Morande.* No; Brissot's pen really did not produce this kind of filth. But it was lucky for him the interrogation was conducted by Lenoir, who was capable of recognizing the ring of honesty in a protest; otherwise he'd still be in chains.

Whatever their provenance, the sheets are out and flying, borne on the breezes, by way of God knows whose windows, or rather pockets, into the study of the King himself.† Some of them—not those against the Queen, but others, attacking Calonne or La Fayette—are the work of a sort of high-class cad, the tax-farmer general Jacques-Mathieu Augeard,** who foams at the mouth whenever the word "reform" is uttered and before whom doors tend to be opened, owing to his position as "secretary of orders" (chief private secretary, a later age would say).[12] But Augeard is not the only generator of smut. The other day Louis XVI found on his desk a pamphlet, highly insulting to Marie Antoinette, that had been printed on a handpress—hence a small run —and he finally lost his temper. He sent for de Crosne. He ordered him to find the authors. The new lieutenant of police rolled fatalistic eyes and raised his arms heavenward:

"Alas, Sire, I fear that will be no easy matter. There are quantities of handpresses in the homes of the high nobility of Versailles, and even in Your Majesty's palace."[13]

---

*A double agent and paid libelist, whom Beaumarchais had gone to see in London in 1774 to kill a broadsheet against La du Barry.

†When the accusers of "the widow Capet" intermingle obscene calumny and true charges at the Revolutionary tribunal, they need look no farther afield, for the bulk of their material, than this arsenal compiled by the Queen's intimate circle ten years earlier.

**Born in Bordeaux in 1731, dies in Paris in 1805. He was not a close associate of the Queen, but he dealt with the correspondence relating to her charities and the administration of her Household. He emigrates shortly after Varennes and leaves some unexceptional *Mémoires*.

# 17

## AUGUST 1785

## *By Order of the Queen*

Then comes her real high point of tactlessness: as though to ensure that the resentful sniping of her entourage would have a firm foundation in the indignation of the people, the Queen insults poverty by instructing the royal treasury to purchase the château of Saint-Cloud, a former Orléans possession, for her. According to Augeard, she did so at the behest of Breteuil:

> The Baron de Breteuil, seeking to render himself agreeable to both the Queen and the Duc d'Orléans [the fat one] and, at the same time, to play a little trick on Calonne, . . . proposed the acquisition of Saint-Cloud to Her Majesty. He urged upon the Queen that this holiday retreat was a thing that must needs please her, by bringing her closer to the amusements of Paris. In this the only reproach one might level at the Baron de Breteuil is not the purchase itself, but that he might have made it cheaper: it is said to have cost 3 million [the deed of sale stipulates 6 million, and improvements and embellishments cost as much again].[1] This matter should not be seen as anything weightier than a ring on the Queen's finger. At that time the income of the King of France was 477 million;* had he not the right to make a gesture for a woman he rightly cherished, without exposing himself to such rabid recriminations?[2]

To those who snort and demand how it is that, with Versailles and the Trianons and Marly, Choisy, Fontainebleau, and Rambouillet to choose from —to mention only those in the immediate vicinity of Paris—the Queen still finds herself cramped for space, her champions retort, with some justification, that her status in all those places is that of the King's boarder and none of them belong to her personally, except the Trianons, which were given to her by official decree but in which there truly is not enough room for her Household and where she is too close to Versailles to escape the perpetual prying of two or three thousand pairs of eyes.

---

*Figures given by a man well placed to know them. In other words, Louis XVI's personal income equaled 3,240 million modern francs [$810 million], and Saint-Cloud cost 84 million [$21 million].

Also, now that, in her opinion, she has fulfilled her contract with France by providing it with two male heirs and really can no longer bear her rare nights in the company of a sleep-ridden Louis XVI, and her "penchant" for Fersen, who is back from America, is turning into a real passion which she would like to keep hidden and enjoy in a setting of her own choosing, she really would like to have a place she could call home. And then, there is the fairy-tale loveliness of Saint-Cloud, the cascade of earth, terraces, and water tumbling down from the superb château all the way to the Seine, two short leagues down from Paris; it will provide her with a base camp for all sorts of little excursions to the home of her beloved Polignac at La Muette; she need only step into the cunning little white-and-gold boat drawn by horses along the bank at the bottom of the Bois de Boulogne and up the river to the landing stage at Passy.

For the Queen, Saint-Cloud is a step toward liberation. But at what a price. It gave Calonne himself the shudders, although he was always bragging about how he could make everything work. The true condition of the treasury stood revealed to his gaze every day; and if he was systematically encouraging spending, even sumptuary spending, it was because he saw it as a way of achieving some degree of balance. The man was not necessarily a bad administrator; he was playing with a broad margin of inflation and, allegations to the contrary notwithstanding, he was neither insane nor irresponsible. For him luxury was the axle that would turn the great economic wheel. But frankly, Saint-Cloud was not going to turn anything; it would simply overload the already bogged-down train of the King's Household. He accordingly did his duty by warning Louis XVI that the purchase was "unseasonable, for the reason that the royal treasury was not in a position to bear the burden. He made highly exaggerated and pathetic remarks to the King," says Augeard, who is about to be the smiling eyewitness to a highly picturesque scene, "with the result that His Majesty gave the Queen to understand that Saint-Cloud was not to be thought of."[3]

Whereupon Marie Antoinette had one of those little childish fits of nerves that were well calculated to make her nobody's favorite.

She sent for Calonne; and this is how she received him:

"I know, Sir, all that you have said to the King to dissuade him from my purchase. If the matter were not public I should most willingly give it up, however agreeable it might be to me; but since your pretext to the King was the state of the royal treasury, I shall provide him with a very circumstantial account of your dilapidations and depredations and the immense sums you have given to the princes of the blood and to my brothers-in-law to build up support for yourself with the King, and all the amounts you have deposited in the purses of the great at Court in order to surround and encircle the King with your toadies and deceive him daily. You may suit yourself, but if I do not have Saint-Cloud I forbid you to appear again before my face, and even more to go to Mme de Polignac's when I am there."

My stricken Calonne then rushes to the King to patch things up, and tells him:

"Sire, this matter is not worth your discussing it with the Queen; I shall manage somehow, and find a way to take care of everything."

Marie Antoinette, however, also has a child's vindictiveness. For her, Calonne is finished, like Turgot before him. Once a person has tried to stand in her way . . . She gets her Saint-Cloud by spring, and she also gets the last word, to Augeard:

"That Calonne is just a great booby."

And the next we know, she is ordering her livery to be worn by

the Swiss Guards at the gates,* the footmen in the château, etc., like those at Trianon, where the concierge of the house had posted certain internal regulations bearing the words "By order of the Queen!" This custom was also adopted at Saint-Cloud. The Queen's livery at the gates of a palace where people expected to see none but the King's, and those words, "By order of the Queen," at the top of the printing near the gates, caused a great sensation and produced a most unfortunate effect, not only among the people but also among those of a superior class: they were seen as an encroachment upon the customs of the monarchy, and customs are close kin to laws.[4]

This is the origin of the vague idea, in the bourgeoisie but also among the people, that the Queen had somehow taken over and was running the country.

She isn't, though. The initiates, the real inner circle, know that Louis XVI is still countering his wife's superficial incursions into politics with opacity, if not authority. Moreover, those incursions are confined to two areas: the promotion of her favorites to specific posts, and her vehement albeit unsubtle support of every initiative taken by the Austrian crown, now sitting on her brother's head.

And in this field too she has had another setback, like the other year when she was agitating to get France to support Joseph II's claims on Bavaria. This time the quarrel is over the Escaut, whose downstream end and mouth are in Dutch hands, thanks to their ancient but still operational fortifications. The emperor, who controls Belgium, is demanding free navigation on the river as far as Antwerp, which could then become a real rival to Amsterdam. On his side he has the opinion of the Flemish, who are easily aroused against their Bavarian neighbors; and he's feeling all frustrated and pent up in his territory,

*According to a witness who, for once, is not inclined to cattiness: Jeanne Louise-Henriette Genet, born in Paris in 1752 and married, by arrangement, to a man named Berthollet (a relative of the chemist) who bore the title of the estate of Campan which had been bought in the Béarn region, and who was the son of a secretary of Louis XV. Mme Campan, after beginning as a "reader" to the daughters of Louis XV, later became a lady-in-waiting to Marie Antoinette.

vast though it is, because Catherine and Frederick have both succeeded in enlarging their pastures and the French have just won a war. Following the Russian example, Joseph is about to begin one with the Turks, in the hope of landing a share of the dismembered Ottoman empire; but in the meantime he'd also like to give a little lesson to that military and mercantile republic of the United Provinces that is thumbing its nose at him to the west.

An armed Austrian barge is cannonaded by the Dutch, who stick as hard to their rights as they do to any other habit. The echo of these few paltry shots resounds throughout the parts of Europe bordering on France. There are sudden noises of baggage trains and cavalry spurs; generals start ordering new uniforms. "If you won't give me the Escaut, then let me have Bavaria!" insists Joseph, returning to his old obsession of a "destabilization" of that part of the world, even if it means ditching the Belgians, among whom the supporters of the "Austrian party" will be much aggrieved when he subsequently does so, and trading Brussels for Munich, and—why not?—Luxembourg for Corsica too. If he keeps shaking Europe around like that, he's going to dislocate its neck. But there are plenty of people on hand to stop him. Vergennes and Louis XVI, as they have just demonstrated to the Genevans, are hostile to any shift of balance anywhere, and at heart they have always been opposed to Choiseul's switch of alliances and the rapprochement with Austria; and on that score the King's marriage has done anything but change his mind. French opinion is on their side. Mirabeau, its barometer, has just published his *Doutes sur la liberté de l'Escaut* ["Reservations regarding the freedom of navigation on the Escaut"—*Trans.*], which has lost him any remaining shreds of favor with the Queen.

The reason why she keeps scratching away at them all over a piddling little thing like the Escaut is not so much her affection for Joseph, who treats her as a nonentity and whom she fears more than she loves—and by now her mother is well and truly dead—it is her image of herself as the incarnation of the raw and tender graft of the Austrian alliance, which is not "taking" in France. She's fighting, instinctively, for herself. But clumsily; her moves are too obvious and, like all weak creatures, she is also devious. She fights openly, by tantrums; and in secret, by plaintive denunciations in letters to her brothers (Joseph, but also Leopold in Florence). For these alone, the French of her day, who never learn of them, would have condemned her for espionage or abuse of influence. How could you call it anything else?

To Joseph, on September 22, 1784:*

*Her letters, like those of Joseph and Leopold, are written in French, the almost universal language of eighteenth-century courts. They were published in Vienna in 1866 and 1872, by Alfred von Arneth, who consulted them in the Imperial Archives but corrected the spelling mistakes.

I shall not contradict you, my dear brother, in regard to the shortsightedness of our ministry. Some of the thoughts you pass on to me in your letter have been in my own mind, and not since yesterday; I have spoken of the matter more than once to the King, but one must know him well in order to judge aright the paucity of resources and means I can prize from his personality and prejudices. He is uncommunicative by nature, and quite often does not speak to me of important matters even when he has no wish to hide them from me. If I mention them first he will reply, but he gives me little information, and when I do learn the quarter of some matter I need much skill to glean the rest of it from the ministers, by giving them to understand that the King has told me everything. When I reproach the King for not having spoken to me of certain matters he does not grow angry, but assumes a rather uneasy air and sometimes replies quite naturally that it did not occur to him. I can honestly admit that political questions are the ones over which I have least influence. The King's inborn mistrust has been fortified, initially by his education, even before my marriage. M. de La Vauguyon quite terrified him of the hold his wife would seek to gain over him, and his black soul delighted in frightening his pupil with all sorts of imaginary ghosts directed against the House of Austria. M. de Maurepas, although with less forcefulness and spite, thought it advantageous to himself to perpetuate that attitude in the King. M. de Vergennes is following the same plan, and may be employing his correspondence in the Ministry of Foreign Affairs for lying and dishonest ends. I have spoken out to the King on this point, and more than once. On occasion he has answered back sharply, and as he is incapable of engaging in discussion I have been unable to persuade him that his minister was misguided or was misleading him. I am not deceived as to my own standing; I know that, especially where politics are concerned, I have not much influence upon the King's mind. Would it be prudent of me to make scenes with his minister over matters in regard to which it is virtually certain that the King would not uphold me?

Without ostentation or lying, I allow the public to believe that I have more credit than I do in reality, because if I were not thought to have so much, I should have even less.[5]

## To Joseph, on November 5, 1784:

The Marquis de Noailles* has informed us that you were going to send 40,000 men to the Netherlands. The King was not surprised and said in his Council that with matters as they now stand you could not do otherwise. If the subject were of less concern to me I should be satisfied with the tranquillity of M. de Vergennes's reception of M. de Mercy† last Tuesday. But I am a little worried by this wordless quietude. I have not wished to send for the minister just yet. I think that by waiting a few days I will find it easier to sort out some of his ideas. Any matter that is of personal concern to my dear brother will never find me wanting in

*French ambassador to Vienna. These are the *Austrian* Netherlands, i.e., Belgium.

†The Austrian ambassador to Versailles and Marie Antoinette's mentor, although he has wielded less influence over her since her mother's death.

application and attention; my heart is too taken up with this one for my mind to admit any other thought.[6]

And to Joseph again, on the 26th of the month:

> You must have been amazed and singularly taken aback by that odious dispatch* that was sent without waiting for your reply to the King's letter, which, even to the eyes of people who are most unpracticed in such matters, makes no sense at all. It was adopted in Council a fortnight ago. I held up the courier's departure for a week but that was the most I could obtain. I was so hoping that your messenger could get here first, with a plan or at least a few words that could have stopped the entire proceeding.
>
> I was enchanted with your last letter, and read it to the King, who was touched by it. It is true that M. de Vergennes, to whom I also read it, seemed cold and indifferent afterwards and had probably made up his mind in advance. His conduct is a tissue of lies, weakness, and fears for this country[7]

—France, that is, "this country" whose sovereign she is.

To Mercy-Argenteau, the Austrian ambassador, the agent of a power with which "this country" might be at war tomorrow, on December 26, 1784:

> I have read all your papers most attentively, M. le Comte, and desire with all my heart that they may produce the effect that their openness and friendly manner should produce. Having thought the matter over, I have decided not to give the King his letter until late this evening or tomorrow morning. It will be impossible for me (and you know him well enough not to doubt this) to induce him to take, alone, a decision sufficiently firm for him to announce it to M. de Vergennes in my presence, and then not change it afterwards. But I believe the moment is essential, and shall try to see M. de Vergennes with the King and there engage them both so thoroughly that the minister, however incomprehensible he may be [*sic*], will find himself at a loss. But for that I must wait until tomorrow, and if I give the King his letter this evening after his Council I am perfectly sure he will not see M. de Vergennes again until after speaking about it to me tomorrow morning, and in that way I shall see more or less what hue his ideas will have taken, and that will determine my actions.
>
> That is my plan; agree that it is a good one.[8]

And just when war seems so close that even the Parisian craftsmen start talking about it, and it looks as though the French army will go to support Holland if she is invaded by the troops Joseph II is massing in his Belgian territories, Marie Antoinette writes to the potential enemy (on February 4, 1785):

> You are quite right, my dear brother, to demand a prompt decision. I am pressing for it too and will not cease to do so. I also believe that your troops would

*From Vergennes, putting Joseph II on his guard against the danger of invading Holland.

not need much time to settle the quarrel with the Dutch, but will they be alone? That point gives pause for thought. Is it conceivable that France, informed of the declaration that you were making to the Dutch in regard to navigation on the Escaut and having almost approved it, or at least having made no motions to the contrary, would then turn round and announce that she intends to send an army to the frontier? That accursed declaration, which I was able to hold up only five days in the hope of news from you, has not been retracted. True, it is not a declaration of war, only an army of observation; but when two armies are so close to each other, marching orders are soon given and obeyed. I hope it will not come to that; but the line that has been followed causes me to fear for the future. . . .[9]

And as though she realized what a case she was building against herself before the courts of History, she adds a postscript:

I hope you will be good enough to burn this letter at once, it is nothing less than a confession.

The emperor will not burn her letters; on the contrary, he has them copied by two secretaries. Out of sheer mindlessness? Or to make use of some day? Or maybe simply out of that sense of family that was the be-all and end-all of the Hapsburgs and has stood them in such good stead. One more sentence from Marie Antoinette (to Joseph, on September 19, 1785) will prove that in this respect she did not fail. The drumrolls are fading; the Dutch, wanting peace in every sense of the word, agree to pay a sort of ransom of 8.5 million florins to their Gargantua of a neighbor, provided that the King of France— as if he had too much money—lends them a quarter of the sum. From the viewpoint of the family honor, however, Marie Antoinette sounds almost disappointed:

Although I have a horror of war, my dear brother, you must be quite sure that I should never counsel you to any kind of patience that would compromise your glory and your consideration.[10]

Leopold, Grand Duke of Tuscany, adds his own lucid footnote in a letter to Joseph on January 24, 1785:

I do see that the Queen [of France] is doing all she can, but that is not much, and her credit, even with the King, has no effect, owing to his lack of ability, firmness, and will. . . . It is a most unpleasant moment for you, and one has to know and feel the ill will and malice of France into the bargain, without daring to let it be seen.[11]

Goodness, weren't they fond of each other, the partners in this alliance!

We know that nobody in France was aware of the existence of these letters. But the mysterious alchemy of "informed circles," which ultimately transforms all the secrets of authority into public knowledge, precipitated a synthesis of the relationship between Louis XVI and the Queen, and of the latter's ventures into the realm of policy, that was inaccurate as to the facts but a faithful reflection of the spirit.

Our old friend Ruault, the Parisian bookseller, was picking up echoes in late 1784, possibly from Beaumarchais but also from a seething mass of whispers in the shadows.

> Negotiations have been started, messengers have been sent from Versailles to Vienna. The King wrote, in his own hand, a very firm letter to his brother-in-law, telling him that he will continue to enforce respect for the treaties and is angry to see him so stubbornly determined to violate them. The emperor, they say, gave Louis XVI a Spartan reply, only two words long: "The Escaut or war." After such a response, it is conjectured that there will be war.[12]

And Ruault knew that the Queen was mixed up in it. A letter to his brother, written a few days later, shows how widely the reputation she was acquiring had already spread, and also contains, incidentally, an allusion to the coarseness now commonly being imputed to the King:

> The lady of the château four leagues from here has no wiser a head nor any better judgment; it is a family affliction, I am told. She has intrigued most energetically on her brother's behalf, against the interests of the House of which she is sovereign mistress. But it was in vain; the master* told her to s——herself, swearing as he is known to do. . . . The lady's sentiments for the foreigner have become widely known to the public, and everyone is remarking upon the lack of attachment she shows to a husband, a House, and a nation that have made her fortune and refuse her nothing for her train and pleasures.[13]

So this is also the start of "L'Autrichienne." Why should Jeanne de La Motte hesitate to pin her little plot onto a person for whom no one, from Versailles to Paris, is showing any sympathy? A Queen who is lesbian, addlepated, extravagant, and authoritarian, and whose husband is the next best thing to a moron and a drunkard to boot. All Jeanne has to do is darken the outlines a little. People were ready to listen to her, from the Grand Almoner of France down to the last pickpocket in the marketplace.

---

*He does not directly name the King and Queen because of the risk of letters being opened in the post. He is writing to his brother the canon.

# 18

## AUGUST 1784*

### *Oh Happy Night!*

By the spring of 1784 Rohan has swallowed Jeanne's fairy tale hook, line, and sinker. She has almost ceased to be his mistress and is fast becoming his secret agent instead.

For years he's been fuming over the Queen's rejection of him, so flagrant that the whole Court has seen it, and it is aggravated by the fact that, for once, Louis XVI shares the sentiments and even the attitudes of his wife.

Why this disgrace for a man who holds—thanks to the King's pusillanimity in his dealings with the Rohan-Soubise-Guéménée clan—the highest ecclesiastical position in the realm? There is certainly no shortage of scandalous prelates at Versailles, and Marie Antoinette, manipulated by Abbé de Vermond, openly shows her own political preference for one of them— Brienne, the Archbishop of Toulouse. Perhaps Rohan was so fatuous that he simply dissembled less than the others; he positively exhibited his vices. When he was the French ambassador to Austria he paraded through the outskirts of Vienna with a carriageful of curious little abbots, so cute and cosmetic that a second look easily revealed them to be pretty young women in drag. "We were unaware that in France the priesthood was open to women," purred the atheist Kaunitz in Maria Theresa's study, and her horrified letters to her daughter, who was still dauphine at the time, had increased and perpetuated Marie Antoinette's instinctive loathing for the cardinal.[1]

Be that as it may, this mitered ass was actually aspiring to no less an honor than the position of first minister. And his entourage encouraged him, if only as a means of preserving their seats at the dinner table in Saverne. Well, there had already been Richelieu, Mazarin, Dubois, Fleury—a fine, sound father-to-son lineage, as the humorists like to say—all those dignitaries of the church who had hopped from the steps of the altar to the steps of the throne. And

*The meeting in the Venus Grove occurs in August 1784, a year earlier than the main events in the "Necklace Affair," which culminate in August 1785. I have deliberately chosen to place it here.

didn't Mazarin end up marrying Anne of Austria? Rohan suffered from the habitual itch of people who have everything: the only appetite left to them is ambition. His is an undying ember, and Jeanne merely blows upon the coals. From her he gains confirmation of the more sensational bits of gossip that are making the rounds. So! his carping Queen is in reality the kind of holier-than-thou prude who can be manipulated by her passions, like the rest. And since he fancies himself gifted along those lines too, his ear becomes ever more open, along with his pocketbook, to the little Valois who decidedly knows how to manage her own affairs. If Louis XVI had had mistresses, people would have had to pursue their careers via them; but times change, so Rohan will work his way into the ministry through a mistress of the Queen.

He starts believing her in earnest when, beginning in May 1784, Jeanne shows him the impassioned letters she is receiving from Marie Antoinette, written "on white linen with gold edges and a pale blue border, with the lilies of France in one corner,"[2] which are carefully burned after being more or less memorized by both of them. Reading them, a bedazzled Rohan sees his name come and go, reappear, remain, yes, the Queen is having second thoughts about her harsh judgment of him; because he helped out his cousin Guéménée in the days of the great bankruptcy, she's ready to grant him "her goodwill," and one of these days she will nod to him on her way to mass; and the poor man takes it into his head that she actually does so one time when she ducks her chin out of the breeze; and then, through Jeanne, she asks the prince to send her a "written justification of his conduct." Twenty rough drafts are required to produce a lengthy memorandum into which, as a self-assured Don Juan, he makes bold to inject "a few sentiments." Hosanna! Back comes the answer: "I am charmed to find you no longer culpable. . . ." But he'll have to wait a little longer for a private audience. He is not forbidden to write, however; he'll be answered.

"And thus began a series of letters and replies. The correspondence, of which no trace has been found,* was subtly organized and slanted, in the feigned letters of the Queen, to make the cardinal believe he had succeeded in inspiring the most intimate trust and lively interest in himself on the part of the sovereign."[3]

Every one of these letters "from the Queen" is inscribed by the quill of Rétaux de Villette, without his understanding much of what was going on, to the dictation of Jeanne de La Motte. That famous blue-bordered, gilt-edged paper

---

*According to Abbé Georgel, grand vicar and confidant of the cardinal; he must have smiled when he wrote this, because it was he himself, on August 15, 1785, who burned all the faked letters from the Queen. Jeanne destroyed most of those Rohan gave her to pass on to Marie Antoinette as soon as she got them, but may have kept a few at Bar-sur-Aube—the ones she lets Beugnot burn on August 18, 1785.

is bought by Deschamps, a trusty footman, either from a perfumer on the rue
Saint-Anastase or a stationer on the rue des Francs Bourgeois—not far from
Rohan's house.[4] All the cardinal or even Abbé Georgel would have had to do
was ask around among the butlers or footmen. But neither they nor the little
group that is eventually let in on the "secret" ever have a moment of doubt.
On the Rohan side, the group consists of his grand vicar, Abbé Georgel; his
chief official parasite, who is a Swiss baron named Frédéric de Planta; Ramon
de Carbonnières, the "head of his council" or more simply "first secretary";* and, of course, his beloved Cagliostro; and on Jeanne's side there is
her husband, her lover Villette, her "almoner" (!) Father Loth, and, of course,
the manservant Deschamps. With the possible exception of La Motte, however, none of them knows any more than his own part in the story, a few
crumbs of which stray into Beugnot's lap; Jeanne alone knows it all.

But even Rohan, dullard though he is, begins to show signs of impatience as
the summer wears on—what about this Queen who's so well disposed toward
me, when is she going to make up her mind to see me? how long is she going
to keep me dangling?—so Jeanne decides to stage a little farce that will clinch
the matter and put him completely at her mercy.

What a resourceful little person she is! She now exploits her husband's
propensity for skirt-chasing in the gardens of the Palais Royal. If you have to
put up with the silly fools, after all, you may as well get some benefit from their
less lovable aspects. Does she just order a girl who can pass for the Queen,
the way she might ask him to pick up a hat at the shop? Or is he the one who
snatches at a sudden windfall? It was certainly he, at any rate, who was buzzing
like an oversized bumblebee around the newly replanted trees of the renovated Orléans gardens, and it was his gaze that fell, early in August 1784, upon
a pretty, full-bosomed girl with long ash-blond hair, "Roman features and
slightly protruding lips," the milliner Nicole Leguay, also known as "Madame
de Signy" in the "Petit Hôtel de Lambesc" on the rue du Four, where she
sometimes returned from her walks with a "friend she had run into." Nicole
is not a whore—just a poor girl, a seed blown about by any breeze, an
orphan† who had been ill-treated in the Legros boarding school "for abandoned infants," too pretty to remain a mere milliner in Paris and too straight
to become a real kept woman. She had one relatively steady companion, the
*écuyer* Jean-Baptiste Beaussire, son of an official in the Paris salt works, who's
about to have trouble with the police because of her, poor fellow, and hasn't
a clue what it's all about. He stays away when she is followed home by

*In 1791 he is elected to the Legislative Assembly for Paris.

†Born in 1761, on the rue Saint-Martin in Paris, child of "Claude Leguay, disabled officer,
and Marguerite David," both of whom died "before she reached the age of reason."

somebody else, whose caresses and gifts she accepts without soliciting them, like a good girl but not like a wanton—witness the fact that she never has more than one at a time and sees him as often as he likes. And when he no longer likes, he walks out, never she. "A gutter slut," Marie Antoinette later calls her, but in the circumstances one can understand her nursing a grudge. A "town girl," says one of the police officers who writes a report on her.[5] A character for Restif de la Bretonne. A sitting duck.

La Motte accosts her. He walks her home and takes over the position as chief suitor without any difficulty. He sees her for about a week before telling her that she is to receive a visit "from a very distinguished lady attached to the Court," who sweeps her off her feet with great gushes of affection and affectation.

> The lady, having seated herself, drew from her portfolio* several letters which she said were from the Queen; she was a very distinguished lady who could not tell her name then, but she [Nicole] would know it one day. ["One day" seems to have been the very next day or the one after that; Nicole soon understands that Jeanne is the wife of La Motte, and he never tries to hide his name.] The letters were read, but [Nicole] said she could make nothing of them; the lady then said to her, "Dear heart, I am the Queen's right hand, she has taken me completely into her confidence, she has instructed me to find a person who will do everything I tell her when the time comes. If you do exactly as you are told, I shall make you a present of 15,000 francs;† that from the Queen will be larger."[6]

Jeanne might have spoiled everything, intimidating the girl with such huge figures. But she apparently possessed an incomparable art of persuasion, and Nicole was no great brain. Dazed by this avalanche of promises, she bites, she positively gulps down the bait.

And runs with it straight to the Venus Grove in the gardens of Versailles, where the Cardinal de Rohan lies prostrate at her feet.

This certainly was an "interview" in the most literal sense ["glimpse," in French—*Trans.*]; one instant of masquerade that gets magnified into a five-act play. It takes place on August 11, 1784, shortly after dark.

The La Mottes have not wasted their time; a scant two or three days have elapsed since the meeting between Jeanne and Nicole. They've got their docile tool, her timidity being another point in her favor. Nicole plays her part without a fault, and the fact that she doesn't know what's going on is so much the better, because there was enough going on to send the most brazen slattern of the Palais Royal scampering away at top speed if she ever tumbled to it. She lets La Motte take her home with him the next day, in the company of Rétaux

---

*Testimony given by Nicole to a Parlement counselor on January 17, 1786.
†100,000 modern francs [$25,000]!

de Villette—not to Paris yet, but to Versailles, to their furnished rooms in the "Belle Image" on the Place Dauphine near the château. There she spends forty-eight hours twiddling her thumbs with the chambermaid or listening to more of their moonshine. They're in the best of spirits—Jeanne has gone to warn the cardinal that the Queen wants to see him in secret, and the great man is trembling like a schoolboy. Perhaps it is during the long wait that Jeanne dreams up the idea of renaming Nicole "Baronne d'Oliva," a truncated anagram of "Valois"; anyway, it was soon done. A touch of whimsy? A precaution, so that even the servants will be unable to identify her afterwards? Who knows?

On the evening of August 11, in the damp unhealthy swelter of the Versailles summer, Jeanne turns up frothier than ever—things couldn't be going better, I have just this moment left the Queen, who is very pleased, now just do as we tell you.

"Nicole d'Oliva" is dressed up like a big doll in a white flecked linen chemise frock with a pink undergown exactly like the one in the Queen's latest portrait; her head is covered with a white *thérèse,* a wing-shaped headdress combining elements of mantilla and mask, whose name Buffon has just given to a Caribbean bird, and which has the advantage of hiding the top of the face. Finally, Jeanne issues her instructions, as brief as they are simple:

"This evening I shall take you into the park. A tall gentleman will come up to you. You will hand him this letter and this rose, saying, 'You know what that means'; that's all you have to do."

Sounds like a scene from the end of the *Mariage de Figaro;* who knows, maybe that's where Jeanne got the idea? Some evenings, like tonight, the gardens are open to "well-turned-out people," and the great dark mass of the famous Hundred Steps coming down from the terrace of the château towers over the Venus Grove (soon to be renamed the Queen's Grove), a sort of little labyrinth, newly planted with rare trees and surrounded by a hornbeam hedge. The sound of water can be heard there, as everywhere else in the grounds, and the footsteps and soft murmurs of people out for a walk, often in twos; at last, a breath of cool air and one carefree hour à la Fragonard.

It's everybody's favorite sport; in the last two or three years several courtiers, even footmen from the château and burghers from Versailles, have run into the Queen around one of these corners, accompanied by her sisters-in-law or her favorite ladies and also by a few men friends—always the same, Vaudreuil, Coigny, Besenval. She's fond of this informal prospect only a few steps away, and has even played blindman's buff and "marriage"* there; Louis XVI himself has joined her when he wasn't too sleepy. It didn't take Jeanne

*A "master of the game" matched players into the most ill-assorted couples imaginable, and they had to avoid all the other couples as long as they could before guessing who was "married" to whom.

long to learn all this, and the fact that she has chosen her time and place so well means that she has definitely wormed her way into the proximity, if not the intimacy, of the Queen.

Jeanne is wearing a black moiré mask. She plants Nicole like a statue in the strategic spot and leaves her there in the dark, alone and petrified, while she goes to fetch a man, or rather a silhouette, equally anonymous, enveloped in a dark *lévite*\* and "hound's ear" hat, which means that the face of Rohan, who has been waiting on the terrace with the Baron de Planta, is also hidden.

But now he bares his head and bows to the very earth, the fake queen holds out her rose and forgets to give him the real love letter manufactured by Villette, but never mind, Jeanne will give it to him later. Nicole stammers out her line, "You know what that means," whereupon, since the sound of her voice must not be allowed to ruin the whole game, Jeanne reappears with Villette, gesticulating like a signalman (the cardinal takes him for a lackey in the Queen's service):

"Quick, quick! Hurry! Madame and the Comtesse d'Artois have come!"

Everybody scuttles away into the night. Was the cardinal dreaming when he thought he heard the "queen" whisper another sentence: "You may hope the past will be forgotten"? Did she for one instant abandon to his lips the hand that was holding the rose, long enough to make him curse the interlopers earnestly for a year? In any event, at the end of this little charade he is more convinced of the Queen's favor, or even "penchant," than he is of the existence of God. Yet Nicole is by no means a perfect double and bears only a vague resemblance to Marie Antoinette; just enough for Beugnot, at that supper with her at the La Mottes',† to be struck by "something in her air" but not to be able to say what it is. All the more reason for Jeanne to choose a dark night, cloudy and close, when the slender sickle of a waning moon is still below the horizon.[7]

For a few days the La Mottes can carouse to their heart's content, with Nicole as dazed as ever; in the end they give her 4,628 livres in five installments, instead of the promised 15,000.[8] But she, like the good girl she is, keeps quiet to the very end, even after they drop her and send her back to her Sieur Beaussire. To her it seems like a lot of money just for letting a stranger hold her hand.

\*A kind of fitted overcoat vaguely reminiscent of a surplice

†He thinks this happened the very evening of the scene in the grove, the exact date of which remains unknown to contemporaries. It would seem more likely that he dropped in on the countess during the brief period when she invites Nicole to her real home in Paris, to spoil her and pet her a little but also to keep an eye on her and make sure she doesn't talk, before placing this compromising witness at a safe remove.

And now, Rohan to the wall! The pear is ripe, it's harvest time. The La Mottes are going to squeeze their victim until even a thirst like theirs is slaked. In one of the letters from cardinal to Queen which Jeanne pretends to rewrite four years later, in a style presumably borrowed from some manual of amorous correspondence, she has Rohan say, on the very evening of the meeting in the grove, "Oh happy night! You were the most beautiful day of my life!"[9]

Notice, however, that at this preposterous point in the plot not one of the protagonists has uttered a word about the "Queen's necklace," for the very good reason that none of them has ever heard of it.

THE QUEEN'S NECKLACE

# 19

## SPRING 1785

### Marie Antoinette de France

Jeanne de La Motte didn't need to reach for that necklace; it dropped ready-made into her lap, wrapped in one of history's neatest swindles. Knowing her, one may assume she would have thought it positively sinful to decline it. No more weekend or year-long stints of obsequious tugging at princes' coattails —one big job and the whole bank's hers, she can retire for life to Bar-sur-Aube and dazzle all those witnesses to her humiliated childhood.

Who does the dropping? Two honest Parisian lawyers—Louis-François Achet, former alternate to the master of requests, and his son-in-law, a parlement barrister named Jean-Baptiste de Laporte. The older man has actually wormed his way into one of the minor parasitic Court functions, as "Honorary Officer of the Wardrobe of Monsieur." Father-in-law and son-in-law are also—what was the term?—"doers of business" [agents, expediters, dealers—*Trans.*] in their free time, to round out their legal fees. It's becoming common practice these days, when even princes of the blood have turned to speculation.

The "reign of Louis XVI" could be defined as a slow process of osmosis between "honors" and money. The attorneys, thus, are equally well-acquainted with the great jewelers on the rue Vendôme and with that intriguing little Valois woman who is, they say—but she doesn't want it bruited about—on the very best possible terms with the Queen.

Böhmer and Bassenge, like every other clay-footed colossus that can be brought crashing down solely by the weight of its immobilized capital, have their backs against the wall. For the last ten years they have been carrying a heavy cross indeed, in the form of the most beautiful necklace in the world —a necklace, or cascade might be a better word, of diamonds* which Louis XV had more or less encouraged them to mount for him—verbally, he certainly did—as a present for Mme du Barry. Twice and thrice they have shown it to Louis XVI since he came to the throne, and at one point, apparently rather half-heartedly, he offered to give it to his wife. She asked to see it, and she visibly fancied it. But that was soon after her investiture, and she had just been severely scolded by her mother and brother for having already bought too much jewelry. And the war with America was about to begin, exacting public sacrifices. The incident gave birth to one of those brilliant historical witticisms that nobody ever actually says,[1] but that are so good for reputations. This one was attributed alternately to Louis XVI and to the Queen: "We need a ship more than a jewel."

Time has passed. We still need ships, if only to replace the ones the English sank at Les Saintes, but they're less urgent now, since no maritime wars are looming on the horizon. And Marie Antoinette turned down the necklace with such bad grace that the jewelers have not quite given up hope. For them, however, time is of the essence: they have invested over half their capital in this gigantic double-or-nothing. Many of the men who are inventing a new career in money are doing the same thing, applying tactics reminiscent of the foolhardy risks taken by the nobility of the sword centuries before, when it was becoming the dominant class . . . You've got to be a bit off your rocker (and the great feudal lords were certainly that, when they built their improbable eagle's nests) to tie up 1,600,000 livres in a single article.† The jewelers are being forced to borrow, and use the necklace as collateral; half its price is already pledged to Charles Baudard de Saint-James, the opulent financier who has just built himself a "folly" at Neuilly that was almost the equal of those at Bagatelle or Mousseaux. Saint-James will have his eyes glued to the proceedings in the necklace affair, you may be sure, if only because he wants to recover his 800,000 livres.

Attempts were made, and failed, to offload it onto the Queen of Spain. And the Queen of the Two Sicilies, and the Queen of England and the Grand Duchess of Tuscany, and Catherine II. But now that Böhmer has been accredited as official jeweler to the Court, he's trying Marie Antoinette again.

---

*647 stones, weighing a total of 2,800 carats.

†This is not an arbitrary estimate—the necklace had been valued by two other jeweler-experts, Maillard and d'Oigny. In modern francs, that makes over 10 million [$2.5 million].

Thus far, all his appointment has gotten him is the right to sell girandoles for the Queen's lying-in. As far as the necklace is concerned, there has been only one audience, a melodramatic one, at which her longing for it made her positively odious to him. The poor man knelt before her, wringing his hands:

"Madame, I am ruined and dishonored if you do not buy my necklace. I have no wish to outlive so much misfortune. I shall go straight from this room, Madame, and throw myself into the river."[2]

According to Mme Campan, the Queen almost wished him a pleasant swim; but she did so with a kind of vague air, a reservation even in her anger that was enough to postpone the drowning. The jeweler no longer felt completely discouraged. And instead of flinging himself into the Seine, he sent his son-in-law to knock at a door in the rue Neuve Saint-Gilles, where Jeanne de La Motte lived.

He knocked twice; on December 29, 1784, and again on January 21, 1785,* encouraged by Achet and Laporte, who introduced Bassenge and sat in on the first two meetings.[3] What a godsend! Jeanne snaps it up. All she's being asked to do is use "her credit with the Queen" to cajole her into buying the necklace. Self-possessed as in every other decisive moment of her life, she decides, at their very first interview, that that necklace is going to be hers. But she has to find some tool or screen, whichever you prefer, and he has to be of very high rank, because she knows full well the jewelers are not likely to put the prize directly into her hands, and insisting that they do so would ruin all her chances. But under the thumb of one of those hands she has an involuntary accomplice who might have been created for the part—Rohan.

And it couldn't come at a better time, because the cardinal is turning querulous again. Why hasn't the Queen given him another rendezvous since the evening in the Venus Grove? Why has nothing been done to begin the grand maneuvers that are to clear his path to the ministry? Jeanne and Rétaux de Villette have kept him in patience with a series of letters "from Marie Antoinette," so cordial that Rohan is almost starting to make love to her in his replies. But such paper transactions are never enough for a libertine, let alone an ambitious libertine. Now here's just the thing to keep him occupied: a highly confidential mission in which he will actually be the Queen's accomplice. It will give him an opportunity to "prove his passion" and, Jeanne insinuates, gain power over the Queen thereafter.

The cardinal returns to Paris from Saverne on January 3. First by word of mouth, then "by letter," he receives the Queen's "good wishes"; by the

---

*Louis XVI has eight years to live. Achet and Laporte were promised 1,000 louis, or more than a 100,000 modern francs [$25,000], as a "commission" from the jewelers for acting as go-betweens; poor guys, they were supposed to be paid out of the first installment.

21st Jeanne is able to summon Bassenge and Achet and inform them that Marie Antoinette has determined to buy the necklace but is keeping the purchase a secret from the King and his ministers, and will use "a great lord" as middleman. Bassenge, drunk with joy, instantly offers her a token of his gratitude, which Jeanne haughtily declines before accepting some bigger ones a month later, when she sends Grenier, her regular jeweler, to pick up earrings, watches, two diamond-studded chains, a medallion, and two solitaires. The rings alone are worth 15,000 and 9,000 livres.*

January 24. The La Mottes sally forth to the rue Vendôme early in the morning, to precede, and identify, the "great lord" in question: the Grand Almoner of France. Could Böhmer and Bassenge hope for better, especially when Rohan in person turns up a quarter of an hour later, demands to see the necklace, asks confirmation of its price, and informs them that he will in any event insist upon payment by installments, and will give them a final answer in the very near future?

On January 29 it is his turn to admit the jewelers to his home on the rue Vieille du Temple and confirm the purchase, to be paid for in four installments of 400,000 livres each at six-month intervals, the first falling due at the beginning of August. They accept, and on February 1, still shrouded in secrecy, they bring him the necklace. Rohan again shows them the text of the agreement entitled "Proposals and Terms of Price and Payment," two sheets he had them sign three days before, on which "a very fine hand" had marked "approved" in three places,[4] and "accepted" under the date of January 29.

"That is the Queen's own writing. Her Majesty has even deigned to sign herself, as you see, 'Marie Antoinette de France.' But the Queen has instructed me to keep this paper by me; it will be transmitted to you if I die."

Böhmer and Bassenge bow their way out, bearing nothing but a letter from Rohan ordering delivery of the necklace. The jewelers do not know the Queen's hand—she always has her jewelry bought by secretaries or ladies-in-waiting—nor do they know that she almost always signs "Marie Antoinette de Lorraine d'Autriche," and sometimes, to abbreviate, "Marie Antoinette d'Autriche" but never, never "de France." And if they had a qualm, Rohan's sweeping conviction would have dispelled it.

But what about him? *He* should have been aware of this detail, of which the counterfeiters themselves were ignorant, and which would have foiled their whole scheme if Rohan had not become so besotted, so utterly bereft of reason since the rendezvous in the Venus Grove and the receipt of a flood of half-demented letters, all written in the same fine hand—a very rough imita-

---

*Or over 150,000 modern francs [$37,500] for the two stones. The total value of the "commission" must have been at least 400,000 modern francs [$100,000].

tion of the Queen's—which sometimes even addressed him as *tu* and were never, ever signed.

After all, if you want to fool somebody maybe it's true that all you have to do is tell him what he wants to hear, like a puppeteer's hand sliding inside the puppet's body. This preposterous tale agrees so exactly with Rohan's notion of women in general, and Marie Antoinette in particular.

That same evening, February 1, Rohan goes to the Place Dauphine in Versailles, accompanied by one manservant. Alone, he climbs up to Jeanne's little furnished apartment where, hidden in an alcove, he witnesses the last link in the whole hypothetical chain. A man enters, duly swathed in a cloak of indescribable hue, and is announced as "coming from the Queen." And Jeanne hands him the big sealed package containing the necklace. Rohan recognizes him; it was the same man who interrupted them in the Venus Grove. Just so, nods the comtesse, that is Desclaux, the Figaro of both Queen and King, being attached to the Queen's chamber and a member of the King's chapel musicians. He is the only man who knows about me . . .* Here is the letter of thanks which the Queen has given me for you.

That evening, as he returned home with swelling heart, the cardinal must have felt that he was prime minister already.

Jeanne and her husband also go back to Paris, and reach the pinnacle of their whole miserable lives when Rétaux de Villette (who was "Desclaux," of course) brings them the magnificent diamond-encrusted gilded copper case worth 100,000 livres in itself.⁵ They open it. Oh, it was a scene worthy of a Rembrandt: those three faces aglow in the candlelight, bending over an imprisoned sun that, freed, could warm thousands of lives; and all its power was being purloined by three petty thieves! Heavy, heavy the necklace, and massive, a tasteless lump of ostentation that would have reduced any woman who wore it to the status of a walking display case. But no woman will wear it, ever —except maybe Jeanne, that night, in front of her mirror, preening before her two accomplices as she turns to let the thousand glimmers refracted from the angles of those clear stones ripple and play. The very next day the river of diamonds is deflected from its course, broken up and disguised as thirty little ponds in suede bags. The cadaver of this object, which becomes known, by an ironic twitch of history, as "the Queen's necklace," is too dangerous to be left intact.

They have very little room to maneuver. They have to play it close. The radical solution would be for all three of them to head for London, with their loot.

---

*Desclaux's role in the King's Household was in fact quite insignificant. He had, indeed, flirted briefly with Jeanne when she first appeared at Versailles, and dined with her once; but he easily proves that he has not seen her in the last three years.

But that would take the lid off the story back here, and it would also mean accepting full guilt and risking official extradition or abduction by secret agents —the French and English police are cooperating again. Besides, Jeanne just can't let go of her childhood dream of becoming the lady of Fontette; it's her obsession. Instead, they'll try to keep their heads down, sell off the necklace a bit at a time, and pacify Rohan and the jewelers until the first payment is due in August. By that time they will already have sold a lot of diamonds and will have plenty of cash in case they have to clear out, but probably that won't even be necessary: Jeanne will tell the cardinal that she has duped him, and he, dreading the scandal, will not prosecute but will pay for the necklace out of his own pocket.

That gives them more than five months to dream in.

The game was nearly up a few weeks later. On February 15, drunk with their success, Rétaux de Villette arouses the suspicions of Israel Vidal and Moïse Adam, two "merchants" in the rue Neuve Saint-Eustache, when he offers them "at any price" three lots of diamonds worth at least 20,000 livres.* The Jewish dealers in that part of town around the Temple, many of whom have been doing business there for generations, are concerned to keep their noses clean and certainly cannot afford to be caught receiving stolen goods. Adam alerts the police inspector of the Montmartre district, who consults his superiors— and it's our old acquaintance Jean-François de Bruguières, "counselor of the King, inspector of police," the one who went up to Holland to collect Mirabeau and Sophie de Monnier, who conducts a crestfallen Villette to be questioned by François Gauthier, commissioner in the Châtelet, on February 16:

"Where did you obtain those jewels?"

"From a lady who instructed me to sell them and to whom I have since returned them; I could not identify her without compromising her, save by the express order of M. le Lieutenant de Police, to whom alone I shall name her, if he insists."[6]

Well, that's no obstacle; he is taken to Lenoir at once, where the "open sesame" works again, when Villette mentions the name of "la Comtesse de Valois" in the course of a "free conversation" of which no record was made. Lenoir is just getting ready to move out, and would not care to jeopardize his new job as administrator of the King's Libraries by importuning a Valois who may be a friend of the Queen's. A search warrant and a trip to her apartment would have blown up the powder keg, for there were diamonds in every drawer. But Lenoir decides that it will be sufficient to have Bruguières ask the security office, for the record, whether any important thefts have been reported. The answer is no; case dismissed.

*140,000 modern francs [$35,000].

It was a close shave for the rue Neuve Saint-Gilles. Villette really is an oaf. The La Mottes put the brakes on the negotiations they had pending with four other Paris jewelers (from whom they ultimately get nearly 30,000 livres even so) and the comte takes a long trip to London,* where he contacts Böhmer's English counterparts Gray, Jefferyes, etc. He thinks up a gimmick that should save a little time: he exchanges his diamonds, at a loss, for stones being offered by the big jewelers, then resells these now impeccably pedigreed gems, still at a loss, to lesser jewelers for hard cash. The lists of these transactions, collated six months later by French investigators in London, could provide a good catalogue for an exhibition of eighteenth-century jewelry, ranging from pearl ropes, swords and toothpick cases, a silk portfolio and its instruments, asparagus tongs and pincers for "lazies" (snails), to watches, pendants, dozens of "naked stones" cut and ready for mounting, bracelets, rings, etc. Nathaniel Jefferyes, a Piccadilly jeweler, is sufficiently impressed by the size and weight of the eighteen enormous stones being offered at a most attractive price by the unknown gentleman "calling himself the Comte de Valois" to betake himself in turn (on April 23) "to the public office at Bond Street to learn if there had been news from Paris of any theft or swindle and, finding that none had been recorded, I left my address,"[7] and is not consulted until five months later.

But what about transferring the money? Nothing simpler: a banker who looks upon the French demimonde of London with an indulgent eye exchanges his English guineas for 123,000 livres† in letters of exchange to one of the rising Paris bankers, Jean-Frédéric Perrégaux, on the rue du Sentier.**

Across the Channel, meanwhile, Jeanne has spent her diamonds on a mountain of furniture. They're all set, they can move on to Bar-sur-Aube and inaugurate their life of ease while awaiting developments. They sell their diamonds so far below the necklace's estimated value that more than half of it is probably gone already; and the rest is in the hands of fences or friends of La Motte in London. No trace of it is ever found in France.

The fumes of triumph go to their heads. How many crooks have brought off such breathtakingly bold, beautifully planned jobs, only to get caught two days later like rank amateurs? Success is not good for them.

---

*The notion of "customs" between countries did not exist for travelers of the "superior class," and their luggage was not searched as long as their passports were in order. The *octroi*, on the other hand, with pay stations at the gates of all the big towns, levied a tax on the most insignificant goods, but it was paid only by the "lower orders."

†About 850,000 modern francs [$212,500].

**Perrégaux is forty-one in 1785. We shall meet him again; he is one of the most influential moneymen of the Directoire and Empire. His daughter marries the future Maréchal Marmont, whose treason, in 1814, is Napoleon's coup de grâce.

On February 2, the day after delivery, Böhmer, his daughter and son-in-law scramble for seats at the royal couple's public dinner. Disappointment: the Queen is not wearing their necklace. They go back to Rohan, still in seventh heaven, who shrugs them off. Come, come now, that necklace is only for the greatest occasions; and you must be aware that the Queen is waiting for a propitious moment to inform the King of her purchase? You will be paid when the first installment falls due in August—what are you complaining of? Patience, prudence, and discretion. And "if you should find yourselves in Her Majesty's presence, convey to her your very humble thanks."*

They resign themselves, but keep hanging around the drawing rooms of Versailles, not daring to address the Queen openly. In February, they are supposed to pay back 200,000 livres to Baudard de Saint-James; they ask him to give them until August, and let him in on the secret. He is not overwhelmed. Saint-James "was a financier in the full meaning of the word.† This man of average size, broadly built and stout, with a very highly colored face and that freshness some people can display at the age of even fifty or more, when they are in good health and happy," stalks out of his mirror-paneled drawing rooms and goes to call on the cardinal, to check up on his debtors' story. They, after all, are mere Jews of Saxon origin. But between us men of the world, Rohan is not above showing off. He lets Saint-James see the famous contract, allegedly signed by the Queen. The financier, being himself a parvenu, has no idea how Marie Antoinette signs her name and, proud to be in the know, keeps mum until August 15, hoping thereby to get into the Queen's good graces, as he had previously sought to gain favor with Mme du Barry.

Rohan is still giving money to Jeanne, who is careful to receive him, on his five or six visits, in a shabbily furnished room, just so he doesn't get any ideas from all the new gewgaws she's bought. She even has him pay off the 5,000 livre loan from Cerf-Beer for which he stood security in 1783. Well, why not?[8] On May 12, she charges him, via "the Queen," to have a good long holiday in Saverne, "the better to forward his career in his absence." That's another month gained. He's back on June 7 and Jeanne is waiting for him, with what she reckons to be a brilliant new ploy. The Queen has come to the conclusion that the necklace really is too expensive. She has decided not to wear it, moreover, until it is fully paid for. Now, if the jewelers would agree to cut 200,000 off the price, they would get not 400,000 but 700,000 livres for the initial installment. At first Böhmer and Bassenge moan and groan, but Rohan reassures them, promising them, in yet another billet-doux on blue notepaper, that the final installment will be adjusted after reassessment of the

---

*At the trial, Rohan's counsel emphasizes this sentence (verbatim), spoken on February 3, which militates strongly in favor of Rohan's innocence.

†According to Mme Vigée-Lebrun.

total value of the necklace, which may well go in their favor. And—another proof of his good faith—he even berates them for not having thanked the Queen for buying it. Perhaps they plead timidity, aggravated by their base condition; to help them, he dictates a note which he advises Böhmer to send Marie Antoinette:

"Madame, we are overjoyed to dare presume that the latest arrangements proposed to us, to which we have eagerly and respectfully consented, may offer fresh proof of our submission and devotion to Your Majesty's orders, and we derive great satisfaction from the thought that the most beautiful of diamond necklaces will serve the greatest and best of queens."[9]

This note is handed to the Queen as she comes out of mass on July 12. Pure Greek to anybody who has not followed the thread unraveled in these pages. But Marie Antoinette has not forgotten the necklace; she has even asked Mme Campan to find out from Saint-James what has become of it. The financier, keeping up the game with a large wink, informs the lady-in-waiting that it has just been sold to "the favorite of the sultan of Constantinople." Is the Queen actually *trying* not to understand these enigmatic lines? Or does everything connected with jewelry nowadays give her a terror of being criticized? In any event, she now commits an act that is held against her forever after, although it seems natural enough for the most spied-upon woman in France, who can't even find a place to hide her private correspondence. Mme Campan says:

"The Queen read aloud what Böhmer had written to her, and could think of no explanation but that the man had taken leave of his senses, not conceiving how he could compliment her on the beauty of the diamonds and ask her not to forget him; she held the paper over a candle that was burning nearby, as she had some letters to seal, and said, 'This is not worth keeping.' "

Something scared her that day, though she didn't know what it was, and her action proves once again that fear is ever a bad counselor.

On July 31 one of the last of the "letters from Marie Antoinette" informs Rohan that the 700,000 livres promised for the next day will not be paid until October 1. He reels, staggers, suddenly begins to suspect that he has been duped, or at least manipulated—and blames the Queen! The jewelers are on the verge of nervous breakdown. And Jeanne decides that the time has come to try her finesse. On August 3 she sends for Bassenge, who finds her packing. The only thing left in the room, in which she receives him standing, is a settee; she delivers her thunderbolt with the voice of an angel:

"You have been deceived, Monsieur. The writing and signature on the paper setting out the terms of the transaction are false. The Queen's hand was forged. But the cardinal is very rich; you must address yourself to him and insist that he make a personal arrangement with you."[10]

In other words, Rohan will cough up.

It wasn't a bad plan. It was ingenious enough, and it might even have worked a few years earlier. The only trouble is that however much of a prince, bishop, and cardinal he may be, Rohan is also a hollow shell, like nine out of ten other great aristocrats, like the Orléanses, and the King's brothers, and soon the King himself. Bankruptcy is their cancer, still invisible but devouring from within that vast generator of extravagance that is the Court nobility. And now, with their heavy borrowing, it is beginning to proliferate. They can no longer talk their way out. In 1782, commenting on the bankruptcy of his Rohan-Guéménée cousins, the cardinal was drawing his own portrait when he said: "Only a king or a Rohan could go bankrupt for so much."[11]

Yes. But his château in Saverne had burned down and was being rebuilt, and in those days there was no more "insurance" for châteaus than there was for peasants' huts. Cost of the reconstruction: 3 million.* And for the last three years the cardinal has also been disbursing over 200,000 francs a year to the armies of the Guéménées' ex-servants and creditors. Every quarter he has to pay off his own debts, too, which have now mounted to a total of 2 million, including 500,000 francs borrowed from Genoese usurers during his term as ambassador to Vienna, to pay for the life style that Maria Theresa found so shocking. His annual income, on the other hand, is "only" 500,000 to 600,000, and he can't sell his vast assets: you don't put an abbey on the market, or the very substantial holdings of the Bishopric of Strasbourg. For years he himself has been borrowing from Cerf-Beer, the most important Jew in the east (200,000 francs, *inter alia,* for the reconstruction of Saverne), which was why he stood surety for Jeanne de La Motte.

The cry is up. But who are the huntsmen and what is their quarry? Confusion reigns. Everybody starts running in all directions at once. On August 4 Bassenge arms himself to confront the cardinal:

"Is His Eminence certain of the agent serving as intermediary between himself and the Queen?"

The jewelers still aren't sure that the agent was Jeanne de La Motte. They are, and they remain, at a loss, until the trial. At this point, however, Rohan starts telling lies, and sinks his own ship. He knows full well that the "interme-

---

*To obtain a relative equivalent in modern francs these figures should all be multiplied by 7, but it should be borne in mind that the positions of essentials and nonessentials have changed substantially on the rungs of the cost ladder.

diary" is Jeanne, and he is slowly coming to realize that part (but not all) of the mess has been her doing.

"If I told you that I had dealt directly with the Queen, would you be satisfied?"

Bassenge: "My mind would be set entirely at rest."

"Well, I am as certain as if I had done so, and I will raise my right hand and tell you so upon oath. Go reassure your associate."*

The evening in the Venus Grove is still inscribed in his flesh. The rose, the hand, the shudder of excitement, the murmured words—*they* were the Queen. That is what he means by "dealt directly." When he is forced to abandon this fairy tale, part of himself goes with it. And it is in the flailings of the death agony of his ambition that Rohan turns to Cagliostro, and the latter, who possesses a goodly dose of common sense beneath his vaticinations, advises him—wrongly perhaps, but with a reflex of honesty—not to pay but to throw himself at the King's feet and confess. "I† was perplexed as to the proper course to follow, uncertain whether to make the whole affair public by denouncing the La Motte woman, or whether it would not be wiser to pay for the necklace and keep the matter quiet."

Böhmer and Bassenge finesse in turn, by going to the horse's mouth:

"Upon the receipt of such alarming news, we determined to go straightaway and throw ourselves at Her Majesty's feet and uncover our position to her; but, not having had the good fortune to obtain an audience at that time, we were unable to give an account of the matter until the 9th of this month, when it pleased Her Majesty to summon the Sieur Böhmer to attend her at Trianon."

Moral: if you ever have to deal with honest people, you can't be too careful. These two Jewish jewelers are about to rock the throne of the Bourbons.

*This dialogue is reconstructed from statements made by Bassenge, Böhmer, and Rohan during the hearings.

†Note written by the cardinal for Target, his lawyer.

BARON DE BRETEUIL

# 20

## AUGUST 1785

### *Arrest M. le Cardinal!*   THE BASTILLE

Versailles, Monday, August 15. Gala occasion at the château, one of the two
big events of the year (the other being the anniversary of St. Louis)—the Feast
of the Virgin, to whom the Kingdom of France has been dedicated. There is
a great procession, instituted by Louis XIII at the birth of Louis XIV to thank
the Queen of Heaven for blessing his marriage with an heir after twenty-two
years of infertility. It is also the feast day of Marie Antoinette's patron saint,
so there won't be many courtiers playing hooky today.

By ten in the morning they're all crowded into the parts of the château
set aside for the "well-dressed" public—the galleries, some of the salons, and
the chapel, where the Grand Almoner is to celebrate mass at eleven o'clock
in the presence of Their Majesties. Outside, the formidable white and blue
deployment of the most impressive show on earth has aligned the Swiss,
French, and Life Guards between the marble courtyard and gate of the Place
d'Armes. The weather is sultry; heavy clouds plod past overhead. From the
carriages parked by the hundreds in the court of honor descend ladies in silk
and satin, encumbered by their huge paniers (still worn on ceremonial occasions), delicately balancing the scaffoldings of their hairdos as humbler women
would balance their jugs; and men of the sword, in long brilliant-hued coats
over waistcoats fastened with gold or diamond buttons, fine lace jabots,
breeches pinched at the knee, white hose, and pumps with jeweled buckles.
Everything that governs France is here and, after passing between the soldiers,
proceeds along at a stately pace in front of short-wigged footmen dressed
predominantly in blue who could be mistaken for gentlemen except that their
immobility makes them look like pieces of furniture instead.

Versailles: eternity.

Slowly the chapel fills. Its style makes one think of a Greco-Roman temple after
a baroque invasion, with grooved Corinthian columns supporting the side

galleries and, at the back, the seats of the royal family, facing the wedding-cake altar "accompanied" by two marble angels inclining affectedly "beneath a heavenly glory in bronze, most excellently contrived."[1]

Underneath and between the two, the public can take turns adoring the King of Heaven and the King of France; all that is needed is a graceful swing of shoulders and head, an art which certain court gymnasts are said to have brought to perfection. "The center of the main vault is occupied by God the Father, promising to send his Son to redeem the world; a host of angels form his court."[2] A mirror reflection of what goes on below.

Around 10:30 a wave of uneasiness ripples over the audience, owing to the unwonted emptiness of the royal gallery. None of the people who ordinarily take their places long before Their Majesties' arrival—the pages and ladies-in-waiting and chamberlains—are there. Fingers point at two empty places in the front row of armchairs and prie-dieux, all gilt and crimson velvet; a rustle of whispering. A few minutes ago, somebody came to fetch the Baron de Breteuil, minister of the King's Household, and Armand-Thomas Huon de Miromesnil, keeper of the seals, and conducted them to the King's "inner cabinet," the room in which he does his real work. Informed circles know that the Queen is already inside it, with her husband, and that she went in "with her hair undressed."

Something's up. But nobody, nobody at all can imagine what. It can't be international, because in that case the Queen would have been kept out and Vergennes sent for instead. Or financial, because Calonne has been "forgotten." And it can't be war, because Castries and Ségur are both out here wondering. It must be something to do with the family, but how can that be, because no prince of the blood has been sent for? This grain of sand in the venerable gears of the great ritual has begun to turn people back, in hesitant little groups, from the chapel to the Oeil de Boeuf, the "Council Room," the "Clock Room," and above all the Gallery of Mirrors, one door of which opens onto the little "inner cabinet"* where four characters in heated altercation, one woman and three men, are keeping a thousand more on tenterhooks.

Marie Antoinette, apprised by Böhmer on the 9th that the necklace has been purchased by the cardinal, or rather delivered into his hands without payment of a sou, and in her name, is beside herself. She is incensed, offended, and aware that she has been manipulated, but, having never exchanged so much as one word on the subject with Rohan himself, has absolutely no idea what for. From beginning to end she conducts herself with the awkwardness of innocence. She orders the jewelers to write a memorandum for the Baron de Breteuil, on whose complete and indeed slavish devotion she knows she can rely, and who expedites and supervises her spending in his capacity as head

---

*Today room no. 130 as you tour the château.

of the King's Household. To her fierce satisfaction, she can also rely on Breteuil's loathing of Rohan, which dates from the time when he took over from the cardinal as ambassador to Vienna and, although he may have been approved by the empress, was ignored by Joseph II and all chic Austrians because of his pretentious manners, his sloppy dress and obsolete wig, and his penny-pinching attitude toward gaming and dinner parties: his term there was like murky night after the high noon of Rohan's extravagance. In 1775 even Maria Theresa could not help writing, "What a boor, by comparison with the gallant Rohan! . . . What pains me most is that the emperor [Joseph II] sets the tone in conversations at Breteuil's expense and has even, upon seeing him, made a mocking sign to Abbé Georgel,"³ Rohan's *âme damnée* and secretary in Vienna before becoming his grand vicar in Strasbourg. Chancellor Kaunitz, moreover, considered Breteuil "a vindictive and arrogant man, with whom one must walk on stilts in order to reduce him to his proper size." Such sayings lose no time making the rounds, and they infuriated Breteuil.

Well, here comes vengeance, and he's not going to miss it. He rejects the last nonviolent solution that could have kept the whole thing quiet—a family council of the Rohans, presided over by the ancient Maréchal de Soubise, patriarch of the tribe. That is Louis XVI's first idea, when he still doesn't have the foggiest notion what is going on and hasn't yet lost his temper. But Soubise is not at Versailles this morning. No, no, there's no time to wait, the Queen and Breteuil want to pierce the abscess here and now, and in front of a qualified witness, since this is undoubtedly a case for the courts. That's why they send for the keeper of the seals, who arrives so white and shaky that he looks sick, with his flaccid, pendulous cheeks hanging like wattles "down to his shoulders," as the spiteful say. The poor man "thought, when he was sent for in the chapel by order of the King, that he was being asked to hand over the seals;* and it was in that persuasion that he followed the Baron de Breteuil."⁴ He heaves a profound sigh of relief when "the King informed him that he had sent for him, desiring to consult him as to the procedure to be followed in a case which he wished to submit to him. It seems that the Baron de Breteuil already believed the cardinal guilty. This was the situation when the King sent for the cardinal, who was at his toilette and who called for his pontifical robes so that he could go on afterwards to mass with the King, whom he was to accompany." This is according to Castries, whose account we must now follow step by step, because the very next day the minister of the navy is appointed to the sort of "jury of honor" that questions Rohan before turning him over to the professionals in the parlement.

---

*That is, being fired from his job as minister. There was indeed talk of doing so, and he had some grounds for alarm, as a member of a government in which ministers were often dispatched without warning.

The cardinal is in the "Council Room"* with the *grandes entrées,* meaning the chief Court dignitaries, and he answers the King's summons in a scarlet moiré cassock under a surplice, or in other words in "preparation for robing" for the mass.

When he came in, the King handed him Böhmer's memorandum, and told him to read and explain it. Having done so, the cardinal said that everything in the memorandum was true and that, the Queen being present, he saw clearly that he had made some mistake; attached to the memorandum was a letter from the cardinal instructing the jeweler to deliver the necklace.

"As to the letter," he said, "I can say nothing about it because this is a copy; I can recall but two or three words of it."

"But," pursued the King, "have you nothing to say to justify your conduct and the guarantee you have given?"

Seeing that the cardinal appeared troubled, he told him:

"Pull yourself together; go alone into my room† and set down in writing what you can say to justify yourself."

The cardinal remained some time there, while the King consulted as to what he should do, and opined [*sic*] to have him arrested.

"But," said the keeper of the seals, "what about his pontifical robes?"

*"Don't talk like a lackey,"*** replied the King with a shrug.

The Baron de Breteuil made no objection to the resolution upon which the King was now determining. The cardinal came in, after writing a few lines which contain nothing but an admission of the accusation against him and an assurance that he had been practiced upon.

At the same time, whether in speech or writing, he seems to have identified Mme de La Motte as someone who had contributed to his deception.

He identifies her, all right: his fifteen rambling lines begin "A woman whom I believed" and end with "Madame Lamotte [*sic*] de Valois."[5] Perhaps he's finally waking up to the fact that she has stolen the necklace. But if there's the devil on one side, on the other, to his utter confusion, is the deep blue sea . . . because he's still completely convinced of the intimacy between Jeanne and the Queen, and the reality of the scene in the Venus Grove—when was it?—a year ago, how time flies. So he thinks that by mentioning the countess's name he will fill Marie Antoinette with consternation and reduce her to silence. But she is even more in the dark than he. She has heard her sisters-in-law and a few of her ladies talking vaguely about this Valois person, whose name nobody could forget, as one of those scores of intriguers swarming on the outer fringes of her circle, some of whom have contrived to wheedle alms

*A small room in which audiences were given, containing a huge globe on a desk.

†To be exact, the sovereigns and ministers went into the King's private library—room no. 133 today—and left Rohan in the "little cabinet."

**Underlined by Castries in his diary.

or a pension out of her. But she truthfully does not remember ever speaking to Jeanne and cannot even recall what she looks like. The misunderstanding is total, and Rohan's hemming and hawing is about to transform it into hysterics on the part of the Queen and a fine fit of temper by the King.

"Where is this woman?" demands Louis XVI.

"Sire, I do not know," answers Rohan, who knows perfectly well that she's at Bar-sur-Aube, having himself, oh irony! financed her trip there "to think things over," after sheltering her and her husband in his own house for two or three days, around August 10.

"Do you have the necklace?"

"Sire, it is in that woman's hands. I shall pay for it."

And about time, too! The poor wretch is in a pretty pickle. He still supposes, even now, that Marie Antoinette could become his accomplice, that by laying the purchase, rightly or wrongly, at Jeanne's doorstep and offering to assume responsibility for it, he is sacrificing himself on the altar of the combined interests of love and state. But then he is a cultural product of the government of the Marquise de Pompadour. He was twenty-five years old when she maneuvered Choiseul into the limelight. His mental structure was fashioned then and there's nothing he can do about it.

He now proceeds to cook his own goose for good. First, he forgets about Louis XVI, who still has control of the situation, albeit in the manner of a bull in a china shop:

"Cousin,* in such circumstances as these I cannot do otherwise than to have the seals placed upon your home and yourself placed under arrest. The name of the Queen is precious to me. It has been compromised. I must let nothing pass."

The nincompoop! The Queen's name is indeed compromised—but only within these four walls. By that decision he compromises it all over Europe. And, starting tomorrow, some people will be insinuating that he doesn't mind half as much as he puts on. But today he has the excuse of having espoused his wife's resentments, and no one can accuse him, at this point anyway, of acting with premeditation.

Rohan implores the King to spare him a public scandal, especially at the very moment he was to officiate before the whole of Versailles and Paris. "Let your Majesty deign to remember his affection for Mme de Marsan, who watched over him in childhood; the glory of the Maréchal de Soubise, the fame of my family name."

Whereupon, in rising irritation, Marie Antoinette herself breaks in:

"How is it possible, M. le Cardinal, for you to conceive, when I have not

---

*Customary form of address used by the King when speaking to all "blue ribbons," i.e., members of the Order of the Holy Ghost, the highest in the kingdom.

spoken to you in eight years, that I should wish your assistance in conducting such a transaction?"

"They say that the cardinal, still laboring under his former delusion, made certain signs* to remind the Queen upon what his belief might be founded, and that these signs destroyed the last shreds of Her Majesty's patience. She told one of her ladies-in-waiting that at that moment she felt such a surge of fright, amazement, and anger that she thought she would faint."

As for Louis XVI, his blood is up, and those who know him know that it's time to get out of his way. Nothing is more fearsome than a mild man's wrath. Enough is enough.

"Monsieur, I shall do what I can to console your family. I desire that you may be able to justify yourself. I am performing my duty, as King and as husband. Leave us."

There follows a moment of great confusion, which has been the subject of much misinterpretation and is not clearly grasped by either eyewitnesses or historians. Rohan leaves the room like a fired flunkey, and drifts through the adjoining chamber, known as the "Clock Room," where he continues his solitary death-walk through a small, distinguished, hypnotized company. He moves on into the "Council Room" and then to the Oeil de Boeuf, crossing the *chambre royale de parade.* It is here that Breteuil, drunk with joy, finally catches up with him, having received official instructions to arrest him and take him to the Bastille—Louis XVI hadn't had the courage to give the order in his presence.

Castries:

"The cardinal walked about for a moment with the Baron [de Breteuil] in the Oeil de Boeuf. He said to him: 'Can't we stay as we are; can you not just keep me beside you as you walk?' so that people won't realize he's under arrest; as yet nothing public has happened. "And, with this, he moved down the hall"—the Gallery of Mirrors, thronged with much less "intimate" people who are pushing and shoving, and some of whom climb up on the chair seats when he appears, livid, followed by a red-faced Breteuil who, "fearing perhaps that he might escape, called a young officer from the King's Guards [in fact, it was Charles de Jouffroy, a lieutenant in the Life Guards] and said," or rather, trumpeted at the top of his lungs, in the most beautiful room in Europe, seventy-two meters long and ten wide,† with seventeen windows and, facing them, seventeen arches completely paneled in mirrors, and also, sixteen me-

---

*According to Castries, confirmed by Besenval and de Crosne.

†For years the story went that the arrest was made, as would have been proper, by the Duc de Villeoir, who was captain of the guard that quarter, but he was in the chapel at the time and didn't get there until the scene was over.

ters overhead, all the battles of Louis XIV painted by Le Brun to intimidate the underlings:

" 'I command you, sir, by order of the King, to arrest M. le Cardinal, and answer for his person.' "

The die is cast. Nothing, now, can stop it from rolling, and nobody knows how far it will go.

Rohan is lost, or thinks he is. But even in calamity there are degrees. A search is to be carried out in his house on the rue Vieille du Temple, where, in the heart of hearts of his private rooms, lie some scores of letters from the Queen, as he still believes, who has just denied him but whose reputation he wants to protect, out of some vestige of love or long-overdue sense of self-preservation, hoping, at least, to avoid the charge of lèse majesté that has cost so many men their heads, including, only thirteen short years ago, Struensee, the prime minister of Denmark and lover of that country's queen.

Perhaps something can be salvaged from the ruins. His sanctified robes, his name, and his carriage have still some power to intimidate. Breteuil has gone off to celebrate his triumph with his friends, which means that he will lose precious minutes in getting to Rohan's house to slap on the seals.

> The cardinal, left standing opposite the officer, asked him whether he would be permitted to write a note.
>
> "By all means!" said the officer, "you're the master."
>
> The cardinal took advantage of this permission, wrote four lines in pencil, stepped out at his house, signaled to one of the servants in the antechamber, and handed him the note. The servant rushed straight away to Paris and got there an hour and three-quarters ahead of the Baron de Breteuil. This gave Abbé Georgel, who lived in his house, time to remove or burn his papers,

which were kept in a large red portfolio.

And thus was born a historic enigma, when one glance at those letters would have revealed their flagrant inauthenticity to every eye. But the very lies they told were of the kind to make one avert one's gaze.

GALLOT

# 21

## APRIL–AUGUST 1785

## *They Are Dying Every Day*

Paris is only sixty leagues from the Poitevin bocage [a *bocage* being mixed woods and pastureland, often with hedgerows, but in this case also with bogs and swampy ground; in England this would be called fen country—*Trans.*] by the King's Highway that crosses the Loire at Ponts-de-Cé below Angers. And the minute village of Saint-Maurice-le-Girard (fewer than a hundred inhabitants), in the middle of this bocage (not to be confused with the far more fertile and extensive Norman bocage further north, toward Caen), is two days from Versailles by rapid post, but nine days by the stagecoach that goes at a snail's pace. In other words, the place in which Dr. Jean-Gabriel Gallot is putting up a devil, or an angel, of a fight against the epidemic that is devastating lower Poitou is on another planet, light-years away from the furor over the Queen's necklace.*

Epidemics, to be exact; three in succession, which have devastated the entire region. The grim reaper always has plenty of work in this unhealthy land, which the sea left sodden and filled with noxious vapors when it absent-mindedly withdrew to Sables d'Olonne, where boats can hardly find water enough to anchor in.

The swathes were overlapping, touched off by a curse in the weather in 1785—a ferocious winter, no spring at all, followed by unending drought. First there was a "catarrhal fever resembling a bilious pseudo-peripneu-monia," according to the reports Gallot somehow finds time to send to the already celebrated Vicq d'Azyr,[1] his eminent colleague in Paris, member of the Royal Academy of Medicine (and former fellow student); in modern language, that would be an infectious influenza carried by an extremely virulent virus. Then came smallpox, and "the extent of the contagion is immense, from the seacoast as far inland as Touraine, Chinon, and possibly beyond."[2]

---

*J.-G. Gallot was born in the village, on September 3, 1744. We shall meet him again in the Constituent Assembly, after he is sent to represent the Poitevin electors on the benches of the third estate at the Estates-General.

And then a raging dysentery with all the appearance of typhus, which extends into upper Brittany as well,[3] where it has been endemic since its importation in 1779 by thousands of sick men returning from the disintegrated armada that ought to have invaded England.

A long face, growing thinner every day, receding hairline, aquiline nose, just time for one roll of graying hair at ear level; pale and gangling in clothes stained by dirt from the pathway or patients' pus, a lace jabot that has worked its way out of his collar, torn and flapping: M. Don Quixote Gallot, trying to hold back an ocean of illness with his bare hands.

"The disease has wrought frightful havoc for the last five or six weeks; the epidemic remains as intense as ever and is spreading with distressing frenzy. In the last two weeks the infection seems to have changed character; nature appears to have chosen sweating as its means of staving off the ravages of the disease. It is useful to encourage this."[4] To do so, he digs into the two leather-covered pharmacy kits suspended on either side of his saddle, which he fills once a week in Poitiers, usually with money from his own pocket but sometimes helped along by the intendant of the province or his colleagues at the hospital. Most of his patients could never pay an apothecary, and besides, where would they go to find one? Their only trips to Niort or Poitiers are for the big annual fairs, and by no means all of them attend those, only the ones with good horses and a wagon they can fill with vegetables, fruit, cheese, or wine to pay for the journey.

One after the other, "to encourage sweating," the white magician tries the potions, powders, or unguents that were already in use in Molière's day but whose names will almost all change or vanish within the next few years:

> acidulated diapnoic potions, sedative powders with Hamburg salts (boric acid-based), vesicants, camphorated boluses, evacuants employed with circumspection. . . . But when the head is implicated from the start and the germ of death grows alongside the disease, nothing is any use. They are dying every day, in thirty-six, twenty-four hours, or less. What must be done, in a case as calamitous as this? The plague itself does not strike more savagely. Contagion appears absolute. Whole families and households are assaulted with amazing swiftness. Many are carried off. . . . In one month I have seen over three hundred new cases.

And thus it goes, from April to June, when the relentless drought bows the head of the man who rides his horse alone from the morning angelus to the evening angelus, between the searing sun that blackens his skin and "the humid, resistant earth, hard to plow and thus to render fertile; and that is the soil of the parish in which I live." When he rides out beyond his home ground, it's even worse—in the other parts of the bocage, where "the clayey, sandy, argillaceous earth, full of ochre [*sic*] and shale, and our boulders of excessively hard vitrescible stone" form a sort of oven for roasting travelers.[5]

He's fighting more than this epidemic. He came back to his native village eighteen years ago, after receiving his diploma as doctor of medicine in Montpellier; as a member of the RPR,* that was one of the few professions he would be allowed to practice. He wanted to be a pastor; but he can hardly be serving the good Lord less wholeheartedly now, in his daily struggle with

> the most frequent diseases, which are those caused by repressed transpiration, such as anginas, inflammations of the chest, congestion of the breast in nursing mothers, diseases occasioned by the patient's manner of life, as dropsy, obstructions, verminous affections, looseness of the bowels, dysenteries; uncleanliness, which causes frequent cutaneous infections such as boils, scabies, scurf, etc. Fevers, especially intermittent, are also commonly met among them.[6]

But, as Gallot writes in ten or twenty letters to the Academy of Medicine, the bocage, and almost the entire kingdom, is no less fiercely infested with "the empiricals, or in other words, the healers and patent-medicine vendors.

> The greatest scourge that is devastating our countryside at present is charlatanism. In the last four or five months the empiricals have prospered and multiplied appallingly. There is no parish that does not have at least one weekly caller. Every fair and marketplace is infested with them and they stand at the door of every church on feast days and Sundays. I have spoken and made representations to the judges in these places; I have shown them the letters patent of 1778 and the Council decree of 1781. They replied that they had no knowledge of either, as the first were registered only at Parlement and the Châtelet, and the second did not have force of law.[7]

Some of the most highly respected of these "empiricals" are the executioners who are attached to every criminal court, and their assistants and retired predecessors. Everybody knows that the shedding of blood has invested them with special qualities. And selling garbage brings in more money than hanging a beggar. According to Jean-Gabriel Gallot, these people account for as many deaths as the disease itself.

> Everybody is setting up to be a physician, as I wrote in one of my previous memoranda. Everyone is a charlatan or quack. The executioners are the most highly renowned; after them come the licensed runners,† and the fairground tricksters roam unchallenged, flouting law and order under cover of a charter that is often counterfeit or stolen, boldly putting the people to ransom before sending them to their deaths. There are others, unchartered, which only makes them the more shameless and impudent, like the man named Deglimne who has been living

---

*Religion Prétendue Réformée* ("so-called" or "allegedly reformed religion") was the term used in royal and ecclesiastical edicts in France to refer to Protestants.

†Here "runner" [*coureur*] means "vagabond."

in Saintes for several years and to whom wonderful curses and miracles are attributed, although it is a proven fact that the man does not know how to read. He calls himself Dutch. I have seen his consultations, which he has written up by a coadjutor who goes about with him everywhere. They proclaim the crassest ignorance and most foolhardy empiricism. And yet he is the Aesculapius of our province. People run after him, they call him from twenty or thirty leagues away.

After these miracle workers of the first order come the farriers, veterinarians, and horse copers, the bone setters and restorers, all recognized doctors of men. And then come the goodwives, "wise" men and women of all conditions, and the vendors of drugs. In sooth, almost the entire population. At this rate, soon the only people who will not be practicing medicine will be the doctors. Such is the state of our profession.[8]

Every night he comes home, groggy with fatigue, to "Les Apprelles," the family house at Saint-Maurice-le-Girard whose firm, square bulk, three stories high, contrasts scandalously with the rest of the village, the score of large thatched blisters made of dried earth and straw, the typical dwelling of this region; they look like beaver's huts, with just enough room inside to be born, vegetate, and die under a lid. The Gallots even have a garden, at the bottom of which cypresses stand guard over the tombs of their ancestors—all Protestants, whose mortal remains were gladly abandoned to their families in order that the Roman Catholic cemeteries might remain unsullied. Jean-Gabriel was baptized, however, on September 4, 1744, by Father Brisson, the parish priest; but he was never confirmed and never goes to mass. This form of "unconsummated baptism," often performed out of tolerance by the local incumbent, was the only way in which Protestants could acquire a legal existence and practice, without too much harassment, the professions left open to them. The father of our doctor, Noé-Mathurin Gallot, and his mother, the daughter of Moïse-Louis de la Morinière—one of the most renowned of the "reformed" (with two pastors in the family) of lower Poitou—were regarded as "notorious Calvinists and heretics, bad Catholics, who perform none of their religious obligations."[9]

The spies are quite right. Baptism and a church wedding are for form; Jean-Gabriel's upbringing and his spiritual life are wholly Calvinist. Group prayer morning and evening, a clandestine but tolerated service on Sunday which was naturally attended—the Gallot house being the most commodious around—by all the neighboring *religionnaires* [the French term for Calvinists —*Trans.*]. His childhood was filled with tales of the dragoonings (of the Huguenots) and attic browsing, for years, among the four or five hundred banned volumes which had been stashed away in trunks since the revocation of the Edict of Nantes.

A century before he and his parents could have lost their lives, or been deported at the very least, for adopting this attitude of passive provocation. But times have changed. The Bishop of Luçon and the intendant of Poitou are prepared to put up with the Protestants as long as they don't start angling for titles or positions and don't proselytize. The land of Noé-Mathurin Gallot was fruitful and multiplied under his management, and he even engaged in a little speculation in local real estate. A just and upright man. "He is esteemed and highly regarded by the gentry of his district, who have adopted him as their sole arbiter in any disputes arising among them. Their confidence in his enlightenment is such that gentry submitting disputes to be settled by him have been known to sign his decision before even reading it."[10]

A father who was something better than a gentleman, thus, and a pious and self-effacing mother who died when Jean-Gabriel was fourteen; and a maiden aunt to finish bringing him up—Suzanne Gallot, whose soul had been seared by the wind from the Camisard "wilderness"* and who sometimes took him to the semi-public "assemblies" at La Fallourdière, a nearby town nicknamed "little Geneva" by the Poitevins "because it contained nothing but Protestants."[11] The "humanities" at Caen, one of the few towns at a reasonable distance where young Poitevin Protestants could find a university that admitted them and fellow Calvinists to lodge with.[12] Paris at eighteen, for the classes in anatomy and medicine taught by the surgeon Antoine Petit at the Jardin du Roi (now the Jardin des Plantes); this was a new, spritely, bright kind of instruction, the very opposite to the outmoded and inaccurate lessons which the Faculty of Medicine was continuing to dispense on the rue de la Bûcherie. It was at the Jardin du Roi that Gallot met Vicq d'Azyr and their friendship began. And after that, Montpellier for his diploma, which was easier to obtain in the "Protestant-infested" capital of French medicine. And, by 1767, he was back in his father's house and out "every day on horseback, often at a canter, sometimes at a trot, along wretched, untended, muddy roads boxed in by dense hedgerows, traveling sometimes more than ten leagues in a day; most of his calls were for the poor in the remote countryside."[13]

The poor. His life. Without ever a boast or self-satisfied smirk. Gallot seems to have been one of the most disinterested men of his age.

In the absolute seclusion in which I live I am not, thank the Lord, a partisan in any dispute; I am attached to no side.† I live in a country house in a very small hamlet with fifteen or twenty hearths. In my parish there is no other individual above the people except the priest, and then the house of my father, with whom I live. I occasionally spend some of my time in a private dwelling of my own, which stands completely alone and isolated two or three leagues from here.** La

*["Le desert" (translated as "wilderness" by contemporaries) referred specifically to the way of life and worship of the Protestants during their time of persecution—somewhat like "underground" during World War II.—Trans.]

†Letter to Dubois de Fosseux, perpetual secretary of the Academy of Arras, whom we shall be meeting on the paths, inter alia, of Carnot, Robespierre, and Babeuf.

**"Le Fief Mignoux" in the parish of Saint-Maurice-des-Noues.

Châtaigneraie, a league away, is a very small town or biggish village in which there is absolutely nothing in any way connected with the sciences—a subdelegate [of the intendant of Poitou], a parish priest and his vicar, a convent with two Dominicans [!], two clerks [taxes], a royal bailliage which has two or three judges, a handful of attorneys, barristers, and *huissiers,* one seigneurial justice, one doctor, and one surgeon. After these notables come ten or twelve houses of gentlemen or people living on that footing.[14]

Such were the country towns, and not only in lower Poitou, as outlined in Doctor Gallot's sociological profile: a thin crust of "elite" beneath which the three "estates of good people"—clergy, nobility, and bourgeoisie—are baked together into a relationship of compulsory tedium, and beneath them scores, or hundreds, of nothings, peasants, farm laborers—Jean-Gabriel's patients, whom he's slogging his guts out to save but without any illusions:

poorly clothed, with bad beds* and mean housing, often among the livestock, lighted by resin candles; for the most part they are black with smoke. Poverty, crude or laxative food, all of it unhealthy and indigestible, and acute want have made the bulk of our peasantry soft and weak, idle, indolent, and gullible.

Very rough and countrified in the marshes, a little less so in the pastureland, not so lumpish in my district, and far more agile, limber, and bright as one moves toward the Anjou and upper Poitou, they are in the main of middle stature. They are neither very robust nor well made. A few good-looking men may be seen, however. Poverty and want interfere greatly with the growth of a strong and handsome constitution. Three-quarters naked all year round, having to run in mud or frost to beg their sustenance, how could such wretched children not be affected in their growth? And this must be understood to apply to the majority, for comfortably off people are the far smaller number in our country districts. After the gentry, ecclesiastics, and well-to-do bourgeois come the manufacturers, merchants, farmers, craftsmen, and laborers, who are, by and large, poor in the bocage and prosperous only in the pastureland. For the rest, the men till the soil and work in the woods and vineyards, etc., and make our flannels and linen; the women spin wool for our coarser fabrics, in which there is a considerable trade.

The staple of all these last-named classes is rye bread, alone or mixed with late barley or *baillarge,* black wheat porridge, chestnuts, vegetable marrows, peas, broad beans and turnips and other legumes, fruit, cooked or raw, and milk products. That is all, apart from butter and eggs for the less needy; only the most prosperous sometimes eat a hen or salt pork. Never wine, or only at the tavern for the drunkards. In years when the fruit crop is plentiful, the people sometimes make cider or a fermented beverage with service apples and plums.[15]

"Nothing can show more plainly (the Poitevin example is one of a thousand) to what degree inequality is the rule.† The bread, sometimes, is bread in name

---

*According to a "Mémoire" he wrote a few years earlier for the Academy of Medicine.

†According to Fernand Braudel, who quotes sources for Poitou going back four centuries earlier, when "the bread of the poor" was already a kind of poison.

alone. Often there is none. White bread is a rarity, a luxury. . . . Even at the beginning of the eighteenth century, a good half of the country population was living on unmillable grain and rye, and there was a high proportion of bran in the maslin of the poor."[16] As far as that's concerned, you might as well say "at the end of the eighteenth century" too, except in large towns where the taste of the people has been refined and some of the bakers are the first graduates of a national school of bakery founded by Necker in Paris in 1780. In any event, "the west of France was still condemned to rye."[17]

When he finally does get home, however, Jean-Gabriel Gallot finds a happy family, formed tardily and almost absentmindedly when, at the age of thirty-five, he was married, by a pastor and in the home of friends (there were no Protestant churches) to Elisabeth Goudal, nicknamed Betsy for her vivacity, the daughter of wholesale merchants from the Bordeaux region. She has given him two sons, Noé-Gabriel* in 1780—a serious child, too clever by half, "gifted" they would say in a later age—and Moïse-André in 1782. Both were baptized "in the wilderness," meaning not in church, a proof that the handicap of Protestant baptism was beginning to lose force. The doctor is loved and admired at home, and his old father is proud of him. But he's got no time for happiness. Late at night he expends his remaining crumbs of energy writing, with feverish intensity, memorandum after memorandum to twenty academies and all the physicians or savants anywhere in France who might conceivably help him to open the eyes of the authorities to the one great basic scourge from which flow all the rest—disease, epidemics, and rising mortality, especially among children: the unbelievable poverty of the people in the west. If something is not done to stop it, whole provinces may die tomorrow.

His brain awhirl with plans and schemes, chief among them the foundation of small country hospitals which would also act as training centers for surgeons and midwives (he wrote Necker about this), and improved bread dough, and massive recourse to potato farming and swamp drainage, and a fairer apportionment of the *dîme* and *corvée* (restored after Turgot's departure), Gallot-Cassandra is flooding France with his writings—outcries, one might better call them. Although still a physician, he already sounds like a politician, if only because he expresses himself with the conviction of a man who knows whereof he speaks:

"The people have so long been beasts of burden that it is time something was done for them!" Or, "What I have said of the bad food consumed by the people is only a part of their indigence; the poor wretches want bedding, clothing, fire, and all as well, and *often hope. . . .*† One would have difficulty

---

*He dies of one of the bocage diseases, in 1792. The Gallots also have a daughter, in 1786, named Anne-Elisabeth, who marries during the Empire.

†Underlined by Gallot.

believing the destitution that has spread through our country districts. I need only say that it is extreme, that it is incredible. . . . To be convinced of it requires but one visit to their hovels."[18]

For the moment, he seems to be the only person daring to accept his own invitation.

HÉRAULT DE SÉCHELLES

# 22

OCTOBER 1785

## *You Shall Suffer Infinitely*

Sunday, October 30, 1785. A fine autumn morning. Cantering on a hired horse through the three leagues that separate Semur-en-Auxois from Montbard, Marie-Jean Hérault de Séchelles might have paused to admire the russet Burgundian forests.* But he hurries forward, keeping his eyes peeled for "the tower of Montbard and the terraces and gardens surrounding it"[1] as a pilgrim scans the horizon for his first glimpse of Jerusalem. And this is a pilgrimage: Hérault is going to see his god in France, there's one left and he's the last— Buffon. He's positively trembling. A "palpitation of joy" surges through him:

> I observed the position of the different places, the hill on which the tower stands, the mounts and slopes above it and the sky over all. I kept looking and looking for the château, I was so impatient to see the dwelling of the famous man to whom I was about to speak. But the château remains invisible until one is virtually upon it, although when you get there you might imagine you were entering some townhouse in Paris instead of a château. There is nothing to warn you of the approach of that of M. de Buffon; it stands in a street in Montbard, which is a small town. For the rest, it is extremely handsome.

To Georges-Louis Leclerc, Seigneur de Montbard et de Buffon, member of the Académie Française and every other noted academy of Europe and America, superintendent of the Jardin du Roi in Paris, this has always been home. He was born here in 1707 and here he composed, in 1746, the first volume of his *Histoire naturelle*. He is now on the thirty-fifth and penultimate

---

*Hérault de Séchelles represents the nobility at the Estates-General before being elected to the Convention, of which he is president twice, and he is also a member of the Committee of Public Safety. He is guillotined with Danton and Camille Desmoulins.

one, and is philosophically preparing to die. He has come to the conclusion of a great adventure of the mind, "a vastly long look at nature,* an immobility in the center of the world, a labor of fifty years performed in a few square feet, a monument of books built upon demolished truths, without remorse and without turning back,"[2] at the bottom of a town so small that the part lying "in the lowlands, on the far side of the River Brenne, is 700 steps long and 250 wide" between crumbling walls, "with no other fortification than a few half-ruined towers." Buffon wears his whole estate on top of his head, so to speak: it rises from the bottom up, beginning with the houses "climbing the slope of a small mountain," a little like in Tonnerre, the Chevalier d'Eon's home five leagues away, twice the distance from Montbard to Dijon.[3]

> How keen was my emotion when I climbed the stairs and crossed the salon hung with all the painted birds as they can be seen in the large edition of the *Histoire naturelle*. † Here I am, in Buffon's room. He entered it from another room, and I must not omit one circumstance that struck me, because it is so revealing of his personality. He opened the door and, although he knew there was a stranger there, turned around most slowly and composedly to close it behind him; then he came toward me . . . majestically, opening his arms. I stammered a few words, being careful always to say "M. le Comte," which is something one must not fail to do.** I had been warned that he was not averse to this form of address. He answered, embracing me,
>     "I must look upon you as an old acquaintance, for you have shown a desire to see me and I wanted to know you as well. We have been waiting some time upon each other already."

One could say more; two worlds were waiting upon each other. Face to face, Hérault de Séchelles and Buffon, a meeting of future and past.

Hérault de Séchelles is twenty-six. He is so good-looking that people catch their breath when he goes by. A fairy child. For the moment, his one shortcoming is that he knows it. As a child, when the young painter Drouais, who studied under the celebrated David,‡ painted him at the age of what?—eight or ten?—in a Pierrot-style satin jacket with big buttons and a lace ruff, wearing a long broad hat that set off his little round nose, round eyes, and round head. He looked good enough to eat.[4] Now he has acquired that slightly haggard air of the handsome man consumed. His identifying marks emerge plainly

---

*As beautifully expressed by Yann Gaillard in his sparkling book on Buffon.

†These are the color plates from the original edition, much prized by modern decorators.

**The Leclercs' nobility was of recent creation; the title of "comte," granted by Louis XV, certified three generations of land ownership.

‡David, launched by the Salon of 1781 and Diderot's last observations on painting, is coming to the fore as the champion of the Classical style.

from history's crossfire, the one point on which friends and enemies agree, and are borne out by his passport: "five feet eight inches tall, brown hair and eyebrows, high forehead, average nose, brown eyes, small mouth." And further borne out by the audience at his pleadings and speeches: "handsome as a demigod, with magnificent eyes, a pale complexion, laughing mouth, admirable carriage, he was the women's idol."⁵

Society women, that is. Hérault de Séchelles is an authentic nobleman who, had he been a few years older and chosen the army instead of the gown, might well have found himself with La Fayette during the American caper. His genealogy, countersigned by the infallible d'Hozier, lies in the Armorial Général [College of Heralds] and certifies that he possesses the requisite number of quarters. His family's roots reach deep into the Avranchin, the country of Mont-Saint-Michel in lower Normandy where the Cotentin begins. In 1380 the Héraults already owned the "sergentrie de Genêts," that is, a "mobile fief granted by the King, but only to nobles." After Louis XIII it was renamed the "Hérault sergentrie." Across their escutcheon waddle three white ducks, "beaked in gold, wings folded, footless, representing three conquered foes, the Imperial, the Spanish, and the English armies."

His grandfather René Hérault, seigneur of Fontaine-Labbé and Vaucresson, was lieutenant general of police in the early days of Louis XV's effective reign, and thus held Paris in his unshrinking fist. A stern taskmaster to evildoers, but also to libertines and Jansenists, moved by a religious fanaticism that smacked more of military ferocity than of evangelism, he was nonetheless remembered with affection by the Parisians for having introduced garbage collection and making the Sabbath a compulsory day of rest even for craftsmen. He did not stint on *lettres de cachet* and was fond of long interrogations conducted in the Bastille. Gloomy and cantankerous at home, he had not made life a bed of roses for his very young wife, Hélène Moreau de Séchelles, who brought him the land called by that name in Picardy and who may, without too many scruples, have accepted the consolations of the Ducs de Boufflers and Durfort. She's still alive, the châtelaine of Séchelles, a pink and white grandmother in a black mantilla, seventy this year.* She married their one surviving son to a descendant of a big Saint-Malo family, Marie-Marguerite Magon de la Lande. But little Marie-Jean, whose young mother had become pregnant almost at once, was born without a father: Jean-Baptiste Hérault de Séchelles was killed, seven months after his marriage, at the battle of Minden (as was La Fayette's father), leading the regiment of Rouergue Infantry of which he had just been made colonel. A swift end to a military career that might have led him to the head of an army.

*And doesn't die until 1798.

Another glorious officer bent over the posthumous infant's cradle, however, and bent even lower over the inconsolable eighteen-year-old widow—
her uncle by marriage, the Maréchal de Contades, upon whom many people,
including Louis XV, laid the blame for the disaster of Minden. Momentarily
disgraced, with a precociously senile wife, he formed a sort of couple with his
solitary young niece, cheerfully brushing aside the fifty-year gap in their ages.
They lived together but, for appearances' sake, in separate apartments—there
was plenty of room in the Maréchal's châteaus. Even before Minden he was
much smitten with his niece; people have whispered, and will continue to
whisper, about Contade's paternal attachment to Marie-Jean, and some are
beginning to find many points of resemblance between the boy and the old
soldier, who, under Louis XVI, is once again in good odor at Court and, as
military governor of Alsace, is still in active service despite his eighty-odd
years.

Hérault's childhood was châteaus—"La Chipaudière" at Montgeoffroy
in Anjou and Livry in Île-de-France; a profusion of footmen, tutors, hunts,
and torches, an old Uncle Sugar-daddy full of tales of the wars, a mother
who was more like an older sister, a quick turn at Juilly with the upper-class
Oratorian fathers, an untroubled future, a choice he can make for himself
between sword or gown. He likes the easy life and is not anxious to run the
risks his father did: name and property must be preserved from any English
or German cannonballs that might stray into the flesh of an only heir. Hérault de Séchelles will be a noble of the gown, a lord of fine talking.
Through his connections he is propelled into this career while still a stripling, just as, had he opted for the army, a regiment would have been precociously bestowed upon him. After all, his mother is related to the Polastrons,
and these days Polastron equals Polignac, and Polignac equals Marie Antoinette. He was presented to the Queen, and she took good note of the
mildly fatuous youth; he was her type. Thanks to her, he has made a dazzling
entry into the parlement. Is it true that Marie Antoinette gave him, on the
day of his promotion to the rank of assistant public prosecutor [*avocat général*],
the belt that magistrates wear round their robes, embroidered by her own
hands? He lets it be said, anyway.

To conquer Buffon when he calls on him at Montbard, "he donned a fine
gold coat such as was no longer worn except by the old lords,"[6] but accompanied by the jabot dictated by modern canons of elegance. Some think he has
"a mild and grave face, a melancholy gaze and an expression of kindliness,"[7]
but these opinions may all come from one sex. What is certain, though, is that
every public gesture, every inflection of Hérault's voice expresses his privileged position: for the last two months he has been one of the three "attorneys
of the King" at the Parlement of Paris. Only two more like him in all of France.
And at twenty-six! Thanks to his family fortune and his protectors in high

places, he has just bought the job from Michel Le Peletier de Saint-Fargeau,* a childhood playmate, a friend, another golden apple of the nobility of the gown who, at the age of twenty-five, has been newly authorized, also thanks to a series of royal exemptions, to move straight into the office and privileges of his father (where've we heard that before), who was mortar president of the same parlement.† Shake hands, princelings of justice.

In 1783 they went together on one of those pilgrimages without which young people of their age and class felt frustrated—the trip to Zurich to meet Lavater, the pastor-author and founder of physiognomy, which taught that everybody could judge everybody else by their eyebrows, skull, jawbone, and wrinkles. "Who am I?" Marie-Jean had asked him shortly before. "Will you pardon my importunity if I take the liberty of sending you two portraits of me that were made this year, and beg that you will be so good as to let me have your physiognomic observations on them?"[8]

"You are endowed with a very exact and delicate tact for all that is good and beautiful and right," replied the "Fénelon of Helvetia."

> You have never sought to win hearts, but you will need to be careful and strong-minded and virtuously discreet, or you will win them too much. Be on your guard, my dear Hérault, women will worship you, tear you apart, annihilate you! You unite too many enchanting qualities; but your heart that is so noble, your feelings that are so human, your ambition that is so elastic, and your goodness that is so grave can save you from this annihilation of yourself, and spare all the greatness of spirit which nature has given you. Your infinitely inflammable imagination will be your joy and your undoing. You shall suffer infinitely, but you will also know how to savor and enjoy as do very few of those who know how to savor and enjoy.

So here we have Hérault across from Buffon—another bon vivant, never doubt it, who has known how to "savor and enjoy" in his day and even now at its twilight some evenings, the old scallywag. A man who has put Man back in his place in Nature, just as Newton put the earth back in its place in the cosmos. He is the creator of the science of life, and has immediately purveyed it to thousands of readers through the medium of an ample, rarefied style; he is one of the most original writers in France,** perhaps the most gifted popularizer who ever lived.

He inhales life as it comes to him, like a good Burgundian, with his big nose stuck firmly in his strong face, reddened by the best vintages, crinkled by air and long outdoor walks and carried at the top of a thick neck. His brains

---

*Member of the Convention and ardent revolutionary, he is assassinated by a Royalist on the evening after the trial of Louis XVI for having voted in favor of the King's death.

†That is, a chief magistrate who wore a mortarboard as part of his officiating costume. There were nine in Paris.

**Victor Hugo later calls Buffon one of the greatest French poets.

leap out of his high forehead, barred by the long wrinkles of reflection; "his black brows shade black eyes, full of movement beneath white hair."⁹

However, Buffon has just been going through hellfire and damnation from an attack of "the most extreme pain from a stone," that gradual obturation of the bladder that is, along with gout, apoplexy, and "catarrh" (meaning chills), one of the chief causes of death among the elderly rich in these days of overeating. Nevertheless, Hérault writes of his "handsome face, noble and calm" in the account of his "Voyage à Montbard" which he will hurriedly compose and have printed without his signature, and will circulate widely among his acquaintances. This eye-catching title—for Montbard is a place all men of letters dream about, like Ferney or the attic of Jean-Jacques a few years ago—will allow him to take his first step, a successful one thanks to his lively descriptions, into the one career that can give him a name outside the walls of the Palais de Justice: *publiciste,* halfway between a commentator on current events and a historian.

Marie-Jean doesn't just want to look good; like many children spoiled too soon, who want to achieve something on their own, his goal is prestige. To read him you'd think he spent at least a week with Buffon, when it was really only two days at most,¹⁰ but he manages to keep the chronology of his story sufficiently imprecise: "I said to M. de Buffon one evening . . . One day he said to me . . . The first Sunday I spent at Montbard . . . A few days later, I left this great man."¹¹

As it stands, his account provides a useful portrait of an illustrious man who would otherwise have been obscured by the enormity of his work.

COMTE DE BUFFON

# 23

OCTOBER 1785

*I Should Be Glad to Massify Myself*

Hérault, testifying for Buffon at the bar of history:

> Despite his seventy-eight years one would not give him more than sixty; and what is even more singular is that, having spent sixteen nights without closing

an eye and in the unspeakable pain from which he was suffering even then, he was fresh as an infant and serene as a person in perfect health. I was told that such was his character; all his life he has sought to rise above his afflictions and emotions. Never ill-humored, never impatient. . . . Ill though he was when I saw him, he had been curled; that is one of his manias, and he admits as much. He has curlpapers put on every day, and the tongs put to them twice rather than once; in the past, after being curled in the morning, he often had himself crimped again for supper. His side hair is dressed in five small loose curls; the rest, tied behind, hung down his back. He had on a white-striped yellow dressing gown strewn with blue flowers. He bade me sit down and spoke to me of his health, complimented me on the lack of indulgence with which, according to him, the public favored me,* and discoursed on eloquence and oratory; while I spoke to him of his fame and could not have done gazing upon his features. The conversation having turned upon the good fortune of knowing, when young, what profession one would subsequently take up, he recited without pause two pages on this subject which he had composed in one of his works. . . . His voice is quite firm for his age, and entirely free from constraint; as a rule, when he speaks, he looks at nothing in particular, his eyes move hither and yon, perhaps because his eyesight is poor, or rather, because it is his manner. His favorite words are *all that* and *egad;* they recur constantly. . . . One of the foremost traits of his character is his vanity; it is all-embracing but open, and with nothing snide. A visitor (M. Target)† said of him, "There is a man who has a vast deal of vanity in the service of his pride."

The public will want to know more of him. I told him that in coming to see him I had read many of his books.

"What have you read?"

"*Les Vues sur la nature.*" ["Views on nature"—*Trans.* ]

"There are some passages of the highest eloquence in that."

Then, contrary to his usual habit, he talked of the news and politics.

True enough; in terms of the evolution of the species, Buffon had reached his culminating point before the invention of religions and politics. Deliberately and uninterruptedly, he stood aside from the quarrels of his century. He has never been a potential inmate of the Bastille, and was much too fond of his little season in Paris, where he went punctually every springtime to breathe the air in the Jardin du Roi and inspect the rare trees and plants he was acclimatizing there.

"Politics" thus for him meant a cautious too-bad-about-Necker, which

---

*Hérault has just made a brilliant debut in his new position (as assistant public prosecutor in a court of appeal, we would now say), on July 27, breaking a will which disinherited impoverished heirs in favor of charities for the poor. The first part of his sentence could also be expressed: "The public is quite right to applaud you."

†A useful reference: Target is one of the top lawyers in the rising generation.

was shared by almost everybody else, and an exchange of letters with Mme Necker on philanthropic matters.

Gods are not made to be seen close up, especially when the sacred tremor does not cloud their disciples' clear gaze or dull their sharp teeth. From the very start of his tale Hérault borders upon disrespect, and sometimes dives headlong into it, at the cost of a quarrel with the Buffon family, including the master himself, before the year is out. Montbard does not forgive him for peeking under the hem of Noah's gown. He should care: he's got his manna.

> The Comte de Buffon *fils* * had just erected a monument to his father in the grounds at Montbard. Near the tower, which is extremely lofty, he put up a column bearing this inscription:
>
>> *Excelsae Turri, Humilis Columna.*
>> *Parenti suo, Filius Buffon, 1785.*
>> To the Tall Tower, the Lowly Column:
>> To his Father, Buffon *Fils,* 1785.
>
> I was informed that the father was moved to tears by this homage. He told his son, "My boy, it will bring you honor."
> He terminated our first interview because the pain from his stone had revived. He added that his son would conduct me and show me the grounds and the column. First, the young Comte de Buffon showed me through the house, which is extremely well kept and handsomely furnished: it has twelve full suites of rooms but is built without regularity, and although this flaw could not but make it more comfortable than impressive, still it is not without beauty. From the house we went through the grounds that rise behind it. They are composed of thirteen terraces, as irregular in their way as the house; but the view from them is vast, with magnificent vistas, grasslands criss-crossed by streams, vineyards, hillsides bright with crops, and the entire town of Montbard.†
> There is a sanctuary in which he wrote almost all his books, "le berceau de l'histoire naturelle" ["the cradle of natural history"—*Trans.* ], as it was baptized by Prince Henri [of Prussia] who insisted upon seeing it, and where Jean-Jacques Rousseau knelt down and kissed the doorsill.** I mentioned this to M. de Buffon.
> "Yes," he said, "Rousseau did homage there." . . .
> The room is square, paneled and hung with paintings of birds and a few quadrupeds from the *Histoire naturelle.* It contains a divan, a few old chairs covered in black leather, a table upon which the manuscripts lie, another small black table;

---

*Guillotined shortly before 9 Thermidor.

†Yann Gaillard writes, at the end of his *Buffon,* a "page of diary, on May 24, 1977": "Those terraces were made by women from the village, who carried the earth up in their grape baskets for three sols a day. At that time, adds the plebeian and resentful guide who shows people around the grounds, a bottle of wine cost thirty sols."

**A plaque commemorating Jean-Jacques's genuflection has since been put up at the entrance.

those are the only furnishings. The *secrétaire* at which he works is at the back of the room near the fireplace. It is a rough piece in walnut. It stood open, showing only the manuscript on which Buffon was then working, a *Traité sur l'aimant* ["Treatise on magnets"—*Trans.*]. His quill stood alongside; above the *secrétaire* was a gray silk cap which he puts on for work. Opposite is the armchair he sits in, a shabby old object over which a white-striped gray dressing gown had been thrown.

Buffon thus was able to visit his own museum in his own lifetime. The rapt contemplation of Hérault de Séchelles, meanwhile, is shifting to sensationalism.

At Montbard, after completing his work, he sent for a young girl, having always been very fond of them; but arose again exactly at five. He saw only little girls, wanting no women who would squander his money. . . . M. de Buffon has always been intensely preoccupied with himself, and in preference to any other thing. As I knew that many women have received the marks of his favor, I asked whether he had not lost time over them. A person who knew him perfectly replied, "M. de Buffon has held unswervingly to three things above all others: his fame, his fortune, and his comfort."
Almost always, he has considered only the physical side of love.

At seventy-eight years of age, heavens above! Tomorrow Paris will conclude that the illustrious Comte de Buffon is nothing but an old *penaillon* or *penard*, the popular term for "a graybeard, meaning a perverse and libertine old man who pursues young girls."[1] "In all likelihood, the root of this calumny was the paternal [?] interest that Buffon takes in two of the village orphans, whom he has brought to the château from time to time to see how their education is progressing."[2] Could be. People in general, and M. Hérault de Séchelles in this particular, have such nasty minds. But deep down in his heart, will Buffon take this snatch of cattiness for "calumny"? At his age he might rather be flattered by it. And he definitely has always been fond of little girls. Once upon a long time ago he had a full-grown woman, a wife, Marie-Françoise de Saint-Belin, a poor but noble girl whom he fetched from the parlor of the Convent of Montbard, where she was living, in order to marry her and let her remain mute for seventeen years to shore up his firm conviction that he made her happy. "No doubt the qualities of this retiring young woman were mildness and moderation. She never showed any sign of impatience; spent her days in her chair, going out but little and speaking less, having never recovered from her one pregnancy, which terminated in the birth of a son. . . . She accepted the traditions of her new family and tranquilly, almost with indifference, played the role of châtelaine of Montbard. That is why affection for her in the neighborhood was rather remote,"[3] until death brought her to the ultimate perfection of silence. Her husband had not wished to grieve over her excessively, lest it interfere with his work. "The great man can be some-thing of a gossip on occasion," Hérault continues, as if *he* never were!

> During his toilette, he has his wigmaker and servants tell him everything that is happening in Montbard, and all the little dramas of his household. Although he appears to be engrossed in lofty thoughts, no one knows better than he all the trivial incidents occurring around him. This also may come from his lifelong predilection for women, or rather girls. He adores tales of scandal, and in a small place their study teaches one almost its entire history.
>
> This habit of little girls, or perhaps also the fear of being governed, has incited him to place all his confidence in a peasant woman from Montbard, whom he has made his governess and who has in the end come to govern him. Her name is Mademoiselle Blesseau, she is a spinster of forty, well made, and must have been quite pretty. She has been with M. de Buffon for nearly twenty years, and looks after him with great devotion. She takes part in the running of the house and, as can happen in such cases, is hated by all the others.

Monsieur de Buffon himself is not exactly worshipped by the 1,500-odd inhabitants of Montbard, who display all the conventional marks of honor and respect, but from a distance. There does not exist, between him and them, the conviviality that is to be found in patches of land that have been defended by generations of possessors' swords while generations of possessors' peasants tilled them. Buffon is a Leclerc, an ennobled rich bourgeois whose colossal opus can mean nothing to his neighbors because they don't know how to read it, and who has removed himself still farther from them by becoming an ironmaster, initially to experiment with the transformation of iron ore but subsequently to make a profit. "He always has one clear year of income ahead of him. His income is thought to be 50,000 écus.* His forges must have added greatly to it. Every year he turned out 800,000 pounds of iron, but against that he made huge investments. This very substantial establishment cost him 100,000 écus to set up. Today, because he is engaged in a dispute with his director, they stand idle; but when they are active they employ 400 workers."

Hérault has his facts straight as far as the initial outlay is concerned, but Buffon corrects him in regard to what he can count on for an old-age pension:

> After having conducted all the operations of these factories for twelve years . . . , I gave them out to farm [i.e., be run by a manager] for 6,500 livres;† thus I do not get 2.5 percent [yield] upon my investment, whereas the tax produces nearly the same amount. . . . I mention these facts merely in order to put anyone who might be thinking of setting up a similar establishment on his guard against

*Just under 1 million modern francs [$250,000] annually.

†Or 45,000 modern francs [$11,250] a year. This is a far cry from the rumors of Buffon's fabulous wealth parroted by Hérault, that drive the Burgundian revolutionaries to sack his house and even open his coffin in An II. When we look at the terms of his inheritance, Buffon's figures would seem closer to the truth.

illusory speculations, and to show at the same time that the government, which derives the clearest profit from them, owes them its protection.[4]

Can the ironmasters be turning "protectionist" and losing momentum even before the heyday of iron? Buffon's forges, consisting essentially of the blast furnace, two reheating furnaces, and a refining works, were built "one league from the town of Montbard and a quarter of a league from Buffon's village, slightly below the confluence of the Brenne and the Armaçon, on the site of a mine; like all the forges of this region,* they produce a granulated ore, although of superior quality, the granules being blacker and more compact."[5]

Buffon is no more of a philanthropist than any other ironmaster. His workers are paid by the day, find their own roofs, and are laid off when ill. Is it the better to persuade them to accept their lot here below that he disguises his bedrock agnosticism in the trappings of religion? Hérault, already a worshipper of reason, does not lose this opportunity to toss a few more darts:

Yes, Buffon, when at Montbard, takes communion every Easter in the lord's chapel. He also attends high mass on Sunday, stepping out sometimes in the course of it to stroll through the nearby gardens, and comes back to put in an appearance at the high points. Every Sunday he also gives the equivalent of a louis to the various alms-collectors.

When he comes out of church he likes to walk about the square, escorted by his son and surrounded by his peasantry. He is especially fond of appearing amongst them in a braided coat.

I have it from M. de Buffon that it is a principle of his to show respect for religion; that the people must have it; that in small towns one is observed by everybody and that no one must be offended.

"I trust," he said to me, "that in your speeches you are careful to suggest nothing that might be found exceptional in that respect. I have always been attentive to this in my books; I have brought them out one at a time, in order that ordinary men [*sic*] should not be able to grasp the whole train of my thought. I have always named the Creator; but one need only take away that word and mentally replace it with the power of nature. . . . It is but a trick, yet men are foolish enough to content themselves with it. For the same reason, when I shall fall dangerously ill and feel my end drawing near, I shall not hesitate one moment to send for the sacraments. One owes that to the public faith. Those who do otherwise are madmen. One must never confront these things head-on, as Voltaire, Diderot, and Helvétius did. . . ."

It is easy to see that the method has worked well for M. de Buffon. His works are the plainest demonstration of materialism, yet they are published by the Royal Printer.

---

*"To reach [today] the old forges [or what is left of them], continue [beyond Montbard] on the Paris road, cross the Burgundy Canal at Buffon, and go by Saint-Rémy."[6]

And as if to make sure he had dotted every *i* Hérault adds, underlining three words in imitation of his host's way of speaking:

> One evening, when I was reading the lines of M. Thomas* on the immortality of the soul to M. de Buffon, he laughed and said:
> "*Egad,* what a fine present religion would be making us, if *all that* were true!"
> The first [and, as we know, the only] Sunday I spent at Montbard, the author of the *Histoire naturelle* called for his son the night before, and held conference with him at great length, and I learned that the object was to get me to agree to come to mass in the morning. When his son mentioned it to me, I replied that I should be glad to massify myself [*sic*] and that it was not worth the trouble of so much conspiracy to bring me to perform a civic action. This reply much pleased M. de Buffon. When I came back from high mass, which the pain from his stone had prevented him from attending, he thanked me profusely for being able to bear up under three-quarters of an hour of tedium, and said once again that in a little town like Montbard mass was an obligation.

So Hérault de Séchelles has not wasted his time at Montbard. In his bags he carries away enough material to erect a statue to his great man and promptly starts throwing rotten eggs at it. His text is of the kind that almost tells us more about its author than it does about his subject.

Paris is awaiting him, the parlement, his orations "in the King's service," each of which, he now knows, will be listened to as in the theater by a favorably predisposed audience. A cloudless life, full of pleasures and honors: all for him. His assets, "comprising various rentals and the fine estate of Epone ten leagues from Paris,† bring him no more than 10,000 livres a year,** but his relatives are unstinting in their assistance, thus enabling him to maintain the requisite standard of living."[7] His ultra-modern turnout alone costs him 4,000 livres a year, and he drives it himself without a coachman, as all the young blades are starting to do, from the stables of the Palais de Justice along the quays on the right bank, around the Palais Royal and down the boulevard to his bachelor's "apartment," a duplex at 14, rue Basse du Rempart in which three servants minister to his needs and those of the 4,000 volumes in his library, among which he has placed a handsomely bound manuscript in his own hand entitled *Livres qu'il faut relire sept ou huit cents fois* ["Books to be read seven or eight hundred times"—*Trans.*] . . . "for the slave reader is no better than the slave citizen" and therefore must attach himself particularly to works "that

---

*A pompous academician then in vogue.

†Near Mantes; it then consisted of 1,200 to 1,300 acres. The château purchased in 1706 by one of Hérault's grandparents still exists, a magnificent structure, originally in the style of Louis XIII but altered to suit that of the eighteenth century, with one main building and two pavilions, all of them three stories high and topped by a steep mansard roof. It stands on a hill overlooking a pretty loop of the Seine.

**70,000 modern francs [$17,500].

make one think, and those which contain facts." In the place of honor, like a Blessed Sacrament, stands the manuscript of *La Nouvelle Héloïse,* four volumes bound in red morocco which he ran to earth and snapped up for 24,000 livres* last year on a trip to Holland. Behind the library is a "boudoir" with walls covered in a yellow English paper (the fashion for wallpaper has just crossed the Channel) edged with scrolls, and cupids on the ceiling; this is not where he does his reading. His lady callers, varied and select, are left in little doubt when they enter it and see the "couch with a mirror running all along one side, and an elastic [*sic*] divan." He doesn't talk about them, and the secrecy of his love affairs helps him to have more of them, since the women he frequents come from circles in which discretion is appreciated. The hour has not yet struck for marriage. Hérault is the type to want to stay single as long as he can. For him, "uninterrupted pleasure is the sign of health, virtue, and wisdom" and "ethics is nothing but the science of intentions or physical predispositions."[8]

So—is he happy with it all? People say so, and people envy him; and he's not complaining. So what is the reason for that aftertaste of bile in his account of his "Voyage à Montbard"?

CARRIER

# 24

OCTOBER 1785

## *His Hatred of the Nobility and His Love of Wine*

Louis, by the grace of God King of France and Navarre, to all who shall these present see, Greetings!

Be it hereby known that, for the laudable account which has been rendered to Us of the person of our beloved Jean-Baptiste Carrier and of his sense, competence, capacity, and experience in the matter of [legal] practice; for these reasons We have given and awarded and do hereby give and award to him the office of prosecuting attorney held and exploited [at Aurillac] by Jean-François Textoris, the latest incumbent, who has voluntarily relinquished it into Our hands, by official declaration dated August 21 ult., in favor of the said Carrier.[1]

---

*Nearly 160,000 modern francs [$40,000]. For such a recent manuscript this is an absolute record, the price alone showing the magnitude of the cult of Rousseau. The first two volumes were lost after Hérault's arrest; the other two ended up in the library of the National Assembly.

Whew! Jean-Baptiste Carrier has finally made it, despite his lack of natural ability and his lack of fortune, at the far end of a long, gray youth. The son of a tenant farmer from Yolet in upper Auvergne obtains his official appointment as prosecuting attorney in the town of Aurillac from Louis XVI shortly before his thirtieth birthday.* He had trouble finding somebody to lend him the money to buy the office from Master [all French lawyers are addressed as "Maître"—*Trans.*] Textoris, whose age is full of affliction and who would dearly like to die at peace and in retirement. Negotiations had been in hand since the beginning of 1785, but it was not until July 5 that Jean-Baptiste managed to extort a promise of 15,000 livres as security for the purchase from his old skinflint of a great-uncle, the former parish priest Guillaume Labouygue, "accredited priest of the community of St. Vincent of Arpajon," a nonagenarian who is also about to kick the bucket on top of a heap of gold —sixty years of accumulated livings—and who quarrels with his kinsman and makes up again as his crotchets inspire him. It was an opportunity Jean-Baptiste had to grab; a Royal Edict of 1779 authorized the appointment of twenty, and not one more, prosecuting attorneys (and eight notaries) for the bailliage of Aurillac.[2] Textoris was selling out cheap and Carrier wormed his way into the crack in order to reach the highest summit accessible to him in his lifetime. To become a man of law: what a leap up for a young man who ought to have considered himself lucky to be selling cheese, seeds, and livestock.

Oh, it's no great shakes being a prosecuting attorney, and there's precious little in common between the Olympian ascension of a Hérault de Séchelles and the kitchen stepladder of a Carrier. This class of unavoidable legal middlemen proliferates on the ramifications of civil lawsuits like mistletoe on oaks. There are whole anthologies of vindictive adages about them running through the gutters: "He who acts by proxy [through a *procureur,* the term usually translated "prosecuting attorney"—*Trans.* ] is often deceived in person."[3] The *Mercure Galant* has a thief telling a *procureur* in the Paris Parlement, "We only snatch, you scalp" [ *"On grapille chez nous, mais on pille chez vous"*]. But in a small provincial town this kind of dig is more like a mark of esteem. For the oldest Carrier boy it means something to don the wide-sleeved black gown worn by "those insects of the Code, always in mourning as though they were the whole world's legatees," and march into court in Aurillac.

Upper Auvergne (Saint-Flour, Aurillac) is the back of beyond, a desert in mid-France. It's not that there are no resources, in both livestock and artisans; but the inhabitants have to carry what they make everywhere on their own

*Carrier represents the Cantal in the Convention, and enters history by virtue of his terrorist activity in Nantes in An II, especially the notorious drownings. Guillotined by the Thermidorians on December 16, 1794. The letter, partly a printed form, is filled in by the intendant of the province and signed by the King mechanically during one of his "Councils on Internal Affairs."

backs or those of mules or horses, or drive their flocks for weeks over impossible roads to fairs in the south, in Rouergue or the Gevaudan—regions that really *are* depressed—or in the north, in the big city of Clermont and the plains of Limagne, so rich that the people there make fun of them and buy their wares out of a sort of pitying taste for the exotic. The stagecoach from Clermont turns off at Rodez for Aurillac twice a week.

There, in the hamlet of Yolet a league and a half north of Aurillac, Jean-Baptiste Carrier was born "in the year 1756 and on the 16th of the month of March, legitimate son of Jean Carrier, tenant farmer, and Marguerite Puech" from the nearby parish of Arpajon, the daughter of a more prosperous peasantry than her husband's family, with "sixteen *journaux* [days, meaning the amount of land that can be plowed in one day] of meadows, sixty *setérées* of land, ten *setérées* of scrubland, four *setérées* of gravel by the riverside,* a two-stone [water] mill, four cows, nine horn-bearing animals, twenty ewes, and three beehives." The baby was baptized the day after his birth in the little Romanesque church of Yolet in the valley of the Cère, where everything is harsh and pure, especially in March when the snow is still lying on the slopes; the air is keen, the earth ochre-hued, miraculous meadows hang suspended between the volcanic alluvia. A devil of a country, where the children who don't die first turn into devils of men, all muscle. But as far as the other kind of culture is concerned, that of the mind . . . "Godmother [of Jean-Baptiste]: Marie Carrier [an aunt], made her mark. Witnesses: Jean Testel and Jean Angelvi, made their marks."[4] "In those days there were four families named Carrier in Yolet, two in the hamlet, one at Lalo and the other at Semilhac. Jean-Baptiste belongs to the last-named, whose origins go back at least as far as 1674, the earliest date at which records were kept in the district of Yolet."

As far as origins are concerned, Carrier will have one of the "basest" extractions to be found among the actors in the Revolution, possessing as many and more "quarters" of peasantry as some courtiers had quarters of nobility.

Parisians, and the natives of Madrid, too, are familiar with the Auvergnats; they're like the chimney-sweep Savoyards or the stonemason Limousins. Traces of Carriers can be found in the parish records not only in Yolet but in Aurillac and neighboring localities as well; the heads of the family are tenant farmers, *brassiers,* sometimes "merchants," at their most successful *hostes,* i.e., keepers of one of those minute inns where travelers could "lie with their horse." Some periodically leave for foreign parts, as *rhabilleurs* [reliners, repairers—*Trans.*] of copper utensils. For the last century this inhospitable

---

*\**Journal, septérée* or *setérée, cartalée* or *punière* were units of measurement in use in the Aurillac region. All told, the Puech parents had the equivalent of about fifty acres.

region, with the Plomb de Cantal towering over it, has been a small pool of migrant manpower for France and beyond.

> The industry of the inhabitants derives in part from the great numbers who leave the province each year to work in other countries, especially Spain. Some five or six thousand travel to Spain annually,* from the region around Aurillac, Mauriac, and Saint-Flour; they bring back seven or eight hundred thousand livres. A great number also come out of the nearby mountains of the Forest [Forez] and Velay every year, and saw trees for planking or clear new land. As for the coppersmiths [the *rhabilleurs* mentioned above], most of them come originally from the outlying districts of the same towns, Aurillac, etc. The numbers of these different kinds of workers are thought to be as large as those of the workers who go to Spain, and they are thought to bring an equal amount of money back to their native provinces.[5]

Jean-Baptiste did the opposite, by putting down his roots not exactly in his native soil but very close to it, in the nearest big town. He owes a goodly share of his social advancement to the hard work of his father, Jean Carrier, a bull of a man who can't have spent much time inside the house except when it was pouring outdoors. In 1768, when Jean-Baptiste was twelve, his father was already in a position to move his family to Aurillac, and rent, from the declining order of Carmelites who had plenty of unused space in their monastery, "a building composed of shops, chambers, and garrets" in which he could set up his trade in seed, fodder, and farm animals. But he also continued to farm the two properties of Barrat and Fontrouge, just outside town, by agreement with their owner, a Demoiselle Delfieux, "mature spinster" who had grown rich in business and didn't mind letting Carrier take the lion's share of the profits during his tenancy, in the form of "all the fruits of the said properties, whether in seed, milk products, fodder, *croît,* † and livestock," provided he brought his landlady "two hogsheads of wine from the vineyard and four cartloads of wood from a league around" every year.

Carrier's childhood, thus, was pure peasant, days and labors in the fields of Barrat-Fontrouge, but under the shadow of the town and within its immediate magnetic field. His initiation to learning was administered by the chaplain of Pesteils, the nearest château, a forgotten priest in an old barony abandoned by its barons. His father could afford to send him early to the collège formerly run by the Jesuits, in which the town's sixty priests and canons dispensed

---

*According to Canon Expilly's dictionary, written at the end of the reign of Louis XV. The amount annually brought home by the itinerants would be equivalent to 5 million modern francs [$1,250,000]. Expilly goes off course in his estimation of the population of Aurillac, which he very precisely sets at—7,000 to 20,000! It was actually 10,000 plus.

†A local expression, although it appears in the official notarized tenancy contract, meaning the fertilizer obtained from manure.

mediocre lessons.* This breakthrough into the world of those who know how to count and read, talk and write—and not only in French, which is almost a foreign language in these parts, but in Latin as well—and this smattering of ancient history and geography, are the seeds of a career "superior" to the peasantry. Carrier begins to climb. Five classes ahead of him in the same collège, and thanks also to a father's determination to have children who will "better" themselves, he makes his first great friend, the one who lasts throughout life and into death—the Milhaud boy, another Jean-Baptiste, from Arpajon-sous-Aurillac,† "son of a merchant-farmer and stallion-keeper." A rough, laughing, loud-mouthed hulk, Milhaud is distinctly cleverer than Carrier as well as ten years his senior, and is planning a career in the only branch of the army open to commoners—like Lazare Carnot, he'll be an engineer. He plays model and ringleader to his young schoolmate and helps him to acquire a taste for learning, which is at first a thankless process. Carrier hasn't a prayer of getting into an "elite" school. If he wanted to be a priest, maybe . . . His father thought of it but didn't insist, and Jean-Baptiste is not enthusiastic. At sixteen, the year his father dies, he's already started to notice the girls.

May 26, 1772, that was, in the Barrat house. He was sick only a few days, "stricken with a physical disease, as an epidemic was raging in the region"; it must have been a lethal one to uproot so stout an oak. Five days before, he dictated his last will and testament, bequeathing "30 livres for masses, 1,000 livres to each of his two daughters [Marie and Catherine, the latter being the second of that name after the first Catherine died in infancy], and 600 livres to each of his surviving sons," Jean-Baptiste and Basile.** His widow remarried two years later, the year Louis XV dies, this time choosing her chief herdsman, Antoine Bronzac. Both newlyweds were "unable to sign" the vicar's paper. The second marriage was a matter of course; Marguerite Puech had to have a man to keep her property together and help her bring up the children. She, too, was a tough woman and a hard worker, who marries both

---

*Carrier's term in the little seminary has been so grossly inflated that some nineteenth-century historians claimed he was an unfrocked cleric.

†Where he was born on November 18, 1766. He dies in Aurillac on July 10, 1833; we meet him again at Carrier's side representing the Cantal and, not far from Marat, on the benches of the Montagne. At heart, he remains a "Mountaineer" (politically), but makes his career in the revolutionary—subsequently imperial—army. He becomes a Comte d'Empire, commands part of the cavalry at Waterloo, and is exiled by the Bourbons from 1815 to 1830. [It may be time to explain *Montagne* (mountain) and the *montagnards* (mountaineers); the Mountain was the nickname for the highest tiers of benches in the National Assembly (Convention), which were occupied by the extremists. They were led by Danton, Marat, and Robespierre, and they became the party that conducted, and was brought down by, the Terror—*Trans.*]

**Say, 200 modern francs for the masses [$50], 7,000 [$1,750] for each girl, and 4,000 [$1,000] for the boys.

daughters "well"—one to her cousin, a tavern-keeper at Yolet, and the other to a "landlord," son of a rich tanner in Aurillac—before dying, on October 2, 1782, at the age of sixty. Jean-Baptiste, her firstborn, was then completing his law studies at the University of Paris, with no honors or awards but adequately enough to be deemed to possess "the necessary practice." In all, he has spent over ten years scratching away at his copybooks, between the priests' school at Aurillac, his apprenticeships to Paris lawyers, and his lectures at the Sorbonne, digested or not, but in any case a reference.

Carrier returns home at twenty-eight without, like so many others, ever having had a youth. September 14, 1785, is his red-letter day, when the King's appointment is officially entered in the records. That makes him a *procoorare-ay*, as the word is pronounced in his country. He marries almost simultaneously, as though defending his first case, and so he is, more or less. Having no mother to look after him, he needs somebody to keep house while he prepares his clients' briefs, and accordingly weds Françoise Laquairie, the daughter of a deceased tradesman who also "made his way up" to the tax-collector's office. She brings him a dowry of 2,000 livres and a hope chest worth another 1,000. Love too? On her side, perhaps; she's nineteen and proves sweet-tempered and devoted. On his? We'll see.

The wedding is a simple affair, all the closest relatives being dead. A few of the bride's brothers, sisters, or cousins, and on Jean-Baptiste's side, friends —has he quarreled with his family?—assemble in the humpbacked church of Notre Dame, the mother hen of Aurillac, for a ceremony which is something like the Lord's blessing upon the new life of Master Jean-Baptiste Carrier, prosecuting attorney at the bar of that town. His path lies straight as a die before him, from here to the cemetery just outside.

On his wedding day, he is a tall man, "very well developed" albeit slightly stooped. His face, "oblong and marked by a very strong personality," is that of a dreamer, with small, deep-set eyes that often seem to be staring at nothing; his skin is very dark, as though tanned by his mountain childhood (this feature recurs in every description); his voice is harsh and his delivery staccato, and he has a way of rolling his *r*'s, or rather pronouncing them like a double *l*, that will strike all his listeners outside upper Auvergne. He is also "all legs and arms," so that the people who don't like him will say that "the protuberance of his hips, coupled with a complete absence of stomach, makes him look as though he had been cut in half, like a wasp"; and the same people add, at the time of his first appearances in court in Aurillac, that "his careless dress corresponds to the unappealing aspect of his physical person" and that "his curly, black, undressed hair stands out displeasingly amid the elegant pow-dered wigs of that day."[6]

His detractors do concede, however, and it would be strange if the son of a canny merchant and farmer from Auvergne were otherwise, "that he lacks neither the vulgar [*sic*] dodges of the legal practitioner nor the prudence of the mountaineer in the ordinary performance of his duties."[7]

The nuptial benediction is given by Abbé Pierre Deconquans, vicar of Notre Dame. The newlyweds move at once into a modest building at the corner of rue Marcenague and rue du Consulat,* apparently monopolized by a lawyers' commune, where they share quarters with three men, a Sieur "Daude, a man of law [?], a Sieur Aude, attorney, and a Sieur Besombes, *huissier.*"[8]

Rich they aren't. Carrier has debts of long standing, even from his Paris days. Until 1789 his attorney's post is taxed at 9 livres, that is, in the third and lowest category, by comparison with most of his colleagues.† On average he pleads no more than thirty cases a year, and one of them is his own defense against two nuns, the heirs of his uncle Labouygue, who accuse him of having extorted the security he needed to buy his position, taking advantage of the old man's senility. He wins, but only just, and the rumor sticks.

Final summing-up of one investigator, after interviewing the survivors of that period: "No instance of cruelty on his part was recorded against him while he was an attorney, but agreement was unanimous as to his taciturn and acrimonious nature, his hatred of the nobility and his love of wine."[9]

GERMAINE NECKER

# 25

## JANUARY 1786

## *As in the Moment of Death*

In the first days of the year 1786 Germaine Necker becomes Madame de Staël, by marrying the King of Sweden's ambassador to Paris. It's like the marriage of an infanta; the only child of a Necker is front-page copy, and Versailles and Paris, Geneva and London alike have been buzzing over it.** Nothing could

---

*Destroyed by fire in 1881

†A symbolic tax equal to 60 modern francs [$15], which certainly did not correspond to a year's real earnings but gave his practice a sort of one-star rating and was levied on top of other taxes.

**Madame de Staël becomes one of the most notorious authors of her age, and one of its most overwhelming personalities as well. Some of her best-known works are *Corinne, De l'Al-*

be more remote from the Carrier nuptials. On January 6 the royal family solemnly endorses the contract, despite Louis XVI's antipathy for Necker, who is still officially in disgrace but is making a strong comeback propelled by the "reformists," and can now return to the proximity of Paris and even rent "a townhouse on a long lease" on the rue Bergère on the right bank (provided he does no entertaining in it).

It is to this house that the young bride returns, "according to custom," to spend five last days with her parents after the wedding, which is celebrated by a pastor on January 14 in the Lutheran chapel of the Swedish embassy. But when they're over, she's going to have to make up her mind to emerge from her enchanted childhood and "take possession of the home of her husband,"[1] meaning the veritable palace in which Staël runs a princely establishment. And what is her attitude to this? No one can tell us better than herself. "This Thursday morning, still in your home, January 19, 1786," she writes to her mother, who's on the next floor:

My dear *maman,*

Tonight I shall not return. This is the last day I shall spend as I have spent my whole life until now. How much it is costing me to endure so great a change! I do not know if there is any other way of life, I have experienced no other, and the unknown adds to my sorrow. Ah, I well know that I may have wronged you, *maman.* At this moment, as in the moment of death, all my actions rise up before me and I fear that in departing I shall not leave in your soul the regret I need so sorely. . . . But I feel in this moment, by the depth of my affection, that it has never altered. It is part of my life and I feel myself troubled and inadequate as the time comes to part from you. I shall be back tomorrow morning, but this night I shall sleep under a new roof. . . . I foresee that I shall miss being here every minute. . . .

I should never end this letter; I have a feeling so strong that it would make me go on writing until death. My dear *maman,* please accept my profound respect and boundless affection.

M. de Staël will bring my letter to you. He has not seen it; I should have had to restrain my words too much, and the keenest emotion of my life should have forced its way to the surface despite my efforts.

This Thursday morning, still in your home.[2]

She closes her letter as she opened it—the last tinkle of a bell that will never ring the same again.

She's changing skin, and all raw and tender underneath. And if this is what she writes to her mother, with whom she has long been at odds, what would

---

lemagne, and *Considérations sur la Révolution française.* She fails to captivate Napoleon, who cordially detests her, but is a great friend of Benjamin Constant, Byron, and legions more. One of the first women of liberty.

a letter to her father, her god, her life, have been like? But it's time she got married. She's nineteen. Another few months and her courage might forsake her; and it would be a strong man indeed who could make such a porcupine marry against her will. Necker, for his part, would probably not even have tried. Yet nobody could seriously imagine the sole heiress to that vast fortune remaining single. Well, it's done now. "His Excellency Eric Magnus, Baron de Staël de Holstein, Chevalier of the Order of the Sword, chamberlain to her Majesty the Queen of Sweden and ambassador extraordinary of His Sovereign Swedish Majesty to the Court of France, married Damoiselle Anne, Louise, Germaine, born in Paris, minor legitimate daughter of Messire Jacques Necker, onetime director general of finance of France, and of the noble Dame Louise Curchod Nass, his legitimate spouse."[3]

For the last two or three years rumor had been betrothing her to the four corners of Protestant Europe, although—again, as in the case of an infanta— the number of aspirants could not be legion. They had to be men of high rank and of the same faith as the Neckers, and of sufficiently substantial fortune not to look as though they were being bought on the nobility exchange.

Over them all, Staël had the superiority of the tortoise. He left the starting gate in 1779 when the child was only thirteen and he himself a mere embassy functionary. The parents smoothly sidestepped, pleading their daughter's youth. He gave them to understand that he would wait. This caused one of the most serious contenders to withdraw: Fersen himself, back from America and Sweden, where he had gone to see the old homestead, his father, and his king, Gustavus III, who was regarding him with an increasingly beaming countenance. She hadn't been the only iron in his fire, however; he was still mulling over the possibilities of the prewar Englishwoman. On April 26, 1783, during the negotiations that would lead to his purchase—generously aided by the Queen—of the "Royal Swedish" Regiment, and complete the process of his "Frenchification" by a firm military commitment to the service of Louis XVI, he wrote to his daddy:

After seeing to my advancement and satisfying my self-esteem, it is now time to think of a more solid establishment; I have reached the age at which marriage, however little vocation I may have for the sacrament, becomes a necessary thing. A union with Miss Lyell would be very advantageous; I have not lost sight of it, and during my stay in America I kept up a correspondence. I wrote her five or six letters but had no replies; perhaps not all my letters reached her. Or perhaps her answers were captured, I have no idea. I have just written her a very pressing letter, and one to the mother. This time nothing can go astray, and I shall have her reply in Paris. I hope it may be favorable; the pleasure which this alliance will give you, dear father, causes me to desire its success all the more ardently, but if it were to fail, if she persisted in her refusal, I have another in view. This will depend entirely upon your desire, I have no interest in it other than that which you may show. She is Mr. Necker's daughter. She is Protestant, her father has a fortune,* she is an only child [thus only heir], she has been brought up in her father's house far from society, and has not yet acquired a taste for it. I have seen her but once, and in passing, and have no recollection of her face; I only recall that there was nothing ill-favored about her and that she is not ill-formed. Everyone speaks of her as well-bred and most carefully nurtured; the mother is a clever woman and very able to give her a sound education.

If this match finds favor with you, I shall put the matter in hand. Staël made an offer for himself before I left but was turned down; I know he has made others since, with no better result. Had he some hopes, I should drop the idea entirely, as I should not like to prevent him from making so very advantageous a marriage, but if he has lost all hope and you consider it suitable, I shall do my best to succeed.[4]

But Staël hung on. And in the last three years, especially after his return to France, Fersen's distaste for marriage in general and this marriage in particular have grown apace with the angle of Marie Antoinette's "penchant." To his father again, in July 1785:

You will already have seen that my idea with regard to Miss Necker could not come to fruition, even had you consented, on account of my friend Staël, for whom it is eminently suitable and much better than for me; I thought of it only to please you, my dear father, and am not in the least dismayed that the thing cannot be.[5]

Throughout his life, Count Axel Fersen casts a cold eye on marriage, and he dies a bachelor.

Well, what about another of those Swedes backed by the Queen, who has a decided predilection for them? Count Stedingk, born just twenty years before Germaine Necker (the same year as King Gustavus), had also drawn his sword for the Rebels during Admiral d'Estaing's first expedition, half successful with the capture of Grenada and half a failure with the check outside Savannah. He came back to Paris on crutches after the latter skirmish and was covered in laurels; Mlle Necker herself produced a few drawing-room couplets in his praise, and maybe, if hers had been the only voice in the matter . . . "But Stedingk was jealous of his freedom,"[6] scented other wars on the horizon of his life, and was not at all anxious to defer to the wish that was being more and more openly expressed by the elder Neckers, namely, that their son-in-law

*The letter mentions no figure. Even for the well-informed it was difficult, at that time, to evaluate the capital under Necker's control; in 1777 it amounted to something like 5 million livres, or 25 million modern francs [$6,250,000], half of which he had lent to the French treasury at 5 percent, when he was director of finance.

should remain within their sphere of influence so that their darling daughter could form, with them, a most respectable *ménage à quatre.*

The Swedes were shelved; what about a German prince—no less a one than Georg-Augustus, brother of the reigning Duke of Mecklenburg in Lower Saxony, between Prussia and Denmark? A fine coat of arms and, for Germaine, a connection with the Queen of England, who is their sister. But despite the principality's rich grazing and the booming trade of the Rostock merchants, the coat of arms was a tarnished one. The prince frankly confessed that he had entered the race "because, being the youngest of the family and for twenty years a major [i.e., top-ranking officer] in the Imperial Army [of Germany, in the service of the Hapsburgs], he had been forced to contract a considerable debt." Necker is not eager to plow both his fortune and his daughter into the Baltic sand. Mind if we change the subject?

William Beckford, for example? At twenty-five, this typical product of a decadent gentry is about to enter the House of Lords; he is heir to a colossal fortune and a name which became renowned during his father's long term as Lord Mayor of London. If he were not so feckless and pleasure-addicted he might become a second Pitt. But by his teens his nervous system, and maybe his mind, had been deranged by the combination of his wondrous beauty and his wealth. His only outlet is writing, and at that he looks better than promising already, in the texts being passed round confidentially among his friends, in which he disguises his erotic and "proto-Sadistic" fantasies in the trappings of the East. George Romney painted him at twenty, already world-weary, leaning languidly against a fragment of a column, a young green ruin among the old ruins of society, slender in close-clinging white hose, breeches, and waistcoat, his hair naturally curly, his head at once so finely cut, gentle, cruel, and sensual that it was enough to send the beauties of both worlds into ecstasies. Without excessive modesty, he drew his own portrait as follows: "His person was that of a young man, whose noble and regular features seemed to have been tarnished by malignant vapors. In his large eyes appeared both pride and despair: his flowing hair still retained some resemblance to that of an Angel of light."[7] We know what happens to angels when they unhook themselves from heaven; Beckford's patron saint is Lucifer, and his disciple is joining Sade to found the dynasty of the mystics of hell.

Much occupied, like Sade at the same age, with ceremonious debauching in the bowels of his châteaus or on trips to Italy, Beckford had stayed briefly with the Neckers early in 1783, shortly before they moved to Coppet. Both families belonged to the cosmopolitan European set whose members paid neighborly calls on each other over seas and mountains. For a tiny elite,

Geneva was a suburb of London. Germaine Necker, precociously passionate, had not been indifferent to his charm, heightened by the fact that his haughtily curious gaze lingered impartially upon youths and debutantes alike. In fact he preferred the former, and had recently had what one might call a hot love affair, if the word "love" has any sense in relation to Beckford, with a lad of fifteen named William Courtenay, the son of a potent lord; but it had not stopped him from abducting Louisa Beckford, his own cousin by marriage (and old Pitt's niece), from a Louis XVI–style husband totally immersed in fox hunting and port. He had swept them both, the boy and the young woman, through the satanical mazes "providentially" provided by the hundreds of rooms and secret corridors of his place at Fonthill, into the whirling incense-scented mists of a liturgy as twisted as the serpents on the three-legged coal-burning braziers they lit around their cushioned "altars." But he also had hundreds of servants to tell the tale. Rumor was beginning to dog his footsteps in Europe and, to mute it, he was thinking of marrying in a hurry, as one might buy a Chinese screen.

Not from the Neckers, though, even though their little girl was vaguely intrigued by him. Beckford would soon have smothered to death in the air they—the parents, at any rate—breathed. He was amused by the daughter, although, according to him, she sang off-key; "I remember her a very symmetrical young lady, who might have . . . made a respectable statue."[8] But as for the tribe of puritans around her . . . the drawing-room doors opened to reveal to him "a synod of pale literati in court dress and a row of dowagers in long pink and yellow bodices, all seated on armchairs covered in the stiffest of tapestries, taking snuff at frequent intervals and seeming determined to submit me to a regular interrogation." In their midst, *Maman* Necker, "part *précieuse ridicule,* part Countess of Escarbagnas." William Beckford fled to Italy, mainly Rome, where, on the feast day of St. Peter, there were "Cannon bouncing, Trumpets flourishing, Pope gabbling, Cardinals stinking and Fish frying on every corner . . . your poor friend is in Pandemonium—stunned with noise and poisoned with sulphur."[9]

On his return from Italy, having understood that boys were decidedly what he liked best, he had politely married an evanescent and tubercular English girl named Mary Gordon,* which merely added a little zest to his flirtation with Germaine Necker when he saw her again in 1784. He gave her his books, not exactly recommended reading for a girl of seventeen. Far from taking offense, she was flattered. "I have not yet finished the extraordinary book you kindly left with me, Monsieur; it is difficult to put it down, for you

---

*On May 5, 1783. She gives him two daughters but dies on May 26, 1786, at the birth of the second. By this time he is being made the scapegoat for every English turpitude and is forced into a long exile "for the avowed crime of sodomy." His political career is over. All that remains for him is to travel and write, which he does for the remainder of his life, until 1844.

move so swiftly from idea to idea, tableau to tableau, that it is impossible to find a moment's respite between one sensation and the next. You dream, when there is nothing left for you to paint. . . ."[10]

He must have been one of the first to treat her as a woman. But he's gone and married somebody else. Farewell, Beckford.

With William Pitt it was a close shave. A serious plan was hatched in 1783 to ally Germaine Necker with the best match in England, the young prince of politics, so impudently successful that all he needed now to become completely enviable was a wife. But we know he was not eager to marry, or rather, that he didn't like to think about it. Not that he too preferred boys; but what with a genetic terrain that was none too strong and had been further weakened by alcohol, he was utterly indifferent to all things sexual.* It wasn't obvious yet. He was investing all his energies in politics and doing so well that on December 19, 1783, he broke the bank. Nobody dared to predict it but it happened: George III, who had been counting on him for the last two years to restore some semblance of absoluteness to his monarchy, called him to the government, which he joins as prime minister and chancellor of the exchequer (thus in charge of finance) at the same time. At the age of twenty-four!

This happened as the result of a sort of legal coup d'état fomented by the king and House of Lords against the Commons, where the Whigs still ruled the roost. Their former chum William Pitt nimbly turned his silken coat; with him and the other new ministers, many not much older than he, the Tory party (the party that had wanted war with America, the party of the great land- and factory-owners) is back in the saddle again. At first, the Whigs try to laugh off this "band of children playing at being ministers. They ought to be sent back to school; in a few days things will return to normal."[11] As it turns out, the schoolboy government lasts seventeen years.

The marriage to Germaine was an idea of her mother's, a woman as hard as iron, as gleaming and well wrought. What better opportunity could her daughter ever have? Other women became queens of this place or that. As Mrs. William Pitt, Necker's daughter would be the queen of enlightened Europe. It would be one in the eye for Marie Antoinette, with her fat lummox of a husband. And what a crown for Jacques Necker, even if he had to spend a few million to get it. For the first time in history one man, and a Protestant to boot, could become the financial adviser to both English and French governments. If he found himself back at the helm in France one day soon, just imagine the bridges across the Channel, the end of the age-old antagonism, the merged budgets of the two liberal maritime powers, Necker as the new

*Pitt governs England uninterruptedly from now until 1801 and again from 1804 to 1806, when he dies of grief upon learning of Napoleon's victory at Austerlitz.

coachman of Europe, holding the reins of the bank and planned trade. There was no veto from Necker, or from Pitt.

In 1783 he went to Rheims and Paris to polish his French, with his friends Elliott and Wilberforce. He had fallen in with that attractive crippled priest, the Archbishop of Rheims's nephew, Maurice de Talleyrand-Périgord, who translated into English for him a large number of French words that could not decently be uttered in either language. That was Pitt's last vacation before shouldering his Albion—he knew perfectly well she would be his before long —and he kept telling his friends, with infectious confidence, that in his country he must be first or nowhere. His name had also crossed the Channel and was beginning to chase his father's round the world.

At that point, however, Germaine and William almost certainly did not meet. There is no trace of an interview—the infanta syndrome again. People met for them; patented matchmakers delightedly shuttled back and forth between Pitt and the Neckers, especially Suzanne, for whom this was the one big deal of her life. William, at least, seemed ready to surmount his distaste for marriage in the interest of an alliance that would bring him a firm position in Europe at a decisive moment, and a more than respectable financial status.

Just then, however, so sorry mummy, pray excuse me gentlemen, Germaine Necker turned her teenaged thumb definitively down. Somebody should have asked her sooner. And as for forcing upon her a husband she didn't want— in her circle those days were already gone forever. And she refused absolutely —not marriage, her only notion of which was that of her parents, nor the candidate, whom she didn't know; but she would not hear of living in England. She subscribed to the current craze for all things English, but was convinced that the best way to see England was from France. She had been marked by Richardson's novels of despair, and she had been—correctly—informed of the fate of English wives, even aristocratic ones. She knew "how little active personal existence they have, being confined to their home and family and accustomed to remain silent when politics were discussed by the men."[12]

That was asking too much of her, even at seventeen. She'd sooner drown. "I shall never be what is called an Englishwoman. Time may show that I have received from nature some few gifts that may earn my pardon; but if an attempt was made to force me, after doing my utmost to free myself from the yoke laid upon me, I feel sure that I should throw myself into the lake on the shores of which my life was chained."[13]

Nobody tried to force her. For the time it takes history to heave one sigh, the possibility of this extraordinary union took form and disintegrated. No one will ever know how Pitt took the news. Necker shrugged. He's not rabid with ambition, all he wants is some terrain in which he can experiment with his ideas. France, which seems to be gently edging back to him, would be quite ample for his purpose. The only person who minded, and she minded a lot, was Mme Necker; her relationship with her daughter never quite recovered. By this pull at the tether, the little goat so soon to be given her head shows her unconscious revolt against an upbringing that was all strictures and groans, the accumulated transmission of a long line of Curchods: we are not here to enjoy ourselves, God made us to suffer in this vale of tears.

Maybe, but not in London, and never mind the inevitable contrition of her adolescent diary; I'm the one who's getting married, not *maman,* although I'm perfectly fond of her in spite of the fact that she behaves like a broomstick: "Why must that wretched England have provoked the stiffness and coldness of *maman?* Accursed isle, source of my present fears, source of my future remorse. . . . Ah, it's certain, I cannot go to England!"[14]

LOUIS XVI

# 26

## JANUARY–
## FEBRUARY 1786

*What an Agonizing Comparison!*    NECKER

Since their disgrace in 1781, accompanied by the customary command that they "remove themselves" from Court, the Neckers have spent quite a lot of time on the road. They have stayed with various friends in Switzerland, on the papal domains near Avignon, at Montpellier, where they went for an—unavailing—attempt to pacify Mme Necker's increasingly unreliable nerves; and, finally they bought the barony of Coppet, near Nyon in the Vaud, from Thélusson the banker. The estate consists of vineyards rising in terraces from the lake. It made Necker a little seigneur, a vassal of Bern. The château, firmly rooted in the town, is "so contrived, following the fashion of the day, that the trees on the grounds obstinately hide from the spectator's view the panorama of Lake Geneva and the Alps, one of the finest of all Europe."[1]

Coppet* . . . You climb up a narrow street with arcades in the Bernese manner along the sides, leaving behind a few placid dwellings with brown tiled roofs and moving in a mist of peace as though you were being enveloped by

*My very warm thanks to M. Jean-René Bory, at that time curator of Coppet, for opening the château and grounds to me outside hours and enabling me to be edified by the excellent exhibition mounted there in 1966 to celebrate the 200th anniversary of the birth of Mme de Staël. Everything has remained as in Necker's day. It's a trip worth making.

the soul of the lake at whose shore the swans tread water, pontificating. Turn right, follow the elm avenue through the big iron gate and into the courtyard in front of a jewel of a château, neither too imposing nor insignificant, three stories beneath a high steep roof, three glass-paneled doors in the middle leading to the hall, an elongated triangular pediment bearing the Necker arms, "de gueule a swan of silver on a sea the same." The beauty of the building derives from its balance, and the restrained proportions that were typical of the eighteenth century. A square tower on the north corner hints at a more distant past; the towers at the other three corners are rounded. On the right a winepress, on the left the stables. A lavish Virginia creeper, blazing red in the autumn, scales the walls. If you carry straight on to the main door after going through the entrance, you may not notice two fountains set in the walls on either side of it, from which a thread of water flows uninterruptedly. Above each is a date, 1766, carved by Necker's order when he bought the château and the barony eighteen years later: 1766—the year of his daughter's birth. Coppet is the château of the infanta, and many an infanta has had less love and care lavished upon her by a doting father.

On the far side of the château, as is often the case, you find relatively unimpressive gardens backed by a high wall. In the center is a large round pool, almost a pond, its still surface dotted with aquatic plants and leaves whirled by the wind from a few purple beeches and more exotic trees—including a sophora —some of which were presented to Mme Necker by Buffon, her lovelorn swain of yore who had them taken from the Jardin du Roi and transplanted here with infinite precautions. Their senior by a century, a monumental cedar, twice the height of the château, majestically stands guard over the tranquillity of this unique site. The pond is ringed by a lawn of brilliant green; a tiny stream tinkles away along one side of the grounds; and there, in 1784, as though for all eternity, were installed the stone benches on which she sat.

It took her a while to get to like the place. "It was at Coppet that my father was happiest," certainly, but "I was mortally afraid that he might wish to spend all his time on his estate. I hope he may forgive me: my store of memories is not yet large enough for me to live on them for the rest of my life. It is not that illusions and pleasures are so precious to me; yet this heart that worships him would quake if the door were to close for good behind the three of us."[2] One can see her point a little, knowing that her mother's nervous complaint, which entailed alternating periods of hysteria and prostration, would have been likely to turn their "tête-à-trois" into No Exit. One reason for choosing Coppet was its proximity to Tissot, the famous Genevan doctor who treated half the dignitaries of Europe, often by correspondence. By the time they moved into the château, though, it was almost too late for Suzanne Necker to consult him; although not fifty years old, she was "subject to attacks of anguish so acute that she became quite unable to sleep; in the daytime, unable to master a surge of agitation, she would remain continually on her feet, even in company," a company whose aplomb was sorely tried on occasion, as when she would enter the salon with "her head covered by a thick black veil falling below her chin." She's not in mourning; maybe it's her way of showing her resentment of her daughter's refusal to marry Pitt. For her complaint, Mesmer might have been a better choice than Tissot.

But her mother's melancholia cannot account for Germaine Necker's indifference to nature, to which many witnesses have testified. At the dawn of Romanticism, she is a pure product of the century of Louis XV, Classical through and through; her one real pleasure is conversation, the thrill of shining in company, the determination to know the largest possible number of interesting people. To her, life is a perpetual salon. "Excepting those entertainments that brought the mind into play, Mlle Necker sought none. Long walks were an ordeal," relates a friend of her own age, who "had the greatest difficulty persuading her to walk out to a windmill two hundred yards from Saint-Ouen, the mechanisms of which I was curious to see."[3] Just now, in the year of her marriage, Germaine has confessed to the celebrated Mme d'Houdetot, Rousseau's mortal friend,* "that she cannot contrive, as her friend does, to unite love of town and love of country. . . . I shall love solitude once I have laid by a store of memories";[4] there she goes, harping on them again—memories of Paris, that is, Paris her childhood paradise, when daddy was ruling the treasury and about to save the kingdom, when Marmontel, Raynal, Grimm, Buffon, all those men who were translating the world, used to sit and explain it to her, paternally titillated by her ardent eyes, full lips, and precocious bosom in the drawing room at Saint-Ouen where she, at fifteen, was the little madame whose opinion they would solicit on this or that. "Perhaps Mme de Staël† was too old when she came to Coppet. A young child's secret passion for a tree, a stream, an old bench, does not develop between nature and a girl of eighteen. The mysterious attraction does not survive, except in someone who has felt it powerfully in early youth. She was wholly intellectual; too committed to the movement of the mind, she had none of that intuition that can bind a soul to an 'inanimate object.' From her mother she inherited a horror of the fens."[5] And if she was so longing for her beloved papa to be returned to power, it is because that would take her back to her beloved Paris.

Marriage might be a shortcut. Anyway, she'll have to face it sooner or later. She's not eager. She knows nothing of men. And she knows nothing of herself

---

*Madame d'Houdetot is only fifty-five in 1785, and lives until 1813. Her interfering and indiscretion did much to envenom the quarrel between Rousseau and the *philosophes.*

†A conclusion of the Baronne d'Andlau in her study *La Jeunesse de Madame de Staël,* cited earlier.

in relation to them either, nothing of the potential of her body and heart. She is totally ignorant of her volcanoes. A few days before the wedding she tells her diary: "I do not yet know what this fault is that a woman can commit, but I shall no doubt be told before the solemn oath"[6]—she who was already discoursing on essence and existence, grace and predestination, political economy and the entry on "superstition" in the *Encyclopédie* . . . But girls, especially in the upper middle classes, were beginning to be brought up in total ignorance of sexuality, the road to which was being cordoned off by the epidemic spread of the quality of *quant-à-soi* [an approximate translation of which might be "I mind my own business and am dignified about it"—*Trans.*] that was replacing, in her class, the unselfconsciousness of the aristocrats and the simplicity of the people, both of whom still called a puss a puss.

All right, if one absolutely has to get married one might as well treat it like a formality, a sort of rite of passage that will put one on a level with the adults. At least she got the chance to eliminate the one she definitely didn't want, the Englishman. But neither was there any question of her being allowed to choose just anybody. Only one had actually given her childish heart a flutter: a pretty posy from the Queen's garden, Comte Louis de Narbonne—the one they said was a son of Louis XV* —who made a few tentative approaches in 1781 or '82. But he was a Roman Catholic, and the parents had politely objected that Germaine was too young, not yet sixteen, and Narbonne married somebody else almost at once.

At the moment, she herself is "leaning" a bit—why should queens have a monopoly on "penchants"?—in the direction of an academician who's one of the youngest of the lot, although twenty-three years older than herself; he's also one of the most attractive, and most illustrious too, the great revolutionizer of the theory of troop deployment: Hippolyte, Comte de Guibert, the last lover of Julie de Lespinasse. A ladies' man who has stayed single because he didn't want to be tied down, and who has paid enough attention to the embryonic Louise-Germaine to plunge her into learned disquisitions on the superiority of the shallow line of battle over the deep one. Perhaps she's a little like Lespinasse? How good it would be to govern men with words! But Guibert makes no move, official or otherwise; to him, the prospect of becoming the Neckers' son-in-law must not have seemed so alluring. And anyway, he too would have been turned down—this way out for Catholics, please.

So the tortoise finally crosses the finish line. After starting out in 1779 as a rather unprepossessing diplomatic councilor whose only strong card was his

---

*His mother, one of Mme Adélaïde's ladies-in-waiting, had certainly been, fleetingly, the mistress of Louis XV. We shall meet Narbonne again in 1792, as minister of war and—lover of Mme de Staël.

membership of a Swedish "good family," "little Staël," as he was called in the early days, takes the thirteenth trick—the actual engagement—late in the summer of 1785, by which time he holds the rank of ambassador. Six years of crawling. He managed to recruit a few ripe and energetic matrons to his cause, such as the Comtesse de Boufflers, who corresponded with both the Neckers and Gustavus III. The king had no special reason to favor Staël but he was extremely suspicious of young women and, perhaps for that reason, would lend an ear to old ones, although even a young woman could be sure of a hearing if she was Queen of France. And Marie Antoinette, advised by the magnanimous Fersen, let on that "little Staël" might be a factor in a reconciliation between Louis XVI and Necker. Like everybody else who saw Germaine's father as the Messiah of finance and had good reason to dread the bankruptcy of Louis XVI, the King of Sweden, copiously subsidized by the French treasury since his rule had become absolute again, wanted Necker restored to power. So if Staël can be a pawn on the chessboard . . .

Creutz* was made Swedish minister of foreign affairs. In two years, from 1782 to 1784, Staël covers the requisite squares on the board—chargé d'affaires, minister plenipotentiary, ambassador—whereupon Gustavus III writes him, "If at the end of all this you marry Mademoiselle Necker, I shall say you have performed an excellent embassy. See whether your negotiations in that quarter cannot bear fruit."[7] When the islands were being reshuffled during the peace treaty negotiations Gustavus even gave up Tobago, which he had coveted for years, in exchange for Saint-Barthélemy, and announced that he had made the sacrifice at the behest of his new ambassador, who was in good odor at Court, and with Louis XVI himself. Germaine Necker must be worth an island.

She is not marrying the embassy, however, but Baron Eric Magnus de Staël. He's tolerable. A better-than-average figure, looking a good five years less than his age (thirty-five), with a symmetrical, hopelessly ordinary head and prettily rolled hair crowning a plump body that is always impeccably attired. Nobody minds him. He says what he should. With a little effort, people find one positive quality to ascribe to him—agreeableness. Necker, whose arm needed quite a lot of twisting because, after all, he's the one who's going to pay, admits that "the man is agreeable and honest, and has a pleasing appearance." His wife, still grieving over Pitt, nevertheless concedes that Staël is "mild, agreeable, honest, and sensible."[8]

What about their daughter, the person whose voice counts for most in the business? She consents with good grace, as long as she's not required to

---

*Swedish ambassador at Versailles during the American war; it was he who notified his king of Marie Antoinette's "penchant" for Fersen.

produce sentiment as well. "He is a perfectly decent man, incapable of doing or saying anything really idiotic, but sterile and lacking in forcefulness.* The only unhappiness he can cause [me] is to add nothing to happiness, but he can do nothing to destroy it."9

Her mother has the last word: "She desired to live in Paris, and M. le Baron de Staël was the only Protestant suitor who could give her a position in that city."10

Any man this girl could marry would have to be a nonentity. The only one she loves is her father, and between them there has never been the shadow of a rift because he took no hand in her upbringing, leaving it all to the reproaches and terrors of her poor mother; so all their daughter's childhood resentments are directed against her. As for Necker—who would believe it? —this solemn personage actually amuses Germaine, he makes her laugh, he roughhouses like a brother with her when La Curchod isn't around, with her crucified airs; if she leaves the two of them alone at the dinner table, father and daughter throw napkins in each other's face.

Germaine's first sexual stirrings were inspired by him, and not long before her marriage, as a sort of reaction to the distaste—or worse—which she felt for her financé.

> There is one moment that will long remain in my mind. My father told him to dance with me and began to sing the tune with charming gaiety. M. de Staël, with his pretty figure and skill in the art of dancing, executed the steps most correctly, but there was no soul in his movements, and the eyes he fixed upon me were animated by neither spirit nor heart. His hand, when he took mine, seemed as white marble, that confined and chilled me at the same time. Suddenly my father said to him,
>
> "Here, Monsieur, let me show you how to dance with a young lady with whom one is in love."
>
> Then, despite his great size and although less young than the other, his eyes, his charming eyes, and his animated movements displayed tenderness combined with grace and energy. Lord, if I should describe the contraction of my heart in that moment, what an agonizing comparison it would be! I could not go on. I fled to a corner of the room and burst into tears.11

Not until after the wedding does she sign herself "*Germaine* Necker de Staël," as though to certify the change in her life; before she tended to write "Louise." Her closest friends call her Minette, but never does her husband use that nickname. Minette is dead, or married—what's the difference? "What a happy creature I should have been if some fourth person, such as my heart pictures,

---

*Note in her diary, August 15, 1785, five months before the wedding; nobody can accuse her of cherishing illusions.

had come to us, if he had been a great man, an admirer of my father, a sensitive soul who loved me and whom I should have loved."[12]

Her father, who has just bestowed upon her an inalienable dowry of 650,000 livres.*

ABBÉ FAUCHET

# 27

## FEBRUARY 1786

### *Contempt for the Poor*

ABBÉ MAURY

We've had the quarrel of the Bouffons and the quarrel of the Gluckists and Piccinists;† now we get the battle of the funeral orations. Three for one man! Of course, he wasn't just any old seigneur, he was the Duc d'Orléans, Louis-Philippe the Stout himself, head of the "junior branch," who departed this life on November 18, 1785, at the age of sixty, thereby confirming the tradition of early deaths on his side of the family. True, he had done nothing to help break the tradition, unless you count hunting every day, but of late even that was from inside a carriage—not enough to melt the fat that was gradually asphyxiating him. The truth was that he ate himself to death: twenty-seven partridge wings, not to mention the trimmings, at one sitting. Indigestion almost killed him eight or ten times before; what finally does the trick is a "climbing gout."[1]

The funeral was unostentatious, bourgeois rather than princely, as befitted his later years in the quietude of his estate of Sainte-Assise on the banks of the Seine near Fontainebleau, where he lived among the literary pretensions of the little coterie of his "morganatic" wife, Jeanne de Montesson. He bequeathed his heart and entrails to the parish church of Seine-Port, which was also the church of his estate, "hoping that the lady of the place would be buried next to him and desiring them to be as united after death as they had been in life."[2] "Are you sure the church is big enough?" the brighter wits were asking. The rest of his body was unceremoniously conveyed to Val-de-Grâce.

---

*4.5 million modern francs [$1,125,000].

†Both having to do with the forms and development of opera.

But three months later came the funeral orations, and wow! The slenderer their argument, it would seem—if I may be forgiven so gross a jest—the more impassioned the orators and their audience. In any event, the deceased himself had little to do with it; three months in the grave are as good as three thousand, for this type of ritual. The ceremony of glorification, before a mausoleum shaped like an enormous wedding cake, was a combination of circus and academy sitting aimed exclusively at the living. The occasion inspired so many speakers that it began to look more like a competition, between the recent winner of the number-one preaching post, Abbé Maury (February 14); an outsider of long standing, Abbé Fauchet (February 20); and a nobody thrown in for good measure, Abbé Bourlet of Vauxcelles. Maury was on a winning streak and looked a safe bet, but he was distracted by a political sugarlump and put off his stride: the sun of the Orléanses, brightened by the advent of a new duke—yesterday Philippe de Chartres—would be sure to warm anyone who would preach on behalf of the new man by talking about the old. And Fauchet beat him by a nose.* The combat of Titans in the previous century, Bossuet versus Fénelon, has shrunk to a contest between the pulpit of Notre Dame and the pulpit of Saint-Eustache. Not that the public believes much of what is proclaimed to it from them, in long, rolling super-sentences; does it even listen? But it reads the gazette next morning and adds up the score. There are seeds of ministers or dauphin tutors sprouting on that marble.

Grimm is self-appointed judge and jury—ruling, of course, as "Tout-Paris" rules:

> Of the three funeral orations given in memory of M. le Duc d'Orléans, that being talked about most in society is, quite properly, the one that left most room for criticism, to wit the sermon of M. l'Abbé Maury [at Notre Dame]. It was so widely taxed with infelicity, insolence, and crassness that, on the strength of the account of it given to the King, the abbé was expressly forbidden to print it. . . . The speech of M. l'Abbé Bourlet of Vauxcelles, reader to M. le Comte d'Artois [in the church of the Dames de Bellechasse, home of Félicité de Genlis, the new duke's ex-mistress and his children's tutor], was less a funeral oration than a simple and touching exhortation to the children of Monseigneur le Duc d'Orléans at their ancestor's tomb. . . .[3]

Diluted holy water, in other words, of no interest at all. As for Fauchet, his effort was both better and worse: "laden with bombast, laced with pointless

*Abbé Fauchet's first success dates from the panegyric on St. Louis which he gave to the Académie in the year of Louis XV's death. He is elected to the Legislative Assembly and the Convention, becomes a Constitutional Bishop of Calvados, is nicknamed "Bishop of the Girondons" when he allies himself with them, and is guillotined in 1793.

taradiddle" was what Grimm called the oration he improvised in a week, at the request of the Orléans heirs, as a riposte to Maury's impertinence.

Maury, ever eager to curry favor with the King and Queen and having no gift for subtlety, had tried to play on their hostility to the ex–Duc de Chartres; he more or less ignored the living Orléanses and concentrated on "singing lengthy hymns of praise to M. le Bailli de Suffren, M. le Comte d'Estaing, M. le Marquis de Bouillé,* M. de La Fayette, etc." His oration was more like the "people" column of a newspaper and, with his rare gift for putting his foot in his mouth, Maury succeeded in vexing not only the new Duc d'Orléans but the royal couple as well, by comparing the dead man's secret marriage to Mme de Montesson with that of Louis XIV and Mme de Maintenon. "This was the big moment, this was the pinnacle of his speech; it has even been said that the sermon might pass muster as a panegyric on Mme de Montesson, rather than a funeral oration for M. le Duc d'Orléans." *Both* branches of the royal family, worse luck for him, were always trying to hush up what was a secret to nobody.

Maury gets his comeuppance; he is temporarily removed from the royal chapels and supplanted by his chief rival in that special category of theatrical soliloquizing known as the sermon. When Claude Fauchet mounts the pulpit of Saint-Eustache, "all of the relief on which is gilded, as are the six virtues adorning its circumference, wrought by skillful carvers after the drawings of Le Brun in the reign of Louis XIV,"[4] he knows he has achieved one of the few moments that count in a career. All Paris, all of clerical, social, and literary France has its eyes upon him; tomorrow he may be more powerful than many a bishop (for bishops reign but nobody listens to them), in his seat in the "Orléans cathedral," as they call this other Notre Dame, built to the same plans as the first one but three centuries later and with a higher central arch, as though the market-district church were trying to thumb its nose at the Mother of the Cité. Saint-Eustache is another vessel of old Paris, and the Orléans family are its very own kings of hearts. "The potent odors of foodstuffs standing outside do not spare that bastion of stone rising amidst the bastions of flesh, vegetables, and fruit, with its superfluity of pilasters and columns, more curious than anything one can imagine,† a sort of Gothic skeleton clothed in Romanesque rags sewn together like the patches on a harlequin's cloak," to which bits are still being added from time to time, such as the banal frontispiece for which Philippe de Chartres laid the first stone when a stripling back in 1754. He feels quite at home here, does His Most Serene Highness Louis-Philippe-Joseph, the new Duc d'Orléans, at the foot of the pulpit immor-

---

*First appearance in the celebrities' hit parade of the rising strong man of the army.
†According to Viollet-le-Duc.

talized only yesterday by the celebrated Fléchier* and today by Claude Fauchet, no one doubts it, and certainly not the interested party himself.

Above the re-embroidered lace surplice, the gold-embroidered violet stole,
and the moiré cassock rises a rather heavy head with already well-rounded
cheeks lengthened by the oval of the face; "impressive stature, a superb torso,
dark brown hair powdered white and dressed in a single roll," big command-
ing black eyes beneath heavy brows, sensual lips, a "Bourbon" nose—they say
he looks a little like the present Duc d'Orléans. A handsome man, to those who
like him and are convinced that "his countenance radiates candor and kindliness," whereas his enemies find his "eye hard and his gaze sinister." Both
groups agree on one distinctive feature: the extreme, almost unhealthy pallor of
the complexion of a man who spends his life in libraries.[5] That's Abbé Fauchet at
forty-nine. It's about time he made the headlines, if he's ever going to.

Until now he has lived like any other priest in the class that gets meat with
its soup. His father was a landowner, pasture and farms in the Nivernais that
brought in 4,000 or 5,000 livres a year.† His mother was the daughter of a
local physician—"surgeon," as people said then. Rural petits bourgeois on
their way up. Nine children, four of whom died in infancy, leaving three girls
doomed to marry in their own circle or enter the convent, and two boys, too
"common" to get into the army, so they had to choose between two gowns,
law and church. In contrast to the usual practice, it is the younger, Guillaume,
who studies law, becomes a judge at Nevers, and undertakes the perpetuation
of the family name. The older boy, Claude, seems actually to have had a
religious vocation, possibly stimulated by the Jesuits of Moulins-en-Bourbon-
nais who were still running the school there before their expulsion.

At sixteen, already tonsured, he was back in his native village waiting for
the "living" that would enable him to advance to the priesthood. He reads a
lot. He writes on religious subjects. He is "highly thought of" by the neighbors. At seventeen he is permitted to preach his first sermon, in a church at
Decize. His subject is the Virgin Mary, and he does so well with her that the
parishioners remember him years later.[6] Perhaps that was the beginning of his
ambition to become a great preacher; he says it was. And preaching was a good
way to move ahead in the church and make money fast:

> When a priest wants to rise above the common ranks** and gain some reputation
> outside his presbytery, he turns to preaching.

---

*A great preacher to high society and a good stylist, contemporary of Louis XIV. He gave
Turenne's funeral oration in Saint-Eustache.
†30,000 to 35,000 modern francs [$7,500–$8,750].
**According to L. S. Mercier in the *Tableau de Paris*.

He tries to be first in line for a good Advent or a juicy Lent. . . . He may earn 100 écus, or he may earn 500.*

The chair-woman [who rents chairs] has great influence on the choice of preachers; in her contract with the parish she stipulates verbally that only accredited orators will be chosen, and her prices fluctuate accordingly. For a beginner's maiden sermon she sets guards at the church door and raises the price of her chairs. It is worth your time to watch her scurry about the place of worship; you can seat yourself nowhere without her leave, she lays down the law.

Go into any church. If the chair-woman has a self-effacing mien, the preacher, you may be sure, is but a poor specimen; but if she is being insolent, take a seat.

Every sermonizer dreams of preaching at Court, they all live on this hope, just as the young rhymer turning his first twenty lines sees himself in the Académie Française. Lent at Court, you see, pays a good thousand écus.†

It takes Fauchet another twenty years to get there, scaling the ladder of episcopal favors—more or less the path followed by his contemporary, Sieys. "In those days he [Fauchet] was affable with everyone, peaceful in his ways, remarkable for the mildness of his features and his height, and, moreover, sincerely pious,"[7] an ideal youth to "go into service" with some great family. The Bishop of Nevers recommends him to a Choiseul-Beaupré who is Archbishop of Besançon and looking for a tutor for one of his nephews and a librarian at Besançon. This Choiseul duly becomes Fauchet's benefactor, and the priest actually grinds out a poem to celebrate some episcopal convalescence or other:

> Dans les champs nivernais, au sein de ma patrie,
> La Loire mugissante, apprenant vos douleurs,
> A suspendu ses flots, et sa rive flétrie
> A vu, dans cet instant, faner toutes ses fleurs.[8]

> [Among the fields of Nivernais, whence I did hail,
> The potent Loire, on hearing of your illness, sank;
> Within the hour did every blossom droop and pale,
> And the waves shrank back appalled from the desert bank.]

One hopes his preaching was better than his verse. In 1766 he becomes a deacon, and in 1769 a priest, still in Besançon, where his reputation was growing. But he wasn't going to molder in the provinces forever. The only place for a preacher to become famous is in Paris, and if he wasn't angling to go there himself his protectors would have angled for him; with adequate backing, priests could hope for as much mobility as army officers. After Nevers and Besançon Fauchet goes back to tutoring—another nephew of the same

*Fees ranged, thus, from 2,000 to 10,000 modern francs [$500–$2,500].
†Around 20,000 modern francs [$5,000]; an écu was worth about 3 livres.

Choiseul-Beaupré and a protégé of the Noailles family which was all-powerful on the right bank of Paris, where the big church of Saint-Roch on the rue Saint-Honoré is more or less their private almonry. Thanks to them, Fauchet can join the "surplice regiment," as it is called, or in plain talk, the "community of priests attached to the parish of Saint-Roch." Fifty-five all told, and room for more: "The community of St. Roch was established in order to bring together all the clergy serving the parish and thereby better enable them to perform the office of their holy ministry or prepare themselves for it. They are not a single body, they simply live together, with the head priest, superior and administrator of the community. Their residence contains sixty-one dwellings, including those in the attics."[9]

And what were all these priests doing, among fewer than 10,000 parishioners? Well, for the most part, nothing. Fauchet, for example, never had any parish work at Saint-Roch. He spent his time there writing and polishing his sermons. "Nearly every son of a good family who, while awaiting the honors of the prelacy, placed himself under the government of a Paris priest, was in a similar situation."[10] Most of them already had a living somewhere, a canonry, priory, or abbey; they paid their chief a modest sum for their room and board, more on principle than out of need, because the parish was overflowing with alms.

Thus by the time he was thirty Fauchet was firmly in the saddle, to borrow an equestrian phrase. His first star role was a sermon to the Assembly of French Clergy in 1773, on the operation of nature and grace in St. Augustine. His presentation of forty sheets closely written in his small hand somehow failed to send his listeners to sleep. The King rewarded this feat with a pension of 1,200 livres.* His next success was the panegyric to St. Louis on August 24, 1774, Louis XVI's first feast day, before the Académie Française; on that occasion he gave "natural religion" a rough time, thereby angering d'Alembert and Condorcet but delighting the King: "Nature is not stronger than nature [sic], and when a man rises above nature he seems greater than it; it being God, perforce, who elevates him."[11]

In addition, he once gave a somewhat startling interpretation of the Crusades, which also pleased Louis XVI's sense of mischief and the champions of the rising middle class, because on this occasion he was casting aspersions upon the nobility in the person of its ancestors, the great feudal barons:

> Europe was purged of so many scoundrels then, and how fortunate it was to have pitted against real enemies [the Saracens] the warring lusts of the lords of that day, who, rather than lying idle, would otherwise have turned against the citizens! Was there any greater service to be rendered to the farmer, the good and useful subject

*About 8,000 modern francs [$2,000] a year; not much, but it was a start, and Fauchet had no personal fortune.

of the realm, than to remove the tyrants who were oppressing him to a safe distance? Alienations,* having become indispensable, abolished the rights of fiefs which were the scourges of liberty.

Is this a twitch of rebellion in Claude Fauchet, shouldering the humiliation of his Nivernais forefathers, the hardworking middle class that was ineligible for honors? In any event, it gets him another 1,200 livres a year from the income of a Benedictine abbey near Luçon, in which he never sets foot. Even in the pulpit it was becoming *de bon ton* in Paris, and profitable as well, to challenge the occasional eternal truth. Fauchet was always careful, however, to deliver his acid in very weak solution. His pulpit is not yet hurling thunderbolts. When he preaches to the Queen, at a meeting of charity dames in 1779, he shows that he knows how to address her:

"Madame, you have mounted the throne of Clothilde, Bathilde, and Blanche, with the graces of nature, the principles of religion, and the gifts of virtue. Like those holy queens, you will make all these beautiful qualities by which you are crowned serve the triumph of virtue. You are made to have altars, but they must not be those of the idolatry of the French; it must be the gratitude of religion that raises them to you."[12] How could he not be appointed "preacher ordinary to the King" in 1781? A purely honorary title, bestowed upon Maury and a few others too, which meant that he would have access to the chapel in Versailles on a limited number of occasions; but it brings in another pension, this time of 1,500 livres, from a Benedictine abbey in the diocese of Boulogne in the far north.

And then a priory at Ploërmel near Saint-Malo; and then a big abbey at Monfort Lacarre, also in Brittany; and then the title of vicar general of Nevers, awarded by his first benefactor, Monsignor Tinseau, the bishop of his youth —another position entailing no further duties than the regular deposit of his checks. Fauchet was becoming no mean moonlighter, without ever leaving his hole at Saint-Roch, except to go out preaching now and then at the request of top-ranking bishops, the ones who play a more or less important political role. In 1785 he's appointed vicar general of Bourges as well, but goes there seldom to preach. "Monseigneur de Puységur [Archbishop of Bourges] had a score of vicars general, but only five or six of that number were actually engaged in the administration of the diocese. The others, advancing toward more lucrative honors, performed honorary functions only."[13]

So for Fauchet it's *la vie en rose?* Well, maybe. Sometimes he seems to be somehow absent, as though he had some private worry. About the rest of humanity, could it be?

On July 18, 1785, for example, although he was fit as a fiddle, he felt the

---

*I.e., the confiscation by the King of estates left by the Crusaders when they came back too many years later or not at all. Note Fauchet's use of "citizens," as early as 1774.

need to make his will, perhaps to mark his entrance into his forties, leaving half of whatever fortune he might have amassed at his death (although he was apparently spending as he earned) to his brother Guillaume and the other half to Abbé Viriot, a friend. His excellent library was to go to Abbé Dupré, another priest living at Saint-Roch. Viriot would get all the manuscripts, by which Fauchet sets great store, with instructions to publish, whenever it might become possible without causing a scandal, a work entitled *Sur les principes* ["On principles"—*Trans.*], which might not be quite "catholic" enough just now.*

His will contains one amusing paragraph: "To Abbé Maury, of the Académie Française, who has perhaps unfairly been taken for my enemy and whom I have always loved, although I have long refrained from telling him so, I bequeath my folio edition of Pliny the Elder."[14]

Written digs are not his only way of avenging himself, however. Sometimes a stifled cry escapes him, as in this letter to an (unidentified) friend, written shortly after his introduction to Versailles:

> I have made my maiden speech at Court, and it was quite as much of a success as I could have wished. I returned from the place highly pleased to have been there, to be able to go back again, and never to remain. The people are a very decent lot, but God preserve a poor man like myself from remaining among them permanently! Compliments cost them nothing; but of virtues one hears never a word. Boredom presides amid opulence there, and feeling is choked by good manners. Long live nature, simplicity, candor, and friendship![15]

However much he may sin by self-infatuation, and in another area perhaps by a weakness for the pretty penitents who cluster around any famous preacher, the man is sincerely a priest in Jesus Christ. As far as the girls are concerned, it is murmured, and reiterated by the scratchy quills of his ecclesiastical biographers, that Fauchet is quite the equal of Maury; except that the latter, a cynic by nature, makes little effort to hide his peccadilloes and will soon acquire the nickname of the "Mirabeau of Notre Dame." Fauchet, on the other hand, respects the secret of the confessional, even his own.

Something, some malaise or presentiment, does seem to be welling up within him at his *mezzo del camin.* He senses the coming storm because he sees that the poor really are too downtrodden. And today, inserting a thistle between two flowers of rhetoric, he's going to say so from the height of his pulpit at Saint-Eustache:

> Monseigneur le Duc d'Orléans respected the exiguous lands bordering upon his own estates; to him the right of a poor man was more sacred even than his own.
> This principle is unqualifiedly just, but it is sometimes cruelly neglected by the powerful, who impudently flout the laws of the nation and of nature. Will

---

*It is brought out in his lifetime, but not until 1789, and is then called *La Religion nationale.*

there never be an end to such frightful abuses and sacrilegious usurpations of the rights of man? . . . What should prevent the coming of the longed-for moment when the equity of the Duc d'Orléans will be the law of those furtive nabobs who, profiting by the powerlessness of the wretched to command the considerable sums needed to take them to task before courts of redress, presume to affect contempt for the poor, independence in their pride, and audacity in their impunity?[16]

On this February 26, 1786, Claude Fauchet kills two birds with one stone. He accepts the relative danger of alienating royal favor, which will soon swing back to Maury anyway—but the "provocateur" is already earning more than he needs, and the provisional suspension of manna from Court will be abundantly offset by the attentive ear of the middle class and lesser clergy, won by his straight talking. And at the same time he concludes a new alliance, switching from the Court of Versailles to the Palais Royal. In praising Philippe the Stout he has pointed an insistent finger at his successor Louis-Philippe-Joseph, sitting in the front row behind the gilded plaster monument in a burning bush of tapers and eddying incense, of all the men in France the one whose heart was most gladdened by his father's death, and who is having some difficulty hiding the fact. This former Duc de Chartres's* accession to the head of the junior branch will enable him to absorb most of his ocean of debts and set out, almost as rich as Louis XVI, in pursuit of fresh intrigues. His dawning middle age has given him a candid, easygoing air, with thick lips under a big nose that is Bourbonian enough to discredit any legends of illegitimacy. His hairline has receded by more than half; his protruding eyes gaze docilely up at his friend and preacher, the sweeping gestures of whose sleeves pour absolution upon his enormous fortune because, of course, he has already announced his intention of devoting it to the relief of the poor, like his father before him, but if possible even more so.

Blessed by Fauchet and pointed toward the vast arena now open to the Orléanses if they have skill enough to manage it, Philippe will spend the next six months and more memorizing every location, dimension, and yield of the appanage bestowed by Louis XIV upon his brother and descendants, a kingdom within the kingdom, so that they can shine brightly enough to dazzle all the princes of Europe but not get in the way of their sovereign cousins: almost the whole of Île-de-France (except Paris), lower Normandy, a bit of Picardy, a piece of Flanders, a lot of Champagne, Bresse, Forez, and Suvergne, the Valaisis, and, of course, the big central estate of Orléans from which their main title derives. Not to mention the Palais Royal in Paris and its commercial exploitation, now that the new shops are built and the gardens open to the

---

*This is, we recall, the future Philippe-Egalité, father of Louis-Philippe, the last King of the French. He is now thirty-nine.

public. Each year Philippe-Joseph will take in a net income (after deduction of outgoings and running expenses) of somewhere between 6.5 and 7 million livres.* And that's not counting the vast holdings of the Penthièvre family in Brittany (mainly), which his wife will inherit.

# 28

FEBRUARY 1786

*The Profession Is Still Respectable*

A few days after her marriage, Germaine de Staël begins to capitalize on her ability to turn a pretty little phrase by becoming, in the wake of Grimm and Bachaumont, one of the unofficial informers dispatching confidential newsletters to foreign sovereigns. After all, she is now the Swedish ambassadress, and so she decides to send Gustavus III, her sovereign-by-marriage, a little monthly diary written just for him. On February 23, 1786, Madame de Boufflers, the old friend of them both, makes the announcement to that peculiar king, "revolutionary" for his own ends only, and only against the Swedish feudal barons, astute, inconsistent, temperamental—one of the last of the age of enlightened despotism: "Madame de Staël has engaged to be your purveyor of news. She will acquit herself extremely well of the task,"[1] not duplicating her husband's diplomatic dispatches but providing the King of Sweden with exactly what he could expect from a gimlet-eyed habituée of the salons: "news of the Court and all the anecdotes of Paris, mainly centered on the people Gustavus had known on his trips to Paris or Versailles in 1771 and 1784."[2]

The job gives her an opportunity, at twenty, to practice her philosophy scales with a music master from a major country. She talks to him almost as an equal, with an aplomb that bodes well for the future—as, for instance, on the subject of her beloved Guibert's admission to the Académie Française: "M. de Guibert is said to have been received rather coolly by the King when submitting his speech. It was found to have too much pathos. That is quite the line of criticism of the people of this Court: the ridicule of ardent spirits by cold ones. They call overdone whatever they do not feel themselves, and say that anyone who is taller than they must be walking on stilts."[3]

*In the neighborhood of 50 million modern francs [$12,500,000].[17]

It seems clear enough—Mme de Staël has risen from the waves.*

If she is backing Guibert so heatedly, it is not only out of personal sympathy for him, but also because the new academician has sided resolutely with the "Necker party." Louis XVI snubbed him at the ritual audience after his reception ceremony because of an incident that occurred during the sitting, after he made a transparent allusion to "administrators . . . whose love of the good accompanies them into retirement . . . and who, if they have conceived great schemes, consign them to immortal writings." Nobody missed that one. "The applause was loud and long, with both hands and feet," and the applauders were looking hard at two guests seated in the gallery, the Comte de Staël and his wife—"daughter of the present-day Sully, still so deeply regretted by the French"†—the disgraced Necker.

In this same lengthy epistle to Gustavus III, Germaine de Staël takes every opportunity to drive home her point: "Monsieur le Marquis de Créqui heard M. Foulon** spoken of the other day as a man likely to take the place of M. de Calonne. 'Gentlemen,' he said, 'do not be deceived. That person [Foulon] goes to great lengths to be thought a clever devil, but I warn you, in reality he is a dolt.' "[5]

Take Calonne's place? Is that really in the wind? On the basis of what—impressions, mishearings, gossip—could this be, as we have yet to see the outline of Calonne's economic design, assuming he's got one, emerge from the mists? Louis XVI doesn't want him out, but since the quarrel over Saint-Cloud Marie Antoinette does. Here and there, just in case, two opposing potential successors are beginning to line up their supporters in the shadows: the conservatives, who blench at the mere sound of the word "reform," even in Calonne's mouth, and the liberals, for whom Necker is still the Savior, with his daughter as their full-time public relations officer.

And she's working overtime on the brick-by-brick demolition of Calonne, beginning in her very next "newsletter" to Gustavus III:

It is said, and very certain, that a short while ago M. de Calonne was conversing at table on the subject of the ministers of Louis XIV. One of his friends remarked

---

*In this she is echoing Guibert himself, who was distinguished from his congealed contemporaries by the warmth of his emotion. He had just written, in his *Eloge de Catinat,* "People in this century have contrived to deride, under the name of enthusiasm, any motion that is noble and generous. The soul is no longer permitted to take flight."[4]

†According to the diary of Hardy the bookseller (folio 290 in the Bibliothèque nationale), whose text, like Ruault's letters, has the merit of expressing the direct and immediate reactions of the Parisian petits bourgeois.

**Jean-François Foulon, born in 1715, former intendant of war and finance, had long had his eye on the office of comptroller general and favored an economic policy of ruthless exploitation of the poor. He is massacred by the Parisians in July 1789.

that in those days ministers could make truly immense fortunes. He referred to
Mazarin and Louvois and complained that it was no longer possible to grow so
excessively rich.

"I beg your pardon," said M. de Calonne, "the profession is still respectable."

Such words ought better to be said in his study than at the dinner table.[6]

Swords will cross, and sparks will fly higher, between Calonne and
Necker.

Who is Charles-Alexandre de Calonne? Where does he come from?
Where is he going?

Born at Douai in Flanders on January 20, 1734, he now carries his fifty years
lightly, apart from "sciatica pains which half paralyze me in the winter" and
have forced him on several occasions to take the waters at Bagnères in the
Pyrenees or Balaruc in Languedoc.[7] The virtuous academician Montyon,
founder of the prize that is beginning to bear his name, couldn't abide Calonne
but sees him as "tall, quite well made, with a lively appearance, his features
not without appeal, a mobile face, its expression changing from moment to
moment, a keen, piercing gaze, but too striking, and tending to inspire mistrust; his laugh is cunning and caustic rather than gay."

Talleyrand, although on his side, certainly does not consider him an
Adonis and adds some qualifying touches to the portrait:

M. de Calonne had an easy and brilliant wit, a sharp and quick mind. He spoke
and he wrote well, he was always clear and full of refinements, he had the gift
of embellishing what he knew and ignoring what he did not. . . . M. de Calonne
was capable of attachment and loyalty to his friends, but it was his mind that chose
them rather than his heart. The dupe of his vanity, he sincerely believed he loved
the men his vanity had sought out. He was ugly, tall, agile, and well made; he
had an expressive physiognomy and a pleasant voice.[8]

Mme Vigée-Lebrun's appraisal was less stern than those of either man. In
the handsome portrait she has just painted[9] there is something undeniably
attractive about the man: clothed in silk and lace, his hair impeccably rolled
and powdered snow white in contrast to black eyebrows, Calonne looks ten
years less than his age, and his gaze, set off by regular features, could truly be
said to pierce the canvas.

These days he is living up to his family motto, *En espérant mieux* [hoping
for better—*Trans.* ], on an azure field with two gold-headed eagles. Calonne's
nobility may be a bit on the meager side, going no further back than the
seventeenth century—first title *"écuyer,"* next "chevalier," next the *seigneurie*
of the estates of Merchin and du Quesne; but it is solidly rooted in Flanders
on both sides of the border, at Tournai, Cambrai, Douai. It was not enough

for a good career in the army, but it enabled Charles-Alexandre to be born into the seraglio of the magistracy, as the sixth of twelve children, almost all of whom died in infancy. His father was Louis-Joseph-Dominique, counselor to the Parlement of Flanders (which sat at Douai), and his mother was Anne-Henriette de Franqueville, whose father was ditto; his godfather was none other than the first president [chief justice—*Trans.*] of that same parlement. If he could survive the grim reaper's sickle in early childhood, his path lay clear before him. He took it: tutors at home, then Paris, the Collège des Quatre Nations (Flanders being one of them, there was no problem about admission) like Condorcet and Lavoisier,* prizes in Latin and Greek and "French discourse." At twenty he returns to Douai and is sworn in as a barrister; a scant three years later he is elected alderman of the town and hence a member of the municipal government. (He is elected by an electoral college of dignitaries —certain franchises had been allowed to survive in "countries of election"; alderman elsewhere were appointed by the agent of the King or local seigneur.)

He spends only five years in Douai, the little county town in a forest imprisoned by Vauban, full of soldiers maneuvering in the shadows of shafts of wood and stone—the belfrys, the collegiate churches, twenty-seven hospitals—one of France's northernmost defenses, perpetually in arms against the Austrian Netherlands. The years of a careful youth with ambition, i.e., Paris, as its focus. Having become chief prosecuting attorney in Douai (his father's job before him), Calonne takes his place at thirty among the twenty-four *maîtres de requêtes* [*rapporteur* for the King's Council of State—*Trans.*].

"The Council of State can lead anywhere, provided that one does not remain in it," Chancellor d'Aguesseau once said, and added, "The *rapporteurs* are like desires in the human heart: they aspire to extinction. It is a condition that is embraced only to be abandoned."[10] Calonne was the type to bounce out of it almost at once, risking a broken neck by meddling too soon between Louis XV's ministers and the famous attorney La Chalotais, the figurehead of resistance by the Brittany parlements against the arbitrary rulings of Versailles. Charles-Alexandre walks straight into one of the great cases of the latter end of the reign, and it teaches him how to answer back after being battered on all sides for presuming to mediate. Compelled to choose, he went to bat for the old King who was so angry with the lawmen for corrupting the docility of a whole province, and in the process he lost half his credit with the magistracy not only of Brittany but of Paris as well. Calonne has not and never will have any of the qualities of opposition, and he always leans toward the winning side. Was he the author of Louis XV's *mercuriale* [speech made at the re-

---

*This school was in the Palais Mazarin, the present home of the Académie Française; for quality of instruction it was one of the best in Paris. Condorcet and Lavoisier were day pupils.

opening of the courts of law—*Trans.* ] of March 3, 1766, so vehement and outrageous in its definition of absolutism that the occasion became known as the "flagellation sitting"? People said he was, and in any event he subscribed to its sentiment:

"It is in My person alone that sovereign power resides, whose particular character is the spirit of counsel, justice, and reason. . . . It is to Myself alone that legislative authority belongs, unconditionally and without fragmentation. . . . The entire order of the state emanates from Me; I am its supreme guardian; my people are but one with Myself."[11]

Calonne got his award for good behavior. In September the King printed a few lines in his own august hand at the bottom of a pleading written by Calonne against Chalotais: "You had no need of justification in my eyes; I attest to your abilities and the uprightness of your conduct. You may count on my full protection." That was just twenty years ago. Shortly thereafter the prize came: "King" Stanislas having died, Lorraine officially became part of the French territory. Calonne was named "intendant of the Three Bishoprics" (Metz, Toul, and Verdun). For twelve years he stared out at the ramparts of Metz and they stared back at him like the ramparts of Douai, except that he was now the viceroy of 300,000 souls. "The town has some fine points, the land around it is charming,* the intendant's residence superb, the secretaries shrewd and intelligent." In this setting he cultivates a love of hard work, preferably performed in surroundings of prestige and opulence.

This was not a job for a bachelor, especially one of thirty-five. February 1769: "I can marry the daughter of a tax master, very rich, his property being in land"—Anne-Joséphine Marquet. True, "the young woman is not pretty, far from it. However, she is well formed. I assure you that it is her homeliness that most holds me back. She is eighteen. I believe I shall be happier with a plain girl who is renowned for her excellent nature and said to be charmingly gentle, however, than with some pert pretty thing who would not be liked by those around me." When the dowry assembled by Anne-Joséphine's father and uncle reached a total of 460,000 livres,† it required little effort to take the plunge. You can do it, lad: "It is one of those sums that neither attract nor repel, one is not overjoyed but then neither is one put off. . . . There is no going back now, my dear father." The wedding takes place on April 12, 1769, at Saint-Gervais in Paris; the splendid château of Hannonville is acquired,** with a huge estate crossed by the Meuse near Saint-Mihiel; a son is born in August of the following year, killing his poor mother within the hour, but there's no time to mourn sweet Anne-Joséphine "with the high, wide forehead and lantern jaw" because she dies smack in the middle of the big squabble with

---

*From a letter to his father. *Ibid.* for the following passages on his marriage.
†About 3.5 million modern francs [$875,000].
**For 173,000 livres, or over 1 million modern francs [$250,000].

the Parlement of Metz. It's 1770, Maupeou and d'Aiguillon in Versailles are directing the deployment of troops for the "royal coup d'état," Calonne's daddy is expelled along with the Parlement of Flanders but his son manages to dissolve the Parlement of Metz before the same thing can happen to him. This did not win him the undying affection of the nobility of the robe, his own, which was increasingly coming to regard him as a "traitor to his class."

Five years later, by the grace of the new King, the exiles were triumphantly returned to Metz and Charles-Alexandre had to make the best of it when re-instating them. How's this: "The stringent orders laid upon me permitted nothing but mute pain, sincere regrets, and wishes that I have not ceased to express since that moment."[12] The returning members were magnanimous enough to pretend to believe him, and Calonne was able to maintain his little regency in Lorraine in the euphoria of the King's coronation until his promotion, in 1778, to the intendantship of Flanders and Artois, one of the biggest in the kingdom.

So it was as lord and master that he came home to his native land. From Lille he administered Douai (Gallician Flanders), Dunkerque (Flemish Flanders), and Artois, where Robespierre and Carnot were still seeking their fortunes. Six hundred thousand inhabitants at his mercy, the great northern markets, French for a scant century, intense rural and industrial expansion, wool, lace, the great mirror and china manufactures, and the eruption into the economy of a novelty that would soon change a whole way of life—the coal mines. An ideal apprenticeship for a ministry, for a man who was skillful, able to compromise, attractive, and in the prime of life.

With an annual paycheck of 40,000 to 50,000 francs a year,* he was beginning to get his hands on some real money. He converted his official residence into a luxury mansion in the latest taste: gorgeous furniture, mirrors all over the place including in his bedroom, and the drawing-room ceiling painted by Louis-Joseph Watteau.[13] He greeted Joseph II at the gates to France, and the Duke of Gloucester,† and the Tsarevich Paul, all of which helped his reputation abroad. On the home front, one whole branch of the highest aristocracy was dealing with him man to man: the Condés, or princes of the north, where they had so much of their property. Calonne danced assiduous attendance upon them, treated them as sovereigns, became the friend of Vaudreuil when he was appointed governor of Lille and, through Vaudreuil, was introduced to the Polignacs and Esterhazys. His name crept into the Queen's ear. Meanwhile, the breeze of bankruptcy was beginning to reach gale force. After Necker's expulsion, Joly de Fleury foundered and was

---

*350,000 modern francs [$87,500].
†Downtrodden brother of the King of England.

replaced by d'Ormesson, who also foundered. The offices of the comptroller-generalship were beginning to be known as "removal house," but a lot of people were still willing to risk that particular removal. The minister's salary was 220,000 francs plus the graft from the farmers general (practiced in broad daylight, as a regular custom) plus a hefty load of gifts from abroad: call it 300,000 francs a year in all.* It did indeed seem that "the profession was still respectable."

Calonne was appointed comptroller-general of finance on November 3, 1783, with the rank of minister and therefore with access to the "High Council," which had been stubbornly denied to Necker. After much calculation—the figures were a pretty mess—he estimated the annual deficit of the royal treasury at 80 million,† which makes a singular dent in the optimistic conclusions of Necker's famous *Compte rendu* of 1781; it would look as if Jacques had fiddled his last balance sheet after all, hoping to stave off disgrace. Plugging a hole like that was going to demand some fancy footwork. Not that Calonne was intimidated by the thought; only he hadn't the first idea how to go about it, and that was the very reason why Louis XVI, mortified after his experience with theorists like Turgot and Necker, had called in a good administrator who had not the ghost of a grand design and who would leave him alone. When Calonne took oath before the Chamber of Accounts, he promised to be a good boy, advocating "a plan for the general amelioration which, founded upon the constitution of the monarchy . . . will banish forever the thought of those empirical and violent remedies, the very memory of which must not be brought to mind."

Breteuil would obviously take kindly to such a tame treasurer. Vergennes had nothing against him, and had just quarreled with poor d'Ormesson, who had stuck his nose into the prime minister's money-making sideline in speculation on seigneurial rights in Lorraine, which he was judiciously selling off cheap to the Crown estates. The Queen was neutral; she didn't like to see a man put into any ministry—particularly the one that held the purse strings—who was not from her own stables, but the Polignacs had sung his praises to her so long and so loudly, too loudly even . . . she did not oppose Calonne, but he never becomes one of her men. So, beginning in late 1783, he has had time and space to breathe in. What has he done with it?

He has groped. He had a lot of trouble finding out what was really going on because he didn't put a team together quickly enough and because the budget

*More than 2 million modern francs [$500,000]. As *rapporteur* he got one-third that amount. The underlings in the office of the comptroller general received a uniform 1,200 livres a year, or 9,000 modern francs [$2,250].

†Or around 600 million modern francs [$150 million].

itself was in such a state of anarchy. "Good accounting, the queen of financial battles, was something the Ancien Régime never possessed."* Failing any bright ideas, however, he did at least have one panacea: keep the money moving. Tease it out of private savings, banks, and investment in far-off places. It is necessary "to spend money in order to attract it; to bring it in from without in order that the money kept hidden within by fear will emerge from the shadows; to adopt an outward appearance of abundance so that the extent of the need will not be perceived." Perhaps those words were the foundation of his reputation as a prestidigitator.

It was his misfortune to take office at the end of the American war. True, the peace treaty had been signed and France had gained by it, but the abyss of extraordinary expenditure, added to the bottomless sea of ordinary expenses (King's Household, pensions, debt amortization), was yawning ever wider at the feet of the budget. Far from reining back, Calonne is making brinksmanship an art, slithering down into the pit with grace—not out of cowardice or servility, but because he is convinced that spending money will beget money.

The avalanche mechanism is often the last resort of decaying societies, and there are plenty of people who can find no cause for complaint. The King's brothers still can't believe their eyes: almost the moment he took over, Calonne ordered the royal treasurer to pay the debts of the Comte d'Artois, some of whose creditors hadn't seen a penny in six years. There was an immediate payment of 4 million, followed in 1785 and 1786 by two more installments, each of about 3 million, and another 5,200,000 francs to round it off in 1787. As for Monsieur, whose debts were almost as great as Artois's despite the latter's prodigality and the miserliness of the former: in 1783 he gets 12 million (seven of them, it is true, were expedited by d'Ormesson before Calonne took office) and a number of "small" payments at intervals until 1786. Between 1783 and 1787 the King's two brothers receive 27 million livres in all.†

"Before the Revolution, a minister of finance might have best been compared to a tree infested by caterpillars, which the vile creatures would not quit until they had devoured it whole."[14] Whoever could have written that? Calonne himself, in 1790, three years after leaving office.

For the first years of his term, however, up till the present, i.e., 1786, everything seemed to be working like a charm. Heavily subsidized literary lights, especially Marmontel, adulated him. The princes of the blood (apart from the Orléanses) protected him. And as he had gratified certain survivors of the old Brittany dispute, a couplet was making the rounds:

*According to Robert Lacour-Gayet in his book on Calonne.
†Or about 200 million modern francs [$50 million].

Tout, jusqu'à la gent bretonne          [Everything, even the Breton
Aime Calonne                                          race,
Aime Calonne . . .                            Loves Calonne's face,
                                                       Loves Calonne's face . . . ]

TALLEYRAND

# 29

## FEBRUARY 1786

### *The True Pleasures of Life*

But he's about to have to put his money where his mouth is. However hard
he works for his millions, Charles-Alexandre de Calonne is not going to be
able to improvise forever. The treasury deficit is growing. Payments are being
delayed increasingly while paymasters juggle with budget subheads, shifting
money for the army to the pensions column and funds for maintenance of the
royal highways to the construction schemes in Paris and Cherbourg.[1] What
will happen when, in the not too far-distant future, we run out of money to
pay the soldiers and, even worse, their officers?

Instead of administering structural chaos on the principle of expediency
alone, we're going to have to reorganize a little. And therefore—with all due
caution, of course—we're going to have to pronounce the word "reform." To
bolster his courage, the comptroller general can now count on a "drawing-
room team" to cover him from attack on that front and conduct a sort of
high-society propaganda campaign in his favor.

"The Calonne set" . . . They meet in his house or in theirs or in those
of other people. They can be recognized by their hostility toward Necker,
the assurance with which they expatiate upon financial matters, and their
fondness for mixing together public and private affairs. Nobles—sometimes
of the highest lineage—grands bourgeois of commerce and banking, a few
senior functionaries in the ministry such as that young man from Rouen and
that other young man from Saint-Denis—Nicolas Mollien, son of a merchant, and Michel-Charles Gaudin, a lawyer's boy—whose precociousness
has already placed them in high positions. Mollien is responsible for inspecting movements of funds in the farmers-general division, and stands one
hundred percent behind Calonne, whom he sincerely admires; Gaudin is

more noncommittal on this point, and is director of a division in the tax department.*

Features in common: pragmatism and a profound mistrust of "ideologies," except for good old Dupont de Nemours, who turns out, rather surprisingly, also to be a member of the "set," more by function than affinity. Its most renowned exponents are the money manipulators Panchaud and Clavière, the latter having returned to Paris after his Genevan debacle. But there's also the Comte de Lauraguais, who's always on the lookout for money;† Lauzun, now kept at arm's length by the Queen but still dreaming of a major role in politics after his interlude in America; and two of his best friends, the Comte d'Antraigues and the Comte de Narbonne—the latter temporarily cross with the Neckers for refusing him their daughter;** and there is Abbé Louis, a young priest with more talent for speculation than for reading his breviary; and finally there's that other lame priest, the greatest seigneur of the lot, who has come a long way since we last saw him gloomily contemplating the coronation of Louis XVI and weeping tears of fury before his ordination: Abbé Charles-Maurice de Talleyrand-Périgord.

So—Talleyrand has become an intimate of M. de Calonne; and through Talleyrand, Mirabeau will come.

At the age of thirty-one the abbé has just had a son, by a twenty-four-year-old comtesse who is personable, attractive, an amateur harpsichordist, amateur poetess, and so forth. The tears of his definitive entrance into the clergy were soon dried. In this century, if you're rich you can survive being made a priest against your will, by treating yourself, for instance, to the joys and honor of paternity without any of its responsibilities. In 1779 Adélaïde-Emilie Filleul had taken it into her head to marry the Comte de Flahaut de la Billarderie, a general forty-six years her senior who had not proved capable, or so she swears, of consummating the union. Never mind; she was not likely to run short of consolers, and her reason for making such an undemanding marriage may well have been that it would leave her free to conduct her affairs unhindered. She had the hot blood of her mother, who had made a few visits to the Parc aux Cerfs before settling down with a farmer general. Emilie's older sister, allegedly a daughter of Louis XV, had married the Marquis de Marigny, Mme de Pompadour's brother, who had arranged the pretty new Elysée

---

*Mollien, in the treasury office, and Gaudin—made Duc de Gaète by Napoleon—become the pillars of finance during the Consulate and Empire.

†He was with Beaumarchais during the first London expedition in 1775.

**We will soon find them in three opposing parties: Lauzun violently revolutionary, Narbonne a moderate Royalist, and d'Antraigues an ultra-Royalist and spy for the émigrés. Abbé Louis becomes Louis XVIII's minister of finance.

Palace for her on the outskirts of Paris. Just the sort of milieu to intrigue Talleyrand.

Like many another, Emilie had become infatuated with the roguish, secretive abbé. "A manner I had of being cold, putting on a reserve, and it caused some people to consider me witty and profound." He can now hold his own in society; an agent general of the clergy is not peanuts. Since 1780 Talleyrand has been one of the two *de facto* ambassadors plying between the French clergy and the authorities in all matters relating to their financial disputes, which were many and thorny; in particular, there were the negotiations with the office of the comptroller general, i.e., Calonne, that terminated in the "free gift" or tax which the clergy voted to pay at every General Assembly; the conflicts with the parlements over the payment of the ecclesiastical taxes with which the clergy relined its pockets after emptying them into the King's coffers; and the fixing of tithes and pensions—all of which are subjects that interest Charles-Maurice passionately. "He already had the reputation of being a clever man; in this position he acquired that of being an able one."[2]

After his thwarted childhood, followed by his interminable adolescence in the seminary of Saint-Sulpice, where he was surrounded by the odor of waxed and incensed virtue and his one divertissement was an occasional quick flit to visit a kindhearted actress on the rue Férou, he is finally breathing free air and beginning to hanker for the high road to the great careers open to prelates of his ilk—a comfortable bishopric, a cardinal's hat, why not? and why not the comptroller general's office, and after that the "principal minister's" job that was the earthly paradise of political priests? "The memory of the Cardinal de Richelieu, whose impressive mausoleum stood in the Church of the Sorbonne, was not unedifying in this respect."[*]

As a name, Talleyrand-Périgord was worth as much as Rohan, and there is little likelihood that Charles-Maurice will ever get himself into the kind of mess in which poor Prince Louis is now floundering. "Then, too, I was in no hurry; I was learning things; I was traveling. . . . I had reputation enough, but by no means acquaintance enough of the world, and I caressed the idea that I had a few more years before me in which to let myself be drawn into all the eddies of society, without having to regulate my movements in the way that a more calculated ambition would require."[3]

Why should he rush? In addition to the services of four secretaries, his position as agent general of the clergy brought him an annual gratification of 30,000 livres,[†] not counting the income from the Abbey of Saint-Denis, which Louis XVI had granted him for life. Since he worked for the clergy as a body

---

[*]According to Talleyrand himself, who confesses to having spent many hours daydreaming in front of the monument in his student years.

[†]210,000 modern francs [$52,500].

he had no specific duties, apart from those of a fictitious vicar-generalship for his uncle the Archbishop of Rheims. The life he led was that of a young jet-set bachelor.

"Upon leaving the Sorbonne I found myself at last under the free and sole government of my own mind. I lived in Bellechasse [Mme de Genlis's neighbor, thus] in a convenient little house.* . . . My first task was to build up a library, which subsequently acquired great value by virtue of the choice of books, rarity of editions, and elegance of their bindings." This was the beginning of "a singular construction of all manner of books, sacred and profane, skeptical or atheistic and Christian or Orthodox; shelves laden with works both pious and frivolous, God and the world, Satan and politics."[4] Four years from now he will lend Gouverneur Morris, the new United States ambassador to Paris, a copy of the most notorious libertine book of the century, *L'Histoire de dom B. . . . , portier des Chartreux, écrite par lui-même* ["The story of the Carthusian porter Dom B . . . , as written by himself"— *Trans.*], which the upright American would not be likely to find on the booksellers' shelves in Philadelphia.[5]

"I sought the friendship of the most distinguished men, whether by virtue of their past life or their writings or their ambition, or of the future that was promised them by their birth, relations, or abilities. Thus placed, through my own efforts within the vast circle in which so many superior men shone so diversely, I permitted myself to indulge in the self-satisfied delight of being the beginning and end of my own existence."

Men only? He's not averse to the other sort, although the ladies' salons had become laboratories for opportunists rather than kingdoms of intellect.

> Every candidate for a ministry could command the doors of a few of the great houses of Paris, and determined the opinions and language of everyone frequenting it. . . . The supporters of M. de Calonne were to be found in the home of Mme de Polignac and the de Luynes house. The Bishop of Arras came to seek out M. Necker in the home of Mme de Blot† and M. de Castries. M. Joly de Fleury was championed by Mme de Brionne. The Baron de Breteuil was second in many houses but first in none. M. de Soubise was the protector of Foulon. Mme de la Reynière** was more or less in favor of everybody, except M. Necker.

It is now that Charles-Maurice begins cultivating his village-gossip side, thanks to which he always knows exactly what he needs to know, exactly when he needs to know it, about absolutely everybody.

*Little? Three stories plus a mezzanine with six windows facing the street. The house still exists, as numbers 9 and 11 of the present-day rue Saint-Dominique (in his day it was number 123).

†A lady-in-waiting of the Duchesse d'Orléans. The Bishop of Arras was the arch-conservative Hilaire de Conzié, born in 1732, much vaunted as an administrator.

**Wife of a farmer general.

I went pretty much everywhere, and, for a mind at all inclined to observation, the spectacle of high society was indeed a curious one.Everyone pretended to more than he was, so that no one was clearly anything any more. . . . Gaming and the artifice of wit had leveled all. . . . Every young man thought himself fit to govern. Every action of the ministers was criticized. What the King and Queen personally had done was subjected to scrutiny and almost always judged with disfavor by the Paris salons. Young women spoke with certain knowledge of every branch of administration.

In the pretty apartment in the Louvre procured for the Flahauts by their relative the Comte d'Angivillier, administrator of the King's buildings, Talleyrand had made himself so much at home that he set up some of his appointments there. And it was not just "administration" that he discussed with the young lady of the house. A stable and attractive mistress forms part of the panoply of a society abbé intent upon a career, especially when the woman regards the liaison as "a marriage of the heart." It's what was known as "settling down" in this class of society, after the age of thirty.

On April 21, 1785, Charles-Joseph de Flahaut is born;* his official father is good enough not to repudiate him. Only the "informed circles" of "Tout-Paris" know that the Abbé de Périgord is his real father. Nobody ever denies it and it is confirmed by physical resemblance and a sort of unofficial adoption.[6]

"No one who was not alive around 1789 can know the true pleasures of life."[7] On the threshold of old age Talleyrand makes his famous comment† to Guizot, the ultra-conservative minister of Louis-Philippe. It is a perfect description of his early adulthood and that of a handful of others. The archetype of the principle that pleasure equals money was evolved in that "little house" on the rue Saint-Dominique when, as morning drew to a close, "luncheon at Belle-chasse" brought together the "Talleyrand set," or "Calonne set"—the two merge into one as the minister becomes increasingly dependent on them. "Those were capital mornings, I should enjoy them again now," sighs Talleyrand in the melancholy of his later "success."

> My room, where we gathered every morning to find luncheon ready laid, presented a singular array: the Duc de Lauzun, Panchaud, Barthès [yes, the great physician come up from Montpellier], Abbé Delille, Mirabeau, Chamfort, Lauraguais, Dupont de Nemours, Rulhière, Choiseul-Gouffier, Louis de Nar-

---

*He becomes one of the more picturesque figures of nineteenth-century historical folklore, a general, aide-de-camp of Napoleon I, ambassador under Louis-Philippe, lover of Hortense de Beauharnais around 1810, and father of the Duc de Morny, who will mastermind the coup of December 2 for his half-brother Napoleon III.

†Reflected into infinity by the converging mirrors of right-wing historians, it has become almost a proverb today, implying that the reign of Louis XVI was a sort of Garden of Eden, desecrated by the barbarians of the Revolution.

bonne* all met there quite regularly, and always with pleasure. We talked of everything, and with total freedom. That was the spirit and fashion of the time. For us all, there was pleasure and edification to be derived, [but] in reality some little ambition in view as well. . . . The news of the day, questions of politics, commerce, administration, and finance all came by turns into the conversation.

The prophet of this little coterie is Isaac Panchaud. If he hadn't existed somebody would no doubt have invented him, to meet the need for an anti-Necker (of sorts). A Protestant banker—whence his biblical first name—and a great money manipulator who was not above sublimating his earnings with doctrine, a cosmopolitan in complete harmony with the atmosphere of his day, born in Geneva of a Swiss father and Dutch mother but having acquired British nationality as a commodity although he was "French by temperament," he became attached, somewhat loosely, to the comptroller general's office after Necker was dismissed from it, with the vague title of "counselor" and a salary of 18,000 livres a year.† His financial expanse is substantially smaller than that of his abhorred alter ego, and his breadth of mind and heart still less comparable; when he concerns himself with politics it is usually to justify the reigning authorities. But he is an incarnation of the New Man in whom Talleyrand was dimly hoping to find a savior, the prophet of the promised land of speculation. How else can one explain the positive paean of praise sung to him by this otherwise icy character in his *Mémoires:*

> M. Panchaud was an extraordinary man: he possessed all at once the most ardent, wide-ranging, and energetic mind, and flawless powers of reasoning. He had eloquence of every form. If genius is the product of the faculties of feeling and thought abundantly and equally imparted to a single individual, then Panchaud was a man of genius.

Gee, is that all? Mollien, who shows considerable common sense for his age and who knew Panchaud at the office several years before Talleyrand met him, deflates the soufflé a little but also makes it clear that the man was not a nonentity:

> I also met a few of the adversaries of M. Necker. The one by whom I was most struck was a Swiss named Penchaud [*sic*], who had spent many years in England. He had set up a banking house in Paris but had little to do with it; he was familiar

*We have seen most of them already, and will soon become acquainted with Chamfort. Choiseul-Gouffier, a nephew of the great minister, becomes ambassador to Constantinople in 1786, and Rulhière is a diplomat and author, best known for his account of Catherine II's coup d'état.

†About 130,000 modern francs [$32,500]—chicken feed in comparison with his income from other sources. I should explain that the reason why I am spending so much time on this (very) small group is that in it we touch the groundwater of finance and speculation that will break surface in 1794 after 9 Thermidor and on 18 Brumaire; with it, money first moves into position as pretender to the government.

with every form of speculation on the markets of London and Amsterdam; he had made a great deal of money and often lost even more; he considered the Paris market too small for his activities, but he had founded a sort of school and a few of those who attended it looked upon him as their master. All hoped to learn in it the high science of finance. . . . One saw courtiers there, abbés, new magistrates. . . . Panchaud had a kind of captivating eloquence and never used it to better effect than when speaking against Necker. . . . One was always imagining that in his definitions one had found the solution to all the great problems, so exact and at the same time so luminous did they seem; and as he habitually attached every discussion to his system of criticism of M. Necker, and as in this way he satisfied a personal sentiment in almost all he said or wrote, one never felt, with him, the weakness of a man seeking to indoctrinate.[8]

As long as it's only talk, and preferably at Necker's expense, this consortium of arrant egotists can believe themselves sincerely bound by ties of friendship. But what will happen to them under fire, in the great ordeal of steady work, by which Talleyrand is already so badly scared?

The intrusion of a new element helps to shatter the overrefined porcelain of "Calonne's set" before he ever gets a chance to use it. Mirabeau joins, bright-eyed and bushy-tailed as ever at first but quickly disenchanted—the spoil-speculator, the "count of storms." He's just back from London and fresh out of momentum again. Clavière, still banished from Geneva, has settled in Paris and Mirabeau grabs hold of his apron strings. For reasons of business and ambition, Clavière is on Panchaud's side against Necker. He introduces Mirabeau to Panchaud, who is immediately suspicious of the big windbag:

"Nobody can speak as well as he on matters of which he knows nothing."[9]

Mirabeau, on the contrary, is dazzled. He says Panchaud has "the gaze of an eagle" and the banker-prophet becomes his latest crush. In his home and that of Talleyrand, whom he feels he's known all his life, he finds one old friend, Lauzun (they were pals during the conquest of Corsica), and makes some new ones, and he also gets his first real chance in a long time: Panchaud or Talleyrand, or both together, introduce him to Calonne just when the minister is looking for some strong-winded polemicists to influence public opinion. Through Clavière he can already count on Brissot, but Brissot's a commoner and unknown. A Mirabeau is something else again, especially since the Aix trial has made him notorious.

The alliance is concluded in the spring of 1785. Calonne plus Talleyrand plus Clavière plus Brissot . . . Playboys of the Western world, unite! Who knows how much you have to lose?

# 30

## JANUARY 1786

## *This Time He Was Not Traveling as a Fugitive*

And that is how Honoré de Mirabeau* finds himself back on the road, from Paris to Berlin in mid-winter, arriving on January 19, 1786. Now, after Switzerland, Holland, and England, it's Prussia's turn; and for once he has a little money and the police are not on his tail. Does this mean an official mission? Not so fast; not even an unofficial one. But after thirty years of dead-end leads on the outskirts of the maze, he's finally found the one that goes somewhere. The bulk of the—still sparse—coins clinking in his purse have been remitted to him on Calonne's instructions. If he's not actually being sent to the Court of Prussia he's at least being a little better than tolerated there, and is hoping to warm up the comfortable seat (as observer–secret agent–*éminence grise* à la Beaumarchais or d'Eon) he's had his eye on ever since his release from Vincennes.

Frederick II, still alive but only just, writes to his brother Prince Henry on January 25: "We have here a M. de Mirabeau whom I do not know. He is to call on me today. So far as I can make out, he is one of those effeminate satyrists [*sic*—the King's French is somewhat eccentric] who write for and against everybody. He is said to be on his way to seek refuge in Russia, where he can publish his sarcasms against his native country without fear of reprisal."[1]

That same day the Comte d'Esterno, French ambassador to Berlin, who is better informed and has been dreading this awkward arrival, writes to Vergennes: "We have here the Comte de Mirabeau, the author of so many pamphlets! I believe he means to settle in Berlin in order to print whatever he pleases without let or hindrance, and if this is his plan he could have chosen no better place in which to carry it out, for so long as he says nothing good

---

*Recap: His full name is Gabriel-Honoré. Sophie de Monnier was the only person to call him Gabriel. On bad terms with his father since the Aix trial, and on no terms at all with his mother, he has vainly tried to make his mark as a polemicist in England before returning to France, where he is partly living by his pen, and finally signing his own name. He has just exchanged blows with Beaumarchais over the financing of the Paris water board.

about the Court of Vienna he can most assuredly say all the evil he likes about God, his saints, and every other king on earth, not excepting the King of Prussia!"[2]

Following in the wake of Voltaire and Diderot, accompanied by less fame but more cynicism, or honesty, than they, Mirabeau takes his turn on the highroad of northern Europe. One possible terminus, it's true, is St. Petersburg, to offer himself to the tsarina. But only if nobody waylays him in Berlin, using the one bait he is sure to swallow these days: Mirabeau is for sale, as openly as if he had a label stuck on his chest, and he's not going to haggle over the price. In his present need, the first buyer to make an offer wins the lot.

He was lucky to get Calonne (with Talleyrand and one or two others) to shoulder the cost of transporting this aristocratic derelict, who has become one of his friends' thirstiest leeches, not least because he's incapable of traveling in anything smaller than a sort of semi-coach with a full complement of inmates, "my horde" as he calls them: one woman, two servants, a little boy of four, and a dog.*

Crack your whip, coachman! (The four horses and their drivers were furnished by the regular posting stations, as they were for almost all travelers, even princely ones.) You are about to turn a decisive page in Mirabeau's life, the one on which he becomes a fringe member of the world of high politics.

One of the servants—the man, the one who rides ahead on a nag to order the changes of horses—is Aimé Legrain, life-and-death valet and buddy since 1781, a character worthy of Figaro, who had assimilated his master's habits so thoroughly way back in Pontarlier that he struck one of the judges there in the face with a whip.† As handy as ever with a wench, Legrain is on the best possible terms with the other servant, Henriette, the "lady's" maid. That makes two women in the coach. The child is Jean-Marie-Nicolas, called Gabriel and, even oftener, Coco. He's not yet four and already behaves like the little man who knows it all.

Mirabeau wasn't going to be able to avoid this kind of fallout forever: the delectable infant has only two traits in common with him, the effervescent head of hair and the inimitable aplomb, but he's indubitably his son, although the sculptor Lucas de Montigny had no choice but to give the baby his own name

---

*Whose name (the dog's), to my eternal remorse—unless some reader can save me—I have been unable to discover, despite a solid half-day of research. Mirabeau seems to have had several dogs, because Henriette de Nehra speaks at one point of "his favorite dog."

†Legrain was hired when Mirabeau came out of Vincennes; he was promised bed, board, clothes and livery, plus 200 livres a year (about 1,500 modern francs [$375]), which he almost never saw.

when his accommodating wife gave birth in 1782, nine months after Mirabeau came to their home to pose for a bust.*

It was not, apparently, the last straw for Mirabeau thus to find himself at the head of a "family." He's fond of Coco; he's always been fond of children —his own, although he never got any joy out of them (the two that were dead, Emilie's son and Sophie's little girl), and those of other people too. And in the general collapse of his inner tower of Babel one whole wall of honor was left standing, the one he inherited from his father: breeding and blood, even when filtered through a bar sinister, were still sacred. He took on little de Montigny as he had often taken on unforeseeable heights and depths before, philosophically, goodnaturedly. One begins to understand the real attraction of this extraordinarily ugly man when one understands that his kindness is not feigned, on the rare occasions when he can afford to show it.

But what about the logistics? At first, he improvised, thanks to the eternal presence of mind of Legrain, who recruited wetnurses while the boy was a baby. The problem could have become serious later, when Coco, suffering from the absence of any stable affection, began to need a real mother with a loving face. After Sophie this seemed pretty unlikely: the women Mirabeau had been devouring since Vincennes, of all classes and ages as long as they were willing, may have had innumerable qualities, but motherliness was not one of them. Besides, he never stuck to one for long.

Then, in 1782, the miracle occurred. The lady on the trip to Berlin is love resurrected. You could call her his "third wife"—possibly the prettiest, very probably the gentlest, and assuredly the most courageous.

Introducing Yet-Lie.

What a guy! How many chances he's had, and squandered! Yet-Lie is the nickname he gave to Henriette-Amélie Van Haren by sticking together the ends of her first names. She is Holland, with all the quiet loveliness of the primitive painters. When Yet-Lie was eleven,† Mirabeau was in her country trying to bring off the impossible feat of persecuted love, Amsterdam, Sophie . . . who knows what part his Amsterdam nostalgia played in this new affair?

> I have a companion to share my fate, a gentle, sweet, good companion whose beauty would infallibly have brought her riches if her excellent moral qualities had not refused them. . . . My companion is beautiful, gentle, kind, even-tempered, courageous, filled with an endearing sensibility that enables one to bear all, even the evils it produces. . . . You will see her angelic features, her penetrat-

*The head, full of vitality, is "one of the best likenesses of Mirabeau in his early thirties," according to the Duc de Castries; it is in the Arbaud Museum in Aix-en-Provence. Montigny remains loyal to Mirabeau and, in 1834, publishes a series of fascinating texts wrongfully called *Mémoires de* [*by*] *Mirabeau,* which are in fact a labor of filial love.

†"Mme de Nehra" was born on May 15, 1765.

ing sweetness, the magical allure that surrounds her. . . . I swear to you, my friend,* I swear by all that is sincere in my soul, that I do not deserve her and that in its tenderness, its delicacy and goodness, her soul is of a higher order."[3]

For once in his life Mirabeau is not exaggerating. This girl really is a peach, a fair flower planted by chance at a crossroads of history, who makes everybody else feel ashamed of themselves without even trying. Honoré, as befits an accomplished libertine, has always been attracted to angel-faced women whose calm waters he could muddy but from whom, at the same time, he could also receive that draft of purity for which Don Juans are always so parched. Like Sophie, Yet-Lie was a virgin when she met him. He could hardly have hoped for such another fountain of youth.

He met her through a former mistress, the Marquise de Saint-Orens, the reheated leftovers of a dish he had partaken of in its prime at Les Saintes, his first garrison, in 1766. She's still diabolically good-looking, and is now rich in experience as well, acquired at the expense of a dyspeptic husband who was as jealous as Georges Dandin.† To add spice to the situation, he had also lived a few weeks of mad passion with her younger sister, Jeanne de La Tour-Boulieu—another smooth skin on which to engrave the first wrinkle—in the summer of 1776, when he was trying to escape the King's men like a big bumblebee knocking against windowpanes, and making up his mind to abduct Sophie. On that occasion he took refuge in the La Tour-Boulieus' château at La Balme in Dauphiné, only to find there, in addition to Jeanne and himself, his own sister, the passionate Louise de Cabris, and her cicisbeo, the Chevalier de Briançon. Incest and orgy. How time flies . . . Eight years later he went back to La Balme, this time with the older La Tour-Boulieu, but the jealous husband pursued them, forced them to return to Paris, and commanded them not to see each other again. To arrange a few furtive meetings notwithstand-ing, and in the most respectable guise possible, Mme de Saint-Orens trans-ferred her unsaintly activities to the home of virtue personified, the Convent of the Petites Orphelines!—where the sisters took in, "on lease," orphaned or abandoned or illegitimate girls or women "of good background" and lodged them in small private apartments. One of the inmates was a childhood friend of the younger La Tour-Boulieu: Henriette-Amélie Van Haren, the natural daughter of an important Dutch politician, who was also something of a poet and author and a bit of a nut, who had "democratic" notions and had stirred up quite a storm in his country during the first part of the century before committing suicide, bankrupt, in 1768. Three years before that he had had, after various bastards, a daughter by Henriette-Amélie Dufour, a French-

---

*The friend is Chamfort, one of the best writers of the day. For this romance Mirabeau had the most clear-headed and least conventional witness of the century.
†Hero of Molière's play of that name.

woman of obscure origin who was said to have been a "nymph from the Palais Royal who had gone north." All that has remained of her is her name, passed on to the little girl who was half-legitimized by an anagram of her father's name. In 1779, when she was deposited in the Convent of the Petites Orphelines following the death of a paternal uncle who had brought her up as a nobleman's child in the stern climate of Friesland but in the French manner, Henriette-Amélie Van Haren became "Mme de Nehra." Thanks to a pension salvaged from the paternal disaster, she pays the nuns well and in cash.

She was not asking for anything, she wasn't complaining, she was just living there holding no grudges against anyone, not even God, for her shriveled existence, when one day the Marquise de Saint-Orens asked to share her rooms, and also asked permission to entertain a lover in them. For Henriette, at nineteen, this was a stellar collision. Saint-Orens was in every respect her opposite, all frills and furbelows, gusto and avid sensuality. And when Henriette first set eyes on the "seducer" whose accomplice she was being made, "I found his features unspeakably off-putting. I drew back in fright."[4] But not for long; the moment she heard those golden tones, the moment that velvet voice swung into the perennial self-justification that had served him so well before, she was lost. He, naturally, was on fire in the instant at the sight of "that slender, deceptively fragile figure, the long, pure, oval face, fine, regular features, a mass of ash blond hair with golden glints dying in its depths, long, bright blue eyes made darker by pale, transparent skin"[5]—happiness in gold and white. Mme de Saint-Orens gets no less than she deserves; that'll teach her to go making love in a convent. When she saw what Honoré was up to, and it didn't take her long, she had enough pride to walk out on both of them without further ado.

Was Henriette attracted to Mirabeau in the same way as Sophie de Monnier? Undoubtedly not. Yet-Lie is intelligent, clear-eyed, and frigid. Her childhood and youth had repressed her capacity for passion. He won her with pity, and he kept her out of kindness—toward her and the little Montigny boy. She explains how it all came about herself,* with a simplicity and dignity that show clearly the kind of person she was:

> I met Monsieur de Mirabeau at the beginning of 1784. All the dangers of persecution and all the woes of destitution were hanging over his head, he had quarreled with his entire family, not one soul was offering him the least assistance, not one friend the slightest consolation. He then attached himself to me with all the fervor so typical of him and, although I sensed very clearly that he was not precisely the man my heart required, I began to sympathize with him in his misfortune, I believed he was born for a better fate, and that with the power I had over his heart

*In a "relation" or account written twenty years later, for an unidentified "former friend" of Mirabeau.

I might succeed in calming the violence of his passions. I should have preferred to remain no more than a friend; people had long since assumed we were united when I was still hesitating; but friendship, and the tenderness born of compassion, caused me to yield. In me these feelings took the place of love; he was often grateful to me, but unfortunately the gentler emotions were not always enough for him.[6]

She duly took charge of the two wild animals, Mirabeau and Coco. It's a little late to do much with the father, and she knows it. But she committed herself to something like the Protestant marriage oath, when she promised "to exist only for him, in good fortune as in bad."[7] Elsewhere she says, "I was all he had left, and I wanted to take the place of everything else." As for little Montigny, she saved at least as much as his life—she saved his sanity. At three years of age he could hardly walk, could not talk at all, and sank his teeth into any friendly hand. Mirabeau despaired: "The soul of this infant is ferocious . . ." By 1786 he is "terrifyingly clever," he is pretty, he's happy with his adoptive mother, and as secure in their improvised household as though it were going to last forever. Mirabeau raves: "You are the first woman to get through to him. With your system of education, he will become more lovable every day."

What system? Tenderness and patience; it's so simple.

They have now been together for two years, and they've already had their fair share of adventures, with Yet-Lie sponging away the sweat of misery and anxiety. This one takes them farther afield, all the way to Prussia, and she gives, in her placid manner, a clear account of it, including one curious incident:

We set out on December 23, 1785. It was intensely cold, but weather never stopped us. Between Toul and Verdun we were in great danger: were the men assassins? We never knew, but they were certainly not robbers.* I offer no interpretation of the event but simply relate it. It was eleven in the evening and the carriage windows were down, despite the snow; everyone inside was asleep except myself. Suddenly a pistol was fired into the coach, which was rolling at a good pace; I moved to wake up the count, saying,

"My friend, someone is firing on us!"

At that very instant, two more shots were fired almost simultaneously; a ball came through, dented the coach, and fell. There is no doubt that the movement I made, and that of M. de Mirabeau as he awoke, prevented either of us from

---

*On the contrary, they almost certainly were. Roads were never quite safe at night, especially near the frontiers, where deserters from the armies formed into bands to prey on travelers. In this text it would seem that Mirabeau may have transmitted a little of his own paranoia to Yet-Lie, because although his pamphlets may have made him enemies, none of them was out for blood.

being injured. These were certainly not robbers, but nor were they practiced assassins. This event remains one of those about which one can only conjecture. The postilion took the wisest course, which was, without waiting to find out whether we were injured or not, to gallop headlong to the next post, only a short distance away. There we found the manservant, who, riding on ahead, had seen nothing but who heard the shots and was calmly telling the tale while waiting for us to come up. The postilion refused to go back over the same road. We had difficulty persuading him that it was not him the people were after, and that as we had been attacked once there would be no second attack, because it was probable that we would report the incident. We continued on our way, only being careful not to sleep anymore. Everyone was very brave, even the poor little boy, although he was not yet four.[8]

Following the usual custom, and to save the cost of rooms, they travel day and night and recover from their exhaustion by making a few long stopovers on one of the fastest roads from Paris to Berlin. Lorraine, the Rhineland principalities, Hesse, northern Saxony, and Prussia: a tangle of customs and currencies in the posting stations across half of Germany, a land that in those days belonged now to some mini-sovereigns, now to the emperor, and now to the King of Prussia: it was like some exceptionally complicated form of solitaire.

In certain seasons, and in snowy or rainy weather [which is what the little "horde" are having] one is often forced to leave the ordinary road, and it is not surprising that the post-masters should try to make up for what they lose in this way, by insisting that travelers take on more horses than the weight of their vehicle requires. When the traveler reaches a post where the roads are better and there is no longer any need for these supplementary horses, the post-master is seldom reasonable enough to give him only as many as he wants, so that he is often obliged to continue his journey with more horses than he has need of; this makes a considerable addition to the expenditure.[9]

Will they have enough gold left—the only kind of money that everybody takes—to change their louis into fredericks (also gold), thalers, and florins when they get to Berlin? Yet-Lie, who keeps a firm hold on the purse strings, is not feeling overoptimistic but Honoré, as usual when he takes a trip, is bubbling over with schemes and has already started building castles in Prussia. Just let him get within earshot of Frederick; he'll seduce him, as he believes he has bewitched Calonne.

After forty-four posts, "we stopped a few days in Nancy," the town that had been renovated for King Stanislas, with its white and gold royal square —one of the most beautiful in Europe—where a bronze Louis XV presides over the wrought-iron gates that set him off like a precious bracelet. The inn there is the "Petit Paris." Meetings with the Freemasons of the "St. John of Jerusalem" lodge. Then on to the "Black Goat" in Frankfurt, the big city in the Main valley where emperors used to be elected (until Maria Theresa);

40,000 inhabitants—"7,000 of whom are Jews," add contemporary travel guides—"a rich town, imperialistic, Hanseatic, full of trade," and with no official overlord. "The government is in the hands of a few families which are called patrician; the choice of the particular individuals who will perform the various tasks, however, is made by the corporation guilds, so that this is an aristo-democratic government."[10]

Another forty-two and a half posts from Frankfurt to Leipzig, still in Saxony but on the edge of Prussia. Perhaps the most lively, the most animated town in Germany, as important a center in the north as Munich in the south: braid, velvet and silks, fairs, mountebanks, rope-dancers, scores of bookseller-publishers, the Society of Concord, the Thursday Society, the Society of the Sixteen, and the Society of the Twenty-One, but most of all, the old university and the *Kaffegarten,* the cellars of the "Italian restaurants, which are something like shops for food" . . . Here they discover a tranquil Germany alive with people, industrious, curious, full of that Saxon bonhomie with which Mirabeau so quickly feels at home. The party stay at the Bavarian Hotel, where the clientele is predominantly French. They hire a gondola—that's right, a gondola—from the fishers of the Ranstedterallee, for a cruise on the three rivers that converge here. "In this last town, M. de Mirabeau associated with savants and made useful acquaintances. This time he was not traveling as a fugitive."[11]

Only twenty-four posts to go, over an increasingly sandy roadbed. The great forests of Dessau, so conveniently squared off for stag hunting. The first Prussian customshouse, where their baggage is more closely inspected than before. Potsdam—Frederick's Versailles—where you pay double for each post and, in return, can clatter down a fine paved road to Berlin in less than three hours. The mecca of *philosophes.* Life's first concession to Mirabeau, who steps out of his coach there on January 19.

FREDERICK II OF PRUSSIA

# 31

## FEBRUARY 1786

## *The Most Beautiful Eyes I Ever Saw*

Unwittingly, La Fayette and Mirabeau have just crossed paths for the first time. When Honoré descended upon Berlin seeking his fortune, Gilbert was on his way back from a visit to Prussia and Austria; all he was seeking were honors

and they came to meet him, but in moderation, far less noisily than two years
before in America, where his triumph had gone to his head. By comparison,
the Old World was a little lukewarm.

He was making his "grand tour," the culmination and conclusion of the
education of all young gentlemen; for him it had begun so long ago and far
away, in the wake of Christopher Columbus. Older than most grand tourists,
Squirrel La Fayette was trying to pretend he wasn't bored as he trotted round
the European cage that had grown too small for him. He even manages to
sound quite pleased when, on February 8, 1786, he writes a lengthy account
of his trip to his daddy, Washington.

"My summer was spent looking at princes, soldiers and post-horses,
. . . going through Kassel, Brunswick, Berlin, Breslau, Vienna, Prague, Dres-
den, and Potsdam"[1] . . . where, six months before Mirabeau, he called on the
grand old man:

> I went to pay my court to the King; and in spite of all I had heard about him I
> was nevertheless struck by his dress and features, which are those of an aged, dirty,
> decrepit corporal littered with Spanish *tomabbo,* * his head so bent that it almost
> touches one shoulder and his fingers nearly dislocated by gout. What surprised
> me even more, however, was the fire, and sometimes the gentleness, in the most
> beautiful eyes I ever saw, which impart to his physiognomy an expression as
> appealing as it can be stern and threatening at the head of his army.

Frederick II, King of Prussia, Margrave of Brandenburg, Arch-Chamber-
lain and Elector of the Holy Roman Empire, Sovereign Prince of Orange,
Neuchâtel, Duke of Magdeburg, Cleves, etc. (eight other duchies), Burgrave
of Nuremberg, Prince of Halberstadt, Minden, etc. (five other principalities),
Count of Hohenzollern, Ruppin, etc. (eight other counties), Marquis of the
Vehre and Flushing, Seigneur (or Baron, they're the same) of Ravenstein,
Rostock, and so many other places that nobody can even count them. A king
of sand and endless fir forests, lost in the unproductive land between the Elbe
and the Baltic; like his father and grandfather before him, he was the shrewdest
manager and estate-builder in the world, piecing together a patchwork quilt
of an empire, a scattering of crumbs from the Niemen to Switzerland and the
banks of the Rhine. "They called him *the King of Prussia,* but the length and
diversity of the list of his titles reflect a complicated history of conquests,
inheritances, conversion of church land, hard-driven business deals, coloniza-
tion, and internal family transactions."†

To tour his possessions without ever setting foot on foreign soil he'd have
to travel by balloon. But for years now he had been curled up motionless in

---

*Perfumed snuff which Frederick II took so often and sloppily that he was covered with it
from head to foot. In 1786 the King of Prussia is seventy-four years old.
   †From Pierre Gaxotte's preface to *Frédéric II, roi de Prusse.*

his armchair in Potsdam, after smashing china all over Europe in his earlier days and imposing the image of himself—thanks to the army, an exclusive creation of his father, the "Sergeant King"—as a generalissimo, a darling of the gods of war, a sort of half-peasant Caesar who kept blundering across his neighbors' boundaries. In the hard year of 1740, when they both came to their thrones, he wrenched Silesia from the grasp of his great enemy Maria Theresa and set in motion the pendulum of wins and losses that swung as high on one side as on the other. Siege, capture, and abandon of Prague. Alliance with the French, but rout of the Maréchal de Broglie; then a switch of allegiances, initiated by Frederick and his often justified fear of being encircled, with the pact between Prussia and England precipitating the pact between Paris and Vienna. In fact, if Marie Antoinette is reigning in Versailles now, the fault is primarily his; but he doesn't care two hoots anymore, having made up his quarrels with everybody—on the surface, anyway.

The peace and quiet of his later years cost him plenty, though, and they cost thousands of casualties even more. That was quite a cyclone, the Seven Years' War in the middle of the century, and what suspense! 1756: the Prussians beat the Austrians. 1757: they have another try at Prague and are beaten in turn. Then they come home again and get trounced by the Russians but give a memorable thrashing, at Rossbach, to the troops of the Maréchal de Soubise (the Rohan clan chieftain) and then turn back on Prince Charles's Austrians to beat his 90,000 men. 1758: they beat the Russians. 1759: they get beaten by the Russians. 1760: two months after losing to the Austrians, they even up the score with them, but the Russians catch them with their backs turned and occupy Berlin in October—the King of Prussia without a capital, for a few months he becomes history's hunted man, Finished Frederick at the end of his rope, the rats are quitting his court, his own generals are conspiring against him, the enemy powers are planning the partition of Prussia. He holds out. He digs in. When he beats the Austrian Marshal Daun at Torgau, only 600 grenadiers are left alive of the 6,000 he sent into battle. But 20,000 of Maria Theresa's men are picked up dead off the field.*

"Ah, the devil of it, inglorious glory, villages burned, whole towns in ashes, thousands of men dispossessed and thousands more massacred, horrors on every side, end it all oneself, let's not talk about it anymore, it makes my hair stand on end. . . . Can you conceive that anyone should want, at the price of the life I lead, to be a King of Prussia so beleaguered and beset as this?"[2] he confided (on April 27, 1758) to Henri de Catt, one of his few, so few friends, and the ones he did have never stayed friends for long. But what the

---

*At the end of the Second World War, Hitler and the other Nazi leaders were haunted by Frederick's grim-death obstinacy. In Goebbel's last notebooks, January–March 1945, the determination to "hold out like Frederick," until destiny can make its miraculous about-face, is referred to no fewer than six times.

hell, "our birth determines our condition. . . . We are obliged to bear the yoke fate lays upon us. . . . Grumbling and revolt are contrary to the laws of the universe. . . . Anyone who is unable to endure bad fortune does not deserve the other kind."[3] The only religion this Prussian knows is Oriental fatalism; whence his tolerance, or indifference if you prefer: "I treat men with kindness, I proffer my humanity impartially to all of my species, of whatever religion and of whatever society they may be.* I assure you, we ought to practice philosophy more and metaphysics less."[4]

1761: The sole aim of Frederick's movements this year was to avoid battle, nobody would give a plugged thaler for his chances, the monarchy of the Hohenzollerns was about to crumple under the blows of two females, the Empress Maria Theresa and the Tsarina Elisabeth; but on January 5, 1762, the latter, the old baba, grandmother of all the Russias, dies and is succeeded by the mad Tsar Peter III, who is German to his very toenails and swears by his friend and god—Frederick, with whom he concludes not just a peace but an alliance as well. Prussia held out the quarter of an hour she had to.

Leaving Austria no choice but to conclude peace too, in 1763, while back there in the west England was bringing France to her knees. End of the Seven Years' War. Frederick retires from the battlefield at fifty, already completely crippled by gout, an old man. Now comes the time for music and philosophy. He is a hereditary Calvinist, ruling, from Potsdam, over a Lutheran people; he's like a little pope of Protestant Europe except that he doesn't persecute Roman Catholics, and at the same time he becomes a sort of Messiah for atheists. In his increasingly lumpy, bumpy armchair, which he occasionally leaves, until the very end, to hunch himself onto a horse and review his troops, he remains the master of the miracle war even though he plays the flute every evening at six, "to assist his digestion"; and he keeps his arms, or rather his army, well polished and oiled so that the world's respect will continue to call it, as it has done for the past thirty years (it's an article of faith), the foremost army in the world.

In 1786, for a bare six million inhabitants, Prussia has 200,000 soldiers —as many as France. It is the only country on earth in which military service is compulsory for every able-bodied man between the ages of twenty and forty, all of whom put in regular periods of service in rotation. "All subjects are born to bear arms and bound to the regiment of the district of their birth.† At the

---

*The word "society" has a very particular meaning here; the passage is from a letter which Frederick wrote to d'Alembert, who was reproaching him for letting in the Jesuits ("Society of Jesus"), as Catherine had also done, and protecting them after their banishment by the Roman Catholic sovereigns.

†According to the regulation of 1753, decreed by Frederick William I, the "Sergeant King."

birth of every male child the pastor baptizing him shall declare him to the authorities and he shall be entered on the military roll at once."[5]

La Fayette's tour included the Prussian army as well as the King of Prussia, as though they were a matching pair of monuments. "I have been to Silesia [from the same letter to Washington] where he [Frederick] was inspecting an army of thirty-one battalions and seventy-five squadrons, totaling 30,000 men in all, 7,500 on horseback. For a week I sat with him at three-hour dinners." And he's off again, the overgrown Boy Scout of Two Worlds who can't resist scoring off a fellow troop member. "The conversation closed between the Duke of York,* the king and myself and two or three others," including dear Lord Cornwallis, small world isn't it, how nice for us all to meet together, victors and vanquished, and drink the healths of the men we kill here, there, and everywhere, Yorktown on this occasion, where Cornwallis surrendered to Rochambeau and Washington, the real conqueror of the English, less than four years ago. In the second row, already relegated to the background, stood La Fayette with his collar as stiff as he could make it, and he's doing the same thing today. "Lord Cornwallis happening to be present, the king took care to seat him by me at table, having on the other side the son of the King of England, and to ply me with questions on American matters."

Poor Gilbert refrains from telling Washington that at the end he got his knuckles rapped like a schoolboy. Far from "plying" him with questions about the Insurgents in America, Frederick was virtually barking with rage at the thought of what was going on across the ocean, and would have called it the devil's work if he had believed in the devil. When La Fayette broke into his usual hymn of praise of the United States, "most energetically maintaining that they would never have either nobility or royalty," the old king roused himself from his habitual torpor and let him have one between the eyes:

"Sir, I knew a young man who, after visiting countries in which liberty and equality reigned supreme, took it into his head to establish the same thing in his own land. Do you know what happened to him?"

"No, Sire."

"Sir, he was hanged."[6]

Whom did he mean? Maybe it was just a parable. And he's not the only "reforming" ruler to lose his cool when he hears the word "republic." On that point he plays in a trio with Catherine the Great and Joseph II, who receives La Fayette in more or less the same tone a few days later: "My stay in Vienna was short;† but I had a very long talk with the emperor, during which we spoke

---

*George III's second son, whom Frederick, who did not like to miss an opportunity to give foreigners an eyeful of his military potential, had invited, along with various lesser lords, to watch the maneuvers.

†This time he's writing to John Jay, the United States ambassador in London.

at length of American trade, and I found him greatly imbued with the British prejudices."[7] So La Fayette isn't having much luck with the sovereigns, in his self-appointed mission as salesman extraordinary for the United States or itinerant ambassador of human rights. What does he care; he's been seen and entertained, and is certain, as so often, that he has also been understood. "I re-established the truth on an infinity of matters. I found the King of Prussia, the emperor, and the important men in both countries either ill-informed or informed by people who were leading them on a false track."

He returns to France, twenty-nine years old, with his head in a whirl of schemes, certain that his true vocation is to overturn the established order. His technique is that of the billy goat, butting in all directions. He already sees himself as liberator of the Protestants, who have been governed by the whims of royal (and royally delegated) prerogative since the revocation of the Edict of Nantes and in whose cause his American and French friends had interested him some months before. He is about to resume the fact-finding tour he began last year on their behalf. Where has it gotten him to have fought for the Virginia planters if people in la Rochelle or Nîmes are still being treated like an inferior species?

> The Protestants in France* are subjected to intolerable despotism. Although there is no overt persecution at present, they are dependent upon the whim of the King, Queen, parlement, or some minister. Their marriages are not legal; their wills have no force of law; their children are regarded as bastards and themselves as fit only to be hanged.† I should like to bring about some change in their situation. For this purpose I am going, under various pretexts and with the consent of M. de Castries and another person,** to visit their chief places of residence. I shall then try to obtain the support of M. de Vergennes and the parlement, with that of the keeper of the seals, who acts as chancellor. This is a task which requires time and is not without some inconvenience for me since no one would give me anything in writing or speak out on behalf of anything. I shall take my chance. M. de Castries could do no more than agree to keep the matter secret, as it is not in his department[8]

—obviously the RPRs (*Religionnaires Prétendus Réformés,* or Protestants) did not come under the Ministry of the Navy but under that of the King's Household, which meant the adamantine Breteuil. The Maréchal de Castries, however, as chief lord of Languedoc, where he followed a policy of broad tolerance, had numerous public and private contacts with the Protestant authorities and would have liked nothing better than to further La Fayette's project.

Our lad, thus, is about to follow up his trip to central Europe with a little trek round France, sticking his nose into whatever he can in order to allay the

---

*From another letter to Washington.

†Hanging was by definition an ignominious form of execution.

**Probably Malesherbes, who retained some hidden influence over the magistracy.

pangs of his growing discomfort—the result of his reaching the full force of adulthood in an icebound land after breaking so much new ground in his earlier years. He continues to spend his huge fortune by the bucket and barrel; money doesn't count so long as he can accomplish something for men, or Man. He has just bought, "in the colony of Cayenne," a plantation costing 125,000 livres,* whose slaves he is going to try to free. And he's knocking himself out trying to secure favorable trade rights for American ships in the largest possible number of French ports. In a sense, he's "double-tracking" Jefferson, and Americans in France and Philadelphia alike are still a little dazed by his zeal. From afar, on the subject of slavery, Washington advocates patience, just as he did six years before when the young general was racing toward the cannon fire:

> The goodness of your heart, my dear Marquis, is shown in every circumstance and I am never surprised when you give fresh evidence of it; your latest acquisition of a plantation in Cayenne, with a view to the emancipation of its slaves, is a generous and noble proof of your humanity. Please God that a similar spirit may come to animate all the people of this country! but I despair of witnessing it in my time. A few petitions were presented to the Congress, during the last session, for the abolition of slavery; they were hardly able to secure one reading. A sudden emancipation would, I believe, bring great evils; but certainly it might, it should be, brought about, gradually, and that by the legislative authority.[9]

Washington has long since understood, and regretted, "that it should always be necessary to democratic states to *feel* before they can *judge.* † That is what causes governments to be slow. But in the end the people return to the true."[10]

The people are even capable of speed, when it comes to a surge of gratitude. The inhabitants of the American port of Nantucket, delighted with the terms La Fayette has obtained for the sale of their whale oil at Dunkerque and Bayonne,

> filled with thankfulness for so great a service which has revived our depressed industry and enabled us to avoid emigration from this island, our birthplace, having assembled municipally, noted and resolved, a short while ago, that each of them would give the milk of his cow for twenty-four hours; that this entire volume would be made into a cheese weighing 500 pounds, which would be sent to M. le Marquis de La Fayette as a token, feeble indeed but very sincere, of the affection and gratitude of the inhabitants.[11]

Until something better comes along . . .

---

*About 9 million modern francs [$225,000]. Jefferson, mentioned subsequently in the text, was then United States ambassador to France.
†His italics.

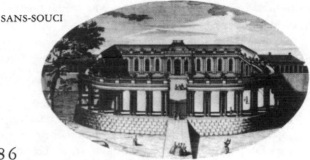

SANS-SOUCI

# 32

JANUARY–
FEBRUARY 1786

## *The Man Is . . . Constantly in Motion*

Mirabeau's turn. As always, he takes the bull by the horns; it's his only resource, being a relative nobody in comparison with La Fayette—not that it would ever occur to anyone to compare them. Five days after moving into the "Hôtel de la Ville de Paris" in Berlin, he sends a letter to Frederick II:

> Sire,
>
> It may be presumptuous on the part of an applicant who has no matter to discuss of particular concern to you to request an audience with Your Majesty. But if you can forgive a Frenchman's desire, after finding the world resounding with your name from birth, to see, at closer range than that from which a king is ordinarily contemplated, the greatest man of this and so many other centuries, you will deign to grant me the favor of coming to pay you my respects at Potsdam.
>
> I am, with very profound regards, yours, etc.[1]

With the letter Mirabeau sends a package of books written (and openly published under his own name) in the last three years—against agiotage, against the Paris water board, and, especially, against Joseph II's claims on the mouths of the Escaut, which is a handy indication that he doesn't belong to the "Austrian party" so abhorred by the king. It is probably this that earns him the chance to be the last foreigner, outside the medical profession, to be received by Frederick before his death. Since the maneuvers and receptions in September 1785 he's been going downhill, and sees almost no one officially anymore. Even as the shades of night close in about him, however, he remains eager to seize upon any grist, even wormy grist, for his anti-Austrian mill. And then, you will never understand the first thing about kings unless you remember that they are, above all else, unutterably bored. A Mirabeau is as good as a circus performer. On January 23 Frederick writes to Count von Goertz, his grand chamberlain:

"In your letter of yesterday I received the books which the Comte de Mirabeau asked you to pass on to me. You will oblige me by thanking him warmly for me. I confess I should be most curious to know what happy chance brings this traveler all this way, and you would please me by letting me know. With this, I pray God, etc."

It would seem that Goertz, possibly impressed by Mirabeau's unbelievable cheek, let the king know forthwith, because Frederick dictates his reply that same evening, January 23:

> Monsieur le Comte de Mirabeau,
>
> I should be very pleased to make your acquaintance and I am touched by the offer you have just made me to come here for that purpose. If you wish to give me this pleasure on the day after tomorrow, the 25th of this month, and ask for Major-General Count von Goertz, I shall be able to see you the same day and, until then, I pray God to keep you, M. le Comte de Mirabeau, under his high and holy protection.

Even that wasn't bad for a beginning; but as Mirabeau always has to make everything bigger, a year later he was cheerfully announcing that "Frederick II called me to his side on his own initiative, when I feared to importune him in his last moments."[2]

Dear liar. Even so, the French ambassador in Berlin, the humorless Comte d'Esterno, is indignant to see so much importance suddenly being attached to an adventurer in connection with whom, as he observes in a sour missive to Vergennes, "I was instructed to complain to this Court following the libels he had printed in Neuchâtel."* The ambassador is also trembling at the thought that his meager funds may be still further depleted by the great sieve: "One major drawback is that M. de Mirabeau has no known means of subsistence and that, being referred [recommended] by France, he will be able to obtain credit here, which will infallibly lead to claims for payment. . . . Please allow me, M. le Comte, to take this opportunity to observe to you that the majority of the French who come here have an adverse effect upon the dignity and esteem in which the nation is held."[3]

This seems to be the usual attitude of the Comte d'Esterno, of whom Mirabeau said, with perfect partiality, that "France's man in Berlin is the natural forwarding address for all malcontents, gossips, and coveters,"[4] but then he might also have been trying to run him down in order to make his own unofficial journey seem more essential. Vergennes hastens to reassure his diplomat by washing his hands of a mission the responsibility for which he lays firmly at Calonne's door: "The letter given to you from me by M. de Mirabeau implies no commitment on your part of any sort in regard to that gentleman, and nothing is to prevent you from conducting yourself, in respect to him, with all the reserve you may deem necessary. You will do very wisely not to grant him access on familiar terms."

A few weeks later, when the informed circles of Berlin cut through the

---

*This refers to *Des Lettres de cachet et des prisons d'Etat* and the *Espion dévalisé*.

clouds of verbiage in which Mirabeau has enveloped himself, the light they imagined they saw was this: the hidden reason for his trip is that he is a sort of harbinger for a new reversal of alliances, France joining forces with Prussia again, cutting herself off from Austria, too bad for Marie Antoinette. The agnostic or Protestant clan, who are accordingly anti-bigot, anti–Roman Catholic and anti-Austrian—Talleyrand, Lauzun, Panchaud, and Clavière, now forming the Calonne set—must be trying to increase the minister's influence and push him into position as the man of the Franco-Prussian-English alliance which would be such a help to the speculations of the great Protestant banks and all manner of financial transactions in the expanding north, to the detriment of the south, which is losing altitude. This year the money manipulators' hour has sounded in London, Berlin, Neuchâtel, Bern, and Paris rather than in Vienna, Rome, Naples, or Madrid. Calonne has therefore agreed, although not without some smirks and simpers of protest because he wants to avoid open warfare with the Queen as long as he can, to a timid revival of a sort of "King's Secret" (so secret that for the moment Louis XVI himself hasn't heard of it)—a parallel diplomacy, alongside that of Vergennes, with Prussia, England, and even Russia. It's a dangerous game, and this comptroller general is not in the same league as the Broglies under Louis XV. *They* would never have put any trust in a Mirabeau. But you have to take what you can get.

Mirabeau, half on his own account and half under orders, has come to Prussia, or thinks he has, to manipulate one of the levers of European policy. At last! But his fingers are trembling. Which of the three Hohenzollerns should he try first? He knows he's been sent out as a sniper, and that his backers will drop him like a hot potato if he can't make his way in Berlin without them —the fate of every secret agent. In theory he ought to put most of his money on Prince Henry, the king's younger brother, whose reputation in Europe has been expanding as Frederick's shrinks. Another of history's short-circuited heroes: as intelligent and learned as his elder, and just as homosexual; as good a general on the battlefield, too, but more sociable, better-liked. He keeps a futile court in his castle at Rheinsberg, and is, like Frederick, childless. At the latter's death the throne will go to the son of the third brother (already dead), a gigantic lump named Frederick William about whom nobody knows anything except that he gorges, guzzles, and screws enough to make up for both his uncles.

The Calonne set also includes most of Prince Henry's personal friends in France.[5] They're betting on him to become a sort of regent, without the title, at Frederick II's death. And they're sure of his love of all things French. But who knows whether the nephew will give him his head? And who knows if Frederick's senectitude is not just the old ape playing one more trick on them all? Has he really said his last word? A Mirabeau ought to be able to make more sense of the situation than that congealed d'Esterno, whose inertia and ignorance have lowered a veil between Berlin and Versailles: Vergennes has stocked the courts of Europe with men as short-sighted as himself, who are sure not to bother him too much. As long as nothing moves . . .

But in Prussia everything's about to move, and this is the kind of situation Mirabeau has been waiting for, an opportunity to show his true colors and at the same time further his own career, without worrying too much about his instructions.

First, he has to find out whether Frederick is really as close to death as they say. The answer is yes. Or almost yes.

On January 25 he duly drives to Potsdam, six leagues from Berlin. A Versailles for men, from which even the queen is excluded—a phantom queen, the Princess of Brunswick-Bevern, whom Frederick married in 1733 under orders from his awesome father and from whom he separated as soon as he came to the throne, undoubtedly without ever having touched her. Few men can have hated women more than he. She's still alive, she has her apartment in the royal palace in Berlin, where he used to call upon her for seven minutes a day in the years when they both inhabited it; and when they appeared together in public he made the regulation gestures. But he certainly never invited her to Potsdam, his true home. "Solomon had a seraglio with a thousand women in it and thought there were still not enough; I have but one, and even that is too many for me."[6]

He's so much more at ease in the company of his beloved hussars, the best-looking men in his guard, culled, one by one, in the course of all those inspections, and now transformed into bedside orderlies. Not so long ago he was still sending for one or another of them when they were on duty (not on guard, nobody stands guard here), seldom the same one twice because he has never wanted an official favorite. He spoke to them roughly, provoking the coarse, overfamiliar backtalk he would take from nobody else; then the shoves and blows in place of caresses, a swift embrace on a sofa behind the screen that always stands open in his study, not another word, and the soldier withdraws, clutching his roll of fredericks, and woe unto him if he utters a boast or risks so much as the shadow of a wink to the king: he'll wake up with marching orders to some garrison in the sticks, unless he is sent to "pull wheelbarrows at Spandau."* Frederick's private life is absolutely no one's business but his own.

Mirabeau rolls past the brand-new château of Potsdam. The king had it built at great expense at the end of the Seven Years' War, to show that the war had not bankrupted him: an ugly rococo building, a monstrous pink-and-green

*A Prussian expression referring to the country's principal military prison.

cake with irregular cupolas and graceless proportions. Frederick spends little time there; you find him further on, in his thirteen-room Trianon—the jewel, or rather jewelbox, of Sans-Souci. Mirabeau, already impressed by the statuary in the grounds (copied after that at Versailles), considers with a wondering but critical eye the "multitudes of gardens, quantities of gilt, a few fine paintings [I should hope so! a little gallery stuffed with Watteaus and Lancrets], a few handsome antiques. I am happy to see this living proof of what can be achieved on a sand dune; perhaps some king will take advantage of it to bring on [in the sense of "cause to grow"] something other than parks and statues."[7]

The inside of Sans-Souci was not decorated by mortal man: white, gold, mirrors, parquet flooring you could skate on, and all of it punctuated with toothpaste moldings that make one want to giggle. This is no solemn, real-life palace: it's lightheartedness personified. [Sans-Souci, the French name of Frederick's *bijou*, means, literally, without care or worry—*Trans.*] The visitor is not shown round the five guest bedrooms, or the little rotunda library, or the king's chamber, or the music room, but is led across the antechamber and official reception room into the study, in which Frederick has planted, like a campaign tent, that famous armchair that has molded itself to his misshapen body and is in the process of becoming a European institution. He's almost never out of it these days, even at night, because he can't breathe lying down.

Face to face, for a few short minutes, Frederick II and Mirabeau. Honoré has a sense of the occasion. This is the first king ever to bestow a semblance of attention upon him; Mirabeau has only seen Louis XVI from afar and has never exchanged a word with him—there was no risk that anyone with his record would be allowed to approach his King. He knows neither the emperor nor the kings of England or Spain, but trusts that he soon will, and since he means to spend his time in their company later, why not begin with the biggest of them all?

All this opulence and artistry have been orchestrated for a heap of old bones, stinking with filth, frighteningly livid, wrapped in a crimson velvet dressing gown liberally sprinkled with tobacco, its legs stuffed into boots that have been slit so he can get them on and then wrapped round with bandages, the whole topped by an ancient plumed hat that has been immortalized in fifty portraits and is so moth-eaten you could take it for the one he wore at Rossbach. From between the folds of his dressing gown peeps the muzzle of one of his darling Italian greyhounds, he's always got at least one of them under his vest next to his skin, to keep him warm. They answer the only need for tenderness he can feel.

Frederick, on the other hand, can have no awareness that this is a historic occasion. He politely lifts his hat two fingers away from his head, invites his caller to sit, and treats him with his habitual courtesy, asking in impeccable French the regulation questions about the weather in Paris this winter and conditions on the journey. But the questions come as though from another planet, the icebound realm of death in which he is taking up his new quarters. From the depths of that vast indifference to all things that marks a long death agony, the velvet eyes of Frederick the Great observe the smallpox-pitted face of this person who is "corpulent, but constantly in motion, whose dark eyes glow like coals and who appears to have suffered much and argued many things."[8]

Is this the "effeminate satyrist" about whom he vaguely recalls some trouble with his police in Neuchâtel? Mirabeau, meanwhile, intimidated and possibly put off his stride by the presence of two chamberlains, seems to have been unable to deploy his usual gamut of seductions. And anyway, what for? It's clear that "Old Fritz" is not long for this world. Better save my talents for his successors, the brother and/or nephew, and try to find a place for myself in the "French circle" of Berlin, which means virtually all the courtiers, French being the common language of the best people.

Silence falls. A pause. The king coughs painfully, almost aggressively. It's called "a catarrh, settling in the chest." You can't get rid of it, especially when there's an unwelcome caller in your presence. Mirabeau bows himself out.

The next day he has another try, on the off chance. What an extraordinary thing, after all, to have been received by Frederick the Great! Whatever else happens, Mirabeau did obtain the historic audience. And you can't conceive how badly he needs money. Since he failed to sell his charm in words, he tries on paper. On January 26 he writes the king all the things he wishes he had said. Have you ever heard a better salesman of himself? In passing, he indicates his readiness to drop Calonne without batting an eyelid. Calonne, who sent him here in the first place.

> Sire . . .
>
> When Your Majesty did me the honor, yesterday, of inquiring whether I was going to St. Petersburg, I replied that it was not my intention to go there yet. I had one, even two witnesses, and my personal circumstances require that my actions not be noised about.
>
> Now that I am speaking alone to Your Majesty, I shall have the honor of informing you that, having been ill-rewarded indeed for the truly great services I have rendered to France in the finance department, my security endangered by the present minister and my reputation nearly so, for the reason that I did not wish to be in any way associated with his latest loan . . . ; compelled, until my father's death, to seek employment for my feeble talents, tormented by the perhaps unreasonable desire to be missed by France, I left that country, with the sovereign's permission, but with the firm resolve not to return to it so long as I should

be young and capable of doing something, except to receive the substantial inheritance which my father will leave to me.*

After the justified curiosity that has led me to Berlin . . . it is my intention, which I confess, Sire, to you alone, to seek employment in that country which, of all those I know, has most need of foreigners. I shall therefore press on to Russia, and I certainly should not have gone to that unformed nation and uncivilized land had it not seemed to me that your government was too highly organized for me to flatter myself that I might be useful to Your Majesty. To serve you, not to sit idly in academies, would undoubtedly have been my first ambition, Sire. But the storms of my early youth and the disappointments of my country have long, too long turned my thoughts aside from that inspiring design, and I fear that it is now too late.[9]

His fears are justified. It is too late. Or else there never was a right time. Mirabeau will not enter the service of the King of Prussia. Frederick's reply, two days later, politely shuts the door in his face:

M. le Comte de Mirabeau,

I could not fail to appreciate the confidence you place in me in your letter of the 26th, when you tell me the reasons that have impelled you, with your sovereign's permission, to expatriate yourself and seek more successful employment of your talents abroad. You may rest assured that I shall keep your secret and shall always interest myself in the career of a man of your merit.

What's one more failure in a list like his? Mirabeau takes up his residence in Berlin, determined to feather his nest there and acclimatize his "horde."

He wore a town coat that made him look absolutely like the people of Court of his own nation; his dress was simple and closely resembled the fashion of the English garment that was to follow. He had black, very vivacious eyes beneath thick brows. . . . He was broad-shouldered, but not fat; he gave the impression of a man who had lived much and among many people. His slightest movements indicated a man full of energy, who examines everything, gets to the heart of everything; he used his lorgnette, and, one might say, his whole self, in the same way. He attended German plays, went backstage, took his own letters every day to the post, where I saw him stand for hours and hours together while a lady and her child, aged eight [*sic*], waited for him in the carriage.† . . .

My father told me he was no one in particular, just the Comte de Mirabeau.[10]

---

*In reality his inheritance would be anything but substantial, because the marquis had named his younger son sole heir and legatee of a fortune which had been totally consumed by lawsuits.

†This portrait of Mirabeau in Berlin in the spring of 1786 is from the pen of a young Berlin Jewess who will soon be the hostess of a famous literary salon and a faithful friend of Goethe: Rachel Levin.

# 33

## APRIL–MAY 1786

## *If It's Dancing You Fancy, Little Count . . .*

On May 1, 1786, on the stage of the Burgtheater in Vienna, Mozart catches the ball tossed by Beaumarchais almost exactly two years before in the theater of the French Acting Company. That day the *Mariage de Figaro,* play of the century, becomes *Le Nozze di Figaro,* most perfect opera ever composed. The spirit of the times, volleying between the offspring of Paris and the scion of Salzburg, sets ringing some strange echoes. Not that the two men ever met, not even during Mozart's unhappy stay in Paris in 1778.* Nor do they correspond, not now, or later; at least, no trace of a letter has ever been found on either side. The two architects of this unique work seem to have been totally ignorant of each other, and the line runs from Figaro to Figaro, from that of Beaumarchais to that of Mozart, via a third, the Figaro of Lorenzo da Ponte.

The theater is part of the ponderous hulk of the Hofburg, or Imperial Palace, right in the center of the city, but that doesn't make it snobbish: anybody can go there, in this town in which the citizens of every class believe that the only thing more important than music is pastries. They are segregated on the inside, however, by the price of the seats, with the *parterre noble* costing 2 florins a seat plus another 40 kreutzers for a *gesperrter Sitz,* or chained and padlocked seat (also in the *parterre noble*), the keys to which are kept by individual music-lovers. A box costs 9 florins; prices in the non-"noble" parterre at the back descend from 24 to 17 kreutzers.† The rather undistinguished amphitheater is in the plain baroque manner. It is full: a large poster, adorned with cascades of fruit, flowers, and cherubs framing the title, has been stuck up on the walls of the old town to announce the first public performance in the

---

*When his mother died. At that time Beaumarchais (although very much a musician, having been harp instructor to Louis XV's daughters) was totally immersed in his dealings with the Americans, and Mozart may not ever have heard his name spoken in Paris. And what did Beaumarchais know of Mozart?

†They were not exorbitant, by present-day French standards. The florin was a silver coin worth 2 French livres in the days of Joseph II, and the kreutzer a copper coin worth 4 centimes.

theater for a week, and the Viennese have been titillated by talk of a thrilling dress rehearsal. It was the first full run-through of the work, and it has been engraved forever in the memory of Kelly, a singer and friend of Mozart:*

> I well remember the first rehearsal with the full orchestra. Mozart was on stage, in his crimson coat and top hat trimmed with gold braid, beating time for the orchestra. Figaro's aria, "Non più andrai, farfallone amoroso,"† was sung by Benucci with the greatest possible animation and power.
>
> I was just next to Mozart, who kept saying, *sotto voce,* "Bravo! Bravo Benucci!" and when Benucci came to the final passage, "Cherubino, alla vittoria, alla gloria militar!" which he sang in positively stentorian tones, the effect was like an electrical discharge, for both the actors on stage and the performers in the orchestra, who, as though moved to ecstasy, were exclaiming "Bravo! Bravo, Maestro! Viva, viva, grande Mozart!" I thought the orchestra would never stop applauding, beating their stands with their bows. The little man thanked them for such exceptional expressions of enthusiasm by bowing several times. . . .
>
> All the principal interpreters had the advantage of having studied with the composer, who transfused his emotions into their souls. I shall never forget his outwardly impassive face, illuminated by burning flashes of genius; to describe it is as impossible as to paint the rays of the sun.[1]

Mozart is thirty years old. He has not become an Apollo since the days when his sour and scrubby adolescent air disappointed the Parisians, who were hoping to see the divine infant of his first trip; but he has taken on weight, aplomb, mystery. His red hair is still strongly rooted above his high forehead and falls straight and thick on his neck. Sometimes, when he's been able to eat one of those fancy meals he so loves, his rather heavy cheeks assume a pinkish hue. "Beneath an appearance of frivolity, he hides his inner anguish . . . in a sort of irony in regard to himself."[2]

One of the performers applauding "the little man in red" is Nancy Storace, a well-known Viennese soprano who is singing the part of Susanna and holds first place in his heart at the moment. In his life too, possibly, but, having married Constanze Weber, Mozart now lives a sedate existence in which there is little room for escapades. It is likely that Susanna's arias were chiseled with even more loving care than the rest, but none was neglected, and especially not those of the pretty Sardy Bussani, who was so disturbingly ambiguous in the role of Cherubino that she became typecast as a transvestite. And there was the Countess's poignant cavatina toward the end of Act III, recalling the moments of mad love shared, in the days of the *Barbier de Séville,* with that same Count Almaviva who has now turned into a lace-fronted boor, half wild with jealousy and half dirty old man: "Dove sono i bei momenti,"

---

*Quoted here by Brigitte and Jean Massin in their *Mozart;* Kelly sang the role of Basilio.
†"You will flit no more, butterfly of love." This is, of course, addressed to Cherubino, when Almaviva punishes him by sending him to the army.

what has become of those exquisite moments of sweetness and pleasure? Where have they fled, the oaths sworn by his lying lip? Why do the memories of that happiness always turn for me now into tears and pain? But the most vigorous, the most incisive passage, the one in which Mozart shows his true colors even more than Beaumarchais, is the redoubtable aria of Figaro, almost at the beginning, when he learns that the Count intends to revive the recently abolished custom of *jus primae noctis* for the sake of his own fiancée, Susanna. "Se vuol ballare, signor contino," if it's dancing you fancy, little count, I'll be the man at the guitar . . .

How did da Ponte manage to bamboozle the emperor into believing that even though Beaumarchais's play was still banned in Vienna, the *Nozze* was somehow an altogether different work, a piece of slapstick, a joke, a bit of fluff? How was it that Joseph II and the entire Austro-Hungarian aristocracy, the Bathyanis, Colloredos, Esterhazys, and Schwarzenbergs, who were sitting in on this assessment of themselves by their servants, failed to see that the violence of Mozart's music had amplified Beaumarchais's message and given the force of an insurrection to a handful of vengeful words that will brand them forever? *Se vuol ballare* . . .

"I must consult only my reason and my heart, and I need no great dame or person of quality to help me do what is right and good, what is neither too much nor too little. Man is made noble by the heart. I am no count, but I may have more honor in my heart than many a count and, footman or count, whoever offends me is a swine."[3] Is that Beaumarchais? Not at all, it's Mozart, in a letter to his father, written in 1781 when he had just broken off with the Bishop-Prince Colloredo, the mini-tyrant of Salzburg, in the most tragicomical manner possible. It was absolutely worthy of Figaro himself: on June 9, 1781, Count Karl Arco, the prince's "master of the kitchens" (we would call him head of staff), gave Mozart a kick in the behind to eject him from the antechamber of his patron, to whom the composer wanted to hand his resignation in person. He had long since had enough of being treated like a lackey, "one grade above the cooks in the domestic hierarchy," compelled to swallow the whims, "the incessant insults, impertinences, and idiocies" continually aimed at him by that coarse brute in a moiré cassock. But the contact of his rump with the chief footman-courtier's shoe was too much, it made him ill, "I had to return home and go to bed for I was all of a fever, I was trembling in every limb and weaving down the street like a drunken man."[4]

*Se vuol ballare, signor contino* . . . The "little Count" Arco is exactly the same age as Mozart. Who knows down what paths that supreme humiliation tunneled through the composer's genius for five years before procuring for him the only revenge possible in those days, the work of art hurled in the teeth of his insulter like a violin smashed over his head? Who knows what shock of emotion, identity, he felt when he read Figaro's outcry in the fifth act—"You took the trouble to be born?" Pierre-Augustin and Wolfgang Amadeus didn't need to be introduced in a drawing room. They met in the hellfire of humiliation imposed by nobiliary systems upon those who could not be their masters' equals and refused to "know their place."

" 'Oh,' Arco said to me,* 'the archbishop accounts you an extremely proud man.'

" 'To be sure,' I told him, with him that is exactly what I am.' I conduct myself with others as they conduct themselves with me. If I see someone treat me with contempt, not appreciate me, then I can be as proud as any monkey."

And, also in the course of this decisive crisis, "I conjure you to be gay, for today my happiness begins! . . . I wish to hear no more of Salzburg.† I hate the archbishop to frenzy." Mozart had broken his chains.

That's why the anger of the *Mariage de Figaro* rose to the fury of "Se vuol ballare." Mozart himself chose the play and imposed it upon da Ponte. The librettist is categorical: "I was [in 1785] calmly meditating upon the drama I was to compose for my friend Mozart. I understood readily enough that the immensity of his genius required a theme that was vast, multiform, sublime. Then, in conversation with him one day, he asked whether it would be easy for me to turn Beaumarchais's comedy the *Mariage de Figaro* into a drama. The proposal was greatly to my liking and I undertook to do it."[5]

Turn it into a drama . . . Little Count Arco will never know how far his kick in Mozart's behind was to travel. "If it is a satisfaction to be rid of a prince who does not pay you and screws you to death,** then yes, it's true, I am satisfied. For were I compelled from morning to night to do nothing but think and work, I should do it gladly if only to avoid living at the mercy of such a ——; I cannot call him by his rightful name. I was forced to take this fatal step and now I cannot draw back by so much as a hair."

He's come a long way since we last saw him at the bedside of his dying mother in the spring of 1778, when the people of Versailles and Paris showed him so little respect that he regretfully turned his back on them. If he had been able to stick it out he might have gained a hearing in the end, but in those days he was still totally dependent upon his two guardians, Leopold and Colloredo, the natural father and the arch-episcopal "benefactor," both equally jealous of Wolfgang and equally tyrannical in their treatment of him; and they recalled him to Salzburg. "You will agree that it is no great good fortune to be driven to that."[6]

---

*Letter from Mozart to his father, June 2, 1781.

†The final quarrels between Mozart and Colloredo and the "scene of the kick" take place in Vienna, where the archbishop was temporarily residing with his court.

**The German is *cuionirt.* [The French is *couillonne.—Trans.*]

He duly returned to the cradle that had become so much too short for him, showing his unwillingness by making many and protracted stops wherever he could give concerts and associate with people who respected him. Nancy, Strasbourg, Mannheim. In the last-named town he gained the esteem of a consequential Rhenish family, the von Dalbergs, one of whom, Herbert, the elector palatine's theater director and minister of state, kept him for six weeks to compose a "duodrama" or "declaimed opera" based on Voltaire's *Sémiramis.* *

Wolfgang played deaf as long as he could to the repeated urgings of his father, who was nagging him to hurry home because of some sordid pecuniary affair—Leopold always did think of his son as a milch cow whose "services" served him to pay his debts.

Then, in Munich, at the Webers', the worst happened.† Until then he had managed to keep smiling because he was hoping to become engaged to Aloysia. For him this was true love, nothing to do with the banter and crudity of his exchanges with the little cousin in Salzburg, whom he was still bombarding with salacious correspondence. But Aloysia was seventeen, and her character was anything but that of the sailor's sweetheart. On Christmas Day 1778, when Mozart came to call wearing a mourning-coat in the French style—red with black buttons—he found himself facing a stranger who pretended she could hardly remember who he was. Whereupon he sat down at the harpsichord to belt out an old folksong in a lusty voice:

"Those that do not love me, they can kiss my ass."7

1778 would have done for Mozart if anything could: his Parisian attempt had failed, his mother's death had come on top of it, and Aloysia had jilted him. On December 29 of that year, for want of anybody else to confide in, he wrote to his father (but without mentioning the Webers by name):

"Today I can do nothing but cry. I really do have too sensitive a nature. . . . In all my life my writing has never been so bad as it is today, because I just can't. There's no room in my heart for anything except the desire to weep."8

1779. In Salzburg, in the month of his twenty-third birthday, he squirmed back into the harness of organ player to the prince-archbishop which he had already been wearing for ten years. "A man of mediocre talent remains medio-

---

*The text of which was hacked to shreds and abundantly transposed to accommodate the ideas of the German *Aufklärung* or Enlightenment. The Dalbergs were great champions of the movement and, with the help of the powerful network of German Freemasonry, the Rhineland's strongest supporters of revolutionary and Napoleonic France. Herbert's brother, the Archbishop Theodor, becomes Arch-chancellor of the French Empire and later prince primate of the Rhine Confederation.

†Reminder: Aloysia and Constanze were cousins of Carl Maria, the future composer of *Der Freischütz.*

cre forever, whether he travels or no, but a man of superior talent (which, without arrogance, I cannot deny being) will go wild if he is cooped up forever in the same place."[9] His little cousin Anna-Maria consoles him for a few months more, until he can at last make a somewhat more auspicious trip to Munich, where the Prince Elector of Bavaria has commissioned him to write an opera on the legendary theme of Idomeneo, King of Crete. There was the warmth of teamwork with singers and musicians, laboring day and night, and the unexpected delight of a big success in January 1781. From then on Mozart was sure of himself, if not of life.

This makes it easier to see how he found the courage to break with Colloredo in 1781 and, in a chain reaction, with his father, although they kept up the appearance of friendliness; but he was more than sick of Salzburg and, above all, he needed to break with himself, with the doll prodigy, the docile automaton of the piano whose dead image still clung to him.

The decisive altercations with the prince-archbishop and his chief flunkey took place in Vienna, the giant town inside its cramped ramparts, whose houses have to be pushed six or seven stories tall in order to contain their 600,000 inhabitants, all a bit bourgeois, all lovers of good food, all musicians.

In July 1782 Mozart was already writing *Die Entführung aus dem Serail* there, and for the same theater; he was working from a German text, i.e., in the line of Gluck, and he wanted to create an operatic art that would express the Germanic patriotism which was one of the strongest features of his personality.* "Then, perhaps, the national theater that has such beautiful beginnings would reach fulfillment; and this would really be a task for Germany, if we Germans would seriously set ourselves to think in German, act in German, speak in German, and even sing in German."[10]

With *Die Entführung,* "the moment Mozart appeared, all our efforts to express the underlying truth of things became vain. *Die Entführung aus dem Serail* towers over us all," Goethe wrote on April 4, 1785.[11]

Having settled in Vienna, he hoped it would be a center from which he could radiate to the largest possible number of German cities; and for a twenty-six-year-old composer who has "arrived," "settle" implies "marry." He edges cautiously forward.

> Who is now the object of my affections? Not a Weber? Yes, a Weber! but not Aloysia, who is a false and wicked person, and a flirt.† Not Josepha, not Sophie, but Constanze, the one in between. . . . She is not homely, nor is she in any sense

---

*The Massins point out that Mozart never once uses the word "Austrian" when talking about himself; he wants to be a citizen of the German empire.

†And who had just married somebody named Joseph Lange.

beautiful. All her good looks consist in two small black eyes and a good figure. She is not quick, but has sense enough to perform her duties as wife and mother. She has no inclinations to extravagance. On the contrary, she is used to being badly dressed because what little their mother was able to do for her children she did for the other two, never for this one. . . . She can make most of the things a woman needs herself. She also does her own hair every day, she knows how to keep house, she has the best heart in the world; I love her and she loves me with all her heart. Tell me how I might hope for a better wife?[12]

Mozart never has much to say about Constanze, and what he does say is almost always in these terms. She was then eighteen.

Their little Raymond was born in 1783. "The child is absolutely calm and good-natured and does everything in abundance, be it drink, sleep, cry, shit, or whatever,"[13] but he dies on August 19. Karl Thomas is born in 1784, followed by Johann Thomas in 1786. The latter also dies in infancy, in the year of *Le Nozze.* *

Like many other great creators, Mozart does not limit his horizons to his family circle, especially not when it consists primarily of the sort of superior cleaning woman whom Constanze remains in his eyes, perhaps as an unconscious reaction to Aloysia's "betrayal." He says little about his children but never a word against them, and he seems to have made sure that they were well looked after. His real life is elsewhere. In Freemasonry, for instance; he joined the movement officially in 1784 and is imbued with its spirit, which is "progressive, anti-mystical, irreligious, rationalistic, socially and politically prerevolutionary,"† and far more markedly so in Germany than in France. But mostly in music, in *his* music, really his own, a sort of gospel (in the sense of good news) of which he now knows himself to be the bearer.

Beginning in 1784, when he writes the six quartets dedicated to Haydn which establish him as the legitimate successor to the father of German music in the eighteenth century, he gets more commissions than he can handle. Possibly because of the Freemasons, he begins to be patronized by the nobility and even by Joseph II, who pats him on the shoulder after *Die Entführung aus dem Serail* and says:

"Very good, very good, except that there are just a few too many notes."

The sovereign, so cold and hard to move, as stingy with his praise as with his thalers, even had a moment of spontaneous enthusiasm at the first performance, in February 1785, of the B-flat concerto for orchestra and the new instrument—the piano—that was creating such a stir and beginning to outdis-

---

*In 1791 the Mozarts have one more boy, Franz Xavier Wolfgang, who survives his parents, as does Karl Thomas; the older boy becomes an official in Milan, the younger one ekes out a living as pianist and orchestra conductor and even composes a few insignificant pieces which he blandly signs Wolfgang Amadeus Mozart. They also had two girls, both of whom died in infancy.
†According to the Massins.

tance the harpsichord. That year (mainly with the D-minor piano concerto) Mozart staved in one or two of the heart's bulwarks, giving the soloists in his concertos notes to play that were the stammering first words of a new language for the expression of the inexpressible. When the performance ended, with himself as soloist, "the emperor, hat in hand, signed to him and called out 'Bravo, Mozart!' " A roar of applause followed.

He was already looking for a librettist for the *Nozze,* although he so longed to "be German" and didn't like the idea of regressing to Italian opera buffa.

He met da Ponte, they hit it off at once; both of them adored feasting, banana-peel stunts at Carnival time, licentious tales, and taking the stuffing out of authority. Joseph II was fond of da Ponte and treated him a little like his jester, so when the production had to be authorized the librettist handled that angle. And here they are; the curtain's going up.

"At the end of the opera [we're back to May 1, 1786], I thought the audience would never stop applauding and calling Mozart back. There were encores after every aria, which made the performance last almost as long as two operas and caused the emperor to decree that no aria could be repeated at the second performance. Never was there a more total triumph," affirms Kelly, "than that of Mozart and his *Nozze di Figaro.* "

And yet

> Almaviva is the only person to risk no more than a passing deflation and some degree of ridicule. The others, Rosina and Cherubino, Susanna and Figaro, are staking a whole lifetime of happiness; Susanna is playing for her self-respect and Rosina for her honor (the women have twice as much to lose), which only intensifies the disparity between the calm, sangfroid, and gaiety preserved by Susanna (and the rest, to a lesser degree) in every crisis, and Almaviva's rage and fury. "You command everything here except yourself," is Figaro's taunt in Beaumarchais. In his music, Mozart demonstrated the contrast so plainly that there was no longer any need for the words. But the underlying dread of the master's threat is much stronger in him than in Beaumarchais, and for good reason, because, with Colloredo, he had felt it in his flesh.[14]

# 34

APRIL–MAY 1786

## *The Wallachians Have Rebelled*

The blaze of triumph of the *Nozze di Figaro,* the crowds of predominantly scarlet-garbed Viennese theatergoers among whom, unlike those of France, few differences can be seen between nobles and bourgeois, the universal acceptance of, even sympathy for, Figaro's misadventures and schemes of revenge: they might all seem to indicate that the battle Mozart was waging in Vienna had been won in advance, and he was simply letting off fireworks to celebrate the victory of Enlightenment.

Says who? The world of art, in Vienna as in Paris, is only an escape valve for noble sentiments, a zoo inside which the weird-looking creatures of the future remain firmly imprisoned. Once you leave the ramparts of Vienna and turn off the broad paths of the Prater, you don't need to travel many leagues to find yourself centuries back in time, roaming, from Danube to Volga, through vast expanses of cruelty. "If it's dancing you fancy, little count . . ." Did Mozart hear any more than vague rumors of the little counts of Hungary who have just hanged or decapitated hundreds of Wallachian peasants? In Deva alone, a little town not far from Buda and Pest, thirty-seven were killed in one day.

In these years of the *Nozze di Figaro,* of *montgolfières* and the founding of the United States, do we really have to bother about what goes on in Wallachia? And to begin with, what Frenchman of yesterday, today, or tomorrow could tell us where Wallachia is? Isn't it some imaginary place from the world of Gargantua? What does the fate of the Wallachians have to do with us?

Nevertheless, while Mozart and da Ponte were spinning the web of *One Mad Day* [the subtitle of Beaumarchais's play—*Trans.*] in the solitude of their candlelit chambers, a French adventurer of the pen, a "Don Quixote of mankind," was writing and publishing—anonymously—a pretty horrifying text about these lost souls in another world. The *Seconde Lettre d'un défenseur du peuple à l'empereur Joseph II, Sur son règlement concernant l'émigration, et principalement sur la révolte des Valaques, où l'on discute à fond le droit de révolte du Peuple* ["Second letter by a defender of the people to Emperor Joseph II on his

regulations concerning emigration, and especially on the revolt of the Wallachians, containing a debate on the substance of the question of the people's
right to revolt"—*Trans.* ], fictitiously described as having been published in
Dublin in 1785, and actually published in Paris early in 1786, undoubtedly
enthralled a far smaller public.

This pamphlet, like another one issued three months before, remains
unknown to the upper echelons of both France and Austria for the simple
reason that both are seized and confiscated from the booksellers' shelves, by
a zealous chief of police who tries to please the Queen every time her illustrious brother is attacked.

Who is this hothead who can fulminate so pertinently about a people of whom
nobody, or almost, has ever heard?

> What is a revolt? Do princes have the right to punish rebels? If they do, must they
> inflict the death penalty, must they invent refined forms of torture for them?
> . . . All who have written of the revolt of the Wallachians appear to have
> conspired against this unfortunate people to encourage you, Prince, to punish
> their leaders by the most horrible tortures, and further to tighten the bonds of
> the people. I saw some who were actually jesting, by the roadside where the
> "demagogue" (as they called him) Hora was to end his days. Fie upon the
> abominable doctrine of such monsters, who prostitute their pens for the people's
> greater woe! May heaven one day heap upon their heads all the horrors of the
> slavery they so villainously preach.[1]

These impassioned lines have just been written by Jacques-Pierre Brissot,* newly released from the Bastille. A fine time for him to start sparring with
an emperor! But Brissot's "vacation" was rained out by what was going on all
those leagues away in a land he will never visit, the endless prairies of honey,
flax, and wheat crossed by powdery trails down which the heavy oxen plod
beneath their carved wooden yokes, the flat interminable horizon that greets
the eye on the far side of the Carpathians, "beyond the great forests"—in other
words, in Transylvania. The peasants there, in bright-colored blouses and
woolen bonnets, talk to each other in a tongue unknown to their seigneurs,
a caricature of rudimentary Latin full of *as* and *us,* a tongue they adopted as
their one capital asset in the long gone days when their homeland, not far from
Byzantium, was called Romania, the other Romanity.†

Their masters, the men who took over the fields, castles, and fortresses
abandoned by the subsiding Turks a century earlier, are Hungarian nobles

---

*Who, when last seen after his return from Switzerland, had just married Félicité Dupont
at Boulogne-sur-Mer and was about to try his luck in England.

†Most of Transylvania, including Wallachia, was attached to Romania in 1945 after Hitler
and Mussolini gave it to Hungary in 1940.

who speak a completely different language brought down by God knows what current from the north. For a final complication, the glittering governors with their escorts of hussars and dragoons, sent out from Vienna by the suzerain of the whole lot, i.e., the emperor, speak German; but to the Wallachians it's all the same.

How are they to know which bunch are to blame for the fact that the bodies of their brothers and fathers are swinging from gibbets at the crossroads, and for the terrifying tales, dutifully read out in church after the sermon, of the executions of Horia Hora, Klocska, and Grisan, who were pinched with red-hot iron tongs and had molten lead poured down their throats before they were broken on the wheel? The Wallachians aren't likely to revolt again for a while.

One lone man in all Europe, alerted, as so many other literate people might have been, by the simple perusal of the newspapers, one lone man starts to bray, and it's Brissot.

> Oh, if I had in hand the documents in this case, had I observed the fate of this people, had I followed them in their daily labors as in their torments, had I but lived in their thatch-covered huts dug into the earth, often their only refuge, had I been present at the conspiracy and witnessed their pleas to the sovereign to put an end to their wretchedness, and their struggles to end it themselves, with what truth, what energy I should defend them! But, far from the theater of this war, having no knowledge of it but the dry or mendacious details of the gazettes, alone, with almost no enlightenment and sustained only by the zeal that impels me to defend the people wherever I see them writhing under the knife of oppression, what can I do but demonstrate, by the very words of the party that has overcome them, that the insurrection of the Wallachians was justified? It is with those words before me that I mean to establish the injustice of their condemnation.
>
> The Wallachians have rebelled; therefore, they were right to rebel. That is my first proof; it will be found strange, when in fact it is only natural.

# 35

## NOVEMBER 1782–JULY 1785

## *A Don Quixote of Mankind*

Jacques-Pierre Brissot, "de Warville,"* was born in the same year as Louis
XVI, 1754, which means that he was twenty-eight in late November 1782
when he sailed by packet from Calais to Dover, unaccompanied by his brand-
new wife, to follow up his recent Geneva escapade by an attempt upon England.

Félicité is a pretty girl five years younger than he, fresh as this morning's
rose, with an oval face, a large, slightly sulky mouth like a child's, and a rather
superficial sweetness in her expression; her gowns and fichus are always neat
as a pin, and she has little Court airs acquired during her two years as "reader"
in the establishment of Mme de Genlis, or in other words in the home of the
Orléans children;[1] her hairdo is a shade severe—a high upsweep as is the
fashion these days—and her "baigneuse" [literally, "bather"—*Trans.*], a
pleated bonnet, sits atop the pile of fair hair drawn back to show all her
forehead and swell out beneath her temples. The reason why she stayed in
Paris rather than going to London with her husband is that she wanted a little
more time at Bellechasse in the home of the other Félicité (de Genlis), where
she had a sinecure and an ideal observation post, her greatest ordeal being a
daily walk with "Mlle Adélaïde" and the new Duc d'Orléans's two adoptive
daughters. (She had no contact with the three boys.)†

In fact, Félicité Dupont was possessed of either true generosity of heart
or a strong passion, because Brissot confessed to her, when they were first
engaged, that although he might look like a staid and steady lad, he was by
no means a free agent; he had a child by a poor girl he had met years before
in the Luxembourg garden, who "worked in lingerie," i.e., went from door

---

*I hope the reader will forgive this "flashback" on Brissot, whom I wanted to link to the
Romanian insurrection. Elsewhere I have explained why he anglicized the spelling of Ouarville,
his birthplace near Chartres.

†A second little girl had lately been ordered from England and rebaptized Hermine, to be
a playmate for Pamela. The Orléans children were steeped in Rousseauism. This Hermine,
married to a man named Capelle during the Empire, becomes the mother of Madame Lafarge.

to door selling lawn, lace, and muslin. Jacques-Pierre is anything but a Don Juan, so maybe it was mere lack of experience that led to this unpropitious pregnancy. Before the lingerie-seller the only other adventure he was known to have had was with another anonymous girl from the opera. Neither of their names is divulged, nor is that of the child, in his *Correspondance* or *Mémoires*. But there it is, the poor little creature, and what is he to do with it? Jacques-Pierre never dreamed of marrying his urban milkmaid—the aristocracy has no monopoly on class pride. As a rising bourgeois who started out from his father's catering shop to become a writer, a thinker, and soon an owner, or almost, of a gazette, such a union would have seemed as debasing to him as for a duke to wed a commoner. Him, marry a girl who "worked in lingerie"? She presumably did not try to force him, either; but she was no streetwalker, and she meant to bring up her child herself, even without marriage.

Upon learning all this, Félicité took, or thought she took, the attitude of a Roman heroine. She offered to have the child along with its father; she would bring it up, they would make a little Brissot out of it. In fact, neither of them treated its poor mother as a human being. And Brissot's contorted recital, to Félicité, of her reaction to the magnanimous offer (this all took place during their betrothal) may rather tarnish his image but it certainly does credit to the poor young woman from the Luxembourg garden:

This Tuesday morning.*
I was pained by your letter, my sweet friend, and once again felt profoundly distressed. I had just been to see the person in question, as it happens, when the letter arrived. I suggested to her the arrangement we had first hit upon, that is, to remove him and have him brought up for three or four years in the country before taking him to live with me. She was upset, I believe, by the fact that I did not want to leave him with her. My answer there was easy, I could not have him with me once he had been seen with her. She asked whether she could come to see him in my home; and whether he would stay there if I married, and whether she could still come. I told her I thought she could because I trusted I was taking a wife generous enough to forget my fault and reasonable enough to give the child a happy life and take an interest in the fate of its mother, especially if its mother were honest and sensible. This seemed to affect her even more, she told me she would not consent to all that because she knew women; and that, moreover, if I were married, she would never have the courage to come to my home. I asked her the reason for that; she did not like to answer, but finally said, "It was because she could never see my wife."† I remonstrated with her, telling her how wrong such a motive was and how, if she cared about her child, she should overcome it, how pleased I should be if I could make her happy with him, if it were possible.

*The letter is undated but was written in Paris late in 1782.
†Meaning "I should never have the courage to become acquainted with her."

I could get nothing from her, she stood her ground. I said my last word: If you will not agree to the arrangement I am proposing, then you can take your child with you but he will never enter my door. However, in due course I shall do whatever may be in my power for him. I gave her the week in which to think it over, and at the end of it I shall see her again and, if she desires, return his papers to her.[2]

Curtain. Brissot's first son, and its mother, are swept away by the waves of time.

1783. So now it's London, and Félicité will join him in the summer. He came over with his friend Marat, who was still prowling around Europe. He stayed with a woman who took in lodgers—a Mrs. Garden, in "Brompton, a pleasant suburb, much sought after by the ill for its healthfulness, far from the city and less subject* to that thick fog, so penetrating and insalubrious, that envelops London for a part of every day; it is close to the home of Swinton and Serres de Latour,"[3] the two owner-partners, one English and the other French, of the *Courrier de l'Europe*. Since the end of the American war the liberal, French-language, London-published gazette had been doing very well: 5,000 subscribers, 25,000 pounds a year clear for each of its owners.†

Jacques-Pierre was approaching the moment of choice. He had been hesitating between "serious" writing and letting himself be frittered to bits by journalism. Serres de Latour, an epicurean who cheerfully squandered every penny of his income, steered him toward the latter.

> Our personalities contrasted singularly. I was ardent, a tireless worker, forever reading, meditating, writing, caring little about fine food, a maniac for the public welfare and a friend to truth, already prepared to sacrifice everything to them both; I was sincerely sorry for Latour, whilst he looked upon me as a madman by whose ravings he was occasionally diverted. He also called me a Don Quixote of mankind, in return for which I would tease him and sometimes preach to him; I berated him for his epicureanism, his nonchalance, but we rubbed along peacefully together. . . . I also cultivated his acquaintance because I hoped to use his paper for my follies, as he called them; that is, for the dissemination of right principles: in this I was not mistaken. . . . Compelled to write, by an imperative urge and by circumstance, I believed that a writer should distinguish between his century and posterity and that one must labor for the one without abjuring the other. There are a score of ways in which one can influence one's century and be useful to one's fellows. One can do it by filling the public papers with one's opinions, by circulating and multiplying useful pamphlets that speak the language

---

*According to Brissot's *Mémoires*. This highroad to the suburbs of old London still exists, having swallowed up three former streets, as Brompton Road.

†The English currency being stronger than the French, this is roughly equivalent to 250,000 modern francs [$62,500].

of the day. Only books that are the fruit of profound reflection and pure writing pass on to posterity. For that, one must etch in bronze and write with the engraver's steel; for the century, one can make do with plaster casts and pastels—they will suffice for the needs of the moment. This was the line of reasoning that prompted me, like all the most distinguished writers of the time, to take up work in periodicals and newspapers.[4]

But Brissot was not devious enough to master all the twists and turns of this marginal London literature with a European vocation. There was a veritable snakepit seething in the shadows of the "French circle." He began by quarreling with Swinton because he (Swinton) was trying to oust Latour, whose cause Jacques-Pierre espoused unreservedly: "The cupidity and baseness with which Swinton sought out the vilest beings, yet feared their influence or their reports; his barbarous speculation on his wife and children [?]; everything rendered him contemptible to my eyes,"[5] and the storm burst when Swinton tried to get Brissot to make friends with the most worm-eaten of all the rotten floorboards in the city, Charles Théveneau de Morande, a Burgundian who had emigrated to London years before in order to put the Channel between himself and the private or public gunmen of the puissant lords and gentle ladies whom he blackmailed with threats of revelations, exhaled by his fetid breath in the *Gazetier Cuirassé* or any of the other tabloid-type rags feverishly devoured by gossips of both sexes on the Continent.

In 1774 Beaumarchais had tethered Morande to the royal hitching post of France with a good strong rope of écus. He stayed on in London and continued belching bile, but never at those whom the French ambassador gave him to understand were in high favor. By now, Théveneau de Morande had acquired a sort of unofficial status as spy of boudoir and bank in England, with one basset ear stretched all the way to Paris and Versailles by correspondents as abject as himself.* One could understand Brissot's revulsion. He didn't write as well as he thought he did, but at least he never dipped his pen in that kind of inkwell. Morande's utter cynicism made the erstwhile champion of criminals, yesterday's champion of the insurgent Genevans, and the champion-to-be of the Wallachian rebels bristle like a hungry wolf:

I saw Morande at Swinton's for the third time, with another hack from the same stable. What impudence! and on my part what stupefaction! To work at a filthy trade and, instead of blushing, boldly to boast of the fact: could there be any greater effrontery or depravity? I was tongue-tied, mute, ashamed, able neither to raise my eyes nor open my mouth. They quoted their most hideous witticisms and vaunted the exaggerations of their imagination, and the fertility of their

*Since his "pact" with Beaumarchais, he was receiving an annual stipend of 4,000 livres (about 30,000 modern francs [$7,500]) paid to him at the French embassy. His name appears in the *Livre rouge* of the King's secret disbursements, published by the Constituent Assembly in 1790.

minds, in concocting the anecdotes they published every day against the most respectable people.

"Now that," one said speaking of himself, "would have been worth a bastinado."

"And wouldn't this be worth the rope?" was the other's reply.

A fine profession, and a pleasant thing, is a gazette written by such people! The victim pays to have his name kept out, his enemy pays to get it put in again; the law protects everything and the public does nothing but laugh. . . .

Leaving them, I felt I was escaping from a den of thieves.[6]

But Brissot is not really wealthy enough to have such fine sentiments, and the enemies he's making now are not amateurs; Swinton has succeeded in detaching Latour from him, and Morande loathes him with the implacable hatred of a demon of hell for his kind of impoverished integrity, and dogs his footsteps even in France with public and private slurs.* At the end of 1783 Brissot tried to revive a publication called the *Lycée de Londres,* which had failed in the hands of Pahin de la Blancherie, that curious fellow with the encyclopedic mind with whom Manon Phlipon had trifled briefly before marrying Roland.† Small world, that of lovers of the human race. Small world of bankrupts for the moment.

On January 17, 1784, the *Mémoires Secrets* announced:

"While M. Brissot de Warville is instituting, in London, a lycée or assembly of correspondence in order that men of letters of all countries may meet and communicate, to be known as the *Tableau périodique de l'état actuel des arts et des sciences en Angleterre* ["Periodic representation of the present state of the arts and sciences in England"—*Trans.* ], the firm of M. de la Blancherie, which is serving as his model in this enterprise, has fallen and collapsed."[7] In Paris there was a vogue for these mixed associations, part club, part academy, part audience for lectures or free courses. They were known as musées or lycées; Condorcet, Marat, and others had been involved in them alongside various Freemasons, who found in them a means of circumventing the official system of education which was still firmly under the ecclesiastical thumb, and they provided a sort of "further education" for adults, as it would later be called —a perpetual supplement to the *Encyclopédie.*

First Blancherie, then Brissot, had wanted to transplant the idea onto English soil, which had been re-opened for cultural relations with literary France since the cessation of hostilities. This implied the publication of a review, to keep up contacts, inform old members, and recruit new ones throughout enlightened Europe.

Having moved, this time with Félicité and one or two of the inevitable

*Some of which are used, unchecked and unadulterated, by the *Montagnards* when they begin their decisive attack upon the "Brissotins."

†Note this first, indirect link between Brissot and Mme Roland.

Dupont sisters, into a large house on Newman Street,* with a ground floor spacious enough to accommodate the "courses," Brissot duly launched his *Journal du Lycée, ou tableau périodique* etc., sixty-four octavo pages published monthly, annual subscription 30 livres.† Through Mme de Genlis he obtained permission from Vergennes to have the *Journal,* which was set up in England, "reprinted in Paris by Périsse-le-jeune, bookseller at the Marché Neuf near the notary's," although it had first, of course, to be subjected to "very severe censorship." Even his mother-in-law got into the act, as agent for the provinces: "Correspondence only may also be addressed to Mme Dupont, rue du Pot d'Etain in Boulogne-sur-Mer."

For him those years, 1782 to 1785, were years of effervescence; sure of his pen, happy in his marriage, at ease in his Franco-English skin, Brissot became an authentic full-time journalist and imagined that he was succeeding where Marat had failed. Month by month his name began to echo farther afield. He's by no means famous yet but he is becoming known, even on the Continent. In Mirabeau's first letter to him, sent on August 11, 1783 from Provence, where he was in the toils of his lawsuit against his wife, he wrote, "I am in a country in which literature is unknown, although several of your works have made their way here."[8]

Brissot's idea was nothing less than to create a London-based "Confédération universelle des amis de la liberté et de la verité" [World confederation of lovers of freedom and truth—*Trans.*]. And in addition to his Lycée, he was also running a *Correspondance universelle, ou ce qui intéresse le bonheur de l'homme et de la société* ["Universal correspondence, or matters of concern to the happiness of man and society"—*Trans.*].[9] It's all happening . . .

But what about money? Subscriptions were not pouring in. The inestimable Clavière had advanced him a little, on a visit to London before returning to settle permanently in Paris after the failure of his attempt to implant a Swiss colony in Ireland. One more hope down the drain—utopia, rather: insubstantial, unplanned, and unprepared. How many such venturesome outlaws have sunk over the millennia, for one tiny handful of emigrants on a *Mayflower* who somehow manage to found a United States? There will be no New Geneva in Waterford, and Brissot was the first to bemoan the fact:

> I should in all likelihood have gone there to live, making myself useful in the field of education, and I should not then have known all the mishaps by which I have since been assailed. The scheme of the Genevan emigrants convinced me that it was hard to bring men, and especially republicans, to give up their former habits,

*The street still exists, off Oxford Street, but none of the eighteenth-century buildings remain. The Brissots and their Lycée lived at number 26. "The five or six months I spent in this amiable society were the happiest of my life" (Brissot's *Mémoires*).

†About 220 modern francs [$55].

and remove them to a foreign land, where everything seems strange to them. The Irish government* was providing substantial financial support, building had begun, but the rainy climate of Ireland, ignorance of the language there, differences in customs, the remoteness of former connections, the lack of harmony among the emigrants, the inconstancy of the leaders who were forever being called back to their affairs in France: everything conspired to defeat this project.[10]

So Brissot remained in London to carry out his own crusade, with the naiveté that was an integral part of his special brand of genius, tinged mildly with prophesy and heavily with provocation. On the one hand he was asking Louis XVI's ministers to authorize the distribution in France of periodicals in which, on the other hand, he was placidly writing (for example):

There is no state, even among the most powerful, that has not some revolution to fear, and it is then that the need of great men is most strong. Where are they to be found, if education has not made them? It is then that hordes of slaves are seen fleeing before a tiny number of republicans. It is then that a glorious Darius is tearfully compelled to acknowledge the puniness of his existence and the inconsequentiality of his pride, it is then that the haughtiest vizier is as a crawling insect at the feet of a free man determined to respect himself.[11]

"Seek (trouble) and ye shall find (it)." Quietude is not compatible with imprecation. The Lycée is censured in France; in London, the creditors attack. The result is debtors' prison, at the behest of his printer Cox (manipulated by Swinton), just as the indefatigable jack-in-the-box is about to launch yet another monthly, *Le Tableau de la situation des Anglais dans les Indes orientales et de l'état de l'Inde en général* ["Representation of the situation of the English in the East Indies, and of the state of India in general"—*Trans.*].

"I had become a father [legitimate this time] only a few days before"; the child was Félix Brissot, born April 25, 1784. More or less everybody in England, nobles included, was in danger of waking up in this kind of prison at the whim of their creditors. "Yet there was nothing sad or gloomy about it; were it not for the bars across the windows I might have thought myself in my own home. It must be admitted that when a debtor is arrested in London he receives the very best care and is at least treated with humanity."

Mme Dupont is enough to make us forgive all mothers-in-law. As soon as she gets the news she sends, from Boulogne, "a payment of 50 guineas," and a few loyal friends chip in for the rest. Cox was paid† and Brissot released after five short days, but good-bye England, Lycée, *Correspondance universelle*, and the whole shebang. His was a cyclical destiny that periodically brought

---

*Read "the English governor of Ireland and the local authorities"; at that point Ireland was merely a British possession.

†A hundred guineas in all. In other words, Cox had had Brissot put in jail for a paltry 2,000 modern francs [$500].

him back to zero. He left for Paris almost at once, hoping to make a fresh start with the support of Clavière and possibly Calonne—only to find himself rejugged, this time in the Bastille, on July 12, 1784, as the result of a denunciation by Morande, who had named him as the author of a spate of filth about Marie Antoinette. Renewed appeal to, and response from, family and friends. Intervention by Mme de Genlis. Understanding nod from Lenoir. Release on September 10, 1784.

Exhausted and gaunt, he spent many months in the Dupont home, whipped by the bitter Boulonnais wind, recovering his physical strength. Morally, on the other hand, he was not only undamaged but full of beans and readier than ever for a fight: he had received the sacrament of the Bastille. He now abhors the whole system, from Morande to Louis XVI, that has brought him so close to suffocation and is still condemning him to abject poverty and semi-speechlessness.

Brissot has turned thirty. He is one of the first true republicans of France. He goes much farther than Clavière, who brings him gradually out of the abyss, first by finding work for him in his new offices in Paris, then by commissioning some of his recent literary essays. He goes farther than Mirabeau, whose acquaintance he finally makes in Paris, but he is repelled by the smell of putrefaction that clings to Honoré, and they never become close friends. These are the months in which Brissot becomes a Brissotin.

Life begins again. "I tore myself away from the study of finance, which I had undertaken with Clavière, and in which Mirabeau occasionally took part with us, to spend the summer of 1785 with an old school friend who was a prior in the Dunois,"[12] one of the easiest of all the easy-living lands in the government general of Orléans, otherwise known as the comte of Châteaudun. Chartres to the north, Vendôme to the south; a rich land glutted with wheat, cider, wine, fruit, but also with "woodlands and fair meadows. Small and large game abound. The inhabitants of this country have great wit and imagination."[13] The priory he went to is in the little village of Lanneray (a good league from Châteaudun), which has 113 hearths (i.e., fewer than 500 inhabitants) and fields "abounding principally in cereals" on either side of a little stream that empties into the Yerre, and the Yerre flows on to the Loire, and the Loire flows on to the Sarthe somewhere above Angers . . .

The countryside where Joliet* lived was not so varied as the enchanting land of Switzerland or the banks of the Saône; but it was at least the country, and scattered woods broke up the tedious panorama of flat ground and limitless horizon. Those

---

*J. H. Joliet, born around 1752, son of a Chartres merchant, prior and priest of Lanneray in 1782; on November 4, 1792, he sheds his cassock. One month before, he was teaching his parishioners "La Marseillaise" (*Patriote* of October 16). He is a public official until An VI and mayor until his death.

solitary woods were conducive to meditation, for which I longed. There, with only the mosquitoes to fear, safe from the importunate and important people of the town, I abandoned myself, with my wife, to the sweet pleasures of observing the movements of our child. My heart thrilled to nature. I have never been in a forest, or any dense solitude, without feeling a tremor, an inner contentment, and a desire never to leave. I looked forward with unmitigated horror to the moment when I should have to part from it and go back to town. The prior's library provided books, with which I could occupy my leisure agreeably. I was free, freer than in my own home, and I took up pen or rake in turns, according to my fancy; some innocent games and frank and friendly conversation refreshed me from my work. Such was the order of my life for the three or four months of my stay in the country with the good prior and a few neighbors. To end my days, I could ask heaven for no more than that modest cottage.

It was under its hospitable roof that I wrote my *Lettres à l'empereur Joseph II* on emigration and the rights of peoples. It was there too that I had the joy of becoming the father* of a second child. I named him Sylvain, to consecrate the rustic setting to which he owed his birth and dedicate him from his cradle, so to speak, to rural life.

Who in Lanneray could have believed that the stranger in town, the "dreamer armed with a rake," was strolling, in his mind, in Wallachia, among hundreds of the tortured, decapitated, and hanged, to whom, that summer, he came closer than anyone else in France, and maybe in Europe?

JOSEPH II OF AUSTRIA

# 36

MAY 1786

## *Little by Little the Fire Spread*

This harried pen-pusher fresh from a prison cell is strangely agitated by a peasant revolt over which its century draws a cloak of silence, just as Catherine II's government did over the Pugachev uprising. Brissot is far more worked up about it, in fact, than is the prime cause of the mess that precipitated the insurrection: the reformer Joseph II. Following events through his letters to his brother Leopold and reconstructing, not without difficulty, the principal

---

*In the original sense of the word: Sylvain Brissot was conceived at Lanneray, but born in Paris on March 14, 1786.

incidents in the saga—virtually all the documentary evidence has disappeared —we obtain yet another measure of the ambiguity of this enlightened despot.

In 1783 Joseph II toured Transylvania and was shocked by the utter wretchedness of the Romanian serfs, and, even more, outraged because they *were* serfs—why, he had, by decree, abolished slavery in all his states! For the right reasons, but with the incidental advantage that doing so provided him with cheap soldiers. He had given orders that the Wallachian peasants in the frontier villages between Hungary and Transylvania, which was a sort of Hungarian colony, were to be registered as volunteers in the imperial army. Registration implied, *ipso facto,* that the peasants were liberated citizens. The consequence was a swelling flood of Wallachians, often in bands, initially peaceful but soon furious when the local administrators, who were all controlled by the Hungarian nobles, refused to register them.[1] The further consequence was sackings and pillage and a rudimentary organization among the peasants, who refused to go back home and be serfs again. And the consequence of that was increasingly brutal reprisals by the Hungarians, made nervous by this tide of erstwhile peasantry "in which religious and social fantasies* mingled with apocalyptic hopes, concrete demands, cruelty, and ingenuousness."[2]

Joseph II was a long way away. At first, sitting in his palace in Vienna, he could only rub his eyes when he read the confused and fragmentary reports sent in by his scattered representatives in Wallachia—a handful of German officers and a few fund-collecting officials—who had dithered protractedly between calls for help from both sides, the Hungarian nobles clamoring for armed intervention by their suzerain the emperor, and the infuriated peasants demanding something to back up his ephemeral promises.

From Joseph to Leopold on October 31, 1784:

> In respect of the Hungarian gentlemen, I have now rather a lot on my plate;† they are opposing conscription irrationally and with impertinence. I may well be obliged to set a firm example to put an end to their arrogance, but am holding off as long as possible.[3]

On November 15, the emperor shows signs of alarm:

> We have a most disagreeable event; there are some Wallachian peasants who, incited by a rascal who sports a Fleece** and carries a letter patent as though he

---

*"On many occasions," according to François Fejtö, in his *Joseph II,* "the rebels demanded that the population in the besieged communities convert to the Orthodox religion. At Abrudbanya they converted 65 Roman Catholics, 468 Calvinists, 41 Lutherans, and 548 Socinians (who rejected the Trinity and divinity of Jesus); 11 persons who would not convert were massacred."

†A reminder that the brothers corresponded in French may not be amiss.

**The Golden Fleece, order of chivalry of the kings of Spain, was awarded, after Charles V, by the Hapsburgs alone; needless to say, poor Hora did not have it.

were sent by me, have formed into bands and are setting fire to the homes of the Hungarian lords, killing them too; in short, they believe they will be soldiers and that the Hungarian lords are their enemies. This is taking place on the frontiers of Transylvania.

By December 3 he has finally begun to see light. No doubt about it, the Hungarian lords are to blame; but, things being what they are, it's the peasants who get punished all the same:

As to matters in Transylvania . . . the outrages of every description which have been perpetrated for many years by the landowners have given rise to widespread complaints from the entire nation and especially the Wallachians    At last, being myself in the country last year, I contrived to delegate a new commission, whose reports were to be sent directly to Vienna. . . . The [Wallachian] subjects having sent a deputation here, they got from the Hungarian chancellery a written assurance that they had nothing to fear; but no sooner had the delegates reached Zalathna than they were arrested and maltreated on the spot. Thereupon one of them, named Hora, ran away, gathered the peasants together, and set them against the landowners and their officers, saying that the way they were being treated was against the orders of the emperor; they also insisted upon being enrolled in the military districts. Instead of smoothing over the affair and bringing them to hear reason, the general in command instructed an officer to confine them, and the officer even exacted a payment for every one and ordered the popes to take up the collection. Then the government informed these men who, claiming to be soldiers, no longer wanted to work for their lords, that their conscription was not valid; but they objected, saying that anyone could see that all the Hungarian lords wanted was to oppress them against my will. After that, they conceived the plan of burning the landowners' houses and driving them out, but took care not to touch the villages or anything owned directly by the sovereign. Little by little the fire spread, and the Wallachians, all very dissatisfied, sent orders from village to village, as though coming from me, to destroy the gentry, and the peasants took good care to obey them.

When these disruptions first broke out, the government and military command spent five days arguing about what was to be done. The delay enabled the movement to gain a foothold and spread, and a host of other disorders followed. At last, the military had to put them down, some drunkards resisted, and several people were killed. Among other things, the government had the regrettable idea that the nobles should join together in a counterinsurrection aided by their Hungarian servants, and move against their Wallachian subjects. I leave you to judge of the lengths to which they went. Among other things, they arrested thirty-seven peasants, whose heads the nobles caused to be cut off in a single day without any form of trial.

On January 13, 1786, however good a prince he may be, Joseph II heaves a sigh of relief.

In Transylvania, it is now finished and done with. I am even sending you the silhouettes of the two rascals* who led the mutiny. They were captured by surprise in a wood, by Lieutenant Colonel Kray.

Leopold's answering funeral oration judiciously adds a few darker hues to the picture:

I confess that it is with the greatest pleasure that I compliment you upon the swift and satisfactory way in which the Transylvanian matters have finally been concluded by the arrest of the leaders of the mutiny. What will be very difficult, now, will be to adjust the peasants' rightful grievances against their masters, and their masters' fears, and the animosity and mistrust that will long reign between them and that it would be indispensable to root out entirely, for the country's peace and prosperity.

Two weeks after the opening night of the *Nozze,* however, on May 14, 1786, the older brother is still burbling with optimism:

My Hungarian affairs are limping along, but always with a laugh [*sic*]; I let the grumbling continue and I achieve my object a little more slowly, yet nonetheless surely. . . . Shipping on the Danube increases daily, for the Levant and the Crimea; there is a watercoach ensured, and a company which, at its own expense, is fitting out twelve seagoing ships to stand at the mouth of the Danube and convoy the products and goods leaving the river there.

Is it true that Joseph II received Hora and a peasant deputation in person three years before, and promised his support against the Magyar exactions? People said so, and continue to say so, but there is nothing in his correspondence to substantiate the hypothesis. The "letter patent" brandished before the crowds from afar by the Wallachian Pugachev may have been nothing more than the emperor's conscription edict. In any event, the ashes of the rebel chief were thrown to the winds and all that remains of his passing, in the depths of the French countryside, is one chief mourner—but what an impassioned one!

Jacques-Pierre Brissot:

Such a people must die of despair or cut its tyrants' throats. . . .
    Their proposals were not accepted. Instead, war was determined upon. An army was sent against them, they were hunted down in their woods and mountains, and at last news came that the uprising had been quelled. Deserted by his comrades, Hora fled, a price was put on his head, he was soon found and handed over, and he died in agonies. . . .
    What could the Wallachians have done, moreover, against trained troops, being without supplies, without money, without a regular army, without leaders, without intelligence? A battle means certain death. Giving in may mean a few feeble rays of life, and a hope of even the most miserable existence appeals

---

*Hora and Klocska. Grisan is caught soon afterwards. The "silhouettes" are profiles drawn around the shadow cast by a face.

strongly to the vulgar. Let us give in, then, and suffer. That is the language of despair spoken by 600,000 Wallachians as I write this letter.

Great God, who can tolerate such an idea? For one man to make millions unhappy and not be overwhelmed with remorse! No, I have no idea what soul a man takes on when he mounts a throne or approaches it, but it seems to me that if it were my misfortune to do so, I should not know a moment's peace until I had dried the tears of these unhappy people. . . .

I am the first to defend the cause of the Wallachians sacrificed to brute force in this uprising, and, I say again, so long as they are slaves and unhappy they have the right to rebel. Whoever punishes them for using that right is punishing them for being human.

CARDINAL ROHAN'S
TRIAL BY PARLEMENT

# 37

MAY 1786

## *News! News!*

From May 22 to May 30, 1786, the Parlement of Paris, assembled in full state, proceeds to judge the accused in the case that no one is yet calling publicly (and mistakenly) "the case of the Queen's necklace." It is known as "the case of the Cardinal de Rohan" or "the case of Mme de La Motte" or even "the Cagliostro case," although the poor magus really has nothing to do with it and is wriggling like an eel on a stick. Since the Grand Almoner's sensational arrest on the morning of August 15, public emotion has stagnated but never completely subsided. If one or two people were ever to begin to understand a quarter of a tenth of what actually happened, however, there was no choice but to allow the investigation to pursue its labyrinthine course before surfacing into the glare of public hearings.

Not that there hasn't been plenty of guessing and supposing going on, from drawing room to gutter. And during the eight days that undermine the monarchy the fever rises steadily, spreading out from Paris to the farthest confines of the realm.

Since the beginning of Louis XVI's reign the highest court of France has not sat in such pomp and ceremony to hear a criminal case. To be sure, there have been *lits de justice*, bittersweet debates over one or another measure adopted by Turgot, Necker, or Calonne, but only among the magistrates of the "Grand'Chambre" or summit of the structure—the only public arena that could permit itself to disagree with, and on rare occasion offer "remonstrances" to, the sovereign of this government in which *As the King Wills, So Wills the Law.* The members of the Paris Parlement are showing more taste for politics than for the law these days; they personify the moods of a nobility of the robe whose robe has shrunk in the wash, and they're determined to make as much capital as they can out of the only field of law left to them: the endorsement of royal edicts.

Ordinarily, criminal and civil proceedings in Paris are handled by police magistrates in the Châtelet or specialized judges sitting in the Tournelle, one of the corner towers of the immense humpbacked turtle of the Palais de Justice. But on this occasion, when the person to be judged is an eminent dignitary, the Grand'Chambre and Tournelle will sit together. They will hear the results of the preliminary investigation carried out by a few chosen counselors, conduct the one and only full public hearing for each of the accused, and deliberate before announcing their joint decision. There are sixty-four of them in all, including the honorary counselors and *"rapporteurs* entitled to pass judgment." The princes of the blood and peers of the realm, both ecclesiastical and lay, who are automatically entitled to sit in parlement on great occasions, have all, understandably, declined the honor.*

The Palais de Justice has become the focal point of the whole kingdom, of Europe itself. For once the Court of Versailles has been reduced to the role of onlooker, like any base commoner. In the last two weeks of August the King could have kept control of the event; on September 5, 1785, when he signed the letters patent transferring the case to parlement, he let it slip from his grasp. Part of his entourage, and especially Castries and Miromesnil, wanted Louis XVI to hold a little private trial of Rohan all by himself, or at most "in his Council," and to close the case by sending the cardinal into a gilded exile on his estates and signing a few *lettres de cachet* for the La Mottes and assorted accomplices. Justice would not have been done, but nor would the prestige of the Crown have been impaired. What difference could be made by one more manifestation of royal prerogative? It would have averted that splatter of "mire upon crosier and scepter" over which one of the rising members of the opposition in parlement, Fréteau de Saint-Just, is crowing so loudly, adding, "A crooked cardinal! The Queen implicated in a forgery case! What a triumph for the ideals of liberty!"[1]

But the King gave the show away to Rohan by allowing him—through

*We meet these "peers" at every one of the monarchy's big events, coronations, *lits de justice,* etc.; but all they have left of their status as the equals of the kings, conferred upon them a thousand years before, is the name. They comprise a handful of nobles (bishops or dukes only) to whom the Bourbons have conceded the appellation, but they display it with ostentation.

Mme de Marsan—to choose. Trial by king, or public trial by parlement? Rohan was no longer the shambles of August 15; he had been thinking, insofar as he was able, and was now convinced that he had been deceived by the comtesse and possibly outraged by the Queen, or by both of them together. His only real fault had been to cherish pretensions to Marie Antoinette. But he knew that very little would be said about that because, after all, nothing concrete had actually happened, except for the incident in the grove, and that was so ephemeral. Abbé Georgel had had time to burn the Queen's letters, real or forged, along with those famous "proposals to purchase" allegedly signed by her.

Therefore, Sire, I am content to be judged by you alone, but not without a confrontation, in your presence and in that of the heads of my family, with the Queen, the jewelers, and the wretches who stole the necklace.

Confrontations, in his presence? The very thought made the King blench. Rohan accordingly settled for trial by parlement, which was authorized to proceed, on September 5, 1785, by a text that has the merit of summarizing the hereafter inalterable—and, as it happens, correct—version of the imbroglio as seen by the royal couple.

> Having been informed that the persons named Böhmer and Bassenge allegedly sold a diamond necklace to the Cardinal de Rohan; that the said cardinal claimed without the knowledge of the Queen, our very beloved spouse and companion, to be authorized by her to purchase this object for the sum of 1,600,000 livres payable in several installments, and produced to that effect alleged proposals which he exhibited to the above persons as being approved and signed by the Queen; that the said necklace having been delivered by the said Böhmer and Bassenge to the said cardinal, and the first payment agreed between them not having been made, they then turned to the Queen; We have been unable to look on without just indignation while a name so august and dear to Us on so many accounts was being impudently misused, and the respect owing to royal majesty was being violated with such unprecedented temerity; We have thought it right and proper to summon before Us the said cardinal and, upon the declaration made to Us by him, that he was deceived by a woman named La Motte de Valois, We have judged it indispensable to arrest him and the said La Motte de Valois woman and to take the measures suggested to Us by Our wisdom with a view to bringing to light all who may have been the authors of or accomplices in an assault of such nature, and We have judged it proper to apprise you accordingly in order that the proceedings may by you be performed and the matter duly judged.

As the Baron de Frenilly, a minor Court figure, writes in his *Souvenirs,* "That was throwing a lighted fuse into a powderkeg and the keg blew up with terrifying force."*

---

*Another solution would have been to have Rohan discreetly summoned before an ecclesiastical court in Rome, Paris, or some "neutral" city; and the pope let it be known that this

So here we go. The first president [or chief judge—*Trans.*], Etienne-François d'Aligre, who has thus become the prime arbiter, possesses, according to Beugnot, "none of the qualities that produce great magistrates, but rather the contrary failings; yet he was singularly adroit in manipulating his entourage and had hitherto shown himself favorable to the Court; but of late it had irritated him, so that while he did not strive against it openly, he did allow opposition to build up." Nevertheless, d'Aligre appoints two counselors "of the Queen's party" to conduct the investigation: Dupuis de Marse and Titon de Villotran. "The latter was not thought incorruptible," at least according to Abbé Georgel; "he acted as *rapporteur* in sensational cases and was reputed to possess, to a supreme degree, the art of presenting a case in the light of his own opinion." However that may be, next August Louis XVI will appoint him *lieutenant civil*,[2] or supreme chief of jurisdiction in the Châtelet, except in criminal matters, with an "advance" on his salary of 100,000 écus.*

In other respects the investigation was relatively straightforward. A royal decree gave parlement temporary jurisdiction over the Bastille, which was a state prison, so that the officials conducting the investigation could have access to the accused, who had been collected together there. "All the documents in the proceedings are complete and bear the signature of both accused and witnesses. The minutes are complete and show no gaps. No detail in the proceedings was kept secret. The accused have all been confronted with each other. They could communicate freely with their counsel and have provided all the particulars they deemed useful to their defense."[3]

We're a long way from torture, or rather the "preliminary question" which Louis XVI abolished only five years ago. But would it have been used in this instance, and on whom? The opening phases proceed courteously, without the slightest insult or reprimand being offered to the persons questioned. An interrogation in kid gloves.

Rohan was interviewed twice, Jeanne de La Motte twice, Rétaux de Villette—abducted in Geneva by special agents, who failed in their attempt to capture the Comte de La Motte in London—three times; only one interrogation for poor Nicole Leguay, alias d'Oliva, who was also abducted, in Brussels, with the complicity of richly rewarded Belgian officials,[4] and now we can tie up the elements of the investigation in a sealed bag for delivery to chief prosecuting attorney Joly de Fleury. Some of the interrogations went on for several days, but they were not made deliberately severe. And although no one actually confronted Rohan, not even Jeanne, she was finally unnerved in the

---

was what he desired, as no cardinal had been tried by a civil court in a Roman Catholic country for many a year. But it was too late.

*Two million modern francs [$500,000].

course of a decisive session with Rétaux de Villette and Nicole Leguay, and showed her chagrin by throwing a tantrum and biting one of the registrars until he bled.

Apart from this inevitable dénouement for the woman who did all the scheming and can no longer wriggle off the hook by dumping everything on the cardinal's doorstep, and a series of increasingly guilty admissions from Rétaux de Villette concerning his role as the forger who imitated the Queen's writing and signature, the rest of the accused never vary their stories by so much as a hair. Rohan declares himself the victim of the comtesse's intrigues; Cagliostro, far from indulging in drawing-room maunderings about his whereabouts over the past thousand years, states that he is "between thirty-seven and thirty-eight years of age, professor of medicine but not at present exercising that profession, orphaned of both parents from the age of three months, and not certain whether he was born in Malta or Medina in Arabia." His fortune? A mysterious inheritance. His occupations? He has traveled the world. His role in the Rohan entourage? That of an intimate adviser, with a sideline in thaumaturgy. As far as the necklace is concerned, his role was confined to putting the cardinal on his guard against the paper signed by the "Queen" and intended for the jewelers, and urging him, before anyone else, to throw himself upon the King's mercy and tell all.*

To these should be added a series of interrogations of witnesses against whom no charge had been brought: the jewelers, the intimates and servants of the La Mottes in Paris (luckily for Beugnot, the enquiry never got as far as Bar-sur-Aube), police inspectors, and a rueful Baudard de Saint-James.

Jeanne de La Motte alone muddies the seemingly placid current of this river of ink. In addition to biting the registrar, she nearly scratches out Rétaux de Villette's eyes. It is true that he offloads everything onto her with a crassness that is perfectly in keeping with the rest of his character. And she actually injures herself with a candlestick, trying to throw it at Cagliostro. Wild with fury against the others, but also against herself, for getting shipwrecked so close to port, she is determined to be a Valois to the end but doesn't really have the stature and is constantly on the verge of hysteria. She ricochets from lie to lie, following her usual method, and ultimately claims that the diamonds from the necklace sold by her husband and Villette were given to her by the cardinal, as a love token!

He, meanwhile, draped in a becoming dignity, does not shrink from the disclaimers demanded by his persona as victim. As a true prince of the church

---

*I am deliberately omitting from this account another case which became attached to the "Necklace Affair" during the investigation; it involved a mythomaniac named Bette d'Etienville and an adventuress who called herself the Baronne de Courville—also "de La Motte"!—both of whom pretended to have extorted favors from the Queen. This tale would only complicate the other one needlessly.

he denies, evidence to the contrary notwithstanding, that Jeanne was ever his mistress. Absurd; why, there was never more than an occasional act of charity on his part. He does admit that he thought she was "favored" by the Queen and might have helped to bring him back into the sovereign's good graces— whence his credulity as go-between about the necklace.

The interrogations glide like swans over the scene in the Venus Grove, although something has got to be said about it because of the testimony of Nicole Leguay and Rétaux. According to the records, no word was spoken, there was nothing but an entrechat of shadows. Nobody mentions the very particular nature of Jeanne's alleged "friendship" with Marie Antoinette, and certainly not she herself. So bold-faced a crime of lèse majesté would mean the gallows for her, although it would also mean utter disgrace for the investigators.

The mute, the one person who is simply absent from the entire proceedings, is Marie Antoinette herself, and it does her no good. Implicitly indicted by the reticence of the accused and the unvoiced questions of all well-informed people, she would lose face if she stooped to defend herself against the suspicion that continues to hang over her head, i.e., that she did after all ask the cardinal to buy the necklace for her in secret. When two counselors respectfully present themselves at Versailles to hear anything she might care to say, they are seen by the Baron de Breteuil, as minister of the King's Household, who informs them that Her Majesty saw nothing and knew nothing of the whole business.

But the more discreet the official investigation, the more clamorous the public one. Counsel for the accused are not allowed to take part in the interrogations; that gives them all the more reason to print and circulate, using whatever euphemisms may be required to avoid seizure, the *mémoires* [in this sense, *mémoires* means submissions, pleadings—*Trans.*] they are busily writing, ostensibly to assist their clients but actually to lay their arguments before the public —which was forbidden by legal usage, even at the final hearing. Target produces five mémoires for the cardinal, Maître Blondel publishes two for Nicole Leguay, Cagliostro perpetrates three—for himself (and sells 17,000 copies in two weeks), and there are three more by poor Master Doillot, whose sixty years are instantly fired with the demon of love the moment he undertakes to defend Mme de La Motte; not counting an avalanche of anonymous pamphlets which the booksellers' police inspectors are powerless to keep from pouring off the backroom shelves.

Toward the end it becomes sheer madness. The hawkers trot down the boulevards crying, "News! News!"[5] as usual, but for once they are telling the truth.

They sell twenty-two portraits (none authentic) of the protagonists in the case; they sell songs about it; they sell "Lives" of Cagliostro—some of which purport to have been printed in Mecca; and when, on May 16, Target's final mémoire for the cardinal comes out, at one écu per copy,* there is almost a mob under the colonnades of the Palais Soubise on the right bank, where three different printers are offering it. The watch is unable to disperse the crowd; they have to call out the Horse Guard.

First prize in the competition is won hands down by Abbé Georgel, however, who has remained at liberty throughout, although everybody is aware that he must be the one person who really knows the ins and outs of the affair. But that's just the point; nobody is eager to challenge him, especially as he has guts enough to defend his boss tooth and claw, and with breathtaking insolence. On Shrove Tuesday morning, for example, the pastoral letter which, being the Grand Almoner's vicar general, he is entitled to issue informing his distinguished parishioners that, as an exception, they will be permitted to eat eggs during Lent, is posted on the doors of the chapels in the châteaus of the King—the Louvre, the Tuileries, Versailles. Just listen to it!

"I, François Georgel, doctor in theology etc., having been sent to you, my very dear brethren, as the disciple Timothy was sent unto the people when Paul, in bondage, could no longer teach, I say unto you that it is permitted to you to eat butter and eggs during Lent."[6]

If Rohan is St. Paul, does that make Louis XVI Nero? The next day a *lettre de cachet,* signed by Breteuil, dispatches Abbé Georgel to eat all the butter and eggs he pleases at Mortagne in Perche. A token chastisement, ending with the trial: at this point the high clergy are solidly behind the cardinal, and they are a reflection of the great majority of the people watching the news. In fact, opinion is not so much in favor of the cardinal as it is against the Queen. "The whole affair," according to Hardy the bookseller, "was no longer thought to be anything more than a rash initiative on the part of the ministry, comparable to the quite unjustifiable imprisonment of the Sieur Caron de Beaumarchais in Saint-Lazare last year."

Most if not all the women are cheering for the new St. Paul and tying red and yellow ribbons in their hair; this spring's fashion note will be "cardinal on the straw."

---

*About 20 modern francs [$5]; but manuscript copies had already been sold for 36 livres, or 250 francs [$62].

# 38

## MAY 1786

## *Even the High Bench Rose*

From May 22 to May 29 the august magistrates listen to the minutes of the interrogations and confrontations. Before making their decision they have now to hear the accused themselves, who are transferred from the Bastille to the conciergerie of the Palais de Justice* during the night of May 29–30.

In the great solemn hall (where mass is said every morning), the colossal, mutilated statue of Enguerrand de Marigny, the famous minister of Philippe le Bel who was executed by mistake, stands as a permanent reminder that justice has been known to miscarry, while a "lion carved in stone kneels with lowered head, to show that he who enters this chamber, however rich and great he may be, must humble himself and obey Justice."[1] Beneath the formidable ceiling, like a forest hung upside down over their heads, the presidents, counselors, advocates general, registrars, and secretaries file in and take their places, some in black velvet mortars, others in ermine-lined scarlet hoods. No public. What actually happens at the two hearings has to be pieced together afterwards from—numerous—indiscretions and the subsequently published memoirs of a few magistrates.

Chief prosecuting attorney Joly de Fleury, brother of the ex–comptroller of finance, begins. Having taken cognizance of the preliminary investigation, it is his heavy duty to name the sentences requested. For Rétaux de Villette and the Comte de La Motte (absent) he demands life on the galleys; for Cagliostro, banishment; for Nicole Leguay, free release, presumably because of her confession; and for Jeanne de La Motte, "the gravest penalty before death." That means a flogging, branding with an iron poker (*V* for *voleuse* [thief—*Trans.* ]) on both shoulders, and life imprisonment in the Salpêtrière.†

---

*Not yet a prison, only an annex to the concierge's rooms; persons awaiting trial were occasionally put there before their hearings in the nearby chambers.

†This was a rare sentence in the Ancien Régime, when "imprisonment" itself virtually did not exist, except as one of the consequences of a *lettre de cachet*. The Salpêtrière, moreover, was a "general hospital"; men who were to be physically confined were ordinarily sent to the galleys, women to a "hospital."

For the cardinal it could be worse, except for his honor: the prosecuting attorney asks that he be condemned to appear before parlement within the week, there to state "in clear and intelligible tones" that he was dealing falsely with Böhmer and Bassenge when he swore to them that the Queen was aware of the purchase of the necklace, and that he repented of his disrespect to his sovereigns; furthermore, he should divest himself of his public offices, "give alms to the poor," and spend the rest of his life far from all royal residences.

But even that is too much; the audience mutters. In the last few weeks every member of parlement has been visited by one or another of the Rohan-Soubise clan. Séguier, the advocate general, almost equal in rank to Joly de Fleury, springs from his seat and begins an exchange that smells of powder—facepowder, that is:

> SÉGUIER: Within a foot of your grave, Monsieur, you seek to cover your ashes in ignominy and compel the magistrates to share it with you.
> FLEURY: I am not in the least surprised to see you so angry. A man as dedicated to libertinage as yourself could hardly do otherwise than defend the cardinal's cause.
> SÉGUIER: Yes, I do visit girls sometimes. I even leave my carriage outside their door. But that's my private business. And I have never been seen selling my opinion, like a craven, to fortune.

Fortunately, duels are not the custom among magistrates. The two men do not cut each other's throats, and, to ease the tension, the trial moves on to the final examinations.

Each of the accused plays his last card, under the hungry gaze of the courtroom. Rétaux de Villette, in black silk, manages to avoid the galleys by reiterating his confession, while the arrogance and insolence of Jeanne de La Motte merely aggravate her position. The trouble with her is that she has never learned how to be humble; she is obsessed with the idea of her blood, especially here, where she might almost believe she is playing Mary Stuart. Sitting "as in an armchair" on the little wooden stool otherwise known as "the seat of ignominy," wearing a bluish gray satin gown and a short embroidered muslin cape, she defies the whole assembly in clipped, tight phrases.

Her first move is to announce, with reference to the cardinal, that she is about to confound a great dastard. "But she made herself heard because she spoke entirely without embarrassment." At first, she is cautious enough to be vague when asked about the alleged letters from the Queen to the cardinal: "I must not speak, to avoid offense to the Queen."

At that point President d'Aligre apparently jettisons his presumed allegiance to the Court. He persists, risking the ultimate scandal: "No possible offense can be offered to Their Majesties, Madame, and you must tell the whole truth to justice."

She doesn't need much persuading. She proceeds to reject Rétaux's state-ments as false and affirms that the letters did exist, that they really were written by Marie Antoinette, that the cardinal had showed her over two hundred of them in which he was addressed as *tu* and several of which mentioned places and times of meetings. Never before has she carried provocation to such lengths. She burns her boats. Even if the majority of her listeners are in the "opposition" her statements don't carry conviction, and a muted clamor shows her that she is going to lose. But she gets the only reward she can, a gratuitous revenge for another lost chance. For a while, at least, some people continue to wonder about that famous correspondence. Jeanne withdraws with a string of curtsies, defying her judges with a blood-chilling smile.

For the martyr himself the wooden stool is removed. Louis-René de Rohan enters, dressed in the long purple gown and short coat worn by cardinals in mourning, his breast adorned by a handsome episcopal cross on a golden chain and traversed by the broad moiré band of the Order of the Holy Ghost. He is livid and shaky, his eyes brimming tears. When the president insists that he be seated, like a colleague, at one end of the gentlemen's bench, there is an approving murmur. He is one of them. He is part of them. He will know how to avoid the traps—that nobody will set for him. According to him, it's all the fault of that little schemer who has just made such a bad impression; but between his justifications one can glimpse something like a sigh of regret that the Queen of France should be a person capable of allowing him to be made a fool of by such a hussy. When he leaves, bowing to the assembly, all the magistrates rise, "even the high bench [where the mortar presidents sat], which is a marked distinction."

His first few weeks of captivity had been mild enough, almost nonexis-tent. On August 15 and 16 he was allowed to sleep at home, and on the 16th passersby saw him through the drawing-room windows, "playing with his monkey." The Marquis de Launay, governor of the Bastille, came to fetch him on the night of the 17th, and conveyed him not into the detention area but into an apartment reserved for staff officers, where he was allowed to keep three servants. The King's Household allotted 120 francs a day* from its own budget for the "catering" of the illustrious prisoner.[2] In this apartment he could command facilities and space enough to give dinners for twenty with oysters and champagne. He had such a throng of callers that the great draw-bridge was lowered permanently and the two leaves of the main door stood open all day long, something that had not occurred within living memory of the people in the Faubourg Saint-Antoine. On August 29, 1785, for example,

---

*About 840 modern francs [$210].

his list of callers was rather short: only the Prince de Condé, the Duc de Bourbon, the Comtesse de Brionne, the Princesse de Carignan and the Comtesse Charlotte (her daughters), the Prince and Princesse de Vaudémond, Prince Ferdinand de Rohan, the Prince and Princesse de Montbazon, the Duc and Duchesse de Montbazon, Prince Camille de Montbazon, Prince Charles de Rohan, the Comtesse de Marsan, the Maréchal de Soubise, the Duchesse de La Vauguyon, the Prince de Lambesc, the Vicomte de Pont and the Comte de la Tour, his equerry. Plus the following members of his own household: Carbonnières, Dubois, Abbé Georgel, Odoran, de Villefond, Sinatery, and Bidot; Louvet and Calès, "in charge of disbursements"; Racle, "in charge of matters relating to Guéménée"; Ravenot; Roth, his valet; Travers, his surgeon; and attorneys Target, Colet, Tronchet, and Bonnières.[3]

Poor fellow.*

The wave of opinion rising around him has brought the Bastille to the notice of France, a thing which hasn't happened since the Fronde. The latest mémoires, falsely attributed to newly released inmates, are selling like hotcakes: there was Le Prévost de Beaumont, a publicist abducted on a whim of Louis XV; Latude, who made many attempts to escape and was only released after thirty-five years; and most of all Linguet, the attorney stricken from the Paris bar out of spite in 1775. Exiled to London, where he has been publishing his *Annales,* he was ambushed by the police on a trip back to France and his reminiscences of captivity, or *Mémoires sur la Bastille,* † published after eighteen months inside, began stirring up the Parisians back in 1783. He made more impact than the others, with his references to the "regimen of this château, which was instituted for the express purpose of rending souls asunder."[4] But even Linguet wasn't enough. Thousands of people for whom the Bastille used to be just part of the landscape are now contemplating the enormous stone monster crouched at the entrance to Paris with startled eyes, and peering along its ramparts in search of a silhouette in scarlet.

The last two interrogations are rattled off like nursery rhymes: the magistrates take a Rousseauist—even more, a Restifian—interest in the affecting testimony of Nicole "d'Oliva," exquisitely appetizing in the studied disarray "of a young mother who has just given the breast to her infant born in prison." She offers no reply to any questions, for the excellent reason that she is sobbing abundantly. Numerous witnesses compare her to the model for Greuze's *Cruche cassée.* She is allowed to retire, "accompanied by the most intense expressions of solicitude."

---

*From March to May, during the interrogations, visiting was restricted.
†His are authentic.

Cagliostro, in his gold-embroidered green taffeta coat, rounds off the play with a comic turn, complete with table-thumping delivery and windmill gesticulations beneath hair falling in little pigtails on his shoulders.

"Who are you?"

"A noble traveler. . . ."

Benevolent chuckles punctuate his tirade to the end.

When he is driven back to the Bastille with the other accused that evening, the crowd besieging the palace cheers him so loudly that he throws them his hat with one lordly sweep of his arm.

Wednesday, May 31. The moment of truth. The judges must sit without interruption until sentence is passed and, as each must have his turn to speak, they commence their deliberations at six in the morning. Being a judge in this case is no sinecure, we see, although their profession is still less arduous than that of loiterer: from five o'clock on, every room in the Palais and every street around it is seething with agitated onlookers, from whom issue wave after wave of rumor for eighteen straight hours. A full contingent of military guards surround the building, but will even they be able to contain an angry mob if the cardinal is convicted? Louis XVI's ineptitude has wrought a miracle, transforming one of the most corrupt prelates of France into the hero of the day.

At the door leading to the Grand'Chambre the sixty-four magistrates file past the members of the Rohan, Soubise, and Lorraine families—nineteen noble personages in mourning, including the Archbishop of Cambrai.

And the interminable palaver begins. Every counselor must present aloud the arguments on which his judgment of the six accused is founded, and reply to objections raised. There is no actual vote; the clerks simply note the opinions in different columns and tot them up at the end.

They expedite the comtesse first, abandoning her to Joly de Fleury: branding and life imprisonment. Ditto for her absent husband: the prison galley. But they let Villette off with banishment from the kingdom. Nicole Leguay, as predicted, is acquitted, and nor is Cagliostro banished; he too is "discharged of all accusation." The only serious legal battle is over the cardinal; it takes place between the majority, who want a pure and simple acquittal, and a large minority who are anxious to placate the Court. A few interchanges raise the temperature a bit, in particular when counselor Robert de Saint-Vincent snaps at the King's prosecuting attorney:

"Since when are ministerial conclusions accepted by magistrates?"

Jean-Marie d'Outremont, a Rohan supporter, proclaims that "he will let himself be hacked to pieces on the spot for the cardinal's innocence." Under the circumstances, the absence of counsel for the defense is no great drawback —what more could they have said?

By ten in the evening there are only forty-eight speakers left in the arena, the rest having been carried out exhausted before the final count. In the end, the Cardinal Prince de Rohan is acquitted by twenty-six votes against twenty-two. He could be released then and there, but he himself chooses to spend another night in the Bastille in order to avoid the deadly embrace of a crowd thousands strong, including the ladies of the market district who are packed in the May Court waving bunches of roses and jasmine and who nearly smother the counselors with kisses, whichever way they voted.

Cagliostro leaves the Bastille around 11:30 that night.

> The night was dark, the district where I lived a deserted one. What was my surprise, when I heard my name being cried out by eight or ten thousand persons! My door had been broken open. The courtyard, staircases, rooms, everything was full of people. I was carried to the arms of my wife. My heart could not encompass all the conflicting emotions competing for mastery of it. My knees sank beneath me. I fell senseless to the floor. My wife uttered a shriek and fainted. Our trembling friends clustered around us, in terror lest the finest moment of our lives should prove to be the last. Anxiety spread, the drums ceased to roll. The joyous din gave way to appalled silence. I am reborn.[5]

Polkas in Paris, *marches funèbres* in Versailles. Louis XVI takes the blow with his customary phlegm. Underneath it all, he may not be too displeased to see his wife put so smartly in her place; her effervescence is a perpetual humiliation to him. Marie Antoinette is visibly upset; she weeps, she feels suddenly giddy and faint in the changeless stage setting of an etiquette that chafes her more and more every day. People go on bowing to the ground before her, but not many of them meet her eyes. Acquitting Rohan means convicting her. War is henceforth declared between her and the Parlement of Paris.

Out of petulance the King sends the cardinal, via Breteuil, a *lettre de cachet* stripping him of all his court offices and most particularly that of Grand Almoner, and exiling him to the "least" of his possessions, the splendid abbey of La Chaise-Dieu, lost in the mountains of the hinterland of Auvergne— Siberia, to Parisians.* Another easy martyrdom. And was it really necessary to top it off by preempting parlement with his royal prerogative and exiling Cagliostro to England?

The punishment of Jeanne de La Motte provides a collective release for all the people who feel somehow frustrated by the court's leniency. On the morning

---

*His stay there is brief. The family is still campaigning for him, and in September he comes back to spend a cosy winter in his abbey at Marmoutiers near Tours. He pays over half the price of the necklace in quarterly installments—ending at the Revolution—to the jewelers, but they die bankrupt even so.

of June 21, almost a thousand voyeurs squeeze up against the iron gates of the Palais de Justice to watch her be dragged to the foot of the "Grand Stairs," the tall flight of steps inside the May Court.

> Until that day she did not know what her sentence was; to make her kneel while it was read out, her knees had to be bent by force. She flew into so great a fury upon hearing it, and uttered such terrible screams, that she was heard all over the palace and around it; to the registrar and executioners she howled, "What have they done to that villain of a cardinal, if this is how they treat me, of the blood of the Valois!" Five hangmen held her while the rope was put round her neck. She writhed full length on the ground in the May Court; she flung her limbs in every direction, shrieking like a fury, and uncovered her whole body, which is superb and most beautiful in shape, according to the accounts of those who witnessed the punishment. The hangmen were forced to lacerate her bodice and chemise in order to bare her shoulders, but she struggled with such rage that the poker slipped on her back and, sliding beneath her armpit, seared her lovely breast. She bit the arm of one of the hangmen; a piece of his coat and flesh stuck in her mouth. Then she fell into an extreme debility.

LOUIS XVI WATCHING THE PLACING
OF A CONICAL TOWER AT CHERBOURG HARBOR

# 39

## JUNE 1786

## *Long Live Yourselves!*

This time it really does seem to be over. True, the waves from the pebble of the "necklace judgment" radiating out in the French duckpond are felt in almost every class of society in the realm except the illiterate. But heads turn quickly at Versailles and Paris, and conversation has moved on.

The lowest stratum of the capital's populace has had its distractions too, however, in the form of two backwashes that have made more work for the constabulary; although totally unrelated to Böhmer and Bassenge's diamonds, and trivial in themselves, they are not without significance.

First, there is that demonstration by the poorest of the poor, the Savoyards as they were called, a subsistence-level people who had emigrated from their "Italian" mountains, where the meadows were not rich enough to feed them, and descended upon Paris and other large towns of France to sweep chimneys

—because, when young, they were small and agile—or serve as private messenger boys. Because of them nobody said "chimney sweep" anymore, only "savoyard," just as "limousin" had become the common word for "stonemason."

They lived apart, speaking a tongue that was incomprehensible to the Parisians, and clung like barnacles to hovels in which no one else would ever have consented to dwell.

> They form, in Paris, a sort of confederation, with complete laws of its own. The oldest act as disciplinarians to the young; punishment is meted out to those who deviate. They have been seen doing justice to one of their number who had stolen something; they tried him themselves, and they hanged him.
>
> They somehow manage to save something from their meager pittances, and send money home to their poor parents every year. These paragons of filial affection are often seen in tatters, while there are many ingrate children who go clothed in gold.
>
> They trot through the streets from morning to evening, their faces smudged with soot, their teeth snow white, their aspect simple and gay; their cry is long, plaintive, and mournful. . . .
>
> It is cruel indeed to see a poor child of eight, blindfolded and with a bag over his head, clamber up the inside of a fifty-foot chimney using only his knees and back; unable to breathe except at the perilous pinnacle, he comes back down as he went up, risking a broken neck if the plaster crumbles beneath his frail bulk; then, his mouth filled with soot, half-choking, his eyelids crusted shut, he asks you for five sous as the price of his peril and his labor.[1]

What has happened is that the Baron de Breteuil, suddenly remembering that he is also the minister responsible for Paris, has founded "a small cartage company" or private postal service, under a special license from the King, to operate inside the capital. Its employees are dressed in green. "Somebody, seeing them pass by, said, 'There go M. de Breteuil's parakeets!' The jester was taken to prison. From this incident the public learned that the cartage company is a financial speculation of the minister of Paris, who is said to have put up the money for it."[2] However that may be, customers are beginning to employ the parakeets in preference to the Savoyards, because they drive little carts and can reach their destinations sooner than the mountain boys on their short legs.

At the end of January 1786, 1,500 Savoyards—the older ones—assembled, made a little noise, and frightened the burghers living around the Hôtel de Ville. Dispersed by the archers, they re-assembled outside the town gates and marched down the Sèvres road toward Versailles, intending to beg their good King to rescind the parakeets' license. A mob of starvelings. A company of the royal gendarmerie was awaiting them on the Sèvres bridge and drove them back. Its captain deigned to receive their clumsily drafted petition and transmitted it to the King, who deigned to drop it into the wastepaper basket.

In doing so, the King was deemed to have "conducted himself well," as in the Grain War, and the Court scampered off to plait him laurel wreathes for firmness. What would become of us if we started paying attention to people "of the lowest order"? In this respect, Louis XVI has diligently followed in his ancestors' footsteps. With equal firmness he tramples on another little guild in difficulty, the hackney-cab drivers. "It was over some reform or other," according to Louis-Sébastien Mercier, that threatened their relatively privileged position. "Almost 1,800 strong, horses, cabs, and men, the drivers agreed among themselves to go to Choisy, where the King was then, to present their petition to him. The Court was quite startled to see 1,800 empty cabs filling the road in front of it, bringing their humble remonstrances to the foot of the throne: it made them feel uneasy. The drivers were sent away as they had come; the four representatives of their guild were thrown into prison, and their spokesman was taken to Bicêtre with his paper and his speech."[3]

A third wavelet, this time in the provinces, would have gone unnoticed except that it agitates a man in the news. A few plebeians undertake to play a little trick on a senior official in the comptroller general's office who is much too wealthy for his position and is known by all who know him at all to have grown even wealthier occupying it. François Foulon has long been ogling the job of comptroller of finance, and threatening to adopt stern tactics when he gets it, to bring in the money. His reputation as a "strong-arm man" has been growing yearly, bringing a satisfied smile to the faces of the privileged and a shudder of dread to the people. Now he goes a trifle too far, by sending Vergennes a mémoire designed to discredit Calonne, and Vergennes promptly makes it public. Calonne manages to have Foulon sent away to think things over on his estate at Doué-la-Fontaine in Anjou, which he seems to have used as a proving ground for his theories.

> Upon the arrival of Monsieur Foulon at Doué, his place of exile, his vassals took up arms, not to show their joy at the sight of a dearly beloved lord, but to insult him. The men, no less angry with him than was the comptroller general, locked him inside his own château. The rebels were not in the least intimidated by the constabulary, and a miniature war ensued, in which men were injured and killed. Five of the vassals were caught and taken to Chinon to prison, where a summary investigation is being conducted.* This insurrection, which is not the first to occur, probably means that M. Foulon was in the habit of trying out his ideas on

*Four of them were hanged.

his peasantry, giving them a taste of what he could do with the docile people of France if, as he still hopes, he were entrusted with the direction of finance.[4]

In Versailles, these movements are perceived like flashes of heat-lightning in an untroubled sky. The governing class is momentarily absorbed by an event of far greater consequence than the "Necklace Affair" or such piffling proletarian murmurs: for the first time in his reign, Louis XVI is venturing beyond the immediate vicinity of Paris. He is going out to the provinces—to Normandy—to tour the works at Cherbourg which, now that the treaty of 1783 permits it to do so, is about to provide France with a formidable military port on the Channel front, where the lack of any military infrastructure had been partly responsible for the failure of the recent attempt against England.

The King's eternal indecisiveness has delayed the trip for over a year: before he could be persuaded to go, the Maréchal de Castries, his minister of the navy, followed by his own brother the Comte d'Artois, had to travel out to Cherbourg and back and insist that the journey would be worth the disruption of his sacrosanct habits and the loss of six or seven days' hunting. All right, then, a pox upon those griping and insolent Parisians and those tittle-tattling Versaillese! Back in the wellsprings of the monarchy, the King will bask in the affection—adoration would be a better word—of the Norman towns and countryside. There he will come face to face with "the real France."[5]

On Monday, June 21, 1786, Louis XVI sets out on a first, longish lap from Versailles, accompanied by his captain of the guard, two ministers—Ségur for War and Castries for Navy—and a dozen other gentlemen, each with three or four servants. The King's own retinue includes equerries; lieutenants of the guard; chamber, mouth, and foot servants; pages; a first surgeon; etc. The little caravan's accommodation requisitions specify twenty-nine "masters' beds" and sixteen "servants' beds," the latter in dormitories (usually abbeys) if need be, plus, of course, the King's apartments. The baggage train numbers thirty-five vehicles, including those for accessories and wardrobe, and the table service and provisions for certain stopping places (one coach is "His Majesty's Second"; it trails behind the convoy empty, in case his first one breaks down). At each posting station eighty-three draft horses are ordered for the carriages and wagons and forty mounts for the outriders and horsemen accompanying the train.

There is no military guard; the King will be protected by local militia and regiments in the garrison towns they pass through. And this is a man's trip—neither the Queen nor any of the gentlemen's wives are in the party; but the numerous receptions along the way are attended by squadrons of dames "of good society."

Louis XVI is in high spirits, behaving like a diligent schoolboy on a study trip. He has nothing to worry about, the only speeches he has to make will be a few gracious remarks in response to the harangues of local dignitaries. In his carriage he has a set of "M. Cassini's maps" and a *vade mecum* written for the occasion by Calonne, giving him the salient economic and demographic particulars of every halting place and "respectfully suggesting" the amount of alms to be distributed to the hospitals and the favors (e.g., tax exemptions) to be bestowed upon specific towns or institutions.

When he leaves, thus, the King already knows that in Normandy, through which he will travel for 180 leagues, there are 1,800,000 souls who bring him 25 million livres annually in direct taxes, and more than 26 million in duties levied by the *Ferme générale* on crops and industry.*

They head for Caen via Houdan, L'Aigle, and Falaise. The *bains de foule* ["crowd baths," a term popularized during the government of General de Gaulle—*Trans.*] start at once; Louis XVI dreads them less than a Court ball. His affability and inarticulateness make him feel positively at home with these friendly hicks, who hem and haw even worse than he does and who, from time immemorial, have been struck dumb by the aura of sacredness surrounding the idol he incarnates, the mere sight of which sends them into ecstasies. In Houdan, one woman embraces his knees, imploring his intercession for her twelve children. He nods. She subsides in tears.

"I see a good King, I can wish for nothing further in this world."

That sets the tone. In Falaise, fifty girls in pink and white welcome him at the town gates and strew flowers before his path. There's a great press around the château of Harcourt, where one of the first families of Normandy, that of the governor of the province and titular tutor of the dauphin, welcomes him on the first night. During her dinner party for a hundred guests the Duchesse d'Harcourt makes bold to beseech his clemency for six deserters sentenced to be hanged in Caen.† Pardon granted; duchess enraptured; general acclamation:

"Long live good King Louis XVI!"

Response:

"Long live yourselves, my children!"

June 22. Arrival at Caen at ten in the morning, in a dangerous crush in which a few people are almost run over by the carriages. The King "grants the inhabitants permission to erect a statue of him."** After Caen, he decides he hasn't been getting enough to eat and gorges himself on butter,

---

*Roughly equivalent to 350 million modern francs [almost $90 million].

†In those days there was, with rare exceptions, only one punishment for desertion: death, even in time of peace.

**This occurs in seven places, but none of the statues is finished by 1789. The only present-day souvenir of the trip is a rue Louis XVI in Cherbourg.

fresh eggs, and black bread in the inn at Sainte-Croix Grand Tonne, the owners of which are almost prostrate with excitement. The entire village crowds around to watch him eat, and the King orders drinks all round. Half-tipsy himself, he signals to a pregnant young woman who is brooding in a corner:

"What's the matter with you, young woman?"

"Monseigneur [*sic*], I am with child by a boy whom my mother will not let me marry; please deign to give him to me."

"Your state is blameworthy," replies the grandson of Louis XV, "but your request is legitimate. I wish you to be married by my return, and I shall give you a dowry."

The village churchbells jangle for joy.*

One in the afternoon: Bayeux, where "His Majesty refreshed himself with a goblet of wine" while the horses were changed. The local dignitaries look a little crestfallen at the brevity of his stay; here as elsewhere, they resemble extras in an opera, standing stiffly in their austere lawyers' or ad-ministrators' garb beside the cushion bearing the inevitable keys to the city, often fashioned for the purpose by local craftsmen. In no place does the King take part in any of their activities, even symbolic ones; most of the time he simply lowers the side windows and doesn't even get out of his carriage.

Behind the giddy façade of one festive hour, though, lies the fen country where, as Calonne warns him, great damage has been done by a terrible drought in 1785. "A small amount of rye is harvested there, some barley and oats, and a great deal of buckwheat. These cereals form the staple diet of the inhabitants of this part of the *généralité* of Caen, from which one may judge of their poverty. And, last year, all these crops failed." Caen's two hospitals are filled, respectively, with 700 old people and 829 foundling children. Lower Normandy is back in the days of Vincent de Paul. The two establish-ments are trying to keep afloat with "excesses of expenditure," or annual deficits, of 43,000 and 20,000 livres.† Calonne has suggested that the monarch might care to make them a present of 10,000. Louis XVI gives 8,000. Almost everywhere, whether on principle or out of parsimoniousness, he shaves some-thing off the amount Calonne was prepared to spend.

Let's hurry away from such cheerless haunts and on to Cherbourg, which they reach after nightfall under "a sparkling sky, with serene weather and a tranquil sea—the sea Louis XVI will see tomorrow for the first time in his life. The whole town is lit up by "4,003 one-sou earthenware cups" filled with

---

*It is memories like this that cause the King, fleeing toward Montmédy five years later, to imagine that the villagers will respond to him the same way again if he is recognized, and so to take the Varennes road.

†Or 420,000 modern francs [$105,000] in all. Calonne's report mentions similar deficits for all the charitable institutions in the towns visited by the King.

1,500 pounds of tallow or lard, placed by eighty worker-days paid at the rate of 30 sous a day.*

Letellier, the worthy mayor of Harfleur, stands in the center of the compact group of men, indistinguishable in the darkness of the night and the third estate, pitch black against the black of their bourgeois coats, as the King's carriage draws up in front of the arch of triumph at the military parade ground, still known as the "Calvary" in these parts. The arch, which was built in eight days, is also illuminated, and it alone requires five hundred of the "cup candles." Letellier prides himself on being a man of letters; a few weeks from now, he produces an account of the *Voyage de Louis XVI dans sa province de Normandie* ["Louis XVI's trip through his province of Normandy"—*Trans.* ][6] in which the lyricism of the provincial notable soars to exemplary heights:

> Toward half-past ten of the evening, the cries of the inhabitants of the mountain† announced that the Prince's arrival was imminent.
>
> Illuminations had been placed along the road leading from the mountain to the town, around the perimeter of the port, and on the countless ships lying at anchor in the roads, and the radiant reverberations multiplied by the crests of the waves created a most brilliant effect. Also, on the square which His Majesty was to cross, a portico had been devised accompanied by artistically lighted pyramids, and these different views, most of which were new to His Majesty, made a most pleasing impression.
>
> . . . All the inhabitants were rushing to and fro and crowding around their sovereign's passageway, singing his praises and hailing his safe arrival; the Church herself appeared in all her majesty, dais and censer in hand, on the principle that a good King on earth is entitled to the same honors as the divinity he represents.

The Church also houses the King, in the abbey of Notre Dame du Voeu. A supper befitting the appetite of Louis XVI is served, to him and his two ministers, the six dukes and peers who came with him or have joined him here, and the Marquis de La Fayette, who is still loftily "resting" and is there solely on the strength of his American laurels, but they're enough to explain his presence wherever an event is in the wind. Does he scent, that evening, the historic odor of an ostensibly commonplace encounter, the meeting of Louis XVI and the military commander of the Cherbourg garrison, the man who has directed the building of the port during the last eight years, and who can almost boast of receiving the King in his own home: Colonel Du Mouriez? Perhaps, but La Fayette's writings, at any event, contain no reference to the presentation of the old soldier to his young monarch.

*About 10 modern francs [$2.50]; in Cherbourg, in 1786, a loaf of bread cost 2 to 3 sous, depending on the quality.

†The "Montagne de Roule" overlooking the town on the south; in 1758, after the English had outflanked the French by disembarking off to one side in the Cotentin, it enabled them to capture Cherbourg after bombarding the town from the heights.

DUMOURIEZ

# 40

## JUNE 1786

### *A Veritable Inn on the Channel*

Chance may have delayed their meeting until now, but Louis XVI knows Du Mouriez by name.* Eight years before, when every head was dizzy with the fever of the "descent upon England" that turned out so disastrously, the King read a memorandum by this strange itinerant colonel, an engineer and spy as well as a warrior, a sort of chameleon who spends his life roaming the Channel coasts and got himself into so much trouble with La du Barry's gang that he found himself in the Bastille for a few weeks shortly before the death of Louis XV. His *Précis sur la défensive de la Normandie* ["Precis on the defense of Normandy"—*Trans.*], an almost unfortified coast that left a gaping hole wide open to any attempted counterlandings by the English, was well timed. His conclusion was that the construction of a full-scale military port somewhere in the region was a crying necessity, and he mentioned Cherbourg as an ideal choice for the purpose. Louis XVI, presumably acting on Maurepas's advice, had written "Du Mouriez, commander at Cherbourg" in the margin of the text. Six thousand livres in salary, plus perks, an expense account, and a private income: Du Mouriez is not one to underrate the usefulness of money, and with a guaranteed income of 23,000 livres—as long as he stays in Cherbourg—he can breathe easy on that score.† For the time being he's not at all tempted to throw in the sponge. He knows about "that attachment of destiny's wings to our most secret desire,"** for which all men yearn without much conviction. He's directing one of the biggest construction jobs of the end of the century, one that will surely turn the English, Dutch, and Danes alike sea green with envy, and he wouldn't mind being hailed as the Vauban of this reign. More often than not, however, all he

*Dumouriez (who incorporates the particle into his name during the Revolution) is Louis XVI's minister in 1792 before becoming a contributor to the victories at Valmy and, even more, Jemappes, where he is commander in chief. A friend to the Girondins but a Royalist at heart, he deserts in the spring of 1793.

†Modern equivalent: 160,000 francs [$40,000].

**Paul Claudel, from the "Second Day" of the *Soulier de Satin.*

actually does is endorse the decisions of Jacques de Cessart, the bridge and roadworks engineer, who has conceived a design even more audacious than that of Richelieu back in the days when he was strangling la Rochelle in order to bring the Protestants to heel.

Cherbourg lies in an open bay, so the idea is to enclose the roads in a rosary of huge wood-framed baskets called "cones," because the part above water narrows toward the sky while the submerged part is splayed out and filled with heavy stones for ballast. The original idea was to sink them side by side, but that would have required a hundred cones and "would have taken a great deal of time and consumed a huge quantity of wood, an all too rare commodity in France," according to Calonne, who informs the King, in his little personal tour guide, that

> the Sieur de Cessart has accordingly proposed that the cones be placed each at a distance of 30 fathoms from the next (at the base), and be linked together by breakwaters of cemented stones; this new endeavor has been equally successful, and it may be hoped now that the first section of the enclosing mole, lying to the east and consisting of eighteen or twenty cones, will be completed by the beginning of 1788, and will afford shelter for forty ships of the line.*

Du Mouriez supervises and helps his technical staff, keeping them supplied with soldiers to do the heavy work and sending blithely optimistic reports to the ministers.

This evening the King tells him "that for several years he has had the drawings relating to the scheme in progress affixed to the wall of his study."[1] And he has come to Cherbourg on purpose to watch one of these famous cones being installed. So tomorrow is the high point of the trip.

The little man Louis XVI is now seeing for the first time is approaching fifty (he was born on January 25, 1739), aquiver with energy, sharp-featured, his skin pitted by Prussian grapeshot that hit him full in the face at his baptism by fire, Klostercamp—Lord, how many years ago that was! The end of his career can't be far off, and he's got no time to waste if he wants to become a second Vauban, so he makes the most of this unique opportunity, wielding the undeniable appeal of a broad forehead, large, gentle mouth, and small, nervous hands —a mixture of refinement and authority in a military although highly distin-

---

*The last cone of the first section is sunk on June 18, 1788, but the structure cannot stand up to the heavy Channel storms; the wooden frames are smashed, the linking stone walls leveled. In 1791 a different team of engineers starts rebuilding it, according to a less original but also less hazardous plan. The port of Cherboug is not finally enclosed and inaugurated until the summer of 1813—by Napoleon and Marie-Louise. Maybe the place was hexed: Napoleon abdicates a few months later.

guished wrapping, complete with elegant dress coat and white-powdered hair.[2]

He was born for the army, and for the northern army. The place was Cambrai, where his father, Antoine-François du Périer du Mourier, commissioner for war,* proudly proclaimed himself a Walloon. So Charles-François, the son, is of better than middling descent, with escutcheon and all. The family hailed originally from the south, though, which may explain his ready gift of gab and his vivacity. Although he grew up without a mother (she died young) and his childhood was rather austere, he loved his father and admired him as a man of unusual erudition, surrounded by mountains of books—many of them ungodly—which conducted his son from mysticism to agnosticism before he reached puberty and helped him to qualify as a secret agent by teaching him languages: Italian, Spanish, English, German. Then, during the Seven Years' War, in which he fought as a very young cavalry lieutenant, the budding *encyclopédiste* was hammered into the sterner stuff of a warrior. He was utterly fearless, performing feat after intrepid feat, and received the Cross of St. Louis at twenty-four.†

The minute the war was over boredom set in, along with professional and emotional frustration. The love of his youth had been a cousin of his, Marguerite de Broissy, a daughter of one of his father's sisters, and the feeling had been mutual. But the parents were in mid-feud, carrying on like Capulets and Montagues, and they forbade the marriage. Marguerite took the veil with shattered heart, while Du Mouriez swallowed a sizable dose of opium, but a last-minute will to live prompted him to grab an oil lamp that was standing near, drink down its contents, and vomit everything up again.

There are similarities between his youth and that of Mirabeau, if we except the latter's terrifying energy. They had the same devouring curiosity, the same fantastic memory, the same attraction for "the military art," the same star-crossed early love. Like Mirabeau, Du Mouriez traveled (Portugal and Spain), feverishly writing about everything he saw in the hope of getting himself noticed by the bureaucrats in Versailles. Also like Mirabeau, he fought in the Corsican campaign, had a keen eye for the wenches, and was not above using his love affairs to further his ambitions. He eased his way into Choiseul's circle and performed a few missions for him in Poland; then, when the wind began to shift, he dropped his first patron and switched his allegiance to the Comte de Broglie. He returned from some picaresque adventures on the

---

*A later age would say "chief of the quartermaster general staff"; it is not known why he changed the *r* at the end of his name to *z*.

†Equivalent to the military medal of the modern French Republic, the only decoration awarded for military action alone.

Russian border to find the Bastille awaiting him, because the all-powerful Duc d'Aiguillon would stop at nothing to get at the man of the "King's Secret."* The one obvious difference between him and Mirabeau is his relative affluence: he inherited a tidy sum, treats money with considerable respect, and has never been short of it.

We first saw him just before the death of Louis XV, when he was released from the Bastille and relegated to the château of Caen for a period of "supervised residence." Chance often makes a mess of things: Caen just happened to be where his cousin was living, "in the convent of the Repentant Sisters," which she had entered immaculate.

> Who would believe it possible to regret having left the Bastille? Yet for him it was the simple truth.† He was living as on a country estate. The château was spacious, the air good, the grounds well wooded, and the company agreeable. He formed a lifelong attachment there, to an infinitely lovable woman named the Vicomtesse de Mathan, who kept a great house. He was quite his own master and could leave the château whenever he pleased to go into town or out to the country. He would have made little use of this freedom, finding more than enough to keep him occupied inside the château, save that his cousin was living in the same town. . . . He considered that in a provincial place, where his cousin had in her way acquired as much notoriety as himself, their actions would be under constant scrutiny and they would become the subject of every conversation. He cursed the fact that out of all the châteaus in the kingdom the choice had fallen upon this particular one of Caen as his place of detention, thus putting him in such an uncomfortable position. It was said throughout the neighborhood that his cousin's excessive piety and many ailments were all the result of her despair at having been abandoned. If he did not see her, he would be taken for a monster, especially by the women. And indeed, why should he not see her? He was no longer in love with her, she was his own first cousin, and she had suffered much for him.[3]

Du Mouriez waited four days before entering the convent locutory to encounter a transformed Marguerite, desiccated by her devotions, scarred by smallpox. She thrust him away screaming and fell into an epileptic fit (a "miliary fever"**). He had had her on his conscience for over ten years. He felt responsible for the "revolution into which their meeting had precipitated her. . . . The convent in which she lived was not cloistered. For twenty-eight days he acted as her self-appointed nurse. He entered her room every morning

---

*Writing about Du Mouriez earlier in this series, I exaggerated his role in secret diplomacy; in fact, he simply did a few occasional favors for the Comte de Broglie, inflating their importance in his *Mémoires*.

†According to the *Mémoires* written by Du Mouriez (and others) in 1794, shortly after emigrating. He speaks of himself in the third person.

**A rash accompanied by high fever, a sort of secondary effect of smallpox.

at seven and did not leave it until eight in the evening; she would take nothing from any hand but his. . . . He was no longer in love with her, but the tumultuous passion of yore had given way to tender affection. He determined to put an end to this state, which was painful to both of them, by marriage," but frankly confesses that although at the time her income was only 1,250 livres, "her mother being aged, they had hopes of at least seven or eight thousand from the inheritance."*

They were married on September 13, 1774, not without a fierce procedural battle and much petitioning to obtain the necessary dispensations: he, as an officer, had to get permission from his minister, while she had to beg all the way up to the pope and pay out 3,200 livres† to various ecclesiastical middlemen, because she had taken the veil and because they were first cousins.

But when did a marriage founded on pity turn out to be a success?

> His spouse's temper had been soured by her sufferings. Piety, when carried to extremes and applied to every little detail, is like clothing that has shrunk; it clings to every imperfection, it covers but does not hide. This couple no longer had enough in common to be a happy one. She saw everything in relation to God, to religion, but even more to their outward trappings. He was neither atheist nor nonbeliever; but to him all forms of worship were variations on one principle, which was the same throughout the universe: the worship of a God.

This discordant union of bigot and agnostic produced a couple separated in mind and bed if not board. By the time Du Mouriez greets Louis XVI in Cherbourg, after weathering, more or less cheerfully, twelve years of storms and scenes, she has dismissed a total of 120 servants! The death of their two children in infancy has not helped, and he is impatiently awaiting that of his mother-in-law, so he can earnestly implore his wife to go off and live somewhere else on her own, once she has her own money. She is not seen at the Cherbourg festivities.

Meanwhile he has made the acquaintance of a woman named de Beauvert-Barruel,** who was married to and is now separated from a Baron d'Angel. She is the definitive woman of his life: "This lady, a paragon of sweetness and amiability, thereafter desired to share his misfortune, and the constance and nobility of her feelings redoubled his pain. This is the strongest bond attaching him to life."[4]

His recent duties, ever since he got stuck in Cherbourg after a vain

---

*Meaning that Marguerite's income would rise from 8,000 modern francs [$2,000] a year to some 50,000 [$12,500].

†Or about 22,000 modern francs [$5,500].

**Her brother is Rivarol, who becomes famous this decade with the publication of his *Universalité de la langue française.*

attempt to give a little flesh to the dream of an invasion of England by planning a landing on the Isle of Wight, have been partly those of a *maréchal de camp* and partly those of a general,* but he is still addressed as "colonel." His relative failure does not seem to have mortified him unduly: Du Mouriez knows how to eat humble pie. Obedient skepticism is his essential quality.

The stint in Cherbourg has been almost a holiday for him, although he has been working like an ox directing the transport of stones, construction of the cone shells, and proper siting of the cannon batteries. The engineer in him has become dominant, and he is specializing increasingly in artillery; although many years older than they, he belongs to the same breed as Carnot and Laclos. The corners of his mouth show, ever so slightly, the latent bitterness of a man who feels he was born for great things but nobody needs him to do them. "He had never commanded a regiment, and even refused a battalion of royal grenadiers. He aspired to become a staff officer, he had traced out a special path for himself, out of the common line,"† and here he is vegetating in his house on the rue des Bastions, where he finds what consolation he can in sharing the creations of his admirable cook with a monotonous little troop of Norman gentry and young lawyers, whose "advanced" ideas keep him from falling asleep.

He has been made honorary president of the Cherbourg literary and academic society, for which his contempt could not be more scathing: "A society of naval and Lower Norman literati, incapable of contributing to either the French language or its literature. The members were admiralty judges, tradesmen, country priests";[5] and as Charles-François Du Mouriez is uncompromising in his judgments, does not suffer fools gladly, insists upon being treated with respect, and is ill at ease in his station in life, he has quarreled with a large proportion of the bourgeois, especially the churchwardens, in his dealings with whom "he defended his rights with great heat."[6] He has thus acquired a reputation as a hard, trenchant man, but of course that enhances his standing among the military. They say he snatched off the hat of one bourgeois who wasn't quick enough about doffing it and threw it in the sea, and that his stick has been acquainted with servants' shoulders.[7] To top it all off, he is not on the best of terms with the trinity who govern Normandy, the Duc d'Harcourt, his father the maréchal, and his brother the Duc de Beuvron, all of whom avoid Du Mouriez because of his "liberalism."

Be that as it may, Cherbourg has changed more in eight years under Du Mouriez's leadership than it had in the preceding eight centuries. At the beginning of the reign of Louis XVI it was a little fishing town. When Du Mouriez arrived the population was 7,300,[8] but in his wake came a swarm of

*To which rank he is promoted in 1788.
†His own words.

carters, sailors, laborers, and clerks to do the work. In another ten years the town will have grown to more than 11,000 souls.[9] Louis XVI sees a lot of new, snow white houses, freshly laid, newly paved streets, and "a face of activity and animation."[10] He does not see, on the other hand, any of the three bad hostelries which are turning people away today, including "La Barque" on the rue du Château,

> a vile hole, little better than a hog-sty; where, for a miserable dirty wretched chamber, two suppers composed chiefly of a plate of apples and some butter and cheese, with some trifle besides too bad to eat, and one miserable dinner, they brought me in a bill of 31 livres.* They not only charged the room 3 livres a night, but even the very stable for my horse, after enormous items for oats, hay and straw. . . . Let no-one go to Cherbourg without making a bargain for every thing he has, even to the straw and stable; pepper, salt and table-cloth.[11]

In 1778 the town's entire trade was still being carried on by three ocean-going ships and thirty coasting vessels—not much for a place situated so neatly at the top of the Cotentin. Du Mouriez has said that he wants to make it "a veritable inn on the Channel," a port of call as important as Portsmouth or Plymouth, halfway between Brest and the Dutch ports. The goal is an exalting one to the Norman middle class but it leaves the lower orders singularly unmoved, because the flood of "foreigners" attracted by the construction work has further depressed their already starvation wage level. "At least one-fourth of the inhabitants must be counted as indigent, being unable to earn enough to buy their own bread,"[12] which costs over 2 sous a pound, and wheat is selling for 7 or 8, and no laborer makes more than 2 livres a day.

June 23 is a red-letter day on the calendars of both Du Mouriez and Louis XVI. They spend it together in the salt sunshine and a head wind. Life at last.

Early rising was no problem for people in those days, if they had reason enough. Three in the morning, on this occasion, but it can't be helped: that is the hour at which the tide (or "new moon high-water," as it was also called), the assistance of which will be enlisted in the sinking of the new cone, begins to flow. It will be at the flood by noon. Despite the hour, however, the King hears mass before setting out, with eighteen dignitaries, including his military ministers, La Fayette, and Du Mouriez, "in a superb twenty-man longboat, its oarsmen dressed in white with red woolen scarves."[13] They embark from the construction site itself, on the Chantereyne bank, wrapped in the pungent aroma of great fresh-hewn timbers, bristling like monsters in parturition in the gathering dawn. The sky is already lightening, as though behind a pane of emerald stained glass; tomorrow is Midsummer, night hardly falls at all in this season. Hundreds of flags have been unfurled, their broad expanses all out of

*Over 200 modern francs [$50]. This account is by the English traveler Arthur Young.

proportion to the launches, brigs, and schooners flying them, and the huge, dim hulks of the ships of the line lie far out in the roads; tomorrow they're going to simulate an easily won naval battle. There are the flags of the King, the admirals, the regiments on board, and the nearby towns (three or four for Cherbourg alone), a forest of fleurs-de-lis against a background of blazing blue and a white so bright that it makes your eyes ache even more than the glinting crests of the lighthearted little waves.

Louis XVI contributes his note to the palette with a broad scarlet coat "bearing the embroidery of the lieutenant generals and strewn with golden fleurs-de-lis" which had been ordered for the event, and which he had also worn the day before, after fastening, over his heart, the omelet-sized golden star of the Holy Ghost. Weighted down by a huge two-cornered hat, also scarlet, with a peak that makes it look like an upside-down broom, Louis the Stout, in the thirty-second year of his life, resembles a sort of roly-poly chimpanzee; his swelling belly is tranquilly displayed in a roll of gilded spare tire beneath the muslin jabot peeking between the two fronts of the scarlet coat with the diamond buttons that will never button anything. How could they? His scarlet breeches are tied under his knees, above white silk hose close-hugging the massive calves that curve stoutly above his buckle pumps. His Majesty offers the irrefutable evidence of fully gratified flesh, with beatific features beaming contentment, the myopic impassiveness of a constantly shifting gaze, and the conciliating smile of a thin, unsensuous mouth under that famous Bourbon nose hooked into place in the middle of his face. Our King . . .[14]

The instant he sets foot in the longboat the royal flag is flown "from both stem and stern and from the mast," but its presence is hailed by no cheers or gun salutes: "the deepest silence was essential in order not to impede the maneuvering of the cone," which, for better effect, was also called "the conic tower." A labor of Hercules. The eyes of the spectators shift from the royal launch, now Lilliputian, to the Gargantuan tub that scores of towing-boats, their oarsmen pouring sweat, are about to unfasten from the strand and drag to its place at the end of the line of eight that have previously been sunk. What a bulk! What a risk! Floats me, floats me not? One hundred and forty-two feet in diameter at the base, 60 at the summit, rising 60 feet above the water line. At this point the flat bottom, which is submerged, contains only enough ballast to prevent it from tipping over. It is ringed round with empty casks to keep it afloat. Floats me? It floats; okay, everybody, you can cheer now. "A triple salvo was then fired by the fort artillery and the maneuvering squadron. The salvos, repeated throughout the day, were accompanied by cries of 'Vive le Roi,' continually uttered by the crews of the ships filling the roads and the construction workers."

The royal longboat follows the enormous object like a water spaniel paddling behind a sea monster. It easily overtakes it and goes on to "the place designated for the sinking" before moving aside as a procession of barges surrounds the cone for two tricky hours: one by one, the belt of casks stabilizing it are replaced by a belt of heavy rocks, then it is crammed with ballast "through thirty openings made at different heights to facilitate the approach of the rock-laden boats. Soon the unchanging mass, consolidated by the gluten [*sic*] of the sea cementing it, the seaweed and shells attaching themselves to it, will turn into a veritable boulder of 2,750 cubic fathoms, weighing an estimated 96 million pounds."* The monster continues to be force-fed for several days before its summit is sealed off at the top with a cement platform. Today, after Louis XVI symbolically commands the cone to be submerged, it takes only twenty-eight minutes to dump enough rocks in it to sink it to the bottom, but not before the shell threatens to tip over at one point, "the knives having failed to cut free all the casks at the same moment," but the engineer-officers manage to set it straight again. A great surge of cheering, 20,000 strong at least, then pours down from the town above, mingling with 600 rounds of cannon fire from the forts and fleet and drowning the cries of three men flung into the sea by the sudden tautening of a slack cable of one of the capstans controlling the cone's balance. Robert Pinabelle is one of them, and is killed instantly. His wife gets a pension from the King, who witnesses the accident through a spyglass and shows earnest signs of grief, standing on the platform of an immobilized cone nearby, on which "an *ambigu* was served to the sovereign and ladies in a tent."†

Tomorrow comes the naval review, then home, by the back roads: Lisieux, Caen, Honfleur, Le Havre, Rouen, the inevitable château of his archbishop at Gaillon, Vernon, Mantes, Meulan, Triel, and Saint-Germain. Louis XVI returns in raptures. Throughout the entire voyage he has not uttered a single arresting sentence or made a single striking gesture, apart from the grunts of satisfaction linking the recurrent "my children" and "my people." Much less exhausting to reign on the road than at Versailles. His longest speech was consigned to an official record:

"I have never savored more the happiness of being King than on the day of my coronation and since I have been in Cherbourg."

So he'll have had one vacation, maybe the only one in his life, before returning to his sea of troubles between Versailles and the Trianons. Calonne is awaiting him with an unwonted air of gravity. The till is empty. Real and radical action will be needed to fill it.

*Once sunk, the conic tower weighed 48,000 tons in all—that is, timbers included.
†An *ambigu* was the name of a cold collation at which meat and sweets were served together.

M. ROLAND

# 41

## AUGUST 1786

## *Workers Against Merchants*

Jeanne-Marie Roland *née* Phlipon is now settled in the Beaujolais country near Lyons, where her husband's career has been crowned by an appointment to the position of inspector of manufactures for the *généralité* of the Lyonnais district. On August 10, 1786,* she writes from their home in Paris:

> My husband is in Lyons; there has been an uprising in that town, workers against merchants, the workers wanting an increase in the making-up.† It was all stones on one side, sabers and guns on the other, I mean the guard; there were twenty injured and about four people killed.
>
> The first protests were directed against the archbishop, who wanted to apply to the letter an ancient right of taxation of the wine merchants. At this they shut their cabarets; and the workers, with no choice but to go to the suburbs to drink, assembled there; then came expressions of discontent, seditious schemings, and the ensuing incidents. . . . Five counts of St. John** acted as negotiators, calmed the people's minds, and brought back inside the town walls a considerable company [of rebel workers] who then took refuge in the Brotteaux [ a part of town] and considered what to do next. The town was overrun with men in arms, and the peace broken on all sides.[1]

And that's all. She says hardly another word about the uprising in her entire correspondence, and she certainly does not fly into an impassioned defense of the *canuts* [silk workers, specifically in Lyons, which was for centuries the center of the textile industry in France; the word comes from *canette,* a spool —*Trans.* ] the way she did for the Genevans or Americans. After all, Manon Roland is a bourgeoise, the daughter of a Parisian artist-craftsman and the wife of an important government official. She reads like a feature story for the local gazette. "Workers against merchants": that much she can see. But she doesn't

*The French monarchy has exactly six years to live.

†That is, in the amount paid for making up a piece of material or a hat. These are the first significant stirrings of the French proletariat. The "guard" she mentions is the local militia.

**These were the canons of St. John Cathedral in Lyons, who ranked as counts and, as we shall see, played an important role in the local society.

know—she who usually has such decided ideas about everything—what to think of it. Note her association of anger and drunkenness, despite the fact that her father Gratien Phlipon the engraver, whom she and Roland support in Paris without ever seeing him, is subsiding at this very moment into an alcoholic stupor. What has become of the Manon Phlipon who was forging a sort of Roman virtue for herself in opposition to her father, all alone in her "asylum" of a few square feet on the Place Dauphine, surrounded by barricades of books overlooking the Seine? Marriage and life in the provinces have benumbed her. "I feel heavy. And despite my affection for everything around me, despite that attraction that makes me care about every detail of the countryside, despite the sense of fond attachment that the spectacle of nature in all her simplicity never fails to arouse in me, I feel myself falling asleep and growing stupid."[2] She sounds as though she's given up hope of the world ever changing. What she's really afraid of is having changed herself.

First, Amiens, after the wedding and a brief transit at the hotel in Paris; four years in the shadow of Mr. Inspector General of Manufactures for Picardy. The bedrooms of their large rented house gave onto the rue du Collège, the dressing room looked over the cemetery, and the perfect lady of the house had plenty of leisure in which to count the convoys of Amiens citizens being buried there without ever having lived, at least not as she understood the word. If she had to be marooned in any big town other than Paris, though, Amiens wasn't too bad an alternative, although it shared the capital's damp climate, made worse here by the marshes and rank gusts of salt air swirling up the Somme.

Just under 45,000 inhabitants, and that's a lot, according to Necker's reckoning in his recent book on *L'Administration des finances de la France* ["The administration of the finances of France—*Trans.* ];[3] Amiens is a town on the move, breathing hard enough through every manufacturing pore to turn the English emerald with envy. The society Mme Roland meets there is, in one sense, less hermetically sealed than that of the Place Dauphine tradesmen's shops. "The Amiens fabric manufacture is one of the most extensive and active of France, with 5,000 looms; more than 30,000 workers, counting the town and the countryside around it, are employed in the production of broadcloth, linen, velvet, serge, satins, silks, and plush, to mention only the most important." Roland had his hands full, being responsible not only for Amiens but for Abbeville as well, where he had to tour the vast works, employing 2,000 people, of the Van Robais brothers, who had more or less swiped their techniques for manufacturing quality broadcloth from the British.

Is the system protectionist, dirigist, or is it obsolete interventionism? These notions are beginning to be the subjects of debate, and will become so increasingly from now on. But whichever *ism* the rules and regulations laid down by Colbert and his successors may represent, they have successfully enmeshed France's entire labor force in a multidimensional spiderweb, woven strong and tight by the manufactures inspectors who, acting through a battalion of clerks and lesser bureaucrats, make sure that not one shuttle flies and not one ell of cloth is folded without His Majesty's permission. The infinite-capacity-for-taking-pains side of Jean-Marie Roland might be comfortable enough in this role as the weavers' official thorn in the flesh, but the humanist in him bleeds from every prick—the tale of his career is a tale of rising indignation. In this respect he deserves his wife's affection; and her admiration, at least, has never flagged. In the course of their interminable premarital indecision he rehearsed to her every thrust and parry of these battles, the only ones he is equipped to fight. Since 1766, when he was transferred from Rouen, Roland has been struggling for every inch of ground that would give a slightly more positive slant to the regulations it is his duty to apply. In Picardy, he contested the privileges of the canons of Amiens in regard to the fulling mills. He defended "cottage" workers, especially in the countryside, against the merchants of the same town who wanted to dictate to them; but he also fought the intendant of Picardy to preserve the rights of "foreign," i.e., non-Picardian merchants; he championed the carpet and velvet workers who were chained to their manufactures by their employers and could not leave without open revolt; he even dabbled in chemistry, when he vainly urged the Amiens academy to endow a prize for indigo dye. There were days when this Don Quixote of planned economy felt like beating his head against a wall:

> I saw, in a single morning, eighty, ninety, a hundred lengths of cloth slashed to shreds, I saw raids by bands of subalterns who invaded the weavers' premises, turned their workrooms upside down, terrified their families; I saw the warp cut from the loom, carried out, and confiscated . . . and all the attendant events, the weeping and moaning, the disgrace and shame . . . and why? Because they were weaving woolen pannes* like those made in England . . . whereas the French regulations said nothing about wool, only linen![4]

If it were for the good of the people, that would be one thing; but it's for the service of the King, and the service of the King is like a dog chasing its tail, like a boarding school in which you learn rules instead of lessons. The treasury itself derives precious little benefit from the system, because the cunning opposition of employers and merchants is automatically and anarchically triggered off by the muscle-bound centralization of the kingdom, theoretically designed to organize the levying of taxes but in reality a perfect jumble of private initiatives. In the France of Louis XVI what counts is not that the regulations should work but that everything should be regulated. In the

---

*Cloth made by the same process as velvet, and of the same width, but with a deeper pile.

spiritual realm, the church has codified every motion of existence and policed every thought, while at the political and administrative levels the structures have been conceived and executed, from Versailles to the smallest backwoods hamlet, so as to throttle any initiative; but there was one large field left uncovered, the brand-new world of manufactured goods, and the buying and selling that went with them. The wind of liberty might have blown this way, and many members of the third estate like to recall how the American rebellion began with a refusal to pay a tax on tea. But in France the third estate is still in the nostalgic phase. There are quite a few men of good will, like Roland, who are spending their lives staunching the perpetual hemorrhage of obeisance to absurdity.

This is preeminently what Jeanne-Marie married; her wedlock bond was built on an illusion of intellectual harmony. What appeals to her most about it is the idea of a partnership of work, the transfer of her pen, now active instead of passive, to the service of Roland, even though it implies a certain loss of loftiness in her subject matter: from the commentaries on Plutarch and Rousseau that she used to send out in installments to the Cannet sisters in Rouen, she has descended to reams and reams of memoranda on "the specification of the days and hours when the inspectors must be at the Amiens markets to visit the bales, trim, and tassels woven in the town; on Thursday, Friday, and Saturday, that is, from eight in the morning until noon and from two in the afternoon until six, between Easter and St. Rémi's day," or the "fine of 100 livres for shearing wool-bearing animals more than three days after their annual washing, the same sum for the sale of their fleece when damp, and 50 livres if that same fleece is tied with more than seven lengths of straw. . . ."

She also helped with the more general essays, several degrees above this humdrum stuff, of which Roland was sending an abundant supply to Panckoucke the bookseller for his monumental *Encyclopédie méthodique* of France in ninety-seven volumes, a sort of polydimensional chain reaction shooting out from the great *Encyclopédie*. Copy and more copy, on the use of fertilizers, the manufacture of hats, improved wool, how to press lace edging, sheep breeding in Picardy, the peat cutter's art, etc.[5] Some of his pages have been of lasting value to historians, by virtue of his clear-sightedness and the precision of his observations—as when he describes the truth of working conditions in

> Picardy, where cloth of wool, velvet, linens, and hose are produced. Of the 25,000 looms working in the region, there are hardly more than 6,500 inside the towns; Amiens contains about 5,000, Abbeville 1,000. Part of the town looms, and all of those in the countryside, stop work during the harvest season; haying, woodcutting, sowing, and other rural tasks also cause them to lie idle often in the villages; and, taken all in all, they may be reckoned to work scarcely eight months in the year. It may be mentioned in passing that this is, beyond a doubt, of all

manufactures the one most felicitously and fruitfully established, in that it permits the hands it employs to turn to farming when they are needed there. This variety in their efforts is a source of good health for the workers, but it also gives them a dual security, through the mutual and reciprocal assistance that each affords to the other. The population is always large where there is a living to be had, and there is always a living to be had where there is earning to be done. In general, from the primary material when it leaves the grower's hands until a length of cloth passes into use, one may reckon that ten persons are employed for every loom.*[6]

Mme Roland is not being ironic when she shares these everyday preoccupations with her new friends in the capital, now that the current of her correspondence has been reversed and flows from the provinces toward Bosc and Lanthenas in Paris. No; she really does care about it all, or puts up a good show of pretending to. Her husband, meanwhile, in the face of constant opposition and setbacks, is also beginning to see himself as the benefactor of Amiens, where

I had given life and encouragement to the muslin makers and a sense of direction to the makers of silk ribbon, conducted divers experiments with broadcloth, worked for seven consecutive years, in the administration, against a powerful corporation, and finally secured the right to set up fulling mills, . . . a water calender and other similar establishments. . . . I say nothing of the projects that were attempted but came to naught: all were judged useful by the administration, but were held up for the most part in the preliminary stages and deferred until a more opportune time. I performed substantial labors in many quarters and on several occasions, acting always impartially, without personal interest, furthering in every case the public good and rendering noteworthy services to the great majority of individuals, while with others I had violent but inevitable crises because the aim of trade, which is to spread knowledge, extend vision, and increase manpower, is always and everywhere in opposition to the aim of the tradesman, whose pleasure comes only from depriving others.

Even in those days, apparently, the lineup was already retailers or middlemen versus producers. A pity Mme Roland does not make the connection between the Lyons workers' uprising, her husband's lucid observations, and their struggles in Amiens. She lacks a sense of synthesis and therefore remains impermeable to whatever might be a sign of a general movement among the laborers, a drive "from below." She has subscribed body and soul to a new form of enlightened despotism, that of middle-class Enlightenment—Roland's, in the last analysis. Nonetheless, the ideological warp of

---

*This passage is quoted *in extenso* by Jaurès, in the first chapter of his *Histoire socialiste de la Révolution française,* where he observes that Roland is attempting "as best he can, to reconcile his passion for the back-to-nature movement preached by Jean-Jacques [Rousseau] with his passion for industrial progress."

their lives in those gray years was a drab and unspectacular revolt against the established order.

But what a change from the wide-eyed letters of her youth! Not only has she become the secretary of Roland, civil servant, and encyclopedic popularizer; she is also the mother of a baby girl and the mistress of a house that she has to manage, with two or three servants, on an average income of about 5,000 livres a year.* Her job, her duty, is to supervise the cellar, bottle the wine, keep a watchful eye on the wood supply, put the clothes away in the attic presses, card the mattresses, prepare the preserves, and preside over the great annual cleaning. She's good at it. She often expresses her pride in the fact in her many letters to her husband, whose frequent absences continue to qualify him as an official correspondent, the one she says *tu* to, but no longer as the recipient of her dissertations on the spirit of the times or Roman history. Gone are the days of sentimental soul-searching. Roland is now the Man, the one to whom you're supposed to render accounts. "I feel heavy . . ." The only erotic touches ever, in their letters, were a few light kisses in Italian; the news of the flesh she has to share with him nowadays tends to be rather on the medical side:

> I do not know whether to be quite pleased with my medicine yesterday; it is true that it purged me thoroughly, but by agitating my intestines it brought a renewal of my pain. I have had a hardworking day; I went to bed at seven very weary; took two eggs, and sleep came of its own accord before nine. My rest was untroubled until two, when the colic returned; nothing that I pass indicates a revival of the illness, but it is pure bile. This morning an oil enema brought some relief. I dined upon a dozen oysters that seemed extremely sweet and good but very small, very thin, making no more than a light repast. I feel quite well this afternoon. I flatter myself that the emotion occasioned by the purge is the cause of my latest ailment and that I am finally about to regain my strength.[7]

> I embrace you with all my heart. Do not fail to apply those poultices to your buttock, I do beg of you, it is very important.
>     What should a woman do before noon if she does not get out of bed until nine o'clock, or sometimes even later, when she is feeling unwell; who needs her toilette to chase away the bugs that have clung stubbornly after her illness; and from there to the child's room to prepare its soup and prowl about while my rooms are being made ready; and who hardly takes possession of them, with cradle, table and writing desk, before eleven. Add to that the interruptions and so forth, and judge for yourself whether there is time for a nice, long chat before the post leaves.

*Say, 40,000 modern francs [$10,000], including Roland's salary, what he earns from his writing, and his wife's tiny inheritance.

Sometimes a sigh escapes her lips, but not of longing for her husband. To Bosc, for instance, on April 1, 1783: "Ah, but it is a mighty unsightly thing, a woman in ill health who goes about rehearsing her ailments. . . ."[8] Not that that stops her from expatiating upon them all at great and enthusiastic length. Roland can't complain, however, because she always eagerly asks for news of his own: "Before and above all other things, my dear friend, tell me about your health; I have half a mind to scold you for being so silent on that point. How are you managing the latter end? Are you careful to apply your poultice? What effect is magnetism having? Is your digestion good? Are you sleeping well? Are you bilious or is your skin clear? How do you feel? Do tell me, and in ample detail, about all these matters."[9]

She hasn't mislaid her spirit of observation, however—tinged with an increasingly acid irony—when she wants to give her friends a picture of her little Amiens society pinned and wriggling on the wall. Sometimes she describes its academic assemblies or drawing-room teas; then, Boeotia is her term for the town, by comparison with her native Paris. A young magistrate she meets is a *Jean-faut-tout-lui-dire* [Johnny-must-tell-him-everything—*Trans.*]. This doctor is an ignoramus. Another medical orator "gabbles" when extolling the virtues of some brainchild of his: "an ingenious instrument which seized hold of the indurated matter, conducted it into the rectum and caused it to pass out through the anus, thereby relieving the unhappy patients who were unable to defecate. Having served up this little trick of his trade in most graceful manner, Master Ancelin spoke no more. . . . He was greatly applauded; I should have followed suit had I found any merit in his discourse, but in the event I never uncrossed my paws."[10]

Such was the celebration of St. Louis's Day in Boeotia. At least she was as ready as ever to call a spade a bloody shovel, but in this case the embers beneath the ash of words were pure boredom.

And despite an affectation of enthralled maternal fascination in the Rousseauist manner, her daughter was not a cure for the condition. She often speaks of Eudora as "the child," moreover, using a word of masculine gender that brings her even closer to Emile. The little girl is allowed to want for nothing, rather the opposite; but at the end of 1786, when we meet the Rolands living near Lyons, Jeanne-Marie issues, again to Bosc, the following highly ambiguous progress report on her motherhood:

> I must now announce that Eudora is reading pretty well, has begun to want no other playthings than her needle, amuses herself making geometrical figures, has no conception that clothing can be tolerated as an impediment, does not dream how much money can be spent on frocks for her, believes herself beautiful when told that she is a good child and has a white dress of unwonted cleanliness; further, that her supreme reward is a sweet offered with a caress, that her moods are

becoming more widely spaced and brief in duration, that she walks in the dark as readily as in broad daylight, is afraid of nothing at all, and cannot imagine that anything could be worth lying about; add to this that she is five years and six weeks old, and that I have never known her to have a wrong idea about anything, or at least about anything important, and you will agree that although I have been wearied by her headstrong nature and worried by her whims, and although her heedlessness has made it difficult for us to exert much influence upon her, in the end our pains have not been altogether wasted.[11]

As for the servants . . . On January 6, 1782, "my new cook has hurt her heel. . . . In consequence of this, we must needs limp, we cannot rise early, we find it difficult to get into the lively way I like to see about me. I rather fear this large female is possessed of the sort of sluggishness that is quite common among people of her height and breadth."[12] By the end of the month the mistress of the house is taking a more lenient view, except that the large female has an equally large appetite:

> Can you imagine that every day we three women consume just under three pounds of meat, and I never eat it in the evening. . . . Our stout cook tucks in so heartily at noon, moreover, that there is not much left for their supper and they would have none at all if the inestimable glutton did not make an effort to restrain herself a little in order to leave some for the rest. I thought I must tell her that I had observed the household consumption rise substantially since her arrival, and that I did not wish to reproach her for having an appetite because I hoped she was not one of those people who eat more meat than bread because they are living at other people's expense.[13]

One can find a good score of examples of this completely unselfconscious class attitude in her postmarital letters. There were signs of it before, though, when her childhood nurse was dying and she was nursing her. In this area, she is incapable of remorse; her class consciousness is as natural as eating. Diderot had it no less than Mme Roland, so did the farmer, and so did the servant himself.

Between 1781 and 1786 Mme Roland became indistinguishable from the average Frenchwoman of good small-town society. Nothing could seem more remote from her than History. Now and then there's the merest ripple, as of a subterranean stream flowing between two stagnant ponds. There was her vibrant letter to the friend of a friend, Albert Gosse, when he fled Geneva for Paris, his heart freshly bruised by the failure of the Swiss revolution. Or the day in 1783, at the end of a convalescence, when she suddenly took it into her head to write to Roland as though he were her fiancé again:

> Vivat! I must be well again, because all the things I like, I like as intensely today as on my best days. I spent all yesterday reading poetry and playing music; scraps

of Sophocles, Anacreon, Sappho, and the other enchanters made me feel delightfully heady; I launched into the glittering chimeras of mythology and was as enthralled as on my first trip among them. I almost believe it is good to be ill sometimes;* those moments of languor that we think of as lost are in truth periods of regeneration, of restorative slumber from which one wakes with renewed vitality. I had no ill effects from my dinner, I slept deeply, I began the day with a little air on the spinet.[14]

And thus, in August 1785, when her departure from Picardy and her discovery, at long last, of a happy, smiling countryside in Beaujolais had restored her appetite for life, she wrote, to Bosc as before but two years later:

I slept in the deep peace and gentle cool that are so essential to good health. Yesterday there was dancing in the home of one of our tenants; I went, and danced two contredanses; note that since two years before receiving the great sacrament [marriage] I had not danced at all; I saw that one's fondness for this pleasant exercise does not fade so quickly, and despite my one-and-thirty years I did not retire until midnight, and then out of propriety rather than because I had had enough.[15]

A little later in the same letter she says, in so many words, "I have hit my stride."

MANON ROLAND

## 42

MARCH–MAY 1784†

## *Which Way the Wind Will Blow*

Thus the Rolands slept away four years of their lives in Amiens town, but were not quite comfortable enough there to stick with Boeotia to the end. She could trust him to get them out; beneath his neurasthenia, Roland was homesick for his roots and the cradle of his family in the Lyons countryside. And when he finally made up his mind to marry, he was looking ahead: M. Roland de la Platière, patriarch, dreamed of founding an ennobled dynasty on the basis of the acres being tended by his kinfolk back home.

*Her health had probably been undermined for several years by the sordid bickering that took place during her engagement, her transplantation to the provinces, and her pregnancy.
†I backtrack in this chapter to explain the Rolands' presence in Lyons in 1786.

It was the dream of a man at the top of the middle class: to dive through the paper hoop that separated him from titled honors, "to obtain the title of *écuyer* [origin of the English "esquire"—*Trans.*], with its privileges of arms and livery, blessed bread, incense and weathercock on the dovecote,"[1] and end his days a laird in his native land, a sword-bearer like Cincinnatus.* As the only one of five boys in the family to escape the priesthood, he rather fancied himself a lesser La Rochefoucauld or Montmorency. With his marriage the dream began to take on consistency; his mother and brothers would be glad to hand over the little estate of Le Clos in Beaujolais to the newlyweds, if they could obtain from the King those indispensable "letters of recognition" that would transform their commonplace vineyard farm into a fief. Way back in 1780, after a (brief) lifetime of sneering at the nobility as a thing beneath her notice, Jeanne Roland becomes field marshal and secretary general of this operation too: after all, when the fate of your own children is at stake . . .

Eudora, being a girl, is a disappointment. For a time her birth calmed the nobility itch, but a fresh rash broke out early in 1784, with a growing appetite for broader horizons. Even if they were to have no more children—and Jeanne's pregnancy and postpartum problems were not an incitement—they could attempt the only mountain left to scale in their position, i.e., a change of state. It would be easier for Eudora to marry nobility if she brought it with her.

In December 1783 Roland made up his mind to apply for "letters of ennoblement" because "there is no other way to obtain recognition;† the titles must be plainer than day. But even to be ennobled demands very great protectors and, by the time one is finished, the disbursement of at least 2,000 écus** for notarization fees, documents, verification, and registration."[2] And he had to go through Vergennes, whose department was gently inflating itself into a "principal ministry" and had just annexed the offices of the "letters patent of ennoblement or confirmation of nobility," which had considerable potential influence.[3]

From Vergennes to the intendant of Lyons:

Versailles, December 10, 1783.
    I am forwarding to you, Sir, a memorandum in which the Sieur Roland de la Platière requests letters of nobility, with the request that you will furnish me,

---

*He already wore one at his side on official occasions, although he had no right to it, but the higher officials in the third estate were increasingly overstepping this boundary. On the wall of his study at La Platière his descendants have piously hung "the sword of Roland."

†His own words, while he was still hesitating; he was so proud that he hated to ask a favor, when in his opinion it was a right that ought to be recognized as a matter of course.

**About 400,000 modern francs [$100,000].

in respect of him and his family, whatever particulars you are able to procure and any comments you may think apposite.[4]

After consulting his deputy in Villefranche, who was also mayor of the town, the intendant issued a firmly noncommital reply.

To obtain a title of nobility by favor of the King, a man in Roland's position had to prove that his family was long-established and had always had sufficient wealth to maintain itself at the summit of the third estate; and he also had to be able to adduce personal services outstanding enough to lend an aura to his name.

For the age and honor of the family, there was no problem: "This is one of the oldest families in our province." You find it at Thizy in 1650: doctors of medicine or theology and counselors of the King, living in a tidy little castellany with a prosperous market in homespun cotton cloth. Lots of Rolands were born there in the château of La Platière, the tower of which bore their arms. They had branched out from Thizy to Villefranche, where the father of our Roland, also named Jean-Marie (he signed himself Seigneur de la Platière in official documents), counselor of the King, civilian magistrate, and alderman, married a daughter of the established nobility of the gown, Thérèse Bessye de Montozan. Ten children, two of whom died in infancy, and three daughters, to be deducted *ipso facto* from the nobiliary project. That left five boys, four of whom were monks or secular priests. In the end, thus, there is only one Roland left to pass on a name and property—Jean-Marie, born on February 18, 1734, and baptized the following day at Notre Dame de Thizy.

So much for the pedigree; but frankly, what about those "exceptional services"? Thirty years spent plowing his furrow from Lodévois in Normandy to Picardy, gauging the weight of cotton and the purity of wool: not in the same league as a Fontenoy or a Rossbach. The intendant of Lyons prudently refers Vergennes to Roland's superiors and colleagues in the inspectorate of manufactures—the men he has spent his entire working life doing battle with —for fuller particulars.

At this, Roland nearly gives up. The regular channel to a title was draining away into the sands of Lyons. What he needs is a second string, the technique adopted by so many other applicants: somebody to troll a parallel line at Court. But who could handle Versailles and Paris? It would have to be someone who knows every word in his file by heart, someone who is capable of seduction, perseverance, patience . . . Did Jeanne volunteer, or was it Roland's idea to delegate this obstinate, eager advocate? In any event, she leaps at the chance to get out and see a bit of the world. Entrusting Eudora, husband, and house to the care of the servants, she speeds off on a mission to a new and unknown world. Oh, something to try, something to stir and shake! From the moment she sets foot in Paris on March 20, 1784, her letters take on a new tone, and maintain it throughout the two months of her visit, which forms a turning point in her life.

She bewitches them all—the grumpy, fussy officials, the intendants of manufactures and trade. She harries and charms and manipulates them so artfully that one can hardly understand how Roland was not made a duke and peer of the realm. He would have been, if it had been up to her and the men she set out to wrap round her little finger . . . When Jeanne Roland has room and scope for her invasive personality, she is irresistible.

She stays at the Hôtel de Lyon, the well-kept lodging house in which she spent her first weeks as a married woman; she takes two rooms for herself and a third for Marguerite Fleury, her favorite chambermaid. There she is reunited with the two loyal and insubstantial friends of her early wedded days: Lanthenas, who lives on the floor above, and Bosc d'Antic, just down the street. The very next day she heads for Versailles, and makes four trips there in the next two months, between hauntings of the comptroller general's offices in Paris. Because of this Paris-Versailles duality, every influential person is possessed of ubiquity; you have to follow two tracks at once. But, fortified by her conviction that she is always right—one of the principal components of her personality—she quickly masters the game. "So here I am turned into quite a solicitress and intriguer! And a foolish trade it is, too, but I work away at it all the same, and in no half-hearted manner. . . . I have seen many people and it has brought me no further forward; I have had delightful hopes, followed by appalling apprehensions; the sum and substance is that I still do not know which way the wind will blow, but I am making acquaintances."[5]

Then comes a cry of victory: "My thirty years have not frightened anyone away!" She was probably imagining that she had already been baked into one of those Amiens meatloaves made of leftovers.

In a few short days she gets her bearings on the terrain and designs her strategy. Vergennes, upon whom the decision ultimately depends, will do nothing without a firm proposal from Calonne who, since the inspectorates of industry and trade come under the authority of the comptroller general, is Roland's hierarchical superior. But Calonne doesn't know Roland from Adam. He must therefore be given a strongly favorable impression of him, either via his social connections or through his professional associates, the intendants of trade:

> The persons having greatest influence with M. de Calonne, as being those most highly regarded, are M. and Mme de Polignac, the Comte de Vaudreuil, the Chevalier de Coigny, M. de Crussol. If any one of these were to become sufficiently involved in our enterprise to make it his own, he would prevail without

a fight. But this eventuality is not easy to bring about. I know no one and have no contacts in the proximity of these five persons, and as you are perfectly aware [letter to Roland, April 5, 1784], it is not by catching at the coattails of valets that one can inspire in their masters an interest as lively as our success would require. . . .

I see only two expedients to be tried, and both are extreme: one is that I should go see all these intendants of trade in person, to sound them out once again, . . . show them our memoranda, arouse their confidence and some sense of justice, if both are not entirely alien to them, and ascertain by this ultimate attempt whether it is possible to count upon them to serve us in this matter, alerting them to the approach that should be adopted with the comptroller general.

The other is far more hazardous: it is, through the secretary of M. de Calonne, to obtain an audience with the minister and put our case to him in the most forceful terms, which I feel myself perfectly capable of doing. If, despite his cleverness, he is but an ordinary man, accommodating everything and never leaving the beaten track, then we are lost; *perditi ma non disperati* [lost but not desperate]. . . . If he has any loftiness of soul or of mind, and the moment is favorable, I can succeed. It's casual;* I feel this and so I dare not undertake it without the help of your judgment; as far as my own part is concerned, I know it so well that I could play it before the King without being intimidated by his crown. . . .

In the mind of a novelist, the thought of an interview with M. de Calonne would be wonderful; for should he chance to grasp the situation clearly and take a fancy to the man, he could adopt him and push him to the fore; but as our task is not to write a work of fiction, and as it most surely is to avoid any unpleasant results, how can one conceive that a new minister, who needs to keep on good terms with everybody and who has not yet any firm plan for anything, should perform some singular act that would indispose the underministers he needs, merely in order to give preference to a subject who is precious to him on account of the general welfare alone; and even then, one would have to assume he were capable of seeing that the general welfare was concerned in the case? Indeed, I am very much at a loss to know what to do.[6]

Dynamic she may be, but not to the point of presumptuousness. There is no interview between Calonne and Mme Roland.

She accordingly lays siege to the solemn, stiff-necked gentlemen who efficiently protect the apparatus enshrined in the vast Gobelin-tapestried chambers and offices in which the doormen make people wait, and wait, and wait some more—the disease of that particular France. All of them—doormen, valets, secretaries, and secretaries' secretaries—are quick to single out the

---

*Then still used in the sense of "as chance will have it; fortuitous; likely to happen or not."

plump, fresh-faced young woman whose steady gaze is seldom the first to be averted, "the indefatigable Mme Roland" who drives them to distraction without sacrificing a whit of her dignity:

> Upon arriving at Versailles I immediately hired a hackney carriage and went to call on a few people; I found a secretary who had just eaten his dinner and who embraced me hard without a by-your-leave. . . . This morning, I sought but did not find a valet of M. de Ségur. . . . All these people who deal in other people's business swear only by me! I have been to see M. de Saint-Romain,* I talked, reasoned, urged, extorted promises; he is very likable, although no longer very young; he is the most conversational, the most likable [again] of all those I have seen in offices. Either I am very much mistaken, or he is the sort of man who would be glad to be paid in a particular currency in which, unfortunately, I do not deal.[7]

The real strongholds are the four intendants themselves, "each one of whom had, in his department, a special service, in addition to a number of general divisions: Tolozan for hosiery; Montaran for linens; Blondel for paper-works and tanneries; Vin de Gallande for silk."[8] Roland had drawn her a terrifying picture of these ogres, and she indulges in a spot of mischievousness by serving them back to him as pygmies:

> My dear friend, these people are not so wicked and diabolical; they were jolted, is all: the harm was done by the asperity of your style, that let them think you had an abominable temper and intolerable pretensions; I assure you, they can be handled; what was needed was to set before these rabid elephants a lamb; now they are appeased.[9]

In the account she sends Roland of her conversion of Tolozan, the fiercest of his opponents, we see her being rather pleased with herself, but also not averse to showing her husband once and for all the image he has created of himself. A piquant scene, nimbly sketched to wreak an imperceptible conjugal revenge:

> When I entered Tolozan's office he was in his nightcap† and, rising with a sort of half-bow and a discontented air, and without giving me a glance, he waved his hand at the armchair awaiting me. I began by thanking him for sparing me a moment of his valuable time, burdened down with work as he was, etc. A brusque "What do you want?" gave me to understand that I had best curtail my compliments. But I was determined not to let myself be put off; I replied quite calmly

*First assistant in the hosiery division, under the dreaded Tolozan.

†In Paris the four chief intendants of trade had, like many other senior officials, a "service apartment" adjoining their offices. Note the functionary's state of dress, or rather undress; it was the custom everywhere in high society, before the midday meal. One received in one's dressing gown, sometimes in one's bath; it would have been thought absurd to "dress" for people coming to ask favors.

that I had come to explain your situation and desires; that I had come to him because, his sagacity being no less well established in the world of business than his equity, I knew I should be able to count upon an accuracy of vision and resolution in him, of the kind needed to take decisions; that, for thirty years, you had given very sufficient proof of your zeal, your abilities, etc. But no sooner had I eloquently placed the trumpet to my lips than he protested, with quite extraordinary vehemence:

"Take care that you do not try to make us see him as a superior man! That is his pretension, but we are far from sharing it."

With that, I was condemned to endure a diatribe against you, but such a diatribe as one cannot conceive! A pedant, insufferably conceited, a perpetual contradictor, a bad writer, a bad policymaker, presuming to run everything, incapable of obeying orders, and so forth and so on. The legend is a colorful one, and the brushstrokes were not laid on with delicacy.[10]

Nor are those in her portrayal of the event; one can well imagine the state of Roland's digestion after he read that particular letter. "In a word, you are [according to Tolozan] a good inspector and nothing more, a worthy man of some ability; but you were forever insisting upon occupying first place, you were good only at giving orders, never at taking them." As for herself, "I can do much good for you, he told me; it was a pleasure to listen to me. He praised my enthusiasm."

She very nearly brought it off. The intendants were one and all her musketeers, and another man, Blondel, who had also been very much against Roland at the start, eked a vague signature out of Calonne one day while he was hard at work, for a letter to Vergennes:

Sir, I have the honor to pass on to you a memorandum presented by the Sieur Roland de la Platière, inspector of manufactures for Picardy. This person is requesting letters of nobility. He states that he has been employed by the administration for over thirty years; that, after traveling in Germany, Italy, and Portugal at the behest of M. de Trudaine, he has enriched our national industry by the sum of all the knowledge he acquired abroad. Sieur Roland has appended to his memorandum details proving that his family is one of the oldest in the Beaujolais and has always occupied a distinguished rank in that province. I can but commend myself to your prudence, Sir, as to that which you will think fit to propose to the King in regard to the request of the Sieur Roland de la Platière; but I cannot refuse him the affirmation, Sir, that he has been truly useful to the manufactures and that, by his character and his long years of service, he would appear to deserve the Council's benevolence and protection.[11]

That's the King's Council, of course. Or, more precisely, the "council of dispatches," in which Louis XVI conscientiously affixes his beautiful calligraphy to the bottom of orders of every description which his ministers slip beneath his quill before sending them out to the four corners of the realm. And there is the rub.

One never knew when and what Louis XVI would read before he signed it. Even if he was feeling particularly lethargic after a heavy meal, he was quite capable of balking suddenly over one or another of his pet issues and, if he thought somebody had been trying to manipulate him, falling into a redoubtable rage. And he was far touchier about people's conditions than he was about some of the weightier problems of state. Few kings can have taken the idea of nobility more seriously than he, whence his deep empathy with the nobiliary backlash that had been confiscating every high office in church and army since Necker's expulsion. And whence the refusal, or rather inertia, of Vergennes, who found Calonne's letter too lukewarm to be shown to the King at the risk of getting hauled over the coals because of some fellow from Lyons who was still a nonentity, whatever he might claim to the contrary. Vergennes accordingly decides not even to submit the request to his sovereign. On May 14, 1784, Mme Roland has lost her last illusions:

> As I have told you before, my friend, we believe, and with some reason, that we have accomplished no small thing in contriving to get ill-humored people to bear favorable witness, and inciting them to write to the minister that you deserve the benevolence and protection of the Council. Assuredly the people who have done this will not be able to refuse you a handsome pension whenever you apply for it; even less can they speak of revocation or anything of that sort, etc. So that is one success: an *ovatio* [*sic*]. As for the honors of the great triumph, I cannot flatter myself that I have carried them off in this campaign. The King's opinion is real and tenacious, as every other that he adopts, and it is very widely known, and in consequence the ministers are loath to propose anything that might oppose it, or that would oblige them to make a special effort to overcome it, or leave them open to a refusal. There is our great difficulty; without it, we might consider M. de Calonne's letter sufficient. But to bring down an obstacle of this size, the letter is not nearly fervent enough; it is but simply, and feebly, fair: it sets you out as a deserving man whereas it ought to present you as a superior and extraordinary one . . .,[12]

and that (in brackets), you really aren't, now, dear, are you? Whose side is she on, anyway, the little lady advocate?

So is it a trip for nothing, defeat, back to the churchyard in Amiens? Not at all, thanks to the curtain-line dénouement. On "Saturday evening, May 22," to Roland, from Paris: "Well, my friend, it is certain, we shall go to Lyons."[13]

A general reshuffle in the inspectorate of manufactures has just vacated one of its most desirable positions, the inspectorate general of Lyons. For that the

King can endorse Roland's transfer without a qualm, even in his sleep. Which is what, at Calonne's behest, he proceeds to do. Jeanne-Marie, having heard about the opening, leaps into the breach, scarcely pausing to ask her husband for permission to act on his behalf and shooing before her her musketeer-intendants, who are delighted to be able to do her a favor that costs them nothing. "Definitively, my dear friend, the Clos, the greenery, the exquisite peace, delicious friendship, we shall have them all, and I don't care a rap about the rest." The "dear friend" doesn't object. He might not be returning to his native land ennobled, but at least he will live out his tenure there as a notability, before subsiding into a scribe's retirement shored up by the savings from a tidy income: 5,000 livres a year plus 600 for a house in Lyons whenever he has to reside there.* Until he retires, he'll have plenty of work to do, and plenty of the disputes and quarrels on which he thrives. At their final interview, Tolozan can't refrain from putting Mme Roland on her guard:

> There were lengthy observations on the manner in which you should conduct yourself in the region, the care you should take in dealing with the manufacturers in town in order not to offend them, and how, at the same time, you must know, without forcing them, everything that goes on, every new technique that is invented, how you should uphold the wool and linen interest in the *généralité;* how you should conform to the administration's views and not offend it by representations put forward with an air of trying to subjugate it, etc. Oh, I have much to tell you, I can promise you that. Great affirmations of interest, promises that there has been no change of attitude toward you and that one had always been on your side but that one found you too hasty, too inflexible, and now assigning to me the task of moderating you.

She is apparently undaunted by the prospect.

On October 3, 1784, thus, the Rolands move to the Beaujolais, she living mainly with her mother-in-law in the big house in Villefranche, but more and more often going to the Clos de la Platière a few leagues away,† and he partly with her and partly in Lyons in a little bachelor's apartment on the Place de la Charité, and the rest of the time on the road, on his long circuits to Saint-Etienne and the other towns in the region that were then in the early stages of industrialization. Their new existence, which they suppose is also

---

*Approximately 50,000 modern francs [$12,500].

†Where we find them in 1789. This is the little country-gentry vineyard I have mentioned before, in the village of Theizé near Villefranche, not to be confused with Thizy, further into Beaujolais, which is the site of the Château de la Platière whose name Roland has transferred to Theizé. The affecting memory of their great-granddaughter Mme Odette Fiérens, to whom I owe so much, has been with me throughout the writing of this page.

going to be their definitive one, is divided between the joys of the countryside and the worries of the largest preindustrial town in France, where, in August 1786, a thunderclap of weavers' bobbins has just rung out.

CITY OF LYON

# 43

## AUGUST 1786

### *A Permanent State of War*

LION or LYON, Lugdunum, Lugodunum, Lucdunum, Lygdunum, Lugdunum [*sic:* Canon Expilly's pen seems to have stuttered with joy, in his dictionary of 1766, before swinging into a hymn of praise to the big city—like the antiphon at lauds], Segustanorum, a city large, rich, beautiful, populous, most active in trade, very celebrated, and the most considerable of the realm after Paris; capital of the Lyonnais and the government-general of that name; with an archbishopric whose archbishop is primate and enjoys the rights of primacy; an academy of sciences, belles lettres, and arts; a public library; a court to try currency offenses, a mint, a presidial court and seneschalsy court, a *généralité,* an intendantship, a commercial tribunal (annexed to the consulate), an *élection,* * a police department, a superintendency of [river] ports, a customs office, a marshalcy, etc.[1]

Lyons, yes. Where the houselights dim once again and nobody in France notices, not even the Rolands, who are sitting in the front row. But you would need a practiced eye.†

---

*Presidial court:* a sort of civil and criminal court sitting in certain major towns; the seneschalsy court could coexist with a presidial court but was lower. *Généralité:* a tax circumscription administered by the local intendant. *Intendantship:* seat of the King's delegated government for the entire province. *Election:* a tax court.

†I cannot resist appending this sonorous rumble from the pen of Jaurès, on the subject of the uprising: "A fantastic bolt of lightning from the stormy heights of the Croix-Rousse, illuminating from afar, beyond the middle-class revolution, that vast and bitter battlefield upon which the dark masses of labor will soon deploy for a further revolution. But it was a fugitive, furtive flash, and soon extinguished! A flickering gleam of wrath and longing, not yet bright enough to guide the infant proletariat scattered through the night! The worker's consciousness had not yet become a self-supporting fire of thought and life; only sparks of passion escaped from it, to whirl an instant in the howling wind above the city before falling back, bleak, ash, to mingle with the sterile dust on the road."[2]

Jeanne Roland's first observation was correct: the trouble starts outside
the taverns at the beginning of August, because of the resuscitation of the
archbishop's "right of *banvin*," although the prelate himself probably knew
nothing about it. But why doesn't he keep a closer watch over his "farmers,"
the swarm of tax-collectors which tradition allots to him, as to some minor
king? In July, these gentlemen suddenly take it into their heads to insist that
the tavern-keepers pay their arrears on the "ecclesiastical right of *banvin*,"
which had more or less lapsed into disuse. It amounted to a tithe of 3 livres
for every ass-load of wine served in jars within the diocese.* Nothing big,
more of an annoyance than a real bite out of the budget, and maybe that's the
way the tavern-keepers took it.[3] But, without batting an eyelash, they shut
their shops two Sundays running—the last two in July. That makes a lot of men
in the streets on the day of rest. And the Lyons weaver puts away plenty of
liquor on Sunday, in order to forget the rest of the week, his six eighteen-hour
days of tedious, repetitive motions in the dark shadows of his cramped lodging, airless and sunless, a galley slave in his own home. Deprived of their "vine
juice," their "piss-stiff,"† the weak reddish poison they down in 6 denier jars,
and also deprived of the warm conviviality of the tavern, where they can pretty
much say what they please as long as they don't play cards (a mortal sin, strictly
forbidden to the poor), between 10,000 and 15,000 *taffetatiers* ** are reduced
to ambling through the streets, where they can find nothing better to do than
pool their depression. And the situation is no different for the milliners and
printers, and the stonemasons and laborers employed on the work sites of MM.
Perrache and Morand, who are in the process of transforming the town,
shifting mountains of sand and stone to build the beautiful houses we will
never live in. On the following Sunday, August 6, the taverns open again, but
not by choice: under orders from the consuls.‡ Sullenly greeted by surly

---

*Measures peculiar to Lyons. An *ânée,* or ass-load, was the average amount of wine
"comprising the load that can be carried by one ass in one trip. It has been fixed at eighty
jars."

†Beaujolais doesn't yet exist as a type of wine, although the region is already producing
some wines of good quality. All are consumed locally, however, not exported; and they would
have been too expensive for the drinkers in the taverns.

**[The source of taffeta, of course—*Trans.* ] The Lyons textile workers are not yet called
*canuts;* that name, presumably derived from the *canette* or spool of the loom, becomes current at
the time of the great uprisings in 1830. A *taffetatier* did a particular kind of work but the word,
along with *tisseur* [weaver—*Trans.* ], was used to describe them all.

‡The consulate of Lyons, which ran the municipal administration, was supposed to represent
the body of working citizens. Composed of the provost of merchants, the four aldermen, the
King's prosecuting attorney, and the secretary and tax inspector of the Chamber of Commerce
—all appointed or co-opted but in no case elected—it actually represented the interests of the
merchants, as opposed to those of the textile producers and their employees.

tavern-keepers, the master weavers and their journeymen spend the day masticating and liquifying their anger. They and the hatters start the ball rolling; they *are* the "Lyons manufactures," and the rest of the workers tend to follow their lead.

The fabric makers (that is, the master weavers) have had it up to here. They sell their cloth at a loss after making it with their own hands and those of their journeymen and apprentices, who are themselves on the verge of starvation. According to Necker,[4] the population now stands at about 160,000 and the "manufacture" consists of 18,000 looms. For every loom there are on average four pairs of hands, including those of the master, who is in fact no better than a kind of "worker-owner." He labors alongside the others and that brings them closer together, but the tiny firm belongs to him and it's his responsibility to sell his finished goods to the merchants, who in turn often supply the raw material he transforms into taffeta, velvet, calico, and chintz, passementerie, satin, damask, lustrine, and those miraculous fabrics woven of gold and silver thread that, since the Renaissance, have conquered half the nobles of Europe and dress the Court of France. What a responsibility, and what a new source of anguish for the laboring economy: selling the act of "making up" a piece of cloth, selling work itself. Every adult weaver usually has a wife and four or five dependent children, not to mention parents; so we're talking about almost one hundred thousand mouths that have to be fed. Six years before, when Maria Theresa died and the Queen's deep mourning draped the whole of Versailles in purple and black for a year, over five thousand unemployed weavers, and their families, were virtually reduced to begging.

This time it's less sudden but more serious, because more widespread; the whole manufacture is feeling the pinch. The journeymen, who earn less than 20 sous a day, literally cannot buy their daily bread—in Lyons, in 1786, the pound loaf costs 8 sous—and the wages they are paid by the masters are fixed by the authorities (the merchants in this case). Over the last two centuries Lyons has become a sort of island within France, specializing in the textile trade and administered by the town's patricians or big burghers, whose staggering profits are derived from the gulf between the rockbottom wages paid for making up their cloth and the high prices they charge their French and foreign customers for buying it. The system is endorsed and made official by royal authority, in the person of the intendant, who simply countersigns the consulate's decisions.

"We have now sketched a general picture of a permanent state of war declared by the merchant class upon the master weavers; the details have been muted and would have been omitted entirely, except that they shaped, by a very natural process, the claims being pressed today.''*

Since the closing of the taverns an endemic strike—not yet known by that name—has been flitting here and there along the *traboules* [specific to Lyons; a *traboule* is a passageway going through a block of buildings and out the other side—*Trans.*] and narrow alleyways between the seven-story houses. On Monday, August 7, the spontaneous caucuses in the re-opened taverns begin to form into a "coalition," the dread specter that the merchant class keeps trying to exorcise throughout industrial history. The lone worker is a domesticated animal, a household pet; united with his fellows, he becomes a power in the play of economic forces. Until now, such a situation has been no more tolerated in France than blasphemy.

But there it is. At opening time on Monday the textile workers leave their looms, cross the new boat-bridge over the Rhône, and assemble in the wasteland of the Charpennes *brotteaux*, † where they have more elbowroom than in the center of town, that narrow pointed tongue where the Saône and Rhône flow together.** Here there are no watchmen-archers or burgher-militia to disperse them. They're not going to hold a regular assembly, with a general discussion led by orators; nothing has been organized yet. It is more like a giant palaver among small groups, the first stammerings of a few hundred voices dominated by that of the master weaver Denis Monnet, who has learned how to write proper French and will prove it, and who has understood the heart of the problem:

> The shameful greed, or rather cupidity, of many merchants of this city has brought despair to the souls of the craftsmen who make up their cloth. Unable to feed themselves, even by working day and night, they have turned to the judge consuls. But the judge consuls are also merchants, and have rejected their remonstrances. . . . The workers have thereupon agreed among themselves that, in order to live by their work, they would make up each particular type of cloth for a price they themselves would set.[5]

A preliminary agreement among workers on the price of labor? That might indeed bring down the pillars of the temple. Tracts are already circulat-

*From the *Mémoire pour les maître-ouvriers, fabricants en étoffes d'or, d'argent et de soie de la ville de Lyon* ["Memorandum for the master weavers, makers of cloth of gold, silver, and silk of the city of Lyons"—*Trans.*], addressed to the King in 1789 and based on the text drafted by Denis Monnet in 1786.

†The *brotteaux* (originally *broteaux*) were uncultivated marshes that gave their name to a large section of Lyons [and to a train station, the other being Perrache, after the great builder mentioned earlier—*Trans.*].

**Still commonly called "the island" in 1786; the works put in hand by Perrache *fils* (who has just died) are giving the district the features it bears today, as well as its name.

ing, in which Denis Monnet and two or three of his colleagues have had a hand:*

> We consider that if representations are not a sufficient means of obtaining a decent rate, we must, firm of mind and sincere in agreement, each acting for himself, raise the price of our work to one full third above the present rates.

After noon that same Monday the weavers are joined by the hatters, more especially the *approprieurs* or dressers, who receive the beaver hides from Canada and process them, washing and scouring, fleshing and brushing until they are soft as modeling clay. When they are done, the finishers, true artists, fashion the "dressed" skins into the thousands of different pointed and rounded forms that are essential to the notable's prestige when he sallies forth outside his walls, "the sword of the head." On weekdays, however, the master hatters are not allowed to wear their own creations but go bareheaded or in bonnets, in their homespun dress which they usually cover with the ample apron that constitutes the uniform of the Lyonnese workman six days out of seven, be he weaver, milliner, or printer, in contrast to the neat outfit, with knee-hugging breeches and a light-colored jerkin, that he purchases once or twice in his lifetime to wear on Sundays and holidays. Merchants and burghers, meanwhile, have five or six suits of clothes for everyday wear hanging in their presses, some with gilt buttons.

Weavers and hatters part around six in the evening, and go home to eat their soup in town without having manifested the slightest collective aggressiveness. But even that is too much for the members of the consulate, who are making a mountain out of this germ of sedition. They're right, too: the disproportion between the handful of members of the ruling and trading class and the mass of their *de facto* slaves is so great that any hint of worker consciousness must be throttled before it sees the light of day.

After glancing at the reports drawn up by the police commissioners on the basis of the accounts of their stool pigeons in the Charpennes, Christophe de la Rochette, the King's prosecuting attorney, issues a "charge for sedition" that evening, and the chief of police begins his careful tracking down of the leaders. By Tuesday morning the consulate's orders are posted at all crossroads, "enjoining all workers, both clothmakers and hatters, and all others who may have left their places of work, to return to them this day; it being forbidden to all persons whatever to appear assembled in the streets, taverns, and other public resorts in groups of more than five."[6]

The consuls can go to hell. This time, a large majority of the workers

*These may be the very first tracts in the history of working-class Lyons. Denis Monnet, youngest of a family of master weavers, learned his letters working for a lawyer. In 1786 he is thirty-six years old. He plays an important role in Lyons's darkest hours during the Revolution, and is guillotined on November 27, 1793, during the terrorist clampdown.

down tools and leave their shops around eight, or as soon as they have finished breakfast, and walk out to sniff the wind of contentiousness. Any lukewarm brothers preparing to set their looms in motion are heard outside their houses and dragged out, none too gently, by groups of five or six of their colleagues. Antoine Bel, a companion of Saint-Just, later reveals that "his master hid him in his bedroom so that his comrades would not find him when they came to search for him."[7]

By noon on Tuesday, August 8, virtually the entire manufacture of Lyons is on strike. There are so many men looking for a name to put to their anger that a split develops: the weavers return to the Charpennes on the south bank of the Rhône while the hatters gather at the southern tip of the tongue between the two rivers, in the dust and clutter of the Perrache works, where the stonemasons catch the bug and decide to desert their building sites. A leader is sifted out of the crowd and becomes the heart and soul of this second movement—Pierre Sauvage, thirty-three, a native of Normandy, onetime soldier in the Lorraine legion and now a dresser in Lyons. In agreement with his fellows, he proposes that they "delegate four or five of their number to present our demands to M. le Commandant." M. le Commandant is Louis Tolozan de Montfort, the provost of merchants, a relative of the Tolozan who was so gallant to Mme Roland and a member of the powerful dynasty that incarnates the rise of big business. The people call him "commandant" because he is, *ex officio,* commander of the bourgeois militia—the only force of law and order immediately available in case of trouble. Lyons is not a military town; the venerable free city has always managed to keep itself unencumbered by governors and garrisons. The nearest regiment of the King's men is at Valence, twenty-five leagues—a three-day march—to the south.

In the late afternoon just under a thousand workers, led by the hatters, "ranged in battle order and marching three by three," having fallen into step behind Pierre Sauvage and his improvised "delegates," pass through the Rhône Gate on their way back from the tip of the "island," and jostle, still without real malice, the *compagnie franche* [free company—*Trans.*]—another local militia company—who are the gate's symbolic guardians.

"We have assembled," calls out Pierre Sauvage, and signs his death warrant with those words: "We want to talk to M. le Commandant, we ask but one minute of his time and then we will withdraw."[8]

All the procession has to do is spread itself along the right bank of the Rhône and it will ambush the commander in his house, a magnificent mansion built by his father and predecessor at the western end of the boat-bridge.* In these days officials are to be found in their residences at least as often as in their

---

*The architect Morand barely manages to replace the boats by stone before he is guillotined, in 1793, not far from the bridge that bears his name today.

offices, where they may go only for ceremonial occasions. They live and work at home. The Tolozan house is the symbol of the new Lyons, the "island"— a sprinkling of distinguished edifices built on the fringes of the Perrache works, on land that is still partly wooded, near rows of tall narrow houses crowded side by side. A good-sized piece of ground offers the crowd a generous welcome between the beautiful four-story façade and the riverfront. The situation is about to become serious, because a far-off rumble and clouds of dust herald the return of the weavers "from the marshes beyond the bridge." Although there has been no official agreement between them and the hatters (notes were passed, no doubt), they too have resolved to state their grievances to the provost of merchants and demand an immediate raise of 2 sous for every piece of work. It's not their fault if the provost's house stands at the end of the bridge and the hatters are already there.

LYON CLOTHMAKERS

# 44

AUGUST 1786

## *As Farmyard Animals*

The weavers make the first move. They're a lot more numerous than the hatters, they've had a lot more to drink in the Charpennes taverns, and they are out from under the thumbs of their temperate wives. At the end of the bridge they roll up against the Tolozan house and encircle it like a flood tide, pushing the hatters into the background. The different guilds are on neighborly terms but do not mingle or have friends on the other team, so the demonstration takes place in two movements and two keys, and it's the weavers' turn first.

The provost, justifiably alarmed, orders his guards inside and bars his doors. All right, if you don't want a dialogue, the stones will do the talking, the stones that pave those streets of Lyons that are paved at all, although what the stones mostly do is twist people's ankles and elicit oaths from men like Arthur Young the traveler. They are large round pebbles collected along the riverbanks and half-buried in the earth but rising several inches above it, and it's easy as pie to dig them up here; they're like rotten teeth wobbling in the gums of a compost as loose and soft as a field. What a temptation to pepper the façade with them, break a few windows! The crowd begins to roar. It mobs

290        AUGUST 1786

and mauls one poor militiaman, Louis Moiron, who was forgotten outside the house by his comrades; but all he gets is a dislocated shoulder. The company of the watch on duty at the theater trots up from the rue du Puits Gaillot but falls back under a hail of stones and, their assailants drawn in their wake, the whole mob pours down the street, past the theater, and into the Place des Terreaux, the very heart of Lyons, where it washes up against the town hall. Tolozan can breathe again. The consulate has been in session inside since noon; it's their turn.

Dusk is closing in; it's going to be a heavy, sultry, misty evening.[1] Way up overhead, in his huge, almost life-size medallion, pawing the granite over the porch of the building's baroque façade, the steed of Henri IV bears aloft the equine profile of the King who knew how to make his subjects love him. But today even he gets stung by a few stray rocks. The "square" which the locals still call "Les Terreaux" [terreau means leaf mold or compost—Trans.] is, as often in old cities, a jumble of odds and ends, an irregular line of houses jutting out in the northwest corner, at the end of the rue Clermont and rue Sainte-Marie, balanced by two big masses, the town hall on the east and St. Peter's Abbey on the south. It can't hold 10,000 people, which only makes everyone in it shout all the louder because they're being pushed from behind by the others crowded into the tangle of streets around the square.

Are they ever going to finish their deliberations in there? Since when does one pennyworth of justice need so many fancy words? The consulate is hedging and dithering; at one point it tries an ill-advised assault, suddenly unleashing a score of mounted gendarmes, its last available cavalry, who bolt out of the town hall stables and into the crowd. It might as well have tried boiling oil. True, the poor gendarmes had orders not "to draw and use their bayonets" but they are so mobbed and their horses so bedeviled that all they can do is gallop away again, down the quay of the Saône, just as Captain de Saint-Didier, a militia officer, emerges at the top of the steps waving a big sheet of paper like a white flag—stop, stop everybody, they've capitulated, victory, we're getting our raise, we've won!

They really have; or at least it looks that way. The consuls have employed the combined tactics of carrot and stick. The officer is indeed waving the text of an order "approving the increase awarded by the masters of the major manufacture, of 2 sous for every ell of English 5–8 and 7–12 taffeta,* the same increase to be granted proportionally in respect of other plain-colored fabrics."[2] But now communications become snarled; the weavers have been infuriated by the gendarmes' charge and are no longer willing or able to grasp the fact that they have gotten what they wanted. One of them, Jean Cléry,

*The figures give the widths of the rolls of fabric when they leave the loom, the ell being their length.

scrambles up the steps, grabs the paper from the captain's hands, glares at it, and melodramatically tears it in two, crying out that the proclamation is meaningless because it hasn't been signed.

Aha, they're trying to put one over on us, are they? The age-old wariness grips the crowd by the guts. A group of overwrought Piedmontese orchestrates the next phase of protest; they crossed the Alps to exercise in Lyons "their skill at weaving the beautiful silks which in their country are made all ready-organized, that is, thrown and prepared to form the warp of silken fabrics,"[3] but all they've gained is one poverty in place of another. Some of the Piedmontese have "knife in hand" and one of them, Joseph-Antoine Dapiano from Turin, outshouts all the rest with the gusto of his twenty years:

"The Piedmontese have done enough, now let the Lyonnese show their stuff!"[4]

Did he add, "We'll have their hides!"—pointing at the rue Saint-Côme that snakes between the abbey and the Luzerne buildings, where the retreating horsemen are still trying to fight their way to the empty banks of the Saône? Joseph-Antoine denies it. Two witnesses say he did. But, Dapiano or not, the soldiers are not in deadly peril when they open fire on a crowd armed with nothing but stones. City workers, unlike peasants, don't even have sticks or clubs.

The crowd scatters at the first shots, fired in sufficient disarray to send a mere seven casualties to the Hôtel-Dieu, and only one of them, Mathieu Bernard, was a silk weaver (although many of his comrades were carried home injured). Because you're not to suppose this is a riot of weavers only. Everybody in Lyons is in the crowd today: Louis-Marie Creuset, a pastrycook's apprentice, is shot in the chest; Joseph Clergé, a tailor's apprentice, gets a bullet in one leg and several saber cuts; Jean-Baptiste Chardonnet, a journeyman joiner, has one lung torn by a bullet; while Benoît Pacalin, locksmith, Antoine Neuville, packer, and Antoine Pitellet, *affaneur,* * get their fill of steel once the gendarmes' fire has cleared enough space for them to charge in—slashes on the head and arms for the last two, and Pacalin receives "two thrusts in the ribs." Mathieu Bernard the silk weaver is the only one to die of his wounds, but another man, Jacques Lavaure, a journeyman cobbler, is picked up dead off the pavement.

Once the weavers are dispersed, the hatters take over. They've also been pelting Tolozan's house, and "one of his secretaries or valets asked them to send a few of their number to the town hall to talk."[5] When they reach the Place des Terreaux, it is full of rubble; better disciplined and at all times more peaceable than their predecessors, they calmly await the return of their "dele-

*Seasonal farmworkers hired for the haying.

gates," led by Pierre Sauvage, who is the very essence of reasonableness in his dealings with the quaking consuls, now supplemented by Tolozan, and who agrees to advise the hatters to disperse, having been assured that a decision in their case will be forthcoming the next day.

Actually dispersing them, however, is another matter, especially as there is a rumor going around to the effect that some of the demonstrators have been put in jail. Look, fellows, you can see for yourselves: the consuls, virtually defenseless that evening against the uprising, order Claude-Joseph Merlino de Boisgrange, ensign-captain of the Terreaux district, "to conduct the seditious to the prisons so they may ascertain for themselves that none of those who were disturbing the peace had been taken into custody."[6]

At Saint-Joseph prison, where the hatters' movement ends that evening, chief jailer Anthelme Fillon and his henchmen, reinforced by eight soldiers of the watch, are in a fine tizzy; they double-bar and triple-bolt the doors on their forty civil and criminal inmates, and unite—as they subsequently declare—"all their forces to withstand the populace." They needn't have bothered; by nine in the evening the workers are falling asleep on their feet; nothing is worse agony for them than a late night. All Fillon has to do is swear, under oath and in front of the recorder, "that none of their comrades are in the prison," and they all troop home to bed.

The next morning, August 8, it's the quick glance from under half-lowered eyelids. The consulate continues its juggling act, pending the arrival of the reinforcements it has called in from the outlying areas, while the workers half-believe they've won and half-fear they've been had. A few weavers go back to work but most return to the Brotteaux, where they froth and fume some more and dream up new demands, this time about how their work should be regulated, how to stop the hiring of lower-paid women workers, and how members of the same guild should have the right of assembly. Their ideas are not worked up into clear statements, but even in this rudimentary form they're enough to convince the merchants that they had better take a firm hand as soon as they can get one. Meanwhile, they'll concede what they must and gain time by holding discussions with the hatters, who have reassembled, as before, around the Perrache works and, because they have some semblance of organization, can be treated as valid negotiators.

Do come for the promised reply, dear friends, you'll be made right welcome. Sauvage, accompanied by Perraud, Berthelier, Villars, and Guinard, goes back into the lion's den. There's already something different in the atmosphere in the town hall antechamber, where a small mobilization of the middle class is beginning to bear fruit. The officers of the marshalcy, the watch, the archers, and the free company are openly awaiting orders "before removing their troops wherever the seditious workers should assemble."[7]

A few of them, in the meantime, are busily noting down the words, attitudes, and identities of the "leaders" now in their clutches, and the discussion drags on so long that the hatters outside begin to worry about their mates. They send Louis Giraud and Jean-Jacques Nerin, an apprentice dresser, to the rescue. Louis Ménard, lieutenant of the watch, observes the latter's keen features and tries to win him over to the right side—a bad choice, Nerin is not the turncoat kind.

> At first he spoke fair and in a manner that gave me some hope of prevailing upon him to dissuade his comrades from their schemes; however, I having sought to make him increasingly sensible of the dreadful consequences of the actions he was undertaking by showing himself in a sense to be the chief of the seditious, the said Nerin then answered me back with a very determined air, saying that he believed what he was asking was only fair, that he meant to have justice, that if he did not he would know how to obtain it in some other way, and that his comrades would not abandon him.

What the officer doesn't realize is that Jean-Jacques Nerin has got a lot more to say . . .

"It is only after having suffered patiently and at length, and having vainly made representations to their immediate superiors, that the master manufacturers of silk of the city of Lyons have at last come to beg justice of you. . . .*

"We can no longer bear this monstrous alliance of labor and poverty, the most industrious worker being condemned to a desolate penury that should rather be the deserts of sloth."[8]

The model budget which a handful of Lyons master weavers drew up together in a cellar, as though they were loading a torpedo, has been passing from hand to hand for the last five years, ever since it was disdainfully ignored by the authorities. From it, most of the poor blighters have at least been able to figure out *why* they are so wretched.[9] The "average annual expenditure" required of each master to keep his loom operating, and also to feed and maintain his dependents, is 2,300 livres. The "product of the worker's hand," as they say, or what will later be called the gross turnover, is 1,944 livres, making an annual deficit of 356 livres† (on average, that is), which is the cost of one year's bread for four people. Now, craftsmen have no more resources "in hand" or "behind them" than have peasants, who are out begging after one bad harvest. For them, the very concept of saving is meaningless; how can

*According to the *Mémoire des fabricants à façon de la ville de Lyon,* written in 1780 and promptly rejected by the intendant and consuls. Printed secretly, in Lyons of course, it is circulating among the strikers of 1786, and serves as their "manifesto."

†Reminder: these figures should be multiplied by between 7 and 10 in order to find the equivalent in modern francs; today, hence, the deficit would amount to about 3,000 francs [$750].

you save a deficit? Nevertheless, this annual budget is frugal unto stringency: three half-bottles of wine a day (for four people), 60 livres a year for laundry, 70 for oil to burn for light "until one hour after midnight in winter"; for the man, "one coat and working trousers every three years, two shirts a year, two pairs of shoes"; for the woman, "one dress and a petticoat costing 36 livres, once in three years"; the annual confinement amounts to 72 livres for midwife, the child's trousseau, and diapers . . .

"In consequence whereof," states the conclusion to this account, also written by the master workers,

> it is most evident that, without any provision for illness, unforeseen accidents, slack times, or cessation of work, the master manufacturers are by no means able to maintain the very moderate level of sustenance and living described above, albeit its being an absolute minimum, without help from their relatives or other compassionate persons: moreover, we are all too aware of the debts they are compelled to contract, to merchants, landlords, butchers, bakers, and others, and which cannot be redeemed, with the best will in the world; and in the end a few, sinking into a piteous state and having no resources of credit, abandon the honorable condition of industrious citizens by turning to the houses of charity for help, which already have many more persons than they can deal with in a similar plight.

It is this bedrock anguish that Nerin and his friends are trying to communicate this morning to the gentlemen who quietly let them talk, keeping one eye on the clock. Not that the workers, having known them all from father to son, have many illusions about their masters; on the contrary, they readily invoke the only arguments capable of making any impression on their audience: we are your geese that lay your golden eggs, and you are killing us.

> Were the silk workers regarded as no more than mechanical instruments needful for the manufacture of cloth, or, ignoring their human condition which should rightly make their fate a concern to the whole of society, were they inhumanly treated as farmyard animals that are fed and kept alive solely for the benefits that can be derived from their labor, it would still be necessary to give them no less than the subsistence one is compelled to give such animals if one does not wish to be soon deprived of the fruits of their work.

# 45

AUGUST 1786

## *The Foxes of Freedom*

A little before noon on August 8, the hatters in the Place des Terreaux burst into cheers. Sauvage steps out "onto the balcony overlooking the square," shaking hands with one of the consulate officers and announcing that the gentlemen inside have melted like the snow in the sun:

"Victory, friends! They've given us the 40 sou day!* Long live the King and magistrates of this town; we'll all be happy now! Follow me to the works, we must tell the others!"

The demonstrators are startled and thrown off guard by the enormity of this sudden capitulation. Sauvage, the unwitting instrument of appeasement, conducts his men "to Perrache," leaving the Terreaux to the gendarmes, who firmly re-occupy it. The hatters who had stayed behind at the works do not share their colleagues' enthusiasm. What proves that we're actually going to get them, our 40 sous? They send Sauvage back to the town hall for a signed decree, which he takes to a printer himself, with Tolozan's consent; the provost has decided to play the game to the end. But when Sauvage returns, waving a handful of posters still wet from the press, he gets a cold shoulder: the "give an inch and they ask for a mile" mechanism has taken over, as it did yesterday among the weavers. Now this bunch have started grousing about working conditions, working hours, terms of hiring, firing, and apprenticeship.

The tide has turned; the mob emotion was at its full yesterday evening, now it is starting to ebb. The hatters have been separated from the silkmakers by the wedge which the consulate has just driven between the two corporations by granting major concessions to the former; and the corporations themselves are being shaken by internal dissension between timid souls and extremists. The fact that promises have been made to them is favorable to the timid, who are suddenly waking up appalled at their own temerity—What are we doing in the streets and on these building sites, outside our lives, outside

---

*Dressers, until then, earned only 32 sous and 8 deniers, so the raise meant almost 8 sous more at one blow. Note, however, that the hatters, unlike the weavers, were asking for an increase for working time, not just for the individual piece.

our everyday setting? For them, obedience is like breathing; out of that element, they suffocate. Their natural inclination is to hurry home and hug their precious, precarious victory. Even now, officers covered with white August dust are knocking at the city gates, announcing the arrival of the Gévaudan light infantry and the artillery from La Fère; and the reassured urban militia has resumed control of the center of town.

If we're going to start behaving ourselves again, we'd better do it fast and all together, in order to avoid the backlash of repression. Careful, friends, these hotheads will lead you to the scaffold . . .

At this point, a singular group of characters steps in and attempts to mediate. Mounting a block of stone as his improvised podium, an imposing but still youthful figure begins to speak, like the preachers of the Crusades of old. His dress is a cross between monk and soldier: dog collar above and breeches below, a moiré capelet but powdered hair, a resounding voice, persuasive gesture, quick eye. Is it a priest, a nobleman, a lawyer? It is a canon of the cathedral chapter, choirmaster César de Clugny by name; and near him stand, similarly attired, his brother Charles-Antoine and his uncle Louis, and Gaspard de Pingon and Anne-Hérault-Paul-Antoine de la Madeleine de Ragny . . . Each and every one a canon! Well, what business is this of theirs? Why, their very own and proper business, and for many a year too: these are some of the authentic counts of Lyons. In their persons, the best of the old nobility and the best of the clergy, hoping to spare the workers, try to arbitrate between them and the merchants.

> The chapter of the church of St. John is one of the most illustrious of Europe and has the King as first canon . . . The canons of this church* take the title of counts.
> The origin of the prerogative is this: in a bull of the year 1157 the Emperor [of the Holy Roman Empire] Frederick I gave to Heraclius de Montboissier, Archbishop of Lyons, and to his heirs, the exarchate [delegation of sovereign powers, usually archepiscopal] of the Kingdom of Burgundy, with all regalian rights over the city of Lyons. There arose upon this occasion a great dispute between this archbishop and the Comte du Forest [modern spelling Forez], who styled himself Comte de Lyons. A transaction was required to end the dispute. In the year 1173 the count ceded his title and all his rights to the archbishopric and chapter in return for 800 silver marks. The archbishop and canons ceded the temporal domain of the city of Lyons to King Philippe le Bel, who confirmed their title as counts.[1]

To bear it in 1786, you most assuredly cannot be a commoner: "Their nobility must be proven in respect of four paternal and maternal quarters. The chapter appoints [co-opts] the canons to be admitted, and the proof [of their

---

*Of which, since 1321, there have been thirty-two. Canons were members of the clergy attached to a cathedral church to celebrate mass like monks and, if need be, assist the bishop in his administrative duties. Laymen could be appointed.

nobility] must be produced upon admission. . . . A count of Lyons may, in less than thirty years' time, come to possess 8,000 livres of income."* These curious canons, who in the last analysis have no master but themselves, actually turn out to be Christians as well.

Etienne Rapou, a police official who was "trying to calm the people," can only blink at this improvised alliance between church and nonentity:

> While he was speaking to them, the Comte de Clugny arrived and entered into negotiations with them and urged them to withdraw peacefully . . ., then asked what they wanted and undertook to present to the consulate himself the memorandum containing their [further] demands. Following this offer and mediation, a table was brought and placed in the middle of the way, and the said Sauvage dictated to the said Comte de Clugny the articles of their demands.† . . . The text having been drawn up, it was read aloud and much applauded.

But then, that afternoon, all the momentum seeps away in foot-dragging negotiations and half-hearted motions. Two of the canon-counts, increasingly alarmed because they know what the authorities have in store, also pay a call on the "workers in silk" who are still hanging around the Charpennes, and that evening they lead the procession back into town, stopping off, as on the previous night, at the prison, where, seconded by the hatters, the crowd is soon 3,000 strong, heckling "the soldiers of the watch commanded by a sergeant and provided with ammunition."

"We have come to get our comrades if there be any inside!"

The same old fear . . . The prison roll is read out to them but they aren't satisfied. One of the canons goes inside with four weavers and four hatters, one of whom, decked out in "a white uniform with green lapels and trim," is brandishing a saber. "The prisoners having been locked up as on the previous night, they called out through the windows to ask if there were any silk workers or hatters among them." Upon being told that there are none, they withdraw for good. If they come back tomorrow they'll have better luck.

August 9. Tension is rising. It's as though the 2 sous a job and the 40 sous a day aren't really true. In the town hall, where he now feels safe again, the King's man of law growls out an ordinance which is posted before noon, proclaiming that "it is forbidden to all persons, craftsmen, journeymen, workers, and members of trades to assemble, gather together, form into groups, or conclude among themselves any agreements contrary to law and order. . . . It is further forbidden to carry canes, sticks, and other weapons,

---

*About 60,000 modern francs [$15,000].

†First occasion on which a spoken demand was put into writing by the pen of a notable. First loose leaf of the thousands upon thousands of notebooks to follow. At the bottom of the sheet, which was preserved in the records of the "case," Sauvage's signature is firm and legible.

and to address one another using such names as 'Companions of duty,' 'ga-vots,' 'droguins' . . ."—huh?

It's out at last. For some time now, secret corporations, otherwise known as *cabales,* have been worrying the improvisers of the capitalist game like a field full of mole holes just made to twist the players' ankles. "The association places on an equal footing those who have been trained, by a body of craftsmen, common and coarse laborers, to destroy each other and wreak savage ven-geances and other extravagances befitting such people.[2] It is here that the officers must enforce order and peace; it is here that firmness, prudence, and force are required. . . ."* "How terrifying the thought becomes,[3] when applied to those creatures who were born to disrupt societies, in whom the passions, less tamed by nurture, combine the raw energy of nature with the spurs they acquire from the unrestraint of towns."†

On September 7, 1778, a police ordinance had been posted at every crossroads, and its terms are reiterated in that of August 9, 1786; the Lyon-ese working class can't say it hasn't had fair warning. "In particular, we forbid all working people to form, have, or maintain any association, under the name of 'Sans gêne,' 'Bons enfants,' 'Gavots,' 'Droguins,' 'du Devoir,' 'Dévorans,' 'Passants,' 'Gorets,' and others,** for the alleged purposes of becoming acquainted with fellow workers, finding work, and affording mu-tual aid." You might as well try to dam an underground river with one hand. The *gavots* are joiners, the *dévorans* locksmiths, the *droguins* clothmak-ers; but in the "disturbances" and "emotions" of Lyons are also mingled, as at some primeval crossroads of all the paths on the journeymen's tour of France,‡ the esoteric rites of the "Enfants du Père Soubise" (carpenters), of "Maître Jacques" (stonecutters), of the "Renards de la liberté" (also carpen-ters), of the coopers or "Petits Brocs"†† . . . Some of those rites were born

---

*According to Panckoucke's *Encyclopédie méthodique,* the very series to which Roland is contributing his *Dictionnaire des manufactures.*

†Remonstrance of the Parlement of Paris to Louis XVI in 1776, criticizing the abolition (by Turgot) of the *jurandes,* which the magistrates regarded as a species of working-class police.

**[*Sans gêne:* rude, brash. *Bons enfants:* good children. *Gavots:* people from the town of Gap. *Droguins:* possibly, as English "drugget" (a coarse cloth or rug made of various fibers), from *droguet,* a diminutive of the old French *drogue,* meaning junk or trash. *Du devoir:* of duty. *Dévorans:* also from "duty," not "devouring." *Passants:* on the move, itinerant. *Gorets:* piglets—*Trans.*]

‡[The journeymen's tour of France was literally that; at the end of their apprenticeships young members of the ancient trades went from town to town to complete their training, and were given food and lodging and assistance in finding jobs by other workers in the same trade. These might have been and occasionally were highly effective groups that could blackball a master and organize a strike, except that there was so much rivalry between them. The *compagnonnages* or fraternal orders of journeymen arose in the late Middle Ages and only waned with the Industrial Revolution; they have never died out, however, and continue in France to this day—*Trans.*]

††[*Enfants du Père Soubise:* Father Soubise's children. *Maître Jacques:* Master James. *Renards de la liberté:* Foxes of freedom. *Petits Brocs:* Little jugs—*Trans.*]

in the Middle Ages and reborn in the Illuminism of the century, and are now linked, through journeymen's sons who have become lodge-attending townsmen, to the rituals of Freemasonry and the Spirit of Enlightenment; and those same rites, if they become the stimuli for collective action, are regarded by the authorities as witchcraft. The reason why the workers are not allowed to carry canes and sticks, moreover, is because, like certain rosettes and ribbons, they are the secret insignia of their concerted action. Every member

> bears a nickname referring to his place of origin, his most salient features, or his first name: Breton-brave-compagnon, Tourangeau-la-tendresse, Tourangeau-l'aimable, Tourangeau-plaisir-de-fille, Nantais-ennemi-du-repos, Angevin-la-fayence, Parisien-va-sans-peur, Alsacien-francoeur, Comtois-sans-chagrin, Angevin-coeur-de-France, Bourguignon-l'incrédule, Poitevin-le-résolu, Suisse-va-de-bon-coeur, Allemand-coeur-content-pour-la-vie, Girondin-craint-l'effort, Bayonne-le-bien-aimé, Béthune-prêt-à-boire.[4]

Some of Pierre Sauvage's fellow hatters call him "Normand-de-Lorraine," because of the term he spent in the Lorraine legion. But wasn't that his nickname in the brotherhood too?

# 46

## AUGUST 1786

## *For Crime of Popular Emotion**

August 10. About five o'clock in the afternoon the two de Clugny brothers, the canon-counts of Lyons, seek out Pierre Sauvage at Charpennes, where the hatters have finally, but too late, joined the weavers. They have wasted the day together, too excited to go home as they were told to do but already too intimidated to begin any more mass marches. In short, sweethearts, you're lost. The chief of police, meanwhile, has not wasted *his* day, he's been poking around the hospital and prisons, and the members of the seneschalsy court have gathered in the courthouse, and warrants have been issued with names

---

*[This might better be translated "incitement to riot" or something similar, but that would miss the irony intended by the author; "emotion" in English did once mean public disturbance or tumult—*Trans.*]

on them and one of them says you, Sauvage, you've stuck your neck out too far, it's time to make yourself scarce, the troops are at the gates.

The row is deafening, it's a shouting match between hawks and doves. Only this morning they wrote "to the hatters in the neighboring towns, to come to Lyons and support them." They sent little cards round to the shops that were still open—the fullers and dyers for instance—saying: "Gentlemen dyers, we mercifully request you to put down your work and leave." By this act, the more determined among them had unconsciously initiated the process that leads from agitation to insurrection. But again, too late. The Gévaudan light infantry has arrived. The canons of St. John, who are shrewd as well as sincere in wanting to help, finally get the kettle off the boil. Demobilization ensues: the workers drift back toward the bridge in small groups with the two canons in front to keep the soldiers from getting ideas, but they needn't have bothered because the soldiers have orders to let potential rioters go home quietly.

What about Pierre Sauvage? The de Clugnys put him on a horse and head him toward Grenoble, with 6 livres for travel expenses and a letter of recommendation to one of their brothers—another canon—who lives at Pont de Beauvoisin on the frontiers of Savoy. In the letter, which is also supposed to serve as a passport, they prudently call him a domestic. They don't even let him say good-bye to his wife and children; the fear of retribution must have been strong that night . . . The night of the day on which Mme Roland writes to Bosc from Villefranche to tell him the news.

Most of the workers thus disperse unmolested, but the guards at the bridges, their numbers trebled, have reinstated compulsory payment of the toll, and they close up ranks around a silent town. At nine in the evening the soldiers of the free company intercept "six persons proceeding together, apparently hatters' boys, who tried to cross the bridge without paying." They are conducted to the town hall, "placed in the guard room," and identified: Joseph Richard, a hat dyer's apprentice, and five hatter-dressers: Pierre Thimonnier, François Deschets, Sylvestre Guillermet, Antoine Charron, Jean-Jacques Nerin.

Nerin? That's the one, that's the devil who had such a loud mouth on this very spot yesterday, when he was so worried about Pierre Sauvage. A good catch, this one's a ringleader. And here come two Piedmontese, picked up at the corner of the rue du Puits Gaillot, right where they whipped out their knives before, Antoine Bel and Joseph-Antoine Dapiano. That second one is another wild animal, dangerous, dangerous. Why, he was shouting about killing the gentlemen.

Maybe we ought to make a few more arrests, even if it means going out and smoking them out of their lairs, raiding the alleyways? No point. Better let sleeping dogs lie, we'd be one against ten again. The consulate will adopt a simpler procedure, the tried-and-true monarchical recipe for maintaining or restoring obedience: a short, sharp terror.

August 11. Better kill off our hostages quick, before the workers wake up to what's happening or those bleating canon-counts come along and start doling out pardons. At dawn the prisoners are transferred to Saint-Joseph where, this time, nobody will come to get them out because there will be no more public assemblies. The judges are in their robes by eight—all members of the presidial court, all closely united by birth and interest, all cousins or the next best thing. The gentlemen of Lyons are about to get even, and they're not going to waste any time doing it.

Justice will not be done on its home ground. "In view of the danger that would result from transferring the prisoners to the courthouse, which lies at some distance from the prisons," the seneschalsy (or special) court decides to transfer itself "to the said prisons, in order that M. *le lieutenant-général criminel* may proceed at once and without any removals to the various stages of the investigation, and the company may rule as to its jurisdiction, apply the special procedures provisions, and proceed to final judgment."

At eleven that morning the gendarmes of the little town of Bourgoin, a regular stopping-off place between Lyons and Grenoble, arrest a man at the end of his tether: Pierre Sauvage, betrayed by his behavior—workmen don't know how to travel. Alerted by the calls for help sent out from Lyons, the authorities in every hamlet between there and the Dauphiné are on the lookout. Instead of protecting Sauvage, his letter from the Clugnys makes him look even fishier. What is this fake servant trying to hide? The counts of Lyons cut no ice outside Lyons, and the Bourgoin magistrates promptly wash their hands of the troublemaker, spy, whatever he is, by packing him off under escort, back to their colleagues in the big city. If his canon chums are so keen to help him, they'll be right on the spot.

Lyons. Saint-Joseph prison. The chief of criminal investigations spends the morning interrogating witnesses, almost all of whom are police, officers, bailiffs, or soldiers. All they have to establish is that some of the prisoners took an active part in the forbidden assemblies of the previous three days, especially the "emotions" on the Place des Terreaux. Once they have been officially identified as having committed this act of disobedience, they can be executed. If the judges had felt like it, they could have hanged 3,000 men. But three or four will be enough to set an example; and in fact we're going to let them off easy, we aren't even going to kill all the ones we've caught, we'll just choose the most obvious. If we hadn't spent so much time eliminating the others, we could have been finished even sooner.

Bel and Dapiano will have to go; they're the only two weavers in the gang, but they're Piedmontese, we can use them to intimidate their fellow countrymen. Bel puts up a good defense, proving that he went to the demonstration under duress and that his master had hidden him when it started. All right, with him we can be magnanimous. But there are too many witnesses against Dapiano, too many people heard him crying murder for anybody to pay attention to his feeble denials. Besides, he admits he was at the Brotteaux on Tuesday, Wednesday, and Thursday. So much for him.

The hatters and dyers make a better showing, and circumstances favor them. They shrewdly point to all the differences between themselves and the weavers, whose agitation struck at the very foundations of the Lyonnese economy and was therefore much more alarming to the bourgeois. They argue that the two groups almost always met separately, that their demands were not the same: "We had nothing to do with the silk workers' revolt. . . . All we wanted was a higher price for our work."

Oh, all right, the chief magistrate decides to charge the whole bunch "officially," but suspends proceedings against Antoine Bel and five others; we'll just keep them in jail indefinitely, as a reminder to their friends. But Nerin will pay for the French, and Dapiano for the Piedmontese. Against these two, at one in the afternoon, "whereas this is a case of sedition and popular emotion," the presidial court declares itself qualified to hear the case without further ado, and does so at once in a room in the prison.

No ceremony, wigs, costumes, or stage sets: just a few black coats seated around a table in front of which the accused are made to stand during a parade of witnesses who re-identify them. Nothing more is asked of them; and of course, there is no counsel present.* Accused and witnesses are simply stood face to face; Dapiano is recognized by four of them, Nerin by four others. They continue to plead not guilty. In his summing-up, the King's prosecutor asks that both be "declared guilty and convicted of being among the principal authors of the sedition and revolt of the journeymen workers . . . of being present at the illicit gatherings and assemblies taking place at the Charpennes and the Perrache works . . . of committing acts of extreme provocation, threats, and violence against the municipal forces of order . . . that, in reparation for the above, the said J.-J. Nerin and J.-A. Dapiano be sentenced to be hanged by the neck and strangled until dead."[1]

The moment he finishes speaking, the prosecutor sends Fillon, the jail-keeper, to the military commander with a letter asking him to make sure that the sentence—which has not yet been passed, and which, he writes, "is made imperative by the need to set an example"—be carried out at once. Nerin and

---

*Give or take a detail, this will be the procedure adopted by the revolutionary tribunal in dealing with "suspects" during the last three months of the Terror, after the law of Prairial An II.

Dapiano, seated, or rather perched, "in the posture of humility" upon the stool of repentance, are questioned one last time. Nerin admits to his actions at the town hall but insists upon his "good intentions" to the end.

They are condemned to death at half-past four.

But they won't be hanged tonight. For reasons of prudence, and not because there was any hope of a change of heart, the leaders of the merchants and marshalcy ask for time. Tomorrow "we shall have the support of an additional battalion, some of the officers of which have just arrived and announced that it will reach Lyons by ten in the morning. . . . The marshalcy and Gévaudan dragoons, moreover, are much fatigued and have no cartridges, which we are taking steps to provide." Meaning: how are the people going to react to the execution? So the condemned men get one last night. Not enough, of course, for the plea for pardon which the comtes de Lyons, firmly barred from the proceedings by the consulate, immediately dispatch to Vergennes. It would take ten days and nights of hard riding to get there and back, even supposing that Louis XVI . . .*

The delay gives the consuls something even better than security: Sauvage is brought in at dawn. Three birds with one stone! He is hustled before the magistrates, who have been unceremoniously tumbled out of their beds, and tried by the same procedure, but even more summarily, in order that the executions can all take place at once. Against him there are plenty of witnesses. He confronts them with the dignity of despair: "Although I led the march, it was not I who called the assembly together. . . . My plan was not to coerce the consulate into raising the price of our workday, but to ask the gentlemen to consider our case. . . . If the hatters had not been granted their request they would have stopped work in their shops, but rather than committing any acts of extremity, their intention was to employ themselves carrying earth for fill at the Perrache works." Sure, sure . . . He is sentenced at three.

At five o'clock on August 12 his body swings between those of Nerin and Dapiano from the gibbets put up on the Place des Terreaux outside the town hall where they waged their only fight, and even that was too much. Three gibbets for two sous. A placard was placed "both in front and in back of the body of Pierre Sauvage, bearing the words: 'Leader of the seditious hatter-dressers.'" The Archbishop of Lyons grants an annual pension of 200 livres to his widow and children. The canons' chapter awards 6 livres a month for life to Nerin's mother, also widowed, "to relieve her in the state of distress

---

*Vergennes replies in a letter dated August 19, congratulating the canons "for their zeal and for the important services rendered by them to the city of Lyons" and informing them that "the intention of the King was that there was to be no more capital punishment."[2]

in which she finds herself through the death of her son." Dapiano is a foreigner; his family get nothing.

The 2 sous a job for the silk workers and the 40 sous a day for the hatters are promptly rescinded. A consulate ordinance issued at the beginning of September stipulates officially that the workers' wages will either remain at or be restored to their figures "prior to the emotion." That same month "le Sieur Denis Monnet"* is arrested, together with a hatter named Philippe, "for the manufacture and distribution of writings, the object of which is to raise the price for the making up of cloth."[3]

In the end, the "additional battalion" they were waiting for doesn't turn up until the morning of August 15, by which time there's nothing for it to do but parade around. It has been detached from Valence by the La Fère artillery regiment, to which, upon his graduation from the military academy, the teen-aged Lieutenant Buonaparte has just been assigned. This short march up to Lyons is his first active duty.

DOCTOR ZIMMERMANN

# 47

## AUGUST 1786

## *Dullness Everywhere, But No Grief*

Old Fritz crosses the bar at three o'clock in the morning of August 17, 1786, "in the seventy-fifth year of his age and the forty-seventh of his reign," but the Prussians do not run howling into the streets, nor does the earth stand still. Some great men's swan songs go on too long. Mirabeau has had six months in which to reserve his front-row seat and "snatch Caesar's portrait from a dauber's hands,"[1] but it looks as though the play is going to be a flop, and the letter he writes Talleyrand that same day is all disgruntlement:

"The event is consummated. Frederick William [the nephew and new king] reigns, and one of the greatest figures ever to sit upon a throne is broken, together with one of the finest molds nature ever framed. . . . There is dullness

---

*In reality, he played a more important part than Sauvage; but having had some previous acquaintance with persecution, he keeps himself better hidden while the heat is on and escapes the death penalty.

everywhere, but no grief; everyone is preoccupied, no one stricken. There is not one face that does not show relief and hope; there is not one regret, not one sigh, not one elegy. And so this is the upshot of so many battles won, so much glory, a half-century's reign filled with so many mighty deeds! Everyone desired it to end, everyone is glad that it has. . . ."[2]

Not glad because they couldn't wait, but because they had grown bored waiting. This is not the spontaneous *oof!* of the libertines at the death of Louis XIV, a prelude to the emancipating effervescence of the Regency: Frederick II had gotten along just fine without a Maintenon and he never played the heavy puritan. Nor is it the backlash of popular virtue offended by the last years of Louis XV, the deathbed merrymaking on the lawns at Versailles. It is the confirmation of a fact, namely, that Frederick has been dead a long time already, and the only people unaware of the fact were Mirabeau and a few Frenchmen in the same circle, the ones who are still talking about "Frederick the Great" far more than his subjects do. The military underpinnings of the Prussian monarchy are so solid that not one boot will stumble nor one salute waver because the crown shifts from a poor old bag of bones to an enigmatic colossus. On the balconies of Europe, though, the spectators incline their heads toward Prussia: two hundred thousand of the world's finest soldiers maintained on a war footing for no apparent reason are now at the orders of the colossus. Holland is snarling and snapping, Austria and Turkey are stripping for a fight. Prussia controls a very large chunk of the chessboard. Is Europe about to destabilize itself?

Naturally, Mirabeau has flapped his wings off over this death. At last, here was something that was worth pretending to be important about. Shortly after his visit to Potsdam he made a lightning trip to Paris to get himself more firmly instated in his post as unofficial informer; at the beginning of the year, he had been feeling decidedly up in the air. He tackled Calonne with his habitual mixture of cajolery and threats, the latter backed up by an explosive hundred-page missive. The two of them are so busy trying to prove that each is cleverer than the other that they sometimes forget they're supposed to be playing on the same team.

But for Calonne, in his big-league match, overtime has run out and it's sudden death: decisive action by him is needed now, to save the country from bankruptcy. He doesn't know where he's going but he's certainly on his way, an Assembly of Notables, the Estates-General, who knows what? He'll need everybody he can get his hands on. He's had two years in which to size Mirabeau up, and he knows that he can count on him exactly as long as he can keep his purse filled; but the public's response to what the crazy devil writes is a sure indication that you'd better have him on your side. Since the trial in Aix, but even more since *Les Doutes sur la liberté de l'Escaut, De la Caisse d'Escompte* (1785) ["On the Discount Bank"], and two broadsheets (also written in 1785) in which he fenced a few rounds with Beaumarchais over the financing of the Chaillot firepump by the Paris water board—a vast swamp of financial literature in which his pen shook out a few bolts of lightning over acres of mud—in other words, during those same two years, Mirabeau has been becoming "a power in the corridors of power." He is read. He is consulted. He is contested. He is feared. He exists.

It would have been so easy to ditch him in Berlin, whither Calonne let him depart in January, under orders yet not under orders . . . But a Mirabeau grudge can cost you plenty. Which brings us back to the explosive missive I mentioned before, a manuscript entitled "Lettre à M. de Calonne"[3] which he dashed off in reply to a reply to his own attacks on a Spanish bank belonging to a gentleman named Cabarrus.* One or two people have been saying that Cabarrus and Calonne are thick as thieves, speculating together for a fall; and if the public hears it from Mirabeau, the comptroller of finance will find himself in very hot water at the worst possible moment. A touch of blackmail will serve him right. Mirabeau sends the draft of his libel to Talleyrand and Lauzun. Half-alarmed and half-amused, his friends transmit the gist of it to the minister, who consents to pay Mirabeau to keep his mouth shut. Tell him to come back to Paris, I'll buy his muck from him, with an endorsement from Vergennes of his status in Berlin, thereby making it official, up to a point.†

At last Mirabeau is becoming a diplomat, albeit a fake one. Ever since he got out of Vincennes he's been snatching at everything that came his way, piecing together a golden cloak out of rags. In a letter to his father he boasts of this blackmail, bitterly negotiated between four knaves, as though it were some high and noble exploit:

> An account, highly injurious to me, is issued by the Banque Saint-Charles. Calonne knows I shall reply, shall publish my reply, and shall strike the speculators and their chief to the ground; he finds it safer to employ me. Frederick II was dying. A few of my letters to friends seemed to imply that I had a pretty clear view of the country. Our diplomacy was dormant. By his own account, and that of my friends who put the wind up him, Calonne gets M. de Vergennes to assign me to a secret mission, at the expense of the Department of Finance. I am called to Paris. I am asked for my preliminary impressions of Prussia, and I deliver myself

---

*Francisco de Cabarrus, born in Bayonne in 1752, is one of the rising moneymen whose center of operations in Spain has overflowed into a good part of France. His Banque Saint-Charles is heavily involved in the secret transactions of the Revolution, and in those of the Empire that succeeds it, and he eventually becomes Spanish minister of finance, first under the Bourbons and then under Joseph Bonaparte. His daughter Theresa is the famous Mme Tallien.

†In so doing, Calonne pretty nearly admits to being implicated in the speculations of the Banque Saint-Charles. How far? No documentary evidence has been found.

of them as a free man, not a courtier. I return to Berlin, with no other ties upon my purse strings than counting from clerk to master.* When asked what payment I desired, I replied in these very words:

"I shall spend nothing save for you; thus you will repay whatever I shall spend. As for the future, since you are putting me in the path of events, it is up to me to conduct myself in such a way that you will not be tempted to remove me."[4]

Back in Berlin, Mirabeau has given them their money's worth, in information, gossip, advice, and prophesy, all the dirty linen of the Court of Prussia mixed with political overviews of Europe and the strategies of the powers, written in the form of a series of thumbnail sketches in letters addressed either to Calonne himself (seldom) or to Talleyrand (more often). He brews them according to a specifically eighteenth-century recipe that might be called "literary tittle-tattle"—the one and only genre for which Louis XVI, like his grandfather Louis XV before him, has any real taste. A few of his efforts, drafted very much with that audience in view, may actually have passed before the King's eyes, after being revised and corrected by Talleyrand and after scooting, like a weasel, from Calonne to Vergennes.† So now he's earning his stripes as a sort of pioneer columnist, on a level, or so he would like to believe, with Grimm. Luck and a sharp nose bring him his first front-page story. As he himself would be the first to tell you, the death of Frederick, recounted by Gabriel-Honoré de Mirabeau, will make history.

Mirabeau to "Abbé de Périgord," on July 12:

"The King is exceedingly ill, that is beyond question; but he is not actually dying and Zimmermann, a famous Hanoverian physician who has been sent for, has declared that if he would spare himself a little he might live yet a while; but he is incorrigible in his intemperance. Even so, the dropsy is said to be most certain."[5]

Of what is Frederick II actually dying? The unspeakable fish and game stews, apparently seasoned with gunpowder, which he stows away by the bucket whenever the fancy takes him, could annihilate his own pet grenadiers, but it would seem that his system was proof against even them. What he mostly complains of is chronic shortness of breath, and it is for that that he summons Zimmermann, the physician of lost causes, in a matter-of-fact letter written on June 6:

---

*That is, on an expense account. No salary, but reimbursement of all outlay.

†Mirabeau later says that Louis XVI read them all. This is far from certain; neither the King nor any of the other addressees confirm it, but he himself sincerely believed he was read by the supreme authority, and Louis XVI would probably not have refused an opportunity to gain information so effortlessly. What *is* certain, on the other hand, is that after 1789 he pays very close attention to any Mirabeau memoranda submitted to him.

Dear Doctor Zimmermann,

For the past eight months I have been suffering from severe asthma. The doctors in this country give me all manner of drugs, but instead of bringing any relief they only make matters worse. The fame of your skill having spread throughout the north of Europe, I should be very obliged if you would take a little turn in this country for a fortnight, so that I might consult you on the state of my health and its circumstances.[6]

Johann Georg Zimmermann is fifty-eight, Swiss by origin (he was born in Bern and practiced there for a few years), German by adoption, when he worked in the English Court of Hanover, and ultimately a British subject attached to the Duke of York; his has been the career Marat once longed for, that of the great cosmopolitan healer. He is a perceptive man and a good observer, he does what he can for the dying king, and he issues a forthright report on the case:*

"After considering that the greatest men, those seated upon thrones and all others so placed as to fix the public eye, have, like the rest of us mere mortals, moments of moodiness and melancholy which they express in a similar manner, I thought it behove me not to conceal the fact that Frederick the Great, the most towering figure of the eighteenth century, said to me, on June 30, 1786, at three in the afternoon:

" 'I'm nothing but an old carcass, fit to be thrown out on the road.' "

That was toward the end of Frederick II's last battle, which he won against his doctor and lost to death. With his habitual blend of courtesy and boorishness, the patient devoted all his energies to finding reasons why he should go on stuffing himself suicidally to the end. The doctor recommended various empirical remedies—chiefly dandelions, the plant that "grows in every field in the springtime and was known to the Greeks and Romans"; its "juice, reduced to the consistency of honey," was vomited up by Frederick with a certain grim satisfaction, just to prove to Zimmermann that all doctors are jackasses. Patiently, humbly, the physician tried to make him stick to a diet, but at every call he was informed that his patient had just partaken, say, of "a clear soup made of the essences of the hottest and strongest ingredients, reinforced by a heaping spoonful of nutmeg and ginger," or "a generous serving of boiled meat à la russe, that is, cooked with half a jug of eau-de-vie," or a polenta of his own invention, "composed of Turkish wheat flour† and Parmesan cheese, to which garlic juice is added before frying the whole in butter until a crust the thickness of a finger forms upon it; and over this is poured a bouillon of the hottest spices." And Zimmermann's forces were further assaulted, dispersed, and routed by "eel pasties so hot that they looked as though they had been cooked in hell," "macaroni" pâtés, "platefuls of

*Published in 1788.
†Corn or maize, that is.

sweets called sour-cream meringues," and such mounds of fresh herrings that you'd have thought they had swum up to the royal tables in shoals.

"Your Majesty's only real enemies are your cooks!"

The reply, which might have come from a four-year-old:

"No one knows how to train a cook like your ministers in Hanover. My own best man comes from that school."

What is he supposed to say to that? On July 10 Johann Georg capitulated, and turned back toward England with tears in his eyes and his fists full of écus.

" 'Farewell, my dear, good Zimmermann; don't forget the old man you saw here. . . .' "

"I was quite beside myself, I thought I must choke. I made a deep bow and left the king's apartments, more moved than I have ever been before or ever shall be again in my life."

Even now, the dear wheezing old ogre's mighty charm does not desert him: irresistible to the last. He is dying of uninterrupted indigestion complicated by catarrh and veering toward dropsy, or in other words of a generalized infection of his entire system, macerated in polluted liquid. " 'Then let all go! I do not fear death, but only pain. Farewell, doctor!' "

"The look he gave me was appalling," Zimmermann adds. "In the great hollows of his cheeks, and in his lips, ordinarily so fine and pleasant, I saw the mark of the blackest and deepest sorrow."

FREDERICK II OF PRUSSIA

# 48

## AUGUST 1786

## *I Have Crossed the Mountain*

From Mirabeau to "Abbé de Périgord" on July 14: "Zimmermann could make no headway against the polenta and eel pasties;* the swelling is everywhere, and it is edematous."

July 21: "The dropsy has reached the stomach, even the chest. The king has known this since Thursday. Some say he took the news with great equanimity; another version has it that he swore and abused the physician for

---

*This shows that Mirabeau was close to the source; he presumably bribed a footman at Potsdam. Zimmermann does not publish the king's diet until two years later, so this is not plagiarized.

being too truthful; he might drag on a while if he would be careful, even, Doctor Baylies says, a year or more, but I doubt he will ever give up the eel pasties."

July 27: "The fine weather is prolonging the king's life, but he is in a bad way. On Wednesday he had himself taken outdoors for a few moments in a cart, but was most uncomfortable and suffered intensely during and after. On Thursday he felt it still more keenly, and was no better yesterday. I continue to think the end will come by September."

July 31: "The king is perceptibly worse; he has had a fever these past two days; that can kill him, or prolong his life. Nature has always done so much for this extraordinary man that it would take only an explosion of hemorrhoids to restore him to life.* His muscular strength is great."

August 8: "The king is extraordinarily low; some people give him only a few hours to live, but this is probably exaggeration. On the 4th, erysipelas set in, with blisters on the leg; that portends an opening, and soon, gangrene; there is now suffocation and a foul stench, and the slightest fever must end the drama. It is affirmed, further, that there is such a fever."

August 12: "The king is very much better; the evacuation afforded by the opening of the legs has reduced the swelling and given relief, but there is weakness and excessive appetite, highly dangerous. Once more, it will not be long."

August 15: "Through the natural evacuation of water through the legs, reckoned at a pint a day at least, the swelling of the scrotum has been quite reduced; the patient even believes that there is less swelling everywhere. It is probable that there is a fever every evening, but efforts are made to keep this hidden. The appetite is so great that most of the time ten to twelve dishes, all the most delicate, are eaten. For lunch and supper there are slices of buttered bread covered with smoked tongue and a liberal pinch of pepper; if there is a feeling of stuffiness from too much food, and this is usually the case, recourse is had to a dose of *anima rhei*† an hour or two after the meal. There is a desire to be purged six or seven times in every twenty-four hours, apart from the regular enemas. You may trust absolutely in every word of this, and the very sure and certain result is that we are in the last scene and it is almost played out."

On Wednesday, August 16, Mirabeau receives a series of intimate reports, beginning at eight in the morning, that leave no further doubt. The curtain

---

*The usual vicious circle of infection in heavy overeaters: the blood is too thick and causes hemorrhoids, whence constipation, risk of occlusion, generalized infection, and fever. By relieving the constipation, the "explosion of hemorrhoids" eased the entire system.

†One of the household purgatives which he took in such variety and so often that they had more than a little to do with the dilapidation of his system.

is coming down. On the previous day the patient's secretaries took up their posts at five in the morning but were not admitted until noon, the king having spent the intervening hours gulping down pints of coffee and milk, followed by "a second breakfast consisting of crabs in a hot sauce." His mind was visibly not on his work, his face was flushed, his tongue thick; but his final dispatches were "clearly reasoned to the end. The excessive uncleanliness of his room and his person, owing to the damp rags he keeps on and never changes, appears to have given rise to a fever of a putrid sort." On Wednesday morning, "a lethargical somnolence" is reported; "there is every sign of dropsical apoplexy and dissolution of the brain."

Honoré calls for his horse. He can't sit still. His is the frenzy of the secret agent (or special envoy, a later age will say) who knows he is at the very nerve center of the event and longs to clutch it in his hand for one moment, so he can be the person to give it to the waiting world. He owes it to Talleyrand first, who might be able to make a nice haul for them all if he knew of Frederick's death before the ministers, before even the King . . . A little trading in certificates, the value of which was dependent upon the old king's caution, and which are likely to plummet if his successor confirms his alleged intention of flattening Holland. The Mirabeau-Talleyrand gang could cut a swathe through the ranks clear to the King's notice: we're quicker off the mark than Vergennes and his doddering civil servants, all hail undercover diplomacy! Gabriel-Honoré quivers like a hound stalking History. Ears and nose atwitch, he prowls back and forth through the big city, so flat that it looks less like a city than a military parade ground for Prussian soldiers, a geometrical design stretching to the horizon. In fact, Berlin is five towns in one—Kölln-zur-Spree, Dorotheenstadt, Neustadt, and Friedrichstadt, each formed of separate smaller towns, are just as substantial as the Berlin that has imposed its name upon them. "The houses are as tall* as in the imperial towns, but the streets are not so wide as in Neustadt or Friedrichstadt, where the houses, on the other hand, are lower and more uniform in style; for even the most modest, often inhabited by very poor people, have a neat and comely air. Vast empty squares may be seen in many places: a few are used for drill and parades, others for nothing at all. Elsewhere there are fields, gardens, boulevards, all within the town walls."[1]

It is this juxtaposition of stones and grass and the odor of leaves that makes the charm of Berlin, a city in a field. Every time the two Fredericks, the "Sergeant King" and the one now dying, snapped their fingers, houses sprang up like thistles in black, stark, rectangular Brandenburg—whence the clean look of this capital, the youngest of Europe (built almost entirely in this

---

*According to Ulrich Bräker, the "Swiss Rousseau," who is here describing in wide-eyed wonderment "the greatest city that I have seen in the world."

century), "in which there are only about six thousand houses, whereas Paris
has nearly thirty thousand.* Within the limits of the town itself are several
gardens and plowed fields. A number of squares as yet barren of buildings
make a singular contrast with the splendor of the edifices elsewhere."[2]

Is it because each town-within-the-town has its own customs and municipal authorities, its own special atmosphere? Whatever the reason, the houses
in Berlin, unlike so many other things in Prussia, do not all stand in straight
lines, even though they were all built at almost the same time. "It cannot be
taxed with that tedious uniformity of edifices that makes towns built on a
regular pattern so unattractive," in the words of a traveler who has no love
for St. Petersburg or Versailles. And the citizens are the same. There's no way
of guessing who lives where. Luther's Reformation, with its affectation of
equality, has left its mark here.

> You are amazed, if you scrutinize closely one of these houses, built in the Ionic
> order with stucco decoration and a stately façade befitting the residence of a
> tax-farmer general or a duke at the very least; you are amazed, I say, to see a
> ground-floor window flung suddenly open and a cobbler busily hang out a pair
> of boots to dry; and before you have time to recover from your stupefaction, a
> window on the floor above opens to show a scourer with a pair of freshly laun-
> dered breeches; the next moment a tailor hangs a suit from an upper window, or
> some old woman empties a plate of potato peelings on your head. You walk on
> a few steps and arrive in front of a Corinthian palace which you take to be at least
> the home of a king's mistress, or the palace of some prince of the blood. Almost
> before you have paused to consider it a Jew bows to you from the top of the
> majestic attic and offers you his wares; you glance lower, and see a shirt hung out
> to dry, belonging to an officer who shaves himself and looks as though he does
> not own another one. You visit two or three more streets, and everywhere you
> find the same sort of inhabitants. At the end you reach a house that actually is
> occupied by a general, as you can easily see by the sentinel posted before his door.
> But do not expect to find here, as you would in Vienna, a Swiss, or all the other
> servants that mark the luxury and opulence of nobility.

This is the Berlin through which Mirabeau rides on the morning of
August 16—four and one-half miles long and three miles wide inside its walls,
their sixteen gates linked together by almost three hundred "passably paved"
streets, many with sidewalks. Back and forth he goes, from the Mills Gate to
Oranienburg, the Bernau Gate to the Potsdam Gate. One hundred and fifty
thousand souls live here,[3] not counting the 26,000 soldiers in the world's
biggest barracks. Their master is dying, their master is dead, and is nothing
changed? The cobbler dries his boots, the cleaner scours his hides, the tailor
stitches, the old woman peels the potatoes that have long since become a staple

*According to the Baron von Risbeck, a painstaking observer, who publishes his *Travels in
Germany* in 1788.

in the diet of this country's poor . . . Mirabeau paces on, back and forth across the big toll-free bridge "in the midst of which rises the life-size equestrian statue in bronze of the old Margrave of Brandenburg; at his feet, some sons of Enoch* with frizzled hair, clinging together in chains."[4]

At one in the afternoon he heads toward Potsdam, going as far as the park promenade on the banks of the Spree:

> The beauty of the woods, paths, and groves is beyond anything that can be imagined. On Sundays, Berlin may be seen there in all her glory. For the people of this town, the park is what the Tuileries are to Paris, except that the mixture of people is more striking here, for the reason that the common people and society are both present together, one can go either on foot or on horseback without the slightest danger. In one or two places in the park, one can see rows of magnificently dressed ladies grouped as in the Tuileries; also as in Paris, one may look them boldly in the face and compare them with one another. At special times, one may meet a great many men of letters, too.[5]

Not today; this is a weekday and there was nothing special about yesterday, August 15, which is the Feast of the Assumption but only in Roman Catholic countries. The little bustle of "populace" is present, however, under the trees, their leaves already starting to turn: wetnurses with babies at the breast, girls glancing sidewise at soldiers. Frederick II is dying a long way from all this, on Sirius.

"Impelled by some strange presentiment, and wishing also to explore the bends in the stream on the right," he presses on, spies a Potsdam groom riding past at full gallop, and intercepts him long enough to learn that he has been sent to fetch one of the physicians the king had been refusing to see, Doctor Zelle, "who was ordered to make haste and set out within the minute. I soon learned that the groom had already ridden one horse to death."

Mirabeau is frantic. Should he send a messenger to Paris to announce the death before it happens? It's a big risk; but he is almost positive that once it does happen the government will shut the gates and prevent everyone from leaving until a public announcement has been made and official messengers dispatched. And yet a shred of caution holds him back: if that old devil turns the tables on him by reviving again, Gabriel-Honoré's great new career will be over before it starts. He has a contingency plan, however, and now orders it to stand by for action: a system of carrier pigeons, recently devised as a means of crossing closed frontiers. Then he "has himself dressed" and goes to the royal palace—a desert inhabited by the queen who has been forgotten by almost everybody, including the dying man, to such an extent that she "had no idea the king was so ill; all she spoke of was my clothes. . . ." Which means, we may note in passing, that he now has regular access to one of the principal

---

*Presumably in the figurative sense of "old male prisoners."

courts of Europe, never mind the fact that it's the court of a comatose princess. D'Esterno, the official French ambassador and fop, and Milord Dalrymple, his English counterpart, have also come round snooping for news. As usual, Mirabeau gets in a dig at the former. "I whispered into our minister's ear that my news came straight from the bedside. . . ."

A short, sleepless night. Dawn (August 17) finds him back on the Potsdam road, just as General Goertz, the aide-de-camp of the king—the late king— whirls into town at half-past six, shouting to the guards at the gates:
"By order of the king, lower the portcullis!"
The last but one of the century's giants is gone. Of that caliber, only Catherine is left, out there in her great Russian North. How could anybody think of calling Prussia's new king "the Great"? No more than they could Joseph of Austria, Louis of France, George of England, Gustavus of Sweden, Carlos of Spain, Maria of Portugal, Victor-Amadeus of Sardinia, Ferdinand of Naples, Pius of Rome, or that hive of Germanic or Italianate princes swarming through their stag hunts and balls. The era of the flat crowns has begun.

Frederick chose to die discreetly. That night there were no guards at the doors of Sans-Souci and there was no civilian or religious regalia around him, just four men: his two favorite hussar-lackeys; Doctor Zelle, pop-eyed and groggy; and Count von Hertzberg, the prime minister.

> Several times he lost both speech and consciousness* and, upon regaining them, asked for no one, summoned no one. At midnight he sank into a painful anguish, cushions were placed beneath his head to elevate it. "All is well," said Frederick, "I have crossed the mountain." What must be terrible in death, that final struggle between life and the disease that was about to annihilate him, was no doubt over; the effusion was ending, he relapsed into a half-sleep; at last, at three in the morning of August 17, 1786, in the words of the physician attending him, the wellsprings animating this extraordinary genius suddenly ceased; Frederick stopped living, and, for his name, eternity began.[6]

He had asked that his dogs be killed and buried with him. "A final proof of his contempt for men," observes Mirabeau.

---

*According to Guibert, the military tactician, who publishes an *Eloge du Roi de Prusse* in 1787, giving details of the death of his most revered master which he gleaned on the spot.

# 49

AUGUST 1786

## *The Naked Truth*

"Sire, you are a king!"

Long before Frederick II is cold in his grave, Mirabeau has tackled his successor with his own unique blend of impetuousness, prolixity, and incongruity. On that very day, August 17, 1786, he sends Frederick William II a letter laboriously recopied in his own hand from a draft written weeks in advance, and he publishes a printed version of its eighty-four pages before the year is out.* At first the event leaves hardly a ripple, but its significance becomes clear a few years later. In it, for the first time in history, a king is given a lecture by a person of no consequence—and what a lecture! His exhortations are a sort of "open letter" to every king in enlightened Europe. Mirabeau's voice is so fierce, so peremptory, and he covers so many subjects, that the disparity between the scope and level of his discourse and the person to whom it is ostensibly addressed—the German colossus over whose shoulder Mirabeau is haranguing and prophesying to all the powers on earth—leaps to the eye. His letter is like the preamble to an Estates-General of the world.

The moving force behind this appeal is the optimism of Enlightenment: "You have come to the throne at a felicitous moment: the century grows more luminous with every passing day, it has labored and is laboring for you, amassing sound and sane ideas for you."[1] Then comes the traditional dash of perfume, its fumes curling up from a rather crass stick of incense and contrasting sharply with the hasty entombment of a Frederick of suddenly diminished Greatness: "Enlightened benevolence has yet to mount the throne pure and unmixed. It is for you to place it there. Your predecessor undeniably won many battles, perhaps too many. For several reigns, for centuries to come, he has dried up the wellsprings of military glory. . . . Frederick conquered men's admiration; never did Frederick win their love. That can be yours undivided." If, that is, you earn it by your actions, because the time for words is over. And

*Its full title being *Lettre remise à Frédéric-Guillaume II, roi régnant de Prusse, le jour même de son avènement au trône, par le comte de Mirabeau.*

for Mirabeau, son of the great Physiocrat, friend of Panchaud and Talleyrand, the way to a man's heart is through "oeconomism." "It is a most remarkable thing that a man such as your predecessor should have embraced a system of political economy so profoundly vicious. . . . Indirect taxation, extravagant prohibitions, regulations everywhere, exclusive privileges, innumerable monopolies—such has been the spirit of his domestic government, to a degree that would appear laughable were it not odious."

Down with Frederick the Dirigiste, long live Frederick William the Liberal. He finishes off the former in passing, not without subtlety.

> Frederick II was an almost unique example of the development of a great personality in its allotted place, far more than a genius whom nature herself has raised to great heights above other men. It is easy to see that, having bent all the force of his talent to the formation of one great military power out of a group of states that were previously disunited, fragmented, and for the most part unproductive, and having determined, to that end, to accelerate the slow pace of nature, he thought principally of money because money was the only means of gaining time. This was the source of his worship of money, his desire to amass, realize, compile. . . . All the tricks and fiscal extortions born in other kingdoms . . . became naturalized, each in its turn, within his frontiers.

Therefore, Sire, the gist of the lesson is: don't be like Frederick II. As regards war, for instance: don't wage it. As regards peace: govern differently. And the panacea, the way to do it, is to give free rein to the money manipulators—the first commandment of their liberal catechism. Take your gold out of its Bastille. Open wide capital's cage. Free men will arrive in the wake of free banking. So goes the gospel that Mirabeau, taking aim at Louis XVI past the ear of his rotund Prussian intermediary, means to preach—not without perceptible nostalgia for the opportunities wasted in Turgot's time, back when the King of France was a lad of twenty. "Sire, the first occurrence shapes the habit. That is why a reign's first moments are so precious. . . . And the first occurrence, Sire, depends absolutely upon you. Acquire none but good habits. Let no frivolous ones gather about Your Majesty." Until something better comes along, he wouldn't mind playing Turgot himself in a "first occurrence" of this kind, and he spends days straining his ears for a reply from the messenger of destiny . . . "Mirabeau, the man who became the Prussian Mazarin." Meanwhile, the candidate for power crams for his exam:

"There are some things which you can carry out at once, and which, by giving the highest opinion of yourself, will enable you to reap the fruits of confidence and facilitate the great reforms in which your reign must abound." He proceeds to enumerate the said "things" with the serenity of the prophet pointing out sycamine trees to be plucked up by the root and planted in the sea. If ye had faith as a grain of mustard seed . . . Mirabeau must certainly have it, anyway, because nothing stops him. That is his nature; that is the quality of the men who change men.

Ready, everybody? The first "thing" is to abandon the militarism of embarracked Prussia. "At the head, I count the abolition of military slavery, that is, the obligation imposed upon every man in your states to serve between the ages of eighteen and sixty or more, that hideous law born to meet the needs of a century of iron and a half-barbarian country; a law that depopulates and desiccates your kingdom, that dishonors the most numerous and useful portion of a nation, the portion without which you and your ancestors would have been no better than painted slaves," the law this, the law that, etc. When he finally stops for breath, it is only in order to create a hyperdemocratic national army to replace the one he's just done away with. "Let the national companies name their grenadiers among themselves, and let the recruits for your regiments be chosen from their ranks. Do not have them selected by your officers, or by the magistrate, but by the plurality of their comrades' votes."

And if there are any old fogeys who can't get used to the new order, why, let them go, and welcome. A country must not be shut in upon itself.

> People must be happy in your states, Sire. To anyone who is not legally constrained by particular obligations, grant the freedom to expatriate himself; bequeath this liberty by a formal decree. . . . The only thing that the most tyrannical laws on emigration ever accomplished is to incite people to emigrate. . . . Man is not attached to the earth with roots; therefore, he does not belong to the soil. A man is not a field, a meadow, a head of livestock; he cannot be property. Hence, he cannot be made to believe that his superiors have the right to chain him to the soil. All the powers on earth might combine their strength in vain, seeking to inculcate in him so infamous a doctrine. Gone are the days, if ever they existed, when those who were masters on earth could speak in the name of God.

Besides, who will want to emigrate, if you follow my advice? The middle classes? By no means. "One of the most pressing operations claiming your attention, and one you can perform with a single word, is a law restoring to the bourgeois the freedom to acquire noble lands" that have been seized for debt but left fallow; in this country, any land ever marked by an aristocratic name is regarded as reserved for noble ownership forever.

And while we're on the subject of "that dreadful prejudice that mutilates the bourgeoisie and stupefies the nobility by making of its honorary rights the exclusive source of its consideration, dispensing it from acquiring any other," we may as well do away with all nobiliary privileges, the ones that stuff land, ranks, positions, functions, commercial rights, and budding industries into the same decadent hands.

> Abolish, Sire, these senseless prerogatives that fill great places with men who are mediocre, to call them no worse, and that sever from you the majority of your

subjects in a country in which they find nothing but fetters and humiliations. Beware, ah, beware this universal aristocracy, the plague of monarchies even more than republics, that oppresses the human race from one extremity of the globe to the other; the interest of the most absolute monarch is encompassed wholly within the maxims of the common people. It is not kings whom peoples fear and shun but their ministers, courtiers, nobles—in a word, the aristocracy. "If the King only knew," they say.

"War upon the nobility and peace to the King" is the battle cry of the Comte de Mirabeau who is himself the son of a marquis, and he has stuck to it since his tract against the Order of Cincinnatus, when he was imploring the Americans not to found a military aristocracy. It's an old French hankering, it goes back to Philip Augustus and Bouvines, the people against the barons. We could use it to

combat the prejudice that drives so great a wedge between military and civilian functions. . . . Sire, it is when facing the enemy that the officer and soldier must be proud; but they are no other than the brothers of the bourgeois, and although they may be defending brothers they are also paid ones. Let civilian officials have more consideration than they did under your predecessor. . . . Let them be better paid, and never forget, Sire, that giving low wages is a poor way to save.

From the middle classes, Mirabeau moves down to those who have nothing at all. "Be the first, Sire, to establish a justice that is truly free. Judges should be paid out of the public revenue, and not by presents from the litigants." The most elementary justice, however, is the right to employment: "Be also the first sovereign in whose states any man who wants to work finds work. Everything that breathes should be fed by its work." He's so sure of this that he makes the leap from unemployment to terrorism, founding the workers' right to insurrection in a single sentence: "any man who receives nothing but refusals for the offer of his work in return for his subsistence becomes the natural and legitimate enemy of other men; he has the right to wage a private war against society."

As he turns the pages his throat tightens, as though some bitter aftertaste were rising up from the cellars of Vincennes. "There are too many poor in your country, especially in Berlin, and these unfortunates are asking for care. In your capital, it cannot be said without sorrow, one inhabitant in ten lives on public charity and the number is rising every year." Following a process which is already that of a statesman, his mind advances quickly from condemnation of the evil to the search for a remedy; nor does he omit a passing thrust at urban overdevelopment: "It is necessary to restrict the growth of towns in which, because of an excess of population, an order develops that corrupts everything. . . . The city's poor are creatures who have lost all, morally as well as materially."

When he reaches the mid-point of his text, his words of advice start crowding each other, opening out like nests of tables, universal education as the panacea for poverty, freedom of the press as a boon to education. "Any obstacle to the progress of enlightenment is an evil. . . . Let everything move, circulate. Read, Sire, and let people read in your states. Would you cry out for the night? Oh no, your great soul will not desire it. You will read, Sire, you will commence a noble association with books. . . ." Culminating in the supreme philosophy that conditions all collective life: the canonization of St. Tolerance. "One great, prime, and sudden operation that I ask of Your Majesty is a prompt and formal declaration, clothed in the most imposing marks of sovereignty, to the effect that boundless tolerance will be forever accorded, in all your states, to all religions. You have a very natural and nonetheless precious opportunity to make such a declaration: consign it to the edict which will grant civil liberty to the Jews"—lengthily prepared under the old king, stuffed aside in some drawer like so many other reign's-end measures deferred to the Deluge, and now awaiting nothing but the new king's signature. "Sire, I implore it of you, take care you do not postpone the declaration of the most universal tolerance." The music swells.

Receding from the heights, he turns to the details of the kingdom's economy, before recapitulating the whole set of measures in numbered paragraphs, each driving home a nail placed earlier in the text. In his conclusion, he tries to explain away the unheard-of cheek of his deed.

> I dare hope that my forthrightness will not displease you. If you are touched by it, O Frederick, meditate upon these lines, free and sincere but respectful, and deign to say:
>
> "Here is what I will not be told, and perhaps the very opposite of what I shall hear every day. Even the bravest offer but veiled truths to kings; here I see the naked truth—Ah, it is more good to me than the venal incense that stifles my nostrils, emanating from the verse makers and academy panegyricists who fastened upon me in the cradle and will scarce quit me in my grave. I am a man, before I was king. Why should I take offense because someone has treated me as a man, because a stranger who wants nothing from me, who will soon leave my court never to see me again, speaks to me without disguise?"

We'll see what comes of it. Whatever comes, Mirabeau cannot, after this, be reduced to his former status—a dabchick paddling in polemics and business, a mercenary of the quill. His powerful torso is bursting the seams of his wornout rags. Asking nobody's permission, he has set himself up as mentor to kings. He has launched his manifesto.

# 50

## AUGUST–SEPTEMBER 1786

## *This Sublime Revolution*

This is all well and good, but the great Mirabeau who feels ready to preach to kings is still being shadowed by his doppelgänger, Mirabeau the Small. On August 15, 1786, the same man who is busily putting the finishing touches to his catechism for enlightened despots issues, in a carefully coded dispatch to Talleyrand, a curious request:

"Prince Henry, great men not being above small means, would like to be sent a blonde, on the plump side, with talents predominantly musical, who might pass as coming from Italy or some such place but not from France, who has had no scandalous intrigue, who would be inclined rather to grant favors than trumpet needs, etc., etc. Bear in mind, however, that the man is a miser."[1]

Which man? The prince himself, Frederick's Francophile brother, the one Mirabeau was hoping would turn into the Uncle Joe of Prussian politics? By no means: it's his nephew, the new king in person. It's for the penny-pincher with the big appetite that the uncle (but we have only Mirabeau's word for this) proposes to import an alluring secret agent and boudoir adornment from the Court of France. This letter must have brought a lot of joy to Louis XVI's private study. Reassuring . . . with Frederick II, the womanless king, diplomacy's special services were deprived of half their resources; now we can bring on the girls again, for Frederick William—about whom Mirabeau has few illusions, however much he treats him as a genius in his homily: "The [new] master: what is he, when all is said and done? One would be tempted to reply, Old King Cole. No wit, no strength, no consistency, no diligence, the tastes of Epicurus's pig, and heroes who are heroes of nothing but arrogance, unless they be rather those of narrow and bourgeois vanity."[2]

What they have to do, since the great Mirabeau can stoop to small means as unflinchingly as Prince Henry can, is speedily unhitch the king's wagon from the star rising over his bed—Julie von Voss, "a girl of twenty, well born, well connected, fair-skinned, fair-haired, with plenty of flesh but little face or mind."[3] She had enough mind to trust to the tried and true methods of women who want weddings, however, by making her Old King Cole sit up and beg for his sugarlump for two years. He, meanwhile, has been trying to get rid of his Pompadour, Mme von Rietz, his manservant's wife who became his official mistress after he had been widowed by his first wife and divorced, by mutual consent, from his second. Whatever happens, the reign of La Rietz is coming to an end. Now, Julie von Voss "feels that it is somehow ridiculous to be German, and corrects this misfortune by an affected Anglomania." In that respect, she might have fitted in with the great scheme of Mirabeau and Co. —the counterreversal of alliances between England, France, and Prussia, designed to abase Austria and "the Austrian woman." But so far, nothing has moved in the direction of a new European realignment and the number-one enemy of the French monarchy is still the United Kingdom, so the Anglomania of a potential favorite must not be allowed to harden into Anglophilia, with its concomitant Francophobia—which, according to Mirabeau, is what's happening to Julie von Voss. Thus, while laying the foundations for his possible accession to the office of mentor of Prussia, Mirabeau finds it expedient to play Nestor on all fronts at once and accordingly divides his attention between an appeal to universal conscience, in his *Lettre au roi-régnant,* and the warrior-king's repose, in the form of "a blonde, on the plump side."

The Mirabeau who was conspiring in Berlin was also a "married man." One gaze—that of Yet-Lie—is fixed permanently upon him and, with the pitiless lucidity of undeluded affection, seizes his every gyration.

> He was prodigiously busy in Berlin. It is inconceivable how much he managed to accomplish in one day; he often went to bed an hour after midnight and, at five in the morning, in midwinter, in so cold a climate and with no other clothing than a quilted dressing gown—no hose, no vest—he would be at work, not even wanting to arouse his servant to light a fire. In addition to his coded correspondence, which took up a great deal of his time, he was also working very hard at his book on the Prussian monarchy, which came out in 1788. On the evenings when he did not go out, he romped about like a child with Noldé* and his secretary, trying to see who could play the most tricks on whom. Mirabeau came off best, not because he was the master of the house but because, being the strongest, everyone feared his rages. He had a [new] valet named Boyer, a nice enough fellow although something of a ne'er-do-well, who had invented a kind of shadow theater and made up plays. The child and I did not always do them the honor of attending their performances, but when we did, I gave warning in the morning and the scenes, in German or French,† were arranged accordingly, deleting whatever was too free in them. Boyer did not like this at all, he com

---

*Baron von Noldé, a young nobleman from Courtland (Latvia), served as a lieutenant in the French Royal Swedish Regiment but occupied his leisure time "studying through travel" and acted as a sort of unpaid henchman to Mirabeau, who found him "honorable, intelligent, knowledgeable, fired with a great respect for the Rights of Man and a great hatred of the Russians."

†Mirabeau wanted the child (Nicolas-Lucas de Montigny), then aged four, to know both

plained that the *fion** of his play had been lost; but when Mirabeau said, "Look out for your ears, if Madame is not pleased," there was no choice but to obey.[4]

This is a rare period in his life, a sort of truce during which things go pretty much the way he wants them. Sambat, the secretary, also gets his share of praise. "Never have I seen more sober, quiet, hardworking, helpful young people" is Yet-Lie's opinion. They have nine servants in all, and a carriage, and fancy clothes for Honoré when he has to make an appearance. Calonne pays up without much haggling over the accounts, especially as Mirabeau roars like a prince whose subordinates are trying to pare down his civil list every time the clerical staff begin clucking in alarm at the hole in his pocket. "I shall spend nothing save for you; thus you will repay whatever I shall spend." Meaning, as he brags to his father, "42,000 livres in eight and one-half months,† including various secret expenses, the opulence of dress required in northern courts, and the horses of every description that are so essential in Berlin."[5] With Talleyrand he doesn't pussyfoot around, that's the charm of their "friendship": "Two hundred pistoles** a month, my beloved master, and a future, or my recall, that is my last word. I was not made to be bargained over. . . . In a word: by birth, I am worth more than most of the King's ministers, and as for ability, you may judge for yourself."

He doesn't spend much time playing house in the gilded cottage of which Sophie dreamed so ardently and which Yet-Lie, the woman who's riding pillion behind him until the next ditch and who asks for nothing more, has made so cosy for him. Berlin high society comes knocking at his door, and if it doesn't knock fast enough he goes out after it. That's what he's there for, after all, to catch every echo as it comes past, be it a whisper of high policy or a murmur of the new philosophies or the clatter of footmen's gossip. "He was such a master of the art of asking questions that it is difficult to give any idea of his ways to someone not familiar with his conversation,"[6] says (later) one member of that society, Christian-William von Dohm, a historian who is also a senior official in the Ministry of Foreign Affairs and his chief guide through the labyrinth of the Prussian elite.

Mirabeau's maieutics . . . He has now grasped the finest points of the art

---

languages: "I have a German maid for my child, who knows both languages equally well, an advantage I do not want him to lose."

  *"A popular word, of very particular meaning," according to the *Dictionnaire du bas langage* of Léopold Collin (Paris, 1808), "approximately equivalent to polish or finish, the final touches given to a piece of work. Ex.: It wants a bit more *fion.*"

  †About 350,000 modern francs [almost $90,000].

  **In France the word "pistole" meant, for accounting purposes, ten *tournois* livres, also called ten francs. What Mirabeau was saying, thus, was that with a monthly working capital of about 20,000 modern francs [$5,000] he could manage not to feel too pinched.

of getting people to talk, knowing how to listen, making them exude the very innermost sigh of their hearts and spearing anything useful in what they say with a ragpicker's pole—an essentially political art. This summer he gives Prussia the third degree. Not just Dohm; he also spends time with the publisher Nicolaï, a Berlinese Panckoucke who is bringing out an *Allgemeine Deutsche Bibliothek* in numerous installments, and most right-mindedly puts the man upon his guard against the first faint rumblings of the *Sturm und Drang,* even though Mirabeau hears in them an echo of his own fierce vitality; but the rationalist in him stiffens against them, perhaps because they are so close. He takes virtually no notice of Goethe, whom he might easily have gone to visit at Weimar and who, on August 30, 1786, packs his bags and takes a holiday from Germany, love, and adulation, seeking the impossible in a long prowl through Italy.* Nicolaï and Dohm, on the other hand, direct Mirabeau's attention to Kant and introduce him to the work of Lessing, the son of a Saxon pastor and the first German author to live by his pen, who died in 1781 at the age of fifty-two after a long struggle for an authentic German theater inspired by Greek tragedy and Shakespeare and absolutely opposed to French Classicism and shapeliness.

What strikes Mirabeau most about Lessing—to such a point that he tries to get his complete works published in France and always speaks of him thereafter as the greatest German author—is his moral and religious philosophy, uncluttered by any dogma including Luther's, and his lifelong quest for a *Christianity of Reason* that begins with his first work (1753), bearing that title, and ends with his last, *Ernst und Falk,* in 1780. The final book is a series of dialogues, drawing on Freemasonry, in which he "contemplates the march of humanity from revelation to revelation, starting at the polytheism of the earliest people. After the monotheism of Moses, the religion of Christ precipitated mankind into a second moral state; and tomorrow may bring the dawn of a third age, in which man, having become fully conscious of his powers, would do good for its own sake."†

If any religion can be palatable to Mirabeau, it is Lessing's.

He also strikes up an acquaintance—again partly for "professional" reasons—with the architect-writer Erman, who is working on the plans for a "city of savants" for the new king, a sort of colony of the Enlightened to be built in Brandenburg.[7] He is taken up by the Jewish elite of Berlin, who appreciate

---

*Goethe's flight, discovery of Italy, and first version of *Faust* will be covered in the next volume. We shall meet Kant when Kant meets the Revolution.

†From the excellent article on Lessing signed "P.G." in volume 9 of the *Encyclopédie universalis;* the author adds, "Lessing was too much of a rationalist to venture into prophesy, but his development of the philosophy of Enlightenment as it came to him from England and France looks forward to the great idealists of German Classicism."

his tolerance: Marcus Hertz the physicist and the endearing Rachel Levin, who becomes the "Lespinasse of Berlin." He hobnobs with the milords at the British embassy. He starts rehearsing for the part of Socrates in the mini-Athens of Prince Henry's château at Rhenburg . . . It's Mirabeau full speed ahead. He plunges in up to the neck but no higher, he keeps a cool head, he feels an ominous sagging underfoot—of the very possibly rotting board of Prince Henry, "a mixture of exaltation and braggadocio, presumptuousness and insecurity, a spate of words from which nothing positive emerges, and it is hard to make out whether he is deceiving himself or trying to deceive others, defending his self-conceit or gorging on illusions."[8]

Above all, he has his eye on the most famous German prince of all, after Frederick II: Charles William Ferdinand, Duke of Brunswick,* Prince-Elector of the Holy Roman Empire. He is independent but allied to Prussia in a relationship that is something like a protectorate.

"Yesterday [July 13, 1786] I dined and supped with the duke. Upon leaving table after dinner, he took me aside into a window seat and we talked there for about two hours, at first with considerable reserve on his part, then more frankly, and at the end with an evident desire to be thought sincere. . . . The duchess made a third." Mirabeau's "art" at work: at his first meeting with this Frenchman whom he's never laid eyes on before the duke opens his heart to him, asks how Vergennes is getting along, whether it's true that his declining health will soon force him to retire, but in that case heaven forbid that Breteuil should replace him as "principal minister," he being "at the head of the Austrian party and for years the obedient servant and ally of the Vienna cabinet. . . ."[9]

This goes on for four pages, in a letter to Talleyrand, which means that we should season his dish with a liberal pinch of salt because it was cooked to suit the palate of the said Vergennes, if not that of Louis XVI himself. It is a fact, however, that Mirabeau is a useful compass for the busy anthill of Versailles politics and finance, and he is pointing to the pole of the body Germanic, as he calls it, toward which many eyes are now beginning to turn.

In Brunswick, an old Hanseatic town fifty leagues west of Berlin, a dynasty of hardheaded princes, descended from the Guelphs who thumbed so many noses at popes, have been skillfully managing a scattered string of fertile fields and ore-rich mountains while they were gradually being encircled by Prussian possessions. All these estates have now taken the name of the town

*A few French monarchists (including Talleyrand) toy with the idea of making him King of France, in place of Louis XVI, after the arrest at Varennes; he commands the Prussian invasion, and, at the beginning of 1792, signs the "Brunswick Manifesto," in response to which Paris revolts and brings down the throne. He is defeated at Valmy and killed at Auerstadt.

ruled over by the elector, a man in his early fifties (the Duke of Brunswick was born in 1735), who became renowned for his bravery and military acumen twenty years ago during the Seven Years' War, in which he rendered loyal service to the King of Prussia, his suzerain in fact if not in name. Public opinion has made him a great general, but that is not what counts for him—Ferdinand of Brunswick wants to be the lord of Enlightenment. He has developed his manufactures and encouraged a new industry based on "a *verd,* discovered in his duchy in 1771, which is superior to *verdet* or *verd-de-gris* * in resistance and beauty; it is a most excellent paint for carriage wheels, iron staircases, and bars."[10] The duke is said to make some 200,000 people happy;† he says so too, and the people don't contradict him. In his capital "the dwellings, stores, and shops are most commodious and rents are low. Large numbers of merchants come from the various provinces of Germany, and even from Geneva, to attend the two great fairs of Candlemas and St. Lawrence and purchase the goods they desire or sell their own; the prince's court is always in town for the fairs; the nobility of the country and neighboring districts also come in then for payments: all these make for much animation. . . ."

A pretty, pleasing German landscape. Thanks to all this coming and going, and soon thanks to Mirabeau, Europe is about to make the acquaintance of this mildly world-weary sovereign who apparently looks like the Comte de Provence, with a majestic allure, large, pensive eyes, and paunchy cheeks. And indeed there is nothing of the field marshal about Brunswick; he is "polite unto affectation; he speaks with precision, even elegance, but it is clear that he is making an effort to do so, and he often cannot find the right word. He knows how to listen, and how to turn an answer into a question."[11]

What is more, the family of Brunswick-Lüneburg is a flourishing nursery for princesses, and even queens, by marriage; kings, too, and not just any old kings. In 1688 when the Stuarts were driven out, a Brunswick became King of England, with Hanover as his stepping-stone, and the two families have remained closely allied. The Duchess Augusta who makes the third during her husband's conversation with Mirabeau is the sister of George III, today's Britannic Majesty. Many currents, including that of the Protestant diaspora which has never forgiven the revocation of the Edict of Nantes, flow together in this family with the well-groomed image.

And

for many years the Duke of Brunswick, seeking to increase the population of his states, has granted great privileges to the French families that have settled in the

---

*Popular name of copper acetate.

†Thirty thousand of whom live in Brunswick itself. These details of the town and duchy are from Peuchet's *Dictionnaire de la géographie commerçante,* compiled between 1780 and 1800.

town of Brunswick, and to any that might wish to settle there, with complete liberty in matters temporal as well as spiritual. In 1750 the reigning duke, wishing even further to accommodate this French colony, authorized all French Protestants, who had previously been confined within the walls and boundaries of the capital, to choose whatever town or place they pleased within his states as their place of residence, with the right of naturalization that would make them the equals of his other subjects.[12]

When Mirabeau walks into this principality of Franco-Germanic osmosis, full of great diplomatic schemes for rattling the rafters of Europe, he takes to it like a duck to water. Among other finds, he uncovers a "German from Provence," Major Mauvillon of the engineer corps, whose father was expelled by Louis XIV. A teacher at the Brunswick military academy, Mauvillon is one of those idealistic pacifist-soldiers of the breed of Guibert or La Fayette, who shake each other's outstretched hands, or pens anyway, across the frontiers. He has amassed a treasure house of erudition on the Prussian monarchy, and its gems arouse the cupidity of our potential pillager; let's be friends, you never know. Bosom buddies, in fact. Mirabeau is on fire: with Mauvillon, "it is a marriage of souls."[13]

As for the duke himself, we'll treat him with the respect that is owed to the future. Again, you never know; there are some oddly shaped storm clouds drifting over the horizon, many an insubstantial monarch may soon find himself confronted by harsh realities. Mirabeau's ears have picked up the early croakings of the frogs that may some day, since they are unable to imagine life without kings, start croaking for new ones. Now, here in Brunswick there is a great and friendly nobleman who might let his arm be twisted into a job as Frederick's true successor in Berlin, should the bull-of-the-bog nephew prove too ponderous. And what if some liberal and resolute Frenchmen should suddenly decide to follow the example set by the English a hundred years ago? Hush, mum's the word.

Meanwhile, Mirabeau shouts out in the direction of Vergennes's rooftop that at last he has met a man capable of sharing and furthering "the idea that has been running through my mind for seven years."[14] "The duke asked me if I would treat as an impracticable chimera the scheme of an alliance between France, England, and Prussia . . ., the greatest difficulty in which may be that one would not dare attempt to carry it out."

Thus groping and fumbling, Mirabeau spends the whole year trying to raise himself, in his correspondence, to the position of Great White Chief of the World. He was born under the sign of Choiseul and nothing will ever change the image of his supreme ambition: to be coachman of Europe. It's no mean stunt he has "running through his mind," after all: the reconciliation of France and England, a thousand years wiped out with one throw of the dice.

He knows he can count absolutely on Lauzun, another nobleman with a diplomatist's instincts and presumptions to statesmanship, who is wilting away in love and war and in whom Anglomania has long sustained a similar scheme; and Mirabeau knows how to rub him the right way:

> I have conversed at length with the Duke of Brunswick, whose wisdom and ability are well known to you, and he speaks of you with great pleasure. I have discussed with him the so-called chimerical idea of an alliance between France and England. He regards it as the salvation of the world, and as presenting no difficulties beyond those of the prejudices of false knowledge and the tepidness of pusillanimity.
>
> I also spoke of it philosophically,* to the English legation, and found Lord Dalrymple [the ambassador] and even his most Britannic secretary of legation infinitely closer to these ideas than I should have dared to hope. The lord told me that the only system for England was a coalition with France, founded upon unbounded freedom of commerce, but that the time was not ripe for this great revolution.[15]

Those three words go dancing through Mirabeau's mind. In his opinion the revolution must be worldwide, not just French, and it must be economic as well as political. On June 3, 1786, he wrote Calonne a report "on the present situation of Europe" and he's thinking now of making that the preface to his letters, whenever he will be able to publish them. Again, he reverts to his scheme of the new alliance: "Is it not time . . . to put an end to our routine by means of this sublime revolution?[16]

LAVATER

# 51

## SEPTEMBER 1786

## *An Artful Insanity*

Between the men in the nucleus of the "Mirabeau nebula" rationalism is one bond, and a good old Diderot-style skepticism is another; for them, too, "philosophy begins with incredulity" [among Diderot's last words]. They join forces, to defend Germany now and Europe tomorrow, against a tidal wave of worshippers of the black suns of every description that are climbing danger-

---

*"Just to see, hypothetically . . ."

ously high in the German heavens and aiming their lethal rays straight at the minds of the men of the new age.

The Illuminati versus the Enlightened.

And versus France as well, she being perceived, by credulous spirits of all persuasions, as an untrustworthy pocket of resistance. Ever since Voltaire and the *encyclopédistes*—and even now, under her present most-Christian King—she remains marked by the seal of reason, and it is as its (and their) heir that Mirabeau bays his cry of warning: "The Rosicrucians, Cabalists, Illuminati, Alchemists, have found supporters, friends, protection and favor everywhere, even in Berlin. . . ."[1] His direct targets here are two names in the news, Cagliostro and Lavater, but they're just an excuse. His attack on them is designed to put the new king's subjects on their guard, if it fails to wake up the man himself. For him it may be too late: Frederick William has already joined the Rosicrucians.

History's pages turn quickly. It is not easy to imagine the heir to the king of the *philosophes* attending the Rosicrucians' annual re-enactment of the Essenian Last Supper, standing with arms crossed and hands flat on his chest before "the all-Wise Arishtrata" and the candelabrum with its seven red tapers, under the Milky Way painted on the temple ceiling, in a jumble of wine vases, silver goblets, and incense burners. A reassuring mixture of Bible and magic, with the refined gratifications of the esoteric: I know, you don't. The masturbation of conceit. I, alone or almost, attain to the topmost summits of knowledge. And thanks to the rose glowing in a circle under the cross as a sign of universal beauty, I can claim kinship with Dante, Luther, and the Templars no less than with Christ, of whom I, the initiate, am the only true confidant. Look at all the hicks outside gaping. Oh, the subtle thrill of being one of the sect, whatever its name—that hovel, misshapen hut still standing atop the mountain of credulity, while the towering walls of established churches begin to totter. And as a secondary attraction, there's always a chance that the alchemy transmitted by the hermeticism of Paracelsus will one day enable me to turn out a few lumps of gold . . .

If there were only the Rosicrucians it might not be so bad; but in fact they are legion, these inoffensive screwballs crouching in the shadows behind their numerous and highly fishy magi. Europe is littered with upstairs rooms full of occultists, hermetics, and mystics diligently searching for supernatural prerogatives under the umbrella of an initiatory Christianism.[2] You can count nine principal movements in the 1780s: the northern school founded by Swedenborg, the school of Avignon of the itinerant Benedictine Dom Pernety, Pasqually's Martinists at Bordeaux, the school of Weishaupt in Bavaria, the school of the Rose Cross of Gold in Vienna, the school of the Rosy Cross in London, and their ramifications in Switzerland—Lavater for Zurich,

Willermoz for the school of Lyons. It is also in Lyons that Claude de Saint-Martin, the "unknown philosopher," has settled this very year, as though to launch an attack upon France's mini-Vatican, the sacred hill of Fourvière, and is preaching—sincerely, in his case—"the highest ambition on earth, which is to remain on it no longer, so alien and out of place is man here below."[3]

Such are the leading houses in the grand multiform order of the knights of alienation, marching alongside the functionless nobles and corrupt prelates of the century's end. And if Mirabeau declares war on them with such vehemence, it's not just because he likes tilting at windmills, nor for the intellectual pleasure of theosophizing more or less orthodoxically—he couldn't care less about their dogmas. Fifteen years ago, on the brink of adulthood, he had his own, very different illumination, that of the atheist finally emancipated from the soft-walled prison of the concept of God.

The doctrines of the diverse illuminations, mixing together the Apocrypha, Egyptian and Coptic tales, and canonical texts, are little more aberrant than those of the official churches, with their Virgin Birth, Immaculate Conception, Resurrection, Assumption, God in three persons, and transsubstantiation. But sects fall even faster and more fatally than churches under the influence of dangerous scoundrels hungry for gold and power. Take, for example, the pair who are now in control of the Prussian Rosicrucians: Wöllner, a tutor, and a rabid foe of the cosmopolitanism and tolerance of Frederick the Great; and the worldly Captain Bischoffswerder, an equally rabid proselyte of Germanic virtues, who believes so strongly that he can work miracles that he uses—possibly in good faith—mechanical and magnetic gadgets to make other people believe he can too.

Bischoffswerder cured Frederick William of some disease, "through the supernatural virtues of a drug whose secret he claims to have received from his order,"[4] and introduced Wöllner to him with a view to the prince's initiation into the Rosicrucians. Wöllner, "forever steeped in darkness, mysteries, intrigues, and accomplices," according to Mirabeau, has just installed a full range of his illusionistic paraphernalia in a room in the royal palace and conjures up on command, before the wondering eyes of the king, Julius Caesar or Marcus Aurelius, Leibniz or poor Frederick II himself, who really deserved better than that. Nothing to it, if you take a little trouble over your lighting effects and make your smoke thick enough: another pal, the ventriloquist Steinart, who is a master at makeup and mime, can play all the illustrious characters in turn. One might shrug, with a pitying smile—except that Wöllner is on the point of "seizing the tiller of finance" and preparing to have the king sign one edict outlawing freedom of conscience and another prohibiting freedom of the press. "Espionage is already being employed. Informers are welcomed, there is muttering against those who disapprove. . . ."

So Prussia might slip over the edge, and Austria is threatened too, because of the addled brain of Joseph II, who may be a candidate for Illuminism. Here is Mirabeau striving for a new balance of power based on a concerted search for progress through reason; and in its place, is the morrow going to bring a vast, retrograde, anti-French coalition? The beacon of European consciousness entering the nineteenth century under a bushel, "in consequence of the suicide of German thought . . ."

The only piece of writing Mirabeau prints in Berlin during his stay there[5] is his *Lettre du comte de Mirabeau à M. . . . sur MM. Cagliostro et Lavater.* Unlike his then still private letter to Frederick William, this one is intended to stir up public opinion, but it is also intended, like everything he writes, to set himself up as spokesman for the enlightened and a potential political translator of the *Encyclopédie:* Voltaire plus Turgot, and one in the eye for Necker. He purposely chooses two figures who are likely to interest a lot of readers. The name of Cagliostro, over whom he glides in his preamble with a sort of condescending contempt, reminds us that the necklace is still mutely embedded in people's minds like a cancer growing in the Court of France; and the name of Lavater, who rhymes with Mesmer, will bring a blush of shame to the faces of those drawing-room habitués who were briefly infatuated with both before tossing them away like grated orange peels.

And since everything is going to be grist for his mill, his rhyming can also encompass Necker the Swiss (Lavater, in Zurich, is an embarrassing champion of his) who occasionally, under his wife's influence, proclaims himself so fervent in his defense of religion that he sounds like a Protestant mystic. This is also a good opportunity to mark the difference between himself and Rousseauists of Brissot's ilk, because the journalist's sentimental deism exasperates Mirabeau. Their half-hearted relationship, begun by correspondence shortly after the quelling of the Genevan uprising and developed in London and Paris in the course of encounters and writings in which they spent most of their time "borrowing" from each other, never quite deepens into friendship; and Brissot admires Lavater. So do the Rolands, who are about to make a special trip from Lyons to Zurich to see him and get their faces explained to themselves, as Abbé Raynal, Hérault de Séchelles, and many more have done before them.* The point about the Reverend Lavater, however, is that he's losing his grip, or his marbles, or whatever you want to call it. The French, who never saw more than the scientific outward trappings of physiognomy, are unaware of this fact, but several months ago some serious Germans, including Dohm and Nicolaï, published critical studies of his more recent work that leave no room for doubt. So Mirabeau into the ring again.

---

*First hint of a meeting of minds which are still scattered at this point but will soon assemble to form a political Rousseauism. The Rolands go to Switzerland in August 1787.

"This Lavater, endowed, in his northern frosts, with all the fiery ecstasies of the south, a weird compound of learning and ignorance, superstition and impiety, sharp-wittedness and insanity; believer and sorcerer, unbending and overflowing, voluptuary and mystic, intriguer and scholar: Lavater, at thirty-six the author of eighty volumes,"[6] has just published five further quarto tomes on

> *Ponce Pilate, ou l'homme sous toutes les formes, ou la hauteur et la profondeur de l'humanité, ou la Bible en petit et l'homme en grand, ou l'ecce homo universel, ou tout en petit* ["Pontius Pilate, or man in all his manifestations, or the height and depth of mankind, or the Bible writ small and man writ large, or the universal ecce homo, or everything writ small"—*Trans.* ]. . . . And this is the man who is giving rise, in a good part of Germany and in a few of the greatest, at least by their titles, to an adulation that looks infinitely like a cult, so prodigious is the force of an overheated imagination, and so capable is a brilliant madness, an artful insanity, when joined to superstition and applied to objects which the imagination alone can grasp, of transforming, on every occasion and in the eyes of people of every class, a madman whom Boerhave would treat for *nerval* fever* into a supernatural person, a man divine![7]

According to Goethe, who visited him with initially fervent but rapidly waning enthusiasm,† Kaspar Lavater is a disconcerting mixture of personal modesty and sectarian arrogance. He lives the life of a Swiss paterfamilias, which is saying a lot, but combines it with an extensive correspondence with the writing cabinets of various princes and Catherine II. "His face, with a long, pointed, probing nose, was adorned by finely drawn brown eyebrows, and his mouth, mild in repose, could become extremely willful in an instant. His great height and loose-jointed stride reminded Goethe of a crane, but did not prevent him from moving with deftness and assurance among the most recalcitrant of men, and winning them to his side."[8] The very model of a founder of a sect: he believes in himself. These days he is performing miracles all over the place, conjuring up not only archangels and guardian spirits but the human great as well. He has pierced the veils of reincarnation. Louis XVI is Henri III, Marie Antoinette is Catherine de Médicis, so why shouldn't Frederick II be St. Luke, since Lavater himself is Joseph of Arimathea?

Is this lunatic doctor really worth all the fuss? What worries Mirabeau most is that this form of collective nuttiness is not just a divertissement for the blasé. The sect disease is spreading to the people.

> Do not believe that I had no motive in observing so many absurdities; moreover, who could dare to criticize me for doing so, in a country that is still resounding

---

*Boerhave, a Dutch physician, was the most famous of his day. *Nerval* fever would appear to mean "of nervous origin."

†In his later years Goethe calls him "a charlatan who deceived both himself and others."

with the wonders of the Tub, the zeal of the Martinists, Cleopatra's little dinners,* . . . and so many other phenomena of our philosophical century? When,
as is beyond any doubt, these follies have gained great favor in Germany; when
Lavater has an infinite number of credulous admirers among citizens of every
class, young ladies and aged bigots, princes and craftsmen, in palaces and taverns;
when his circular letters or sermons, his abettors and disciples, supporters and
friends are seeking to infect every rank, every country, every communion with
a philosophico-cabalistic Christianism that leads straight to fanaticism and intolerance; when any who do not believe in him are scarce suffered admittance to
certain German courts, and are irremediably looked upon as most immoral atheists; when heads grow heated and feverish; when the agitation is such that Protestant and Catholic have already begun to mutter against one another, to offer
insults and accusations and reciprocal calumnies, then these absurdities have become all too significant.[9]

Mirabeau is scared. One can get no purchase on madness. Everything that
the men of his time, and especially those of his own country, have edified, or
at least laid the foundations of, in the way of a new society whose emergence
he can feel at his fingertips, can be swept away overnight, like a sandbank, by
a movement of collective fanaticism. The choice is between the Dark Ages and
the Age of Reason, there can be no middle road.

And if these wretched charlatans, ever impelled by their thirst for gold or intrigue,
were to drive away from the courts they infest all wise and good citizens, who are
never eager for the company of adventurers and quacks; if, by turning the princes'
attention aside from the true sources of public prosperity, they were to contrive,
through the almost irresistible force of habit or the allurements of self-conceit that
is never fond of admitting to error; if, I say, they contrived to circumscribe them,
to enchain and bewilder them in the ghoulish and sterile round of their deceptions
and their practices; if hatred sprung from resistance, the contagious and deadly
affliction of all absolute rulers, were to transform these obscure fantasies into a
system of intolerance and persecution—ah, what would become of us then? We
should be the playthings and victims, the predicants and satellites of the most
shameful superstitions that ever infested the earth!

It may be said that my imagination has run away with itself, that I have
overstepped the bounds of the possible. The bounds of the possible! Ah, do you
then know the bounds of superstition, fanaticism, the dreams and deliriums of the
imagination? Poor human creatures, whose fate in one hemisphere as in the other
depends solely upon the tiny number of beings to whom your enslaved peoples
are delivered up like so many flocks of sheep; poor humans, who expend such
volumes of adulation and vials of corruption to sour, blind, and paralyze the senses
and moral faculties of your leaders! Are you then persuaded that even religious

*He's speaking of France, of course. "Cleopatra's little dinners" were organized by
Cagliostro.

tolerance (for no other form has hardly been heard of) has made such great strides upon earth?[10]

Tolerance, again. He hammers away at it; it is his religion. "Tolerate Cagliostro, tolerate Lavater; but tolerate, too, those who denounce them as insane."

Frederick William carries his intimacy with Mirabeau no farther than the tolerance of decent manners. He thanks him for his letter on August 20, in a note in the palace-scribe style that is the same the world over, and Mirabeau vainly awaits any further response. Once or twice, at official receptions, the big lout of a king proffers a couple of superficial jabs about despotism, enlightened or otherwise, as though he might have leafed through Mirabeau's diatribe. "He gave a silly little laugh, someone came to say the play was about to begin, and that was the end of it."[11] Frederick William has other fish to fry. He shares out his favors between his beloved Illuminati and Julie von Voss, and that takes up all the space for intrigue at his court. He makes ministers of a couple of the former, but without giving them full power, and before the year is out he makes a "left-hand wife" of the latter, but by no means a Maintenon. Like a Prussian Louis XVI he keeps, and guards, a private domain of apathy for himself.

Mirabeau went too far. He can do nothing without overdoing. He referred to Prussian state counselors by name and suggested that the king appoint them to be his ministers; he expatiated to him at dithyrambic length upon Prince Henry's qualities, as though the Hohenzollern family affairs were any business of his. Such things really are not done, and from October on he is made to feel that they are not done by a general cooling off. D'Esterno moans to Vergennes about how the intruder has damaged the French image and influence. Mirabeau himself starts sinking into those fits of lassitude that always smother his bursts of energy in the end. Sick unto death of Prussia. And Prince Henry, bah:

> Now bloated, now agitated, he can govern neither his features nor his impulses; he is false and does not know how to dissemble; gifted with ideas, wit, and even some talent, he has not one opinion that is his own. Petty parts, petty counsels, petty passions, petty views, everything is petty in the soul of that man, whilst there are things gigantic, but no method, in his mind; haughty as a parvenu, vain as a man who has no title to consideration, he can neither lead nor be led. He is one of those living proofs, encountered all too frequently, that a mean character can kill the highest qualities.[12]

Berlin will not see Mirabeau into his grave. "Rot before ripeness; that, I very much fear, is the motto of Prussian power."[13]

# 52

## SEPTEMBER–OCTOBER 1786

## *He Would Not Sign*

Blérancourt. Summer is slipping away. The dawn of September 15, 1786, caresses the Saint-Just home—more than a farmhouse, less than a manor, no third floor but a dozen rooms on the corner of the rue de la Chouette and the rue du Jeu d'Arc near the rampart walk.* This is twenty-five leagues northeast of Paris, in a big Soissonnais village surrounded by forest and fertile land, still reminiscent of the Île-de-France but already in Picardy. The morning mist clings round the yellowing foliage and muffles a chorus of birds.[1]

Louis-Antoine de Saint-Just ran away in the night, three weeks after his nineteenth birthday. He couldn't take anymore.

His mother wakes up to find him gone. She is "incredibly grieved."[2] Indignant might be a better word. My firstborn child, do that to me! And as if it wasn't enough to inflict such humiliation upon me without a thought for my two girls —and the neighbors, what will the neighbors say in the little town in which Nivernais-born Marie-Anne de Saint-Just *née* Robinot has always felt she was being stared at—no, running away wasn't enough for him, he had to rob me too! Oh, if only his father were alive!

She might have allowed the culprit a few extenuating circumstances; his heart has just been broken and he hasn't a sou to his name, as she should know because she doles them out one at a time. But you won't find so much as a tremor of tenderness or compassion in the call for help she addresses to the Chevalier Joseph Brunet d'Evry, godfather of one of her daughters and owner

---

*Two centuries later the house still stands but is almost in ruins, except for a restored outbuilding; the street has been named after Saint-Just. A sign points to the "Charmille de Saint-Just"—a scrap of garden. The road from Paris to Blérancourt is unforgettable. We drove it on August 25, 1967, for Saint-Just's 200th birthday. You take the N 17 to Compiègne, then the D 130 and N 134, through magnificent forests. The Franco-American Museum at Blérancourt (Aisne), in the handsome remains of the Château de Gesvres, has a Saint-Just room, lost in a welter of World War I souvenirs; there are also mementos of the American Revolutionary War.

of the big house in Nampcel, a neighboring village where her deceased husband once lived. He's a nobleman with a long arm, an officer in the French Guard, living for the moment in Paris in his home on the rue Ventadour on the Saint-Roch hill; and through him the royal police can be mobilized without making too many waves, and she can obtain a *lettre de cachet,* the solution to all upper-class family quarrels. The letter Saint-Just's mother sends Brunet d'Evry sets in motion the machine employed by the society of that day to bulldoze proud youths into submission, and it operates as implacably now as it did against Mirabeau a few years before, and at roughly the same age. There are the standard ingredients: an angry parent + a friend in high office + the police commissioner + the minister + the King. All that remains is to bake the rebel in the prison oven.

> My son came to spend a fortnight with me [on vacation from the Louis-le-Grand Collège in Paris where he was finishing his studies and where he had been kept under close surveillance since the beginning of the year to make sure he did not see Louise-Thérèse Gellé until they got her married, virtually by force, to the notary Thorin] and he left, for Paris, in the night of Friday-Saturday last [September 14–15], without my knowledge, taking with him a new silver bowl marked with an *E* and an *R,* a silver goblet with the foot turned up at the bottom, marked with the name of Saint-Just, a drinking cup with gilt stem and edge that holds half a bottle and is marked with the name of Robinot, parish priest of Decize,* three cups with a very high silver content, packets of silver braid, a brace of gold-inlaid pistols,† a good ring set with stones in the shape of a rose, and several other small articles in silver; all these objects he took without my knowledge, presumably in order to sell them and get money for no good purpose. As these goings-on have grieved me sorely and it is in my interest to try to recover these valuables and give the alarm so that my son can be arrested and his misconduct brought to an end, I should be very obliged, Sir, if you could trouble yourself to see M. le Lieutenant de Police and obtain from him an order to begin a search for my son at once, recover from him the objects he took away, and have him put in a safe place so that he will no longer be tempted to behave so badly and will have time to repent of his wrongdoing.

The letter, signed "Robinet, widow of Saint-Just," is dated September 17— which means that the petitioner took time to suck her pen before she wrote it. But it leaves the Chevalier d'Evry in something of a quandary; how can he put the police on the trail of a phantom? The mother's intuition is probably

---

*In fact, Uncle Robinot was parish priest of Verneuil, not Decize, as she perfectly well knows; but more people had heard of Decize.

†The braid and pistols had belonged to Louis-Antoine's father and were his anyway. One of them was found, as we shall see, and he carried it at Fleurus; today it is in the Musée Carnavalet in Paris.

correct, her son very likely is in Paris, which is the only town in which a runaway and his stolen trinkets might pass unnoticed. But you might as well send the men out after a needle in a haystack. Having no address to start from, Brunet d'Evry sits tight.

A week later the horizon clears. The inconsolable parent sends a second letter: here's the address, we've got him, the scoundrel has cooked his own goose by giving it to me, haste ye, haste ye, Chevalier! Antoine is staying at the Hôtel Saint-Louis on the rue Fromenteau, between the Tuileries, Louvre, and Palais Royal; it's the hottest street in Paris, teeming with streetwalkers, who have been relegated to it since the days of St. Louis.

> It is noteworthy for this ancient attribution.* As it was outside the walls of Philippe-Auguste, St. Louis permitted public women to reside there. The pious king, who would have liked to extirpate every vice from his realm, ordained in 1254 that all such women should be driven out of Paris, their goods seized and even their clothing removed, and that whoever should rent a house to them would be sentenced to pay a fine equal to one year's rent. But he gave permission for streets in the suburbs to be set aside for the public women.[3]

The town's grown some since. In the days of Louis XVI, its walls enclose the Champs Elysées all the way to the gate at the Etoile, and the rue Fromenteau, situated across from the Palais Royal like a filter placed to trap libertines and girls of easy virtue as they emerge from the gardens, is no longer in the suburbs. But its vocation has not changed, and the manager of one lot of furnished rooms on it has named his establishment after the holy king, as though it might bring him luck.

This is where Saint-Just came to roost after climbing down from the Noyon stagecoach, which he caught at the end of a nocturnal walk (or ride) of three leagues, starting in Blérancourt. One of the first things he does there is to give himself away by writing his mother a perfect fairy tale of a letter, signed by a "Doctor Richardet" of whom nobody has ever heard or ever will.† The writing slants backwards as though the writer were trying to disguise his hand, and the letter is studded with spelling mistakes, especially in the technical terms. "Doctor" or no, its author is no great shakes as an advocate:

> I am the innocent cause of [your son's] foolish act. Some time ago I cured him of an affliction in the temple, highly dangerous and new to all my colleagues in medicine, whom I questioned about it. The treatment amounted to 200 francs, which he did not pay me. . . . Your son, fearing to alarm you by asking you for 200 francs for a doctor, went to your house and took away what he needed to

*According to Le Géographe parisien, a two-volume guide to Paris published in 1769.
†During his interrogation Saint-Just does not mention this imaginary character, and his name is seen no more.

pay my fee.* He sold 200 francs' worth of silver and brought me the money at Sceaux. He has confessed all his actions to me and told me he would never in his life dare to appear in your presence again, but said he would prefer even that to being taken for a knave by me. I hastened to the Jew who had bought his silver, but unfortunately he had given it all to be melted down except a goblet, which I got for 39 livres. I have returned it to your son, who has promised me to give it back to you, with a brace of pistols and a ring. . . .

Next installment (dated September 20): Antoine has tried to join the Oratorian fathers but they quite rightly refuse him, "the priestly estate befitting him very ill," and now "he wants to embark at Calais." A loving pardon will catch him in the nick of time, because he means to set out from Paris on October 7 or 8 and on foot, "which would heat his blood still further, and he would never reach his destination." Dying is what your son is, Madame, and nobody knew it! The "affliction of the temple" was caused by "his blood that has been burnt out by study," he "must not be made to work for a few months," he should have a diet of dairy products and vegetables, because if he goes on working, "he has no more than a year to live."

"... I was unable to persuade him to return home to you, Madame, but do you write him yourself and urge him to come back, as he is stubborn. . . . He forbade me to write to you or tell you his address, but I give it to you anyway: Hôtel Saint-Louis, rue Fromenteau. Write to him, but with affection, for I have never seen a sensitivity to equal his."

By way of "affection," Marie-Anne, not in the least taken in, forwards the hypothetical doctor's nonsense straight to the Chevalier d'Evry. The trick was much too childish, Richardet didn't even offer his own address, for the excellent reason that he had none, and only said he had a practice somewhere near Sceaux.

D'Evry learns that the runaway is a couple of hundred yards from his own door; the rue Ventadour and the rue Fromenteau are in the same district, on opposite sides of the Palais Royal. It would be so easy for the chevalier to show a little chivalry for once and help the orphan without vexing the widow. A little man-to-man conversation, some cordially offered advice, a purse forgotten on the corner of a table, and I shall be glad to accompany you to the coach for Noyon whenever you like, my friend, but not before notifying your mother, who will be glad to see you . . . Instead of which, making no attempt to contact the youth, Joseph Brunet d'Evry goes to the hotel, questions the manageress and a servant on the sly and, having done his job as spy and informer, proceeds to tighten the net around Saint-Just by

*Proof that Saint-Just hadn't asked his mother for money—hadn't crossed the family barrier of silence.

writing Thiroux de Crosne, the chief of police, on September 27. Same club, y'know; easier to talk to.

> Sir,
>
> Authorized by a mother who is a respectable person in herself and who has brought up her children in a respectable manner, sacrificing herself entirely for them and seeking to increase their small fortune, and deserving, by virtue of these qualities, that I should interest myself in her, I solicit your kind assistance in redressing the wrongs her son has done to her; he left her home on the night of the 15–16 of this month, without saying a word, and he took with him various items,

a list of which follows, copied from Marie-Anne's first letter. Further particulars:

> The name of the young man's mother is Saint-Just and she lives at Blérancourt near Noyon in Picardy; the young man has the same name. His father is dead. He reached Paris on the evening of the 16th of this month and is living in the Hôtel Saint-Louis on the rue Fromenteau. The mistress of the hotel saw him with a silver bowl that had no cover, a long-stemmed silver goblet engraved with the name Saint-Just, and two finger rings, and the chambermaid in the same hotel also saw the three silver cups which she calls cupping bowls.* The mother, fearing that this conduct of her son's might lead him to more serious misdemeanors, and desirous of having her jewels and other property restored to her, asks, through me, that justice should be done by you, by obliging him to return the articles listed above and *putting him in some safe place,*† where he may have time to see the error of his ways. Commissioner Chenu has already been apprised of the matter, and might undertake to carry out whatever orders you may care to give.

Chenu? The very man, the chief commissioner of the right bank districts between the Hôtel de Ville and the Tuileries—the one who knocked at Beaumarchais's door last year to arrest and ceremoniously conduct him to Saint-Lazare. As a close associate of the lieutenant-chief of police, he is one of the four or five magistrates who can reel off the seamy side of Paris by heart. He's not a man whose door you can fling open just like that. D'Evry, playing his unsavory part to the bitter end, humbly queues up for an appointment in his offices in the Châtelet but fails to persuade the officer to take the case on his own say-so. Chenu has seen so many plaintiffs in his day that he can work up little enthusiasm over a tale of bowls and cups stolen from a mother by a grown son; before bestirring himself, he'll wait for orders from above. It'll be that much time gained. So d'Evry duly tackles the little god of all these saints,

*Cup used by surgeons when they bled their patients; they held about a half-pint.
†Italics by d'Evry himself, as in his next letter.

the chief of police himself, whose position is actually comparable to that of minister of the interior.

Thiroux de Crosne is another not-so-bad baddy. In the wake of Sartines and Lenoir, he's the reign's third repository of secrets, and his judgment, like theirs, has been tempered by daily commerce with vice, crime, and misery. It takes a matter of grave consequence to upset the King's top cop, especially so soon after the "Necklace Affair." At first he too plays for time, asking d'Evry to produce documents in support of his allegations. On September 29 d'Evry tries to needle him into action, with a plaintive missive in the following terms:

> Dear Sir,
>
> I append hereto the letter from Mme de Saint-Just which you require; I had not enclosed it before, supposing it would be of no use to you. You will see from it that the mother desires her son to be arrested and incarcerated, as punishment for his wrongdoings. I second her request, Sir, that you apprehend, as soon as may be, the young man who is now living on the articles he took from her home and who will soon have no resources at all if you delay.
>
> I also enclose another letter, written to his mother by a presumed doctor in Sceaux. I believe the letter counterfeit, as the young man has not been ill and is merely seeking to lessen his blame in his mother's eyes by means of this pretext. I would further make bold to remind you, Sir, that Commissioner Chenu has already been informed of these circumstances.

The fellow seems desperate for results, maybe we'd better give him some . . . De Crosne must have shrugged and sighed, on September 30, when he signed an order dispatching Inspector Saint-Paul of the Palais Royal district to "the Hôtel de Petit Saint-Louis, rue Fromenteau, there to arrest the Sieur Saint-Just and conduct him to the commissioner general to be heard and, if appropriate, released." And if they really can't let him go, Crosne has another idea, which he explains to Chenu in the same letter:

> Sir,
>
> I have just given instructions to arrest and bring before you the Sieur Saint-Just, charged with running away from his mother's home after taking silver and other valuables. You will please question him regarding the charges laid against him. Should you deem it necessary to detain him, you will have the Sieur Saint-Paul take him to the home of Dame Marie, mistress of the pension at Picpus, where he will be admitted upon presentation of the enclosed letter. For the rest, I trust to your good judgment to determine what had best be done, after hearing the Sieur Saint-Just.

They take their time; there's no fire on rue Fromenteau. Six more days go by, time enough for Chevalier d'Evry to utter another howl—he seems to be making a personal issue of the thing. As a courtesy, Crosne had told him what he intended to do; the result was the following brisk exchange.

From d'Evry to Thiroux de Crosne, on October 2:

"I am pleased to thank you most humbly for ordering the arrest of M. de Saint-Just, but as his mother is by no means affluent, having the barest competence to keep herself and her other children, I beg you will be good enough to have him sent to Saint-Lazare and at the lowest rates, rather than to a private home where the board must be dearer and which must be less secure . . .

"I further beg to inform you that the matter is most urgent."*

At this, Crosne irritably scribbles in the margin:

"Replied: Saint-Lazare would be more expensive than the place chosen for him on account of the subsistence fees and, moreover, the place where he will be is as safe as Saint-Lazare, etc."

On October 6, 1786, Saint-Just is interrogated by the police.†

Interrogation conducted in the presence of the undersigned, Gille-Pierre Chenu, commissioner at the Châtelet of Paris and royal censor.

By the Sieur de Saint-Just, brought before us by the Sieur de Saint-Paul, inspector of police.

In pursuance of orders received, I proceeded as follows:

On Friday, October 6, 1786, at nine in the morning.

Firstly, asked his name, first names, age, condition, country of origin, and residence?

To which he replied, having sworn to tell the truth and promised to answer categorically, that his name was Louis-Antoine de Saint-Just, of no condition or estate, born in Decize-en-Nivernais, age nineteen years, ordinarily residing at Blérancourt in Picardy in the home of his mother and temporarily in Paris, Hôtel Saint-Louis, rue Fromenteau.

Asked why and for how long he had absented himself from the maternal residence?

Replied that he left his mother's home about six weeks before,** because she had sent him to Paris.

Asked whether, upon leaving his mother's home, he had not taken away with him a new silver bowl [etc., etc.] . . . of which he had possessed himself without his mother's knowledge, and what had become of the said valuables?

Replied that he had taken the articles, no longer had them, and had sold them.‡

---

*All the fuss over "Beaumarchais's spanking" in 1785 had made this prison highly fashionable among the "spare the rod and spoil the child" faction.

†For the first and last time in history, if we except his identification on the morning of 10 Thermidor An II, less than eight years later, before he mounts the scaffold.

**Three too many. Why?

‡False. Except for the pistols, he had given them as collateral to a moneylender but didn't say so because he hoped to be able to recover them later.

Asked to whom he had sold them?

Said he had had them sold by an agent he met in a café.

Asked where his personal belongings were?

Said he had brought none with him.

Asked how he was supporting himself in Paris?

Said he had his meals from a caterer whom he paid with the money received for the above valuables.

Asked what he intended to do after spending this money?

Said he was about to be taken into the guard of M. le Comte d'Artois, until he grew tall enough to enter the Life Guards.*

Asked whether he had been presented for that purpose?

Replied no, but he was about to be.

Asked why he had not returned home to his mother?

Said he had not dared.

Asked whether he was prepared to believe witnesses with firsthand knowledge of the facts [presumably d'Evry]?

Said there could be none.

Asked if he had ever been in prison?

Replied no.

After the above questions and replies had been read out to him, said that his answers were the truth, he would stand by them, and would not sign.

Saint-Just's first refusal. He is facing the world mother-naked, not one hand outstretched, not one thing he can call his own, and his only freedom, springing out of the depths of his discomfiture, is a refusal to sign his name.

Naked, but armed with great beauty. It is his nature to say nothing, to exude a kind of silence that imposes silence on others. He has the carriage, the bearing, the collectedness, the air of an adolescent with something to say who is not going to say it until the moment is right because he wants to be heard. "Of average height, a healthy body, its proportions expressing strength."[4] He loves to ride, and his seat is a pleasure to behold; his "voice is strong but muted," another sign of restraint. His complexion has been spoiled by boarding-school food,† and his features, so delicate as to be almost effeminate, are crowned by a storm of curly black hair, dragged to either side by a straggling center part and tumbling in disarray over forehead and ears. Long brows and high eyelids form a setting for enormous dark eyes that stare straight out and batten upon their object. A long, straight nose is a—fortunately, scaled-down—reminder of the anteater's appendage that adorned his father's face. If you like, if the ladies like, you could say that the entire

---

*The King's Life Guards had to be two inches taller than those of his brothers. But did Saint-Just, at nineteen, imagine he would go on growing? This is more likely to have been made up on the spur of the moment.

†As were those of Robespierre and Desmoulins.

saturnine oval of his elongated head culminates in the slightly swollen, unprudish fruit of his mouth.

Imprinted overall is "a general cast of anxiety":[5] Saint-Just in his twentieth year, on his way to jail.*

SAINT-JUST

# 53

## SEPTEMBER–OCTOBER 1786

### *Humbly and in Imploring and Respectful Terms*

He was born at Decize in Nivernais, his mother's country, but Saint-Just's real home, the one you leave when you set out to live, the one the prodigal son ran away from, is Blérancourt, the center point of a handful of villages strewn between the Oise and Aisne rivers—Coucy, Morsain, Nampcel, Vassens, and Attichy—and equidistant from the great forests of Compiègne, Laigue, Ourscamp, and Villers-Cotterets. The region's big town is Noyon, a little to the north, and he went to secondary school in Soissons, a little to the south. He grew into manhood on this rectangle of twenty square leagues where his forefathers had put down firm family roots and edged their way, generation by generation, toward the lesser nobility. The "plain of Soissons."

They were still commoners, however, when the father, Louis-Jean de Saint-Just, was born in Morsain, two leagues from Blérancourt, in 1715, the year of Louis XIV's death. The grandparents' village, Chelles sous Attichy, stands in the middle of the rectangle I have described, near Pierrefonds. There were Saint-Justs in these parts in the sixteenth century, all listed as "farmers" in the parish records. Patiently they moved northwards, from the relatively poor banks of the Aisne to the fertile valley of the Oise; purchase by purchase, dowry by dowry, they become farmers for the gentry of Montplaisir and Attichy, and the grandfather, Charles-Adam "the Younger," was "tax-collector for the land and seigneurie de Nampcel," part of the d'Evry estates, before

---

*Taine seized upon the incident, or rather what he chose to know of it, to settle his score with Saint-Just in an ineffable passage in the *Origines de la France contemporaine,* which remains the breviary of conservative historians today: "Saint-Just, who stole the silver plate from his own home and went to sell and eat it [sic] on a street for prostitutes in Paris, and who dared, after that, to talk of an idyllic life and virtue."

farming the little property that came to him from his wife, at Morsain. That puts the Saint-Justs in the midst of some fair acres.

> This brief summary will establish their rural origins and social ascension in the region. . . . They were upwardly mobile.* The combination of a good-sized farm and a "charge" [office] as collector of seigneurial taxes entailing, as was the custom, various lucrative services and profitable transactions on the side, classes them in what one might call the rural patriciate. Whence the adjectives "bourgeois" and "sieur" applied to the grandfather in the parish records; and whence the family tendency to ennoble itself *de facto*, never omitting the particle before its name and, in the case of Saint-Just's own father, adding a second particle and the qualification "messire" on his marriage certificate.[1]

The end of the name was dropped when it was spoken locally, so that it was pronounced "Saint-Ju" or "Saint-Jeu," and this leads to many a vagary in the spelling of the name of its most famous member. What was its origin? The sainted fourth-century bishop of Lyons whose legend was adopted by forty or more convents and fortified towns in France, or another saint martyred in the Beauvais country? There are three villages named Saint-Just in the region.

Antoine's father, thus, takes the next step in his family's rise. He is the first, apart from a few priests, to have any book learning. At twenty he chose a military career, enlisting in the first Berry light-horse brigade; he became, that is, a slightly superior gendarme in a superb red uniform resplendent with the famous silver braid subsequently pinched by the son . . . The gendarmerie of France, offspring of the ancient ordinance companies, marches at the head of the light-horse parade, immediately after the King's Household; and Berry is a duchy for royal princes. In other words, the company is as good as those of Monsieur or Artois. So let's hike our collar another fraction of an inch higher—from his enlistment on, Louis-Jean styles himself "de Saint-Just de Richebourg," taking over the name of a hamlet of Commelancourt in the parish of Morsain,[2] which actually belongs to one of the gentry by whom his father had been employed as estate manager. But not even two particles can guarantee a career. He stagnates. A mere brigadier in 1751, and chief sergeant (in mounted arms, and with the title of captain) in 1760. At last, the Cross of St. Louis in 1762 for valor in Germany; now he can defend his "chevalier."[3] But he was also beginning to turn gray in the harness, twiddling his thumbs at the war's end in a garrison at Cusset in the Bourbonnais and whiling away his boredom in the company of the Duc d'Orléans's gendarmes who were stationed over twenty leagues away, at Decize.

---

*According to Maurice Dommanget, who points out that holdings in this region were relatively larger than in other parts of the country, thus facilitating the accumulation of wealth. Because of this aspect of his background, Saint-Just (always attentive to rural economy) is distinctly more lenient than other Conventionnels toward the concentration of holdings.

And at Decize, aching with idleness, he met Marie-Anne Robinot, in 1766.

That makes him fifty-one. She's thirty-one herself. He has a fine pair of eyes. He's "handsome," or at least personable, and all of five foot six inches tall. But the face with its lofty brow is completely deformed by a catastrophe of a nose, plunging down over a wide, thin mouth. Even so, he's a godsend for a young woman in imminent peril of spinsterhood, who is also gifted with an overhanging nose in a homely, disenchanted face.[4] She has reason to be disenchanted: unwed at thirty in a century when girls marry at fifteen. Not that she's a bad match, as the daughter of a robust line of master bakers, pastrycooks, tanners, and butchers in the Nivernais town of Decize, where the Robinots are somebody. Her grandfather, the last of the bakers, drove two of his ten children into the church. The tenth, Léonard, Marie-Anne's father, incarnated the rise of the Robinots by becoming a notary, then a prosecuting attorney, then manager of the Decize salt warehouse,* and finally alderman.[5]

But his twenty years as a hardened widower seem to have soured his temper. To begin with, he robbed his eldest daughter of her youth by making her into his housekeeper. Then, perhaps because of his cantankerous opposition to her marriage to Captain de Saint-Just, she moved out and began living alone in Decize. Or had father and daughter already quarreled? In any event, Marie-Anne was forced to resort to an exceptional procedure† which the law provided to assist adult children balked by parental opposition in such circumstances, known as the *sommation respectueuse.*

First, she had to enlist the support of the *lieutenant général* of the bailliage at Saint-Pierre-le-Moutier, and mobilize a triumvirate of important persons: Notary Grenot, her father's rival in Decize—what an affront!—flanked by a couple of witnesses, one of whom was a captain of the Duc de Nevers's hunt, and the other a member of the local gentry and captain in the Auvergne regiment. All's fair in love and war. The attack took place on three successive days in May 1766, between four and six in the afternoon, in the entrance to "the house and home of the Sieur Robinot, situated in this town close by the bridge, in the parish of St. Aré."

Cordiality was not the keynote. On the 21st,

> Demoiselle Robinot, in all respects dutiful and respectful, reiterating several verbal prayers and supplications which she previously addressed to the said Master Robinot, her father, abundantly prayed and requested of him his consent to and

---

*That is, administrator of the *gabelle,* or compulsory salt tax.

†But relatively inexpensive: the total of the fees paid to the notary and bailliage officials amounted to 15 livres, or 130 modern francs [$32].

approval of her marriage with Messire Louis-Jean de Saint-Just de Richebourg, Knight of the Royal and Military Order of St. Louis, Captain of Cavalry, Chief Sergeant of the Company of Gendarmes of Berry, quartered at Cusset, native of Nampcel in Picardy, who is a favorable and advantageous match for her; whereupon the said Master Robinot, after the prayers and requests of the said demoiselle, which he heard out in part, withdrew at once without offering any reply, albeit summoned to do so, by which the said demoiselle was moved to declare most respectfully that she would continue to make further representations to him.[6]

## On the 22nd,

in speech with Simone Juge, servant of the said Master Robinot in the absence of her master, upon whom we attended with the witnesses enumerated below from the hour of half past five until the hour of half past six, during which Simone Juge told us that she did not think her master, the said sieur, had a mind to come or present himself in a hurry, upon seeing which the said demoiselle, in all respects dutiful and respectful, said, reiterating several verbal prayers and supplications which she had previously addressed to the said Master Léonard Robinot, that she was come a second time to ask and request his consent to and approval of her marriage.

And, on the 23rd day of the month of May, 1766, at the fourth hour after noon, reiterating the summations above, and those of the other parties, in the presence and company of the undersigned notary of the King . . ., being and speaking to the said Master Robinot, the said demoiselle Robinot, in all respects dutiful and respectful, said, reiterating several verbal prayers and supplications . . ., that she was come once again to ask and request his consent to and approval of her marriage with Messire Louis-Jean de Saint-Just de Richebourg . . ., who is a favorable and advantageous match for her, and, indeed, spoke to the said Master Robinot, her father, whom she beseeched humbly and in imploring and respectful terms to consent to her marriage to the said Sieur de Richebourg, whereupon Master Robinot, after the prayers and requests of the said demoiselle, which he heard out in part, withdrew at once without offering any reply or signing any paper whatsoever;

but who cares, that's enough, and the very next day she herself can sign her marriage contract in front of the same Notary Grenot and in the presence of a fair crowd of Robinot uncles and cousins, but not, of course, her father, or her two surviving brothers, who also turn their backs on her for a while. Her contribution to the contract is 400 livres in furniture, linen and clothing,* and both parties undertake to invest in their marriage whatever "rights and entitlements fall to them" at their parents' death. In all, not counting two houses, one in her name at Decize and one in his name at Morsain, and a few adjoining scraps of land, they have a fortune in "expectations" of nearly 10,000

---

*About 3,500 modern francs [$875].

livres.* Until then his soldier's pay, and later his pension of 600 livres a month, would keep them in relative comfort.[7]

There was a quiet wedding on May 30 at Verneuil, a hamlet near Decize, where a pet uncle named Antoine Robinot, the very opposite of Léonard, was the parish priest. In her hometown, when there was a big difference in the newlyweds' ages, it was customary for well-wishing hecklers to wait outside the church and greet them when they came out by banging as loudly as possible on pots, pans, and other kitchen utensils, and they preferred to forgo this pleasantry. The couple set up housekeeping at Decize, and Louis de Saint-Just resigned his commission forthwith.

Fifteen months later, on August 25, 1767, in the parish of St. Aré at Decize (unique in France in being served simultaneously by four priests), comes the baptism of Louis-Antoine, "born this day, the legitimate son of Messire Louis-Jean de Saint-Just de Richebourg, etc. and of Jeanne-Marie [the record is wrong] Robinot." The parish priest–uncle from Verneuil stands godfather, and as he also made his niece a wedding present of 1,700 livres, the child's usual name will be Antoine.† The grandfather is as little in evidence here as at the wedding. The baby is put out to nurse at once, in the sugar-daddy uncle's parish of Verneuil, and it is the uncle who presides over his first contacts with the world because his parents leave for Picardy to look after family matters soon after his birth, and stay there four years. They settle at Nampcel, part of the Brunet d'Evry estate, and the chevalier, like his father before him, is hired to manage it. For Saint-Just, life's first mollification, and the only one ever to come from his kinfolk, is an old man in a cassock, the Byzantine portal of whose church opens just across from the house in which he is nursed and learns to lisp, the "Locaterie des Marches" as it is known, on the road from Cercy to Champvert.** His early childhood was lulled by the mild murmur of the heart of France, meadows, animals, a little stream called the Aron at the end of the field where he toddled, a soft leafy silence broken by the bells from the little church. But until he was four years old, no father, mother, brother, or sister; nothing but Father Robinot, whose big gilt bowl with the name engraved

*Say, 80,000 to 100,000 modern francs [$20–25,000]. Saint-Just's father's pension would amount to about 4,000 francs a month today [$1,000].

†There has been quite a controversy about the actual house in which he was born in Decize, and in the end nobody has been able to settle the question. A plate has been affixed, on the off chance, to the site of the old salt warehouse—where Léonard Robinot never lived; and his grandson was certainly not born in his house, wherever it was, but in one which his parents had rented somewhere in town. The uncle's present was worth 15,000 modern francs [$3,750].

**Still standing.

on it he steals fifteen years later, as though denying his mother's title to his childhood.

Two sisters arrive, both born in Picardy, in 1768 and 1769—Louise-Marie-Anne and Marie-Françoise-Victoire*—and are brought to Decize at the beginning of 1772 by the parents who have decided to return to the Nivernais, possibly because Antoine, the priest, has now died. The son is also reunited with the family. They finally patch things up with Léonard, the grandfather, for the four years he has left to live, so they can all move into a wing of his big house.

Saint-Just accordingly reaches the age of reason at Decize, where the Aron flows into the Loire at the halfway mark on its course, before subsiding languidly into the sands of Touraine and Anjou—a swift river here, and the pretty family house stands on its bank like a small mansion, "the east front giving onto the bridge, the south facing the street that runs from the bridge to the rue du Paville, the west looking onto the rue des Pêcheurs and the north, onto the home of the Perrin heirs."[8]

The youngster's experience was that of a scion of the upper middle class, in a tangle of "rooms below-stairs and rooms above, with an attic on top and cellars, courtyards and stables and then more outbuildings, two wells and a cesspool."† Perhaps he already has the proud head-carriage for which he is so sharply criticized later—after all, he is the grandson of an alderman, the son of a captain and chevalier—as he explores the five annual fairs or watches the work on the new stone bridge begun in front of his house in 1774 by the architect Robert Arnault, "executor of the King's works" (and a witness at his parents' wedding). The old bridge, a little higher up the stream, was on its last legs. "It was made entirely of stone but part of it had fallen down and the ruins of the pilings were used to support a wooden bridge, for which the town had paid. Near this town are mines of mineral coal, which is soft, black, and viscous, and burns as readily as charcoal, but with a hotter fire."[9] They're beginning to scratch at the earth here and there, two or three forge masters are building furnaces and swearing—with reason—that there's iron, too, in the island beneath the old town weighed down by its massive priory. The word "mine" is about to enter the vocabulary of the 2,000-odd inhabitants, too few as yet to supply manpower on an industrial scale. The Decize that Saint-Just leaves behind is still rural.

---

*They play almost no part in Saint-Just's life and are involved in neither his struggles nor his woes. Married to Blérancourt dignitaries, they feign ignorance of his very existence and survive him into the Restoration undisturbed. Marie-Anne, the mother of all three, dies on February 11, 1811, at Blérancourt.

†The house stood at the corner of the present-day Place Saint-Just and the rue des Pêcheurs. Before it was razed, in 1857, it was a hotel, known successively as the "Nation," the "Cheval Blanc," and the "Grand Cerf." A bank has since occupied the site.

The first page of his childhood is turned before his ninth birthday:* Grandfather Robinot departs this life in January 1766. After converting the inheritance into cash, largely through the sale of the big house, the Saint-Just family settles in the north for good. On October 16, 1766, they're already at Blérancourt buying their new home. Less than a year later, Saint-Just's father dies at the age of sixty-two.

# 54

## SEPTEMBER–OCTOBER 1786

## By Heart

History surges into Saint-Just's life like fresh blood into the heart. He's ten, the age at which inner dikes crumble before the tidal waves of thought. History becomes his pastime, his passion, almost his self.† He has his "historical crisis" as other children do their "spiritual crises," at puberty, when the antibodies of the adult are not yet operational and the protective self-centeredness of the child begins to splinter apart. The age of the child-prey. In him, history fills all the space left empty by his indifference to religion, his indecision as to a career, and the disappearance of his father.

Did he love him? Not enough to be badly damaged by his death, but certainly more than he ever loved his mother. And he admired him unreservedly.** For Antoine, the Chevalier de Saint-Just was more of a grandfather than a father; he was the old man, proud and strong. The Elder. The Cross of St. Louis was the one decoration that could be won only on the battlefield, and the portly and majestic parent had plenty of time to tell the boy how he earned his during that last year at Blérancourt when, perhaps already sinking,

---

*Saint-Just's historians long thought he spent only a few months at Decize, after his birth. It required exhaustive excavation work in the archives of the Nièvre and Aisne, conducted mainly by O. Boutanquoi in 1926, to discover that he lived so many years in the region.

†The same precocious intellectual awakening takes place at the same age, and almost the same moment in time, in the young Buonaparte, two years his junior, and leads to the same fascination for past glory.

**When, as member of the Convention, Saint-Just writes his strongly Roman text on education, he incorporates two private obsessions into it: the primordial role of older men and the importance of military training.

he spent most of his time sitting in the shade and pacing the hedgerow planted along the banks of the Feuillants that ran past the bottom of their garden.[1]

His first approach to history was through those images of a war in which his father shone like Mars, and the war was one waged against the Germans. For him, the bad men are the ones on the other side of the Rhine; they're the ones his father fought, even if the English were behind them. At this point Antoine wants to be a soldier too, that's why he starts riding so early, galloping bareback down the road to Noyon or Coucy. He also learns to talk like a soldier; his father was not sparing of oaths and curses and the goodwives of Blérancourt sniff and tut-tut at a coarseness of speech in his son that sends his sisters scurrying from the room. For years, in the village, they tell how he used to smash the little girls' dolls when they tried to get him to play with them. In fact, this seems to be the neighbor's only memory of his first year in the march of Picardy, where the natives are all infused with a prodigious pride, the heritage of a past so glorious and so remote that it has made them close-mouthed, as they say in those parts. From Noyon to Soissons this land of woods, streams, and wheat was once the heart and shield of ancient Neustria, the Kingdom of the West, in the centuries when the Franks were groping for the future shape of France as they engaged in their muddled wrestling match with the devils from Austrasia, or the East, where the sun and the Goths both rose.

When little Antoine was taken to the big town of Noyon, 6,000 strong and less than an hour away at a trot, Paris suddenly shrank in his mind. For his folks, and everybody in that part of the world, Noyon was the true capital of France, and so it had been in the "olden days," long before Paris and King Henri's mass. The Parisians prattled and crowed about the deeds of the Valois and Bourbons while the Noyonnais stared down upon them unmoved from the causeway of giants: ever heard of Hugues Capet? It was in Noyon that he was proclaimed king, in 887, by his peers. We gave France the Capetians. And that's not all. Still further back in the gleaming mists of old, when King Pippin the Short was dead and his two young sons were proclaimed kings of his divided empire, it was here, at Noyon, that the eldest, Charles—later *magnus* [Charlemagne—*Trans.*] was crowned King of the Franks on October 9, 768, at the age of twenty-six, in the "320 foot nave of Our Lady of Noyon, the cathedral church built by Pippin the Short, its portal adorned by two stout towers 200 feet tall; the town's two other patron saints were St. Médard and St. Eloi."[2] On that same day, that unique October 9, Carloman, the younger brother, was crowned king of the other half of Pippin's subjects at nearby Soissons.* There are ten leagues between the two towns by the Bléran-

---

*Carloman conveniently dies of "languor" on December 4, 771, and Charlemagne becomes the sole heir of Pippin the Short.

court road, and Blérancourt stands almost in the middle, astride the provisional frontier between two worlds that merged to produce the Holy Roman Empire.*

One year earlier and Saint-Just would have been born on the thousandth anniversary of the dual crowning; between Charlemagne and him, a thousand years of forest had nursed the legends flowing into his brain. There was that mighty beard of the emperor's, of course, who has become so much an inmate of his mind that he calls him Charlie as often as Charles;† but there was Roland too, and Ganelon and Turpin, the Bishop of Rheims and Noyon who is credited with the founding of scores of abbeys and priories in the region, when they're not made to go all the way back to St. Eloi—who is also, naturally, buried in the cathedral at Noyon, where the Universal Church has held no fewer than six councils. Is that all? Far from it. "That same town has been visited at divers periods by the greatest misfortunes. The Normans took and sacked it; they even made a prisoner of Ismon, who was then bishop. It was burned six times, in the eleventh, twelfth, and fifteenth centuries. It also suffered greatly in the time of the League." And it was in Noyon that a child was born in 1509, and from Noyon that he set out forever, sometime around the age of twenty, upon a redoubtable career in teaching, preaching, and burning at the stake: the son of the ecclesiastical prosecutor Cauvin, a young man in a rage against his town's compliance with the crass stupidity of the clergy, a roving flame called John Calvin who was to give the French a Bible by translating it, for the first time, into a "vulgar" tongue of incomparable beauty.

Such is the breed of Saint-Just, on his father's side and in his childhood. There's plenty of lung power behind his historic breath, and, at twelve, he starts exuding little puffs of it onto pieces of paper.[3]

Next page: school, in Soissons, the region's other great historical center, where the Oratorians kept a highly reputed collège, having taken over the Jesuits' premises there as everywhere else after their expulsion.

At Soissons Saint-Just can root his pride even more deeply in the past; for instance, in the marriage of the Christian princess Clothilde to Clovis, the chieftain of the barbarian Franks who had just crushed Syagrius, the local Roman king. Soissons was also the site of the famous sharing out of spoils after which Clovis was said to have broken a soldier's head on account of a broken vase—and is still said to have done so today [The soldier broke the vase because it could not be shared, so Clovis did the same to the soldier; the expression "Who broke the vase of Soissons?" is commonly used in French

---

*The line is marked today by N 334 and D 6, which meet at Blérancourt.
†At least twenty times in the great lyric poem I discuss later.

families to end a sharing dispute—*Trans.* ]. Meanwhile, over in Rheims, a short distance to the east, the holy Bishop Rémi was standing poised to sprinkle his baptismal waters over the heads of a converted people. Then, for a hundred years, Soissons was the capital of a kingdom founded by Clotair, one of Clovis's four sons. In 1780 the town's 7,000 or 8,000 inhabitants all swear they were 40,000 strong in Charlemagne's time, when the monks were building the formidable abbey of Saint-Médard, a town within the town, in whose cellars you can see the cubicle in which Charles's son Louis the Debonnaire [or the Pious—*Trans.* ], the emperor dispossessed by his son Lothair, etched his lamentations on the wall with his dagger. Later, the descendants of those Soissonnais almost stoned to death Abélard, the learned doctor and Abbess Héloise's great love, at the end of the council that was convened on purpose to condemn him, in 1121, and get him to recite, against his conscience, St. Athanasius's creed on the Trinity. "He did it sorrowfully, and the tears flowed from his eyes; every couplet he uttered was broken with sighs,"[4] before the porch of the town's oldest temple, the cathedral built in the early days of Constantinian Christianity on the site of the martyrdom of the two sainted shoemakers who evangelized Soissons: Crispin and Crispinian.

Saint-Just may also have daydreamed outside the great creaking gate to the thousand-year-old ruins of the refectory of the canons* who, until the sixteenth century, were entitled by royal privilege to receive "body servants, on the same basis as the other items comprising the ecclesiastical estates; one might as soon have called them human tithes. Henri, Comte de Brie et Champagne, for example, gave them a man as alms; Helvide, abbess of Notre Dame, gave them a woman from Ressons named Liette, in exchange for another one named Pomeline."[6] All this France of orgies, mysticism, and cruelty eddies round Antoine's footsteps as he goes to sit tamely behind his desk at school, where the Oratorians undertake to weed, prune, and discipline his childish fairy tales but fail—not that they really try—to sterilize the loamy soil of his earliest discoveries, on which their seedlings rise like a second crop.

Six years of "humanities," 1779 to 1785. The word would be more fitting in the singular because, thanks to the Oratorians who provide a sort of transi-

---

*It was to outlast him by very little: revolutionary vandalism, followed by the "black band" of vendors under the Empire, devastated Soissons. In 1810, according to Reichard, "the former abbey of Saint-Médard is in a state of utter ruin; the abbey proper, every aspect of which proclaimed its venerable antiquity, and which contained many precious monuments, is now the property of a tanner; the church has been partly torn down, but the vaults, drying room, and old tannery still exist; the tomb of St. Médard is a wine cellar, that of Clotair I, with its chapel, has become a stables, and the last remains of the palace of the kings of the first dynasty will soon be demolished. The prison of Louis the Debonnaire can still be seen, with the writing carved on the wall in his own hand."[5] Then came the battles of 1814 and, for good measure, heavy bombing during World War I.

tional semi-religious semi-secular instruction, humanity now enters the world of Saint-Just and begins to organize itself inside his head. The Oratorians were not exactly an order; they were more like regional groups of priests assembled under the authority of their bishop. They were individualists and, depending on the individual, they tended to radiate either a delectably sensuous mysticism like that of their founder, the great Bérulle,* or a healthy indifference to dogma; the choice was theirs to make. Little proselytism. Many of their more gifted pupils shed their faith toward the end of their time in the Oratorians' care as painlessly as they might discard their outgrown socks, not at the end of a lengthy conflict but almost as a matter of course.† The one passion they all had in common was teaching. Their taste for the exact sciences and the "arts" made them a church-tolerated educational conveyor belt for the *Encyclopédie.* "They were very much inclined to accept modern concepts. They taught natural science, mathematics, and geometry in French," unlike the Jesuits, who worked in Latin, "and the instruction they gave in history and geography was quite adequate."[7]

The ones in Soissons, who taught in the hospital of the poor clerics of Saint-Nicholas, are a good lot. The school is not too big: it has a principal, Father Sulpice-Marie de Molis, who also teaches philosophy; a prefect; and eight regents (or teachers), two of whom, Father Mannes and especially Father Silvy, do Saint-Just the inestimable service of giving him a solid grounding in rhetoric. Thanks to them, he can both write and speak by the age of fifteen. Better still: if, at the same tender age, he also knows how to keep still, listen, and think, it is thanks to one of the Oratory's most brilliant hopes, a puny twenty-two-year-old (only six years older than Saint-Just) named Pierre-Claude-François Daunou, who was his professor of logic in 1783 and 1784 and who had himself been so excellently taught, from the age of seven, by the fathers in Boulogne on the stormy shores of the Channel, that he was admitted "as a brother to the institution of the Oratory of Paris on December 4, 1777, being only sixteen years and three months old"—an almost unprecedented exception.**

*Cardinal Pierre de Bérulle (1575–1629) founded the Oratory under Louis XIII and might have played a major political role if his sweet and persuasive ways had not contrasted so sharply with those of Richelieu that the latter was afraid of being outmaneuvered by him. Bérulle left some delightful spiritual writings, made known by Abbé Brémond in his *Histoire littéraire du sentiment religieux en France.*

†Gilbert Romme, the future Montagnard, for instance, who studied under the Oratorians at Riom; his intellectual background is very similar to Saint-Just's and, like him, he later takes part in the drafting of the revolutionary education bills.

**Daunou was born on August 18, 1761, on the Place Saint-Nicolas (today the Place d'Alton) in the old town of Boulogne-sur-Mer near the home of Brissot's in-laws; he was the son of a "master in surgery, demonstrator in the art of child delivery" and a chemist's daughter. We shall meet him again at the Convention and then among the Five Hundred, where he sits with

Daunou's passion for study had left him nothing but skin and bones. A day-student at Boulogne, "he went from his father's house to the school twice every day. He was so eager to learn that he spent most of his recreation periods preparing his homework. Even in winter, when there was no fire in his little room, he would thrust his feet between two mattresses to feel the chill less acutely, because it was very sharp so close to the sea, and that way he could study more comfortably. On his way to school he had to cross a great open expanse where the wind blew fiercely. His schoolmates, taking pity upon so small and sickly a creature, would pick him up and carry him across this place."[8]

Saint-Just's adolescent schooling was burned by the same bitter salt, and it left him unable ever to live in an ivory tower. Here he first got his *idée fixe: only the whole world counts.* In Soissons his military ambition—to be like his father—began to give way to a professorial ambition—to be like Daunou. The combat of learning bade fair to be as stern as that of war, and besides, on the threshold of the modern world it was itself a sort of war. Not everything is a lie, perhaps—at least not at a deeper level—in the imaginary Dr. Richardet's letter to Mme de Saint-Just after the flight from Blérancourt; maybe her son really did think seriously about entering the Oratory at nineteen, although if he did it was because of the hunger for learning that he shared with his friend and teacher and certainly not out of any religious vocation. At sixteen, Daunou had tried to resist the paternal pressure that was being applied to him on all sides, by both his physical father and his religious fathers. He wanted to go to Paris, yes, but to be a lawyer or writer, not a priest. But by what means, and *with* what means? In the end, he resigned himself, primarily because the Oratorian library in Paris offered more treasures than any other. Daunou sowed and milled his life's grain in books. In the Book. "The thought of having continually at his disposal the rich libraries of the congregation enabled him, too easily perhaps, to overlook the drawbacks of the ecclesiastical life."[9]

Daunou, Silvy, and Saint-Just's other teachers did effect one conversion: the child who used to read stones in Blérancourt, Coucy le Châtel, and Noyon now became a reader of books in the library of Saint-Nicholas—10,000 volumes strong, both ancient and modern authors. The grim white stone building hugged the ramparts of Soissons, broken by a monumental gateway on either side of which, looking through the window of the reading room,

---

the moderate Montagnards and is principally concerned, like Saint-Just, with schemes for universal education. A prolific author and historian, he dies a much-honored peer of the realm in 1840. We shall also see more of Silvy, who leaves the church and marries in 1791. A Montagnard and Jacobin, he becomes the public prosecutor of the criminal court of the Aisne and sides with Saint-Just until 9 Thermidor. He later becomes a lawyer in Laon, then in Soissons, and, under the Restoration, he supports one of the spokesmen for liberalism, General Foy—who was a pupil of his at Soissons shortly after Saint-Just.

Antoine de Saint-Just could see the figures of Pallas and Ceres held up by two Doric columns.

And so he fed the bulimia of his fifteen years, that extraordinary age—Lord, how a kid can read if he's a reader! Antiquity in quarto cartloads: Pliny, Tacitus, Plutarch; the two philosophers too, Aristotle and Plato. And the great orators: Demosthenes and Cicero. The Middle Ages, as recounted by Joinville and Froissart and in the nine volumes of the chronicles of Matthew Paris.* The heroic tragedies of Corneille and the ironies of Molière, whom nobody knows how to stage anymore, as Saint-Just is soon to complain. The wisdom of Montaigne, of whom, Antoine indignantly expostulates, there is no statue in Paris. And the truculence of Rabelais,† so seldom found in the baggage of eighteenth-century scholars, that somehow sanctions the rough talk of the old soldier of Blérancourt.

A balanced diet of moderns. Beneath his later musings on civil society and its rules there is, first of all, Montesquieu, whole pages of whom he can quote from memory five or seven years later, the Montesquieu of the *Esprit des lois,* but always seasoned by the spice of the *Lettres persanes.* [11] With Montesquieu the spirit of obedience and respect for tradition go by the board, and from him Saint-Just learns a realistic approach to political problems, human rights, forms of government, and the role of opulence in states.[12] Rousseau? Of course, as amplified by Daunou, who is beginning to distill from him a comprehensive theory of education. Above Rousseau, however, there is Voltaire, for whom Antoine shows a distinct preference and whom he tends to allude to or quote at the drop of a hat once he gets out of school.** The Voltaire of the tragedies, but even more the Voltaire of the *Siècle de Louis XIV,* the pioneer historian of modern times; and above all, the Voltaire of the *Dictionnaire philosophique* and *La Pucelle,* large portions of which Saint-Just learns by heart, if only because the presence of that outlawed erotico-sarcastic poem about Joan of Arc on the shelves of a "bourgeois" library could be dangerous. All honor to the Oratorians, among whom he could find such a book in more or less camouflaged form! And this represents his first application of a theory of rote learning from which Saint-Just never departs: none of those file cards, notebooks, and abstracts that

---

*A thirteenth-century English Benedictine whose *Chronica majora,* commencing at the creation of the world and ending in 1259, served as the standard textbook of world history until the Revolution. This curious compilation, in which facts and legend are woven nimbly together, is not lacking in either breadth or lusty vitality. In his great poem Saint-Just speaks of Matthew Paris as one of his favorite authors. Here again Daunou was his initiator, and later publishes a *Discours sur l'état des lettres au XIIIe siècle.*

†In An II, Saint-Just takes *Pantagruel* along when he goes to join the Rhine army and reads it aloud between bivouacs to Joseph and Henriette Lebas.[10]

**Eight times in his poem, often referring to him familiarly as Arouet; and on two occasions he incorporates into his verse alexandrines from Voltaire's tragedies *Oedipe* and *Irène,* quoted verbatim and complete with references.

trail in the dusty wake of so many scholars. "He needs only to read a passage through twice to carry it engraved forever in his mind. That is what explains how, at so early an age, he was able to know so much."* He's absolutely convinced on this point:

"The method of abstracts is of no use at all. When you are struck by a maxim or a development or by some other thing in a book, read it through twice: you will remember it. If you consign it to writing, your memory will rely on your copy and become lazy and idle, and all your learning will be in cardboard boxes."

And if somebody points out to him that "the studies of the ancients consisted solely in learning passages from the great masters," he closes the debate with a sweeping,

"Yes, but by heart."[13]

The Saint-Just who has just turned nineteen is a Voltairean.

He tells us so himself, in the "bits of verse" he's been playing with since his first year at the collège, forming a sort of undated diary, in lyrical or epic code, of his intellectual development. "He was forever writing them. His schoolfellows had nicknamed him 'd'Assoucy,' and as they also conscientiously explained to him that d'Assoucy was a very bad poet, this drove the boy wild but did not prevent him from aligning his rhymes."[14]

D'Assoucy? The nickname was more than a coincidence: he was a burlesque poet and translator of Ovid who played court fool during Louis XIV's childhood, roamed Europe with his two pages scratching on a lute, got himself imprisoned by the Roman Inquisition for a satire, and, like so many others, was huddled into his grave by one word from the merciless Boileau, who dubbed him "Scarron's chimpanzee."

Ah yes, Boileau: he is the subject of the first literary essay to be published (in 1787) by the precocious Daunou—*De l'influence de Boileau sur la littérature française.* In it he defends d'Assoucy and one or two other poets and wits against the ferocity of the great leveler, who had been impervious to certain forms of whimsy. Who but François Daunou could have taught his pupils enough about d'Assoucy for them to turn him into a nickname? And who else —perhaps in revenge against his compulsory clergyhood—could have introduced into Saint-Just's reading list the "secret masters of king Voltaire," the libertines of the age of Louis XIII, who were "known only to a small number but, by the vigor, or at least the boldness of their thought, did much to turn doubters into negators, and discreet adversaries of religion into insolent ones?"[15] There was Pierre Cuppée, for example; Dumarsais; the Freret of

*According to Barère, whose *Mémoires* contain this engaging conversation between Saint-Just and himself on "the best method of learning and retaining what one learns."

*L'Epître à Thrasybule;* the *Testament du curé Meslier,* * the parish priest who never believed in God; and also, going still further back, Bayle, Fontenelle, Saint-Evremond, Abbé de La Fare; and, above all, that most singular character Guillaume Anfrye, Abbé of Chaulieu, the Duc de Vendôme's favorite scoffer in the reign of Louis XIV and new Epicurus of the *Anacréon du Temple,* the *Ode contre l'esprit,* the *Stances sur la Goutte,* a man who spared neither God nor the Devil . . . Chaulieu adds so much brightness to the intellectual universe of Saint-Just that when he comes to sum up his nascent philosophy in verse, he defines himself in one of those formulae which is already almost a pithy epigram:

"When I read Plato, I love Chaulieu."[16]

He might just as well have said, "When I read Voltaire, I love Rabelais." Saint-Just? And how!

PLACE ST.-PIERRE IN SOISSONS

# 55

SEPTEMBER–OCTOBER 1786

## *A Lover and His Lady Fair*

Saint-Just often drops over from Soissons to Blérancourt, on Sundays, or on the thirty-two holy days dedicated to Christ, the Virgin, and the saints, or during those unscheduled bits of the summer when the collèges (which never close) give their pupils a little surprise "vacation." In fact, he is almost a half-boarder, and although his mother and sisters and the village people see him imperceptibly changing into a handsome young man, always neatly turned out, they don't really notice the fact until the crisis forces their eyes open. Such a good, quiet boy, our little Antoine, immersed in his rambles and his scribbling. When did he decide to embark upon a literary opus, assembling the fragments written during his study periods into a single long epic-satiric poem? When he was still at Soissons, no doubt; because it was in the chronicles of Matthew Paris that he found the legendary character of the Chevalier Organt, bastard son of Archbishop Turpin in Charlemagne's day, with whom he identifies himself in a fictionalized autobiography that serves as a safety valve for

---

*At the time known only through Voltaire's references to him.

his obsessions and an escape from reality, as well as a proving ground for his creative powers: if he doesn't turn into an officer or a professor, writing might do as a third choice, after all.* For practice, and to prove to himself and everybody else that he's no mere drawing-room rhymester, he spends the whole of 1785 collecting material for and writing a monograph on the château of Coucy.†

One hundred and twenty-six pages, from which we can reconstruct the milestones of his youth: the cool, fresh walks over four leagues of country to Coucy, by way of Saint-Aubin and Trosly, crossing the Oise at Guny;** the long nostalgic sigh of the ancient tree-filled ruins crowning the Coucy hill like the top of some huge escutcheon, and "leaving so powerful an impression upon those who see them close up";[1] the romanticism of his vision; the rigor of his research.

So unquestioning, this essay by a diligent schoolboy; Saint-Just records without a murmur the demolition of his beloved château, which Mazarin ordered because the Coucy clan had to be stopped from preying upon the Soissonnais roads. "Since those days, the ruined portions have expanded considerably. The last earthquake in France, which occurred on September 18, 1692, sundered the great tower from top to bottom. . . . Most of the vaults that supported several stories of suites of rooms have collapsed. This celebrated castle, one of the wonders of France a hundred years ago, and perhaps the most impregnable fortress in the kingdom, is now no more than a mournful monument to the splendor of its former lords," Antoine observes—and moves on. In fact, all that remains of the château of the Enguerrands, lords of Coucy (there are four or five Enguerrands in *Organt*) is one tower—but what a tower. "Remarkable for its height, its solidity, its stoutness. On the tower one may see the figure of one of the Enguerrands of Coucy, who is depicted saber in hand, protected by a shield, fighting a lion which he is said to have slain in single combat and which had been wreaking great destruction in the lord's forest. The lion had apparently been brought from Africa,‡ and had subsequently escaped."[2] Which Enguerrand was it, Saint-Just wonders? The first of

*Organt* is published in the spring of 1789, and gets its author, as we shall see, into very hot water. Saint-Just never repudiates the work and even has it reprinted in 1792, with a different title: *Mes passe-temps, ou le nouvel Organt, par un député à la Convention nationale* ["My hobby-horse, or the new Organt, by a delegate to the National Convention"—*Trans.*]. He is (to my knowledge) the only man of liberty to have produced any serious poetry before turning twenty.

†A copy of the manuscript was made by the curator Caix de Saint-Amour and is on display in the Saint-Just room at the Blérancourt Museum. The original, long kept in the family of one of Saint-Just's sisters, seems to have gone astray. In 1979 it had still not been published in full, and nobody knew it existed for over a century.

**Today, national Route 334, running east from Blérancourt.

‡This is the deduction of Canon Expilly, whose *Dictionnaire géographique* became a basic reference work, after 1760, in every well-stocked library.

the dynasty, "who had no other weakness but his penchant for the fair sex" and "who was a man of honor, respectable for his good qualities"? or was it his son, "the most wicked and cruel man of his century? From early youth he became habituated to brigandage, and this predisposition later drove him to such enormities that one is ashamed to read them [in Latin] in the works of the authors who attempted to recount them in detail, and they could not be tolerated at all in our language."

On the whole, the essay is extremely conventional: the Crusaders are right and the Turks are wrong; kings are respected to such a degree that Antoine praises Charles V for putting down the revolt of the Maillottins in 1383, in "Paris, a factious town, for it is no light matter for a citizen to resist his prince"; and he considers Enguerrand VII to have done well in helping that prince to crush the rebels, "who carried their fury to the uttermost lengths." Even the popes are right. Schoolboy Saint-Just seems a very proper little person, deeply imbued with a sense of law and order.

What about the other Saint-Just, the solitary stroller? When he gives his horse and his rhyming bent their heads, there is a change of key.

> He ambled his way, an indolent moth,
> And chance, that rules all here below,
> Led him on, past wood and hedgerow,
> Toward a castle built by some Goth.
> Scant shrubs and hawthorn its realm reclaimed,
> Feebly cheering its ruins dire.
> Afar, a tower, its turrets maimed,
> Cowered beneath a lofty briar.
> Here, time had tapestried with ivy thread
> A leaning parapet's littered bones.
> Beyond stood Gothic statues, dull stones,
> Of ancient heroes, beauties long dead. . . .

The poet's vision of history is more sincere, hence less credulous, than that of the student:

> This old palace may once have embraced
> Licentiousness and Inhumanity,
> Held a tyrant who laid earth to waste,
> An ingrate false to amity. . . .

Let's not spend all our time in the past, however; or rather, let it serve the present.

> The forsaken and tranquil tower soon heard
> The moans of a lover and his lady fair,

And their kisses, sounds that were made by no bird—
Ah, where are they now, those pleasures rare?

Among the ruins of the château of Coucy, life, the rarest mistress of all, was waiting to give Saint-Just the one lesson without which the labors of all the Oratorians in the world would have been so much wasted breath: love and sorrow. Thérèse.

She's blond, plump, gentle, has freckles and unforgettable breasts, and is simple and smiling.[3] For History with a capital *H,* she is also mute; we have not one word of hers. All we know is what Organt is pleased to tell us and what we can glean from the four official records in which we try to imprison a woman's life: birth, marriage, divorce, and death.

She's a year older than Saint-Just. They fall in love, thus, when they are about eighteen—for her, in those days, a woman's age. Not puppy love.

She is an illegitimate child; no churchbells rang on her baptismal day:

"In the year one thousand seven hundred and sixty-six, on Tuesday the fourteenth day of the month of October, was baptized by me, the undersigned parish priest [of Blérancourt] Louise-Thérèse-Sigrade,* born yesterday at seven in the evening to Marie Marguerite Sophie Sterlin, merchant woman of this parish, who presented to me a declaration, brought by Marie Jeanne Mennessiasse, midwife of this parish, and made, in accordance with the regulations, to Master François Thorin, royal notary in the bailliage of the provincial seat of Soissons, residing at Blérancourt." Godfather and godmother? The gatekeeper and the wife of a gardener employed in the magnificent château of Blérancourt which Mansard built a century before and in which the fortune of the Marquis de Gesvres and his family is slowly being engulfed.

The father? Everybody knew he was Louis-Antoine Gellé, the notary of Coucy and "widower of his second wife," who waits eight more years, or until August 1778, before marrying Sophie Sterlin almost secretly in the church of Saint-Leger of Bieuvy, a parish of Soissons, and recognizing little Louise-Thérèse, again in an official document notarized by his colleague Thorin. When it comes time for them all to start browbeating her because she goes for a roll in the hay without benefit of clergy, her parents, at any rate, look a little foolish.

Saint-Just meets her at her father's house, where he is a regular caller beginning in 1784, when he starts compiling his documentation on the château and surrounding properties.[4] In the pocket handkerchief of that provincial society, a notary's daughter and an officer's son would have been acquainted as a matter of course, and at first the young people's arm-in-arm excursions to

---

*Sigrade is a first name but I can find no other instance of it in the region. Fortunately for her, it wasn't used; she was usually called Thérèse, sometimes Louise.

the château are watched by their families with dewy-eyed approval. Touching, aren't they? After all, one never knows, maybe later on, when he's found himself a situation . . .

But they don't behave, and he doesn't have a situation. She is no goody-goody herself, and the local folks are badly taken in by his prim and proper airs. His large eyes do not remain chastely downcast, and his father has taught him how to talk. When he holds out a hand to help Thérèse over the fallen stones and tree roots, in halls standing open for them alone, what he sees moving toward him is everything a bright young man dreams of.

> I want a mistress sweet and kind . . .
> I do not mean some dame enshrined,
> For mine I'll find among the heather.
> I want her waist to be friendly-shy,
> Open her heart, she fifteen forever,
> Mild her temper, sparkling her eye.
> I want her to have a quick little smile,
> Nothing bold, but a hint of wile.
> And, above all, when she's by my side,
> Let her blush. . . .

And so she does. What else is she supposed to do, with his gaze riveted upon

> Her ivory arms outstretched and limp,
> A breast of milk by a sigh made shake,
> On which two floating berries quake,
> And that little pink mouth for kisses to print,
> Where coral gleams and pearls glint?
> . . . Her gaze was wild but it was gay;
> So should be ever Reason's way;
> One glimpse of nipple, if she could show,
> Would win her more servants than dim Plato.

Those nipples, by the way, take over the whole stage, damning monks, upsetting battle orders, and skewing the imperial crown on "Charlie's" head, when the magnum opus finally gets cast into twenty stanzas. Their recurrent invocation hints at a sort of mammary obsession:

Of these was Nice* possess'd:

> 'Neath a wispy bodice, two sweet breasts;
> The cloth had innocently dropped to show

---

*Nice or Nicette is the name Saint-Just uses for Organt's beloved, but in a wink to the reader he gives his own name, Antoine, to his hero.

Their tender curve: that's how I know.
And, quite unwittingly too, no doubt,
Let peep two cunning niplets out.

With what hawk's eyes he watches her!

A sweet smile she wore, and bright, and wide;
It had, like her blue eyes, nothing to hide.
Her short white petticoat, when it would whirl,
Showed lathe-turned legs beneath the swirl.
. . . Her two arms were firmed and plumped by love.
Enchanting she was, and quite unaware,
As she danced through the house, below, above,
How that wicked petticoat would flounce and flare. . . .

Does she see him as he thinks he is? He mirrors himself in those blue eyes
without excessive modesty.

Twenty times Antoine Organt had beheld
The fresh hay flower, the dry hay felled.
Turpin's blood throbbed through his veins.
His glowing eyes from his mother had come,
But of her traits that was the sum,
For his lofty brow was not one that feigns.
E'en then a vigorous growth of down
Turned his young jawline a darker brown.
With mastery he wielded his lance;
His tutors had all a soldierly stance,

and, like his father, they also had

The look of a Picard and a man of France.
His father, a Neustrian man of war,*
Was unknown but pure, great although poor,
Great in himself, not through some ancestor,

in contrast to that mother whom he bore like life's burden, that "bigot"
observed by her son's implacable eyes as

. . . she rises from her bed,
Conjuring the devils that threaten her head;
Then, matronly cape around her spread
When the first churchbell tolls through the town,

---

*He's talking about the archbishop, we recall; but those were the days of soldier-
monks . . .

> Prayerward she flies with yapping dog,
> Her missal clutched firmly upside down.

Tight-fisted, Marie-Anne Robinot?

> In the road lies a wretch who has nowhere to sleep;
> But she is praying, there's no time to weep.

It is unlikely that the old folks formed the chief subject of conversation between him and Thérèse. The ruins of Coucy were their refuge, outside every time and age.

The preliminaries are dispatched in short order.

> My virtue, showing a blush indiscreet,
> Revealed to him its fatal defeat,
> And on his amorous brow I could read
> His emotions, with which mine well agreed.
> Ah, I did not know that to love was a crime!
> And it would seem, no more did he,
> For my faith I gave him, he his to me.
>
> "Princess of my life . . .
> I am not here a war to declare,
> And Heaven alone knows what sort of strife
> My arms would wage, if you thought fair."
> The girl turns rose. He bolder grows.
> Her smile glows. And so does his.
> Her hand he brings to his lips and 'tis
> A confession in the plainest prose:
> "Nicette mine, I love thee true,"
> He now delivers. Unoriginal, too,
> I grant you that. But let it pass:
> Nicette was a village lass
> And our hero not given to impudence.
> She speaks: "Now, please, none of your sass!"
> But her blue eyes belied that innocence.
> One kiss, furtively, Organt stole;
> The second was easier, 'pon my soul.
> There was a third, then there were four.
> In the end she returned them and wanted more. . . .
> What quantities of kisses now mingle
> That left their owners' lips quite single.
> Kisses rushed, repeated, endless. . . .

Without trace of shame or backward glance,
The lovers plunge into the burning dance.

The only witness to this unrobed wedding is Voltaire; but Rabelais is not far from the young wit's thoughts:

That hour is love's hour, Arouet says.
In marble palace or hut in glen,
In that moment all men are men.
Though her skin be brown and features plain,
More joy may flow from the shepherd's Jane
Than the king in his canopied bed can know
In the arms of his queen with all her show.
Her buttocks' skin is old and rough,
Her breasts are withered, her thighs are tough,
And the sex with which he bends to play
Has cuckolded him seven times that day.
Brave Bill, meanwhile [the shepherd], sips a nipple firm,
A throat—enchanting is the only term,
And he can trust, though he may want wit,
That his neighbors never tasted it.*

His neighbors will pay him back, though—if you're caught and get spanked, it's always the neighbors' fault, there's always one lurking somewhere on your path to freedom. Antoine and Thérèse soon feel the hellfire in the eyes that follow them out of town and scorch them on their way back, peering from behind the edge of a twitching curtain. Saint-Just has a good ear for the hiss of bigotry, maybe he's already heard it at home:

The charms you sigh for are born to sorrow,
Their glow is frail, their strength is vain,
Worms will feast on them tomorrow.
Those firm, pink lips, those breasts you crave,
Soon will founder in the grave.

He's got his answer ready:

*After a critical perusal of *Organt* in 1979, it is intriguing to read the riot of over- and understatement in which nineteenth-century historians wallowed when writing about this adolescent work. "Obscenity," "odious pornography," "a work grubbed up in the gutter," "so risqué that it is impossible to quote it in full" is how the conservatives saw it, while for the champions of the Revolution it became "a regrettable error of youth," "irresponsible mischief" to be endured with averted gaze . . . The historians of that period must have been a powerfully frustrated lot!

> Then what must we do, if life is a dream?
> At least let us dream we are happy.

He makes his choice, and never regrets it:

> One day, if I'm damned by the powers above,
> I'll read again these rhymes I have penned
> In a transport of requited love.
> If for my sin I must weep one day,
> If the judgment sends me straight
> From the arms of a girl to th'infernal gate,
> Then let love now make me drunk, make me gay.*

THE SAINTE-COLOMBE HOUSE
ON RUE DE PICPUS

# 56

## JULY–OCTOBER 1786

## *The Dead Against the Living*

Lightning strikes the lovers of Coucy in the spring of 1786, when the nature of their relationship has become evident to all. They presumably made no attempt at secrecy, and, thanks to the Lamotte sisters, Marie-Madeleine and Françoise, amiable thirty-year-old "landowners" who had lived there since childhood, they were often meeting in Blérancourt itself.†[1]

A coalition of distinctly notarial cast is formed, between Madame de Saint-Just; the Gellés; the Notary Thorin (the one who notarized Thérèse's birth and subsequent recognition by his colleague in Coucy); the Chevalier d'Evry, seigneur of Nampcel and benefactor of the widow Saint-Just; Grenet de Marquette, the brand-new seigneur of Blérancourt—a wealthy landowner who bought the château from the Marquis de Gesvres; and a young notary named Decaisne, from a well-to-do family whose imposing house stands next to the Thorins' across from the orphans' home—he has just married a Thorin

---

*The next volume will cover, at the time of *Organt*'s publication in 1789, the political and historical superstructure Saint-Just added to this biographical story line.

†Françoise Lamotte has just married Charles-Marie Bigot, one of Blérancourt's fourteen (!) tavern-keepers. It is conceivable that Thérèse's visits to the inn were what finally drove the families into action. In April 1790 Saint-Just stands godfather to the Bigots' baby, and Thérèse is godmother of one of their nephews, born the same year.

girl and been taken on as junior partner by his father-in-law/neighbor.* Thorin himself is a widower, and he still has a son to dispose of, hardly older than Saint-Just (François-Emmanuel Thorin is twenty-one), but *he,* as the son of a notary in his father's employ, has a situation. Just what the doctor ordered. The obvious solution is to marry him off to Thérèse, and she can shut up and do as she's told.

What about Antoine? Out of sight, out of mind is the course prescribed for him; we can send him to Paris to learn the ropes and complete his education. To a hick society like his, Louis-le-Grand is a name to conjure with. They pack him off to school there for a few months,[2] presumably as a boarder, and then appear to forget all about him until he emerges from the mists like the Commendatore's statue for those famous two weeks with his mother at the end of August. When he walked into Blérancourt did he already know what had taken place there a month earlier, or wasn't he told until after he got home? In either case—

> In the year 1786, on Tuesday, July 25, after posting of the bans announcing, for the first and final time, the marriage to take place between François-Emmanuel Thorin, minor son of Master François Thorin, royal notary, authenticator of documents, and lieutenant of justice in the marquisate of Blérancourt, and of the deceased Marie-Anne Chèdeville, his father and mother, born in this parish on December 25, 1765 . . . and Louise-Thérèse-Sigrade Gelé [*sic*], minor daughter of Sieur Louis Antoine Gelé, royal notary and tax-collector of the same justice, and of Marie Marguerite Sophie Sterlin, her father and mother, born in this parish on thirteenth October one thousand seven hundred and seventy . . . on the 15th of this month and at mass, in both this church and in that of Villers-Cotterets, during the announcements following the sermon at the parish mass for the sixth Sunday after Pentecost, no impediment or opposition having been found. . . . Being exempted from the posting of two further bans, as appears from the document signed on the 19th of this month . . ., and after the celebration of the betrothal in this church, I, the undersigned priest of this parish, received in this church the mutual consent of the two parties and gave them the nuptial blessing.[3]

The marriage certificate is signed Flobert, priest of Blérancourt, and witnessed by Brunet d'Evry-Grenet-Decaisne—small world! Why the rush? Why the waiving of the other two bans? Why so few people, or at least signatures? It looks as though they were in a terrible hurry to get it over with before that boy in Paris starts making trouble—but what trouble could he make? Thérèse isn't pregnant, her new husband is not going off to war. And she's consenting, at least for the time being.†

In August 1786 Saint-Just keeps quiet too; but that doesn't stop him from

---

*Widowed in 1789, Decaisne marries Saint-Just's older sister on February 11, 1790.

†The Thorins' divorce is registered on 2 Thermidor An II by the mayor of Blérancourt. The divorce law was enacted by the Legislative Assembly at its final sitting on September 29, 1792.

thinking. He bides his time. No trace of an outburst has come down to us, but as far as marriage and the social pressures on women are concerned, his credo is forged during those days and at white heat:

> All things partake of nature and rest upon her as the sea upon its shores. Outside nature, everything is sterile and bleak as in those deserts in which nothing lives.
>
> In their natural state men are in no way unequal or else they must be imagined to live isolated, like monsters, each alone of its species. In nature all are equal because all have a heart which has come from the same womb and it is in the attraction he feels for his fellow that each person finds a guarantee of his equality.*
>
> [But today] there is nothing of nature left in man; love, so legitimate and sweet to his author, has become a dreaded law engendering nothing but torture. Brute force has leagued tyrants and gods against love. Man, rather than following the natural relationship that unites him to his fellows, has become dependent upon them; the law girds him round with traps and dubs him a criminal at every move, and divine law offers him nothing but torment.
>
> The nature of marriage is that man and woman unite themselves freely and engage in their possession [of one another] on the same condition and for as long as it shall please them. . . . the way to stop crimes is to remove the torment; the way to make marriage moral is to make it free. . . .

Something it certainly is not, at that point.

> A woman cannot unite herself to what she loves without also giving herself a master; and that is the least of her life. But if she is united perforce to what she does not love, or if she no longer loves what is no longer lovable, and if, in her slavery, a gentle hand dries her tears, then that woman is guilty, is an adulteress! The law is more adulterous than she, though: by what right has it disposed of her property?
>
> The contract that bestows a woman does not violate only nature, it violates her virtue and her peace of mind. An innocent virgin hears talk of her death; the law bears witness to her favors, her caresses, and points out her tomb.

Enough? No; listen to some more of Saint-Just's fulminations, the obstinate rhetoric of a gagged child, the sob of Blérancourt:

> The cruelest law sells a woman—sells her unconditionally. But on this earth no one should command. All power is illegitimate. No sex should be above the other. That is a truth of nature. Crime is born from force. It is not in the human heart to do evil, but it is in the heart of the slave to break his bonds. Whoever dares to say that one sex is subject to the other is lying to his own heart. In the social

---

*This quote and those that follow, unfamiliar save to readers of the *Annales de la Révolution française,* are written by Saint-Just six years later, in the winter of 1792–93, when he enters the Convention and, as Albert Soboul puts it, begins to interest himself "in the general problems of government and matters of doctrine"; but the notes he uses were written some time before and antedate the divorce law.

state, man and woman are equally sovereign. [Under present law] the man can freely break his [marital] undertaking, and the law threatens only the delicate breast of his wife whom the law has sold.

Wretches that we are! like incompetent architects who, ignoring the art of proportion, must reinforce our buildings with iron in order to make them stand.

And finally:

Might made law; and law is ever and always contradictory to nature. The civil laws it has made are codes for savages. The laws of fear are the tyrant's weapon against the people, the father's against the son, the husband's against the wife, those of the dead against the living. They are nothing but pressure and repression. The very idea of justice is perverted. It is no longer the rights of men founded upon equality: only the right of the strongest. In this sense, the earth is now peopled entirely by savages. Whatever may be the source of the present order, it is impure, it is a work of darkness, because the world is unhappy. . . .

I am no more austere than the ordinary. Do not condemn unheard a strong and sensitive soul that wishes no harm.[4]

They do, though, and without a trial. So there were those two weeks of secret agony at Blérancourt, followed by his flight and the rue Fromenteau, and here he stands, white-faced, in front of Commissioner Chenu, who only half-represses his sympathy for the boy's clumsy attempt to brazen it out. "Would not sign."

They don't mean to do him any real harm, the people he later calls "savages." He doesn't have to face a judge, and for that he has his mother and the gentlemen officers to thank. His fate will not be that meted out to the Chevalier de La Barre, also in Picardy, the year before Antoine's birth. No prison, no magistrates, no ogling crowds outside the bailliage court at Soissons, his school town. No defamatory sentence. His case proceeds in a discreet hush, in Paris, the great muffler.

Beyond the Faubourg Saint-Antoine, the town is slowly engulfing the houses—many still standing in gardens and orchards—that were formerly part of a village inflicted, in the fifteenth century, with a sort of hereditary scabies. The Parisians treated its inhabitants with contempt and left a wide berth around this hamlet where the fleas seemed to bite so perdurably. Picquepusse, Piquepus, Picpuce—in 1786 there were still several ways of spelling what eventually became* the Rue de Picpus, although by then its reputation had changed. In the new reign it is claimed to enjoy clean air and healing waters, and four "educational homes" have been opened in it by masters and mistresses who undertake to improve and "finish" young people whose families

---

*And remains today. The Saint-Colombe house stood on the site of numbers 4 and 6. [*Puce* = flea, *piquer* = the sting or bite of an insect—*Trans.*]

have reasons for not wanting to bring them up at home. They're beginning to be called *pensions* [partly but not exactly equivalent to boarding schools—*Trans.*], and, on the whole, they have a good name—all except one. Marie de Sainte-Colombe, its owner and headmistress, is a sort of distinguished procuress or madam in the employ of the forces of justice, an invaluable adjunct to the Châtelet magistrates. She takes in youths who need "time to repent," and boards them in circumstances far superior to any prison: Saint-Just has his own room, books, writing materials, decent food, a fire, and, like the other twenty boarders, the use of the household domestics, in exchange for payment, by his family, of 800 francs a year.*

There's less regimentation than in a collège—no lessons, the inmates are left to their own devices. But when you've been living on the rue Fromenteau you can't help feeling a little confined, because you're not allowed visitors and it's forbidden to leave the premises. And yet there are no guards, although they do bolt the doors at night. If the compulsory boarder departs without permission, however, woe unto him and he knows it: that would constitute an act of lèse majesté and means a prison cell, judge, and galleys, when they catch him.

His legal status is that of "an involuntary guest of the King," and the chief of police undertakes to make it official by applying to the minister of the King's Household for a retroactive *lettre de cachet*. This would no longer be granted as a matter of course: they've stopped handing them out like lollipops since they've become so unpopular as symbols of the King's gracious pleasure. Presumably for that reason, and to increase the likelihood of obtaining the minister's assent, Thiroux de Crosne drops another gratuitous blot onto poor Antoine's reputation:

October 15, 1786

To M. le Baron de Breteuil,

M. le Chevalier d'Evry, officer in the regiment of French Guards, in the name and as authorized representative of Mme de Saint-Just, residing in Blérancourt, having informed me that the Sieur de Saint-Just, her son, aged nineteen, had run away from his mother's house, taking with him a considerable quantity of silver and other valuables, *together with current coin,*† and gone to Paris, where the consequences of his misconduct were feared for, I caused him to be brought before a commissioner to be questioned in regard to the allegations against him. The young man having admitted to removing the above-mentioned articles from

---

*Roughly 7,000 modern francs [$1,750]. The Chevalier d'Evry advances the money, in installments of 200 livres a quarter. He also, despite the outcries of Madame de Saint-Just, who "wishes no further responsibility for her son's debts resulting from his wild spending," settles the bill of the hotel-keeper on the rue Fromenteau, who was charging Saint-Just 10 écus a month (about 3,000 modern francs [$750]).

†My italics.

the home of the said lady, his mother, and to having subsequently sold them, I have dispatched him, subject to the minister's gracious pleasure, to the house of Madame Marie, mistress of a pension at Picpus, where he is now regularly detained, his mother bearing all costs and undertaking to pay his board.

M. le Baron de Breteuil is requested to forward the proper orders, dated September 30, 1786, authorizing the apprehension of the Sieur Saint-Just and his detention in the house of Madame Marie.[5]

"Current coin"? That means cash. But nobody has accused Saint-Just of pinching money, and there is no mention of it in the transcript of his interrogation. The chief of police of the whole kingdom has just plain made it up on the spur of the moment, but, by virtue of the entry on page 169 of Volume 12 of the records of the lieutenant general, it promptly becomes historical fact:

"The Sieur de Saint-Just:

"Detained at the behest of his mother for having run away from her house, taking with him a considerable quantity of silver and other valuables, together with current coin.

"Order of September 30, 1786, issued through M. le Chevalier d'Evry. Madame Marie."[6]

It remains for Mme de Saint-Just to pronounce her funeral oration for a truncated youth, in a—for the time being—final letter to her inestimable "authorized representative," the Chevalier d'Evry:

> Sir,
>
> I have received, with no less gratitude than satisfaction, the letter you have done me the honor to write, informing me that my son has been arrested and put in safekeeping, by which my mind has been greatly relieved. I thank you, Sir, for all the trouble which you have taken and which I shall never forget.
>
> I should very much have liked this circumstance to have caused my son to repent of his wrongdoing and show some sign of remorse. But I perceive with renewed pain, from your letter and from the one by him that was enclosed with yours, that he looks with indifference upon the event to which he has exposed himself; it must be hoped that his detention in a place of enforced residence will inspire him to behave himself more creditably hereafter, and that in acknowledging his wrongs he will seek, by the use of his reason, to situate himself so as to afford greater satisfaction to me and secure a solid position for himself.
>
> I shall observe how he goes on now, and whether he deserves my affection sufficiently for me to have him released from his retreat, which I shall never resolve upon until I have sought your opinion and the good account of him that you may give me, and until I shall be fully assured that he will conduct himself correctly in the future.[7]

We'll see. For the moment, Saint-Just has plenty of leisure in which to begin polishing his *chanson de geste* on the Chevalier Organt. This winter, that will be all he *can* do.

A beautiful chimera I would build,
myself to please, my idle time keep filled.
This little while, king of the earth I'm willed.

BILLAUD-VARENNE

## 57

### SEPTEMBER 1786

## *When One Has Fiery Blood*

Jacques-Nicolas Billaud, on the other hand, manages to marry as he pleases, on September 12, 1786. Not that there haven't been ups and downs. But he's thirty, after all, and he's a lawyer, and he's making a marriage of love and almost of reason too, and it smoothly turns the page of a rather zigzag youth. In other words, there's not much in common between his fate and that of Saint-Just, who runs away from home the same week. On the surface, that is, because if you look a little deeper . . .*

"The purpose of everything that exists in nature is related to man, and all things seem to have been created solely for his use and happiness," Billaud wrote almost ten years back, in the opening lines of his *Tableau du premier âge* ["Images of Youth"—*Trans.* ], in which he fictionalized his childhood at the age at which Saint-Just was poeticizing his. And if you're going to be anthropocentric you might as well go the whole hog: "The earth, the sea, the elements, the seasons, all preserve the wonderful harmony that reigns among them for no other reason than to foster his existence." We should take "man" here in a literal—and sexual—sense. Imperturbably, Jacques-Nicolas proceeds to place "woman" at the same level as "earth" and "sea": an element, neither more nor less. "It is solely to raise to their highest dimension the delights experienced by his [man's] soul, that that bewitching sex, the masterwork of the Supreme Being, has been endowed with grace and beauty."[1] Whatever

---

*Billaud-Varenne is a member of the Convention and the Committee of Public Safety, and one of the most important figures in the Terror. He quarrels with Saint-Just, whose heart he "sears" in the night of 8–9 Thermidor, and, the next morning, finds himself among the Thermidorians alongside Collot d'Herbois; the latter's name is linked with his thereafter in every French history textbook. Both are deported in prairial An II, by those same Thermidorians. His stature enhanced by his rejection of Buonaparte and his loyalty to the Revolution, Billaud-Varenne never returns to France and dies at Port-au-Prince, Haiti, in 1819. Just now, in 1786, Collot d'Herbois is managing a theater in Lyons.

could the "bewitching" sex find to complain about? It's harmony all round. God's in his heaven in a neatly ordered universe. This is the *Weltanschauung* that was Billaud's first lesson from the Aunis.

A little province fifty leagues square in the west of France, the ancient Terre des Aulnes [alders—*Trans.*] is itself a paragon of harmony and good manners, a careful compromise between the Poitou marshes, the ocean, and the Gironde. Its colors shift from yellow to green according to the ever-changing light, and its inhabitants are tutored from birth in the art of the subtle shade. "The Sèvre, Charente, and Vendée are the principal streams. The climate is most temperate and in the main wholesome, but along the coast lie many marshes causing much sickness in the summer. There is abundance of fruit, vegetables, wood, and grazing,"[2] and therefore profit to be made from the little farm of Varenne that belongs to Attorney Billaud, Jacques-Nicolas's father, near la Rochelle. "Game and fish also abound. Large quantities of salt are manufactured in the salt marshes and it is thought to be the best in Europe for preserving meat or fish. That which is made in warmer countries is too strong, while that produced in less temperate ones is not strong enough." It must be the salt that gives the Billauds their temperate self-assurance, and also "renders the inhabitants of the Aunis, as far as their character is concerned, quick, courteous, active, and hardworking."

History has stepped in on several occasions, however, to disrupt this entente between earth and sea. Jacques-Nicolas was born on April 23, 1756, in la Rochelle, the smiling but firm stronghold of armed commerce that had stood poised for centuries between marshes and open sea, ready to thumb its nose at the English; yet two kings of France, Charles IX and Louis XIII, had broken its back. For the latter, Richelieu choked off the besieged town with

the famous mole 747 fathoms long that must, moreover, be regarded as a prodigious achievement of the art.* It stood about 700 fathoms out to sea, and its ruins are still visible when the waters withdraw.† Louis XIII made his entry into la Rochelle on All Saints' Day, 1628. To punish the town for its rebellion he ordered its fortifications razed, its privileges abolished, and the priests and Roman Catholic religion, which had been banished from it, reinstated. . . . It is certain that la Rochelle would have remained loyal to its legitimate princes had the new opinions [of the Protestants] not been introduced into the town. From then on la Rochelle became, so to speak, the metropolis of the Calvinists in France, a haven for the

*According to Abbé Expilly, whose pages on la Rochelle are a rather endearing illustration of Roman Catholic bad conscience in the eighteenth century.

†A few twisted wooden forms, the foundations of the mole of 1627, can still be discerned at low tide today, lying off the old port. Their place is marked by a little tower—naturally called the Tour Richelieu. I have written the town's name "*la* Rochelle" on purpose, because the capital *L* was not used before the Revolution.

seditious, and a formidable bulwark which they were ever ready to throw up against royal authority. . . .³

That's what the youngsters of la Rochelle had been taught for the last century and a half.

"Thus it is," Jacques-Nicolas Billaud writes in his notebooks sometime around 1780, "that in every century the thirst for vengeance and resentment have cloaked themselves in the mantle of religion to enlist the aid of fanaticism in destroying an abhorred foe." In this passage he's talking about the St. Bartholomew's Day Massacre, but what France did to la Rochelle was no less, except that it was methodical and military.

> The people most deeply attached to the principles of honor, the people held to be the most peace-loving and civilized on earth [he's talking about the French], armed themselves in the name of God when their only object was to destroy a powerful party and sallied forth in cowardly guise to cut the throats of their defenseless fellow citizens, under cover of night. . . . Their very King was seen taking hideous delight in firing his harquebus from the windows of the Louvre upon his own subjects,* who came crying out loudly and imploring his aid against barbaric murderers.⁴

You are not to conclude from this that the Billauds are in any way associated with the RPRs. Their orthodoxy goes back as far as anyone's can, through a sound lineage of the gown: presidial court attorneys, notaries, a few aldermen;⁵ and the courts of Richelieu, followed by those of Louis XIV, had so painstakingly uprooted and neutralized every last weed, by exile and forced abjuration, that la Rochelle is now one of the most purely Catholic cities in the west.

But the Billauds are also firmly implanted in the town with the subtle smile and they identify with it body and soul. Jacques-Nicolas shows impatience and irritation whenever the talk turns to religion; he simply doesn't like the subject, and neither do the children he grows up with.

> The Place des Petits Bancs is situated in the best part of town and surrounded by pleasant homes. In the middle of the square stands a fountain, erected at the birth of the dauphin, son of Louis XIV, and known on that account as the Fontaine Dauphine. The fountain's basin is octagonal. Each side was originally faced with large bronze plaques depicting the most noteworthy exploits in the siege of la Rochelle, with inscriptions referring to the town's rebellion, conquest, and capitulation. One night, in 1718, these inscriptions were removed, and the military commander was never able to learn the identity of the author of so daring a feat.⁶

---

*He's referring here to the notorious incident attributed to Charles IX, on the eve of St. Bartholomew's Day, when he was said to have fired upon the Protestants cast into the Seine beneath his windows.

Nights in la Rochelle can be busy, on occasion.

Not far from the Place des Petits Bancs, on the corner of the rue de l'Escale and the rue de l'Abreuvoir, stands* one of the prettiest and most picturesque houses in town, in a neighborhood of arcades and half-timbered façades. That's where the Billauds live, in "the house of Nicolas Venette," and have been living since grandfather Simon at the beginning of the century; and that's where Jacques-Nicolas was born, the son of another Nicolas, deputy chief prosecuting attorney in the *cour des aides,* and Henriette-Suzanne Marchand, "also of honorable family."[7] The second story of the Venette house, built about 1660, sports six gray stone busts of famous physicians, including Aesculapius and Hippocrates, looking very dignified in their round bonnets and resembling the quaint carvings on cathedral porches; Latin sayings recommending tolerance to the passerby are carved between the tall windows with their small square panes.[8]

The memory of Nicolas Venette, however, "professor of surgery and anatomy," is not cherished by the Oratorian fathers who cultivate the mind of Jacques-Nicolas:

> In 1589, under the name of Salocini of Venice, he had a book printed in Amsterdam entitled *La Génération de l'homme, ou le Tableau de l'amour conjugal* ["The generation of man, or the image of conjugal love"—*Trans.*], a work highly pernicious to young minds, in which the author proffers many a futile and dangerous precept. The book went through several printings in French and was translated into German and Flemish; that is to say, it was far more successful than it deserved to be.[9]

Did Jacques-Nicolas ever get a glimpse of this abomination, which may have been written in the room in which he was born? There is no proof that he did; but the first texts produced by his own pen exude, alongside the regulation legal pathos, a distinctly salacious flavor, as though Dr. Venette's spirit of ribaldry had impregnated the very walls of his birthplace. When he reviews the relatively humdrum phases of his own "first age," which he outlines in a rough draft for a biographical novel, his governess does nothing "but chatter and flirt" and he describes his own mother as being both pious and bemused by the ambivalent attentions of her father confessor. And when they set out to find a tutor to teach him his ABCs, they have no better luck:

> At the very first enquiry that was made to find such a person, Rose, my mother's chambermaid, proposed an abbé whom she described as her cousin. She was a pretty girl, which means that my father could not refuse her, and so her kinsman was engaged to teach me what he himself did not know.
>
> Following the custom, this young man was making a rather mediocre prepara-

---

*And it still stood there in 1979, in the pedestrian precinct that has turned the center of town into a delight.

tion for the priesthood, but Providence had another fate in store for him, so chance sorted everything for the best. The room designated for my lessons led into the room where Rose worked, and while my parents were trustingly imagining the tutor engaged in the assiduous cultivation of my mind, he was in fact engaged in paying assiduous court to his cousin.

Curiosity is an attribute of every age. One day, impelled by it, I tiptoed to the door that stood ajar, to see what was going on between the two cousins. As I looked, M. l'Abbé was kissing Rose and, imitating Dr. Pangloss, no doubt,* rehearsing to his cousin the lessons in experimental physics he had received at his school; but I was too young to understand the objectives and charms of the tête-à-tête.[10]

Was it to this same libertine pair that he was sent, in the *pension bourgeoise* they may have opened in la Rochelle, with financial assistance from Billaud's father, after it became impossible to keep them in the house? In any event, he complains of the food there. "Going without meals is the most common form of punishment in such houses, and it is easy to guess the reason why: it means a saving for the master. But the child's stomach, already spoiled by the inferior quality of what food he is given, is yet further enfeebled by this additional measure of economy. For three consecutive years my parents seem almost to have forgotten my existence in this pernicious retreat. At last, they remembered it, and removed me,"[11] only to enroll him, presumably as a day pupil, in the town collège, whose archives have preserved the record of a prize won by him for a Latin prose composition. This was a relatively modest establishment with a principal and five teachers, the Oratorians having, once again, taken over the facilities of the Jesuits. They had occupied the three parish churches in town the moment it was reclaimed for Rome, and conducted themselves with their customary urbanity as missionaries among the heathen.

"Upon the revocation of the Edict of Nantes, the Oratorian priests strove to good effect in la Rochelle to bring back a great many Protestants to the Roman Catholic Church, employing for this purpose the method of public and private disputations and lectures, conducted by their ablest people."[12]

Billaud makes his first great friends there; a few of the fathers exert themselves to make him feel wanted and compensate to some extent for his parents' lack of affection—not that they actually neglected him, but they were certainly remote. He always speaks of them with respect, never anything stronger.† For the Oratorians, on the other hand, he has nothing but praise, at least in 1786:

*So Billaud is also a reader of Voltaire, whose Pangloss, in *Candide,* is a very colorful figure.
†Until his deportation to Cayenne in 1795; thereafter, he maintains an affectionate but never emotional correspondence with them until their deaths—in 1804 for his mother and 1809 for his father.

"At last [in the heyday of the Jesuits], a new order arose, founded on sincere devoutness, zeal, and a love of doing good to others; seeking no attachment other than that formed by good will, having no desire beyond that of being useful and no laws other than those dictated by honor and virtue, it became at once an object of jealousy to the Society of Jesus. The Congregation of the Oratory could count among its members men of the very highest merit."[13]

His tune changes when he writes about the Collège d'Harcourt, where his parents send him to put the traditional Parisian polish on his education. This was the great uprooting—the trip to Paris alone in the stagecoach, the excited embarrassment of finding himself, before his fifteenth birthday, squeezed into a jolting box against the bodies of unknown women. In his head he spins a whole fairy tale out of the journey: one of these creatures, hardly more than a child herself, is traveling disguised as a boy; and, can you imagine, she mistakes his room in the inn for her own, and if the poor boy had not been so scared—

Young Billaud has plenty of imagination. It would be equally unwise to take at face value everything he says about his arrival at the old school at the top of the rue de la Harpe near the Sorbonne—a venerable place, its reputation strongest in the provinces—which had been founded by Canon d'Harcourt in 1280 and maintained for many years by secular priests from the diocese of Paris.* Hérault de Séchelles and Talleyrand both attended it. In his tale of his abrupt sexual initiation and the picaresque mishaps that allegedly accompanied his first communion, how much is invention, how much reality? Despite the clouds of fantasy in which Billaud envelops his account of his youth, we should listen to it: he may not actually have experienced those scabrous incidents in the Collège d'Harcourt, but he certainly dreamed that he did. Like that other Nicolas at the opposite end of the social scale, Edme-Nicolas Restif de la Bretonne, the writer-peasant-laborer who embroidered so many and such varied versions of his early loves and who composed his "scandalous" books on type in his printshop and sold them himself, a stone's throw away from the school in which the Billaud child is becoming a very undeluded young man. Any schoolboy who had a little pocket money and spent a few terms on the Montagne Sainte-Geneviève in the 1770s will have had plenty of opportunity to read *Le pied de Fanchette, Le Paysan perverti,* or *La Vie de mon père*[14] ["Fanchette's foot," "The perverted peasant," "My father's life"—*Trans.*]; and there is a distinctly Restifian flavor about Billaud's Parisian escapades:

---

*Two brothers were born during his childhood in la Rochelle: Henri in 1762 and Benjamin in 1768. His departure for Paris cannot be dated exactly, but took place sometime in 1770 or 1771.

Our arrival was now imminent, and every heart beat faster as we drew near the capital. The conversation was all of the pleasures and rare things to be found there. As for me, who had heard tell such marvels of it in my province, I expected to see nothing but palaces and noble edifices. What was my amazement, then, when I beheld, within the town, small shacks built of mud and roofed with straw, hovels, narrow, twisting alleyways, and then houses the only noteworthy feature of which was their enormous height; because in those days I had not learned that a painting must have shadow, to throw its finer features into relief.[15]

This is not exactly Brissot's rapturous discovery of the Paris he saw when the King had just turned twenty and he stepped out of the stagecoach from Chartres. And for poor Nicolas-Joseph, or the character in which he cast himself, this is only the beginning:

On my second day in the Collège d'Harcourt, the schoolfellow to whom I was closest—for this is a place in which acquaintances are soon struck up—asked if I wanted him to come see me at night, when everyone was asleep. I gladly accepted his offer and awaited him, sitting fully dressed on my bed. He came about eleven.

"Not in bed yet?" he asked.

"No, I was afraid of falling asleep, and besides, we'll be more comfortable for talking this way."

"But I've come to play with you."

"What kind of play?"

"Get in bed, my friend, and I'll teach you."

Indeed, a few minutes more and I was, unfortunately, only too edified. The ensuing nights saw me repeating the lessons I had learned; I even moved beyond those of my first friend, and other schoolmates soon became the companions of my pleasures, or rather, I joined in their debauches and infamies.[16]

Restif or Rousseau? In its exhibitionistic earnestness, the story of Billaud's first communion is very much in the line of the *Confessions:*

In every letter, my father never failed to ask why I did not make my first communion, and I took great care not to tell him that a wretched sin of habit was the only obstacle; but now there was no drawing back. No one can leave the school without consummating this sacrifice, and I had only six more months to go. One day I finally made up my mind, and went to present myself at the tribunal of penitence. After charging myself with all my sins, I was told by my director that I would have to make a general confession, and he gave me one week in which to prepare for it.

Why cudgel one's brain for hours on end to remember some sin committed last month or a year ago? It is far easier to consult those little manuals that are made to assist one's memory by presenting tables of every conceivable error. I thought they might help me. I turned over the pages of chapters entitled "against God," "against one's neighbor," etc., etc., without the slightest risk of a stumble or a fall, but gad! when I came to the one called "against the self," how I shuddered! How is it possible, when one has fiery blood and an imagination that can be kindled by a spark, to read without gasping particulars of which the obscene and waggish Grécourt* offers but a bare outline?

Upon the instant, the fibers of my brain quailed, a thousand burning darts inflamed my heart. I lost all control, the book fell from my hands.[17]

The poor lad wrestles like an angel; away he speeds to throw himself at the feet of his director, who, with the best of intentions, sends him reeling from Scylla to Charybdis:

"You have one refuge. Commit yourself into the hands of the Mother of God, invoke her aid, that she may grant unto you her wisdom and chastity."

I entered a chapel dedicated to her. The first thing to strike my sight was a painting in which she is depicted suckling her child. Lord, how beautiful she was! With what artistry the painter had invested his work! What a bewitching pose! A gown, admirably indicating the beauties it hid, showed the half of a naked, alabaster bosom crowned by a rosebud which the most adorable fingers in the world seemed to be pressing softly in order to extract from it a few drops of milk. With her head tilted carelessly to one side, she seemed in that state of happy abandon that so often corresponds to sensual pleasure. A childish smile played expressively over her countenance. In my deranged condition, it seemed to me that her eyes, filled with soft languor, were fixed amorously upon me.

I stared at her enthralled. My soul flitted to my lips, seeking to mingle with the partner it cried out for. Beloved, sinister illusion! I was infatuated with an inanimate object. What impetuous desires that cold and lifeless image inspired in me! It was too much. I could bear no more; nature triumphed over reason and I succumbed.[18]

In church! A fine way to behave. The poor boy expected the temple walls to come crashing down on his head. He'd sooner die than confess the place in which this sin was committed—to his director, that is, because he doesn't have much difficulty talking about it to one of his friends, who finally delivers him from his anguish:

"There's no getting round the fact that you have chosen a rather unusual theater in which to gratify your pleasures. But if it is true that we become guilty when we satisfy desires that God has given us, then, He being everywhere, the deed cannot be made worse by the place."

Well, then, what about that confession? A bagatelle!

"When one has on one's conscience a deed one thinks is serious enough to warrant the refusal of absolution, one doesn't confess it."

"Heavens, my friend, what are you advising me to do?"

*Joseph Willart de Grécourt, 1684–1743, an author of light verse. According to the *Dictionnaire de Lebas,* "Few eighteenth-century poets better illustrated the dissipation, gaiety, and immorality of the period known as the Regency." Billaud was a widely read youth, it seems.

"What I do myself when I am forced to take communion. If I sin in doing so, it is those who have compelled me who must take the responsibility."

"What! You have never had the slightest remorse?"

"Never."

So this boy, who may have been Billaud and with whom he certainly identifies himself, duly communes in a state of mortal sin, and loses his faith by the end of the story. After dutifully ingurgitating the catechism of his day, he fails to digest it, and presents his conclusions in a sort of historic panorama at the close of which Jacques-Nicolas's philosophy is stated plainly for all time:

Religion is the work of priests. To achieve their ends, they took the name of the God they served. Credulity and superstition came hard on the heels of ignorance and it was easy for them to dazzle gross and stupid people with a stern frown, a superficial morality, and, above all, a great deal of magic and charlatanism. In short, their wealth increased, their power became boundless, kings themselves were little better than their slaves and held authority from them alone. At last, after centuries of darkness, a new dawn came to enlighten the world. Man acquired knowledge and learned how to think. He opened their books, and what did he find in them? Truth and falsehood all jumbled together. At once the philosophers set out to write, bringing the absurdity of their dogma into the light of day. Then, ashamed of being their dupes for so long, we changed from fanaticism to irreligion and, after believing too much, ended by believing nothing.[19]

FONTAINE DE LA CAILLE AT LA ROCHELLE

# 58

SEPTEMBER 1786

## Icily Regular and Honest

1774: back to the West. Billaud, still buffeted by the winds of family tradition, studies law at Poitiers. He doesn't really have the "stuff" to make a barrister, if only because his delivery is dispassionate and plodding. He wants to write; he begins an "epistolary novel" and a diary of his childhood, in a beautiful molded script with big bars crossing his *t*'s to assert his worth, and quite unusually good spelling for his day, showing only an occasional hesitation, which was universal, as to the doubling of consonants. Then he returns to la Rochelle and, sometime around 1778, when he is twenty-two, steps into the profession and practice of his father. He prepares briefs. He negotiates suits between ship outfitters and agents. Beneath the ashes, the embers glow. His mind is on other things.

He composes, for his private perusal, angry pages on the condition of the peasants, the injustice of which he can see at firsthand as he strolls around the farm at Varenne. "I confess that everything I observe is far from my former idea of the countryside. After reading the engaging works of Virgil and Horace I fancied that true anguish was to be found only in gilded halls. But today. . . . Can joy exist for a class of men, consumed by poverty, who feel themselves to be the mere calamities of a state?" He gives attentive consideration to the misfortunes created by the *corvée*—a labor tax for the upkeep of the roads—in the poorest hamlets, where roads are always laid for the convenience of the powerful. He recounts the suit brought by a poor wine-growing woman against the royal subdelegate* "who bought a country home a quarter of a league from here" and then sent "men armed with long poles to lay a new road down the middle of our vines." She and her husband protested, while their servant, with the good sense of the downtrodden, chided them:

"You were wrong. We must flatter the powerful even when they do us injury, and when the Good Book commands us to kiss the hand that smites us [*sic*], it is so that it will not smite us even harder."[1]

So,

At first we swallowed our sorrow. But my husband, knowing that our seigneur had been paid damages for the loss of his right of *huitain,*† thought he could ask for damages too, but he was refused, with threats. Then, beside himself, he cried aloud against the injustice, and would you believe, Sir, what they did to silence him? They decided to ruin us utterly by forcing us to sell this little property. They put us down for double on the *tailles*** and, at the time of year when we needed our horses and wagon most, they ordered them to work on the *corvée*. My husband was desperate, and refused. But that was just what the barbarians were waiting for, and they sent for him with four horsemen of the marshalcy, to each of whom we had to give 6 francs a day for the trouble it took them to carry him to prison, where he remains today.[2]

Billaud then had his first and long-lasting—lifelong—taste of middle-class bad conscience in regard to the "fourth third" of the nation, 15 to 18 million miserable wretches:

*This might today be a subprefect (in France). Since Turgot's time the *corvée,* reckoned in man-hours, was often paid in cash, but that was not much use to the majority of the peasants who had none (to put it mildly) in 1786.

†A sort of "value-added tax," we might say today, amounting to an eighth of the retail price of produce sold by farmers, particularly in the *généralité* of la Rochelle.

**"They doubled our direct taxation."

I am appalled to see beings who were born my fellow-creatures and are condemned, from the first breath they draw, to live eternally in want and be harassed
ignominiously without so much as the right to complain.

A second self, the other voice in the dialogue you invent as you go along,
answers:

You have just condemned yourself unknowingly; you have a share in this injustice
against which your soul rises up. It is we, it is the utility of men of our rank, that
necessitates the poverty of those you pity: if they were well off and could live
without working, then you and I would want bread, and the nabob, despite his
gold, would either starve or be compelled to grasp a sharp, heavy pick in his soft
and effeminate arm and go out with the dweller of the countryside to brave wind
and storm and force the earth to bring forth fruit.

These lessons were at least as much good as those I learned at school.

Something is wrong somewhere. Jacques-Nicolas is somehow unable to
fold himself up in the Billaud linen cupboard, between his father, mother,
brothers, servants, and clients. He writes a play about the woman of his
dreams, ineffably pure, of course, La Femme comme il n'y en a plus [A true
old-fashioned girl"—Trans. ]*—not to be confused with the women for whom
one can feel contempt (even if one secretly swoons in front of a painting of
the Virgin) because they sleep with men other than oneself. There are ladies
of the latter sort in la Rochelle, for example, and he pillories them with perfect
small-town spitefulness, using the Lysistrata of Aristophanes as a model.[3] It was
presumably that little whiff of scandal that got the play staged by local actors,
and hissed by audiences. He and his town have had a falling-out. He and his
parents too? A cooling off, at any rate—assuming, that is, there ever was any
warmth between them before. He'd caught a glimpse of Paris beyond the
windows of the Collège d'Harcourt. In 1781, he goes back.

He vegetates for a few months in the waiting rooms of parlement attorneys and barristers on the King's Council, drafting a memorandum here and
a brief there. He's worth more than this sort of hand-to-mouth existence. The
Oratorian fathers come through: they had seen in him the makings not so much
of a teacher as of a good administrator, the kind of quiet, precise person who
keeps the wheels turning. And then, he had a habit of keeping and filing every
scrap of paper he saw. The la Rochelle Oratorians get him a recommendation,
from their bishop, to the directors of their mother house, the Oratory of Juilly
where Bérulle and Condren worked—their Vatican, their Mecca! In March
1783 Billaud is engaged there as prefect of studies, which means he is the
syllabus and timetable man, the man of discipline and contacts with the pupils.
But does it also mean that he has to become a priest? His younger brother

*The text has apparently been lost. Here at least is one thing in common between his youth
and that of Collot d'Herbois: they both wrote for the theater.

Benjamin is staggered at the thought, and puts the question to him straight. Just the right kind of sharp, sensitive little brother, that Benjamin. He's twelve years younger than Jacques-Nicolas but already chafing at the paternal bit, while the middle brother, Henri, stolidly prepares for an uneventful life as a judge. In Benjamin, the muted social indignation of his elder is radicalized into open protest.* All the more reason to give the big brother a jolt, in the standoffish form of address *(vous)* that was customary in upper-middle-class families:

> My dear brother,
>
> Two years of absence have done nothing to efface from my heart the memory of a brother who will reign in it forever. You might, it is true, have found my own long silence unpardonable, if you had not been so fully aware of the sincere attachment I have always felt for you.
>
> One by one, I have learned all the things that have happened to you since your departure from la Rochelle. Your entrance into the Oratory, in particular, pained no less than it astonished me. I had always thought you nursed a great disrelish for such places. The reasons inducing you to go there must have been potent indeed. Although I do not know that it is true, I do fear that in this new estate you will not be so happy as I should desire.[4]

Benjamin can relax. Nicolas does not even take the minor orders, and neither does another teacher at Juilly, Joseph Fouché, who also hails from the west (Nantes).† He wears the severe black coat and little collar, but no cassock. He is a brother, not a father of the Oratory. This tolerance is a new development, an option not open to poor Daunou; the reason for it was the staggering teaching load they had to shoulder when they became the more or less universal successors to the evicted Jesuits. The shortage was so acute that they had no choice but to resort to "assistant masters," men who need not have a vocation or take vows but who would promise to obey the superiors and remain celibate, if not chaste, as long as they taught in the Oratory.

So for a time there was a sort of "Père Billaud," as they called him, at Juilly; he was popular enough for a fellow teacher to write, years later, "He seemed a very good man, and perhaps he was so; perhaps, indeed, he was so all his life. . . ."** He even taught the top classes. He showed some ability as an amateur physicist, helping with the construction and launching, in 1784,

---

*He becomes one of the most fiery leaders of the Jacobins of la Rochelle.

†"Fouché de Nantes," he is later called. I shall analyze his childhood and youth in the next volume, and shall also describe the Oratory of Juilly in more detail, when Fouché enters it in September 1787, after leaving Vendôme. That date alone is enough to quash the legend, which a few historians accept as truth, of a meeting between Billaud and Fouché at Juilly; the former had already left when the latter arrived.

**Written by Arnault, a rabid counterrevolutionary, in his *Mémoires d'un sexagénaire;* most of the time he cannot speak of the men of those days without choking on his spleen.

of a *montgolfière;* and the rather endearing lines to the King attached to the cradle slung from the balloon are attributed to him:

| | |
|---|---|
| Les globes de savon ne sont plus de notre âge; | [Our infant soapbubbles we've left behind, |
| En changeant de ballon, nous changeons de plaisir. | This larger sphere is our new delight. |
| S'il portait à Louis notre premier hommage, | Should the breezes wafting it King Louis find, |
| Les vents le souffleraient au gré de nos désirs.[5] | They will be following our fancy's flight.] |

But he's still cramped. He's marking time, not living. He's the wrong sort of material for the teacher factory. Father Petit, his director, and one of the most experienced "priest makers" in France, shows considerable acumen in the regulation report submitted to the superior general of the congregation to decide the fate of probationary staff. What shall we do with "Father Billaud" at the end of his trial year?

> Judging from the manner in which he reads Latin, he does not know it very well. Is he clever? I have not sufficient evidence to say. He is well endowed with self-love, however, and I consider him a worldly person* clothed in Oratory dress, icily regular and honest, who has been at pains not to compromise himself, especially in the last few months, for at the outset he was not among the most industrious. Although he is judicious in his conduct I do not believe, having regard to his years, what he has been, and what he is, that he is suitable for the Oratory.[6]

A view in which the party himself concurs, although he may have tried to extend his term in this haven of security where he was well fed and looked up to but where, "being more worldly than was commensurate with the modest society to which he then belonged, he was in truth avid for literary renown and was secretly employed by the theater."[7] Still stage-struck, eh? How did he make contact with such people, ones an Oratorian brother cannot properly frequent: actors, players, minstrels, people who are still refused the comfort of "Christian burial," however famous and feted by the great they may be before they die? Was it through Larive, "actor ordinary to the King," i.e., one of the top people in the French Acting Company? Or was it Granger, the male lead in the "Italian" company? Billaud submits a tragedy to the former and a comedy called *Murgan* to the latter; both are politely rejected. Is it true, as they whisper at Juilly and will later print in Paris, that Jacques-Nicolas, not content with getting a play on the boards in la Rochelle, takes a real leap into the unknown by

---

*His meaning here is "a man made to live in the contemporary world," hence without the aspiration to ego-annihilation on which the doctrine of Bérulle and Condren is founded.

sharing for a few months, as adviser and possibly stage director, the adventures of a company that was touring between Nantes and Bordeaux? Would that be why his parents pushed him off to Paris? And could that be the explanation of the Delphic "what he has been" in Father Petit's report? Billaud never tells us. He talks a lot about his childhood but never about his youth, as though he didn't have one. True, a youth spent at Juilly . . .

1785. Here he is in Paris, in January, not exactly thrown out of Juilly but, let's say, encouraged to resign. He's made it up with his dad, life is now the color of the Aunis pastels; he wasn't really cross with him *but,* just as he hadn't been sacked by the fathers *but,* and he tried teaching *but*; anyway, here he is now, for good, at the bar, an attorney in the Paris Parlement, how could his parents not be pleased by that? All three of their sons will sail hand in hand over the ocean of jurisprudence. All's well that ends well.

There remains a little problem about the name of the firstborn. Billaud is a bit skimpy for the Parisian gentlemen, so Jacques-Nicolas does like everybody else and fabricates a touch of rustic nobility for himself. Daddy's farm comes in handy here: the name entered on the parlement records in 1785 is Billaud de Varenne.

At first he lives very modestly and on a shoestring, "at the home of Master Thiellement, cabinetmaker" on the rue Saint-Etienne-des-Grès running up from the rue Saint-Jacques to the site of the new Church of Sainte-Geneviève on the hill bearing the same name,* "which is frequented by all manner of artisans. There are quantities of butchers' shops, upholsterers, and old-clothes dealers. This is also the district of erudition; the many schools, the well-deserved fame of their professors, and the abundance of skilled engravers, printers in character and copperplate, booksellers, and print vendors have made this part of town celebrated. It is on their account that it has come to be called the Latin Country."[8] What a perpetual party, when your head is swimming in little libertine tableaus and you've come from la Rochelle via Juilly! These are happy hunting grounds for Jacques-Nicolas, who grumbles at having to forsake them for the right bank, even if it's only for a few months, when he camps rather than moves into lodgings in the Marais, at 2, rue de la Corderie, almost in the shadow of the tall tower of the Temple.

Around September 1785 he crosses the Seine again for good, back to the big village on the left bank where he can finally slough off the skin of solitude that had grown too small for him. This time it's the rue de Savoie, running from the rue Pavée to the rue des Grands Augustins, just behind and parallel to the quay of the same name, between the big monastery of monks who gave

*Today, rue Cujas. The building being completed at the top of the hill is the future Pantheon; it was originally meant to be a sort of second left bank cathedral, Saint-Sulpice having already become too small.

their name to that bit of town and the curious building that housed the fraternity of shoemakers "who take no vows and work for the public."9 Their building is tall and skinny, like every other one in the old part of Paris, and in it he dwells, close to the roof, in keeping with the hierarchy of fortune that divides the world by floors and allocates the most flights of stairs to the poorest. On the floor below him live two women, the Widow Doye and her daughter, who are endowed with affecting dignity and sweetness. The widow is a German from Osnabrück in Lower Saxony, whence her husband* brought her and their little girl when he came to die in Paris. The daughter is a creature of striking beauty, and how could her name be other than Anne-Angélique? "She is one of the most beautiful women one could ever hope to see."10 A queen's carriage, dimples, a hint of Germanic plumpness, dazzling skin, and just ten years younger than he—nineteen, as he's about to be thirty. This is the not-to-be-missed miracle. Without a hint of coyness she turns upon him that limpid gaze of true old-fashioned girl. She "knows how to behave,† has a gentle nature, unflagging good temper, and the loftiest soul. This is, in one word, what I cherish."11

He himself is no Valentino, however, for "although his face shows character" he is usually deemed to have "regular and insignificant features, a yellowish complexion, a narrow brow, staring eyes that squint slightly, and a long knife of a nose above an embittered and secretive mouth."12 But that's just the thrill of it; who knows what that mouth is so secretive about? Angélique does not see him the way the others do—it's what you call preference. And when, like thousands before them, the two have to pierce the protective shell that their families have secreted around their plans, the old parental egg indurated by years of opposition to chicks who must peck themselves free, Jacques-Nicolas uses that very word in his mollification of one of Angélique's brothers: "Your sister will never have occasion to repent of the preference she has deigned to bestow upon me. She will forever remain my life's companion, the adored wife chosen by my heart."13 Of course, Billaud Senior is also railing against this alliance with a dowerless child born a Protestant in the hinterland of Germany. All the better: it'll give the son another chance to deliver some home truths to the people in la Rochelle:

> My father, your name is the title that gives me some claim upon your affections. In this moment I am invoking that claim—would you refuse to acknowledge it? For two years I have had an inclination.** The match was not, in your eyes, a suitable one; Mlle Doye's lack of fortune made you doubt your son's happiness.

*Of—to my knowledge—undetermined occupation, but not a soldier. He may have gone to Germany as tutor.

†According to Billaud, in a letter to his father.

**He's cheating a bit: eighteen months at the outside, assuming he had already met Angélique when he was living on rue Saint-Etienne-des-Grès. But la Rochelle is a long way away.

And perhaps you also imagined that this was the effect of a passing whim, and so refused to bind the ties between us. But two years of constancy are proof that I shall never change. As for fortune: what price fortune, weighed against virtue? Besides, father, one is always happy when one can satisfy one's needs oneself.[14]

On the religious side, Billaud doesn't push provocation to the point of contracting marriage with a follower of the RPR. When they first began "keeping company," the young woman converted to the Roman Catholic faith and, under the law promulgated by Louis XIV for such cases, receives an annual pension of 150 francs, paid by the diocese out of the income of the Paris clergy.*

Jacques-Nicolas and Angélique are duly married, on September 12, 1786, by Father Debois de Rochefort, in front of the four evangelists painted by Restou in the choir of the tottering old Gothic church of Saint-André-des-Arts†—not, as one may imagine, in the presence of the parents, as this was obviously a "regularization" which they could not condone, but with the signature of some respectable witnesses: a cavalry captain, a parlement attorney, and two "bourgeois of Paris."[16]

They move, permanently as they fondly suppose, into rooms on the fourth floor of number 42 of the street which is also called Saint-André-des-Arts (because of the artisans) or des-Arcs (because one of the artisans made and sold bows), as you prefer; unless the name was derived from the vines of the Laas, a vineyard stretching back into the mists of time, that lay between the little bridge and the abbey of Saint-Germain, before Philip Augustus ordered a road put through it. Laas, Ars, Arcs, Arts? Who knows.

Billaud has his work cut out for him. Loved and admired at home, supplied by colleagues with jobs enough to pay the rent and buy their food, he can now sit down and write some of the things he has on his mind. Against religion, for example: *Le Dernier coup porté aux préjugé et à la superstition* ["Prejudice and superstition put out of their misery"—*Trans.*]. Or, on a more down-to-earth level, *Le Despotisme des ministres de France combattu par les droits de la Nation, par les lois fondamentales, par les ordonnances, par les jurisconsultes, par les orateurs, par les historiens, par les publicistes, par les poètes, enfin par les intérêts du peuple et l'avantage personnel du monarque* ["The despotism of the ministers of France, opposed by the rights of the nation, fundamental laws, statutes, men of law, orators, historians, publicists, poets, and, lastly, the interests of the people and the personal advantage of the monarch"—*Trans.*]. The labor of a Benedictine in revolt, on a scale commensurate with those years of thinking in dark corners. The first of these works is four hundred pages long, the second

---

*Reduced to 60 francs after the nationalization of the clergy's assets, and paid by the national treasury; she continues to receive this amount until 1793.[15]

†Torn down between 1800 and 1808. It stood on the site of the present-day Place Saint-André-des-Arts near the Pont Saint-Michel. Voltaire was baptized there.

over a thousand, three volumes worthy of its interminable title. Will they be published one day,* or must they remain meticulously packed away in his drawers alongside the sketches of his fictionalized childhood?[17] The future will tell. In the present what counts is, at last, to be. Billaud is dead and gone, Billaud-Varenne has begun—and why not, as he now makes bold to style himself, "Monsieur de Varenne"?[18]

# 59

## DECEMBER 1786

## *When the Hollow Mountain Comes Crashing Down*

And then, at the end of the year, in the flat grip of mid-winter, Louis XVI turns a page. It's all going to happen. After the convening of the notables, which he makes into his own private Versaillese coup de théâtre, nothing will ever be the same again. Everybody has been vaguely expecting something, but how could anything new come from him? So everybody is completely stunned when it happens, apart from the three ministers who've been pushing and prodding him for the last few months—Vergennes, Miromesnil, and, above all, the manufacturer of the Pandora's box unwittingly opened today by the King's chubby little hands: Calonne. Calonne's hour has come.

The French Revolution begins at about five o'clock in the afternoon of December 29, 1786, when the footmen place the lighted tapers in the King's *grand cabinet* for the *Conseil des Dépêches.*† At first it is a revolution within the monarchy. The straw, the fatal flick of a finger.

The minutes (not ordinarily kept), written afterwards in preparation for the Assembly of Notables, are unusually solemn and ceremonial, as though Calonne, in dictating them, did have some awareness that he was writing a rather spectacular opening paragraph:

"In the year of Grace one thousand seven hundred and eighty-six, thirteenth of the reign of Louis XVI, King of France and Navarre, on Friday, December 29, following the dispatch council, His Majesty announced that he

---

*They will, in 1789, allegedly in London and Amsterdam, and are swept along unnoticed in the floods of ink that then begin to pour.

†Cabinet meeting at which decisions were announced and instructions dispatched.

intended to convene an assembly of the most qualified persons of various conditions in his State, to communicate to them his intentions in regard to the relief of his people, the ordering of his finances, and the reform of several abuses."[1]

Less sonorous, more appropriate to the style of the reign, is the little statement that Louis XVI himself insists on reading out just before the Council rises—the literal text, so to speak, of the pebble that sends all the frogs flying.

> I am concerned with matters very important to the relief of my peoples, to the reform of several abuses, and to the ordering of my finances. Before giving orders to carry out my proposals, I have resolved to consult an Assembly of Notables. I have selected the persons who will compose it. Each secretary of state, acting for his department, will dispatch without delay the letters giving notice of the meeting, a model for which will be issued by M. the Keeper of the Seals. The proposals I shall have brought before the Assembly will be examined beforehand in my Council,[2]

the last sentence having been added to smooth the predictably ruffled feathers of the ministers not in the know—Castries, Ségur, and Breteuil. And indeed, at first all they can think is that nobody told them about it, Calonne's the fair-haired boy. The very next day the Maréchal de Castries consigns his hysterics to a letter to the King:

> Sire,
>     It is more respectful, and more in my character, to show Your Majesty the sharp grief I feel, rather than allow it to dishearten me in the performance of my duties, or my devotion to be weakened by it; I have served Your Majesty, and the King your grandfather, for forty-seven years, in different careers and in the most honorable employments; for six years, Sire, I have been ruining my health. I have the advantage of being seated first in Your Council; I have never showed any other concern there but for Your glory; and the kindness, esteem, and confidence of Your Majesty have been the only rewards I coveted; and nevertheless, Sire, You have determined upon the most outstanding event of Your reign without deigning to try my discretion and loyalty, and it is in public that I first learn of it.
>     There are matters, Sire, which appertain more directly to one or another department, but those affecting essentially the constitution of the State do not belong exclusively to any, and when Your Majesty deigns to show preferences from which I am excluded, in discussing matters of such moment, it gives me (through the rank which I see Your Majesty assigning to me) a wound which I do not believe I have deserved.[3]

Why, whoever said you could talk to the King of France in such a tone? Gone are the days, apparently, when Turgot was sacked for no more. Who would have dared to write a letter like that to Louis XIV? But then, would Louis XIV have written back the same day, and in so propitiating a vein?

I answer at once, M. le Maréchal, to set at rest your anxiety and your pains; I do not know why you say that you learned my decision in public when I myself announced it yesterday in the Council meeting. I know your administration and I have been satisfied with it; I have given you to understand so several times when you were worried about your health.

You are mistaken if you think there is any question of debating my projects; I may confide to you that they relate solely to arrangements for the allocation of taxes and have to do with absolutely nothing but finance.[4]

"Nothing but finance!" That's what Louis XVI thinks; and they let him think so. And in the proximity of the throne they go on wanting to think so for a long time to come. Here begins another great misunderstanding. For the first time in a century and a half the King "goes to the country," but he is under the impression that the subject of his going is a chicken in every pot. No question of condescending to talk politics to him, any more than to a pretty woman in a salon. But every individual in France who has his or her ears peeled for the heavy tread of the march toward *la Nation,* as people are already beginning to say, is firmly preparing, very much to the contrary, to talk about nothing but politics. It isn't just money that's at stake now, it is power.

Otherwise, why the notables? Calonne is anything but reckless; it's not a thirst for adventure that has impelled him to slip a dangerous explosive into the King's fumbling hands. Beginning with the summer of 1786, however, the royal treasury has been a hair's breadth away from bankruptcy. The deficit is over 100 million a year, repayment of the debt is 250 million in arrears; in other words, almost half of every year's income is virtually spent before anyone sees it. Payments of pensions, annuities, civil servants, sailors and soldiers, and the King's own creditors are beginning to lag and falter for want of cash in the till.

Borrow? From whom? People have lost confidence and parlement—the same parlement that has just acquitted Rohan and is thus *politically* at war with the Crown already—will not ratify any borrowing decrees without fresh security. And when we learn that in the last three years Calonne has appealed to direct and indirect savings to the tune of 653 million . . .*

Well, in that case, what about reducing expenditure—in the King's Household, for instance? By all means. We've been waiting long enough; but cuts there, even amputations, will not suffice. And what about new levies on the present taxpayers? "This was equally out of the question,† especially as 'the people' had been misled by a mirage of immediate relief at the end of the American war, and responding to their hopes by an increase in their tax burden would have exasperated even taxpayers as resigned as those of this regime."[5]

*For a rough equivalent in present-day terms, multiply by seven.
†According to Robert Lacour-Gayet, from whom I have also taken the following analysis.

Besides, parlement is on guard there too. "In short, it was necessary to enlarge the terms of the problem and create new taxable raw material, rather than adding to the pressure on that which already existed." To do this, the criteria for the levying of taxes on the wealthy and productive would have to be reorganized from top to bottom of the social scale. It was a matter of justice, ergo of organization, ergo of power, ergo of politics. Turgot had seen it clearly. Calonne had tried not to see it, and gone on improvising expedients in his own limited domain. But "his term in the government offers a striking illustration of the inability of a minister of finance to obtain effective results when his technical decisions, however excellent they may be, are not supported by an overall policy. So long as the system of taxation had not been revised by a general reform, the public coffers were doomed to empty faster than they could be filled."[6] France is living beyond its means.

Like M. Jourdain speaking prose,* Calonne is making revolutions but is totally unaware of the fact. He's acting as in a dream. On the one hand, he wants the cream of the kingdom, the biggest and the fattest, feeling flattered by his request for help and honored by a doff of the regal cap, to join him in intimidating the parlements and extracting from them the emergency measures needed to plug the most urgent financial holes. And on the other, he is counting on the King's authority and the majesty of the ritual of fealty to induce that very same cream voluntarily to desist from the "abuses" alluded to in the King's statement to his Council—that is, its own political, administrative, and fiscal privileges, which are successfully blocking any reordering of society.

As soon as they've untied their purse strings, of course, we'll send the notables back to their notability, and the Capetian monarchy will continue to wield a power that will be as absolute as ever but a little less lonely because it will be supported by provincial assemblies with a purely economic brief and a single function, the allocation of taxes. Calonne has had the devil of a time getting Louis XVI to consent to even this hypothetical delegation of sovereignty. Nothing's settled, all the work has still to be done, and even defined. But, after December 29, the comptroller general becomes the man who has stuck the tip of the scepter into the gears and therefore the target of mingled roars of hatred and acclaim. A reformer in the government? Darling, you can't mean it! Dear heart, I do: a reformer. One who has contrived to do what Turgot and Necker could not, i.e., advance upon the wealthy with outstretched hand, shoving the King before him like a hostage.

What a to-do! In the first days of 1787 Versailles, followed by Paris, begins to buzz like an overturned beehive.

On December 31 the *Journal de Paris* and *Mercure* try to set the tone for

*The main character in Molière's *Bourgeois Gentilhomme.*

later commentators with a text inspired by Calonne. At least the priests can use it in church after the sermon, which is how nine-tenths of the population first hear the news:

> The resolution upon which the King has determined, to communicate to an Assembly of Notables of his kingdom the great designs which His Majesty has elaborated for the good of his state and the relief of his subjects, can but be universally applauded. The nation will be overjoyed to see its sovereign deigning to move closer to it, becoming increasingly one with it. Nothing could be better calculated to raise to enthusiasm the feelings by which it is already animated; nothing could better nourish and sustain its patriotism. . . . There is every reason to believe that we may look forward to the most fruitful results; never has an event aroused greater and more justified interest.[7]

So much for the official attitude; but it's so baldly obsequious that the "sovereign deigning to move closer" raises a general outcry (one figure of speech already dead, thus), and two days later Calonne has to send both papers a revised version, but it reaches them too late for the first editions.[8] Of course it ought to read "sovereign moving closer," you numbskulls!

A little more reserved, firmly committed to the "happy medium," the unknown editor of the *Correspondance secrète* judiciously weighs the pros and cons for his noble foreign subscribers:

> The great news of the day is the convening of a national assembly [*sic*]; it is producing a most lively sensation in the public. That our monarch should call the nation to his side, like a father sending for his children to inform them of his intentions, is received with no less admiration than gratitude: one likes to see him rise above the ill-founded fears that, for one hundred and sixty years, have seemed to separate the sovereign from his subjects. . . . A better system of taxation appears to be the main occasion for the event, and M. de Calonne, more adept than his predecessors, has put into practice the ideas of M. Turgot and M. Necker in such a way as to avoid making the enemies they created for those men, while at the same time achieving the same ends. There is much conjecture as to what will be discussed in this august assembly. There is talk of territorial taxation, alienation of demesne, simplification of tax collection, etc. . . . One malcontent said recently, at the close of a lively speculation as to the true reasons for the assembly:
>     "Do you know with what it most certainly will be concerned? I shall tell you: with the means of taking as much money as possible away from us."[9]

Still more reserved, yet resolutely pro, is the reaction of Jean-Sylvain Bailly,* the most famous astronomer of France, who is becoming a sort of "Buffon of the stars." He shows the restrained quiverings of those who are keeping their imaginations in check:

*Born September 15, 1736 in Paris; became famous in 1775 with the publication of the four volumes of his enormous *Histoire de l'astronomie ancienne.* We shall be meeting him often in the next volume, when he becomes president of the first National Assembly in May 1789, and

On Friday, December 29, 1786, I dined with M. le Maréchal de Beauvau;* that was when the news of an Assembly of Notables first reached me. I was deeply stirred. I foresaw a great event, a change in the present state of things and even in the form of government. I did not foresee the Revolution as it actually came about, but that, I believe, no man could have done; yet the deplorable state of the treasury made my conjectures credible enough. Want of money had rendered the government weak and dependent. This gave a great advantage to the governed, and I presumed they would be quick-witted enough to make use of it. Such an assembly, of 150 of the most distinguished citizens, from all classes [?], who were occupied with the most important affairs of state, could not fail to effect a great reform. This assembly, this meeting, was an image of the entire nation; these were citizens deliberating less upon matters of state than upon their own interests. For a number of years the finest minds had been expending their energies in meditating upon political economy, and the assembly, convened to give opinions and views upon the administration of the kingdom, must unite all minds upon this point as a matter of course, and draw to it the attention of the whole nation. Now when, after long sleep, or rather absence, one turns to reflect upon one's affairs and finds them in a dilapidated condition, it is hard to forget that one is entitled to set them in order. I accordingly foresaw, not a revolution, but a change, which, although I could not define its nature, must be to the nation's advantage. When, in a century of enlightenment, recourse is had to reason, then reason must ultimately prevail.[10]

La Fayette is delighted to find himself among the notables, but for once in his life he shows caution. Maybe because the event will deprive him of another grand tour and one last enlightened despot to add to his collection: he will not meet Catherine the Great in the same year as Frederick II.† France is calling me, my dear general . . .

To Washington, on February 13:

The Empress of Russia is traveling to the Crimea and has kindly invited me to come; but I have suddenly been prevented by an event that has not occurred in France for many a long year. The King has convened, for the end of this month, an Assembly of Notables composed of the principal persons of each order of the kingdom who have no office at Court. There will be 144 members, archbishops, bishops, nobles, presidents of the different courts, and mayors. Your only ac-

---

then first mayor of Paris. After sharing with La Fayette the responsibility for the fusillade of July 17, 1791 on the Champ de Mars, he is guillotined on October 10, 1793. At this point (1787) he has shown no signs of a political itch and is dividing all his time between science and philanthropy.

*Prince and maréchal of France since the promotions of 1783, he distinguished himself at the siege of Prague during the Seven Years' War. He becomes a minister for one short moment in 1789.

†Catherine's notorious trip to the Crimea will be recounted in the next volume.

quaintances in this assembly are the Comte d'Estaing, the Duc de Laval,* and your humble servant, who are among the thirty-six representatives of the nobility. The King's letter announces his plan to submit to the notables for consideration the financial situation, which must be improved, the means of relieving the burdens upon the people, and many abuses that need to be reformed. You will easily understand that the root of all this is the desire to get money, in some form or another, so as to restore the balance between income and expenditure, for extravagance has made the latter monstrously large. But to achieve this end no way could be more patriotic, more open, or more noble. The King and his minister, M. de Calonne, very much deserve our thanks, and I hope that a tribute of gratitude and good will will reward this popular† measure. My most ardent and fondest hope is that the outcome of this meeting may be assemblies of the people in the provinces, the abolition of many impediments to trade, and a change in the status of the Protestants, all things for which I mean, with my friends, to strive with all my heart, and to which I shall devote my meager energies. . . . I shall keep you informed of the proceedings at the assembly, not only because nothing that concerns me can be foreign to my dear general, but also because anything that affects the happiness of twenty-six million people is interesting in itself.[11]

Talleyrand, acting for Calonne, sends a sort of "for publication in your columns" notice to the German press via Mirabeau, who is still in Berlin; to Versailles, thus, his chief value these days is as a public relations man:

Here, my dear Count, is the substance of what one would like to see in the German papers, and the French-language publications circulated in Germany, on the Council's deliberations last Friday the 29th as regards the convening of the notables of the kingdom. It is desired that this information should appear without delay. You cannot too highly praise the subject [King] for this enterprise. He must be supported by unanimous acclaim so that he may succeed in this great undertaking; above all, he must be shown how much glory will redound to his credit. If the articles are to have any effect, however, they must not be all alike; so you can rearrange the material as you think most fit, taking only the gist of what I send . . . ,[12]

and since what he sends is the text for the gazettes of December 31, including the "deigning," the need for adaptation and amplification is all the more acute.

Mirabeau paws, snorts, rears, and he's off. Let me out of here! This is the news he's been waiting for in the very marrow of his bones. They can't really imagine he's going to go on playing boy scouts in Berlin.

My heart has not aged, and if my enthusiasm has been somewhat dampened it is not yet dead. I felt it today; I look upon the day on which you inform me of the

---

*He served in America under Rochambeau.
†[To be taken here as meaning both "involves the people" (a few of them, anyway) and "finds favor with the people"—*Trans.* ]

convening of the notables, no doubt shortly to be followed by that of the National Assembly, as one of the happiest of my life. I see a new order of things, which can regenerate the monarchy. I would think myself a thousand times honored to be the least of the secretaries of that assembly, the idea of which it was my good fortune to have first, and which has great need that you should belong to it, or rather that you should become the life and soul of it. . . . To remain here, condemned to the torments of brutes, to plumb and probe the slimy sinuosities of an administration that distinguishes each day of its existence by some new act of pusillanimity and incompetence, is what I no longer have strength to do, because I see no use in it. So have me recalled at once, dear master. . . .[13]

You're not going to make the world over without me! As for his copyright in the matter, the idea of the Assembly of Notables "which it was my good fortune to have first," there is no confirmation of this, but Calonne's little clique had been tossing it around for months. And Mirabeau sticks to his claim to the end, even if he is speedily forced to accept the fact that he is not going to be so much as the least of the secretaries, the intermediaries between the event and posterity: "Whatever rights I may appear to have over the issue of an idea that was mine alone and for which, I may say in passing, I have worked out all the details, I cannot believe our government has reached such a degree of enlightenment as to desire that I should form part of an assembly of notables, and even less in the position to which the public voice [?] is calling me, that of secretary."[14] But never fear, I'm on my way, and will in my own person play all the parts of an alternate France, if need be in the wings. The horses are at the door.

Somewhere between the Cévennes and the sea, a man made of purity and candor is almost unable to contain his hopes; it's too much. Jean-Paul Rabaut, the still youthful pastor of the Protestants of Nîmes, who is known as "Saint-Etienne" in the Lower Languedoc underground where he went to school with the birds,* is the son of Paul Rabaut of glorious memory, the "pastor of the Wilderness." Jean-Paul has watched the erosion of the country's finances, and Calonne's crabwise approach to the Assembly of Notables, with the acuteness of gaze that is peculiar to all provincials, whom the Parisians are always putting down because "they're not there and don't know," but who, by virtue of their very remoteness from the event, can often see more clearly how things come about. Especially when, as in the case of Rabaut, the essential conditions of their lives and those of their fellows hang upon the breath of fresh air that this

---

*Rabaut Saint-Etienne, born in 1743, plays a major role among the men of liberty, beginning in the next volume. He "comes up" to Paris in 1787 to help La Fayette obtain civil status for the Protestants, becomes a delegate to the Constituent Assembly and then to the Convention, and remains in the foreground of the Revolution until his proscription in June 1793, for siding with the Girondins. Guillotined December 1793.

assembly may, at long last, blow into the civic jail inhabited by the followers of the "reformed" religion.

> Never did the Court have a happier time, for it was the Court that was consuming the greater part of the public substance; the festivities and prodigalities there beggared description. The Court was entertained, the people were destitute. But there is, in states that live by borrowing, a hidden regulator, the product of the interrelations of all who speculate in trade, and that is public credit; it is composed of the confidence of every individual, it looks down upon administrations from above, penetrates their intentions, and divines their most secret thoughts. And public credit was gone. Borrowing, which had been so easy under the virtuous ministry of M. Necker, found no takers under that of M. de Calonne; taxes could be raised no higher; and the King, moved by the people's distress, spoke the word that precipitated the age of the Revolution:
>
> "I want no more taxes or borrowing."*
>
> M. de Calonne, therefore, laboring under an immense burden, sought in his bold and fertile mind a means of saving the situation and preserving his credit. Secretly, for several months, he prepared his plans for reform, which granted one or two of the people's demands and sacrificed the clergy, and he arranged his accounts so that the enormity of the deficit should fall upon his predecessors' shoulders. In this way his own name was saved, and he hoped to embellish it further by persuading the nation that he was the rejuvenator of France.
>
> But schemes that were in truth quite vast in scope could not be carried out by a single minister: moreover, he felt that if he put them forward alone and unsupported, he would be unable to hold out against the host of enemies his plans would create for him. He therefore conceived the idea of obtaining support for his aims in the form of a sort of national fiat; and, not wishing to convene the Estates-General, the very thought of which frightened him, he hit upon an Assembly of Notables, and, at last, presented his ideas to the King. Louis XVI always desired the people's happiness. He was most impressed by the useful reforms the minister was submitting to him and often worked on them together with their author, taking pleasure in a task from which the skillful courtier had removed all the thorns. The King was looking forward to the Assembly of Notables as the purest delight that could be experienced by his well-intentioned heart, and, in the end, he ordered it to convene.
>
> It is impossible to convey the nation's amazement at this totally unexpected event.[15]

On the con side, the drumrolls are at first decently, but barely, muted. Richelieu, the decrepit libertine, roams the salons asking what fate Louis XIV would have visited upon the minister who had dared to propose an Assembly of Notables to *him*. The Vicomte de Ségur, despite the fact that he had been one of La Fayette's companions in America, goes around saying, "The King has

---

*There is no other trace of this statement. It is an act of charity on Rabaut's part, prompted by the spirit of the moment.

resigned . . . ," but maybe, when you come to think of it, that was his way of being pro.[16]

Breteuil is silent, and, more to the point, so is the Queen; and as her silence automatically means the silence of the Polignacs and all their clan, that makes a lot of mutes, especially if we add the King's brothers and the Condés. Orléans, too, perhaps mute with astonishment, is saying nothing for the moment. Is it the Queen's thoughts that Mercy-Argenteau, ambassador of Vienna to France, is expressing when he writes to his master that all he sees in Calonne's initiative is "a few little tricks to get money, the one and only credible object of everything that is now going on"? His reply from the Queen's brother runs along the same lines; the least one can say is that Joseph II the Reformer is not exactly panting with enthusiasm:

"I personally believe that it is a trick by the ministry and the comptroller general who, needing support and having to propose objectionable and unpleasant measures, want to be able to lean upon the opinion, or at least the semblance of an opinion, of these 140 assembled gentlemen; but they are not the Estates-General, and so their opinion will not be that of the nation."[17]

The old conservative Kaunitz, who is still chancellor of the Empire and still keeps up with the news, proves on this occasion that his tongue has lost none of its acerbity although the rest of him is virtually mummified in inertia:

"I assure you [to Mercy] that I look upon this absurdity to which the King has been forced to consent as a harlequinade. In my view, this assembly is, with respect, what is commonly called a lot of balls."*

Is Louis XVI aware that both the Austrians in general and his own "Autrichienne" in particular are worried? Or is he in the state of euphoria of the congenital abulic who has actually taken a decision? In any event, the small hiccough of contentment which he utters to Calonne—who may have taken it to mean that his worries were now over—on the morning of December 30, the morning after he had said, "It is my will," is strange and almost unprecedented:

"I did not sleep last night, Monsieur, but pleasure was the cause."[18]

More clear-sighted than all the pros and cons together, Ruault the bookseller, a man of the third estate, is among the first nonnotables to hear the news, which takes some time to trickle down to the "depths" of France. It is he, in a letter to his brother, who finds the right words for this curtain-raiser:

Money there must be, and there's an end to it; money for expenditure known and unknown; money for the ordinary and for the extraordinary; money for the five or six kings reigning in France who dip so generously into the public treasury; money for the king of Paris, the king of finance, the king of war, the king of the

---

*Couillonnade* in French, the language of the original.

fleet, the king of foreign affairs, and the King of all these kings, who, they say, would be the thriftiest of them all if it weren't for his wife, his brothers, his cousins, and so forth. . . .

Finance has grown so powerful, so proud, so despotic that one must believe it can go no higher and must infallibly perish before many years have passed. When finance is honored, says Montesquieu, the state is lost. A fearful revolution is very imminent; we are very, very close to it, at any minute we are going to reach a violent crisis. Things cannot go on longer as they have been, that is self-evident. There is nothing but speculation, finance, banking, discount, borrowing, wagering, and payment. Every head is glued to money, crazy with speculation. A little patience, and we may see some pretty goings-on in 1800! In the meanwhile, though, we must live and contrive not to be carried away by the coming débâcle.

Farewell, dear friends, do not take my prophesies too much to heart. Curl yourselves up tightly in your little den, let the madmen get on with their folly, and let us try to remain simple spectators when the hollow mountain, that groans beneath the weight of all these thousands of brainless fools who are crawling over it, finally comes crashing down.[19]

COMTE DE VERGENNES

# 60

**FEBRUARY 1787**

## *He Was Not an Angel*

Deciding to convene the "notables" is one thing—but who, when, and how? From the 1786 edition of the dictionary of the Académie Française we glean the following: "NOTABLE: remarkable; considerable. Notable deeds. A notable statement. A notable case. That is notable. A notable pity. A notable sum. In France and in several other countries the principal and most considerable persons of a town, province, or state are called NOTABLES. An assembly of notables"[1]—ah, here we are!

If he had gone by the book, Louis XVI could have invited over 10,000 persons to Versailles. But the King and Calonne are both firmly resolved to avoid anything that smacks even remotely of a "national assembly," however much the words keep swimming to the surface. No crowds, no mob. None of those tribunals that always seem to throw up tribunes. What we want is a sort of enlarged cabinet meeting, a conclave, not a congress. So Louis XVI's choice, in which he takes intense personal interest and shows himself extremely jealous of his prerogative, proceeds far more by elimination than by election, and follows his own perfectly arbitrary ideas. For every notable convened he creates scores of malcontents, but for him that's half the fun. He spends weeks drawing up lists, in consultation with Vergennes, Calonne, and Miromesnil, but never with the Queen, the other ministers, or his brothers. These clandestine preparations are one of the reasons why the secret is not unveiled until December 29, and also why it is then possible to move at once from the announcement to the act, that is, the convocation. Castries, Breteuil, and everybody else, left standing at the gate, are unable to put forward a single name from their own clans. The assembly? Sorry, sold out. "I want an assembly of notables," Louis XVI said, "not of [all] the notable."

Beginning that same evening [the official minutes go on], and the following morning, the letters of convocation were dispatched by the secretaries of state to the different provinces of their departments; they went by courier [special messengers on horseback] to the places farthest away and by regular mail coach to the rest. There were some variations in the wording, as the offices had not had time to consult together and ensure complete uniformity [the object of this explanation being to forestall the waves of outcries from feelings hurt by differences in the terms of their letters; the poor gentlemen are so terribly sensitive]; but for the most part they read as follows:

"Having considered it necessary to the welfare of my affairs and my service, that the measures I am proposing to carry out, for the relief of my peoples, the ordering of my finances and the reform of various abuses, should be communicated to an assembly of the most qualified persons of various conditions in my state, I have thought, in consideration of your rank, that I could choose no one better than yourself, and I trust that on this occasion you will give me fresh proof of your loyalty and attachment. I have set the opening of this assembly for the 29th of the month of January next, 1787, at Versailles, where you will be present to attend the opening session and hear what will be proposed on my behalf; trusting that you will not fail to be there, in accordance with my desire, I pray you may remain in God's holy keeping."[2]

So who gets them? One had hoped to send out a bare 100 and one is already sorry that the number has been allowed to creep up to 144. Well, are they in any sense representative of anything? They're more like the catch of a fishing game at the fun fair, or a few haphazard crabs culled from the top of a creel.

Except for the seven princes of the blood, of course; they had to be there and they all are: Monsieur, Comte de Provence, Artois, Orléans, Condé, Bourbon, Conti, Penthièvre.

But when you turn to the churchmen, it's already a fairly random choice. There are fourteen elect, including Talleyrand-Périgord (Rheims); La Luzerne (Langres); Juigné, Archbishop of Paris and Duc de Saint-Cloud; Dillon (Narbonne), "hereditary president of the Estates-General of the province of Languedoc"; Boisgelin (Aix-en-Provence); Champion de Cicé (Bordeaux); and Brienne, the Archbishop of Toulouse and the greatest intriguer in the Church of France, whose crosier has been scratching at the door of power in the Queen's antechamber for years.

The nobility of the sword? Thirty-six gentlemen, including the Ducs d'Harcourt, de Noailles, de Choiseul (adopted son of the great minister), de Guines, de Nivernais, de Broglie, de Clermont-Tonnerre, de La Rochefoucauld (not Liancourt the economist, the one at La Roche-Guyon), the Maréchal de Vaux who conquered Corsica, and the Marquis de Bouillé. Names picked out blindfold by sticking a pin at random in the book of French heraldry. Only two concessions to public opinion, because of the American war—but Lord, that seems a long time ago: the door is eased open to admit Charles-Henri, Comte d'Estaing and vice-admiral of France, and Marie-Paul-Joseph-Roch-Yves-Gilbert du Motier, Marquis de La Fayette, who was written in by Calonne, scratched out by Louis XVI, and restored by Calonne at the last minute. No invitation for Rochambeau, none for Suffren, and even less for de Grasse, who has just been acquitted by a council of war for the disaster of Les Saintes.

The nobility of the gown? Thirty-eight magistrates, including a Lamoignon, a d'Ormesson (both in the Paris parlement), the first presidents of the parlements of Paris, Toulouse, Bordeaux, Grenoble, Dijon, Rouen, Provence, Brittany, Pau, Metz, Franche-Comté, Flanders, and Nancy, and the "sovereign councils" of Alsace and Roussillon ("lands reputed alien," in language and customs, since their conquest by Louis XIV), the first presidents and chief prosecuting attorneys of the court of audits and the tax dispute courts, supplemented by a sprinkling of chief prosecuting attorneys from here and there, and the *lieutenant civil* of the Châtelet.

> Singular idea! The sole justification for convening the notables was the desire to circumvent opposition from the parlements, and yet, to carry out this plan directed against them no better agents could be found than thirty-three of their own number, plus two from the audit chamber, two from the tax dispute court, and the *lieutenant civil,* making a total of thirty-eight magistrates, all of them of the highest rank, the ones most imbued with *esprit de corps,* the ones longest steeped in the cult of tradition![3]

As for the third estate, to them the door was almost completely barred. Oh, the list does stoop to twelve ordinary delegates from the *pays d'états* * and

---

*The *pays d'états* are regions in which the three orders still assemble annually to approve (almost a foregone conclusion) the taxes demanded by the King. Brittany and Languedoc are examples. The rest of the county is divided into *pays d'élection,* in which nobody has anything to approve or disapprove because the estates have been discontinued there. "Ordinary" delegates means that they sit regularly in their province's estates.

twenty-five municipal leaders of towns, but the great majority of these are noble anyway. "At the end of the eighteenth century, the chief municipal authorities of the towns of France, especially the large towns, were royal officials who were either noble, ennobled, or aspiring to ennoblement, and almost none of them had ever shared the ideas or interests of the third estate." These invitees in sheep's clothing include Tolozan (the one who just hanged the three workers in Lyons); Conrad-Alexandre Gérard, France's first ambassador to America (invited in his capacity as mayor, or more precisely "royal praetor," of Strasbourg); and a man named François-Pierre Gobelet, an alderman of Paris, whose name becomes the occasion for a festival of puns. "One lone goblet for all those jugs," etc. [= jugheads—*Trans.*]. Punning has become the rage at Versailles, by the way, since the King began to set the example. The other day, at the Queen's gaming tables, he deliberately brought the conversation round to the Illuminati so that he could place his latest:

"But can you tell me this, gentlemen: to which sect do fleas belong?"

"???"

"Why the Epicurean, of course!"*[4]

To weight down the government side, twelve counselors of state are added, one of whom is Lenoir, the former chief of police, and another Berthier de Sauvigny, the intendant of Paris who has been hated by the people ever since the Grain War. The ministers themselves will attend sittings but without being invited as notables.

The net result, thus, is a mass of colorless pottage, the scum from the top of the salon stew. Except for La Fayette, there is not one proven brilliant personality in the lot, which automatically makes him the one-eyed king in this country of the blind. Not one savant, not one man of letters, not one industrialist, not one lawyer. Nonentities incorporated. They might easily have invited Condorcet, for example, the director of the mint, academician, and companion of Turgot—a biography of whom he has just published; he is certainly the man who has written and said most in the last ten years about the possible form of the society of the future. What's more, he is still fiercely opposed to Necker. But there you are: however much Calonne himself may be borrowing Turgot's ideas, the very sound of the man's name sends Louis XVI into fits. If any Turgoting is going to be done, it'll have to be anonymous. Inviting even Condorcet would mean a partial rehabilitation of the big boy who was shown the door when the King was twenty-two. Besides, Condorcet has consolations elsewhere: he got married last Christmas, to the delectable Sophie de Grouchy. What, him? Who could have believed it? If his bachelorhood could

*[In French, *d'Epicure;* the pronunciation is identical to *des piqures.* A *piqure* is a bite or sting —*Trans.*]

come to an end, there is no such thing as a bachelor.* May he be happy all his days, and let the Court get on with more serious matters.

And yet Turgot's ghost is not entirely banned, "the King having chosen, to hold the pen for the assembly, the Sieur Hennin, secretary of the Council of State and His Majesty's private office; and the Sieur Dupont, commissioner general of trade. They were appointed secretary-registrars by royal warrant, dated January 26."

Dupont de Nemours, the very man. The one who, thirteen years ago, at the beginning of this story, was setting out with the catechism of Enlightenment to convert Poland and hurtling back to sink up to his neck in the Turgot experiment. He survived the exhaustion and then the heartbreak of those days. He endured. He negotiated the Necker period, followed by those of the ministerial ephemera, by floating through a series of important jobs in the comptroller general's offices, with the elasticity of reflex, in the face of rebuff and disappointment, that is second nature to him—and has its source, some say, in ambition, while others call it goodheartedness. After years of true conjugal felicity, Pierre-Samuel Dupont has recently been widowed. He enters the loneliness of the heart just as his friend Condorcet leaves it. He is still ready for the eruption of the new world, which he has been awaiting since youth with messianic fervor and which he has helped to bring about by efficiently seconding Calonne, for the last six months, in the drafting of the reform bills, visibly "Turgotizing" them as he went along. The pen he will wield is not only that of the notables, as we shall see; it is that of the minister too. Dupont, the man of shadows. At least two of the actors in this grand circus of skeptics are going to play their parts as if they meant them: he and La Fayette.

And there's another figure on the sidelines, gliding smoothly through the chiaroscuro: Abbé de Périgord, as he is most commonly called. He has become indispensable to Calonne because of his inimitable talent as go-between in the comptroller general's dealings with every Tom, Dick, and Harry. To his official position as agent general of the clergy he has added an unofficial one, as liaison agent extraordinary between the reign, the Church of France, and the big speculators: his uncle the archbishop on one side, Mirabeau on the other. Like the latter, he is a master at the art of reconciling things with words, or rather getting other people to reconcile them—because he has a whole factory of scribes at his beck and call and it is to him, and them, that Calonne turns for help when the dreaded moment finally comes and he has to sit down and actually write his speech:

*The opening chapters of Volume V will cover his marriage and intellectual evolution in the years leading up to the big upheaval; we will catch up on Dupont de Nemours in the chapters on the debates at the Assembly of Notables.

Eight days before February 22, 1787, when the assembly was to open, M. de Calonne sent a note enjoining me to spend the week with him at Versailles and help him to draft certain of the memoranda he was to present to the assembly. He added that I should find all the material I might need on the questions for which I should agree to take responsibility. He had written similar letters to M. de la Galaizière, Dupont de Nemours, M. de Saint-Genis, M. Gerbier, and M. de Cormerey.* We all met on the same morning in the study of M. de Calonne, who handed us sheaves of papers on each of the questions we were to cover. It was from these that we were to extract the memoranda and drafts which had to be printed and ready to submit to the assembly for discussion eight days later. On February 14, thus, not one word had been written. We shared out this Herculean labor. I undertook to write the memorandum and draft the bill on grain, and wrote every word of both myself. I worked with M. de Saint-Genis on the memorandum on the payment of the debt of the clergy, and with M. de la Galaizière on his text on the *corvées*. M. de Cormerey did the whole of the bill on the replacement of the barriers.† Gerbier was contributing paragraphs on all sides. My friend Dupont, who believed that some real good could come of it all, lavished his imagination, intelligence, and faith upon the questions more closely allied with his own opinions. In one week, thus, we made a fairly passable job of the work which M. de Calonne's presumptuousness and carelessness had caused him to neglect for five months.[5]

Talleyrand is blowing his own horn a little here, no doubt, by pretending that what was actually a heavy (and belated, to be sure) labor of organizing and polishing was actually the preliminary brainwork; he wrote that last paragraph when Calonne was no longer around to defend himself against a reputation for irresponsible idleness that sticks to him from now on. But his description is still valid as a reflection of the little fever that swept through circles close to the seat of power in February 1787. At last, something is happening. This is action. This is motion. In the enchanted forest of Versailles, the sleeping beauty's eyelid has twitched.

But—why February? Didn't the letters of invitation say something about January 29? Why this two-month gap between the announcement, on December 29, and the event? It is always a bad idea to make the future wait. And since piling on the bandwagon is almost everybody's favorite sport, rumor

---

*The Marquis Chaumont de la Galaizière was born in 1697; intendant of Soissons, chancellor of Lorraine (1737), counselor of state (1766), member of the royal council for finance (1776), he dies in 1787. Pierre Gerbier, a renowned lawyer in the Paris Parlement who was born in Rennes in 1725, is one of the few who consented to plead before the commission set up by Maupeou during the parlement interregnum. He dies in 1788. Saint-Genis and Cormerey are smaller fry who often act as Talleyrand's secretaries.

†These were internal duty collection posts, which Calonne wanted to abolish and relocate at the frontiers.

blames the delay on the indecisiveness of the King and the irresponsibility, even incompetence, of Calonne. That is unfair.

The fault, in this case, is in the stars. In January, the ministry is stricken by a curious visitation: an "affliction of the guts" and rheumatism nail Calonne to his bed, which he has to "have set round with tables" so he can go on working regardless; Ségur is suffering from "very acute gout"; Miromesnil is coughing his lungs out at the bedside of one of his daughters, herself consumptive; and Vergennes is dying. Now, the Assembly of Notables really cannot take place without the chief cabinet ministers. Mirabeau, zooming round the palace like a homeless hornet, calls it "a crisis in the ministerial healths."[6] A twentieth-century psychiatrist might be tempted to see in this epidemic a collective shrinking from action—but if it is so, then in one case at least it is a mortal shrinking, because Vergennes actually departs this life on February 13, 1787, after thirteen years as minister of foreign affairs and, since Maurepas's death, principal minister without the title.

A discreet death, like the life that preceded it. "Of a rising gout," they say. In fact, of overwork. He killed himself at his desk; that was his battlefield. In his younger days he represented his King from Stockholm to Constantinople, but when he was given a seat in the spider's web he edged his way to the middle of it and never stirred again. Not one trip, and almost no social life. He waited for the world to come to him, and it pretty much did. As for his reputation: hard workers are always respected in the end, grudgingly or not. And as for his fortune: he was born poor and he dies very rich,* although not as rich as the obituary whisperings claim him to be:

> This minister has left his family something better than his position, namely, 15 million in hard cash, 9 million of which are held by Laborde, onetime banker to the Court and now guardian of the royal treasury. . . . Item, twenty-two good pieces of land. M. Gravier de Vergennes was a very hardworking man, extremely frugal and unattracted by ambition, honors, and dignities. He preferred to be paid in money for every act he performed, be it good or bad. People of quality say he thought like a bourgeois, like his grandfather the timber merchant (who gave his name to a measure of firewood), but the people of quality who censure him are almost all losing face and going bankrupt themselves.
>
> The prince alone seems to regret his passing. He was not an angel, but he

---

*According to Vergennes's will, dated August 1, 1784, which is shown to Louis XVI when the noise about his wealth reaches earsplitting proportions, the bulk of his assets in land, valuables, buildings, and offices, plus the "presents received from the courts of Russia, Holland, Sardinia, England, Portugal, and Vienna," amounts to a little over 2,600,000 livres, or about 25 million modern francs [$6,250,000]. Louis XVI nevertheless grants Mme de Vergennes a widow's pension of 20,000 livres [$5,000] a year and two pensions of 10,000 [$2,500] each to their two sons.

had a long experience of the business of his department, and that can take the place of, and perhaps be worth more than, all the speculations of an overexcited man of genius.[7]

"You see me now," he says to his family two hours before his death; "to this we all must come. One day we must render our accounts for all our actions."[8] Never were last words more absolutely in character with the line of a life: irrefutable and commonplace.* His name remains linked to the greatest glory of the reign—the victorious peace treaty of 1783 with England, ending a war declared against his will; and to his vilest deed abroad—the crushing of the freedom of Geneva, which he achieved all by himself. His friend the Comte de Caraman, who kept a diary of Vergennes's last days, writes, on the evening of his death, a measured eulogy that would make a good epitaph: "He spoke the particular language of international relations, which was understood by all nations; and for that reason he enjoyed greater consideration in the rest of Europe than he did in France."[9]

His death is not so great a tragedy for France as it is for Calonne, who has had a hard enough time extorting the tough-hided conservative's consent to the convening of the notables and his reformist program, and who desperately needs him as an ally, on the Council and at Court, to keep the other ministers in order, Breteuil quiet, the Queen intimidated, and, above all, Louis XVI's nose to the grindstone during the decisive weeks. Vergennes was a sort of soft rock, and would have shamed the King into sticking to his guns. But with him dead Calonne stands alone in the front line, advancing over the shifting sands of royal inconsistency. His friend Jean-Jacques Vidaud de la Tour, one of the twelve counselors of state to sit among the notables, already feels the ground giving way beneath his feet: "It is a grave loss that we have suffered, especially at this time when he [Vergennes] could have held great sway over the Assembly of Notables. He and the keeper of the seals were the only ministers who had been consulted in regard to all of M. de Calonne's plans, and, by virtue of the respect that he inspired, he might have smoothed over dissensions, resolved difficulties, and determined upon the course to take. This resource is now wanting. The comptroller general is abandoned to his own resources."[10]

Meanwhile, it's roundup time at Versailles, the sheep pen into which have crowded the 144 dignitaries who have been imperatively invited to present themselves at the end of January, only to be left dangling there, with families and servants, and who are greatly exaggerating the adversity of their situation. Most of them are hardly at a loss for board and lodging; they all have friends

---

*Vergennes's tomb in the Church of Notre Dame in Versailles is decorated with a medallion by Blaise, the sculptor, which contains one of the best portraits of him.

and relations, and besides, the King's Household has been instructed to see to their accommodation if necessary. But* the delay gave "the notables time to discuss among themselves the questions to be placed before them (to which they had easy access, owing to the great number of people employed in their drafting), and to form parties to oppose those that would affect their assets or privileges."[11] The streets are echoing with epigrams and songs. The atmosphere is quintessentially French; people are laughing before they know what the joke is. Mirabeau is shocked. "On the most solemn occasion that has ever riveted a nation's attention, all we hear is a torrent of jest. . . . Ah, are we then so congenitally incapable of seriousness?"[12]

The fact is, they're caucusing. Little unofficial assemblies are being held on all sides, and their proliferation is going to paralyze the big one. The provincial magistrates are being catechized by their colleagues from Paris, all of whom are in a state of latent revolt. The prelates are foregathering at the home of the Dillons—friends of the Queen—around Arthur-Richard Dillon, Archbishop of Narbonne and president of the Estates of Languedoc, one of the strongest voices in the upper reaches of the church. "As for the nobility, a few visits to the salons in Versailles and Paris, and they were emboldened to the point of resistance and steeped in the spirit of opposition."[13] "Evil tongues," according to a bleak letter from La Fayette to Washington, "are beginning to speak of an assembly of *not ables*," a pun upon which the Anglophiles could fasten with glee.[14] Everybody's got a story to sell, and "there is no idea so wild that someone does not believe it. Ill-assorted women are convinced that they have but to ask for their divorce; nuns, for husbands; priests, for wives; monks, for pensions and their freedom, and all will be granted."[15]

And there are ants tickling cruelty's wings, too. Calonne, they say, spat blood the other day. "Was it his own, or that of France?"[16]

*According to Besenval, a close friend of Marie Antoinette for many years.

# 61

**FEBRUARY 22, 1787**

## *Innumerable Fleurs-de-Lis*

The big white sun of February 22, 1787, should be able to clear away all these wisps and fumes. Everything happens in France, even change. A beautiful bright winter day, pale as a glass of Aÿ wine, coolly illuminates Versailles and the glitter of coaches and costumes, the giddy carnival of the whole coopful of shimmering, sleek, bright-hued barnyard fowl beplumed, cravated, booted, belted, and strutting like so many turkey gobblers in mating season, but what for? There's not a female in sight. At *lits de justice,* at least, the Queen and a few other ladies get a gallery in a corner; but on this occasion, sorry, members only—not one smile, gaze, or gown will distract the gentlemen from their appointed duty. But how forlorn they look all by themselves, ranged around the two stoves camouflaged as columns, in the brand new hall that was built for the purpose in a month in the Menus-Plaisirs on the Avenue de Paris, and is much too big for them.*

No women and no crowds. The Assembly of Notables has not yet reached the consciousness of the lower strata.

The Menus-Plaisirs is like a huge rummage closet: it's a storehouse for the costumes, draperies, costume jewelry, candelabra, girandoles, partitions, and flats used in Court ballets, masques, and balls.[1] The administration of the demesne built it, wing by wing, on a lot bought in 1748 alongside the most stately avenue of the royal town, the one from which you see the château dead center in the distance, and the sight gives you the same jolt every time you come out from Paris and find yourself stepping into the perspective drawing that reaches from Montreuil to the reservoirs in an urban geometry designed to domesticate history. In the last twenty years these festivities have required so many and such divers props that the Menus, as they're called for short, are overflowing with clutter and claptrap. But they had to have their stupid assembly somewhere, and Louis XIV thought of everything, when Versailles was

---

*The Estates-General also meet there in 1789.

laid out, except a room big enough to hold 200 subjects. There are the chapel and theater, of course, but those would be out of the question. So, like one more warehouse, they stuck this rectangle onto the rest of the Menus-Plaisirs building, absolutely plain and terrifically tall: the unpainted ceiling, four or five times a man's height, rests upon four cant walls wide enough for the skylights that let in the day. To please the King, large tapestries, borrowed from the Gobelins works, have been hung up to enliven the walls with hunting scenes. A huge dais, raised three steps from the floor, stands at one end, for the throne and princes' armchairs; in front of it is a long cloth-covered table for the speakers designated by the King; and two or three rows of chairs run along the sides and far end, for the notables. In the middle, empty space, so vast you could hold a ball in it. It's a five-minute walk from the château, but in the eyes of protocol a King has no legs.

In this instance, protocol will scrupulously copy every detail of the procedure followed at the most recent precedent, which was the Assembly of Notables called by Louis XIII in 1626, where Richelieu stood twice as tall as everybody else. But since there is no Richelieu this time, minds have gone back a step to the occasion before that, the assembly convened by Henri IV in 1596, also for strictly financial purposes. There's a little feeling of the old boy in the air today too, as there always is when the monarchy returns to the wellsprings of its popularity. "The King kindly undertook to settle all points of rank and ceremony himself, and gave his instructions accordingly, to M. le Marquis de Dreux de Brézé, grand master of ceremonies, and to the masters of ceremonies MM. de Nantouillet, father and son; and the account of [the first sitting of the assembly] consigned to these minutes has been drawn from their notes."[2] Why not treat ourselves to the pleasure of reading them in full, in their noble and excellently descriptive style: they are the swan song of the monarchy of divine right.

On Thursday, February 22, the day set by the King for the opening of the Assembly of Notables, the hall and all adjacent rooms were closed from early morning and no one was allowed to enter either them or the rooms of the apartments reserved for the King.

At half-past nine in the morning His Majesty's guard, comprising one company of the French Guard detached from the château and a similar detachment of the Swiss Guards, proceeded to the door opening onto the Avenue de Paris; they took up their positions outside, and occupied the entire outer perimeter of the courtyard and adjoining buildings.

A few moments later, the Provost Guards, Gate Guards, Cent-Suisses, and Life Guards arrived and took up their positions.

The King himself had assigned all the seats and marked them with his own hand several days beforehand, on a plan which the masters of ceremonies had the honor to present to him; His Majesty also settled various other matters arising and gave the most exact orders to the officers in charge of the ceremonies.

Pursuant to His Majesty's decisions, the gentlemen prelates and notables of the nobility had been notified by the grand master of ceremonies of the day and hour of opening of the assembly, and the form of dress upon which His Majesty had determined.

Around half-past ten in the morning, His Majesty left his private cabinet in coat and mantle, preceded by Monseigneur the Duc de Penthièvre, Monseigneur the Prince de Conti, Monseigneur the Duc de Bourbon, Monseigneur the Prince de Condé, Monseigneur the Duc d'Orléans, Monseigneur the Comte d'Artois, and Monsieur, also in coat and mantle. The princes were accompanied by the principal officers of their households, and His Majesty was preceded and followed by his great and lesser officers and mace bearers. His Majesty went down to the chapel and heard a low mass. . . .

The grand master of ceremonies placed the people in the chapel and accompanied His Majesty inside. Meanwhile, the master of ceremonies had gone to the assembly hall to prepare the sitting there and inform each of MM. the notables of the place His Majesty had assigned to him.

At this point, Monseigneur the Keeper of the Seals arrived, with the members of the Council also seated in his coaches; he was escorted by two brigadiers and twelve provost guards, etc.

At the same time, MM. the notables began to enter, through the door on the rue des Chantiers. They were all in ceremonial dress; that is to say, MM. the prelates were in cassock, rochet, cape, and square hat; MM. the notables of the nobility, in coat and mantle with cravat and plumed hat. His Majesty had decided that MM. the notables who were knights of his orders would not wear the dress of their order on this occasion. Nor did these gentlemen wear the necklace of their order outside their mantle. MM. the presidents and prosecuting attorneys were in black gown and square hat; MM. the municipal officials of towns were each in the ceremonial raiment appropriate to their station as head of a municipal body. MM. the delegates of the *pays d'états* were each in the dress of their order, and MM. the members of the King's Council in their ceremonial robes. . . .

The King emerged from the château at eleven, being in his ceremonial coaches, and escorted by detachments of his military Horse Guard. With His Majesty in his coach were Monsieur, Monseigneur the Comte d'Artois, Messeigneurs the Duc d'Orléans, Prince de Condé, and Duc de Bourbon. The King was greeted, upon alighting from his carriage, by Messeigneurs the Prince de Conti and Duc de Penthièvre, etc.

The only persons to enter the King's private room with him were those possessing the rights of entry.

His Majesty, having taken a few moments' repose and been notified by the officers of ceremony that the meeting was ready, proceeded to the assembly.

His Majesty, entering the assembly hall, went to his throne, on a platform raised two steps from the floor and covered with a carpet of velvet strewn with innumerable fleurs-de-lis; His Majesty's throne was surmounted by a violet canopy also strewn with fleurs-de-lis, and the King had two bricks placed beneath his feet.

Monsieur sat upon a folding chair at His Majesty's right, on the first step of the platform; Monseigneur the Comte d'Artois on a folding chair similarly placed on the left side. Monseigneur the Duc d'Orléans, Monseigneur the Duc de Bourbon, and Monseigneur the Duc de Penthièvre sat on folding chairs on the right side, and on the same level as that of Monsieur, but beyond the carpet. Monseigneur the Prince de Condé and Monseigneur the Prince de Conti were placed similarly on the left side, on folding chairs beyond the carpet and on the same line as Monseigneur the Comte d'Artois.

No other person entered the hall, His Majesty having expressly forbidden it; he had, however, permitted a few persons belonging to the Menus-Plaisirs and wardrobe to be placed at the back of the hall behind the guards, so that they might perform such services as might be needed.

The King, after seating himself upon his throne, removed and replaced his hat, and made the following address:

"Gentlemen, I have chosen you among the different orders of the state, and I have assembled you about me, in order that I may make known my intentions to you.

"Such has been the custom of several of my predecessors, and in particular of the head of my branch,* whose name has remained dear to every Frenchman and all of whose examples I shall glory in following.

"The projects that will be communicated to you on my behalf are great and important. On the one hand, they are designed to improve the revenues of the state and ensure their total liberation by means of a more equitable apportionment of taxation; and on the other, to free trade from various impediments hampering its movement, and insofar as circumstances may permit me to do so, to relieve the most needy portion of my subjects: such, gentlemen, are the designs which I have in mind and upon which I have determined after the ripest consideration. As they will all increase the public weal, and as I know that all of you are zealous in my service, I have not feared to consult you as to the manner of their application; I shall hear and attentively examine the comments you may consider them to warrant. I trust that your views, all conspiring to the same end, will readily agree, and that no particular interest will rise up to oppose the interest of all."

The mace bearers, master of arms, and pages of arms ought, by rights, to have knelt throughout the sitting; but His Majesty thought it proper for them to rise when he had finished speaking.

After the King's address, Monseigneur the Keeper of the Seals approached the throne, making three deep bows: the first before leaving his place, the second after taking a few steps, and the third upon the first level below the throne; he then knelt and received His Majesty's instructions.

*Henri IV, first reigning Bourbon.

Which apparently are to pronounce an unintelligible and tedious speech that sounds like a sermon, and then to "sign to M. the Comptroller General, who, having saluted, taken his seat" at the long table on which he has spread his files and folders, "and replaced his hat," intones his challenge to a hallful of men waiting to eat him alive. "Messire Charles-Alexandre de Calonne, Grand Treasurer, Commander of the Order of the Holy Ghost, Minister of State, and Comptroller General of Finance" now takes the floor, as one might dive into the water to retrieve a drowning man—this unmoored kingdom adrift in the stream.

*Notes*
*Index*

# Notes

Titles appearing in Volumes I, II, and III, where fuller descriptions will be found in some cases, are marked with an asterisk (*) upon first mention here.

## I

* 1. *Histoire de Beaumarchais* by Gudin de la Brenellerie, p. 355; also Nicolas Ruault, *Gazette d'un Parisien sous la Révolution, lettres à son frère*, presented by Anne Vassal (Paris, Perrin, 1976), p. 54—a fascinating and well-documented text.

2. Gudin, *Histoire de Beaumarchais*, p. 157.

* 3. *Oeuvres complètes de Beaumarchais*, p. 279.

4. This detail and those that follow concerning takeoffs of the *Mariage* come from the catalogue of the Beaumarchais exhibition at the Bibliothèque nationale in 1966, pp. 104 ff. Exact references to the manuscripts are given. For the play by Des Fontaines, see Grimm's *Correspondance littéraire*, XIV, 74.

5. Bibliothèque nationale, Imprimés, 2, 2935[8].

6. Gudin, *Histoire de Beaumarchais*, p. 341.

* 7. Jean and Brigitte Massin, *Wolfgang Amadeus Mozart*, p. 439.

* 8. Reichard, *Guide des voyageurs en Allemagne, en Hongrie et à Constantinople*, III, 145.

9. J. and B. Massin, *Mozart*, p. 440.

10. Gudin, *Histoire de Beaumarchais*, p. 342. I have not been able to find confirmation of any contemporary translation of Beaumarchais into one of the languages of India, and there appears to be none now either, although I am not at all sure of this.

*11. This and the following two quotes are from the Duc de Castries, *Figaro, ou la vie de Beaumarchais*, p. 377. *Ibid.* for the lines from Suard's "tract" at the end of the chapter.

## 2

1. Dominique-Joseph Garat (the critic alluded to earlier), *Mémoires sur la vie de M. Suard, sur ses écrits et sur le XVIIIe siècle* (Paris, 1820), published by A. Belin, printer-bookseller, I, 133.

2. *Ibid.*, I, 277.

3. *Ibid.*, I, 298.

4. *Ibid.*, II, 295; *ibid.* for next quote.

* 5. Lescure, *Correspondance secrète*, I, 536.

6. Excerpts from Suard's letter published under a—transparent—priest's alias in the *Journal de*

* *Paris* and reprinted verbatim by Meister in his *Correspondance littéraire,* XIV, 117.

7. Beaumarchais, *Oeuvres complètes,* p. 136: preface to the *Mariage de Figaro.* Other quotes in this text are from the same source. The letter to du Paty is quoted in
* Louis de Loménie, *Beaumarchais et son temps,* II, 581 (appendix).

8. Bibliothèque nationale, Imprimés, 4° Lc², 80.

9. Ruault, *Gazette d'un Parisien,* p. 54.

## 3

1. Ruault, *Gazette d'un Parisien,* p. 53.

2. Pierre Manuel, *La Police de Paris dévoilée* (Original edition of "the second year of freedom," 1790, by Garnery, rue Serpente), I, 189.

3. Dulaure, *Nouvelle description des curiosités de Paris* (1791), II, 151. *Ibid.* for the next quote.

4. Jacques Hillairet, *Gibets, piloris et cachots du vieux Paris* (Paris, Editions de Minuit, 1956), p. 303.

5. Dulaure, *Nouvelle description,* II, 152. *Ibid.* for the description of the painting in the church.

6. Hillairet, *Gibets, piloris et cachots,* p. 304. *Ibid.* for the following quotes and notes on the number of prisoners in Saint-Lazare.

7. Grimm, *Correspondance littéraire,* XIV, 122. *Ibid.* for the following lines, mainly the captions beneath scenes showing "Beaumarchais's spanking."

8. Unpublished letter from Gudin to Beaumarchais, dated March

16, 1785 (private collection, exhibited at the Bibliothèque nationale in 1966, cat. no. 416, and falsely attributed to someone named Gomel).

9. Gudin, *Histoire de Beaumarchais,* p. 358.

10. Bibliothèque nationale, Estampes [Prints], Vinck Collection, 896.

11. Arnault, *Souvenirs d'un sexagénaire,* quoted in the 1966 Beaumarchais exhibition catalogue under no. 417. The following quotation from the *Nouvelles à la Main* is taken from Loménie, *Beaumarchais et son temps,* II, 368.

12. Gudin, *Histoire de Beaumarchais,* p. 357.

*13. Letter quoted in Anne and Claude Manceron, *Beaumarchais, Figaro vivant,* p. 83.

14. Gudin, *Histoire de Beaumarchais,* p. 360. *Ibid.* for the following passage. The list of major prisons of state in the footnote was taken from E. le Mercier, *Le Prévot dit de Beaumont, prisonnier d'Etat* (Bernay, by Miaulle-Duval, 1883), p. 338.

*15. Unpublished text by Grimm, quoted by the Duc de Castries in his *Figaro, ou la vie de Beaumarchais,* p. 390.

## 4

* 1. Gilbert Lély, *Vie du marquis de Sade,* p. 385.

2. *Ibid.,* p. 388.

* 3. *Histoire économique et sociale de la France* (PUF, under the direction of Fernand Braudel), II, 492.

4. According to information given to Gilbert Lély in 1964 by Mr.

André Hurtret, keeper of the château of Vincennes.

5. Frantz Funck-Brentano, *Légendes et archives de la Bastille* (Paris, 1898), p. 43. The author presents these statements by Launay, the governor of the Bastille, as replies to Linguet's *Mémoires sur la Bastille* (see note 7 below).

6. Letter from Sade to his wife, dated March 8, 1784, quoted by Lély, *Vie du marquis de Sade,* p. 380. *Ibid.* for the following quote.

7. *Mémoires sur la Bastille et sur la détention de M. Linguet, par lui-même* (fictitiously printed in London by T. Spilsbury, Snowhill, 1783), p. 85.

8. Funck-Brentano, *Légendes et archives,* p. 60.

9. Letter of September 23, 1779, hence addressed to Vincennes, quoted by Lély, *Vie du marquis de Sade,* p. 316.

10. This reply, whose truculence makes one long for enough space to print it in full, was written on October 4, 1779, and caused one of Sade's lady friends to say, "M. le Marquis is well, as I judge from a quite totally delirious letter he has written to 'La Jeunesse.' " The complete text is *ibid.,* pp. 318–20.

11. Letter by Sade, written from Vincennes in September 1778, a fortnight after his second arrest: *ibid.,* p. 294.

## 5

1. An excerpt from the certificate of baptism of Barère's child

bride was published in *La Liberté des Hautes-Pyrénées.* She was born at Vic-en-Bigorre on July 21, 1772, and baptized the next day at the parish church of Saint-Martin.

2. Barère, *Mémoires* (Paris, Dentu, 1838), p. 240.

* 3. Expilly, *Dictionnaire,* IV, 162: "Lavedan."

4. Bertrand Barère, *Eloge de J.-B. Furgole, avocat au Parlement de Toulouse* (by Lavesse, bookseller at Toulouse, quarto, ten sheets, 1784.)

5. Robert Launay, *Barère de Vieuzac, l'Anacréon de la guillotine* (Paris, Tallandier, 1929), p. 10. Most of the details concerning Barère's family background come from this book.

6. J. Bourdette, *Notice sur les seigneurs de Biéouzac,* p. 63, quoted in Launay, *Barère de Vieuzac.*

7. *Ibid.,* p. 39.

8. Jean-François Soulet, *La vie quotidienne dans les Pyrénées sous l'Ancien Régime, du XVIe au XVIIIe siècle* (Paris, Hachette, 1974), p. 231.

* 9. Arthur Young, *Travels in France,* II, 95. [Retranslated from the French—*Trans.*]

10. Soulet, *La vie quotidienne dans les Pyrénées,* p. 78.

11. Barère, *Mémoires,* p. 30.

*12. Mme de Genlis, *Mémoires,* II, 161.

13. This patchwork of Barère's recollections of his background and youth has been based on two sources: his *Mémoires,* pp. 203–27, and a little unpublished manuscript dated

1797 and entitled "Pages mélancoliques," a few excerpts from which are quoted on pp. 28–30 by J. Leflève, author of the introduction to the *Mémoires.*

14. G. Mauran, *Sommaire Description du païs et comte de Bigorre* (Paris, Auch, 1887), quoted by Soulet, *La vie quotidienne dans les Pyrénées,* p. 175.

15. According to Soulet, *ibid.,* p. 173.

16. Bertrand Barère, *De la pensée du gouvernement républicain* ("imprimé en France" in Floréal, An V), p. xxxiii.

*17. *Encyclopédie,* XVI, 451: "Toulouse." The short quote that follows on the Dominican inquisitor is from the same source.

18. Gustave Bord, article in the *Correspondant* for May 25, 1906, entitled "La conspiration maçonnique en 1789."

19. According to Reichard's guide, volume II, *France,* p. 166.

20. J. Bourdette, *Notice sur les seigneurs de Biéouzac,* quoted by Launay, *Barère de Vieuzac,* p. 15.

# 6

1. Benjamin Franklin, *Dialogue between Franklin and the Gout,* written and printed by himself on his private press during an attack of gout in Passy in 1780. Quoted by Carl Van Doren, *Benjamin Franklin* (New York, Viking Press, 1938; reprinted 1973 by Greenwood Press), p. 633.

2. Van Doren, *Franklin,* p. 635.

3. Excerpts from Franklin's little travel journal, quoted *ibid.,* p. 724. Other excerpts from Franklin's journal are from the same source.

* 4. Quoted by Bernard Fay, *Benjamin Franklin, citoyen du monde,* II, 270.

5. (Unpublished) correspondence between Franklin and Mme Brillon, quoted by Van Doren, *Benjamin Franklin,* pp. 642 and 643.

* 6. *Histoire des environs de Paris,* II, 127.

7. Expilly, *Dictionnaire,* III, 540: "Gaillon." The description of the château that follows, priceless now that the building itself has been destroyed, is from the same source.

* 8. Saint-Simon, *Mémoires,* VI, 356.

# 7

1. Ruault, *Gazette d'un Parisien,* p. 59.

2. Marie-Victoire Monnard, *Les Souvenirs d'une femme du peuple,* published by O. Boutanquoi (Imprimeries réunies de Senlis, 1928). The passages quoted thus far and those that follow, on Marie-Victoire's childhood and the episode of the procession, are from pp. 4–13. The excerpt from the record of baptism in my footnote is reproduced in full on p. 4 n.

* 3. *Histoire des environs de Paris,* II, 184; and Expilly, *Dictionnaire,* II, 531: "Creil."

4. Monnard, *Souvenirs d'une femme du peuple,* pp. 16 and 17.

# 8

1. "Reflections on the Increase in Wages Which Will Be Occasioned in Europe by the Revolution in America," unpublished text by Franklin found in his papers and printed in full by Jacques Ahrweiller in *Benjamin Franklin, premier savant américain* (Paris, Seghers, 1965). In this clear and concrete text Franklin is already foreseeing the massive immigration that forms the demographic fabric of the United States a century later, thanks to the lure of the wages paid to workers, which he considered substantially higher in his country in 1785 than those paid in England, where they were still higher than in France. "I have taken these figures," he wrote, "from Adam Smith's book on *The Wealth of Nations.*" [Retranslated.]

2. Printed anonymously, presumably on Franklin's presses in Passy, and dated 1782; it bears the traditional fictitious city of publication, in this case Amsterdam. See in this connection Van Doren, *Benjamin Franklin,* p. 425.

3. Article by J. Quentin-Bauchart, "Guillotin et la guillotine," in the *Nouvelle Revue* (1905), xxxiv, 484–93. Other details relating to Guillotin are from the same text, and from no. 18 of the *Revue de la Révolution française* (article by Charles Vellay on the relations between Franklin and Guillotin).

\* 4. Franz Anton Mesmer, *Le Magnétisme animal* (works,

published by Robert Amadou), p. 243, end of a letter to Franklin dated August 20, 1784. When he writes it he has not yet seen the committee's report, which was drafted the previous week and which will annihilate him, but he has a pretty good idea of its contents. This sermon and threat to Franklin are on the order of a last-ditch skirmish for honor's sake, and typical of Mesmer.

5. *Ibid.,* p. 277. The secret report of which I speak later in the text, which intimates a close link between magnetism and eroticism, was written by the same committee and is published in full in the following pages of the same book.

6. *Mémoires* of the Général Baron Thiébault, published by F. Calmettes (Paris, Plon, 1896), I, 26.

\* 7. Louis-Sébastien Mercier, *Tableau de Paris,* IV, 151.

8. Page from an unpublished manuscript on Mesmer by M. P. Vinchon which will, I hope, appear shortly; I thank its author for letting me see and make use of it.

# 9

\* 1. Gaston Maugras, *La Disgrâce du duc et de la duchesse de Choiseul,* p. 391. Other particulars concerning Choiseul's bankruptcy and death are from the same source, pp. 392–400.

2. Archives nationales, Ancien Régime, 04841, folio 6, "Théâtre des Italiens."

3. Reminiscences of Abbé Barthélemy, an intimate of the Choiseuls, quoted by Maugras, *Disgrâce du duc*, p. 393.

* 4. Bachaumont, *Nouvelles à la Main*, XXXII, 25.

5. *Lettres du comte Valentin Esterhazy à sa femme, 1784–1792*, published by Ernest Daudet (Paris, Plon, 1907), p. 61. Same source, pp. 62–7, for the following quotations.

6. Bachaumont, *Nouvelles à la Main*, p. 27.

7. Comte Dufort de Cheverny, *Mémoires* (Paris, Plon, 1909), I, 470.

8. Bachaumont, *Nouvelles à la Main*, p. 29.

## 10

1. Lescure, *Correspondance secrète*, I, 548.

2. *Ibid.*, p. 562.

3. *Ibid.*, p. 568.

4. Comte Beugnot, *Mémoires, 1779–1815* (Paris, Hachette, 1959), p. 28.

5. *Ibid.*, p. 62.

6. The dialogue has been reconstructed from Beugnot's *Mémoires*, p. 65.

7. Beugnot, *Mémoires*, p. 67. The unreferenced quotations that follow are from the same source, pp. 66–72, including those relating to the Abbot of Clairvaux.

8. Expilly, *Dictionnaire*, II, 357: "Clairvaux." I have taken some of the details concerning the abbey at the time of its founding and in 1785 from the same source.

9. Beugnot, *Mémoires*, p. 67.

10. *Ibid.*, p. 20.

11. *Ibid.*, p. 66.

12. Reichard, *Guide*, II, 122: "France"—the road from Paris to Basel.

13. Funck-Brentano, *L'Affaire du collier, d'après de nouveaux documents* (Paris, Hachette, 1901). This is one of the most comprehensive and careful accounts; it has aged hardly at all and all sources are given, e.g., p. 232 for the weather and time of day at Clairvaux.

## 11

1. Dialogue taken verbatim from Beugnot's *Mémoires*, p. 69.

* 2. Barras, *Mémoires*, p. 97. The other unnumbered references to this meeting between Jeanne de La Motte and Barras have been taken—with the necessary grain of salt—from the same passages of this dubious text, which was edited by Rousselin de Saint-Albin, a Restoration pen-pusher, from material supplied by Barras.

3. The letter requesting an audience is reproduced in full in the *Mémoires* of Barras, p. 98. By cross-checking it is possible, thanks to the reminiscences of poor Saint-Rémi, to confirm the contacts between Barras and the La Mottes in the summer of 1785. See in this connection Jean Savant, *Tel fut Barras* (Paris, Fasquelle, 1954), p. 40, and n. 47 to the same page. Jean Savant has no love for Barras and spares none of his fairy tales, but

concludes that the "betrothal" scheme and the dinner party related here actually did exist. Even so, Barras's story should not be taken at face value, and I have by no means done so, especially when he claims that Jeanne explicitly confided to him her apprehensions concerning the cardinal and the necklace. All other indications agree, and Beugnot confirms, that she believed herself absolutely safe until the evening of August 17 at Clairvaux. As for the marriage between Barras and Marie-Anne: not only was nothing concluded, but in fact nothing had really been begun; the La Mottes had several other irons in the fire. See Archives nationales, AB XIX 3073 D4.

4. Beugnot, *Mémoires,* p. 69 and *passim* for the story of the destruction of her papers.

5. Brief of Target, Rohan's counsel, in the Paris Municipal Library.

## 12

1. Beugnot, *Mémoires,* pp. 21–3.
2. *Ibid.,* p. 30. Same reference for the next two quotes.
\* 3. Paul d'Estrée, *La Vieillesse du maréchal de Richelieu,* p. 206.
4. Beugnot, *Mémoires,* p. 36. *Ibid.* for the following quote.
5. *Ibid.,* p. 47. The description of Cagliostro is on p. 53.
6. Beugnot's story of his meeting with Mlle d'Oliva is on pp. 58–61 of his *Mémoires.*
7. Archives nationales, X², B/1417: interrogation of the Cardinal de Rohan.

8. Expilly, *Dictionnaire,* I, 450: "Bar-sur-Aube." Other particulars relating to the town are from the same source.

## 13

1. The tale of the burning of the papers is in Beugnot's *Mémoires,* pp. 70–2.
2. Funck-Brentano, *L'Affaire du collier,* p. 162. *Ibid.* for the subsequent description of the house and footnote relating to it.
3. Beugnot, *Mémoires,* p. 22.
4. *Ibid.,* p. 72.
5. Beugnot's terrors are openly confessed on pp. 74–6 of his *Mémoires.*

## 14

1. Bibliothèque nationale, Mss. français, 10364, folio 217.
2. Manuscript notes by Jeanne de Saint-Rémi, found in London after her death and quoted by Funck-Brentano, *L'Affaire du collier,* p. 5.
3. *Ibid.,* p. 67.
4. *Ibid.,* p. 66.
5. *Vie de Jeanne de Saint-Rémi de Valois, ci-devant Comtesse de La Motte,* by Garnery (rue Serpente, Paris, An I of the Republic), I, 106. This text, written or dictated in England, is, of course, full of exaggerations and falsehoods and can be used only after cross-checking, especially in matters relating to the necklace. But there is a certain ring of truth in these passages on her childhood and youth, and they have been confirmed by Beugnot

and other contemporaries, as has the philandering of the Marquis de Boulainvilliers, to which Jeanne's tardy placement in a convent, which ought "normally" to have occurred at least five years before, can reasonably be attributed.

6. *Affaire du collier: Mémoires justificatifs de la comtesse de La Motte écrits par elle-même* (Paris, Frison, 1789), p. 10. She gets so entangled in her own lies that in another pamphlet she says this expression of petty vindictiveness took place after the death of the marquise, on a visit—which she never made—to the widower.

7. Archives nationales, CI 199, folios 140 and 142. The decree awarding the allowance from the King's privy purse is in the same file.

8. Funck-Brentano, *L'Affaire du collier,* p. 70.

9. Archives historiques du ministère de la guerre. Pensions sur le trésor royal, II, 592.

10. According to Bougainville, member of the Académie and cousin of the navigator, quoted by Abbé Sicard, *L'Ancien Clergé de France,* volume I, *Les Evêques avant la Révolution* (Paris, Victor Lecoffre, 1905), p. 98.

11. According to the *Mémoires* of the Marquis d'Argenson, quoted *ibid.,* p. 99; and (by Abbé Sicard himself) the following quotation as well.

12. *Souvenirs du marquis de Valfons,* from which details of the Saverne hunting parties are also taken, in Sicard, *L'Ancien Clergé,* p. 100.

13. See the Rohan of this period as engraved by Cathelin and Campion de Terson from a portrait by Rossin; there is also one by C. N. Cochin. Other portraits of the cardinal were painted by Captellan, Chapuy, Klauber, and François.

*14. Baronne d'Oberkirch, *Mémoires,* p. 115.

15. Premier intérrogatoire de M. le Cardinal de Rohan, Archives nationales, X² 257.

16. According to the Boulainvilliers's steward, quoted by Funck-Brentano, *L'Affaire du collier,* p. 85.

## 15

1. Based on a manuscript note from Rohan to his counsel Target. See Chapter 10, note 11.

2. Declaration made by Police Inspector J. F. de Bruguières— that's right, our old acquaintance from the days of the abduction of Mirabeau and Sophie in Holland—on April 11, 1786, to the officials of the Parlement (Archives nationales, X, B/1417). The Châtelet had instructed Bruguières to keep a discreet eye on the La Mottes after 1782, when there were numerous complaints from creditors.

3. Emile Campardon, *Marie-Antoinette et le procès du collier d'après la procédure instruite devant le Parlement de Paris* (Paris, Plon, 1863), p. 44. This collection contains the main official items in the investigation conducted by the Parlement

magistrates after Rohan's arrest. A little later, Inspector Quidor refers graphically to Rétaux as "Mme de La Motte's bull."

4. Mme Campan, *Mémoires sur la vie privée de Marie-Antoinette, reine de France et de Navarre, suivis de souvenirs et anecdotes historiques sur les règnes de Louis XIV, de Louis XV et de Louis XVI* (Brussels, Wahlen et Cie, 1823), in three volumes (this is the first and fullest edition); II, 17, n. by Mme Campan herself.

5. Testimony of Madame Pothey. first lady-in-waiting to Mme Elisabeth.

6. Abbé Georgel, *Mémoires pour servir à l'histoire des événements de la fin du XVIIIe siècle* (Paris, 1806), quoted by Louis Hastier, *La Vérité sur l'affaire du collier* (Paris, Fayard, n.d.), p. 140.

7. *Mémoires justificatifs de la comtesse de Valois de La Motte.* (See Chapter 14, note 6.) This quote is on p. 12, and those that follow on pp. 14, 17, 18, and 19.

# 16

1. Lescure, *Correspondance secrète*, I, 595.

2. From the *Souvenirs de Madame Vigée-Lebrun*, published by Pierre de Nolhac (Paris, Fayard, n.d.), p. 45.

3. This comes from the mysterious Demoiselle de Mirecourt, the authencity of whose *Mémoires*, recently exhumed by Claude-Emile Laurent (Paris, Albin Michel, 1966) and published under the rather cursory title *L'Autrichienne*, is

often contested. One is tempted to wonder whether their author actually existed. I therefore use them only for passages that are obviously accurate as regards the setting and hazards of Court life under Louis XVI, and are confirmed by many other sources. Even if this is no more than a compilation of reminiscences or pamphlets about the Queen, the unity of tone and precision of detail bespeaks the work of a master craftsman who was also very well acquainted with his material. The excerpt quoted here, and the following one, are on pp. 132 and 133.

4. Charles-Joseph, Prince de Ligne, *Fragments de l'histoire de ma vie* (Paris, Vergiol et Audiat, 1928), p. 208.

* 5. Abbé de Veri, *Journal*, I, 470.

6. Jean-Louis Giraud, alias Soulavie, *Mémoires historiques et politiques du règne de Louis XVI* (Paris, An X), III, p. 8. This ex-priest wrote at second hand, using texts supplied by émigrés, Richelieu in particular. But his story, published during the Consulate, has the advantage of being "hot," still close to events.

7. *Ibid.*, p. 13.

8. Lescure, *Correspondance secrète*, I, 569.

9. *L'Autrichienne* (see note 3 above), p. 163.

10. Pierre Manuel, *La Police de Paris dévoilée par l'un des administrateurs de 1789*, I, 37: catalogue of books deposited in the Bastille under the seal of M. Lenoir.

* 11. Brissot, *Mémoires*, II, 7.

12. *Mémoires secrets de J.-M. Augeard,*
    *secrétaire des commandements de la*
    *reine Marie-Antoinette, 1760–1800,*
    published by Evariste Bavous
    (Paris, Plon, 1866). He
    confesses his share in the libel
    writing on pp. 133 ff.
13. Felix Rocquain, *L'Esprit*
    *révolutionnaire avant la Révolution,*
    *1715–1789* (Paris, Plon, 1878),
    p. 418 n.

## 17

1. From the *Mémoires* of the Comte
   de Saint-Priest, quoted by Sabine
   Flaissier, *Marie-Antoinette en*
   *accusation* (Paris, Julliard, 1967),
   p. 228.
2. Augeard, *Mémoires,* p. 134.
3. *Ibid.,* 136. The unnumbered
   quotes that follow, referring to
   the dispute between the Queen
   and Calonne, are from the
   same source, beginning on that
   page.
4. Mme Campan, *Mémoires,* I, 322.
5. *Correspondance de Marie Antoinette,*
   *Joseph II et Leopold II,* published
   by A. von Arneth (Leipzig,
   Vienna, and Paris, Jung-Treuttel,
   1866), p. 38.
6. *Ibid.,* p. 45.
7. *Ibid.,* p. 51.
8. *Ibid.,* p. 62.
9. *Ibid.,* p. 73.
10. *Ibid.,* p. 94.
11. *Correspondance* between Joseph II
    and Leopold, published by A.
    von Arneth (Vienna, 1872),
    p. 265.
12. Ruault, *Gazette d'un Parisien,*
    p. 47 (dated December 1,
    1784).
13. *Ibid.,* p. 49.

## 18

1. See, in the index to volume III
   of the *Correspondance de*
   *Marie-Thérèse avec Marie-Antoinette*
   *et le comte de Mercy-Argenteau,*
   references to eighty-three
   passages of anti-Rohan spleen in
   the letters of the empress or her
   daughter.
2. According to notes prepared by
   Rohan for his counsel Target,
   preserved in the Paris Municipal
   Library (also chapter 11, note 5).
   Hereafter I shall refer to these as
   the "Target file."
3. Abbé Georgel, *Mémoires,* II, 42.
4. Interrogation of the Cardinal de
   Rohan and Father Loth (the
   monk attached to the La Mottes)
   on March 16, 1786, Archives
   nationales, $X^2$, B/1417.
5. Campardon, *Marie-Antoinette et le*
   *procès du collier,* 1. There is a
   minor mystery concerning
   Nicole Leguay's exact age. The
   record of a transaction between
   her and the heirs to the Legros
   boarding school, in 1783, shows
   her as born in 1761 (Archives
   nationales, Y, 5110). But why
   does the record of her first
   interrogation (on January 19,
   1786, by Pierre Titon, counselor
   at Parlement [Archives
   nationales, $X^2$, 257]) make her
   say she is "thirty-four years old,"
   which would mean she was born
   in 1751? I have been unable to
   trace her life far enough into the
   past, and hereby bequeath this
   enigma to future research. As far
   as her looks are concerned, a
   police description in 1785 says
   she was "twenty-six or

twenty-seven years old"
(Archives des Affaires Etrangères
[Foreign Affairs], Mémoires et
Documents, France, 1785,
volume 1399, folio 230). Marie
Antoinette will be thirty on
November 1, 1785.

6. Interrogation of Nicole Leguay
by Pierre Titon, reference in
preceding note. The full text
may be found in Campardon,
*Marie-Antoinette et le procès du
collier,* pp. 350–5.

7. According to notations in the
Paris Observatory, quoted by
Hastier, *La Vérité sur l'affaire du
collier,* p. 158 n.

8. According to the *Mémoire pour la
demoiselle Leguay d'Oliva* [*sic*] by
her lawyer, Blondel, in
Campardon, *Marie-Antoinette et le
procès du collier,* p. 7.

9. *Mémoires justificatifs de la Comtesse
de Valois,* evidence in her
defense, p. 242.

## 19

1. That is, at any rate, the
considered opinion of Louis
Hastier, in *La Vérité sur l'affaire
du collier,* p. 178.

2. Mme Campan, *Mémoires,* III, 5.

3. To make the end of this story of
the necklace move a little more
quickly, I have drawn the
following text from the
combined investigations of
Funck-Brentano, Campardon,
and Hastier, whose works I have
cited on many occasions, and
from the *Mémoires* of Mme
Campan, when it has been
possible to cross-check her
statements. Specific references

will be given only where other
sources have been used. On the
first two calls the jewelers were
represented by Bassenge alone;
the countess first sees Böhmer on
the rue Vendôme.

4. Archives nationales, X² B/1417,
128, folios 3 and 4.

5. As estimated by the goldsmith
Régnier: statement made by
Bassenge to a Parlement
attorney, in Campardon,
*Marie-Antoinette et le procès du
collier,* p. 108.

6. Archives nationales, 12076.

7. Brief of the trial, "Evidence in
favor of M. le Cardinal,
accused," quoted by Campardon,
*Marie-Antoinette et le procès du
collier,* p. 93.

8. Target file in the Paris Municipal
Library.

9. Bassenge kept a copy of this
note and gave it to the
Parlement attorney who
questioned him. Rohan did not
deny either the terms of the
missive or the responsibility for
dictating it.

10. An even fuller account of the
episode has been preserved,
through the curious whims of
documentary destiny, in the
Dijon Municipal Library, Mss
1189, folios 162–5. It contains
the two jewelers' story of their
dealings with Rohan and
Jeanne de La Motte, as handed
to the Queen on August 12,
1785.

*11. According to the diary of the
bookseller Hardy, quoted by
Felix Rocquain, *L'Esprit
révolutionnaire avant la révolution,*
p. 402.

## 20

1. *Voyage pittoresque des environs de Paris, ou description des maisons royales, etc.,* by M. D. (Paris, De Bure *aîné,* 1755), p. 50.
2. *Ibid.,* p. 53.
\* 3. *Correspondance secrète de Marie-Thérèse,* letter to Mercy-Argenteau, March 4, 1775, II, 303. Kaunitz's opinion of Breteuil is quoted by the empress in the same letter.
4. For the complete text of the Maréchal de Castries's account, in the abundantly documented book the Duc de Castries has published (France Empire, 1978), see *Papiers de famille,* p. 388. I thank him very warmly for permission to quote from them.
5. From this point on Castries's account can be supplemented by that addressed by Breteuil to Thiroux de Crosne, lieutenant chief of police (published by Peuchet, *Mémoires historiques,* III, 158–61) and by the *Mémoires* of Besenval, to whom the Queen spoke the same day.

## 21

1. Letter from Gallot to Vicq d'Azyr, March 28, 1785, in Dr. Louis Merle, *La Vie et les oeuvres du Dr. Jean-Gabriel Gallot, 1744–1794* (Poitiers, Société des Antiquaires de l'Ouest, 1961), 4th ser., volume V. Despite the date of his death, Gallot was not a victim of the Terror; he died of a typhoid fever contracted among his patients, to whom he returned after his incursion into politics during the Constituent Assembly. His letters to Vicq d'Azyr are on pp. 253–97 of the book.
2. *Ibid.,* letter to the same, April 21, 1785.
3. See in this connection Jean-Pierre Goubert, *Malades et médecins en Bretagne, 1770–1790* (Paris, Klincksiek, 1979).
4. Letter from Gallot to Vicq d'Azyr, April 21, 1785 (see note 1 above).
5. "Mémoire sur les maladies régnantes à Saint-Maurice-le-Girard, près la Châtaignerie (Bas-Poitou) et aux environs, avec des observations sur la nature du climat, les productions du sol, les habitants et les épizooties," Archives of the Academy of Medicine, Gallot Papers.
6. *Ibid.* The fourteen pages of this memorandum are unnumbered.
7. Letter to Vicq d'Azyr, November 26, 1787, in Merle, *La Vie et les oeuvres,* p. 284.
8. Another excerpt from the Gallot "Mémoire" (note 5).
9. Archives nationales, TT 445A. Memorandum by M. de la Mauvinière on the bocage Huguenots.
10. Said by a dignitary from la Rochelle, in Merle, *La Vie et les oeuvres,* p. 5.
11. *Ibid.,* p. 6.
12. See the work by M. Gaufrès, *L'enseignement protestant sous l'Edit de Nantes.*
13. Mercier du Rocher, "Notice sur Gallot," published by Dugast-Matifeux in *Annales de la*

*Société d'émulation de la Vendée,* 1878, ser. 2, VIII, 25.

14. Letter to Dubois de Fosseux, August 29, 1787. These letters are published by Merle, *La Vie et les oeuvres,* and follow those from Gallot to Vicq d'Azyr.

15. Continuation of the "Mémoire" cited in note 5.

*16. Fernand Braudel, *Civilisation matérielle et capitalisme,* I, 105.

17. *Ibid.,* p. 106.

18. Document found among Gallot's papers, preserved in the Nantes Municipal Library under the title "Réflexions ou Discours sur les causes principales des maladies populaires ou épidémiques en bas Poitou, avec des vues de soulagement public pour le peuple des campagnes" and, published by L. Merle, *Le Service des épidémies et l'Hygiène au Poitou avant la Révolution* (Niort, 1913).

22

1. Hérault de Séchelles, "Voyage à Montbard," in his *Oeuvres littéraires,* edited by Emile Dard (Paris, Perrin, 1907), p. 5. All unnumbered quotations in this chapter have been taken from the fifty-page account of which Hérault publishes a first version on his return to Paris, in November 1785, falsely dated September.

2. Yann Gaillard, *Buffon, biographie imaginaire et réelle* (Paris, Hermann, 1977), p. 146. It contains the complete text of Hérault's "Voyage à Montbard."

3. Details from Expilly's *Dictionnaire,* IV, 811: "Montbart" [*sic*]. In the original version of his story Hérault uses all three spellings: Montbar, Montbart, and the modern Montbard.

4. The portrait is owned by the Polignac family and is reproduced in Ernest Daudet, *Le Roman d'un conventionnel: Hérault de Séchelles et les dames de Bellegarde* (Paris, Hachette, 1904). The details of the relationship between the Maréchal de Contades and Hérault's mother are taken from this book.

5. Albert Descoqs, "Les Origines avranchinaises du conventionnel, Hérault de Séchelles," in *Revue de l'Avranchin,* 1930, no. 141, p. 124. *Ibid.* for the particulars of his coat of arms.

6. Daudet, *Le Roman d'un conventionnel,* p. 46.

7. *Ibid.,* pp. 49 and 64.

8. Letter from Hérault to Lavater, July 29, 1784, written almost a year after his visit, which was on October 3, 1783. At that time Lavater told him that he would only pass physiognomic judgment upon "immobile faces." This letter and Lavater's reply are in the Zurich Stadtbibliothek and are published in full by Emile Dard, *Un épicurien sous la Terreur: Hérault de Séchelles, 1759–1794* (Paris, Perrin, 1907), pp. 37–41.

9. The best portrait of Buffon must be the bust by Houdon, made in 1781. Hérault refers to it.

10. Some people, troubled by the vagueness of the text, have

426

wondered whether Hérault ever
went to Montbard at all—which
is high praise for his powers of
fabrication. But a letter from
Buffon's son to Mme Necker,
dated October 30, 1785 (the
very day), attests to the reality of
the visit and also restricts its
duration. (Buffon's
correspondence, Lanessan
edition, volume XIV, 324).

11. Dard, *Hérault de Séchelles,* p. 49.

### 23

1. *Dictionnaire du bas langage ou des
   manières de parler usitées parmi le
   peuple* (Paris, Léopold Collin,
   bookseller, 1808), p. 215.
2. Gaillard, *Buffon,* p. 55.
3. *Ibid.,* p. 27; from the biography
   of Buffon by his secretary
   Humbert-Bazile.
4. Buffon, *Oeuvres* (Auguste Comte
   edition), II, 237 n.
5. According to the *Journal de
   voyage de M. Jars, Inspecteur des
   Forges de Bourgogne,* quoted by
   Germain-Martin in *Buffon, maître
   de forges* (Le Puy, Régis
   Marchessol, printer, 1898), p. 3.
6. Gaillard, *Buffon,* end of the
   "page of his diary for May 24,
   1977," on p. 174.
7. Dard, *Hérault de Séchelles,* p. 8.
   Same source, pp. 9–12, for the
   following description of his
   domestic life.
8. Maxims from the *Codicille
   politique et pratique d'un jeune
   habitant d'Epone* which he
   publishes in 1788 (in his *Oeuvres
   littéraires,* published by Dard, pp.
   66–149).

### 24

1. Archives nationales, ser. VI, 523.
2. This detail, with many others, is
   taken from the exhaustive paper
   on the "Origines sociales de
   Carrier" written by Michel
   Leymarie for a symposium held
   at Riom and Clermont on June
   10 and 11, 1965, by the
   Department of Literature and
   Science of Clermont-Ferrand, on
   "Gilbert Romme et son temps";
   it was published by PUF in
   1966. I have based this chapter
   on his text (pp. 43–62) because
   it corrects and qualifies the
   mistakes in an earlier work
   which was used as a reference by
   most of Carrier's biographers.
   This was Jean Delmas, "La
   Jeunesse et les Débuts de
   Carrier" in *La Révolution
   française,* May 14, 1895, pp.
   417–39. From the latter article I
   take only material confirmed by
   Michel Leymarie. See also, by
   the same author, "Documents
   nouveaux sur la jeunesse et les
   débuts de Carrier" in *La Revue de
   la Haute-Auvergne,* 1954–5, pp.
   425–74.
3. Philibert-Joseph Le Roux,
   *Dictionnaire comique, satirique,
   critique, burlesque, libre et
   proverbial, etc.,* published in Lyons
   by the heirs of the "Beringos
   frates" [*sic*], p. 138:
   "procureur." In subsequent
   references this book is
   abbreviated as *Dictionnaire
   comique.*
4. Carrier's record of baptism was
   first published in the *Dictionnaire*

*des Parlementaires* by Robert, Bourloton, and Coigny.

5. Expilly, *Dictionnaire*, I, 392: "Auvergne."

6. Alfred Lallié, *J. B. Carrier, représentant du Cantal à la Convention, 1756–1794, d'après de nouveaux documents* (Paris, Perrin, 1901), pp. 5, 6, and 17.

7. Marcellin Boudet, *Les Tribunaux criminels et la justice révolutionnaire en Auvergne* (Clermont-Ferrand, 1873), containing a number of statements by the last living eyewitnesses to Carrier's youth.

8. According to the An II census, preserved in the Aurillac Municipal Archives, found by Michel Leymarie and used in his "Origines sociales de Carrier," p. 59, n. 84.

9. Letter from Marcellin Boudet to Jean Delmas, Saint-Flour, January 22, 1894, quoted by Leymarie, *ibid.*, p. 60, n. 89.

## 25

1. According to a letter from Coindet, a former secretary of Necker who became a family friend, sent on January 23 to Paul Moulton-Cayla (Bibliothèque Publique et Universitaire, Geneva, acq. 1945/35).

2. Letter from the admirable *Correspondance générale de Madame de Staël* published by Beatrice W. Kasinski at J.-J. Pauvert, beginning in 1962. This is from volume I, *Lettres de jeunesse*, first part (1777–August 1788), p. 58. Other references will be

abbreviated *Correspondance générale*.

3. Baronne d'Andlau, *La Jeunesse de Madame de Staël, de 1766 à 1786* (Geneva, Librairie Droz, 1970), p. 101.

\* 4. *Lettres*, Axel Fersen to his father, p. 177.

\* 5. Lady Blennerhasset, *Madame de Staël et son temps* (Paris, Westhausser, 1890), I, 238.

\* 6. A. Geffroy, *Gustave III et la Cour de France*, I, 354.

7. William Beckford, *Vathek* (1786 Translation, New York, Scholars' Facsimiles and Reprints, 1972), p. 194. Romney's portrait (from the Bearsted Collection, Upton House, Banbury) is reproduced as the frontispiece to Marc Chadourne, *Eblis, ou l'enfer de William Beckford* (Paris, J.-J. Pauvert, 1967). "Eblis" or "Yblis" is the equivalent of Satan in sacred Arabic texts. To learn more about Beckford, I recommend the monumental book by Professor André Paneaux, *William Beckford, auteur de Vathek* (Paris, Nizet, 1960).

8. C. Redding, *Memoirs of William Beckford of Fonthill*, 1859, II, 353. Beckford's further comments on the Neckers [retranslated from the French—*Trans.*] were taken from the *Correspondance générale* of Mme de Staël, I, 20 n., 21 n.

9. Lewis Melville, *The Life and Letters of William Beckford of Fonthill* (London, Heinemann, 1910), p. 157, letter from Beckford to his cousin Alexander Hamilton, from Rome, on June 29, 1782.

10. Letter from Germaine Necker (signed "Louise") to William Beckford, late February 1784, in *Correspondance générale*, I, 19.

*11. Allegedly said by Elliott, a well-informed Whig member, related by Jacques Chastenet in *William Pitt*, p. 83 [Retranslated from the French.—*Trans.*].

12. Madame de Staël, *Considérations sur la Révolution française*, in the first edition of her *Oeuvres complètes* (Bern, Treuttel and Wirtz, 1820), XIV, 286.

13. *Correspondance générale*, I, 471 (letter to M. de Staël, July 30, 1791).

14. Quoted by Lady Blennerhasset, *Madame de Staël*, I, 202.

## 26

1. Lady Blennerhasset, *Madame de Staël*, I, 204.

2. *Ibid.*, 217, from Haussonville's *Mémoires* on "Le salon de Mme Necker."

3. Catherine Rilliet-Huber, "Notes sur l'enfance de Madame de Staël," in *Occident et cahiers staëliens*, March 1934, p. 142.

4. *Correspondance générale*, letter to Madame d'Houdetot, May 18, 1785, I, 35.

5. Baronne d'Andlau, *La Jeunesse de Madame de Staël*, p. 69.

6. "Journal de jeunesse de Madame de Staël" in *Occident*, October 15, 1932, p. 238.

7. Lady Blennerhasset, *Madame de Staël*, I, 235.

8. Letters, from Necker, November 10, 1785, and from his wife, October 23, 1785, to their friend Paul Moultou, in Francis

de Crue, *L'Amie de Rousseau et des Necker, Paul Moultou* (Paris, Honoré Champion, 1926), p. 181.

9. "Journal de jeunesse" in *Occident*, p. 236.

10. Letter to Madame de Portes, quoted by Béatrice Jasinski in the *Correspondance générale*, p. xxviii n.

11. "Journal de jeunesse" in *Occident*, p. 237.

12. *Ibid.*, p. 239.

## 27

* 1. Britsch, *La Jeunesse de Philippe-Egalité*, p. 450.

2. *Ibid.*, p. 451.

3. Grimm, *Correspondance littéraire*, XIV, 340 and 342. The quotes relating to Fauchet are from the same text, also p. 342.

4. The description of Saint-Eustache which, as I write these pages, rises impressively from the ruins of the market district in Paris, is taken from two previously cited
* works, the Larousse *Dictionnaire*
* *de Paris* (480) and Dulaure's *Nouvelle Description des curiosités de Paris* (1791), I, 322.

5. This bouquet of descriptions was assembled from p. 357 of volume II of the fullest biography of Fauchet, J. Charrier, *Claude Fauchet, évêque constitutionnel du Calvados, député à l'Assemblée législative et à la Convention, 1744–1793* (Paris, Honoré Champion, 1909). The book was written by a priest from the diocese of Nevers, who was something of a masochist in his choice of subject;

unfortunately, his style is infuriatingly "priestly" and he is forever bemoaning Abbé Fauchet's "ideological deviations" from unconditional allegiance to throne and altar.

6. *Annales de la ville de Decize,* published by M. Trevaux de Bertaux (Moulins, Enaut printers, n.d.).

7. Charrier, *Claude Fauchet,* I, 3.

8. *Ibid.,* p. 5.

9. Abbé Delarc, *L'Eglise de Paris pendant la Révolution,* I, 256 n.

10. Charrier, *Claude Fauchet,* I, 10.

11. *Panégyrique de Saint Louis, roi de France, prononcé dans la chapelle du Louvre,* August 25, 1774 (Paris, Dorez, 1774), 74 octavo pages, Bibliothèque nationale, Lb 18/136. *Ibid.* for the next quote.

12. Manuscript sermon, quoted by Charrier, *Claude Fauchet,* I, 19.

13. *Ibid.,* p. 25.

14. Text confiscated with the rest of Claude Fauchet's papers at his arrest, and returned to his family by the Thermidorians, quoted by Charrier, *Claude Fauchet,* I, 26–9.

15. Edmond and Jules de Goncourt, *Histoire de la société française pendant la Révolution,* definitive edition published under the supervision of the Académie Française (Paris, Flammarion et Fasquelle, 1928), p. 179 (letter copied from a catalogue of autographs, April 8, 1844).

16. *Oraison funèbre de Louis-Philippe d'Orléans, prince du sang,* 31 quarto pages (Paris, Imprimerie Lottin, 1786), Bibliothèque nationale, Ln. 27/15 506.

17. Figures given in the outstanding book by Béatrice Hyslop,

*L'Apanage de Philippe-Egalité, duc d'Orléans, 1785–1791* (Paris, Société des Etudes robespierristes, 1965) (with the cooperation of the CNRS). See in particular the table on p. 77.

## 28

1. *Lettres de Gustave III à la comtesse de Boufflers et de la comtesse au Roi, de 1771 à 1791,* published by Aurélien Vivié (Bordeaux, 1900), p. 372.

2. *Correspondance de Madame de Staël,* I, p. 61, n. 1. The passage in quotes is by Gustavus III himself.

3. *Ibid.,* letter to Gustavus III, March 15, 1786, I, 63.

4. *Eloge de Catinat,* passage quoted by E. Forestié, *Biographie du comte de Guibert* (Montauban, 1855), p. 29. *Ibid.* for the other passage from Guibert's speech below.

5. *Correspondance de Madame de Staël,* I, 70.

6. *Ibid.,* "newsletter" to Gustavus III, November 1786, p. 145.

7. Letter from Calonne to the Maréchal de Ségur, August 28, 1783, in Robert Lacour-Gayet, *Calonne, financier, réformateur, contre-révolutionnaire, 1734–1802* (Paris, Hachette, 1963), p. 68, n. 1. The bulk of my documentation on Calonne, and unnumbered passages in quotes hereafter, are also from this work.

\* 8. Talleyrand, *Mémoires,* I, 103.

9. Today in Windsor Castle in England; it is reproduced on the cover of Lacour-Gayet's *Calonne.*

10. Lacour-Gayet, *Calonne,* p. 14.

11. M. Antoine, *Le discours de la Flagellation* (Paris, 1955), Festschrift for M. Clovis Brunel.

12. *Procès-verbal de la séance de M. le Maréchal de Broglie au Parlement de Metz, accompagné de M. de Calonne, jeudi 3 octobre 1775* (Paris, no date or publisher).

13. V. Champier, *L'Art dans les Flandres françaises au XVIIIe siècle* (Roubaix, 1926), p. 127.

14. *Mémoire de M. de Calonne, ministre d'Etat, contre le décret rendu le 14 février 1791 par l'Assemblée se disant Nationale* (Venice, 1791).

## 29

1. R. Chéroy, "Les Transferts de postes budgétaires dans les dernières années de l'Ancien Régime," in *Annales économiques et historiques du Gâtinais,* IV, 72.

* 2. G. Lacour-Gayet, *Talleyrand,* I, 63.

3. Talleyrand, *Mémoires,* I, 58. Other passages written in the first person, including the one above, are from the same source.

4. Ch. Place and J. Florens, *Mémoires sur M. de Talleyrand, sa vie politique et sa vie intime* (Paris, 1838), p. 82. The authors of this pamphlet had the good fortune to consult all three catalogues of the Talleyrand library sales—in London in 1793, again in London in 1816, and lastly in Paris in 1838, two months after his death. The catalogue for the last sale contained 412 items. Cf. Bibliothèque nationale, 35145.

5. *Journal de Gouverneur Morris pendant les années 1789–1792* (Paris, Plon, 1901), p. 174.

6. See in this connection the demonstration by Lacour-Gayet, *Calonne,* I, 73–4, the *Journal de Gouverneur Morris,* and A. Marcade, *Talleyrand, prêtre et évêque* (Paris, 1883), p. 139.

* 7. Guizot, *Mémoires pour servir à l'histoire de mon temps,* I, 6. The author claims actually to have heard Talleyrand utter the sentence. The end is often deformed and has Talleyrand say "la *douceur* de vivre" instead of "plaisir" ["sweetness" instead of "pleasure"—*Trans.* ].

8. *Mémoires d'un ministère du Trésor public, 1780–1815* (Paris, 1845), I, 70.

* 9. Alfred Stern, *La Vie de Mirabeau,* I, 227. *Ibid.* for Mirabeau's remarks on Panchaud.

## 30

1. Frederick II, *Correspondance,* official edition (Berlin, Deckern, 1854), XI, 13.

2. Archives des Affaires Etrangères [Foreign Affairs], Prussia, volume 205.

3. From letters written by Mirabeau to Chamfort in 1784 and 1785, quoted by Nicolas de Montigny
* in *Mémoires de Mirabeau,* IV, 145–6 nn.

4. Madame de Nehra, *Souvenirs,* published in part by Nicolas de Montigny. This sentence is
* quoted by Antonina Vallentin, *Mirabeau avant la Révolution,* p. 302.

5. This synthesis of descriptions of Mme de Nehra is by Antonina Vallentin, *ibid.,* p. 301.

6. Reproduced in full in an article

by Léo Mouton, "Madame de Nehra et Mirabeau," in the *Revue des études historiques* (86th year), 1920, pp. 528–35.

7. Vallentin, *Mirabeau,* p. 306. The next two quotes are on pp. 305 and 308.

8. Quoted by Nicolas de Montigny in *Mémoires de Mirabeau,* IV, 286.

9. Reichard, *Guide,* III, 188: "Germany."

10. *Encyclopédie,* VII, 282: "Frankfurt-am-Main."

11. This is the end of Henriette de Nehra's travel notes; the reference is the same as for note 8, p. 288.

### 31

* 1. *Mémoires, correspondances et manuscrits du général Lafayette* [*sic*] *publiés par sa famille* (Paris, 1838), II, 130. Unnumbered quotes later in this passage are from the same letter to Washington, dated February 8, 1786. When I take other texts from this source (six volumes in all), I give the title as *Correspondance de La Fayette.*

2. Conversations of Frederick II with Henri de Catt, excerpts published in *Frédéric II, roi de Prusse,* texts compiled for the "Mémorial des siècles" collection of Gérard Walter (Paris, Albin Michel, 1967), preface by Pierre Gaxotte, p. 178.

3. Excerpts from letters quoted by Pierre Gaxotte in his preface, *ibid.,* p. 68.

4. Letter to d'Alembert, March 13, 1771, *ibid.,* p. 61.

5. Gaxotte, *ibid.,* p. 94.

* 6. *Courrier de l'Europe,* September 8, 1785, XVIII, 154.

* 7. Charavay, *Le Général La Fayette,* p. 123, n. 2. The letter was written by La Fayette in Paris on February 11, 1786.

8. *Correspondance de La Fayette,* II, 121, letter to Washington, May 11, 1785.

9. *Ibid.,* p. 152, letter from Washington to La Fayette, May 10, 1786.

10. *Ibid.,* p. 125, Washington to La Fayette, July 25, 1785.

11. Collection of the *American Cultivator* (Boston), III, 385.

### 32

1. *Correspondance de Frédéric II, roi de Prusse,* X, 457. *Ibid.,* p. 458 for Frederick's reply and his letter to von Goertz (note 1, chapter 30).

2. Foreword to the *Lettre remise à Frédéric-Guillaume II, roi régnant de Prusse, le jour de son avènement au trône par le comte de Mirabeau* (Paris, 1787), p. 4.

3. Archives des Affaires Etrangères [Foreign Affairs], Prussia, volume 205. *Ibid.* for Vergennes's reply.

4. Vallentin, *Mirabeau,* p. 362.

* 5. This aspect of Mirabeau's mission and its possible implications are clearly brought out by Dauphin-Meunier in *Autour de Mirabeau,* in the chapter entitled "A la conquête du roi de Prusse," pp. 160–2.

6. Letter from Frederick II, August 8, 1769, to the Dowager Electoress of Saxe.

7. Vallentin, *Mirabeau,* p. 363.

8. According to Rachel Levin, wife

of a famous Berlin physicist
named Marcus Herz, a few of
whose classes Mirabeau attended.
Quoted by Alfred Stern, *La vie
de Mirabeau,* I, 239.

9. *Correspondance de Frédéric II,* X;
*ibid.* for the reply.

10. Vallentin, *Mirabeau,* p. 369.

# 33

1. According to his brother-in-law
Joseph Lange, who sketched a
good portrait of him in 1783.
See also the wax medallion of
Mozart at thirty-two by Leonard
Posch. Portraits of the composer
as an adult are very scarce; the
two I mention here are in the
Mozart Museum in Salzburg.

2. B. and J. Massin, *Mozart,* p. 448.

3. Letter from Mozart to his father,
June 20, 1781, quoted by the
Massins, *Mozart,* p. 345.

4. Most of the quotes relating to
the "kick episode" come from
Mozart's letters to his father and
are quoted by the Massins,
*Mozart,* pp. 340–2.

5. Laurenzo [*sic*] d'Aponte [*sic*],
*Mémoires d'un coureur d'aventures*
(Paris, 1884), p. 122. Lorenzo
da Ponte has always been the
accepted spelling.

6. Letter to his father, September
11, 1776, in B. and J. Massin,
*Mozart,* p. 271.

7. According to his friend Nissen,
who was an eyewitness (*Ibid.,* p.
290). The Rabelaisian words
were those of an old folk *lied* by
Goetz von Berlichingen.

8. B. and J. Massin, *Mozart,* p. 293.

9. To his father, September 11,
1778, *ibid.,* p. 302.

10. Letter from Mozart to the
librettist Anton Kelin, March 21,
1785, *ibid.,* p. 347.

11. *Ibid.,* p. 389.

12. To his father, December 15,
1781, *ibid.,* p. 363.

13. Also to his father, December 15,
1781, *ibid.,* p. 363.

14. Note by the Massins in their
analysis of the *Nozze,* in *Mozart,*
p. 1021. And while I'm stealing
from Brigitte and Jean Massin, I
may as well pay full homage to
the brilliance of their
interpretation, by reproducing
this excerpt which concludes
their commentary on the opera:
"Hence the function of
Cherubino in the plot, always at
the center of the action,
unpredictable, useless, disrupting
every scheme of either camp but
loved by one side and loathed by
the other: youth incarnate.
Almaviva, who spends his life
being overwhelmed by the
turbulence of reality, personified
here by the enterprising
adolescent, cannot abide him.
And yet who was Almaviva
himself when he was
Cherubino's age, abducting his
Rosina from Bartholo a few
years before; isn't that what the
self-important, fatuous character
whose authority has no power
over reality hates so much in
Cherubino—the image of his
own youth, free and full of
promise?"

# 34

1. I want to express my very
sincere thanks to Professor Pavel

Apostol, dean of the Department of Languages and Literature of Bucharest, for procuring for me the most important passages from this fiery essay by Brissot, which is preserved in the Biblioteca Academiei Romane in Bucharest. They were selected by Paul Desfeuilles and Jacques Lassaigne, and published in an anthology of texts edited by the Romanian State Press in 1937, entitled *Les Français et la Roumanie.* Brissot's two pamphlets are wrongly attributed to Mirabeau in the catalogue of the Bibliothèque nationale in Paris, and are here re-assigned to their rightful author.

## 35

1. The best portrait we have of her is in the museum of Chartres; it was painted before the Revolution.
* 2. Brissot, *Correspondance,* pp. 36 and 37.
3. Brissot, *Mémoires,* I, 302.
4. *Ibid.,* I, 307.
5. *Ibid.,* I, 312.
6. *Ibid.,* I, 315 and 316.
7. Quoted in Claude Perroud's preface to Brissot's *Correspondance,* p. xxvii. *Ibid.* for the following details on the price and circulation of the *Lycée de Londres.*
8. Brissot, *Correspondance,* p. 65; the letter is headed "Château de Mirabeau," where Mirabeau was staying with his uncle. The two men had not yet met.
9. Twelve numbers came out between December 1782 and

November 1783, bound in two octavo volumes inscribed "London and Neuchâtel, 1783."
10. Brissot, *Mémoires,* I, 337.
11. Brissot (unsigned), *Correspondance universelle,* etc. (see note 9), issue of February 1, 1783.
12. Brissot, *Mémoires,* II, 45; *ibid.* for the rest of the quote, after the description of the countryside.
13. Expilly, *Dictionnaire,* II, 709: "Dunois." Details relating to the village of Lanneray are from the same source, IV, 135: "Lanneray."

## 36

* 1. See Victor Tapié, *Monarchies et peuples du Danube,* pp. 261–4.
* 2. François Fejtö, *Un Habsbourg révolutionnaire: Joseph II,* p. 273.
* 3. This and the following quotes are from the *Correspondance de Joseph II et de Léopold de Toscane,* pp. 228–64.

## 37

1. Quoted by Funck-Brentano, *L'Affaire du collier,* p. 245. In this chapter I also borrow from other works to which I have already referred in peeling off the layers of this "affaire": Louis Hastier, *La Vérité sur l'Affaire du Collier;* Emile Campardon, *Marie-Antoinette et le procès du collier* (this contains the records of the interrogations); and Mme Campan's *Mémoires.*
2. Lescure, *Correspondance secrète,* II, 63.
3. According to Funck-Brentano, *L'Affaire du collier,* p. 265,

4. Archives des Affaires Etrangères [Foreign Affairs], France, 1785, volume 1399, folios 244, 273, and 278.
5. Hardy, *Journal,* July 12, 1786.
6. *Ibid.,* March 13.

## 38

1. *Le Géographe parisien, ou le Conducteur chronologique et historique des rues de Paris* (no author's name) (Paris, 1760), I, 100.
2. Bibliothèque de l'Arsenal, Ms. Bastille, 12 457, folio 63.
3. *Ibid.,* folio 59.
4. Linguet, *Mémoires sur la Bastille,* p. 55.
5. Quoted by Funck-Brentano, *L'Affaire du collier,* p. 316. *Ibid.* for last paragraph of the chapter.

## 39

1. L. S. Mercier, *Tableau de Paris,* IV, 92.
2. Lescure, *Correspondance secrète,* II, 5. See also p. 7.
3. L. S. Mercier, *Tableau de Paris,* I, 134. The "coachmen's uprising" took place in 1782.
4. Lescure, *Correspondance secrète,* II, 34.
5. Warmest thanks to my friend the historian R. G. Nobécourt for obtaining this rare work for me: *Le Voyage de Louis XVI en Normandie, 21–29 juin 1786* (Caen, Caron et Cie, 1967), in which J. M. Gaudillot has assembled the main texts and documents I have used in this chapter, is accompanied by handsome illustrations that give

one a sense of actually seeing the trip.
6. It claims, weirdly, to have been printed in Philadelphia; dated 1787, 16 mo., 95 pages. It was actually printed in the offices of the *Affiches de Normandie* and the least one can say is that it contains nothing seditious! The Bibliothèque nationale's copy disappeared in 1948; the only copy now known is in the Rouen Municipal Library (Normandie, 57/26).

## 40

1. According to Du Mouriez himself, in a (manuscript) "Journal de la visite de Sa Majesté Louis XVI à Cherbourg," Cherbourg Municipal Archives, BB.5.
2. Arthur Chuquet, *Dumouriez* (Paris, Hachette, 1914), p. 51.
3. *Mémoires du Général Dumouriez* (Paris, Firmin Didot, 1862), p. 185.
4. *Ibid.,* pp. 190 and 191.
5. Comment by Du Mouriez, quoted by Georges Lefebvre, *Cherbourg à la fin de l'Ancien Régime et au début de la Révolution* (Caen, Cahier des Annales de Normandie, 1965), p. 98.
6. *Ibid.,* p. 103.
7. See, by J. Renard, *Dumouriez et les marguilliers de Cherbourg* (Caen, 1842).
8. Census conducted at the behest of the *gouvernement de Normandie,* Cherbourg Municipal Archives, BB.16.
9. Verusmor, *Cherbourg à quatre*

époques, and Municipal Archives, *ibid.,* BB.5, folios 325 and 331.

\*10. Young, *Travels in France,* p. 81.

11. *Ibid.,* p. 82.

12. According to the diary of a Cherbourg savant, Voisin La Hougue, quoted by Lefebvre, *Cherbourg,* p. 112 (see note 5). Same reference for the price of bread and wage figures.

13. Gaudillot, *Le Voyage de Louis XVI,* p. 41. Unreferenced quotes at the end of this chapter are from the same source.

14 See the painting by Lemonnier in the Rouen Museum, "Louis XVI Receiving the Dignitaries of Rouen," one of the best portraits of the King at this period in his life (reproduced as plate XXII, *ibid.*).

## 41

\* 1. Mme Roland, *Lettres,* published by Claude Perroud, I, 625, letter dated August 10, 1780.

2. *Ibid.,* to Bosc on June 10, 1783, from somewhere near Corbie in Picardy, p. 255.

3. Figures re-used and authenticated in An VII (i.e., 1799) in the *Dictionnaire universel de la géographie commerçante* by J. Peuchet, one of the most assiduous contributors to the *Encyclopédie méthodique,* on which he worked with Roland for Panckoucke (Paris, Blanchon, Testu, printers, An VII), I, 327: "Amiens." Other unreferenced information about the town in this chapter is from the same source.

\* 4. Quoted by Georges Huisman,

*La vie privé de Madame Roland,* p. 103.

\* 5. Madeleine Jacquemaire-Clemenceau, *Vie de Madame Roland,* I, 152.

6. Jean-Marie Roland, *Mémoire des services donnés dans la généralité d'Amiens,* exhumed by Claude Perroud from Appendix E to Volume II of the first series of *Lettres de Madame Roland,* p. 609. Same source for the next quote, also by Roland.

7. Mme Roland, *Lettres,* I, 88 (to Roland, from Amiens, on December 28, 1781). *Ibid.* for the following quotation.

8. *Ibid.,* p. 242.

9. *Ibid.,* to Roland from Paris (where she had gone to agitate for a patent of nobility, see next chapter), March 26, 1784, p. 301.

10. *Ibid.,* to Roland from Amiens, in a long letter dated August 25, 1783, p. 264.

11. *Ibid.,* to Bosc on November 10, 1786, from Villefranche, p. 640.

12. *Ibid.,* to Roland, p. 117.

13. *Ibid.,* to Roland, p. 173.

14. *Ibid.,* p. 216.

15. *Ibid.,* on August 8, 1785, to Bosc, from Villefranche, p. 530.

## 42

1. Ambition attributed to Roland by the Marquise de Créqui in her *Souvenirs,* quoted by M. Jacquemaire-Clemenceau in *La Vie de Madame Roland,* I, 164.

2. Roland papers in the Bibliothèque nationale, letter by J.-M. Roland dated November 16, 1782, MS. 6240, folio 91.

3. *Almanach royal* for 1784, p. 246.
4. Lyons Municipal Library, Coste Archive, J. 14719, *Ibid.* for the intendant's reply.
5. Mme Roland, *Lettres,* to Roland, April 4, 1784, I, 319.
6. *Ibid.,* p. 322, to Roland on April 5. This long passage is typical of her.
7. *Ibid.,* to Roland on May 12, 1784, p. 393.
8. *Ibid.,* I, note by Claude Perroud at the bottom of p. 255.
9. *Ibid.,* to Roland on April 20, 1784, I, 350.
10. *Ibid.,* to Roland on April 19, 1784, p. 346. Same source for the next two brief quotes.
11. The letter was drafted jointly by Blondel and Madame Roland. The Roland papers in the Bibliothèque nationale contain two copies, MS. 6241, folio 267, and MS. 6243, folio 55, one in the hand of Lanthenas and the other in that of Jeanne-Marie— her first text for a minister.
12. Mme Roland, *Lettres,* I, 400.
13. *Ibid.,* p. 429. Same source for the following quotes.

## 43

1. Expilly's *Dictionnaire,* IV, 275: "Lyon."
2. Jean Jaurès, *Histoire socialiste de la Révolution française,* edition revised and annotated by Albert Soboul (Paris, Editions Sociales, 1968), I, 174. In the errata to his first edition Juarès was scrupulous enough to observe that "the allusion to the Croix-Rousse is partly anachronistic, because in those days there were few weavers' houses on the heights above Lyons."
3. The basis of my documentation on the "two sou uprising" is the very full article by J. Beyssac in the *Revue d'Histoire de Lyon,* 1907, VI: "La Sédition ouvrière de 1786." He gives a great many exact references and shows (see his first three pages) how the archbishop's ill-advised restoration of the "right of *banvin"* was no more than a token manifestation of the general bullying attitude of the ruling class toward the poor; it was not the cause of the uprising, only a convergent factor.
4. In his *Administration des finances de la France,* published in 1784, II, 61.
5. *Doléances des maîtres-ouvriers, fabricants en étoffes d'or, d'argent et de soie de la ville de Lyon,* texts collected and presented by Fernand Rude (Lyons, Editions Fédérop, 1976), introduction, p. 7. *Ibid.* for the quote from the note in the following paragraph, a copy of which was seized by the consulate police.
6. Lyons Municipal Archives, BB 347.
7. Rhône *département* archives, Criminal Seneschalsy Court, August 1786; proceedings instituted at the behest of the King's prosecuting attorney against Jean-Pierre Sauvage, Jean-Jacques Nerin, and Joseph Dapiano; item 11.

8. *Ibid.,* item 27: testimony of a sergeant and a soldier of the watch.

## 44

1. *La Gazette de Lyon* (full title: *Nouvelles extraordinaires de divers endroits*) publishes several letters referring to the events in Lyons in its issue of August 25, 1786. One of them makes a point of mentioning the extreme sultriness of the weather during the three days of the uprising.
2. Lyons Municipal Archives, archive no. IV, box VII, folio 190.
3. Peuchet, *Dictionnaire de la géographie commerçante,* IV, 391: "Piedmont."
4. Documents in the proceedings referred to earlier (note 7 to chapter 43), item 27, testimony of the first and sixth witnesses.
5. *Ibid.,* item 7.
6. *Ibid.,* item 11.
7. *Ibid.,* item 27. Other unreferenced quotations later in this passage are taken from the same documents in the case.
8. *Mémoire des fabricants à façon de la ville de Lyon en 1789,* Archives nationales, F 12, 1441, quoted by Maurice Garden, *Lyon et les Lyonnais au XVIIIe siècle* (Paris, Les belles lettres, Bibliothèque de la Faculté de Lyons, n.d.), p. 298.
9. "Tableau des dépenses journalières qui forment les charges annuelles des maîtres-ouvriers fabricants, et calcul d'icelles pour la nourriture et entretien des personnes à leur charge et le paiement des travaux du compagnon," in *Doléances* (see note 5 to chapter 43), text I, 17. This account and the text by the master workers (previous note) are reproduced word for word in the notebooks of grievances of the Lyons third estate in 1789.

## 45

1. Expilly's *Dictionnaire,* IV, 281: "Lyon."
2. From the text of the *Encyclopédie méthodique,* in just under one hundred volumes, published by Panckoucke; Roland wrote the three volumes of his *Dictionnaire des manufactures* for it. This extract is quoted by Germain Martin in *Les Associations ouvrières au XVIIIe siècle, 1700–1792* (Geneva, reprinted by Slatkine-Megariotis, 1974), p. 43.
3. *Ibid.,* p. 51, quoted from Flammermont, *Remonstrances des parlements au XVIIIe siècle,* p. 310.
4. Edmond Soreau, *Ouvriers et Paysans de 1789–1792* (Paris, Les belles lettres, 1936), p. 28.

## 46

1. Readers are reminded (see note 7 to chapter 43) that these excerpts are taken from the trial papers; the address by the public prosecutor is item 35.
2. J. Beyssac (see note 3 to chapter 43), p. 454.

3. Lyons Municipal Archives, IV, box VII, 190.

pp. 212–36 of Gérard Walter's book.

## 47

1. Henri Welschinger, *La Mission secrète de Mirabeau à Berlin, 1786–1787* (Paris, 1900), p. 37. The merit of this book, which begins with a wildly inaccurate introduction on Mirabeau's life, is that it contains the complete text of his letters to Talleyrand, much abridged in the scandalous publication of 1789. The full text published here is based on the collection in the Archives des Affaires Etrangères [Foreign Affairs].
2. *Ibid.,* pp. 169 and 173.
3. Unpublished, and understandably so. But the original manuscript, repurchased by Calonne via Talleyrand, is in the Archives des Affaires Etrangères [Foreign Affairs], Mémoires and Documents, volume 1889.
4. Quoted by Welschinger, *La Mission secrète de Mirabeau à Berlin,* p. 22.
5. *Ibid.,* p. 104.
6. Letter quoted by Gérard Walter in *Frédéric II, roi de Prusse,* p. 210. Two years after the king's death, Zimmermann published his account of his fruitless attempt to save him in "Uber Friedrich d. Gr. und meine Unterredungen mit ihm kurz vor seinem Tode," the text of which he translated into French himself. Unreferenced quotations later in the chapter are from the same text, which appears on

## 48

1. Uli Bräker, *Le pauvre homme du Toggenbourg* (Lausanne, Editions de l'Aire, 1978), p. 133. This is the unprofessional but beguiling autobiography of a humble peasant-craftsman from Toggenburg in the principality of St. Gall who, like Rousseau or Restif, had a bad case of writer's itch but whose notebooks were not published until after his death, thanks to a pastor who discovered them in 1788. The best edition of his works now available (in German, published by Birkhäuser Verlag, Basel, 1945) includes three volumes of private diaries interspersed with philosophical dialogues, parts of plays, reflections on Shakespeare's theater, a rough draft of a novel, etc.
2. *Voyages en Allemagne du baron de Risbeck,* translated from the English and revised on the basis of the original German (Paris, chez Regnault, "Bookseller, rue Saint-Jacques vis-à-vis celle du plâtre," 1788), II, 241. *Ibid.* for the next quote.
3. According to Peuchet's *Dictionnaire de la géographie commerçante,* III, 12: "Berlin," the population of the city in 1784 was 145,021.
4. Bräker, *Le pauvre homme du Toggenbourg,* p. 134.
5. *Voyages en Allemagne du baron de Risbeck,* III, 47.

6. *Eloge du Roi de Prusse* by the author of the *Essai général de tactique* (London, 1787), p. 300. This is the original edition, actually printed in Paris, but anonymously, because Guibert, being a circumspect man, did not fancy a quarrel with the Court of Versailles over a few allusions to Frederick's religious tolerance.

## 49

* 1. All the excerpts from the *Lettre remise à Frédéric-Guillaume II* are taken from volume II of the *Oeuvres de Mirabeau*, pp. 411–55, which reproduces everything in the original edition of 1781, allegedly printed in Berlin but actually published in Paris. The people in Mirabeau's proximity are soon claiming that this text, like so many others, is not really his at all and was largely composed by his Parisian friends (Talleyrand, but even more Clavière, according to the Swiss Dumont). We can eliminate the former; prophetic exhortation is not his style. It is conceivable, on the other hand, that Clavière had some share in the *Lettre,* but anyone familiar with Mirabeau's prose cannot attribute the bulk of it, enriched by firsthand knowledge of the subjects, to anybody but himself. On the contrary, this, along with his letters to Talleyrand and Mauvillon, is one of the few writings by Mirabeau of which it can confidently be affirmed that it is *not* a plagiarism.

## 50

1. Welschinger, *La Mission secrète de Mirabeau en Prusse,* p. 163. On this sordid business of the French attempt to cut out Julie von Voss by imposing a homegrown mistress on the new King of Prussia, see Dauphin-Meunier's chapter "A la conquête du roi de Prusse" in *Autour de Mirabeau,* p. 155.

2. Vallentin, *Mirabeau avant la Révolution,* p. 397.

3. Dauphin-Meunier, *Autour de Mirabeau,* p. 163. *Ibid.* for the following quotation.

4. "Mémoires inédits de Madame de Nehra," affectionately quoted by Nicolas de Montigny, little Coco himself, in *Mémoires de Mirabeau,* IV, 343.

5. Vallentin, *Mirabeau avant la Révolution,* p. 392.

6. "Dohm sur Mirabeau, abstraction faite de ses Mémoires," in *Lettres à Vertuch* published in Berlin by L. Geiger in the *Akademische Blätter,* I, 13.

7. Stern, *Vie de Mirabeau,* I, 238.

8. Mirabeau's words quoted by Vallentin, *Mirabeau avant la Révolution,* p. 368.

9. Welschinger, *La Mission secrète de Mirabeau en Prusse,* p. 106.

10. Peuchet, *Dictionnaire de la géographie commerçante,* III: "Brunswick."

11. Same reference as note 9.

12. Same reference as note 10.

13. Vallentin, *Mirabeau avant la Révolution,* p. 382.

14. Duc de Castries, *Mirabeau,* p. 240. The author gives some

extremely useful general notes on changing French attitudes in this connection.

15. Letter to Lauzun, July 21, 1786, in Welschinger, *La Mission Secrète de Mirabeau en Prusse*, p. 146. Mirabeau tried to get an invitation from Brunswick on his way to Paris but only succeeded at his return, on the road to Berlin. On the outward journey, on the other hand, he requested and obtained a second and final audience with Frederick II, in the course of which the two men exchanged a few commonplaces on tolerance; Mirabeau tries to inflate this into a sort of last will and testament of the dying king.

16. Welschinger, *La Mission secrète de Mirabeau en Prusse*, p. 97.

## 51

1. *Lettre du comte de Mirabeau à M. . . . sur MM. Cagliostro et Lavater*, in *Oeuvres de Mirabeau*, IV, 522. The complete text is on pp. 463–536. Subsequent references will be given under the shortened title *Lettre sur Lavater*, the essay having much more to do with him than with Cagliostro.

2. François Ribadeau-Dumas, *Les Magiciens de Dieu: les grands illuminés des XVIIIe et XIXe siècles* (Paris, 1970), p. 173. My information on the different spiritual movements has been taken from this source.

3. *Ibid.*, p. 162.

4. Vallentin, *Mirabeau avant la Révolution*, p. 396. *Ibid.* for the following quotes.

5. In Berlin, by F. de la Garde, inscribed "terminé le 25 mars 1786"; this is the French-language edition, however, the two thousand copies of which were immediately dispatched to Paris under diplomatic cover and sold at once, thanks to the names of Cagliostro and Lavater. Nicolaï brought out the first German translation in the *Allgemeine deutsche Bibliothek* (appendix to volume 53–86, part III, 1608) two months later, when Mirabeau no longer had any illusions about gaining favor with Frederick William.

6. *Lettre sur Lavater*, p. 493.

7. *Ibid.*, p. 494.

8. Richard Friedenthal, *Goethe, sa vie et son temps* (Paris, 1967), p. 157.

9. *Lettre sur Lavater*, p. 510.

10. *Ibid.*, p. 521. And p. 523 for the following quote, which is the last sentence of the text.

11. To Talleyrand, on January 8, 1787. in Welschinger, *La Mission secrète de Mirabeau en Prusse*, p. 474.

12. To Talleyrand, on August 29, *ibid.*, p. 188.

13. To Talleyrand, on November 7, *ibid.*, p. 343.

## 52

1. The *Gazette de Paris* for September 20, 1786, rejoices in the beautiful weather by which France has been blessed during the previous two weeks. At Blérancourt, on fine autumn days, the mist lingers in the

mornings because of the nearby forests.

2. The exact words of Saint-Just's mother at the beginning of her letter to the Chevalier d'Evry, quoted in full by Alfred Bégis in his article "L'Emprisonnement de Saint-Just sous Louis XVI" in the *Curiosités révolutionnaires,* 1892, pp. 7–50 (Bibliothèque nationale, Ln 27/40675). In the nineteenth century, hagiographers of Saint-Just like Ernest Hamel (*Histoire de Saint-Just,* Paris, 1859) tried to prove that he never ran away from home or was imprisoned at all. Unfortunately, Albert Ollivier follows their lead in his *Saint-Just et la force des choses* (Paris, Gallimard), a fine book although full of inaccuracies. The discovery by Alfred Compardon and Alfred Bégis, in 1869, of the evidence in the Brunet d'Evry file in the Archives nationales (ser. F7, box 4701) removes the runaway episode from the realm of polemics. It did happen. For the facts, readers are referred to the relevant file, and for the context, to the following: Ralph Korngold, *Saint-Just* (Paris, 1937); D. Centore-Bineau, *Saint-Just* (Paris, 1936); Emmanuel Aegerter, *La Vie de Saint-Just* (Paris, 1929); and the article by Jean-Pierre Gross, "Autour de Saint-Just," in *Annales historiques de la Révolution française,* 1962, XXXIV, 218. All unnumbered quotes in the following pages are from the documents in the Archives nationales. I have received valuable help from Mme Madeleine-Anna Charmelot, who knows everything there is to know about Saint-Just, and whose *Saint-Just ou le chévalier Organt* (Paris, 1957) contains information on his romance with Louise-Thérèse Gellé which has not been published elsewhere; my heartfelt thanks to her.

3. *Le Géographe parisien, ou le Conducteur chronologique et historique des rues de Paris,* II, 68.

4. Noted by Paganel, delegate to the Convention, quoted by Albert Ollivier in *Saint-Just et la force des choses,* p. 38. Four portraits exist, from which we can form some idea of Saint-Just's physical appearance; they are by David, Prud'hon, Greuze, and an anonymous portraitist working in pastels (in the Musée Carnavalet, reproduced in Centore-Bineau, *Saint-Just,* p. 144). Greuze prettified and romanticized him, of course, underlining his girlish aspects; the anonymous portraitist restores his virility by thickening his jaw; Prud'hon strikes a balance. There are a host of other portraits around, more or less good likenesses.

5. According to Paganel; for us the value of this description, written seven years later, is that it shows the eternal boyishness of Saint-Just, and shows that he preserved it to the end: apart from the self-confidence he subsequently acquired, Saint-Just is the same in 1786 as at his death in 1793.

## 53

1. Maurice Dommanget, *Autour de Saint-Just* (Paris, 1971), pp. 78 and 80.
2. O. Boutanquoi, *Le Conventionnel Saint-Just et sa famille* (Compiègne, 1927), p. 18.
3. Archives Administratives de la Guerre [War], file on L. J. de Saint-Just, inspectorate of the gendarmerie, ordinance companies, volume 3, beginning in 1757.
4. (Anonymous) portraits of Saint-Just's parents can be seen in the museum at Blérancourt.
5. J. Hanoteau, *Les Ascendances nivernaises de Saint-Just* (Nevers, Imprimerie de la Nièvre), Bibliothèque nationale, 4° Ln 27/80655. This article, the product of an impressive piece of digging, establishes beyond question Saint-Just's presence in Decize until the age of nine.
6. Nièvre *département* archives, Decize acts notarized by Grenot, from the inspectorate records, folios 24, 25, 61, 62.
7. Full text of the contract appended to the *Ascendances nivernaises* (see note 5 above).
8. From the description in the deed of sale (for 5,200 livres) of 1776, in *Ascendances nivernaises,* p. 47.
9. Expilly, *Dictionnaire,* II, 608: "Decize."

## 54

1. The reconstruction of Saint-Just's relations with his parents, like that of his intellectual background, which is the subject of this chapter, is based on the many accounts of contemporaries whose statements were noted down at Blérancourt under the Empire and Restoration, largely in the Decaisne (the name of Antoine's two sisters following the marriage of the first and remarriage of the second), Thorin, and Fouquet-Dutailly families. The last-named kept the archives, which were extensively consulted by Madeleine-Anna Charmelot. Ernest Hamel, on the other hand, whose *Histoire de Saint-Just* must be used with circumspection because of its hagiographical aspect, had "family connections" at Chauny and Blérancourt (p. 22), so his material on these points is accurate.
2. Expilly, *Dictionnaire,* V, 268: "Noyon." *Ibid.* for other unnumbered references to Noyon.
3. According to Silvy, his teacher at the Oratory, and his friend Pierre-Germain Gateau, who sticks by him in Thermidor (cf. Archives nationales, F7, 716), Saint-Just began writing bits of a large lyric poem in 1780.
4. According to the historian Dormay in *Histoire des environs de Paris,* IV, 24 (history of Soissons).
5. Reichard, *guide,* volume II, *France,* "Soissons," p. 132.
6. Dormay, *Histoire des environs de Paris,* IV, 22.
7. Emmanuel Aegerter, *La Vie de Saint-Just,* p. 25.
8. M. A. H. Taillandier, *Documents*

*biographiques sur P. C. F. Daunou* (Paris, 1847), p. 3. *Ibid.* for the following quote, p. 2.

9. *Ibid.,* p. 5.

10. Centore-Bineau, *Saint-Just,* preface by Gérard Walter, p. 40.

11. According to the statements of a fellow pupil at Soissons, who was interviewed in his eighties at Coucy-le-Château by the historian Fleury. Cf. Edouard Fleury, *Saint-Just* (Paris, 1851), 2 volumes.

12. Cf. Daniel Mornet, *Les Origines intellectuelles de la Révolution française* (Paris, 1938), p. 33.

13. From Barère's *Mémoires,* quoted by Edouard Fleury, *Saint-Just,* I, 18. I don't like to force comparisons, but in the matter of memory's role in the formation of the intellect I cannot avoid associating, once again, Saint-Just and Buonaparte.

14. *Ibid.,* p. 19, also from the account of Saint-Just's former schoolmate.

15. Mornet, *Les Origines intellectuelles,* p. 27.

16. Saint-Just, *Organt,* 1789 edition reprinted in his *Oeuvres complètes,* published by Charles Vellay, p. 173.

## 55

1. Excerpts from the monograph, analyzed by Dommanget in *Autour de Saint-Just,* pp. 31–58. This is the source of all my material on the work, the Blérancourt copy of which I have consulted.

2. Expilly, *Dictionnaire,* II: "Coucy-le-Châtel."

3. Thérèse's portrait and the story of her gun-point wedding are examples of the durability of village oral tradition. By assembling and combining local commentary, much of it kept alive in Blérancourt for three or four generations, Hamel, Fleury, and Mmes Centore-Bineau and Madeleine-Anna Charmelot (the last-named drawing mainly on the Fouquet-Dutailly family) have been able to reconstruct the essential points.

4. Saint-Just documented himself extensively before writing his monograph. Dommanget has identified in it references to, and actual passages from, the *Histoire de la ville et des seigneurs de Coucy* by Dom Toussaint-Duplessis, the *Miracles de Sainte Marie de Laon* by Brother Hermann, and the *Histoire généalogique de la maison de Coucy* by A. Duchesne, which he consulted in the notary's house.

## 56

1. According to Charmelot, in *Saint-Just ou le chevalier Organt,* p. 26. See also, for the Lamottes and Bigots, the same historian's article "Les habitants de Blérancourt en l'An IV" in the *Annales historiques de la Révolution française,* 1959, XXXI, 61–75.

2. The date is uncertain. To my knowledge, moreover, and until some researcher takes up the trail, Saint-Just's stay at Louis-le-Grand (attested to by his own statements during the Revolution and by tradition at Blérancourt) remains shrouded

in total darkness. His name occurs nowhere in the examination lists for the end of the 1786 academic year.

3. Marriage certificate given in a footnote by Charmelot in *Saint-Just ou le chevalier Organt,* p. 27. See also the article in the *Annales historiques* mentioned above in note 1.

4. Antoine de Saint-Just, "De la Nature, de l'Etat-civil, de la Cité, ou les règles de l'indépendance du gouvernement." This text, which was never published, is in the Bibliothèque nationale, manuscript 12947 in the French collection (recent acquisitions). It consists of 138 sheets, 99 of them blank, in a leather binding; the title appears on the title page, in Saint-Just's own hand, and he also wrote, as a subtitle on p. 1, "Du droit social, ou principe du droit naturel." Albert Soboul published the complete text, with commentary, in the *Annales historiques de la Révolution française,* 1951, XXI, 321–59. For the exact dating of this text, between the publication of *L'Esprit de la Révolution* (1791) and the *Fragments sur les institutions républicaines* (Floréal, An II), see the exhaustive study by Jean-Pierre Gross, "L'Oeuvre de Saint-Just, essai de bibliographie critique," in *Actes du colloque Saint-Just,* June 25, 1967 (Paris, Société des études robespierristes), p. 350.

5. Article by A. Bégis on "L'Emprisonnement de Saint-Just," p. 23 (see note 2, chapter 52).

6. *Ibid.,* p. 24. These records survived the fires of 1871 and are kept in the prefecture of police.

7. *Ibid.,* p. 24.

## 57

1. *Mémoires de Billaud-Varenne,* published in full by F. A. Aulard in the *Revue de la Révolution française,* 1888, XIV, in four installments, p. 753. I have compared this text, which is often inaccurate owing to carelessness on the part of the copyist, with the original in the Archives nationales, F7, 4582; it was among the boxes of papers seized in Billaud-Varenne's home when he was arrested in Germinal An III. The whole consists of two sheaves of manuscript on unnumbered pages, one entitled *Lettres recueillies par J.-N. B.,* and the other entitled *Tableau du premier âge.* The first is an attempt at a novel in letter form, the second an autobiographical novel written in the first person. There is such constant interference and overlapping between the two that one is tempted to wonder whether they were not mixed together and some pages of one put in the other by mistake. In fact, the first is more or less a draft of the second. The beginning of *Porphyre* is dated 1775; some pages of the *Tableau du premier âge* are marked 1786 on the back; thus we can determine the extreme dates of this long, unfinished effort. Both

texts break off in mid-sentence. But Billaud must have set some store by these reflections upon his youth, because they lay side by side with his most important later papers. Be this as it may, it was quite unjustified of Aulard to call his publication "Mémoires" of Billaud-Varenne: they are literary fragments, written in youth, on the basis of which certain biographical relationships may, with great caution, be elaborated, and one or two psychological traits inferred. Nevertheless, here I shall, for convenience's sake, refer to the text in the *Revue de la Révolution française* as *Mémoires de Billaud-Varenne*.

2. Expilly, *Dictionnaire*, I, 356: "Aunis." It contains a gratifyingly detailed description of the salt-refining process in the marshes.

3. *Ibid.*, VI, 351: "Rochelle (la)," and *passim*. Other unnumbered quotations relating to la Rochelle are from the same source.

4. *Mémoires de Billaud-Varenne*, p. 1043.

5. La Rochelle Municipal Library, 355, folio 13, and 609, folio 215.

6. Expilly, *Dictionnaire*, I, 353.

7. Jacques Guilaine, *Billaud-Varenne, l'ultra de la Révolution* (Paris, Fayard, 1969), p. 4. This book, the only modern biography of Billaud-Varenne thus far, is a conscientious summary of everything now known about him.

8. There are some beautiful photographs of the façade in the album by Rémi Béraud, *La*

*Rochelle, ou la douceur de vivre* (La Rochelle, 1973). Warm thanks to my friends Bernadette and Christian Raspiengeas for enabling me to make this unforgettable excursion.

9. Expilly, *Dictionnaire*, I, 355.

10. *Mémoires de Billaud-Varenne*, p. 755.

11. *Ibid.*, p. 757.

12. Expilly, *Dictionnaire*, I, 354.

13. *Mémoires de Billaud-Varenne*, p. 849.

14. See dates of the first publication in the monumental biography by J. Rives-Childs, *Restif de la Bretonne* (Paris, 1949).

15. *Mémoires de Billaud-Varenne*, p. 843.

16. *Ibid.*, p. 929.

17. *Ibid.*, p. 1034.

18. *Ibid.*, p. 1036. *Ibid.* for the following dialogue.

19. *Ibid.*, p. 1032.

## 58

1. *Mémoires de Billaud-Varenne*, p. 1032.

2. *Ibid.*, p. 1033. Also for the following quote.

3. A. Aulard, *Les Orateurs de la Révolution* (Paris, 1907), II, 486: "Billaud-Varenne."

4. Letter published by A. Bégis, *Mémoires inédits et correspondance sur Billaud-Varenne et Collot d'Herbois* (Paris, 1893), p. 4. The book's great value lies in its account of the second part of Billaud-Varenne's life in Cayenne and Haiti.

5. Also quoted by Arnault and requoted by Guilaine, *Billaud-Varenne*, p. 14.

6. Aulard, *Les Orateurs de la Révolution,* II, 487.
7. End of Arnault's account; see note 5.
8. *Le Géographe parisien,* II, 126.
9. *Ibid.,* I, 252.
10. According to Georges Duval, in his *Souvenirs thermidoriens,* quoted by Bégis in *Mémoires sur Billaud-Varenne,* p. 6. A curious rumor, amplified by the gossipy Lenôtre, attributes the paternity of Anne-Angélique to Jean-Jacques de Verdun, one of the richest farmers general in France. In 1793 we shall see that even here there is no smoke without fire. But I can find no trace of such an insinuation at the time of Billaud-Varenne's marriage.
11. Letter from Billaud-Varenne to his father, undated but probably written in July 1785.
12. According to Aulard in *Les Orateurs de la Révolution,* II, 485, and Guilaine, *Billaud-Varenne,* p. 17.
13. Bégis, *Mémoires sur Billaud-Varenne,* p. 9.
14. *Ibid.,* p. 7.
15. Archives nationales, ser. F 7, 565.
16. Text of the marriage certificate published by Bégis in *Mémoires sur Billaud-Varenne,* p. 9.
17. Both books are in the Bibliothèque nationale: D2, 5976; and Lb 39, 1321.
18. Archives nationales, ser. F 7, 4582/2.

## 59

1. *Archives parlementaires de 1787 à 1860* (Paris, Librairie administrative de Paul Dupont, 1879), I, 182. As a rule, I shall take the texts of the official speeches or writings of the Revolution from this collection in ninety-six volumes. It is a more authentic source than the *Moniteur,* where speeches were summarized and often rewritten. The simplified reference will be *Arch. parlem.*
2. "Projet d'annonce de l'Assemblée des notables à faire au Conseil du Roi," Archives nationales, K 677 (III).
3. Duc de Castries, *Le Maréchal de Castries,* p. 144.
4. *Ibid.,* p. 145. In fact, the minister was not being altogether truthful, because the Duc de Castries tells us (in the same book) that Calonne had informed him of the King's intentions, although only, it is true, on December 26, presumably to avoid a scene at the Council meeting. Anyway, that didn't change the main reason for his tantrum, which was that Louis XVI had not taken him into his confidence.
5. Lacour-Gayet, *Calonne,* p. 169.
6. *Ibid.,* pp. 170 and 132.
* 7. Quoted by Bernard Fay in *Louis XVI ou la fin d'un monde,* p. 283.
8. Joseph Droz, *Histoire du règne de Louis XVI pendant les années où l'on pouvait prévenir ou diriger la Révolution française* (Paris, 1860), I, 359.
9. Lescure, *Correspondance secrète,* II, 92 (dated January 3, 1787).
10. Bailly, *Mémoires* (Paris, 1821), I, 2. After a few introductory lines this text opens the unfinished

*Mémoires* that Bailly had time to begin after withdrawing to Nantes, between his resignation as mayor of Paris on September 19, 1791 and his arrest during the Terror.

11. *Correspondance de La Fayette*, II, 190.

12. Welschinger, *La Mission secrète de Mirabeau à Berlin*, p. 448, letter from Talleyrand, January 1, 1787.

13. *Ibid.*, p. 479, letter to Talleyrand, January 13, 1787.

14. Letter from Mirabeau to Major de Mauvillon, quoted by Aimé Chérest, *La Chute de l'Ancien Régime* (Paris, 1884), I, 113.

15. Rabaut Saint-Etienne, *Précis de l'histoire de la Révolution française*, in his *Oeuvres complètes* (Paris, 1826), I, 264.

16. Chérest, *La Chute de l'Ancien Régime*, I, 127.

17. Exchange of letters from the *Correspondance de Mercy-Argenteau*, quoted by Lacour-Gayet in *Calonne*, p. 179. Same source for the remark by Kaunitz that follows.

18. Lacour-Gayet, *Calonne*, p. 187.

19. Ruault, *Gazette d'un Parisien*, p. 78.

## 60

1. *Nouveau dictionnaire français composé sur le dictionnaire de l'Académie française* (Paris and Lyons, chez Delamollière, 1793), II, 156.

2. *Arch. parlem.*, I, 184.

3. Chérest, *La chute de l'Ancien Régime*, p. 132. *Ibid.* for the next quote.

4. Lescure, *Correspondance secrète*, II, 108.

5. Talleyrand, *Mémoires*, I, 105.

6. In a letter to Mauvillon, February 13, in Chérest, *La Chute de l'Ancien Régime*, I, 137.

7. Ruault, *Gazette d'un Parisien*, p. 80, letter to his brother, February 21, 1787.

8. Charles de Chambrun, *Vergennes*, p. 416.

9. *Ibid.*, p. 417.

10. Letter to his mother-in-law, February 16, 1787, quoted by Jean Egret, *La Pré-Révolution française, 1787–1788* (Paris, PUF, 1962), p. 11.

11. Quoted by Chérest, *La Chute de l'Ancien Régime*, I, 135.

12. *Ibid.*, p. 137, letter to Mauvillon, February 6, 1787.

13. *Ibid.*, p. 134.

14. *Correspondance de La Fayette*, II, 194.

15. According to Bachaumont, quoted by Lacour-Gayet, *Calonne*, p. 187.

16. *Ibid.*, p. 185.

## 61

* 1. Fernand Evrard, *Versailles, ville du Roi*.

2. *Arch. parlem.*, I, 186. *Ibid.* for the text of the minutes, which are given almost complete.

# Index

## A

Abélard, Pierre, 351
Académie Française, 8, 9, 10, 56, 65,
  87, 137, 170 *n.*, 174, 178, 179,
  181 *n.*, 396
Academy of Sciences, 49, 50, 51
Achet, Louis-François, 112, 114,
  115
Adam, Moïse, 117
Adams, John, 37
Adélaïde, Mme (daughter of Louis
  XV), 65, 95
agriculture: drought and famine, 42,
  44 *n.*, 45, 58, 255
  food and diet, 44, 46, 135, 152,
    255; bread, 135–6; potatoes,
    45 *n.*; prices, 58
  land, measurement of, 151
Aguesseau, Henri-François, 181
Aiguillon, Duc d' (Emmanuel-
  Armand de Richelieu), 183, 260
Alembert, Jean d', 35, 174, 203
Aligre, Etienne-François d', 240, 245
Amboise, Cardinal Georges d', 34,
  40 *n.*
American Revolution, 4, 19, 158, 167,
  185, 204, 269, 388, 398, 403
Amiens, 267, 268, 269–70
Amsterdam, 100
  publishing, 96, 149, 373, 386 *n.*
Andlau, Baronne d', 165 *n.*
Angivillier, Comte d', 190
Anne of Austria, Queen, 107
Antraigues, Comte d', 187
Arco, Count Karl, 216, 217
Armand, Nicholas, 77 *n.*
Arnault, 381 *n.*
Arnault, Jean, 17
Arnault, Robert, 347

Arneth, Alfred von, 101 *n.*
Artois, Comte Charles d' (later Charles
  X), 14, 121, 170, 185, 341 *n.*
  Assembly of Notables, 395, 397,
    407, 408
  and brother, Louis XVI, 93, 253
  and Marie Antoinette, 10, 94, 95,
    96
Artois, Comtesse d' (Maria Theresa of
  Savoy), 90, 95
Assembly of Notables (1596), 406,
  408
Assembly of Notables (1626), 406
Assembly of Notables (1787), 305,
  386–409
  composition of, 397–9, 400
  meeting, 405–9; dress, 407
Assoucy, Charles Coypeau d', 355
Auersperg, Prince of, 7
Augeard, Jacques-Mathieu, 97, 98, 99,
  100
Austria: and Bavaria, 100, 101
  and France, 100–5 *passim*, 202, 209
  and Holland, 100–1, 103–4, 105,
    207
  and Prussia, 202, 203, 207, 305
  and Turkey, 101, 305
  Wallachian revolt, 222–4, 233–7
  *see also* Joseph II
Austrian Netherlands (Belgium), 100,
  101, 102, 103, 181

## B

Babeuf, Gracchus, 134 *n.*
Bachaumont, Louis Petit, 178
Bache, Benjamin, 38 *n.*
Baden, 19, 85, 87
Bailly, Jean-Sylvain, 49, 50, 51, 390–1
Balbi, Comtesse de, 10

# N

# O

# P

# Y

# W

# Z

A NOTE ABOUT THE AUTHOR

Claude Manceron is the Head of the French Ministry of Culture and the Director of all details concerning the celebration in France of the French Revolution. Born in 1923, he is the son of a French naval officer and a Greek princess. His formal schooling ended after he was crippled by polio at age eleven, but he continued to read and became a teacher and a writer—at first of historical novels. His research, undertaken to make the characters' backgrounds authentic, led him to give up fiction and become a historian. He has been working on the Age of the French Revolution series since 1967, and has now completed the fifth and final volume, *The Blood of the Bastille*.

## A NOTE ABOUT THE TRANSLATOR

Nancy Lipe Amphoux was born in Rockford, Illinois, and was educated by the cornfields there, at Vassar and Carnegie-Mellon, and in Europe, where she has lived since 1959. Her interests and activities include teaching and social work, horses and tropical fish, and Zen. Some of the books she has translated are Henri Troyat's biographies of Tolstoy, Pushkin, and Gogol; Edmonde Charles-Roux's biography of Chanel; François Ponchaud's *Cambodia Year Zero;* and an earlier volume in the Age of the French Revolution series, *The Wind from America.* She now lives in Strasbourg, France.

## A NOTE ON THE TYPE

The text of this book was set, via computer-driven cathode-ray tube, in Garamond, a modern rendering of the type first cut by Claude Garamond (c. 1480–1561). Garamond was a pupil of Geoffroy Tory and is believed to have based his letters on the Venetian models; it is to him we owe the letter we know as old-style.